Sustainable Development Goals (SDG) and Its Intersection With Health and Well-Being

Sandeep Poddar
Lincoln University College, Malaysia

Waliza Ansar
Behala College, India

IGI Global
Scientific Publishing
Publishing Tomorrow's Research Today

Vice President of Editorial	Melissa Wagner
Director of Acquisitions	Mikaela Felty
Director of Book Development	Jocelynn Hessler
Production Manager	Mike Brehm
Cover Design	Phillip Shickler

Published in the United States of America by
IGI Global Scientific Publishing
701 East Chocolate Avenue
Hershey, PA, 17033, USA
Tel: 717-533-8845
Fax: 717-533-7115
Website: https://www.igi-global.com E-mail: cust@igi-global.com

Library of Congress Cataloging-in-Publication Data

Names: Poddar, Sandeep editor | Ansar, Waliza editor
Title: Sustainable development goals (SDG) and its intersection with health and well-being / edited by Sandeep Poddar, Waliza Ansar.
Description: Hershey, PA : IGI Global Scientific Publishing, [2025] | Includes bibliographical references and index. | Summary: "This book will explore the economic, environmental, healthcare and social facets of sustainable development, delving into its many components"-- Provided by publisher.
Identifiers: LCCN 2024055617 (print) | LCCN 2024055618 (ebook) | ISBN 9798369397558 hardcover | ISBN 9798369397565 paperback | ISBN 9798369397572 ebook
Subjects: LCSH: Sustainable development
Classification: LCC HC79.E5 S861885 2025 (print) | LCC HC79.E5 (ebook) | DDC 338.927--dc23/eng/20250618
LC record available at https://lccn.loc.gov/2024055617
LC ebook record available at https://lccn.loc.gov/2024055618

British Cataloguing in Publication Data
A Cataloguing in Publication record for this book is available from the British Library.

Table of Contents

Detailed Table of Contents

Green infrastructure is a crucial strategy for climate change adaptation, enhancing health, air quality, and patient outcomes. It also offers ecosystem services that improve human health and well-being. However, the benefits of green infrastructure have not been thoroughly assessed. Geographic Information Systems (GI) in the context of climate change can provide economic and public health benefits. Green infrastructure, including sustainable building techniques, water management systems, and renewable energy systems, reduces reliance on finite resources and promotes environmental sustainability. Advancements in technology, such as early warning systems, telemedicine, and health data analytics, enhance operational effectiveness, disaster preparedness, and service delivery. This book chapter explores the potential of green infrastructure and technology in constructing resilient health systems in developing nations, highlighting the need for a comprehensive strategy that combines innovation and sustainability to address climate change.

Rapid urbanisation, fueled by population growth and industrialisation, poses significant threats to public health, particularly in densely populated areas. This chapter explores the interplay of pollution, overcrowding, and industrial activities in exacerbating health disparities in urban settings. Drawing from evidence-based research and case studies, the chapter highlights innovative approaches to mitigating urban health risks, including green infrastructure, integrative health interventions, and policy reform. The chapter also examines how sustainable urban planning and community-driven initiatives can align with SDG 3 (Good Health and Well-Being) and SDG 11 (Sustainable Cities and Communities), emphasising the need for equitable, resilient urban health systems.

Tuberculosis (TB) remains one of the most deadly infectious diseases worldwide, with accurate notification playing a critical role in its control. This chapter explores the importance of TB notification in public health, focusing on international guidelines from the World Health Organization (WHO) and their implementation in high burden of TB, such as Indonesia. Several factors associated with TB notification, such as patient demographics, healthcare provider characteristics, and notification-system challenges, are discussed. The chapter also highlights the problem of under-notification in private healthcare settings and examines how technological advancements can improve notification systems. Finally, it provides policy recommendations for enhancing TB notification, emphasizing private-public partnerships and regulatory reforms.

Embracing change in the context of climate change and diversity challenges is crucial for fostering resilience and promoting sustainability. Rising temperatures, extreme weather events, and sea-level rise are not just environmental issues; they amplify social inequities and economic disparities, disproportionately affecting marginalized communities. Addressing these challenges requires a commitment to environmental sustainability and the integration of diverse perspectives. Additionally, fostering cultural diversity enhances our collective knowledge and adaptive capacity, allowing for innovative solutions rooted in varied experiences and traditions. Governments and organizations must collaborate to create adaptive policies that prioritize resilience, equity, and inclusivity. Embracing change means recognizing the interconnectedness of climate issues and social dynamics, ultimately fostering a holistic approach to create a sustainable and equitable future for all. By understanding these challenges, we can navigate the complexities of change and emerge stronger together.

Industry 5.0 is on the horizon representing a big change, focusing on combining advanced technologies with a people-centred approach. Industry 5.0 incorporates technologies such as artificial intelligence (AI), big data analytics (BDA), the Internet of Things (IoT), machine learning (ML), robotics, and virtualization to pave the way for innovative ways of doing things. The goal is to attain equilibrium between humans and machines, all while ensuring our growth occurs in an environmentally sustainable manner. In healthcare, Industry 5.0 aspires to build resource-efficient and user-friendly solutions. In this chapter, we explore how Industry 5.0 can work together with Sustainable Development Goal 3 – Good Health and Well-being by analysing the optimal use and the collective potential of numerous technologies that might aid in achieving the targets of SDG 3. We examine the optimal utilization of various technologies to attain the objectives of this goal.

Achieving health equity is central to the Sustainable Development Goals (SDGs). This chapter examines how gender inequality and poverty intersect to create systemic barriers to equitable healthcare. It explores the multifaceted impacts of social discrimination and marginalisation on health outcomes, drawing on global and regional data to highlight disparities. Strategies for addressing these issues are discussed, including policy reform, community-based interventions, and the integration of intersectional approaches. The chapter underscores the urgency of addressing gender and socioeconomic inequalities to foster sustainable, inclusive health systems that leave no one behind, aligning with SDG 3 (Good Health and Well-Being) and SDG 5 (Gender Equality).

This chapter explores how green infrastructure strategies can improve health and well-being for ageing populations through sustainable urban design. With a focus

and offering best practices. Many nations lack recycling infrastructure & specific policies, which makes managing e-waste particularly difficult. Community education & stricter regulations are demanded. A concerted worldwide strategy is needed to properly manage e-waste, lessen its negative effects on the environment, & promote sustainable development.

This study explores the spiritual well-being of incarcerated individuals, a topic less examined compared to the relationship between criminality and religiosity. Data were collected from 259 inmates in Tamil Nadu's Central Prisons, Special Prisons for Women, and Open Air Prisons, using the Spiritual Well-Being Scale. This tool encompasses five dimensions: Divine Connectedness (DC), Self Connectedness (SC), Other Connectedness (OC), Nature Connectedness (NC), and the Spirituality Rating Index (SRI). Employing a descriptive research design, the study combined qualitative and quantitative methods, with SPSS version 23 used for analysis. Statistical techniques included descriptive and multivariate methods such as frequency, mean, standard deviation, and correlation, focusing on the Spiritual Rating Scale across dimensions.

This chapter examines the transformative impact of technology, artificial intelligence (AI), and information proliferation on healthcare and allied sciences. It explores advancements in telemedicine, wearable devices, and AI applications in diagnostics and drug discovery. The role of big data analytics in identifying health trends and informing policy is discussed, alongside ethical considerations of AI-driven healthcare. The chapter also addresses future trends, including genomics-AI integration and quantum computing in drug development. This overview illuminates how these

Marine ecosystem is facing threats of pollution from heavy metals and pesticides that have the propensity to bioaccumulate and biomagnify through food chains, putting biodiversity and human health at risk. This chapter focuses on bioaccumulation and trophic transfer of heavy metals and carcinogenic effects that have their pathway in marine organisms to humans via seafood consumption. Objectives include examining the mechanisms of bioaccumulation, evaluating ecological disruptions, assessing cancer risks from prolonged exposure, and analysing the shortcomings of current legal frameworks. The chapter underscores the persistence of heavy metals in aquatic ecosystems, their toxic impacts on marine species, and the severe health risks, including cancer, linked to contaminated seafood. The study urges strong discharge controls, improved water quality standards, and integrated monitoring systems to lower heavy metal contamination, preserve biodiversity, and protect human health from carcinogenic risks. It also calls for international cooperation, public awareness, and strong regulations.

Foreword

It is my great pleasure to introduce the book entitled, "Sustainable Development Goals (SDG) and its Intersection with Health and Well-Being" edited by Dr. Sandeep Poddar and Dr. Waliza Ansar and published by IGI Global Scientific Publishing, USA.

The book comprises 19 chapters by distinguished authors from various countries. The primary focus of the publication is the United Nations Sustainable Development Goals (SDGs). Within a comprehensive perspective, the book fosters global collaboration on scientific innovative research and green infrastructure strategies. The book having a multidisciplinary global framework that encourages nations to collaborate in order to establish a more sustainable and improved future. The importance of finding creative solutions to ensure a sustainable future and the urgency of addressing environmental concerns are both emphasized in this substantial study. Careful research into current sustainability practices has allowed the authors to provide an in-depth examination of how these developments contribute to better Global health.

Sustainable development is not to be viewed in a vacuum, but rather as an integral component of a broader agenda that seeks to enhance human health and well-being. This holistic perspective highlights the importance of this integration. Emphasizing the need for innovative problem-solving and interdisciplinary teamwork, the delicate balance between health and environmental stewardship is highlighted.

The pursuit of sustainable development is an ancient endeavor; however, the objectives were novel and unavoidable. By fostering informed action and cooperation, we can establish the foundations for a more prosperous, resilient, and equitable global community. This book serves as an exhaustive manual, providing practical solutions and insightful perspectives to assist in the attainment of this significant objective by enhancing health outcomes.

Lalitbhushan S. Waghmare
Datta Meghe Medical College, DMIHER campus, India

Preface

The United Nations created the Sustainable Development Goals (SDGs), which act as a multidisciplinary worldwide guide for nations to work together to build a better, more sustainable future. These goals are intended to conceptualize, surpass/meander a number of integrated and coherent issues, such as social stability, public health, climate change, promote health, well being, peace and security, and the growing needs for food, shelter and energy justice. The need for revolutionary action is more important than ever as the world deals with interrelated problems including pandemics (Pre and post era), harsh weather, and ecological destruction.

Chapter 1 details the findings of a study analyzing the health and psychological well-being of convicts in the Central Prison of Tamil Nadu. The study investigates personal, economic, health, familial, psychological, and general well-being factors, personality traits and their correlations, psychological characteristics, offense-related variables, age, leisure activities pre- and post-incarceration, marital status and well-being, among other elements. This descriptive study employed both qualitative and quantitative methodologies. The chapter also explores the potential interventions and strategies to improve the overall well-being of the incarcerated population.

Bridging the Climate Gap chapter 2, focus on green infrastructure which helps adapt to climate change by improving health, air quality, and patient outcomes. Its ecosystem services benefit human health and well-being. However, green infrastructure benefits have not been fully studied. Geographic Information Systems (GI) can improve climate change economics and public health. Green infrastructure—sustainable building, water management, and renewable energy—reduces resource use and improves environmental sustainability. Technology including early warning systems, telemedicine, and health data analytics improves operations, disaster preparedness, and service delivery. This book chapter discusses how green infrastructure and technology may build resilient health systems in developing nations and the need for an innovative, sustainable climate change strategy.

Population growth and industrialization generate rapid urbanization, which risks public health in densely populated places. Chapter 3 investigates how pollution, overcrowding, and industrialization aggravate urban health gap. Green infrastructure, integrative health interventions, and policy reform to lessen urban health hazards are discussed using evidence-based research and case studies. This chapter emphasizes equitable, resilient urban health systems and how sustainable urban planning and community-driven initiatives can support SDG 3 (Good Health and Well-Being) and SDG 11 (Sustainable Cities and Communities).

TB is one of the worst infectious diseases, and accurate notification is key to controlling it. This chapter 4 discusses the importance of TB notification in public health, concentrating on WHO standards and their implementation in high-TB countries like Indonesia. TB notification considerations include patient demographics, healthcare provider characteristics, and notification-system problems. The chapter also discusses private healthcare under-notification and how technology might enhance notification systems. Finally, it suggests private-public collaborations and legislative reforms to improve TB notification.

Embracing Change: Understanding Climate Changes and Diversity Challenges, chapter 5 depicts change is needed to address climate change and diversity issues and build resilience. Climate change, extreme weather, and sea-level rise aggravate social and economic inequality, affecting the poor. Environmental sustainability and diversity are needed to fix these issues. Fostering cultural diversity boosts our knowledge and adaptability, enabling innovative solutions based on varied experiences and practices. Governments and groups must collaborate on robust, egalitarian, and inclusive policies. Change promotes a holistic, sustainable, and equitable future by addressing the connection of climatic and social issues. Understanding these challenges helps us adapt and grow.

Chapter 6 discusses on industry 5.0 which will integrate new technologies and a people-centered strategy. Industry 5.0 uses AI, BDA, IoT, ML, robotics, and virtualization to enable new methods. Authors want to balance humans and machines while growing sustainably. Industry 5.0 aims to provide resource-efficient, user-friendly healthcare solutions. This chapter examines how Industry 5.0 might support Sustainable Development Goal 3 – Good Health and Well-being by analyzing the optimal usage and aggregate potential of many technologies. The optimal use of various technologies to achieve this goal is examined.

Gender Inequality and Health Disparities chapter deals with the Sustainable Development Goals prioritize health equityin chapter 7. Gender inequality and poverty constitute systemic impediments to egalitarian healthcare, as shown in this chapter. It examines the complex effects of social discrimination and marginalisation on health outcomes using global and regional data. These concerns can be addressed through policy reform, community-based interventions, and intersectional approaches. To achieve SDG 3 (Good Health and Well-Being) and SDG 5 (Gender Equality), the chapter emphasizes the need to address gender and socioeconomic inequities to create sustainable, inclusive health systems that leave no one behind.

Green Infrastructure Strategies for Ageing Populations in chapter 8 examines how sustainable urban design and green infrastructure might improve health and well-being for aging populations. The chapter discusses ageing in place and how green spaces reduce loneliness, improve mobility, reduce falls, and promote holistic care for those with chronic conditions like oncology, chronic kidney disease (CKD), and frailty-related issues that require specialized moving and handling. It targets fair access to urban health solutions, sustainability, and social inclusion, providing creative urban design solutions to improve older adults' mental and physical health in line with Sustainable Development Goals (SDGs).

Chapter 9, discusses how digital transformation drives sustainable growth across industries. It shows how the Internet of Things, AI, and big data analytics improve operational efficiency and decision-making, boosting environmental sustainability. The links between digital transformation and environmental sustainability and the implementation obstacles firms confront are examined. Digital technologies have been used to reduce air and water pollution and conserve resources in the chapter's case studies. It stresses ethical leadership and stakeholder participation for digital efforts with genuine sustainability aims. Finally, the chapter provides a complete framework for using digital transformation to promote sustainability and meet global sustainability goals.

Non-communicable diseases (NCDs) remain a major global health concern, causing significant morbidity and mortality. Chapter 10 discuss on the WHO Global Action Plan 2013-2020 reports that 36 million people die from NCDs, 14 million of whom are under 70. India's NCD rate has risen in the past decade. NCDs pose a serious public health danger and require global surveillance, prevention, and control. Understanding these illnesses' health issues is essential to developing effective prevention and management strategies. Cancer, CVD, respiratory illnesses, and diabetes are the four main NCDs mentioned in this chapter. It will cover these diseases' prevalence, risk factors, healthcare costs, economic repercussions, health inequities, and socioeconomic influences that increase their occurrence and management.

Chapter 11 discuss on heavy metals contamination in river water and sediments of Ganga and Hooghly in India. Industrial effluents, agricultural runoff, cultural practise, idol immersion, and domestic waste pollute the Ganga and Hooghly rivers in India. Heavy metals (Pb, Hg, Cd, and Cr) in river water are repeatedly above the safe limits (above maximum admissible & desirable limits), making them toxic, hazardous to aquatic life, ecosystem, biodiversity health, and livelihood of people who drink, irrigate, pasture, and use the rivers. Heavy metal-contaminated fish and other aquatic species can cause retardation, chronic and acute toxicity, carcinogenic effects, liver and lung damage, neurological and skin diseases, cancer, and gastrointestinal disturbances. Thus, all Indian government departments, companies, and communities must work together to address pollution and protect human and environmental health.

Chapter 12 examines how health, water, food security, sanitation, and livestock productivity relate to sustainable development. This research emphasizes risk management and intervention options for these interrelated sectors to create a resilient and sustainable future by aligning with the UN Sustainable Development Goals (SDGs). The chapter has various sections, each focused on a crucial subject and its issues, hazards, and solutions, especially in developing nations with limited resources and socio-economic and environmental restrictions.

The chapter 13 on the Mental Health Crisis Among Kattunauakan Tribal Adolescents in Kerala, South India examines Kattunayakan tribal adolescents' mental health and the causes and variables affecting it. 93 tribal teenagers from Kattunayakan, Wayanad district, Kerala, were randomly selected for this study. The teens' self-rated anxiety, mental stress, and social interaction were assessed using a self-administered interview questionnaire. The findings shed light on tribal teenagers' unique challenges and help build interventions and support systems for them.

Solid waste management: E-waste Management for Environmental Sustainability, chapter 14 focuses on the critical issue of solid waste management, particularly e-waste, and its implications for environmental sustainability. The chapter explores various strategies for sustainable e-waste management, including recycling, reuse, and responsible disposal practices, highlighting the importance of implementing effective policies and regulations to minimize the environmental footprint of electronic waste.

The spiritual well-being of jailed people is less studied than the relationship between criminality and religiosity has been discussed in Chapter 15. Using the Spiritual Well-Being Scale, 259 convicts in Tamil Nadu's Central, Special, and Open Air Prisons provided data. It measures Divine Connectedness (DC), Self Connectedness (SC), Other Connectedness (OC), Nature Connectedness (NC), and Spirituality Rating Index (SRI). The descriptive research study employed SPSS version 23 to analyze qualitative and quantitative data. Focusing on the Spiritual Rating Scale across dimensions, descriptive and multivariate statistical methods included frequency, mean, standard deviation, and correlation.

The chapter 16 on technology, AI, and information proliferation in healthcare and allied sciences discussed on telemedicine, wearables, and AI breakthroughs in diagnostics and drug discovery. AI-driven healthcare ethics and big data analytics' significance in health trends and policy are examined. Future trends include genomics-AI integration and quantum computing in medication development. This review shows how these interrelated factors are transforming healthcare, precision medicine, and healthcare professionals in a tech-driven world.

Chapter 17 discussed on the SDGs are vital to addressing health disparities. These goals address health inequalities' social, economic, and environmental causes. SDG 3, “Good Health and Well-being,” seeks universal healthcare and disease reduction, especially for vulnerable people. SDG 1 “No Poverty,” and SDG 10 “Reduced Inequality,” aim to remove economic barriers to healthcare. SDG 2, “Zero Hunger,” targets malnutrition as a health factor. SDGs 13 and 6 address climate change and clean water, which disproportionately affect underprivileged communities. The SDGs address these interconnected aspects to achieve global health equity in an inclusive and equitable manner.

The chapter 18, Unseen Stressor-How Pollution impacts Mental Health, provides a systematic assessment of 2007–2024 research on the complex relationship between environmental pollution and a variety of mental illnesses. The chapter concludes that integrated public health policies, strict pollution control, sustainable urban planning, and targeted interventions are needed to reduce the widespread negative effects of environmental pollution on population mental health and support resilient communities.

The chapter 19 Toxins in the Food Chain, emphasizes heavy metals' persistence in aquatic environments, their harmful effects on marine animals, and the serious health concerns, including cancer, of polluted seafood. The report recommends tight discharge limits, enhanced water quality standards, and integrated monitoring systems to reduce heavy metal contamination, biodiversity loss, and carcinogenic concerns. It emphasized on international cooperation, public awareness, and strict rules.

This book will foster the comprehensive need for substansive outcomes to guarantee a sustainable future and highlights the urgency of tackling environmental challenges. The writers have painstakingly investigated the most recent achievements in sustainability, offering an encompassing analysis of how these advancements interact with and revitalize health outcomes.

We express our gratitude to all members of IGI Global, particularly Jocelynn Hessler, Managing Editor of Book Development at IGI Global. We express our gratitude to all the reviewers for evaluating the book chapters in accordance with the instructions to ensure the quality of the articles meets global standards and publisher requirements. This edited volume is considered to have substantial implications for the United Nations Sustainable Development Goals (UNSDGs), focusing on health and well-being and targeting a broad audience that includes academics, researchers, students, corporate professionals, policymakers, investors, and the general public.

Sandeep Poddar
Lincoln University College, Malaysia

Waliza Ansar
Behala College, Kolkata, India

Chapter 1
An Analysis Health and Psychological General Well-Being Among Convicts Central Prison of Tamil Nadu

S. Srinivasan
https://orcid.org/0009-0002-0179-9849
Department of Humanities and Social Science, Graphic Era University, Deharadun, India

R. Vallipriya
https://orcid.org/0009-0008-6692-603X
Department of Physical Science, Institute of Education, Tamil Nadu Teacher Education University, India

Ajay Kumar Singh
https://orcid.org/0000-0003-0429-0925
Department of Humanities and Social Sciences, Graphic Era University, Dehradun, India

ABSTRACT

The study emphasizes the health and well-being of convicts in the central prison of Tamil Nadu. The incarcerated population is highly vulnerable and often neglected. There are studies on health and well-being, but there is limited research specific to this region. The significance of the study mainly focuses on health and well-being, specifically on factors such as personal factors, economic factors, health, familial characteristics, psychological general well-being, personality traits and their

DOI: 10.4018/979-8-3693-9755-8.ch001

relationship to psychological general well-being, psychological characteristics, offense-related factors, age and psychological general well-being, leisure time activities before and after imprisonment, marital status and well-being, extraversion and psychological general well-being, and emotional stability. The study utilized a descriptive research design, employing both qualitative and quantitative methods. A purposive sampling technique was used, with a total sample size of 173. The study was conducted in various prisons, Central Prisons.

INTRODUCTION

As per the WHO report, improving the health and well-being of prison inmates is essential. The report recommended improving the health concentration of prison inmates. It can cover various aspects of prison inmates' human rights, medical ethics, communicable diseases, and non-communicable diseases. Europe Health and (WHO,2019) report provide the Health in Prison Programme (HIPP) to share information related to best practices and health for the prison. The HIPP is the main resource for researchers, policymakers, and public health concerns to provide concrete support for them. The WHO report believes that prisoners can benefit from receiving the same standard of medical care as the general community. The health and well-being of prisoners depend on the prison regime and ethical aspects (Lines, 2008). The health concept for prisons reinforces the health and well-being of prisoners; it is not solely the responsibility of those providing healthcare for the prison. It also involves the dependence on the prison setting to be established (Woodall & Freeman, 2021).

There are other factors involved in prison health conditions, such as mental health, continuity of care, dental care, and non-custodial measures.

Mental Health: Mental health is common for everyone; however, mental health disorders are especially prevalent among prison inmates. The psychiatric care can provide more comprehensive support for the prison inmates and ensure equitable care (Ndindeng, 2024).

Continuity care: Half of the prisoners have access to community health care services (Roberts et al., 2004).

Dental care: Prison inmates face dental issues, which can deteriorate their health due to age and long-term incarceration (Amir, 2017).

Non-custodial measures: Some of the prisoners face health and human rights problems, which need to be improved through non-custodial measures (Grow, 2022).

The Tamil Nadu Prison Department supports various aspects to provide services such as health and psychological well-being for the prison inmates. It includes:

Medical Care: The prison setting in the central prison provides a nearly 50-bed hospital with medical support equipment, including X-ray, ECG equipment, and other blood analyzers. The prisoners also benefit from treatment for leprosy and TB (Guin, 2015).
Mental Health: In the central prison, psychologists and counselors are deputed to treat prisoners who experience depression, stress, anxiety, and violent behavior. They can be admitted to psychiatric care at the government hospital, which provides support for specialized treatment (Srinivasan & Rajavel, 2025).
Health camps: Inside the prison, health camps are regularly conducted to screen all the prison inmates and provide proper medical treatment support for them.
Nutritional Food: Prisoners can receive nutritional support and proper hygienic food, including a special diet for vulnerable prisoners and those who are sick and isolated, especially those affected by TB. Additionally, nursing women can receive extra care and support for their children (Bray, 2024).
Cleanliness: The food is cooked in stainless steel vessels, proper plates are provided, and clean, hygienic trolleys and mugs are used for better hygiene.
Smoking ban: Smoking is still prohibited inside the prison, but in some exceptional cases, prisoners use tree leaves to make and smoke for field observation.
Ambulances Services: Central prison ambulance services are available, especially for the special prison for women and women's sub-jails.
Clinical Laboratories: In central prisons, specific clinical laboratory tests are available for diagnostic purposes.
Sanitary napkins: Female prisoners can use sanitary napkins during their menstrual period.

The study mainly emphasizes the psychological general well-being of Tamil Nadu prison inmates to identify their personal characteristics, family background, economic status, and offense-related factors that can be linked to psychological general well-being.

RESEARCH GAP, RESEARCH QUESTIONS

The incarcerated population is highly neglected in contemporary society. This study aims to address prison inmates' health and psychological general well-being, providing concrete policy implications that can offer support for this vulnerable community. The incarcerated population faces numerous health and psychological problems. The study can address the problems and provide significant solutions, which can be used for further policy implications. The vulnerable population can benefit and achieve better advancement in their lives.

1. What is the socio-economic background of the prison inmates?
2. What psychological problems affect the respondents?
3. What offences have the respondents committed?
4. How does prison life affect the health problems of the inmates, and what are the identified causes?
5. How do the personal characteristics of prison inmates associate with their psychological general well-being?
6. How does family support associate with the psychological general well-being of prison inmates?
7. What is the relationship between the psychological characteristics of prison inmates and their psychological general well-being?
8. What is the association between offence/prison-related characteristics of prison inmates and their psychological general well-being?

FACTORS AFFECTING WELL-BEING IN PRISONS

Complete mental health is a combination of subjective well-being, comprising emotional well-being as well as objective well-being, consisting of social well-being and psychological well-being (Keyes, 2005).

CONCEPTUAL FRAMEWORK

Psychological general well-being of prison inmates results from an interplay of multiple factors. The pre-imprisonment variables considered under the study as influential factors upon psychological general well-being are personality and familial characteristics such as age, gender, income before imprisonment, marital status and place of origin, land ownership, housing and atmosphere in the parental family (Albertie et al., 2017). The other characteristics such as psychological/spiritual/personality characteristics are applicable to situations of the respondents before imprisonment as well as after imprisonment. Offence/prison related characteristics are post imprisonment variables. The background variables constitute the personal, familial, psychological, spiritual and offence/prison related characteristics of the inmates which can indirectly influence psychological general well-being. Personality traits, psychological general well-being and its dimensions, spirituality and its dimensions such as divine connectedness, self connectedness, other connectedness and nature connectedness as well as spiritual well-being comprising religious well-being and existential well-being constitute the key variables which can directly impact psychological general well- being (Thauvoye et al., 2018).

Background of the Study

The prison population in India has seen a steady increase over the years, with Tamil Nadu being one of the states with a significant number of incarcerated individuals. Central prisons, which house long-term convicts, often present unique challenges in maintaining the physical and psychological well-being of inmates. Prisoners are subjected to confinement, restricted social interaction, limited access to quality healthcare, and institutional routines that may adversely affect their general health and mental stability. Convicts, particularly those serving extended sentences, often face issues such as chronic stress, anxiety, depression, and deteriorating physical health due to the restrictive environment. These challenges are compounded by over-crowding, inadequate medical facilities, lack of recreational activities, and limited opportunities for rehabilitation and social reintegration. Despite various reforms and programs initiated by prison authorities, there remains a gap in understanding the holistic well-being of prisoners, especially from a psychological perspective.

In Tamil Nadu's central prisons, the situation reflects broader national trends but also includes unique regional dynamics related to prison administration, healthcare access, and cultural attitudes towards incarceration. Examining the health and psychological well-being of convicts in these settings is essential not only for upholding human rights but also for formulating effective intervention strategies that promote mental health, reduce recidivism, and support reintegration into society. This study aims to analyze both the physical health conditions and the psychological general well-being of convicts in selected central prisons across Tamil Nadu. It seeks to identify prevailing issues, assess the adequacy of existing health and mental health services, and explore correlations between prison conditions and inmate well-being. The findings will contribute to evidence-based policy formulation and better implementation of inmate welfare programs.

RELEVANT LITERATURE

Psychological General Well-Being Among Prison Inmates

Shri. S.K. Dogra, the former Additional Director General of Prisons, Tamil Nadu had considered prison as an ashram where one abstains from unhealthy habits and is reformed. The former ADGP had organized mediation, yoga and green thumb therapy in Puzhal Prison.

Providing physical and mental health care in prisons cannot be compromised even though correctional institutions come across various challenges in this endeavor (Klingele, 2015). Inmates are mostly influenced by staff who act towards them in a friendly and considerate tone and manner, who treat them with fairness and predictability (Pandelie, 2015). From the late nineteenth century onwards, the function of imprisonment had explicitly evolved from simple punishment to a process of moral reformation (Eadie et al., 2003). The above discussion lays a good evidence base on the significance of spirituality in enhancing well-being in general and among prison inmates.

Loss of Identity and Feelings Related to Social Stigma:

This sensitivity with regard to the terms used is important for an interviewer in correctional settings as this sets the quality of interaction with the prisoners. Social stigma, sense of social isolation, feeling that she is a convict and the biggest failure in the world and 'People treat me like dirt and slowly I am learning to live with that' were some of the expressions of the respondents (Middlemass, 2017).

FEELINGS RELATED TO LIFE IMPRISONMENT

As per the Supreme Court Judgment on November 25, 2012 *life imprisonment* means imprisonment for the entire life of a convict. Portugal was the first country in the world to abolish whole life imprisonment in 1884 (Gomes et al., 2018). The verbalisations of the respondents such as "Who is longing for the luxuries here sir, we are expecting release. According to Nicholson (1998), individual behavior reflects personality traits. But Scott & Codd (2010) has critically analyzed the idea that life imprisonment is given to dangerous offenders. According to him dangerousness could also be due to the harsh and brutal treatment and prison experiences. Some who might have been labeled 'dangerous' in one prison have settled down without doing any harm to others in another prison environment. In United States volunteers set up hospices in prisons to ease the condition of dying persons who were confined to life imprisonment. The review reveals a higher level of distress and poor well-being among prison inmates undergoing life imprisonment.

FEELINGS RELATED TO PUNISHMENT

A significant 60% view physical punishment as ineffective for crime control (Jacob & Jackson, 2010), while 74% prefer imprisonment. Only 8%, mainly older individuals, find physical punishment helpful (Rao, et al., 2018). Dscribes severe torture in prison cells, such as injecting petrol into the rectum, a practice also reported by Panthic.org (2011) as a major cause of anxiety (Kumar, 2013). From 2001–2010, over 14,231 deaths occurred in police and judicial custody in India, averaging four deaths daily (Asian Centre for Human Rights, 2011). Discipline is often linked to punishment, but effective prison management rarely relies on severe penalties (Nair, 2013). The Indian Prisons Act (2000) abolished degrading practices like handcuffs, fetters, and penal diets (Anderson, 2007). Complaints against police often result in severe reprisals, such as a prisoner being set ablaze for raising concerns (Aston, 2020). Another instance in 2004 involved police torturing a laborer who failed to pay a bribe, injecting petrol into his rectum and admitting him to a hospital under a false name (Davis, 2004). Custodial torture, unrest, group clashes, and jailbreaks compound prison tensions. Pandey, (2019) sheds light on life in Indian prisons, exposing extortion by gangs like the 'bladebaaz,' torture chambers, preferential treatment for influential inmates, sexual assaults, prolonged under-trial detentions, and the plight of innocent prisoners released without compensation after years of suffering.

RELATIONSHIP WITH STAFF AND INMATES

The study by Thompson, (2008) indicated a strained *relationship between the police and the prison inmates.* However, though 90 per cent of them had unfavorable opinion about police men, 90 per cent of them opined that the treatment of prison officials in the jail was kind/ friendly. A majority of 80 per cent of the prisoners of Bangalore central prison had a favorable attitude towards their co-inmates though *carrying tales and quarrels* were pointed out as the major problem in the study by Leask (2017). After a few years of stay, the initial fear about prison too vanishes. Some of them could *learn new crime techniques* from others (Jacobs & Helms, 1996). A favorable as well as unfavourable opinion about relationships in prison is evident from the review.

PAROLE VIOLATIONS AND RECIDIVISM

Houser et al. (2019) evaluated *parole violation rates* among inmates who had mental health problems and those who did not have mental health problems. The results revealed that 23 per cent of the inmates who had mental health problems returned to the prison sooner indicating the higher probability of recidivism among persons with mental health problems. Bakken and Visher (2018) found that more than 8 in 10 men and 9 in 10 women returning prisoners, recidivists of USA had chronic physical, mental or substance abuse conditions requiring treatment and management. Lamb and Weinberger (1998) too found that 24 per cent of the prison population had severe mental illness. The findings once again reinforce the role of poor psychological well- being as well as substance abuse in increasing recidivism.

SUBSTANCE ABUSE

Jeter, (2008) found that two-thirds of U.S. prison inmates had active substance abuse issues six months before incarceration. Inmates with psychological distress were 3.129 times more likely to have a history of alcohol use (Rossetti et al., 2014). At Bangalore Central Prison, 51.5% of prisoners reported alcohol use, nearly double the national prevalence (21%), and smoking rates increased significantly during incarceration (Math et al.,). Among substance users, most expressed a need for help: 85% of smokers, 73% of tobacco chewers, 99% of alcohol users, and 71% of drug users (Welle-Strand, 2015).

Various studies confirm widespread substance abuse issues among inmates (Fazel et al., 2006). Norway's "Narkotikaprogrammet" (Narcotics Programme), introduced in 2006, offers court-mandated treatment and follow-up for addicts and remains in practice (Bondurant, 2018). This underscores the need for counseling and de-addiction programs in prisons.

ATTEMPTS TO SUICIDE

The existing study had instances of attempt to suicide as well as attempts to escape validating the theory of Liebling, (1999) which states that the pains of imprisonment cannot be viewed only as pertaining to loss of liberty, but also related to frustrations and social causes (Ross, 2017). Baid (2015) stated that some of the prison inmates had attempted suicide due to external and internal stressors. Long period of isolation coupled with stigmatisation further aggravated suicidal behaviour.

FAMILY WELL-BEING

Incarceration impacts families through crises (Fishman, 1990), loss of dignity (Schneller et a., 2023), and victimization of children (Bloom, 1993). Weaver and Nolan (2015) highlighted how family well-being affects inmates' well-being. Parental imprisonment leads to emotional, social, financial, and developmental consequences for children, influenced by factors such as the offense, care arrangements, and socio-cultural context. Fishman (1991) showed how imprisonment disrupts spousal relationships, with wives coping creatively while facing hardships. Sfendla et al. (2022) found inmates with psychological distress were significantly more likely to experience fears about family acceptance and a history of family distress.

Children of prisoners fall into three categories: those staying with mothers in jail, those with caregivers, and self-reliant children. Murray (2007) reported that parental imprisonment causes social exclusion, loss of capital, and stigma. Aggarwal et al., (2022) found 62% of inmates had 1–3 children, with 82% being under 15 years old, requiring significant support. Bhandari (2016) emphasized placing women in prisons closer to their families and noted that caregivers are typically maternal grandmothers or family members. These findings underline the need for family-centered social work interventions to improve inmate and family well-being (Simons et al., 2016).

LINKAGE WITH FAMILY AND OUTSIDE WORLD

Prisoners maintain outside connections through newspapers, television, visitors, and family visits during bail, parole, or court appearances. Social relationships are eroded by stigma, financial strain, and when family or friends are victims of their crimes (Homer, 1979). Regular contact with prisoners can foster positive changes (Ronel et al., 2013). Non-official visitors help bridge prisons and communities, raising awareness of jail issues (Renford, 1979). Woods (2011) found that 62% of female inmates wrote letters, 73% maintained good relationships with relatives, and 60% received visitors on festive occasions. Most (67%) were satisfied with family contact. Bhandari (2016) emphasized the need for family-oriented programs, nearby prison placements, subsidized calls, and post-release support. Bhatt (2015) reported that 54.55% of female inmates in Bhopal Central Prison were never visited by family.

PSYCHOLOGICAL DISTRESS AND PSYCHOLOGICAL GENERAL WELL-BEING

Prison managers must see that the inmates use their time to re-engineer their minds (Jain, 2020). The study by Combalbert et al., (2019) revealed that the prevalence of *psychological distress* among male inmates was found to be 51.04 per cent. Choudhury (2017) questioned the primary purpose of imprisonment, namely, reform and rehabilitation as her narratives bring to light the stress, strain, pain and anxiety of prison inmates, particularly those in high security cells and those who have not got any privileges, inferring well-being among prison inmates is relative. Overall, the studies reviewed unveil the distressed mental status and poor psychological general well-being of the prison inmates in India as well as in other countries (Picken, 2012).

PSYCHIATRIC DISORDERS AND PSYCHOLOGICAL GENERAL WELL-BEING

India has the highest global rate of lifetime major depressive episodes (Kessler et al., 2012). A study in Kashmir found higher depression rates among women, the non-literate, married individuals, and those in nuclear families (Burnette, 2015). Women generally score lower on psychological well-being scales, with variations by age, and well-being is linked to health issues like cardiovascular risk and migraines (Diamond, 2007). Prisons, being stressful environments, exacerbate distress and affect inmates' well-being.

In the U.S., 8% of annual jail bookings involve individuals with severe mental illness (Haney, 2012). Indian studies reveal prisoners often suffer from depression, neurotic disorders, and feelings of worthlessness, worsened by isolation and lack of social support (Ramanjam, 2022). In Bangalore Central Prison, 12.7% experienced major depressive episodes, and 2.2% had psychosis, primarily schizophrenia—double the rates in the general population (Murugesan et al.,2021).

PROGRAMMES THAT HAVE ENHANCED WELL-BEING AMONG PRISON INMATES

Honawar (2019) emphasized the role of professional social work in providing legal support and psycho-social rehabilitation for prisoners post-release. Goal attainment contributes to well-being (Bahrami Ehasan, 2015). May, (2023) found that prisoners in maximum security focus on maintaining sanity and self-preservation to aid societal reintegration. Paseda, (2024) demonstrated that self-awareness, regulation, and motivation programs significantly benefit inmates, with gender differences observed.

Van Ginneken, (2016) noted that imprisonment could serve as a turning point for inmates, fostering positive adjustment and recovery from negative circumstances like addiction. The study advocated promoting self-efficacy and optimism over risk reduction. Van der Kaap-Deeder et al. (2017) concluded that enhancing autonomy and choice improves prisoners' quality of life.

PSYCHOLOGICAL GENERAL WELL-BEING

The term *psychological* refers to affective and cognitive processes that reflect well-being, while *general* indicates these states are derived from various subjective, non-condition-specific experiences. *Well-being* reflects the overall impact of psychological forces on an individual (Srinivasan & Rajavel, 2025). General well-being is the harmonious functioning of physical and psychological aspects, bringing personal satisfaction and societal benefit (Srinivasan & Rajavel, 2025).

HEALTH CARE FACILITIES

Every Central Prison has a hospital equipped with medicines, X-Ray, ECG machines and automatic blood analyzer. During emergency, inmates are referred to outside hospitals for specialized treatment. The prison hospital has two assistant surgeons with supporting paramedical staff. The health camp under 'varumun kappom thittam' (preventive camp) is conducted to screen the prisoners. Prisoners who need specialized treatment such as leprosy and T.B. are segregated and given treatment at the prison hospital or at Government Hospitals. To eradicate TB among prisoners, DOTS Centers have been established at Central Prisons, Vellore, Cuddalore, Tiruchirappalli, Salem and Puzhal and Special Prisons for Women at Tiruchirappalli and Vellore.

Objective of the study

- To understand the socio-economic conditions of the prison inmates
- To examine the psychological issues among prison inmates
- To identify offence-related and health problems among prison inmates
- To assess the relationship between psychological general well-being and the personal characteristics of prison inmates
- To explore the association between familial characteristics and the psychological general well-being of prison inmates

- To identify the association between selected psychological characteristics, offence-related characteristics of prison inmates, and their psychological general well-being

Main Objective of the study

The aim of the study is to examine the psychological general well-being of the inmates of the Central Prisons, Special Prisons for Women, and Open Air Prisons of Tamil Nadu, with specific reference to spirituality.

METHODOLOGY

The study adopted a cross-sectional analysis and was conducted in Tamil Nadu central prisons. The sample size was 173 respondents, and the study was conducted in various prisons in Tamil Nadu. The research design used was a descriptive research design. The sample used was a purposive sample selected from prisons. The study utilized SPSS version 23 and analyzed the data using various methods, such as simple frequency and t-tests. The study provides a comprehensive analysis and identifies results to determine further implications (Narayan et al., 2023; Srinivasan & Rajavel, 2025).

Limitation of the study

The limitation of the study mainly focused on the psychological general well-being of convicts in central prisons of Tamil Nadu. The study used a very limited sample size, which may affect the generalizability of the findings for the incarcerated population across different types of prison inmates. The health and psychological well-being may introduce bias in the study, as it focuses on prison inmates' experiences of stigma and their lack of awareness. The cross-sectional analysis captures data on health and psychological well-being over time and can analyze the relationships between various variables. The social and cultural context of prison inmates can influence the health and psychological well-being of the incarcerated population. The limitation of the study is its focus on relevant factors affecting health and psychological well-being, such as trauma and abuse, which could provide a better understanding of their psychological problems. The stigma associated with prison inmates, their mental health problems, and health issues affects the accuracy of the data. These limitations provide insight into the psychological problems of the incarcerated population and help understand the findings, offering implications for future practice.

HEALTH CHARACTERISTICS

Effective prisons provide health care which is equivalent to the standard available in the open community for which understanding is needed among the prison staff too (WHO, 2021). Table 1 sreveals a better health status of prison inmates as only 31.9 per cent of the respondents stated that they have one or the other health problem and a vast majority of 68.1 per cent of them had no health issues. The highest stated health problem was Blood Pressure (20.1 per cent) followed by diabetes (10.4 per cent), mental illness (8.7), heart problem (4.2 per cent), skin disease (2.3 per cent), surgery (2.1 per cent), cancer (1.4 per cent), Lung related problem (1.4 per cent), HIV (1.2 per cent), Tuberculosis (1 per cent) and disability (0.6 per cent).

Table 1. Health Characteristics of the Respondents

Sl. No.	Health Problems	Frequency N = *173*	Per cent
1.	**Health Problems** Has health problems Does not have health problems	*55* *118*	*31.9* *68.1*
1.	**Mental Illness** Yes No	*15* *158*	*8.7* *91.3*
2.	**Tuberculosis** Yes No	2 *171*	*1* *99*
3.	**HIV** Yes No	2 *171*	*1.2* *98.8*
4.	**Cancer** Yes No	2 *171*	*1.4* *98.6*
5.	**Blood Pressure** Yes No	*35* *138*	*20.1* *79.9*
6.	**Diabetes** Yes No	*18* *155*	*10.4* *89.6*
7.	**Skin Disease** Yes No	*4* *169*	*2.3* *97.7*
8.	**Heart Problem** Yes No	*7* *166*	*4.2* *95.8*
9.	**Lung Related problems** Yes No	*3* *170*	*1.4* *98.6*
10.	**Surgery** Yes No	*4* *169*	*2.1* *97.9*
11.	**Disability** Yes No	*1* *172*	*0.6* *99.4*

The fact that s (8.7 per cent) interviewed had episodes of mental illness reveal the poor psychological well-being of prison inmates. As many as 16 per cent of the world population suffer from mental disorders. In Tamil Nadu, the population of persons with mental disorders is found to be 77 lakhs (www.tnhealth.org).Among the 5203 prison inmates who suffer from mental illness in India, 2744 (52.7 per cent) inmates are convicts. Among the 51 respondents who suffer from mental illness in Tamil Nadu, 19 prisoners (37. 3 per cent) are convicts (National Crime Records Bureau, 2016). As per this study, among the 173 respondents, 15 prison inmates (8.7 per cent) reported to have a history of mental illness. The fact that the three highest reported health problems are blood pressure, diabetes and mental illness indicate the prevalence of stress among these prison inmates. It also indicates the need for diet food.

PSYCHOLOGICAL CHARACTERISTICS

Table 2 shows that the usual thinking pattern of a vast majority of 81.9 per cent of the respondents is about the future indicating their reluctance to dwell in the past which might activate unpleasant and traumatic memories of crime and arrest, their inability to find meaning in the present life in prison as well as their eagerness to move out of the prison all of which reflect a poor well-being that they experience behind bars. This is further substantiated by the fact that the major concern of a majority of 83 per cent of them is about home and the major concern of a majority of 83.6 per cent of them is on release. The rehabilitation package for prison inmates needs to incorporate mindfulness training which can set the here and now mental-mode among them, characterized by maximum attention to the present-moment experiences, being devoid of judgment, elaboration or emotional reactivity. Mindfulness is a way of holding attention 'on purpose' (Sanyal, 2015).

Table 2. Psychological Characteristics

Sl.	Psychological Characteristics	Frequency N = *173*	Per cent
1	**Feeling** Felt accepted Did not feel accepted	*103* *70*	*59.8* *40.2*
2	**Usual Thinking** Thoughts about the past Thoughts about the present Thoughts about the future No thoughts at all	*11* *13* *141* *8*	*6.4* *7.3* *81.9* *4.4*
3	**Thoughts of Concern – Home** Yes No	*143* *18* *12*	*83.0* *10.4* *6.6*

continued on following page

Table 2. Continued

Sl.	Psychological Characteristics	Frequency N = *173*	Per cent
4	**Thoughts of Concern – Release** Yes Somewhat No	*144* *19* *10*	*83.6* *10.8* *5.6*
5	**Experience of trusting** Yes No	*127* *46*	*73.6* *26.4*
6	**Challenges Faced in Prison** Stage in life and Live with them Try to escape from them and avoid Too exhausted and depressed to face them All the above	***96*** *36* *40* *1*	*55.4* *20.8* *23.0* *0.8*
7	**Daily activities stress** Mostly able Sometimes Mostly unable	*132* *16* *25*	*76.3* *9.5* *14.3*
8	**Mode of Responding to Clashes** Withdraw/Give in to the others' views Dialogue Argue strongly/ Shout and use violence	*72* *80* *21*	*41.7* *46.5* *11.8*
9	**Alcohol Use** Yes Sometimes No	*83* *44* *46*	*48.3* *25.3* *26.4*
10	Substance used Yes No	*16* *157*	*9.5* *90.5*

Positive psychological setting: 59.8% of prison inmates feel accepted by their families, and 73.6% have experienced trusting relationships.

Resilience: Defined as effective coping and bouncing back (Singh & Gupta, 2015; APA, 2018). While 76.3% of inmates manage daily activities despite stress, 44.6% struggle with challenges, indicating a need for resilience training.

Conflict management: 46.5% use assertive strategies like dialogue and compromise, while 41.7% adopt submissive methods, and 11.8% rely on aggression. Assertiveness training is needed for rehabilitation.

Substance use: 73.6% report alcohol use, with 25.3% being social drinkers. Drug abuse is less prevalent (9.5%). These findings highlight the influence of substance use among inmates.

Offence Related Characteristics

Prison type: Most respondents (69.7%) are from central prisons, consistent with Tamil Nadu's high central prison population (95.95%). A smaller proportion are from special prisons for women (22.6%) and open-air prisons (7.7%).

Prison experience: 66.8% have been confined to only one prison, and 94.4% are first-time offenders.

Criminal classification: Nearly all respondents (99%) are criminal prisoners, with very few political (3) or civil prisoners (2).

Sentencing: A majority (62.7%) are serving life imprisonment; 78.5% of respondents were convicted of murder-related crimes, including attempt to murder, abetment to suicide, and culpable homicide.

Other offenses: Include sexual assaults (7.5%), theft/robbery (4.8%), dowry-related crimes (2.9%), offenses under arms/explosives/goonda acts (2.5%), narcotics-related crimes (2.1%), and forgery/property offenses (1.5%).

Table 3. Offence Related

Sl. No.	Offence Related Characteristics	Frequency N = *173*	Per cent
1.	**Type of Prison**	*120*	*69.7*
	Central Prison for Men	*39*	*22.6*
	Special Prison for Women	*14*	*7.7*
	Open Air Prison		
2.	**Number of Prisons entered**	*115*	*66.8*
	Nil	*44*	*25.3*
	1-2	*12*	*6.8*
	3-4	*2*	*1.2*
	5 <		
3.	**Number of Times Sentenced to Imprisonment**	*163*	*94.4*
	First offender 2-3 times	*7*	*3.9*
	More than 3 times	*3*	*1.7*
4.	**Frequency of Crime Based Category**	*163*	*94.4*
	First Offender	*10*	*5.6*
	Sentenced more than one time		
5.	**Legal Category**	*171*	*99.0*
	Criminal Prisoner	*1*	*0.4*
	Civil Prisoner	*1*	*0.6*
	Political Prisoner		
6.	**Duration of Sentence**	*65*	*37.3*
	Determinate Imprisonment	*108*	*62.7*
	Life Imprisonment		
7.	**Lawyers Engaged**	*113*	*65.4*
	Private	*50*	*29.0*
	Government - Legal Aid Self	*10*	*5.6*
	No Facility available		
8.	**Legal Support**	*29*	*16.4*
	Good	*48*	*28.0*
	Average	*96*	*55.6*
	Poor/No response		

continued on following page

Table 3. Continued

Sl. No.	Offence Related Characteristics	Frequency N = *173*	Per cent
9.	**Imprisonment Completed Time** < 4 years 5-12 years 13-20 years >21 years	*82* *58* *29* *4*	*47.7* *33.8* *16.2* *2.3*
10.	**Parole Availed** One week > 10 days > 20 > 30 days	*117* *27* *11* *7* *11*	*68.0* *15.4* *6.2* *3.9* *6.6*
11.	**Privileges Availed –Convict Official** Yes No N/A	*24* *85* *64*	*13.7* *49.0* *37.3*
12.	**Good Conduct** Yes No	*81* *92*	*46.9* *53.1*
13.	**Privileges availed – Personal Cash Property** Yes No	*127* *46*	*73.6* *26.4*
14.	**Prizes won any event in priosn** Yes No	*75* *98*	*43.2* *56.8*
15.	**Educational Qualification** Nil Secondary 10th Standard Higher Secondary/Technical course UG/PG	*110* *6* *25* *19* *13*	*63.7* *3.3* *14.7* *10.8* *7.5*
16.	**Occupation in Prison** No Job Farming Convict Warder/librarian/ Teaching prison inmates/ Hospital care Electrician/ Barber Cooking work/Cleaning work/Gardening maintain Student	*34* *61* *18* *26* *25* *9*	*19.5* *35.3* *10.2* *14.9* *14.7* *5.4*
17.	**Daily Wages at Present** Not applicable weekly > 30 Quarterly Does not know	*132* *193* *92* *34* *67*	*25.5* *37.3* *17.8* *6.6* *12.9*
18.	**Frequency of Visit by Family Members** Every week Often Sometimes Rarely Never	*41* *42* *36* *54*	*22.8* *24.3* *21.8* *31.1*

continued on following page

Table 3. Continued

Sl. No.	Offence Related Characteristics	Frequency N = 173	Per cent
19.	**Visitors – Parents** Yes No Not applicable (Aged/Passed away)	44 85 44	25.7 49.0 25.3
20.	**Visitors – Wife** Yes No Not applicable (Unmarried)	154 218 146	29.7 42.1 28.2
21.	**Type of Visitors – Sons/Daughters** Yes No Not applicable	35 105 33	20.3 60.6 19.1
22.	**Category of Visitors – Friends/Relation** Yes No	7 166	3.9 96.1
23.	Family Members visiting Yes No	21 152	11.8 88.2
24.	**Visitors** Do not get visitors Has Visitors	55 118	31.5 68.5

A large proportion (69.7%) are confined in central prisons for men, with fewer in women's prisons (22.6%) and open-air prisons (7.7%). Most (66.8%) have not been transferred to other prisons, indicating stability in placement. The majority are first-time offenders (94.4%), with very few repeat convictions, suggesting a relatively low rate of recidivism. Nearly all are criminal prisoners (99%), while civil and political prisoners are rare. More than half (62.7%) are serving life sentences, indicating the seriousness of offences. Most engaged private lawyers (65.4%), though 29% used legal aid. However, over half (55.6%) reported poor or no legal support, pointing to a gap in legal aid effectiveness. Almost half (47.7%) have served less than 4 years, while 33.8% have completed 5–12 years. Parole usage is high (68% for one week), but long-term parole (>30 days) is limited. Less than half (46.9%) are recognized for good conduct, while only 13.7% reported accessing official privileges. On personal entitlements, 73.6% have availed cash/property privileges, and 43.2% won prizes during prison events, suggesting some engagement in constructive activities. Educational backgrounds are mostly low, with 63.7% lacking formal qualifications, though a few possess higher secondary or UG/PG degrees. Occupationally, 35.3% are involved in farming, while others work in maintenance, healthcare, or teaching roles. A smaller group (19.5%) remain without work. Wages vary, with some unaware of their income or receiving it irregularly, highlighting transparency or literacy issues in wage systems. Family contact is uneven; 31.1% rarely receive visits, while 22.8% are visited weekly. Only 25.7% receive visits from parents and 29.7% from spouses. Visits from children (20.3%), friends (3.9%), or relatives are limited. Notably, 88.2% do not have family members visiting, and 31.5% do not receive visitors at all, indicating social isolation.

DISCUSSION

Health Characteristics of the Respondents

Effective prisons ensure healthcare equivalent to community standards, requiring staff awareness (Varghese et al., 2019). A survey revealed that 31.9% of inmates reported health issues, while 68.1% had none. Common health problems included blood pressure (20.1%), diabetes (10.4%), and mental illness (8.7%). Less common issues were heart problems (4.2%), skin diseases (2.3%), and tuberculosis (1%).

Psychological Characteristics of the Respondents

A significant majority (81.9%) of inmates focus on the future, avoiding past memories of crime and imprisonment, reflecting poor well-being. Concerns about home (83%) and release (83.6%) further highlight their distress. However, positive psychological experiences are evident as 59.8% feel accepted by their families, and 73.6% experience trusting relationships. Resilience is notable among inmates, with 76.3% managing daily activities despite stress, and 55.4% accepting challenges as part of life. Despite low psychological well-being (mean score: 52.34 ± 21.647), many continue their responsibilities, demonstrating resilience. Regarding conflict management, 46.5% use healthy assertive skills, while others rely on submissive (41.7%) or aggressive (11.8%) approaches (Srinivasan et al., 2025). Alcohol use is self-reported by 73.6% (48.3% regular users, 25.3% social drinkers), while drug abuse is reported by 9.5%. Similar trends have been observed in previous studies.

Offence Related Characteristics of the Respondents

Most respondents (69.7%) are from central prisons, with fewer from women's prisons (22.6%) and open-air prisons (7.7%), reflecting a distribution that differs from the state-wide prison composition. A large majority are first-time offenders (94.4%) and are serving life sentences (62.7%). Most have been incarcerated for less than 12 years (81.5%), while a smaller portion (19.5%) have served between 13 and 29 years. The most common offence is murder (78.5%), followed by sexual assault

(7.5%) and theft or robbery (4.8%). In terms of legal representation, 65.4% hired private lawyers, while 29% relied on legal aid. However, 58.6% rated their legal support as poor, highlighting the challenges faced by prisoners from economically weaker backgrounds (Srinivasan & Rajavel, 2025). Only 32% availed parole, with reasons for non-eligibility including pending appeals, lack of eligibility, or absence of family support. Access to leisure and educational opportunities is limited. A majority (67.6%) reported the absence of structured leisure activities, and 63.7% had no formal educational background. Activities such as prayer (47.7%) and watching television (52.5%) are the main forms of daily engagement.

Approximately 75.1% are engaged in work within prison, including farming, maintenance, and support services, though only 55.1% reported receiving wages. Many contribute their earnings to support their families outside prison. Social connections remain weak for many, with 68.1% reporting no visitors. Among those who do receive visits, spouses (29.7%) and parents (25.7%) are the primary visitors. Relationships within the prison appear more positive—63.1% describe their interactions with fellow inmates as cooperative, and 50.6% report good relationships with prison staff. Emotional challenges are prevalent, largely due to long-term incarceration, limited social interaction, and weak family bonds. Despite this, some inmates have shown resilience by helping others financially to access legal aid or apply for parole, indicating strong internal solidarity and coping strategies among some individuals (Ballaret, 2025).

Factors Influencing Psychological General Well-Being Other

The respondents' mean Psychological General Well-Being Index (PGWBI) score was 52.34±21.647, indicating overall distress. A majority (78.2%) reported severe psychological issues, while only 13.1% experienced positive well-being, and 9.7% reported marginal well-being. Gender differences were significant ($t = 3.167$; $p<.01$), with males (53.95±22.423) scoring higher than females (46.81±17.743) across all six PGWBI dimensions—anxiety, depressed mood, positive well-being, self-control, general health, and vitality. The lowest scores were on positive well-being (7.14±3.982), reflecting severe distress. Anxiety and depressed mood also showed high distress levels, while vitality, self-control, and general health indicated marginal well-being (Valdebenito et al., 2024).

Personal Characteristics and Psychological General Well-Being

Apport: Inmates without supportive friends scored lower (48.42±22.581) than those with support (58.84±20.401) ($F = 12.064$; $p<.01$).

Economic Characteristics and Psychological General Well-Being

Below Poverty Line (BPL) respondents reported the lowest well-being (47.36±9.066) ($p<.01$). Inmates who frequently experienced starvation had poor well-being (49.45±20.865) ($p<.01$). Other factors like land and house ownership or occupation before imprisonment showed no significant influence on well-being (Western, 2018).

Familial Characteristics and Psychological General Well-Being

Variables related to marital family such as marital family atmosphere ($F_{=}4.227$; $p<.01$), children's occupational status ($F_{=}4.730$; $p<.01$), caretaker of children ($F_{=}4.149$; $p<.01$) as well as variables related to both parental and marital families, that is, imprisonment of family members (($F=3.319$; $p<.01$) and feeling of acceptance by the family ($F_{=}4.227$; $p<.05$) significantly impacted the psychological general well-being of the respondent prison inmates. A higher level of psychological general well-being was observed among those whose marital families were conflictual, among those whose children are students, among those whose children are taken care of by either the spouse or other family members, among those whose family members are not imprisoned and those who felt accepted by their families. On the other hand, variables such as parental family atmosphere, respondent being the head of the family, alcohol/Drug abuse by the family members did not have a statistically significant influence upon the psychological general well-being of the respondents.

Personality Traits and Psychological General Well-Being

Extraversion: A vast majority of inmates, both male (90.5%) and female (82.9%), exhibited low levels of extraversion, contradicting Eysenck's theory that crime is linked to extraverts. This aligns with studies suggesting personality changes over time and with environmental influences (Srinivasan et al., 2025).

Other Traits: Most inmates scored low on openness to new experiences (79.9%), extraversion (88.8%), and emotional stability (87.1%), reflecting reserved, anxious, and tense personalities in prison. However, many scored moderately high on:**Agreeableness** (54.6%, mean 5.25): Reflecting warmth, sympathy, and adaptability, likely influenced by the prison environment. **Conscientiousness** (77.8%, mean 5.70): Indicating dependability, discipline, and systematic behavior shaped by "prisonisation."

Gender and Traits: No significant gender-based differences were observed in personality traits. **Well-Being Association**: Emotional stability, agreeableness, and conscientiousness—more interior traits—positively correlated with psychological well-being, whereas openness to experience did not. The findings highlight how prisonisation fosters conforming, conscientious, and introverted traits, challenging traditional theories linking deviance with impulsive and aggressive personalities.

Psychological Characteristics and Psychological General Well-Being

There is a highly significant association between inmates' usual thinking patterns and their Psychological General Well-Being (PGWB) scores ($F=4.725$; $p<.01$). Those who focused on the present reported the highest PGWB (mean 61.32), while individuals who concentrated on the past (51.88) or future (52.23) showed lower well-being. The lowest PGWB scores (40.13) were recorded among inmates who reported having no particular thoughts, indicating a state of severe psychological distress. The ability to face frustrations is also significantly related to PGWB ($F=26.167$; $p<.01$). Inmates who accepted frustrations as part of life had the highest PGWB scores (58.29). Those who tended to avoid frustrations scored lower (50.82), while inmates unable to cope with such situations recorded the lowest scores (38.99), reflecting considerable emotional strain (Ellin et al., 2023).

A similar pattern is observed in handling responsibilities under stress. There is a strong relationship between the ability to maintain responsibilities despite stress and PGWB ($F=43.239$; $p<.01$). Inmates who managed to uphold their responsibilities scored higher in well-being (56.09), while those who could not maintain routines under stress had the lowest PGWB (32.45), signifying deep psychological distress. Finally, there is a strong positive correlation between sound sleep and PGWB ($r=0.688$; $p<.01$). This suggests that inmates who experience better sleep tend to report higher psychological well-being, and improved well-being in turn promotes better sleep quality, indicating a mutually reinforcing relationship (Srinivasan & Ilango, 2015).

Offence Related Characteristics and Psychological General Well-Being

Inmates housed in open-air prisons reported the highest levels of psychological general well-being (PGWB) with a mean score of 81.95, indicating a notably positive mental state. Conversely, inmates in Special Prisons for Women showed the lowest PGWB scores (46.81), while those in central prisons fell in the mid-range (50.85), with a statistically significant variation among these groups ($F=50.083$; $p<.01$). The term of sentence also had a significant impact on well-being. Inmates with determinate (fixed-term) sentences reported better PGWB (57.26) compared to those serving life sentences (49.42), highlighting how clarity around sentence duration contributes to psychological stability (t=4.049; p<.01). Access to cash property in prison proved to be a strong determinant of well-being. Inmates who possessed prisoner's cash property (PCP) had significantly higher PGWB (54.88) than those without such resources (41.28), suggesting that financial independence or control correlates with better psychological outcomes (t=4.531; p<.01).

Participation in prison work was another significant factor. Working inmates had notably higher PGWB (54.96) compared to their non-working peers (41.50) (t=5.779; p<.01). Among various occupations, farm workers enjoyed the highest PGWB (79.06), while those involved in prison industries had the lowest scores (46.44), demonstrating a clear variation across job types (F=35.082; p<.01). Engagement in leisure activities was linked with higher PGWB scores (54.53), whereas those without leisure engagement scored lower (47.77), suggesting that meaningful pastimes contribute positively to inmates' psychological state (t=3.359; p<.01). Relationships played a crucial role in well-being. Inmates reporting positive relationships with co-inmates had significantly higher PGWB (63.51) than those without such connections (44.12) (F=30.024; p<.01). Similarly, good relations with prison staff also correlated with better mental well-being (58.14 vs. 49.31) (F=15.400; p<.05). However, certain variables such as the type of lawyer engaged, leave (parole) availed, and frequency of visitor interactions did not show any significant association with PGWB, suggesting these factors may have less direct impact on psychological well-being in the prison context.

Age and Psychological General Well-Being

Among the dimensions of psychological general well-being, the highest negative correlation is observed to be between age and general health (r=-.364; p<.01) indicating the highest impact of ageing upon general health followed by self control, vitality, depressed mood, positive well-being and anxiety indicating a comparatively higher level of physical distress with ageing. A highly statistically significant inverse relationship exists between age of the prison inmates and psychological general well-being (r=-.208; p<.01) as measured by the Psychological General Well-Being Index (PGWBI) inferring rejection of null hypothesis.

Gender and Psychological General Well-Being

There exists highly significant association between gender and psychological general well-being (t=3.167; p<.01). A lower level of psychological well-being is indicated among women as the mean score on PGWBI for women was 46.81± 17.7443 while men inmates had a higher mean psychological general well-being, that is, 53.95±22.423. While considering the various dimensions of psychological general well-being, a highly significant association is indicated between gender and general health based well-being ($t = 4.451$; $p < .01$), followed by depressed mood based well-being ($t = 2.943$; $p < .01$) and vitality based well-being ($t = 2.845$; $p < .01$). A significant association is found between gender and anxiety based well-being ($t = 2.335$; $p < .05$) followed by self control based well-being ($t = 2.324$; $p < .05$). No significant association is found between gender and positive well-being based well-being ($t = 2.324$; $p > .05$). The male respondents reported higher levels of well-being in terms of the six dimensions of psychological general well-being compared to female respondents. The null hypothesis is rejected (Muring'u et al., 2021).

Marital Status and Well-Being

A statistically significant variation is signified by one way ANOVA between marital status of the prison inmates and their psychological general well-being ($F = 5.968$; $p < .05$). A higher level of psychological general well-being, higher than the overall mean PGWB is reported by the unmarried prison inmates (59.58 ± 18.581) and married prison inmates who are living with their spouses (59.72 ± 22.678). The respondents who are widowed/widower/divorcee/separated demonstrated a lower level of psychological well-being, that is, 49.55 ± 21.621. The finding reflects the poor psychological general well-being of the respondent prison inmates who have strained marital relationships and who are single parents. The finding is significant at .05 level and hence the null hypothesis is rejected.

Extraversion and Psychological General well-Being

No statistically significant association was observed between extraversion and psychological general well-being ($t = .806$; $p > .05$). The finding infers that being enthusiastic and sociable in prison may not indicate a high level of psychological general well-being. The null hypothesis is accepted.

Emotional Stability and Psychological General Well-Being

A statistically highly significant association is observed between emotional stability and psychological general well-being ($t = 7.238$; $p < .01$). The prison inmates whose emotional stability indicated a low level had a lower score on psychological general well-being index too (49.81 ± 20.257) while those who had a higher level of emotional stability indicated a much higher level of psychological general well-being (69.37 ± 23.122). The finding reflects the significance of maintaining emotional stability in effectively coping with stressful situations which can enhance their well-being. The null hypothesis is rejected.

Duration of Sentence and Psychological General Well-Being

Justice Mulla Committee (1983) and various prison reform committees have advocated for determinate sentence rather than indeterminate sentence. Prison inmates undergoing determinate sentence were hypothesized to have a higher level of psychological general well-being than those undergoing life imprisonment. The respondents who were awarded determinate sentence are found to have a higher level of global psychological general well-being, that is, 57.26±22.881, compared to those who are sentenced to indeterminate or life imprisonment (49.42±20.358) substantiating the adverse repercussions of life imprisonment. The certainty of release is thus proved to be an incentive that raises hope for those under determinate sentence whereas hopes fade away in the uncertainty of life imprisonment behind the bars. The finding is statistically significant at .01 level ($t_{=}4.049$; $p<.01$). The null hypothesis is rejected.

Implications and Recommendations for Government and Policy Formulation

Life Imprisonment and Determinate Sentences 62.7% of respondents are serving life imprisonment. 89.2% suggest determinate sentencing for life convicts, as seen in countries like Portugal and Norway that have abolished life imprisonment. Reviewing life sentences and introducing phase-wise reform programs or general amnesty is recommended.

First Offenders and Open-Air Prisons: 94.4% of respondents are first-time offenders, emphasizing the need for probation and alternative forms of imprisonment, like open-air prisons. Only 0.82% of inmates are in open-air prisons, yet they show the highest psychological well-being. More such prisons should be established, even for life convicts.

Humane Treatment in High-Security Prisons: High-security facilities cause severe social deprivation, leading to psychological issues. A call for more humane treatment and efforts to reduce poverty and unemployment to prevent crime is emphasized.

Social Workers in Prisons: Few states (e.g., Tamil Nadu and Kerala) employ social workers in prisons. All states should integrate social workers to facilitate rehabilitation and reintegration.

Family Support and Counseling: Governments and NGOs should enhance family bonds through counseling and training programs to prevent crime and support rehabilitation. Prisoner Family Support Cells should assist families with legal, educational, and welfare needs (Hasan, 2017).

De-addiction Programs: Alcohol and drug abuse are common among inmates. A comprehensive strategy to tackle addiction, beginning with awareness campaigns and curriculum integration, is necessary.

Family Visits: Liberalizing prison rules for family visits is crucial. Accommodating inmates in prisons close to their hometowns and fostering family interactions can reduce depression and improve discipline.

Training for Prison Staff: Regular training in management, counseling, and stress management should be provided to staff to enhance inmate and staff relationships. Adequate relaxation time and access to counseling for prison staff are essential to their well-being.

Reformative and Rehabilitation Programs: Long-term reformation programs addressing all stages of inmates' lives are critical. Establish aftercare homes for reintegration, supported by government and NGOs.

Crime Prevention: Addressing poverty and unemployment through robust poverty alleviation programs is key to reducing crime.

Substance-Free Society: A national strategy against substance abuse, involving education, monitoring, and awareness, is essential for long-term impact. These recommendations advocate for systemic changes to improve rehabilitation, well-being, and the humane treatment of prison inmates.

IMPLICATIONS AND RECOMMENDATIONS FOR CORRECTIONAL ADMINISTRATION

To improve the well-being of prison inmates, several key measures must be prioritized based on the study findings. The psychological state of inmates, particularly in high-security settings, remains critically low, marked by heightened anxiety and depression. This underscores the urgent need for therapeutic interventions such as counseling, yoga, physical exercise, and outdoor activities, with a specific focus on inmates in maximum security facilities. Inmates housed in open-air prisons exhibited significantly better psychological well-being, highlighting the benefits of a less restrictive and more rehabilitative environment. Expanding this model, especially to Special Prisons for Women and Central Prisons, could greatly enhance mental health outcomes across the prison system. Spiritual engagement emerged as a powerful contributor to well-being. Initiatives that promote prayer, religious involvement, nature-based engagement, and emotional counseling can foster a deeper sense of inner peace and connectedness. Alongside this, structured rehabilitation programs incorporating mindfulness, resilience training, and conflict resolution techniques can equip inmates with tools to manage stress and interpersonal relationships more effectively.

Health care services must be strengthened, with particular attention to elderly and mentally ill inmates. Specialized services, including mental health support and trained psychiatric professionals, are essential to address their complex needs. Employment within prison, especially in areas like farming, was shown to enhance psychological well-being. Broadening occupational opportunities can keep inmates engaged, build their skills, and support rehabilitation. These work programs should be linked with occupational therapy strategies to maximize their benefit. Legal and family support systems require considerable reinforcement. Many inmates lack access to adequate legal aid due to financial constraints. Strengthening legal assistance and enhancing family counseling and communication channels can ease legal burdens and support emotional stability, particularly for reintegration after release. Leisure activities remain underutilized despite their strong correlation with improved well-being. Encouraging inmates to participate in creative, social, and physical activities—such as drawing, group discussions, or fitness sessions—can significantly boost their morale and mental health.

Integrating spirituality into rehabilitation offers a holistic path toward healing. Programs should promote not only physical and psychological wellness but also spiritual growth, creating a balanced and positive outlook among inmates. Innovative initiatives, such as inmate-led organic farming and other prison industries, present valuable opportunities for vocational training, income generation, and self-esteem building. These projects deserve institutional support as part of long-term reform strategies. Lastly, empowering inmates with greater autonomy over their work, education, and leisure choices can lead to increased satisfaction and well-being. Encouraging self-direction within structured programs can foster a sense of agency, making rehabilitation more meaningful and sustainable. Collectively, these measures form a comprehensive strategy aimed at transforming prison environments into spaces that promote healing, growth, and successful reintegration into society.

Future Implication of the study

The future implications of the study on health and psychological well-being among the incarcerated population in Tamil Nadu. The findings of the study can help policymakers develop solutions for the health and psychological problems faced by the incarcerated population. The study leads to targeting people to provide interventions, improve policies, and enhance the well-being of the incarcerated populations. The study highlights the various gaps in health services in the prison setting to promote prison administration's allocation of resources to improve medical services and enhance psychological support for prison inmates. This can increase equitable access to health care for the incarcerated population. Rehabilitation programs can support and consider the psychological needs of the incarcerated population and provide successful reintegration into society upon their release. The study can improve prison inmates' awareness campaigns, such as those targeting prison staff, inmates, and the general community, regarding the importance of health and mental health in the context of well-being. The study's outcome provides a comprehensive understanding of prison staff and mental health awareness for crisis intervention and techniques for addressing the psychological problems of prison inmates. The results of the study can address the prison inmates' needs in the prison setting by providing individual counseling, vocational training support, and mental health care services. Longitudinal studies can support the health and psychological well-being of the incarcerated population by providing interventions. The holistic approach can adopt the prison inmates' health and their physical, mental, and social well-being in the care and practices within the prison system. The study can provide prison inmates the opportunity to advocate for the health and psychological aspects of their rights and human rights. The study can address the need for more support for the rehabilitation of prison inmates and benefit not only individuals but also society and the incarcerated population as a whole.

CONCLUSION

The conclusion of the study on psychological general well-being for the incarcerated population in central prisons in Tamil Nadu highlights that the study plays a vital role in improving the overall well-being of the inmates. The prison inmates face challenges related to vulnerable individuals, including mental health disorders, physical health problems, and socioeconomic factors. The findings of the study on health and psychological general well-being relate to their personal characteristics, family conditions, and economic situation. The study examines the association between health and psychological well-being in healthcare services in the prison setting. It can support mental health conditions, medical situations, and promote various rehabilitation programs, benefiting the incarcerated population. The health and psychological support are important in the prison setting, as they can strengthen the correctional policy in prison administration. The study ultimately enhances the health and psychological well-being of convicts in correctional settings. The study emphasizes the quality of life for the incarcerated population and provides the necessary support for their reintegration into society.

REFERENCES

Aggarwal, K., Gupta, J., Kaur, R. K., Bansal, D., & Jain, A. (2022). Effect of anxiety and psychologic stress on periodontal health: A systematic review and meta-analysis. *Quintessence International*, *53*(2). https://web.p.ebscohost.com/abstract?site=ehost&scope=site&jrnl=00336572&AN=156241338&h=dZtpMPPrrdm4w8K PMID: 34595909

Albertie, A., Bourey, C., Stephenson, R., & Bautista-Arredondo, S. (2017). Connectivity, prison environment and mental health among first-time male inmates in Mexico City. *Global Public Health: An International Journal for Research, Policy and Practice*, *12*(2), 170–184. DOI: 10.1080/17441692.2015.1091023 PMID: 26465257

Amir, N. (2017). *Exploring oral health and dental care experiences, perceptions and behaviours of adults whose parents were incarcerated during their childhood* (Doctoral dissertation, University of British Columbia). DOI: 10.14288/1.0354451

Anderson, C. (2007). *The Indian Uprising of 1857-8: Prisons, Prisoners, and Rebellion*. Anthem Press. https://www.google.co.in/books/edition/The_Indian_Uprising_of_1857_8/FBrFfrIDOtEC?hl=en&gbpv=1&dq=+The+Indian+Prisons+Act+(2000)+abolished+degrading+practices+like+handcuffs,+fetters,+and+penal+diets+(Roy,+2003).&pg=PR7&printsec=frontcover

Aston, J. N. (2020). *Torture Behind Bars: Role of the Police Force in India*. Oxford University Press., https://www.google.co.in/books/edition/Torture_Behind_Bars/IOrkDwAAQBAJ?hl=en&gbpv=1&dq=Complaints+against+police+often+result+in+severe+reprisals,+such+as+a+prisoner+being+set+ablaze+for+raising+concerns+(Asian+Legal+Resource+Centre,+2004)&pg=PT10&printsec=frontcover DOI: 10.1093/oso/9780190120986.001.0001

Bahrami Ehsan, Z. (2015). *Psychological predictors of well-being in relation to goal attainment* (Doctoral dissertation, UNSW Sydney). DOI: 10.26190/unsworks/18444

Baid, S. (2015). Mental health and psychiatric morbidity in prisoners. *IOSR Journal of Nursing and Health Science*, *4*(9), 67–72. DOI: 10.9790/1959-04346772

Bakken, N. W., & Visher, C. A. (2018). Successful reintegration and mental health: An examination of gender differences among reentering offenders. *Criminal Justice and Behavior*, *45*(8), 1121–1135. DOI: 10.1177/0093854818774384

Ballaret, J. R. (2025). Behind the Bars and Beyond: A Qualitative Exploration of Filipino Families Embracing Returning Prisoners. *The Family Journal (Alexandria, Va.)*, *10664807251325557*, 10664807251325557. Advance online publication. DOI: 10.1177/10664807251325557

Bhandari, A. (2016). Women prisoners and their dependent children: A study of Jaipur and Jodhpur central jails in Rajasthan. *Sociological Bulletin, 65*(3), 357–379. DOI: 10.1177/0038022920160304

Bhatt, A. (2015). Study on the need of prison reforms in India. https://elibrary.ddn.upes.ac.in/bitstream/123456789/1970/1/Anjali%20Bhatt.pdf

Bloom, B. (1993). Why Punish the Children. *A Reapraisal of the Children of Incarcerated Mothers in America/National Council on Crime and Delinquincy*. https://core.ac.uk/download/pdf/71342923.pdf

Bondurant, S. R. (2018). *Essays on Health and Abuse* (Doctoral dissertation). https://oaktrust.library.tamu.edu/items/a9cf26cc-da77-4aab-9427-3931551a55f3

Bray, P. K. (2024). *Health Status of Prison Inmates: A Qualitative Study of Akuse Prison in The Lower Manya Krobo Municipality in The Eastern Region of Ghana* (Doctoral dissertation, Ensign Global College). https://repository.ensign.edu.gh/handle/123456789/228

Burnette, D. (2015). Help-Seeking for 'Memory Loss' by Older Adults in India: Patient, Caregiver and Health Providers' Perspectives. https://run.unl.pt/bitstream/10362/15216/1/Burnette%20Denise%20TM%202015.pdf

Choudhury, S. (2017). *Behind Bars: Prison Tales of India's Most Famous*. Roli Books Private Limited. https://www.google.co.in/books/edition/Behind_Bars_Prison_Tales_of_India_s_Most/1qohEAAAQBAJ?hl=en&gbpv=1&dq=Choudhury+(2017)+questioned+the+primary+purpose+of+imprisonment,+namely,+reform+and+rehabilitation+as+her+narratives+bring+to+light+the+stress,+strain,+pain+and+anxiety+of+prison+inmates,+&pg=PT10&printsec=frontcover

Combalbert, N., Pennequin, V., Ferrand, C., Keita, M., & Geffray, B. (2019). Effect of age, time spent in prison and level of education on the perceived health and quality of life of elderly prisoners. *International Journal of Prisoner Health, 15*(2), 168–180. DOI: 10.1108/IJPH-09-2018-0048 PMID: 31172858

Davis, C. C. (2004). *So close to goddess: Myth, history, and the power feminine in Ana Castillo's novel "So Far From God"*. University of California., https://www.proquest.com/openview/ddde6827f46f0ed2a40db39d124ce6bd/1?pq-origsite=gscholar&cbl=18750&diss=y

Diamond, M. (2007). The impact of migraine on the health and well-being of women. *Journal of Women's Health, 16*(9), 1269–1280. DOI: 10.1089/jwh.2007.0388 PMID: 18001183

Eadie, T., Morley, R., Baldock, J., Manning, N., & Vickerstaff, S. (2003). Crime, justice and punishment. *Social Policy*, •••, 541–573. https://books.google.co.in/books?id=6WqcAQAAQBAJ&newbks=0&printsec=frontcover&pg=PA369&dq=From+the+late+nineteenth+century+onwards,+the+function+of+imprisonment+had+explicitly+evolved+from+simple+punishment+to+a+process+of+moral+reformation+(House+of+Commons,+2009).+&hl=en&source=newbks_fb&redir_esc=y#v=onepage&q&f=false

Ellin, M. R., Ramoo, V., Yahaya, N. A., & Pin, T. M. (2023). Association between affiliate stigma and psychological well-being among caregivers of patients with dementia: A quantitative report. [MJN]. *The Malaysian Journal of Nursing*, *14*(4), 132–141. DOI: 10.31674/mjn.2023.v14i04.014

Fazel, S., Bains, P., & Doll, H. (2006). Substance abuse and dependence in prisoners: A systematic review. *Addiction (Abingdon, England)*, *101*(2), 181–191. DOI: 10.1111/j.1360-0443.2006.01316.x PMID: 16445547

Fishman, L. T. (1990). *Women at the wall: A study of prisoners' wives doing time on the outside*. State University of New York Press.https://books.google.co.in/books?id=Ico9Gw4SUrgC&newbks=0&printsec=frontcover&pg=PR9&dq=Incarceration+impacts+families+through+crises+(Fishman,+1990)&hl=en&source=newbks_fb&redir_esc=y#v=onepage&q&f=false

Fishman, L. T. (1991). Treacherous trysts, tender trade: Prisoners' wives as contacts and contraband carriers. *Women & Criminal Justice*, *2*(2), 45–70. DOI: 10.1300/J012v02n02_04

Gomes, S., Leote De Carvalho, M. J., Oliveira, R. V., & Duarte, V. (2018). Trends and challenges in the Portuguese penitentiary system: from law to practice. *Antigone, 13*(1/2), 61-102.https://irep.ntu.ac.uk/id/eprint/44519/

Grow, M. (2022). A Prosecutorial Duty to Seek Non-Custodial Sentencing. *Geo. J. Legal Ethics, 35*, 805. https://heinonline.org/HOL/LandingPage?handle=hein.journals/geojlege35&div=36&id=&page=

Guin, S. (2015). *Prison inmates living with HIV in India: case studies from prisons in Maharashtra*. Springer. https://www.google.co.in/books/edition/Prison_Inmates_Living_with_HIV_in_India/wfVICAAAQBAJ?hl=en&gbpv=1&dq=l+with+medical+support+equipment,+including+X-ray,+ECG+equipment,+and+other+blood+analyzers.+The+prisoners+also+benefit+from+treatment+for+leprosy+and+TB.&pg=PR5&printsec=frontcover

Haney, C. (2012). Prison effects in the era of mass incarceration. *The Prison Journal, 0032885512448604*, 0032885512448604. Advance online publication. DOI: 10.1177/0032885512448604

Hasan, S. S. (2017). Impact of Health Educational Program upon upon Care Givers Knowledge and Practices for Psychosocial Problems of aCUTE Leukemia Adolescent Patients. [MJMR]. *Malaysian Journal of Medical Research, 1*(4), 12–17. https://ejournal.lucp.net/index.php/mjmr/article/view/276

Homer, E. L. (1979). Inmate-family ties: Desirable but difficult. *Federal Probation, 43*, 47. https://heinonline.org/HOL/LandingPage?handle=hein.journals/fedpro43&div=12&id=&page=

Honawar, M. (2019). Social Work Intervention with Women Offenders: A Pathway to Prevent Recidivism. *Asian Social Work Journal, 4*(4), 35–46. DOI: 10.47405/aswj.v4i4.112

Houser, K. A., Vîlcică, E. R., Saum, C. A., & Hiller, M. L. (2019). Mental health risk factors and parole decisions: Does inmate mental health status affect who gets released. *International Journal of Environmental Research and Public Health, 16*(16), 2950. DOI: 10.3390/ijerph16162950 PMID: 31426341

Jacobs, D., & Helms, R. E. (1996). Toward a political model of incarceration: A time-series examination of multiple explanations for prison admission rates. *American Journal of Sociology, 102*(2), 323–357. DOI: 10.1086/230949

Jacobs, D., & Jackson, A. L. (2010). On the politics of imprisonments: A review of systematic findings. *Annual Review of Law and Social Science, 6*(1), 129–149. DOI: 10.1146/annurev-lawsocsci-102209-152933

Jain, K. R. R. (2020). Effective and Humane Restoration of Prisoners With Special Reference to India. *Journal of Victimology and Victim Justice, 3*(1), 113–127. DOI: 10.1177/2516606920904296

Jeter, K. (2022). *Returning Home: The Role of Recovery Management Checkups on Housing, Employment, Abstinence Self-Efficacy and Quality of Life Among Formerly Incarcerated Black Women with a History of Substance Use Disorder* (Doctoral dissertation, UC Berkeley). https://escholarship.org/uc/item/3zd6s847

Kessler, R. C., Birnbaum, H. G., Shahly, V., Bromet, E., Hwang, I., McLaughlin, K. A., Sampson, N., Andrade, L. H., Girolamo, G. D., Demyttenaere, K., Haro, J. M., Karam, A. N., Kostyuchenko, S., Kovess, V., Lara, G., Levinson, D., Matschinger, H., Nakane, Y., Browne, M. O., & Stein, D. J. (2010). Age differences in the prevalence and co-morbidity of DSM-IV major depressive episodes: Results from the WHO World Mental Health Survey Initiative. *Depression and Anxiety*, *27*(4), 351–364. DOI: 10.1002/da.20634 PMID: 20037917

Keyes, C. L. (2005). Gender and subjective well-being in the United States: From subjective well-being to complete mental health. *Psychology of stress*, 1-15. https://www.google.co.in/books/edition/Psychology_of_Stress/G0W7P3Sxt1QC?hl=en&gbpv=1&dq=Complete+mental+health+is+a+combination+of+subjective+well-being,+comprising+emotional+well-being+as+well+as+objective+well-being,+consisting+of+social+well-being+and+psychological+well-being+(Ryff+and+Keyes,+1995).+&pg=PA1&printsec=frontcover

Klingele, C. (2015). The promises and perils of evidence-based corrections. *Notre Dame L. Rev., 91*, 537. https://heinonline.org/HOL/LandingPage?handle=hein.journals/tndl91&div=17&id=&page=

Kumar, J. (2013). In Search of New Scene of Crime: A Need of Forensic Science in Investigation of Custodial Crimes. *Indian J. Criminology, 41*, 141.https://heinonline.org/HOL/LandingPage?handle=hein.journals/idnjlocmly41&div=13&id=&page=

Lamb, H. R., & Weinberger, L. E. (1998). Persons with severe mental illness in jails and prisons: A review. *Psychiatric Services (Washington, D.C.)*, *49*(4), 483–492. DOI: 10.1176/ps.49.4.483 PMID: 9550238

Leask, A. (2017). *Behind Bars: Real-life stories from inside New Zealand's prisons*. Penguin Random House New Zealand Limited. https://www.google.co.in/books/edition/Behind_Bars/2fCcDwAAQBAJ?hl=en&gbpv=1&dq=+favorable+attitude+towards+their+co-inmates+though+carrying+tales+and+quarrels+in+prison+imates&pg=PT12&printsec=frontcover

Liebling, A. (1999). Prison suicide and prisoner coping. *Crime and Justice*, *26*, 283–359. https://www.journals.uchicago.edu/doi/abs/10.1086/449299. DOI: 10.1086/449299

Lines, R. (2008). The right to health of prisoners in international humanrights law. *International Journal of Prisoner Health*, *4*(1), 3–53. DOI: 10.1080/17449200701862145 PMID: 18382849

Math, S. B., Murthy, P., Parthasarthy, R., Kumar, C. N., & Madhusudhan, S. 2. PRISON AND HEALTH. https://d1wqtxts1xzle7.cloudfront.net/7331010/chapter_2-_h_h_in_prisons-libre.pdf?1390850955=&response-content-disposition=inline%3B+filename%3D2_PRISON_AND_HEALTH.pdf&Expires=1732892156&Signature=AsmXoipVMYQ71X~uxggEaTD3ODEnckpaDO-

May, A. (2023). In the Shadow of the 'Big House'Redefining halfway houses within the debate over incarceration.https://open.uct.ac.za/items/50af7db9-f594-46b2-b24a-646b8aea707a

Middlemass, K. (2017). *Convicted and condemned: The politics and policies of prisoner reentry*. NyU Press. https://www.google.co.in/books/edition/Convicted_and_Condemned/DVi1DgAAQBAJ?hl=en&gbpv=1&dq=ocial+stigma,+sense+of+social+isolation,+feeling+that+she+is+a+convict+and+the+biggest+failure+in+the+world+and+%E2%80%98People+treat+me+like+dirt+and+slowly+in+prison+setting&pg=PP9&printsec=frontcover

Muring'u, P. N. U., Kariuki, M., & Njonge, T. (2021). Influence of physiological stress coping strategies on the psychological well-being of life-sentenced inmates in maximum-security prisons in Kenya. *Editon Consortium Journal of Psychology. Guidance and Counseling*, *3*(1), 242–258. DOI: 10.51317/ecjpgc.v3i1.283

Murray, J. (2007). The cycle of punishment: Social exclusion of prisoners and their children. *Criminology & Criminal Justice*, *7*(1), 55–81. DOI: 10.1177/1748895807072476

Murugesan, M., Damodharan, D., Naik, S. S., Parthasarathy, R., Kumar, C. N., & Math, S. B. (2021). Prison Mental Health. *FORENSIC PSYCHIATRY IN INDIA*, 126. https://www.researchgate.net/profile/Shalini-Naik/publication/351902644_Forensic_Psychiatry_in_India_-_Interface_of_Indian_Laws_and_Mental_Health/links/611500671e95fe241ac6a293/Forensic-Psychiatry-in-India-Interface-of-Indian-Laws-and-Mental-Health.pdf#page=133

Nair, N. (2013). Beyond the 'communal' 1920s: The problem of intention, legislative pragmatism, and the making of Section 295A of the Indian Penal Code. *The Indian Economic and Social History Review*, *50*(3), 317–340. DOI: 10.1177/0019464613494622

Narayan, G., Vasudevan, K., Rajagopal, A., Gunasekaran, K., Savla, H., Suvvari, T. K., & Gunasekaran, K.Jr. (2023). Active Screening for Pulmonary Tuberculosis Among Jail Inmates: A Mixed Method Study From Puducherry, South India. *Cureus*, *15*(5). Advance online publication. DOI: 10.7759/cureus.39749 PMID: 37398710

Ndindeng, A. N. (2024). Mental health and well-being in prisons and places of detention. *International Journal of Prison Health*. Advance online publication. DOI: 10.1108/IJOPH-07-2024-0035 PMID: 39465264

Nicholson, I. A. (1998). Gordon Allport, character, and the" culture of personality," 1897–1937. *History of Psychology, 1*(1), 52–68. DOI: 10.1037/1093-4510.1.1.52 PMID: 11620320

Pandeli, J. (2015). *Orange-collar workers: An ethnographic study of modern prison labour and the involvement of private firms* (Doctoral dissertation, Cardiff University). https://orca.cardiff.ac.uk/id/eprint/83532/

Pandey, A. (2019). *Movement allies: the politics of civil rights activism in India (1960s-1980s)* (Doctoral dissertation, University of Oxford). https://ora.ox.ac.uk/objects/uuid:4290038a-e5d4-48f6-a915-9f795b167f24

Paseda, O. K. (2024). *"I'ma Person Beyond My Past": An Interpretive Phenomenological Analysis of Black Women Reentry After Incarceration* (Doctoral dissertation, University of Georgia). https://www.proquest.com/openview/154edee0343f7377816b6d340ef88f6b/1?pq-origsite=gscholar&cbl=18750&diss=y

Picken, J. (2012). The coping strategies, adjustment and well being of male inmates in the prison environment. *Internet Journal of Criminology, 2012*, 1-29. https://d1wqtxts1xzle7.cloudfront.net/80111102/b93dd4_63ebd332965f40f9b28f85d9bc37e63f-libre.pdf?1643878436=&response-content-disposition=inline%3B+filename%3DThe_Coping_Strategies_Adjustment_and_Wel.pdf&Expires=1732894287&Signature=PkExj3z3VEAQ6uKSSQCBx5jH2IXXu3hAbUcPv79aGC2mistxA4P1DU9KhJyQnm2e-vTlJ-

Ramanjam, S. N. N. (2022). The Imprisoned Prisoner: Interpreting Ways to Facilitate Recovery and Growth for Prisoners. How Do Rehabilitative Services in Prisons Support Prisoner Well-Being? A Hermeneutic Literature Review. https://openrepository.aut.ac.nz/items/d432e6ee-ff52-4b61-943e-af75ffdf242b

Rao, G., Manaf, R. A., & Minhat, H. S. (2018). A Review on Determinants of Depression among Adult Prisoner. *Malaysian Journal of Medicine & Health Sciences, 14*(2). https://www.researchgate.net/profile/Rosliza-Manaf/publication/326007537_A_Review_on_Determinants_of_Depression_among_Adult_Prisoner/links/5b32ebc00f7e9b0df5ccc450/A-Review-on-Determinants-of-Depression-among-Adult-Prisoner.pdf

Renford, R. K. (1979). *The Non-Official British in India, 1883-1920*. University of London, School of Oriental and African Studies., https://www.proquest.com/openview/3c8747f285e19b004c05349e9bbed506/1?pq-origsite=gscholar&cbl=2026366&diss=y

Roberts, C., Kennedy, S., & Hammett, T. M. (2004). Linkages between in-prison and community-based health services. *Journal of Correctional Health Care, 10*(3), 333–368. DOI: 10.1177/107834580301000306

Ronel, N., Frid, N., & Timor, U. (2013). The practice of positive criminology: A Vipassana course in prison. *International Journal of Offender Therapy and Comparative Criminology, 57*(2), 133–153. DOI: 10.1177/0306624X11427664 PMID: 22094598

Ross, C. E. (2017). *Social causes of psychological distress.* Routledge., DOI: 10.4324/9781315129464

Rossetti, C., Spena, G., Halfon, O., & Boutrel, B. (2014). Evidence for a compulsive-like behavior in rats exposed to alternate access to highly preferred palatable food. *Addiction Biology, 19*(6), 975–985. DOI: 10.1111/adb.12065 PMID: 23654201

Sanyal, N. (2015). Mindfulness meditation: The essential stressbuster in military life context. *Positive Psychology: Application in Work, Health and Well-being, edited by Kumar, U., Parkash, 2015*, 134-147. https://www.google.co.in/books/edition/Positive_Psychology/3YnCCwAAQBAJ?hl=en&gbpv=1&dq=Mindfulness+is+a+way+of+holding+attention+%E2%80%98on+purpose%E2%80%99+(Chaskalson,+2011+as+cited+in+Sanyal,+2015).&pg=PA134&printsec=frontcover

Schneller, H., Kasdan, D., Kaufman, R. E., & Wilson, A. (2023). Dobbs v. Jackson Women's Health Organization: Reckoning with its Impact and Charting a Path Forward. *U. Pa. J. Const. L., 25*, 1002. https://heinonline.org/HOL/LandingPage?handle=hein.journals/upjcl25&div=36&id=&page=

Scott, D., & Codd, H. (2010). *Controversial issues in prisons.* McGraw-Hill Education (UK).https://www.google.co.in/books/edition/Life_Imprisonment/aCd9DwAAQBAJ?hl=en&gbpv=1&dq=But+Stern+(2006)+has+critically+analyzed+the+idea+that+life+imprisonment+is+given+to+dangerous+offenders.&pg=PP1&printsec=frontcover

Sfendla, A., Martinsson, B., Filipovic, Y., Senhaji, M., & Kerekes, N. (2022). Psychological distress in a sample of Moroccan prisoners with drug-dependence. *International Journal of Offender Therapy and Comparative Criminology, 66*(10-11), 1093–1108. DOI: 10.1177/0306624X211010286 PMID: 33882747

Simons, I., Mulder, E., Rigter, H., Breuk, R., van der Vaart, W., & Vermeiren, R. (2016). Family-centered care in juvenile justice institutions: A mixed methods study protocol. *JMIR Research Protocols, 5*(3), e5938. DOI: 10.2196/resprot.5938 PMID: 27619801

Srinivasan, S., & Ilango, P. (2015). The Elderly Inmates in the Indian Prisons–A Psychosocial Perspective. In *The 2nd International Social Work Conference*. https://www.researchgate.net/profile/Srinivasan-Sekaran/publication/374628926_Perpustakaan_Negara_Malaysia_Cataloging-in-Publication_Data_The_2nd_International_Social_Work_Conference_2015_-Celebrating_Diversity_in_One_World/links/652783cd82fd2a6bab881311/Perpustakaan-Negara-Malaysia-Cataloging-in-Publication-Data-The-2nd-International-Social-Work-Conference-2015-Celebrating-Diversity-in-One-World.pdf

Srinivasan, S., & Rajavel, N. (2025). A Study of the Psychological Well-Being of Tamil Nadu Prison Inmates With Special Reference of AI. In *AI Technologies and Advancements for Psychological Well-Being and Healthcare* (pp. 219–254). IGI Global., DOI: 10.4018/979-8-3693-9158-7.ch009

Srinivasan, S., & Rajavel, N. (2025). Artificial Intelligence Approach to Psychological Wellbeing Among the Ageing Population. In *AI Technologies and Advancements for Psychological Well-Being and Healthcare* (pp. 187–218). IGI Global., DOI: 10.4018/979-8-3693-9158-7.ch008

Srinivasan, S., Rajavel, N., & Mahmoudi-Dehaki, M. (2025). Elderly Inmates Living With Dementia in Central Prisons. In *Assistive Technology Solutions for Aging Adults and Individuals With Disabilities* (pp. 343–404). IGI Global Scientific Publishing., DOI: 10.4018/979-8-3693-6308-9.ch015

Srinivasan, S., Rajavel, N., & Sanchez, N. K. (2025). The Impact of AI on Elderly Inmates in Central Prison. In *Exploration of AI in Contemporary Legal Systems* (pp. 281–314). IGI Global Scientific Publishing., DOI: 10.4018/979-8-3693-7205-0.ch013

Thauvoye, E., Vanhooren, S., Vandenhoeck, A., & Dezutter, J. (2018). Spirituality and well-being in old age: Exploring the dimensions of spirituality in relation to late-life functioning. *Journal of Religion and Health*, *57*(6), 2167–2181. DOI: 10.1007/s10943-017-0515-9 PMID: 29063369

Thompson, A. C. (2008). *Releasing prisoners, redeeming communities: Reentry, race, and politics*. NYU Press. https://www.google.co.in/books/edition/Releasing_Prisoners_Redeeming_Communitie/vnEmtS2pRqIC?hl=en&gbpv=1&dq=+90+per+cent+of+them+had+unfavorable+opinion+about+police+men,+90+per+cent+of+them+opined+that+the+treatment+of+prison+officials+in+the+jail+was+kind/+friendly&pg=PR7&printsec=frontcover

Valdebenito, V., Benjumeda, I., Hadler, V., & Guzmán, S. (2024). The high costs of freedom: Subjective well-being and mental health in prisoners in Chile. *International Journal of Prison Health*, *20*(4), 434–449. DOI: 10.1108/IJOPH-12-2023-0087

Van der Kaap-Deeder, J., Audenaert, E., Vandevelde, S., Soenens, B., Van Mastrigt, S., Mabbe, E., & Vansteenkiste, M. (2017). Choosing when choices are limited: The role of perceived afforded choice and autonomy in prisoners' well-being. *Law and Human Behavior, 41*(6), 567–578. DOI: 10.1037/lhb0000259 PMID: 28771016

Van Ginneken, E. F. (2016). Making sense of imprisonment: Narratives of posttraumatic growth among female prisoners. *International Journal of Offender Therapy and Comparative Criminology, 60*(2), 208–227. DOI: 10.1177/0306624X14548531 PMID: 25182466

Varghese, F. P., Israel, T., Seymour, G., Becker Herbst, R., Suarez, L. G., & Hargons, C. (2019). Injustice in the justice system: Reforming inequities for true "justice for all". *The Counseling Psychologist, 47*(5), 682–740. DOI: 10.1177/0011000019892329

Weaver, B., & Nolan, D. (2015). Families of prisoners: A review of the evidence. https://strathprints.strath.ac.uk/68426/

Welle-Strand, G. K. (2015). Opioid maintenance treatment in pregnancy: Maternal and neonatal outcomes. https://www.duo.uio.no/handle/10852/48185

Western, B. (2018). *Homeward: Life in the year after prison*. Russell Sage Foundation. https://books.google.co.in/books?hl=en&lr=&id=oDBUDwAAQBAJ&oi=fnd&pg=PT7&dq=Other+factors+like+land+and+house+ownership

Woodall, J., & Freeman, C. (2021). Developing health and wellbeing in prisons: An analysis of prison inspection reports in Scotland. *BMC Health Services Research, 21*(1), 1–9. DOI: 10.1186/s12913-021-06337-z PMID: 33827565

Woods, T. E., Jr. (2011). *Rollback: Repealing Big Government Before the Coming Fiscal Collapse*. Regnery Publishing. https://www.google.co.in/books/edition/Rollback/GInmAgAAQBAJ?hl=en&gbpv=1&dq=Boyapati+(2014)+found+that+62%25+of+female+inmates+wrote+letters,+73%25+maintained+good+relationships+with+relatives,+and+60%25+received+visitors+on+festive+occasions&pg=PA1&printsec=frontcover

World Health Organization. (2019). Status report on prison health in the WHO European Region. https://iris.who.int/bitstream/handle/10665/329943/9789289054584-eng.pdf

World Health Organization. (2021). The WHO Prison Health Framework: A framework for assessment of prison health system performance.https://iris.who.int/bitstream/handle/10665/344561/9789289055482-eng.pdf?sequence=3

Chapter 2
Bridging the Climate Gap: Leveraging Green Infrastructure and Technology for Resilient Health Systems in Developing Nations

Priya Makhija
https://orcid.org/0000-0002-7436-2798
Jain University, India

Anita Walia
Jain University, India

R. Thanga Kumar
https://orcid.org/0000-0003-2594-7543
Jain University, India

A. Vyshnavi
https://orcid.org/0000-0003-4508-6904
Jain University, India

Shankar Prasad Prasad
https://orcid.org/0000-0002-7008-3361
Jain University, India

ABSTRACT

Green infrastructure is a crucial strategy for climate change adaptation, enhancing health, air quality, and patient outcomes. It also offers ecosystem services that improve human health and well-being. However, the benefits of green infrastructure have not been thoroughly assessed. Geographic Information Systems (GI) in the

DOI: 10.4018/979-8-3693-9755-8.ch002

context of climate change can provide economic and public health benefits. Green infrastructure, including sustainable building techniques, water management systems, and renewable energy systems, reduces reliance on finite resources and promotes environmental sustainability. Advancements in technology, such as early warning systems, telemedicine, and health data analytics, enhance operational effectiveness, disaster preparedness, and service delivery. This book chapter explores the potential of green infrastructure and technology in constructing resilient health systems in developing nations, highlighting the need for a comprehensive strategy that combines innovation and sustainability to address climate change.

INTRODUCTION

Green infrastructure is defined as "an interconnected network of green space that preserves the values and functions of natural ecosystems and offers related benefits to human populations (Canzonieri, 2007) and has been identified as an effective adaptation strategy for climate change (Byrne & Jinjun, 2009). The implementation of green infrastructure as a climate adaptation strategy has promise for mitigating the many health hazards associated with climate change, encompassing both mental and physical health and wellness. For dangers associated with excessive heat, this is especially true. High temperatures raise the chance of both death and illness (Field, 2014). From an adaptation standpoint, it offers several advantages, including as improved air quality, cooling, and less floods. It also offers a variety of ecosystem services that enhance human health and well-being and make cities more livable (van den Berg et al., 2015). Human civilizations can profit from the preservation of the ecological system and the integration of biodiversity and ecological mechanisms into territorial design and execution, according to the theory behind green infrastructure. One of the two main features of green infrastructure is multifunctionality and interconnectedness (Phillips et al., 2022).

Human health is being seriously impacted by climate change, which opens up new problems and raises the need for robust health systems. Heatwaves, wildfires, droughts, floods, and storms are among the climate-related disasters that are occurring more frequently, which has a wide variety of negative health effects. These include ailments brought on by the heat, wounds, mental health issues, vector-borne infections, food and water-borne infections, and disorders of the heart, lungs, and kidneys. Because of the increased demands for services, the strain on infrastructure, the disruption of supply chains, and the resulting costs, healthcare systems must become more resilient in order to adjust to climate change (Okara, 2024). The ability, competence, and capacity of the health system to anticipate, avoid, prepare, absorb, adapt, and change when subjected to shocks and pressures and provide regular health services continuously during crisis management is known as health system resilience (Ezzati et al., 2023). In order to achieve long-term gains in population health despite an unstable environment, a climate-resilient health system must be "able to anticipate, respond to, cope with, recover from, and adapt to climate-related shocks and stress" (World Health Organization, 2021). Expert opinions on the urgent need to strengthen health system resilience in the face of climate change, especially for vulnerable populations including remote communities and those in developing nations, were highlighted at a roundtable discussion hosted by Economist Impact Events. In the long term, investing in health systems can greatly lower carbon emissions, improve patient outcomes, and yield substantial financial returns by enhancing healthcare infrastructure, streamlining the supply chain and waste management, and promoting the development and application of cutting-edge medical devices. Infrastructure, innovation, supply chains, and labor skills must all be strengthened for a better global healthcare system, and this requires a concerted, community-led effort to match data systems with creative finance (Okara, 2024)

The usefulness of green infrastructure as a climate change adaptation approach is supported by a sizable body of research. This is due to the fact that green infrastructure may, among other things, enhance water management, control the temperature, and lessen air pollution. It has still to be thoroughly ascertained, nevertheless, to what degree these quantified physical advantages lead to better human health outcomes. The advantages of employing green infrastructure as a climate change adaptation strategy for human health have not yet been thoroughly assessed or quantified (K. J. Bowen et al., 2014). Recent innovations like green walls and roofs have received little attention in the research on the health advantages of green infrastructure, which has mostly focused on green areas and natural settings. The lack of a consistent scientific framework for assessing the economic health value of green infrastructure projects makes it challenging to compare and analyze financial estimates in a methodical manner. This assessment highlights the pressing need to strengthen the financial case for green infrastructure and standardize methodologies in order to enable fair and sustainable city growth (Kathryn J. Bowen & Lynch, 2017).

Green infrastructure is essential for enhancing human and environmental health as well as for creating habitats for animals. To reduce environmental effects, compact design techniques have been adopted and metropolitan areas have grown as a result of urbanization. This might weaken networks of green infrastructure and turn urban space into a battlefield. Potential trade-offs and synergies between wildlife support and mental health are revealed by a thorough assessment of the features of urban green areas. A One Health-based paradigm is put out, including the connections among wildlife support, mental health, and green space quality. This all-encompassing viewpoint could offer helpful advice for better green space management and design that enhances all aspects (Felappi et al., 2020). The influence of human activity on global environmental systems, of which climate change is a major element, is referred to as the Anthropocene. There are serious risks to human health and welfare from this, and those risks are expected to increase over the next several decades. Increased health-related adaptation efforts are needed to lessen these risks, taking into account various policy and demographic groupings as well as regional sociocultural contexts. Because of the complexity of climate change risks and their connections to other global health challenges, a worldwide effort is required to address underlying problems and mitigate the consequences of climate change (Thomas, 2017). The scientific community is becoming more interested in planning GI to support sustainability in the global context of climate change, according to a report by (Sokolova et al., 2024) According to the study's findings, GI may play a significant strategic role in tackling the environmental and socioeconomic issues that cities face globally. The relationship between GI and climate change was another significant finding, with climate change being one of the most often used phrases. Thus, it is clear from this viewpoint that the scientific community supports the use of GI as a strategy for mitigating and/or adapting to the negative consequences of climate change. The use of Geographic Information Systems (GI) to solve the environmental and socioeconomic concerns posed by climate change is gaining traction in the scientific community. New approaches are required to assess GI's advantages from an economic and public health standpoint, since it may be used as a tool for adaptation and mitigation. (Caparrós-Martínez et al., 2021).

Ying et al., (2022) found that the US leads Europe in green infrastructure publications and publishing houses, followed by the UK, Italy, and Sweden. However, the lack of research in South America, Asia, and Africa may restrict how broadly applicable the conclusions of green infrastructure may be. Given their growing urbanization and ecological environmental problems, the report recommends that future research concentrate on emerging regions. There isn't a widely accepted definition or assessment criteria for green infrastructure in the literature, which is essential for planning and scientific study. A study conducted by (Arzo & Hong, 2024) reveals the significance of the connections between environmental sustainability, skill development, policy stability, and green policies in accomplishing Sustainable Development Goal 13. Stable policies are necessary to address environmental challenges, as evidenced by the high association found between skill development, stable policy, and green technology innovation. With a focus on the importance of skill development in improving environmental sustainability outcomes, this research also examines the dynamics surrounding global events such as the COP27 and G20 Summits. The Change Initiative is an international research fund dedicated to healthcare that is climate resilient. It seeks to lessen the need for resource-intensive therapies and treatments, lessen the impact on the environment, and enhance population health. The project is also looking into financial incentives and performance-based measures as means of encouraging green healthcare practices. Identifying environmental pressure points, mapping the global healthcare landscape, and investigating trade-offs between environmental, financial, and health outcomes are the objectives of the study. The project is utilizing each stakeholder's distinct capabilities to solve important health issues and dismantle barriers between them (Charlotte Ashton, 2024).

According to a study by Zuniga-Teran et al., (2020) there are five main obstacles to the deployment of green infrastructure: design standards, regulatory channels, socioeconomic trends, financeability, and innovation. It recommends a systematic design procedure that takes into account social and ecological purposes as well as multifunctionality. Performance may be enhanced through certification programs and engagement from stakeholders. Socioeconomic problems continue to exist, including gentrification and low public engagement. Although it's unclear who finances the investment and how to measure the results, financial viability is vital (Nassani et al., 2023). Many developing nations are striving to meet GI targets in the next ten years, which is fueling the green versus blue infrastructure debate. It offers information on various results that ought to be regarded as important elements in the mainstream literature. In the current study, a framework for improving GI performance in the business contexts of developing, demanding energy enterprises was presented. This framework was based on pollution reduction, green and blue infrastructure, and the role of green technology. using a quantitative approach to gather data and validate the relative importance of the research variables. An important contribution was made by green and blue infrastructure, which shed light on the notable effects of green technology's moderating function and pollution reduction's mediating role on GI. Furthermore, without green technology's crucial role, GI cannot become a reality. Making health systems climate adaptable requires sufficient funds and resources. Health expenses rise as a result of climate change's detrimental consequences on people's health. A sustainable budget is also necessary to improve the health system's resilience and adaptation. In poor nations, the annual cost of adapting to climate change is around USD 70 billion, and by 2030, it is expected to reach USD 140–300 billion (Neufeldt, Henry; Christiansen, Lars; Dale, 2021).

A climate change resilient health system requires good governance, evidence-based policymaking, strategic planning, and cooperation with a range of stakeholders, particularly those involved in sectors that impact people's health, such as urban planning, energy, nutrition, and water and sewage (Mosadeghrad & Shahsavani, 2023). The development of strategic health policies and the strategic management of climate-related shocks to health systems depend on leadership and governance actions. The national plan and policy for climate change should prioritize health. In order to address present and future health hazards, several nations have created national health and climate change policies as well as national health adaptation plans. Additionally, national and local inter-sectoral coordination should be improved. However, it has been noted that multi-sectoral partnerships and the execution of plans are difficult (*Health and Climate Change: Country Profile 2021: Czechia*, n.d.). Health services and policy should take climate change into account. To address the health consequences of climate change in other sectors' initiatives, political leadership is also crucial. Therefore, in order to address the underlying causes of climate change and its effects on health, there is a need for more cooperation between the health sector and other sectors that determine health, such as agriculture and urban planning. Expanding institutional capabilities to deliver improved health care may also be accomplished by involving a variety of stakeholders (Sen et al., 2017).

The inclusion of climate change strategies into regional development plans in Europe, namely in Greece, is the focus in the study (Kalogiannidis et al., 2024) conducted by which focused on Economic stability, environmental sustainability, and social well-being are all seriously threatened by climate change. Regional growth is higher in areas with more options for climate change initiatives, according to the study. But obstacles to integrating climate change continue to have a big impact on regional development. Barrier-ridden regions are more likely to implement conventional climate change policies, such reducing emissions and switching to renewable energy sources. In order to support long-term sustainability objectives, environmental sustainability, and economic growth, this study emphasizes the significance of incorporating climate change solutions into regional development policies. The role of civil society in mitigating climate change is examined in the research conducted by Angel P. A., 2024, with particular attention paid to their initiatives in grassroots projects, policy reform, and community empowerment. Using a mixed-methods approach, the study examines both qualitative and quantitative data in Kerala's Ernakulam district. Civil society uses resource distribution, capacity building, and education to promote community ownership of climate action. In addition, they encourage sustainable farming methods and renewable energy initiatives while holding governments responsible for climate pledges. According to the report, civil society fosters cooperation between communities, governments, and the private sector, resulting in more successful mitigation methods for climate change. The creation of workable mitigation and adaptation strategies is imperative in light of the current climate emergency. Radiative forcing geoengineering, negative emissions technologies, and traditional mitigation technologies are the three primary approaches. All technologies should be used if they are both technically and financially feasible, but there is no one-size-fits-all answer to climate change. Alternative strategies are required to accomplish the objectives of the Paris Agreement, as decarbonization initiatives alone are not enough. Although it could stabilize greenhouse gas concentrations, radiative forcing geoengineering is not a sustainable solution. When combined with ongoing decarbonization initiatives, negative emissions technologies—like biogenic-based sequestration techniques—offer a sound option. However, governments and policymakers should provide suitable policy tools and support structures because carbon pricing for negative emissions is still in its infancy. Market-based procedures and more financial assistance should be made available by the financial sector to encourage carbon removal initiatives (Fawzy et al., 2020).

Methodology: This chapter employs a qualitative research methodology anchored in literature mapping to explore the interdisciplinary connections among Climate Resilient Health Systems, and their implications within the context of developed nations.

LITERATURE REVIEW

As public health demands and global climate goals converge, the relationship between health systems and climate change has drawn more attention. In order to improve health system resilience and support climate action, a substantial body of research now highlights the necessity of integrated and transformative strategies. At the macro level, (Chan et al., 2021) proposed a catalytic framework that links climate ambition with sustainable development, emphasizing the co-benefits of integrated climate-health coverage methods. This units the foundation for fitness structures to behave no longer simply as responders, but as proactive marketers in climate mitigation and adaptation efforts. Their framework promotes a systems-wondering technique, where sustainability, fairness, and climate ambition are interconnected levers for transformation.

Ridde et al., (2024), through case studies in Bangladesh and Haiti, exemplified the contextual complexity of embedding resilience in health systems. His paradigm acknowledges that resilience isn't a destination or end point but a more fluid phenomenon conditioned by social, political and environmental inputs. The experience of these countries is illustrative of the broader reality faced by many low- and middle-income countries where vulnerabilities are compounded by underdeveloped infrastructure and governance limitations.

Even systematic reviews keep underpinning the crucial need for preparedness. A review conducted in 2023 in *the*Gkouliaveras et al., (2025) suggested that the world was not prepared for a major health crisis, with significant health system readiness deficiencies, including deficits in early warning systems, inter-agency coordination, and community awareness and engagement. Such findings highlight the importance of climate risk assessments as part and parcel of public health planning.

Moreover, adaptation strategies are increasingly seen not as reactive mechanisms but as transformative opportunities. Teshome, (2023) argued for health systems that are adaptive by design—responsive to shifting climate baselines, technologically empowered, and community-oriented. Their research stressed the role of anticipatory governance and cross-sectoral collaboration in building future-ready systems.

Regional knowledge sharing has also emerged as a strategic enabler. Fears et al., (2023) emphasized that inter-regional collaboration is vital for capacity building, especially in areas with shared vulnerabilities. Platforms for exchanging data, practices, and innovations can bridge gaps in implementation and reduce duplication of effort.

In terms of actionable interventions, Braithwaite et al., (2024) detailed how decarbonization of healthcare operations—through green procurement, energy-efficient infrastructure, and low-emission care delivery—can significantly reduce environmental footprints without sacrificing service quality. This approach aligns with a global movement toward planetary health, where environmental stewardship is integrated into medical practice.

Zurynski et al., (2024) concentrated more on human capital, emphasising that the foundation of resilience-building must be skill development and workforce planning. This entails educating administrators about data literacy, preparing frontline staff in climate-health risk management, and creating flexible staffing models that adapt to disruptions brought on by climate change. Technology innovation is also becoming more important. In a study in 2023 Lokmic-Tomkins et al., digital health equipment promoted adaptation by reducing telemedicine convenience and travel and paper use under climate conditions.

On the one hand, the Sánchez Rodríguez & Fernández Carril, (2024)review highlighted the significance of context-driven climate-resilient development in the context of developing nations. It promoted participatory planning processes that involve local communities, incorporate (Corvalan et al., 2020; Lokmic-Tomkins et al., 2023) indigenous knowledge and prioritize co-benefits (e.g., poverty reduction and gender equity). These techniques, along with the principles of design proposed for sustainable health infrastructure, form a comprehensive roadmap for a climate-ready healthcare future (Corvalan et al., 2020).

Climate change presents a formidable challenge across sectors, necessitating integrated approaches to mitigate its adverse impacts while ensuring sustainable development. The healthcare sector, often overlooked in climate discourse, has been identified as a significant contributor to global emissions. Salas et al., (2020) emphasize that healthcare systems themselves must transition towards sustainability, presenting a comprehensive roadmap for achieving net-zero emissions. Their study highlights the necessity for healthcare organizations to measure their carbon footprints and implement systemic changes across energy usage, procurement, waste management, and clinical practices to align with broader environmental goals (Rodríguez-Jiménez et al., 2023).

In developing countries, the role of the private sector is critical in building climate resilience, especially given the limited capacity of public institutions. Biagini & Miller, (2013) investigate the extent of private sector involvement in climate adaptation. They identify substantial barriers, including policy uncertainty, lack of information, and financial constraints, while also noting that private actors possess the innovation and investment capabilities essential for adaptation efforts. The authors advocate for stronger public-private partnerships and supportive regulatory environments to facilitate private engagement in climate initiatives (Biagini & Miller, 2013).

Extending the scope to a more holistic framework, (Singh & Chudasama, 2021) propose the integration of human well-being with ecological boundaries to guide climate-resilient development. Their "safe and just space" paradigm emphasizes balancing planetary thresholds with social equity, arguing that development pathways must simultaneously ensure environmental sustainability and meet the basic needs of all individuals. The paper provides a multidimensional assessment model that connects climate policy with health, education, gender equity, and poverty alleviation (Singh & Chudasama, 2021)

Together, these studies provide a multi-layered understanding of climate resilience, underscoring the urgency for cross-sectoral collaboration, inclusive policy frameworks, and sustainability-driven transformation across healthcare, governance, and development domains.

The intersection of climate change and finance has emerged as a crucial area of inquiry in recent years, driven by the growing recognition of climate-related risks to global financial systems. Scholars and practitioners alike are exploring how financial strategies can support climate resilience and sustainability, particularly through infrastructure investment, insurance mechanisms, and financial risk assessment.

Meyer & Schwarze, (2019) provide an in-depth analysis of financing climate-resilient infrastructure by focusing on the fundamental challenges of determining risk, reward, and return on investment. Their work highlights that the unpredictability and long-term nature of climate change make conventional investment appraisal techniques insufficient. This leads to a disconnect between infrastructure needs and available financial resources, as traditional investors often seek short-term returns that do not align with the extended payback periods of climate-resilient projects. The authors argue for a recalibration of investment evaluation metrics to account for non-monetary benefits such as avoided damage, social stability, and environmental preservation.

A significant contribution of their study is the framing of climate resilience as both a risk management and value creation strategy. By integrating climate considerations into early planning stages, infrastructure can be designed to withstand environmental shocks, which in turn protects investor capital and enhances long-term performance. Moreover, Meyer & Schwarze, (2019) emphasize the role of public-private partnerships (PPPs) and blended finance in addressing funding gaps, as public actors can absorb some of the risks that private financiers are unwilling to bear.

In a broader financial context, the paper aligns with literature that advocates for climate-informed decision-making in capital markets. The incorporation of climate risk into financial disclosures and ratings is becoming more prevalent, propelled by global initiatives such as the Task Force on Climate-related Financial Disclosures (TCFD). Investments that account for climate resilience are increasingly seen as not only ethical but also financially prudent in the face of systemic risks posed by climate variability.

In summary, Meyer & Schwarze, (2019) contribute a critical perspective on aligning financial instruments with climate resilience goals. Their work underscores the need for adaptive financial frameworks that transcend traditional risk-reward paradigms, enabling sustainable development through resilient infrastructure financing. The online sector intends to implement green products, which will benefit the industry in the long run even if they might not be simple in the near term. Although green marketing is still in its infancy in Indian businesses, there are prospects in both domestic and foreign markets. According to a factor study, factors including prompt delivery, flexible payment plans, affordable costs, brand recognition, product availability, and ratings and reviews all have an impact on customers' decisions to purchase eco-friendly items online (Ghosal et al., 2021, Chand, K.K., 2019)

Green finance has emerged as a vital mechanism in addressing climate change and promoting sustainable development. It encompasses financial instruments and investments that aim to generate environmental benefits, particularly through supporting low-carbon and climate-resilient projects. Recent scholarly works underscore the evolving dimensions of green finance, from policy frameworks to the integration of digital technologies.

Corfee-morlot et al., (2012) emphasize the necessity of a comprehensive **green investment policy framework** to guide investments towards **low-carbon, climate-resilient infrastructure**. They argue that aligning public and private financial flows with climate goals requires clear policy direction, risk-sharing mechanisms, and capacity building. The study highlights the gap between climate objectives and existing financial incentives, suggesting reforms in investment planning and regulatory frameworks to mobilize green finance at scale.

Digital innovation, particularly **blockchain technology**, is increasingly recognized for its potential to enhance the transparency, accountability, and efficiency of climate finance. Schulz & Feist, (2021) explores how blockchain can be leveraged to support innovative financial mechanisms under the **Green Climate Fund (GCF)**. By enabling traceability and trust in the flow of funds, blockchain is seen as a tool to attract private investment and improve stakeholder confidence in climate finance mechanisms.

Further expanding on this digital trajectory, another study investigates how **blockchain technology** contributes to the **governance and implementation** of sustainable development initiatives (Schulz & Feist, 2021). The authors argue that blockchain facilitates decentralized decision-making, improves monitoring and verification processes, and can bridge the trust deficit among stakeholders. These capabilities are crucial in the context of green finance, where transparent impact tracking is essential (Schulz K.A. et al., 2020; Schulz K.& Feist, 2021).

In the context of financial services, Puschmann et al., (2020) focuses on **Green FinTech** and its role in mitigating the impacts of climate change. Using Switzerland as a case study, the paper demonstrates how financial technologies can promote sustainable consumer behavior, support green investment products, and create innovative financing solutions. Green FinTech, thus, represents a convergence of environmental and financial objectives through technology-driven models.

Together, these studies reveal a multidimensional view of green finance that integrates policy reform, technology adoption, and financial innovation. While policy frameworks lay the foundational ground, emerging technologies like blockchain and Green FinTech are expanding the reach and effectiveness of green finance initiatives, making sustainability not only a regulatory necessity but also an opportunity for financial innovation.

Decentralized Finance (DeFi) represents a transformative shift in the global financial ecosystem, challenging traditional financial systems by leveraging blockchain-based smart contracts. It seeks to offer open, permissionless, and transparent financial services including lending, borrowing, trading, and asset management without reliance on centralized intermediaries. The emergence of DeFi protocols has brought both opportunities and significant risks, necessitating a deeper exploration of its underlying architecture, benefits, and vulnerabilities.

The study *Carter & Jeng, (2021)* offers critical insights into the paradoxes that define the DeFi space. On one hand, DeFi promises to enhance financial inclusion and reduce reliance on centralized financial institutions. On the other hand, it introduces new vectors of systemic risk due to the interdependence of smart contracts and the composability of DeFi protocols. The paper argues that while decentralization reduces certain traditional risks, it simultaneously amplifies new ones, particularly in terms of security vulnerabilities, protocol design flaws, and governance limitations (Schär, 2020).

One of the paradoxes highlighted is that although DeFi systems are designed to be trustless, users often end up placing significant trust in the code and the developers behind it. This reliance poses a contradiction to the core philosophy of decentralization. Furthermore, the open-source nature of DeFi protocols, while enabling innovation and composability, also makes them susceptible to exploitation by bad actors through mechanisms like flash loan attacks or oracle manipulations (Carter & Jeng, 2021; Schär, 2020)

The research also emphasizes the implications of composability—where different DeFi applications interact and build upon each other, forming a "money lego" structure. While composability fosters innovation, it also creates fragility, as a vulnerability in one protocol can cascade and compromise multiple interconnected systems. This interconnectedness mirrors the complexity of traditional financial systems, suggesting that DeFi is not immune to systemic risk despite its decentralized structure (Carter & Jeng, 2021; Shamili & Muruganantham, 2022).

Moreover, governance remains a critical area of concern. While many DeFi protocols promote decentralized governance through token-based voting, there are questions around voter apathy, concentration of token ownership, and the effectiveness of such mechanisms in managing risk or responding swiftly to emergent threats (Carter & Jeng, 2021).

In summary, the literature reveals that while DeFi represents a revolutionary approach to finance, it is still in its nascent stages, facing challenges that stem from its technical complexity, evolving regulatory landscape, and reliance on a community-based governance model. Further research and development are necessary to address the paradoxes within DeFi, particularly those related to systemic risk, code security, and protocol interdependencies.

DISCUSSION

The intersection of climate change, healthcare systems, and green finance is receiving increasing scholarly attention, yet significant research gaps remain. While existing literature offers robust frameworks for health system resilience, decarbonization, and adaptation (Chan et al., 2021; Ridde et al., 2024), there is limited integration between health resilience planning and climate finance mechanisms. Studies on green finance and technological innovations like blockchain and Green FinTech (Puschmann et al., 2020; Schulz & Feist, 2021) highlight their potential for sustainability, but their application to healthcare infrastructure remains underexplored. Particularly in low- and middle-income countries, research rarely addresses how financial tools—such as blended finance or decentralized finance (DeFi)—can directly support climate-resilient health systems. Moreover, while health system reforms stress anticipatory governance, regional knowledge sharing, and workforce preparedness (Teshome, 2023; Zurynski et al., 2024), operational challenges in implementing these frameworks across diverse socio-political contexts are not sufficiently studied. There is also a noticeable underrepresentation of the private sector's role in climate-health initiatives, despite evidence of its potential in adaptation and innovation (Biagini & Miller, 2013). Additionally, governance models that align financial regulation, health priorities, and environmental sustainability are still evolving, with limited empirical evaluation of their effectiveness. Finally, while DeFi and blockchain technologies offer transparency and decentralized decision-making in finance (Carter & Jeng, 2021), their risks and ethical implications—especially in managing sensitive health data—warrant further investigation. Thus, there is a pressing need for interdisciplinary research that bridges health systems, climate policy, and financial innovation to inform integrated, context-specific solutions. Such work should prioritize inclusive governance, technological feasibility, and financial accessibility to ensure equitable, climate-resilient healthcare futures. The stability and efficacy of health systems depend heavily on the health workforce's resilience. Providing high-quality and effective healthcare, especially in light of climate change, requires a workforce that is informed and well-prepared. Since public health is still at serious risk from climate change, healthcare workers need to be thoroughly educated, trained, and mentored on climate-related health issues. Giving health workers the tools they need to identify, avoid, and manage health hazards related to climate change can help health systems become more adaptable and improve healthcare delivery under challenging environmental situations. Building cross-sector collaboration is a key component of creating a health system that is climate resilient. In addition to its effects on health, climate change has an impact on a number of other areas, such as environmental health, disaster management, vector control, and legislation. To develop a comprehensive response to health concerns brought on by climate change, intersectoral collaboration must be strengthened. The establishment of health and climate change departments should be spearheaded by government organizations, especially the Ministry of Health. These departments would be in charge of creating national health and climate change policies, organizing and overseeing climate-resilient initiatives, and fostering collaborations with important stakeholders to guarantee thorough policy implementation. By destroying vital infrastructure, such as hospitals, clinics, and supply networks for medical supplies, extreme weather events including heat waves, droughts, and floods can seriously impair healthcare services. Furthermore, vital utilities like water, power, and sanitation can be interrupted, which would increase the hazards to one's health. Thus, making investments in climate-resilient infrastructure is essential to ensuring that healthcare services continue to be provided without interruption. In order for hospitals and other healthcare facilities to continue operating even during climate-related disasters, they should be built or renovated to withstand severe weather. This entails putting in place energy-saving measures, environmentally friendly water management plans, and disaster preparation procedures that enable prompt crisis response.

In order to improve the health sector's decision-making procedures, health information systems are essential. Identification of climate-related health trends, vulnerability assessments, and the development of evidence-based policy all depend on timely and accurate data gathering. By fortifying health information systems, policymakers and medical practitioners would be able to foresee health issues connected to climate change and create suitable reaction plans. In order to prevent future health emergencies, authorities can monitor illness trends, evaluate environmental changes, and enhance early warning systems by incorporating climate-related health indicators into current health surveillance systems.

CONCLUSION

Strengthening health systems globally is imperative given the rapid rate of climate change and its harmful effects on health. Governance, policy creation, public involvement, and resource allocation are all components of a multidimensional strategy needed to create a health system that is climate resilient. Investments in emergency preparedness, illness prevention, and risk reduction techniques connected to climate change must be given top priority by governments. Additionally, improving research capacities in the relationship between climate and health is crucial to creating novel solutions that tackle new health risks. Service delivery, health workforce, information systems, access to necessary medications, funding, and leadership/governance are the six fundamental elements of health systems that should be in line with a comprehensive plan for creating a climate-resilient health system. Sustainability, inclusiveness, and equity should be prioritized in policies that improve these elements to prevent disadvantaged groups from being disproportionately impacted by climate change. Both domestically and internationally, governments may enhance health outcomes and save lives by enacting well-thought-out policies and carrying out focused initiatives.

Strong national and international leadership and governance are necessary to create a health system that is climate resilient. In order to include climate issues into health policies and initiatives, ministries of health should set up specialized climate change and health divisions. Increased public awareness initiatives are necessary to inform communities about the health hazards associated with climate change and to encourage adaptable behavior. In order to support training initiatives, emergency response plans, and infrastructure development that improves the resilience of the health system, budget allocation must also be streamlined. An emergency preparation plan is another essential element of a health system that is climate resilient.

For health institutions to efficiently handle climate-related catastrophes, they need to have backup plans. The provision of clean water and power backup systems, the storage of necessary medications, and the education of healthcare personnel in disaster response and management are all examples of this. Health systems will be better equipped to react quickly to climate-related emergencies and reduce the negative health effects on impacted communities if local and regional emergency response capabilities are strengthened. Health-focused actions are equally crucial for mitigating climate change. Incorporating green building designs, encouraging sustainable waste management techniques, and reducing the carbon footprint of healthcare facilities through the use of renewable energy sources may all help mitigate the effects of climate change. Furthermore, preventative healthcare practices including immunization campaigns, vector control projects, and health awareness campaigns can improve community resilience and lower the prevalence of climate-sensitive illnesses. Research and innovation must also be consistently funded for a strong and climate-resilient healthcare system. The development of innovative technologies that improve healthcare delivery in climate-sensitive areas, the identification of successful adaption techniques, and research institutes' investigations on the health effects of climate change should all be encouraged. Cooperation between government bodies, academic institutions, and international organizations may promote evidence-based policymaking and information exchange. In conclusion, immediate action is required to enhance health systems globally due to the rising threat posed by climate change. To create a climate-resilient health system that can endure and adjust to environmental changes, a thorough and integrated strategy is needed. This entails strengthening the health workforce's capabilities, making investments in robust infrastructure, advancing health information systems, encouraging intersectoral cooperation, and putting policies in place to deal with health issues connected to climate change. Governments and stakeholders may safeguard public health, lessen climate-related vulnerabilities, and guarantee sustainable and equitable healthcare delivery for future generations by giving priority to these important areas. In the face of a changing environment, a well-prepared health system will not only save lives but also promote general community well-being and economic stability.

REFERENCES

Angel, P. A. S. (2024). Empowering change: The crucial role of civil society in climate change mitigation. *American Journal of Economics and Sociology*. Advance online publication. DOI: 10.1111/ajes.12577

Arzo, S., & Hong, M. (2024). Resilient green infrastructure: Navigating environmental resistance for sustainable development, social mobility in climate change policy. *Heliyon, 10*(13), e33524. DOI: 10.1016/j.heliyon.2024.e33524 PMID: 39035491

Ashton, C. (2024). *How health economics is redefining climate-resilient healthcare | World Economic Forum*. World Economic Forum. https://www.weforum.org/stories/2024/06/how-health-economics-is-redefining-climate-resilient-healthcare/

Biagini, B., & Miller, A. (2013). Engaging the private sector in adaptation to climate change in developing countries: Importance, status, and challenges. *Climate and Development, 5*(3), 242–252. DOI: 10.1080/17565529.2013.821053

Bowen, K. J., & Lynch, Y. (2016, November). Bowen, Kathryn J., & Lynch, Y. (2017). The public health benefits of green infrastructure: The potential of economic framing for enhanced decision-making. *Current Opinion in Environmental Sustainability, 25*, 90–95. DOI: 10.1016/j.cosust.2017.08.003

Bowen, K. J., Parry, M., Barrett, M. A., Miller, D., Frumkin, H., Peen, J., Schoevers, R. A., Beekman, A. T., Dekker, J., Sandifer, P. A., Sutton-Grier, A. E., Ward, B. P., Gascon, M., Triguero-Mas, M., Martínez, D., Dadvand, P., Rojas-Rueda, D., Plasència, A., Nieuwenhuijsen, M. J., & Newell, J. P. (2014). The evidence base for linkages between green infrastructure, public health and economic benefit. *Ecosystem Services, 11*(2), 1–15. http://www.pubmedcentral.nih.gov/articlerender.fcgi?artid=3993093&tool=pmcentrez&rendertype=abstract

Braithwaite, J., Smith, C. L., Leask, E., Wijekulasuriya, S., Brooke-Cowden, K., Fisher, G., Patel, R., Pagano, L., Rahimi-Ardabili, H., Spanos, S., Rojas, C., Partington, A., McQuillan, E., Dammery, G., Carrigan, A., Ehrenfeld, L., Coiera, E., Westbrook, J., & Zurynski, Y. (2024). Strategies and tactics to reduce the impact of healthcare on climate change: Systematic review. *BMJ (Clinical Research Ed.), 387*, e081284. Advance online publication. DOI: 10.1136/bmj-2024-081284 PMID: 39379104

Byrne, J., & Jinjun, Y. (2009). Can urban greenspace combat climate change? Towards a subtropical cities research agenda. *Australian Plants, 46*(4), 36–43. DOI: 10.1080/07293682.2009.10753420

Canzonieri, C. (2007). M.E. Benedict and E.T. McMahon, Green Infrastructure: Linking Landscapes and Communities. *Landscape Ecology*, *22*(5), 797–798. DOI: 10.1007/s10980-006-9045-7

Caparrós-Martínez, J. L., Milán-García, J., Martínez-Vázquez, R. M., & Valenciano, J. de P. (2021). Green Infrastructures and Grand Environmental Challenges: A Review of Research Trends by Keyword. *Agronomy 2021, Vol. 11, Page 782, 11*(4), 782. DOI: 10.3390/agronomy11040782

Carter, N., & Jeng, L. (2021). DeFi Protocol Risks: The Paradox of DeFi. SSRN *Electronic Journal*. https://doi.org/DOI: 10.2139/SSRN.3866699

Chan, S., Boran, I., van Asselt, H., Ellinger, P., Garcia, M., Hale, T., Hermwille, L., Liti Mbeva, K., Mert, A., Roger, C. B., Weinfurter, A., Widerberg, O., Bynoe, P., Chengo, V., Cherkaoui, A., Edwards, T., Gütschow, M., Hsu, A., Hultman, N., & Shrivastava, M. K. (2021). Climate Ambition and Sustainable Development for a New Decade: A Catalytic Framework. *Global Policy*, *12*(3), 245–259. DOI: 10.1111/1758-5899.12932

Chand, K. K. (2019). Agripreneurship: A Tool For Economic Development of India in The New Millennium. [IJRTBT]. *International Journal on Recent Trends in Business and Tourism*, *3*(4), 19–25. https://ejournal.lucp.net/index.php/ijrtbt/article/view/871

Corfee-morlot, J., Marchal, V., Kauffmann, C., Kennedy, C., Stewart, F., Kaminker, C., & Ang, G. (2012). *Towards a Green Investment Policy Framework*. OECD Publishing., DOI: 10.1787/19970900

Corvalan, C., Prats, E. V., Sena, A., Campbell-Lendrum, D., Karliner, J., Risso, A., Wilburn, S., Slotterback, S., Rathi, M., Stringer, R., Berry, P., Edwards, S., Enright, P., Hayter, A., Howard, G., Lapitan, J., Montgomery, M., Prüss-Ustün, A., Varangu, L., & Vinci, S. (2020). Towards Climate Resilient and Environmentally Sustainable Health Care Facilities. *International Journal of Environmental Research and Public Health 2020, Vol. 17, Page 8849, 17*(23), 8849. DOI: 10.3390/ijerph17238849

Ezzati, F., Mosadeghrad, A. M., & Jaafaripooyan, E. (2023). Resiliency of the Iranian healthcare facilities against the Covid-19 pandemic: Challenges and solutions. *BMC Health Services Research*, *23*(1), 1–16. DOI: 10.1186/s12913-023-09180-6 PMID: 36859284

Fawzy, S., Osman, A. I., Doran, J., & Rooney, D. W. (2020). Strategies for mitigation of climate change: a review. *Environmental Chemistry Letters 2020 18:6, 18*(6), 2069–2094. DOI: 10.1007/s10311-020-01059-w

Fears, R., Canales-Holzeis, C., Caussy, D., Harper, S. L., Hoe, V. C. W., McNeil, J. N., Mogwitz, J., ter Meulen, V., & Haines, A. (2023). Climate action for health: Inter-regional engagement to share knowledge to guide mitigation and adaptation actions. *Global Policy, 15*(S5), 75–96. DOI: 10.1111/1758-5899.13210

Felappi, J. F., Sommer, J. H., Falkenberg, T., Terlau, W., & Kötter, T. (2020). Green infrastructure through the lens of "One Health": A systematic review and integrative framework uncovering synergies and trade-offs between mental health and wildlife support in cities. *The Science of the Total Environment, 748*, 141589. DOI: 10.1016/j.scitotenv.2020.141589 PMID: 33113695

Field, C. B. (2014). [*Impacts, adaptation, and vulnerability : summary for policy-makers*. <bound method Organization.get_name_with_acronym of <Organization: Intergovernmental Panel on Climate Change>>.]. *Climatic Change*, •••, 2014.

Ghosal, I., Gupta, B., Dey, M., & Prasad, B. (2021). Impact of Outlining Factors Towards Online Green Products: An Empirical Investigation on Consumers' Awareness. [IJRTBT]. *International Journal on Recent Trends in Business and Tourism, 5*(1), 1–7. DOI: 10.31674/ijrtbt.2021.v05i01.001

Gkouliaveras, V., Kalogiannidis, S., Kalfas, D., & Kontsas, S. (2025). Effects of Climate Change on Health and Health Systems: A Systematic Review of Preparedness, Resilience, and Challenges. *International Journal of Environmental Research and Public Health, 22*(2), 232. Advance online publication. DOI: 10.3390/ijerph22020232 PMID: 40003459

Health and climate change: country profile 2021: Czechia. (n.d.). Retrieved November 30, 2024, from https://www.who.int/publications/i/item/WHO-HEP-ECH-CCH-21.01.13

Kalogiannidis, S., Kalfas, D., Papaevangelou, O., Chatzitheodoridis, F., Katsetsiadou, K. N., & Lekkas, E. (2024). Integration of Climate Change Strategies into Policy and Planning for Regional Development: A Case Study of Greece. *Land 2024, Vol. 13, Page 268, 13*(3), 268. DOI: 10.3390/land13030268

Lokmic-Tomkins, Z., Borda, A., & Humphrey, K. (2023). Designing digital health applications for climate change mitigation and adaptation. *The Medical Journal of Australia, 218*(3), 106–110. DOI: 10.5694/mja2.51826 PMID: 36625463

Meyer, P. B., & Schwarze, R. (2019). Financing climate-resilient infrastructure: Determining risk, reward, and return on investment. *Frontiers of Engineering Management, 6*(1), 117–127. DOI: 10.1007/s42524-019-0009-4

Mosadeghrad, A. M., & Shahsavani, A. (2023). Strengthening the resilience of Iran's health system against climate change. [Health Monitor]. *Payesh, 22*(4), 479–482. DOI: 10.61186/payesh.22.4.479

Nassani, A. A., Yousaf, Z., Radulescu, M., Balsalobre-Lorente, D., Hussain, H., & Haffar, M. (2023). Green Innovation through Green and Blue Infrastructure Development: Investigation of Pollution Reduction and Green Technology in Emerging Economy. *Energies 2023, Vol. 16, Page 1944, 16*(4), 1944. DOI: 10.3390/en16041944

Okara, L. (2024). *Building resilient health systems: adapting to climate change.* Economic Impact. https://impact.economist.com/sustainability/resilience-and-adaptation/building-resilient-health-systems-adapting-to-climate-change

Phillips, D., Jamwal, P., Lindquist, M., & Gronewold, A. (2022). Assessing catchment-scale performance of in-stream Provisional Green Infrastructure interventions for Dry Weather Flows. *Landscape and Urban Planning, 226*, 104448. DOI: 10.1016/j.landurbplan.2022.104448

Puschmann, T., Hoffmann, C. H., & Khmarskyi, V. (2020). How Green FinTech Can Alleviate the Impact of Climate Change—The Case of Switzerland. *Sustainability (Basel), 12*(24), 10691. DOI: 10.3390/su122410691

Ridde, V., Barua, M., Bonnet, E., Casseus, A., Clech, L., De Allegri, M., Kabir, M. M. S., Goudet, J.-M., Henrys, D., Islam, M. N., L'Heureux, Y., Masselot, C., Mathon, D., Meistre, S., & Sarker, M. (2024). Improving an Integrative Framework of Health System Resilience and Climate Change: Lessons from Bangladesh and Haiti. *Earth ArXiv*. DOI: 10.31223/X5MH6F

Rodríguez-Jiménez, L., Romero-Martín, M., Spruell, T., Steley, Z., & Gómez-Salgado, J. (2023). The carbon footprint of healthcare settings: A systematic review. *Journal of Advanced Nursing, 79*(8), 2830–2844. DOI: 10.1111/jan.15671 PMID: 37198974

Salas, R. N., Maibach, E., Pencheon, D., Watts, N., & Frumkin, H. (2020). A pathway to net zero emissions for healthcare. *BMJ (Clinical Research Ed.), 371*, m3785. Advance online publication. DOI: 10.1136/bmj.m3785 PMID: 33004403

Sánchez Rodríguez, R. A., & Fernández Carril, L. R. (2024). Climate-resilient development in developing countries. *Current Opinion in Environmental Sustainability, 66*, 101391. DOI: 10.1016/j.cosust.2023.101391

Schär, F. (2020). Decentralized Finance: On Blockchain- and Smart Contract-based Financial Markets. SSRN *Electronic Journal*. https://doi.org/DOI: 10.2139/SSRN.3571335

Schulz, K., & Feist, M. (2021). Leveraging blockchain technology for innovative climate finance under the Green Climate Fund. *Earth System Governance*, *7*, 100084. DOI: 10.1016/j.esg.2020.100084

Schulz, K. A., Gstrein, O. J., & Zwitter, A. J. (2020). Exploring the governance and implementation of sustainable development initiatives through blockchain technology. *Futures*, *122*, 102611. DOI: 10.1016/j.futures.2020.102611

Sen, B., Dhimal, M., Latheef, A. T., & Ghosh, U. (2017). Climate change: Health effects and response in South Asia. *BMJ (Clinical Research Ed.)*, *359*, j5117. DOI: 10.1136/bmj.j5117 PMID: 29146578

Shamili, P., & Muruganantham, B. (2022). Blockchain based Application: Decentralized Financial Technologies for Exchanging Crypto Currency. *Proceedings - IEEE International Conference on Advances in Computing, Communication and Applied Informatics, ACCAI 2022*. DOI: 10.1109/ACCAI53970.2022.9752485

Singh, P. K., & Chudasama, H. (2021). Pathways for climate resilient development: Human well-being within a safe and just space in the 21st century. *Global Environmental Change*, *68*, 102277. DOI: 10.1016/j.gloenvcha.2021.102277

Sokolova, M. V., Fath, B. D., Grande, U., Buonocore, E., & Franzese, P. P. (2024). The Role of Green Infrastructure in Providing Urban Ecosystem Services: Insights from a Bibliometric Perspective. *Land (Basel)*, *13*(10), 1–20. DOI: 10.3390/land13101664

Teshome, M. (2023). The Transformative Role of Adaptation Strategies in Designing Climate-Resilient and Sustainable Health Systems. *Journal of Prevention*, *44*(5), 603–613. DOI: 10.1007/s10935-023-00740-4 PMID: 37544936

Thomas, F. (2017). Climate change and health. In *Encyclopedia of the Anthropocene* (Vol. 1–5). Elsevier Inc., DOI: 10.1016/B978-0-12-809665-9.09791-3

van den Berg, M., Wendel-Vos, W., van Poppel, M., Kemper, H., van Mechelen, W., & Maas, J. (2015). Health benefits of green spaces in the living environment: A systematic review of epidemiological studies. *Urban Forestry & Urban Greening*, *14*(4), 806–816. DOI: 10.1016/j.ufug.2015.07.008

World Health Organization. (2021). *Operational framework for building climate resilient health systems*.

Ying, J., Zhang, X., Zhang, Y., & Bilan, S. (2022). Green infrastructure: Systematic literature review. *Ekonomska Istrazivanja*, *35*(1), 343–366. DOI: 10.1080/1331677X.2021.1893202

Zuniga-Teran, A. A., Staddon, C., de Vito, L., Gerlak, A. K., Ward, S., Schoeman, Y., Hart, A., & Booth, G. (2020). Challenges of mainstreaming green infrastructure in built environment professions. *Journal of Environmental Planning and Management, 63*(4), 710–732. DOI: 10.1080/09640568.2019.1605890

Zurynski, Y., Fisher, G., Wijekulasuriya, S., Leask, E., Dharmayani, P. N. A., Ellis, L. A., Smith, C. L., & Braithwaite, J. (2024). Bolstering health systems to cope with the impacts of climate change events: A review of the evidence on workforce planning, upskilling, and capacity building. *The International Journal of Health Planning and Management, 39*(3), 781–805. DOI: 10.1002/hpm.3769 PMID: 38308433

Chapter 3
Cities Under Pressure:
Addressing Urban Health Threats in the Era of Industrialisation and Sustainable Development Goals

Tiago Manuel Horta Reis da Silva
https://orcid.org/0000-0001-5220-1718
King's College London, UK

ABSTRACT

Rapid urbanisation, fueled by population growth and industrialisation, poses significant threats to public health, particularly in densely populated areas. This chapter explores the interplay of pollution, overcrowding, and industrial activities in exacerbating health disparities in urban settings. Drawing from evidence-based research and case studies, the chapter highlights innovative approaches to mitigating urban health risks, including green infrastructure, integrative health interventions, and policy reform. The chapter also examines how sustainable urban planning and community-driven initiatives can align with SDG 3 (Good Health and Well-Being) and SDG 11 (Sustainable Cities and Communities), emphasising the need for equitable, resilient urban health systems.

1. INTRODUCTION

Urbanisation is a multifaceted phenomenon that significantly impacts public health, particularly in the context of pollution, population growth, and industrialisation. As urban areas expand, they often experience increased levels of air and water pollution, which are directly linked to various health threats. The rapid influx of populations into cities exacerbates these issues, leading to overcrowded living conditions and

DOI: 10.4018/979-8-3693-9755-8.ch003

increased exposure to environmental hazards. This chapter aims to explore these interconnected themes, highlighting the health implications of urbanisation and the urgent need for effective public health strategies.

The relationship between urbanisation and health threats is well-documented. Urban environments are often characterised by elevated levels of pollutants, including particulate matter, nitrogen dioxide, and sulphur dioxide, which are primarily emitted from vehicles and industrial activities. These pollutants have been linked to a range of health issues, including respiratory diseases, cardiovascular problems, and even premature mortality (Li & Zuo, 2022; Çiftçi et al., 2021). Furthermore, the industrialisation that accompanies urban growth contributes to environmental degradation, with waste disposal and industrial emissions posing significant risks to public health (Mucchielli, 2023). The cumulative effect of these pollutants creates a public health crisis, particularly in low-income urban areas where regulatory oversight may be lacking.

Population growth in urban areas further complicates health outcomes. As cities expand, the demand for housing, transportation, and services increases, often outpacing the infrastructure needed to support such growth. This can lead to inadequate sanitation, poor air quality, and limited access to healthcare services, which disproportionately affect vulnerable populations (Bahri et al., 2022). For instance, studies have shown that migrant workers in urban settings face heightened health risks due to their precarious living conditions and exposure to hazardous environments (Guan et al., 2022). The intersection of urbanisation and population growth thus creates a perfect storm for public health challenges, necessitating comprehensive planning and intervention strategies.

Industrialisation, a key driver of urbanisation, also plays a critical role in shaping health outcomes. The establishment of industries in urban areas often leads to increased job opportunities; however, it also introduces a range of health risks associated with occupational hazards. Workers in industrial settings may be exposed to toxic substances, ergonomic challenges, and unsafe working conditions, which can lead to both acute and chronic health issues (Bijekar et al., 2022; Ameen & Abdulsahib, 2022). For example, research has indicated that long working hours and exposure to hazardous materials significantly increase the likelihood of mental health disorders among industrial workers (Tran et al., 2019). The need for robust occupational health and safety regulations becomes paramount in mitigating these risks and ensuring the well-being of the workforce.

Moreover, the food industry, which is often a significant component of urban economies, has been implicated in the rising prevalence of non-communicable diseases (NCDs) due to the marketing of unhealthy food products (Kim et al., 2016). The corporate political activities of food industry actors can undermine public health initiatives aimed at promoting healthier dietary choices, thereby exacerbating health disparities in urban populations (Lawani, 2023). This highlights the importance of integrating public health considerations into urban planning and industrial policies to create healthier urban environments.

The environmental health challenges posed by urbanisation are further compounded by the socio-economic inequalities prevalent in many urban settings. Low-income communities often bear the brunt of environmental hazards, facing higher exposure to pollutants and limited access to healthcare resources (Mialon et al., 2016). This inequity necessitates targeted public health interventions that address the specific needs of these populations, ensuring that all urban residents have the opportunity to live in healthy environments.

2. POLLUTION AND URBAN PUBLIC HEALTH

Urbanisation has led to significant increases in pollution levels, particularly in urban areas, where air and water quality have deteriorated markedly. The rise in industrial activities, vehicular emissions, and population density has contributed to this environmental crisis, posing serious health threats to urban populations. Air pollution, characterised by the presence of harmful substances in the atmosphere, has been linked to a range of health issues, including respiratory and cardiovascular diseases, as well as mental health disorders (Reis da Silva, 2025a). This section will explore the impacts of air and water pollution on public health, emphasizing the need for urgent interventions to mitigate these effects.

Air pollution is a critical public health concern, with the World Health Organization (WHO) estimating that nearly nine out of ten individuals living in urban areas are exposed to polluted air (Kurt et al., 2016). The primary pollutants include particulate matter (PM), nitrogen dioxide (NO2), sulphur dioxide (SO2), and ozone (O3), which can originate from various sources, including transportation, industrial processes, and residential heating (Ghorani-Azam et al., 2016). Research indicates that exposure to these pollutants is associated with increased morbidity and mortality rates, particularly for respiratory and cardiovascular diseases (Bräuer et al., 2021; Li et al., 2020). For instance, studies have shown that long-term exposure to PM2.5 is linked to a higher incidence of chronic obstructive pulmonary disease (COPD) and lung cancer (Saini & Kumar, 2022; Grigorieva & Lukyanets, 2021). Furthermore, air pollution exacerbates existing health conditions, leading to increased hospital admissions and healthcare costs (Liu & Ao, 2021; Zhong et al., 2019).

The respiratory system is particularly vulnerable to the effects of air pollution. Fine particulate matter can penetrate deep into the lungs, causing inflammation and impairing lung function (Priyankara et al., 2021). Children and the older citizens are especially at risk, as their respiratory systems are still developing or are already compromised (Shi et al., 2021). A study conducted in urban settings found that children exposed to high levels of air pollution exhibited a higher prevalence of asthma and other respiratory conditions (Kim et al., 2018). Additionally, the impact of air pollution on mental health is gaining recognition, with evidence suggesting that exposure to pollutants may contribute to anxiety, depression, and cognitive decline (Ramírez, 2024; Akbar, 2023). The complex interplay between air quality and mental health underscores the need for comprehensive public health strategies that address both physical and psychological well-being.

Water pollution is another significant health threat in urban areas, often resulting from industrial discharges, agricultural runoff, and inadequate waste management systems. Contaminated water sources can lead to a range of health issues, including gastrointestinal diseases, reproductive problems, and neurological disorders (Santos, 2024). The presence of heavy metals, pathogens, and chemical pollutants in drinking water can have severe health implications, particularly for vulnerable populations such as children and pregnant women (Krishnamoorthy et al., 2021). For example, exposure to lead in drinking water has been linked to developmental delays and cognitive impairments in children (Anwar et al., 2019). Moreover, waterborne diseases, such as cholera and dysentery, remain prevalent in many urban settings, exacerbated by poor sanitation and inadequate access to clean water (Ruziyev, 2024).

The intersection of air and water pollution creates a compounded health risk for urban populations. Pollutants in the air can settle on water bodies, leading to the contamination of drinking water sources (Zulfikri, 2023). Additionally, the health impacts of air pollution can be exacerbated by poor water quality, as individuals with compromised health due to respiratory issues may be more susceptible to infections and diseases transmitted through contaminated water (Czermański, 2024). This highlights the need for integrated approaches to urban planning and public health that consider the interrelated nature of environmental factors.

3. POPULATION GROWTH AND HEALTHCARE ACCESS

The rapid growth of urban populations has led to significant challenges in healthcare access, particularly in the context of overcrowding and the strain it places on urban health systems. As cities expand, the demand for healthcare services often outpaces the available resources, resulting in increased pressure on healthcare facilities and professionals (Reis da Silva, 2025a). This section will explore the implications of population growth on healthcare access, particularly for marginalized groups who experience health disparities.

Overcrowding and Strain on Urban health Systems

Overcrowding in urban areas is a direct consequence of population growth, leading to increased demand for healthcare services. This phenomenon can overwhelm existing health systems, resulting in longer wait times, reduced quality of care, and increased stress on healthcare providers (McMaughan et al., 2020). Studies have shown that higher population density correlates with greater challenges in accessing healthcare, as facilities become inundated with patients, leading to a decline in service quality (Cu et al., 2021). The strain on urban health systems is particularly pronounced in low-income neighbourhoods, where healthcare resources are often scarce, and residents face additional barriers to accessing care (Chen et al., 2023). For instance, a study in Nairobi found that traffic congestion significantly impacted access to healthcare services, exacerbating the challenges faced by urban populations (Mutono et al., 2022).

Marginalised Groups and Health Disparities

Marginalised groups, including low-income individuals, racial and ethnic minorities, and immigrants, often bear the brunt of these challenges. These populations frequently encounter systemic barriers that hinder their access to healthcare, resulting in significant health disparities (Reis da Silva, 2024a). Factors such as socioeconomic status, language barriers, and lack of insurance coverage contribute to these inequities (Parak et al., 2022). Research indicates that marginalised groups are less likely to utilise healthcare services, even when they are available, due to fears of discrimination, cultural insensitivity, or financial constraints (Al-Sheddi, 2023; Reis da Silva, 2024a). For example, a study examining healthcare access among immigrant populations in the United States found that many individuals faced significant obstacles in navigating the healthcare system, leading to unmet health needs (Sadler et al., 2021).

The impact of these disparities is profound, as marginalized groups often experience worse health outcomes compared to their more privileged counterparts. Chronic conditions such as diabetes, hypertension, and mental health disorders are more prevalent in these populations, exacerbated by barriers to accessing preventive care and treatment (Tripathi, 2024; Reis da Silva, 2024b). Moreover, the COVID-19 pandemic has highlighted and intensified these disparities, with marginalised communities experiencing higher rates of infection and mortality due to systemic inequities in healthcare access (Doetsch et al., 2023). This underscores the urgent need for targeted interventions that address the specific barriers faced by these populations.

Efforts to improve healthcare access in urban areas must consider the unique challenges posed by overcrowding and the needs of marginalised groups. Strategies may include increasing the availability of healthcare facilities in underserved areas, enhancing transportation options to improve access, and implementing community-based programs that address the social determinants of health (Jumadi, 2024). Additionally, fostering culturally competent care and increasing the diversity of healthcare providers can help bridge the gap in access for marginalised populations (Haque, 2023).

4. INDUSTRIALISATION AND OCCUPATIONAL HEALTH

Industrialisation has been a significant driver of economic growth and urban development, but it has also introduced a range of workplace hazards and contributed to environmental degradation. The interplay between these factors has profound implications for occupational health, as workers are often exposed to hazardous conditions that can lead to acute and chronic health issues (Reis da Silva, 2025a). This section will explore the various workplace hazards associated with industrialisation, the environmental impacts of these hazards, and case studies of industrial health crises that illustrate the urgent need for improved occupational health standards.

Workplace Hazards and Environmental Degradation

Workplace hazards in industrial settings can be broadly categorised into physical, chemical, biological, and psychosocial hazards. Physical hazards include exposure to noise, vibration, and extreme temperatures, which can lead to conditions such as hearing loss, musculoskeletal disorders, and heat stress (Ndejjo et al., 2015; Abokhashabah et al., 2021; Reis da Silva, 2023a). Chemical hazards arise from exposure to toxic substances, including heavy metals, solvents, and pesticides, which can result in respiratory illnesses, skin disorders, and even cancer (Zebrak et al., 2022). Biological hazards are particularly relevant in healthcare settings, where workers may be exposed to infectious agents, leading to increased morbidity and mortality among healthcare professionals (Ndejjo et al., 2015). Psychosocial hazards, including workplace stress, bullying, and harassment, can also have significant impacts on mental health and overall well-being (Hsieh, 2023; Wijaya et al., 2022; Reis da Silva, 2025b; Reis da Silva, 2025c).

Case Studies of Industrial Health Crises

The environmental degradation associated with industrialisation further exacerbates these workplace hazards. Industrial activities often lead to air and water pollution, which can have direct health impacts on workers and surrounding communities. For instance, the release of pollutants into the air can contribute to respiratory diseases among workers and residents alike, while contaminated water sources can lead to gastrointestinal and other health issues (Gatto, 2024). Moreover, the cumulative effects of environmental degradation can create hazardous working conditions, particularly in industries such as construction and manufacturing, where workers may be exposed to hazardous materials without adequate protective measures (Onguto et al., 2020).

Case studies of industrial health crises provide stark examples of the consequences of inadequate occupational health standards and environmental management. One notable example is the Bhopal gas tragedy in India, where a gas leak from a pesticide plant exposed thousands of workers and nearby residents to toxic methyl isocyanate. The disaster resulted in immediate fatalities and long-term health consequences, including respiratory problems, neurological disorders, and increased cancer rates among affected populations (Badri, 2023). Similarly, the Flint water crisis in the United States highlighted the health impacts of lead exposure from contaminated drinking water, disproportionately affecting low-income and minority communities (Oche et al., 2020). These case studies underscore the critical need for robust occupational health regulations and environmental protections to prevent such tragedies from occurring in the future.

In addition to these high-profile cases, many workers in various industries face daily exposure to hazardous conditions without adequate protections. For example, research has shown that construction workers are often exposed to a range of physical and chemical hazards, including falls, noise, and exposure to harmful substances like asbestos and silica (Reis da Silva, 2024c; Reis da Silva, 2023b; Jian et al., 2023; Sharma et al., 2021). Despite the known risks, many construction sites lack proper safety protocols and training, leading to high rates of occupational injuries and illnesses (Jovanović et al., 2017). Similarly, agricultural workers are frequently exposed to pesticides and other chemicals, with limited access to protective equipment and training on safe handling practices (Tolera, 2024).

The need for improved occupational health and safety measures is further emphasised by the growing recognition of the psychosocial aspects of workplace health. Studies have shown that workplace stress and harassment can lead to significant mental health issues, including anxiety and depression, which can in turn affect job performance and overall quality of life (da Silva, 2022; Uddin et al., 2023; Macdonald, 2024; Reis da Silva, 2024d; Reis da Silva, 2024e; Reis da Silva,

2025d; Reis da Silva, 2025e). Addressing these psychosocial hazards is essential for creating healthier work environments and promoting the well-being of workers (Reis da Silva et al., 2025).

5. AGEING AND URBAN HEALTH

The intersection of ageing, urban health, and the unique challenges faced by older populations in urban environments is a critical area of study (Reis da Silva, 2025a). As urbanisation continues to rise globally, the health and well-being of older individuals in cities have become increasingly important. This section will explore the health challenges faced by older people in urban settings, the factors influencing their health outcomes, and the implications for urban health policy and planning.

One of the primary health challenges faced by the elderly in urban areas is the prevalence of chronic diseases (Reis da Silva, 2024b). Studies have shown that older adults living in urban slums often experience a higher burden of morbidity, with conditions such as arthritis and visual impairments being particularly common (Barua et al., 2017). The urban environment can exacerbate these health issues due to factors such as pollution, limited access to healthcare services, and social isolation (Reis da Silva, 2024f). For instance, research indicates that older adults in urban settings are at a higher risk of developing mental health issues, including depression and anxiety, often linked to social isolation and the stressors associated with urban living (Lee & Lee, 2019; Liu et al., 2021; Reis da Silva, 2024f).

Access to healthcare services is another critical factor influencing the health of the elderly in urban areas. Many older adults face barriers to accessing necessary medical care, including financial constraints, transportation difficulties, and a lack of awareness about available services (Bhan et al., 2017). In urban environments, the availability of healthcare facilities does not always translate to accessibility, particularly for marginalised populations. For example, studies have highlighted that elderly individuals living in low-income urban neighbourhoods often have limited access to quality healthcare, resulting in unmet health needs (Banerjee, 2021). This disparity underscores the importance of addressing social determinants of health in urban planning and policy.

Moreover, the living arrangements of older adults significantly impact their health-related quality of life (HRQOL). Research has shown that elderly individuals living alone or with limited social support are more likely to experience poorer health outcomes compared to those living with family or in supportive community environments (Zhou et al., 2018; Reis da Silva, 2024f). In urban settings, where traditional family structures may be disrupted due to migration and changing social dynamics, the need for community support systems becomes paramount. Urban design that fosters social interaction and community engagement can play a crucial role in enhancing the well-being of older residents (Qiu et al., 2021; Somsopon et al., 2022).

The role of urban green spaces in promoting the health of the elderly cannot be overlooked. Access to parks and recreational areas has been linked to improved physical and mental health outcomes among older adults. Green spaces provide opportunities for physical activity, social interaction, and relaxation, all of which are essential for maintaining health and well-being in later life (Lee & Lee, 2019; Sazali et al., 2022). Urban planners must prioritise the creation and maintenance of accessible green spaces to support the health of ageing populations.

Innovative approaches to urban health challenges for the elderly include the integration of technology and smart city initiatives. The development of smart health care platforms can enhance access to health services and improve the overall quality of care for older adults (Hou et al., 2022). For instance, telehealth services can provide remote consultations and health monitoring, reducing the need for elderly individuals to travel to healthcare facilities (Reis da Silva, 2025f; Reis da Silva, 2025g; Reis da Silva, 2025h). Additionally, community-based interventions that involve older adults in the planning and implementation of health programs can empower them and ensure that their specific needs are met (Bhan et al., 2017).

6. INNOVATIVE APPROACHES TO URBAN HEALTH CHALLENGES

Innovative approaches to urban health challenges are increasingly recognised as essential for creating sustainable and healthy cities. Among these approaches, the integration of green infrastructure and urban design, alongside community-based interventions and participatory planning, plays a pivotal role in enhancing urban health outcomes. This section will delve into the significance of these strategies, supported by relevant literature, to illustrate their potential impact on urban health.

Role of Green Infrastructure and Urban Design

Green infrastructure refers to the strategically planned network of natural and semi-natural features in urban areas that provide ecosystem services and enhance the quality of life for residents (Reis da Silva, 2025a). The incorporation of green spaces, such as parks, green roofs, and urban forests, has been shown to positively influence public health by improving air quality, reducing heat islands, and promoting physical activity (Puig-Ribera et al., 2022). For instance, a study conducted in Barcelona highlighted how integrating health considerations into urban planning led to the creation of green spaces that not only improved the aesthetic appeal of the city but also contributed to the physical and mental well-being of its inhabitants (Puig-Ribera et al., 2022). Access to green infrastructure has been linked to lower rates of obesity, cardiovascular diseases, and mental health disorders, emphasising the need for urban planners to prioritise these elements in their designs (Rupprecht, 2017).

Moreover, the design of urban environments can significantly affect social interactions and community cohesion, which are crucial for mental health. Research indicates that well-designed public spaces encourage social engagement and physical activity, thereby fostering a sense of community and belonging among residents (Spencer et al., 2023; Reis da Silva, 2023b). The potential for green infrastructure to serve as a catalyst for social interactions is particularly important in densely populated urban areas, where social isolation can be a significant risk factor for mental health issues (Yu & Ahlgren, 2023; Reis da Silva, 2024f). By creating inviting and accessible green spaces, cities can enhance the overall quality of life for their residents.

Community-based Interventions and Participatory Planning

Community-based interventions and participatory planning are equally vital in addressing urban health challenges. These approaches emphasise the involvement of community members in the decision-making processes related to urban planning and health initiatives. Participatory planning allows residents to voice their concerns, preferences, and ideas, ensuring that urban development reflects the needs and desires of the community (Ampatzidou et al., 2018; Reis da Silva, 2023c). For example, participatory budgeting initiatives have been implemented in various cities, enabling residents to allocate funds for community projects, including health-related initiatives and green space development (Palla, 2024). This not only empowers residents but also fosters a sense of ownership and responsibility towards their environment. The effectiveness of community-based interventions is further enhanced when they are tailored to the specific needs of diverse populations. Research has shown that engaging marginalised communities in the planning process can lead to more equitable health outcomes and improved access to services (Hussein et al., 2020). For instance, participatory mapping exercises have been used to identify socio-environmental determinants of health, allowing communities to collaboratively address issues such as pollution, access to healthcare, and availability of recreational spaces (Meyer et al., 2018). By incorporating local knowledge and experiences, urban planners can develop more effective and culturally relevant health interventions.

Additionally, the integration of technology in participatory planning processes has the potential to enhance community engagement. Digital tools, such as mobile applications and online platforms, can facilitate communication and collaboration among residents, planners, and policymakers (Prior, 2023; Reis da Silva, 2025i; Reis da Silva, 2025j). For example, participatory e-planning models have been developed to enable residents to contribute to urban planning discussions and decisions through interactive platforms (Reaver, 2023). This approach not only increases transparency but also encourages broader participation, particularly among younger populations who may be more comfortable using digital technologies (Reis da Silva, 2025k).

7. INTEGRATIVE HEALTH SOLUTIONS

Integrative health solutions in urban settings are becoming increasingly important as cities grapple with the complexities of urbanisation, population growth, and the diverse health needs of their residents. This section explores the role of traditional and integrative medicine in urban environments and discusses strategies for promoting emotional resilience and well-being among urban populations.

Traditional and Integrative Medicine in Urban Settings

Traditional and integrative medicine encompasses a wide range of practices that prioritise holistic approaches to health (Reis da Silva, 2024g). These practices often include herbal medicine, acupuncture, yoga, and mindfulness, which can complement conventional medical treatments. In urban settings, where access to healthcare services may be limited or fragmented, traditional and integrative medicine can provide valuable alternatives for managing health conditions and promoting overall well-being (Ramírez-Rubio et al., 2019). For instance, integrative health approaches have been shown to improve health outcomes for chronic conditions such as diabetes and hypertension, particularly in underserved populations (Yang et al., 2018). The integration of these practices into urban health systems can enhance the accessibility and effectiveness of healthcare services, addressing the unique needs of diverse communities.

Moreover, the incorporation of traditional and integrative medicine into urban health policies can foster a more inclusive approach to health promotion. By recognising the cultural significance of traditional healing practices, urban health initiatives can better engage communities and encourage participation in health programs (Fathi et al., 2020). For example, community health programs that incorporate traditional medicine have been successful in improving health literacy and promoting preventive care among marginalised populations (Lu et al., 2022). This approach not only respects cultural diversity but also empowers individuals to take an active role in their health management.

Promoting Emotional Resilience and Well-being in Urban Populations

Promoting emotional resilience and well-being in urban populations is another critical aspect of integrative health solutions. Urban environments can be stressful, with factors such as noise pollution, overcrowding, and social isolation contributing to mental health challenges (Peponi & Morgado, 2020; Reis da Silva, 2024f). To address these issues, cities can implement programs that foster social connections and community engagement. Research has shown that social integration is positively associated with mental health outcomes, highlighting the importance of creating supportive environments where individuals can connect with one another (Larter, 2024). Community-based interventions, such as support groups and recreational activities, can help build social networks and enhance emotional resilience among urban residents.

Additionally, urban design plays a crucial role in promoting emotional well-being. The creation of green spaces and public areas that encourage social interaction can significantly improve mental health outcomes (Reis da Silva, 2025a). Studies have demonstrated that access to nature and green infrastructure is linked to reduced stress levels and improved mood (Puig-Ribera et al., 2022). Urban planners should prioritise the development of parks, community gardens, and recreational facilities that foster social engagement and provide opportunities for physical activity. By integrating health considerations into urban design, cities can create environments that support the emotional and physical well-being of their residents.

Furthermore, the use of technology in promoting emotional resilience is gaining traction in urban health initiatives. Digital mental health platforms and mobile applications can provide accessible resources for individuals seeking support for mental health issues. These tools can facilitate connections to mental health professionals, offer self-help resources, and promote mindfulness practices (Zhao, 2024). By leveraging technology, urban health programs can reach a broader audience and provide timely support to those in need.

8. LINKING URBAN HEALTH TO SDGS

Aligning Urban Health Strategies with SDG 3 and SDG 11

The Sustainable Development Goals (SDGs), particularly SDG 3 (Good Health and Well-being) and SDG 11 (Sustainable Cities and Communities), provide a comprehensive framework for addressing urban health challenges (da Silva and Rodrigues, 2023). Aligning urban health strategies with these goals is essential for creating healthier urban environments that promote well-being for all residents. SDG 3 emphasises the need to ensure healthy lives and promote well-being for all at all ages, while SDG 11 focuses on making cities inclusive, safe, resilient, and sustainable (da Silva and Rodrigues, 2023; Thondoo, 2024).

To effectively align urban health strategies with SDG 3, cities must prioritise access to quality healthcare services, particularly for marginalised populations. This includes implementing policies that reduce health disparities and improve healthcare accessibility through community health programs and integrated service delivery models (Rahaman, 2023). For instance, urban health interventions that target chronic diseases, mental health, and maternal and child health can significantly contribute to achieving SDG 3 targets (Weeks, 2023). Moreover, the incorporation of traditional and integrative medicine into urban health strategies can enhance the overall health system by providing culturally relevant care options that resonate with diverse communities (Ren et al., 2016).

In relation to SDG 11, urban health strategies should focus on sustainable urban planning that incorporates green infrastructure and promotes active transportation. Research has shown that urban environments designed with health in mind—such as those featuring parks, pedestrian pathways, and bike lanes—can lead to improved physical and mental health outcomes (Barron et al., 2019). By integrating health considerations into urban design, cities can create environments that encourage physical activity, reduce pollution, and foster social cohesion (Lo et al., 2020). Furthermore, participatory planning approaches that engage community members in the design process can ensure that urban spaces meet the needs of all residents, thereby enhancing the inclusivity and sustainability of urban environments (McEwan et al., 2019).

Metrics for Evaluating Urban Health Interventions

To effectively evaluate urban health interventions and their alignment with SDGs, it is crucial to establish robust metrics that capture health outcomes, accessibility, and community engagement. Metrics should encompass both quantitative and qualitative indicators to provide a comprehensive assessment of health interventions. For instance, health outcome metrics could include rates of chronic diseases, mental health status, and access to healthcare services (Rahaman, 2023). Additionally, metrics related to environmental factors, such as air quality and green space availability, can provide insights into the broader determinants of health in urban settings (Puig-Ribera et al., 2022).

Community engagement metrics are also essential for evaluating the effectiveness of participatory planning approaches. These metrics could include the level of community involvement in decision-making processes, satisfaction with urban health initiatives, and the perceived impact of interventions on community well-being (Moll et al., 2019). By employing a multidimensional approach to metrics, policymakers can gain a deeper understanding of the effectiveness of urban health strategies and make informed decisions to enhance health outcomes (Wang, 2024).

9. RECOMMENDATIONS

Policy Reforms for Resilient Urban Health Systems

To build resilient urban health systems that effectively address the challenges posed by rapid urbanisation, policymakers must prioritise comprehensive reforms that integrate health considerations into all aspects of urban planning and development. This includes fostering collaboration between health, urban planning, and environmental sectors to create cohesive strategies that promote health equity and sustainability (Baum et al., 2017). Additionally, investments in green infrastructure and community-based health initiatives should be prioritized to enhance the resilience of urban health systems (Davis et al., 2022).

Furthermore, addressing social determinants of health through targeted interventions is essential for reducing health disparities in urban populations. This may involve implementing policies that improve access to education, employment, and housing, as well as enhancing transportation options to facilitate access to healthcare services (Yiga et al., 2022). By adopting a holistic approach that considers the interconnectedness of health, environment, and social factors, cities can create healthier and more equitable urban environments.

Future Directions in Urban Health Research and Practice

Future research in urban health should focus on the long-term impacts of urbanisation on health outcomes, particularly in the context of climate change and environmental degradation. Investigating the effectiveness of innovative interventions, such as nature-based solutions and digital health technologies, will be crucial for developing evidence-based practices that enhance urban health (Tuson et al., 2021). Moreover, research should explore the role of community engagement in shaping urban health policies and interventions, ensuring that the voices of marginalized populations are heard and considered (Chaet et al., 2016).

Additionally, the development of standardised metrics for evaluating urban health interventions will be essential for assessing progress towards SDG targets and informing policy decisions. By establishing a comprehensive framework for urban health metrics, researchers and practitioners can better understand the effectiveness of interventions and identify areas for improvement (Bartoll-Roca, 2024).

10. CONCLUSION

This chapter underscores the urgent need for comprehensive, multisectoral strategies to mitigate the health risks posed by rapid urbanisation, pollution, population growth, and industrialisation. It advocates for a holistic and sustainable approach to urban planning that integrates public health priorities, including stricter environmental regulations, equitable healthcare access, and improved living conditions. The detrimental health effects of air and water pollution demand targeted interventions, such as clean energy investments, waste management enhancements, and public awareness initiatives.

The discussion also highlights the compounded health vulnerabilities among marginalised populations, particularly due to overcrowding and systemic barriers in healthcare access. This necessitates inclusive urban health policies that promote equity and social justice. Industrialisation is presented as a critical area of concern due to its occupational health risks and environmental degradation, calling for stringent safety regulations, worker protections, and a culture of occupational health.

Older adults in urban settings face multifactorial health challenges, including chronic illness, inadequate healthcare access, and social isolation. The conclusion calls for age-friendly urban planning that fosters healthcare access, social engagement, and physical activity. Furthermore, it emphasises the role of innovative solutions, such as green infrastructure and participatory community planning, in addressing urban health disparities. Integrative health strategies, including the incorporation of traditional medicine and emotional resilience-building, are presented as essential for holistic urban health management.

Finally, aligning urban health initiatives with the Sustainable Development Goals (SDGs), fostering intersectoral collaboration, and implementing health-focused policy reforms are deemed crucial for achieving sustainable, resilient, and equitable urban health systems.

REFERENCES

Abokhashabah, T., Jamoussi, B., Summan, A., Abdelfattah, E., & Ahmad, I. (2021). Effects of heat stress exposure and climate change on health and safety of outdoor workers. *Current World Environment, 16*(3), 836–847. DOI: 10.12944/CWE.16.3.15

Akbar, D. (2023). Pollution and stunting (case study at Dki Jakarta). *Interaction Jurnal Pendidikan Bahasa, 10*(2), 764–776. DOI: 10.36232/jurnalpendidikanbahasa.v10i2.4899

Al-Sheddi, A., Kamel, S., Almeshal, A. S., & Assiri, A. M. (2023). Distribution of primary healthcare centers between 2017 and 2021 across Saudi Arabia. *Cureus*. Advance online publication. DOI: 10.7759/cureus.41932 PMID: 37583734

Ameen, B., & Abdulsahib, S. (2022). Association between morbidity patterns and chemical hazards among industry workers in Iraqi Kurdistan region. *International Journal of Health Sciences*, 2046–2058. DOI: 10.53730/ijhs.v6nS9.12863

Ampatzidou, C., Gugerell, K., Constantinescu, T., Devisch, O., Jauschneg, M., & Berger, M. (2018). All work and no play? facilitating serious games and gamified applications in participatory urban planning and governance. *Urban Planning, 3*(1), 34–46. DOI: 10.17645/up.v3i1.1261

Anwar, A., Ayub, M., Khan, N., & Flahault, A. (2019). Nexus between air pollution and neonatal deaths: A case of Asian countries. *International Journal of Environmental Research and Public Health, 16*(21), 4148. DOI: 10.3390/ijerph16214148 PMID: 31661852

Badri, F. (2023). Work-related de quervain's tensosynovitis (DQT): The diagnosis dilemma. *Cureus*. Advance online publication. DOI: 10.7759/cureus.33458 PMID: 36751202

Bahri, M., Al-Harthy, T., Hashmi, K., & Rishidi, I. (2022). Noise measurements in industrial areas in north a' Sharqiyah region -Oman. *International Journal of Research and Innovation in Applied Science, 07*(06), 43–47. DOI: 10.51584/IJRIAS.2022.7603

Banerjee, S. (2021). Determinants of rural-urban differential in healthcare utilization among the elderly population in India. *BMC Public Health, 21*(1), 939. Advance online publication. DOI: 10.1186/s12889-021-10773-1 PMID: 34001026

Barron, S., Nitoslawski, S., Wolf, K., Woo, A., Desautels, E., & Sheppard, S. (2019). Greening blocks: A conceptual typology of practical design interventions to integrate health and climate resilience co-benefits. *International Journal of Environmental Research and Public Health, 16*(21), 4241. DOI: 10.3390/ijerph16214241 PMID: 31683765

Bartoll-Roca, X., López, M. J., Pérez, K., Artazcoz, L., & Borrell, C. (2024). Short-term health effects of an urban regeneration programme in deprived neighbourhoods of Barcelona. *PLoS One, 19*(4), e0300470. DOI: 10.1371/journal.pone.0300470 PMID: 38630702

Barua, K., Borah, M., Deka, C., & Kakati, R. (2017). Morbidity pattern and health-seeking behavior of elderly in urban slums: A cross-sectional study in assam, India. *Journal of Family Medicine and Primary Care, 6*(2), 345. DOI: 10.4103/2249-4863.220030 PMID: 29302545

Baum, S., Machalaba, C., Daszak, P., Salerno, R., & Karesh, W. (2017). Evaluating one health: Are we demonstrating effectiveness? *One Health, 3*, 5–10. DOI: 10.1016/j.onehlt.2016.10.004 PMID: 28616496

Bhan, N., Madhira, P., Muralidharan, A., Kulkarni, B., Murthy, G., Basu, S., & Kinra, S. (2017). Health needs, access to healthcare, and perceptions of ageing in an urbanizing community in India: A qualitative study. *BMC Geriatrics, 17*(1), 156. Advance online publication. DOI: 10.1186/s12877-017-0544-y PMID: 28724399

Bijekar, S., Padariya, H., Yadav, V., Gacem, A., Hasan, M., Awwad, N., Yadav, K. K., Islam, S., Park, S., & Jeon, B. (2022). The state of the art and emerging trends in the wastewater treatment in developing nations. *Water (Basel), 14*(16), 2537. DOI: 10.3390/w14162537

Bräuer, M., Casadei, B., Harrington, R., Kovacs, R., & Sliwa, K. (2021). Taking a stand against air pollution—The impact on cardiovascular disease. *Circulation, 143*(14). Advance online publication. DOI: 10.1161/CIRCULATIONAHA.120.052666 PMID: 33506685

Chaet, A., Morshedi, B., Wells, K., Barnes, L., & Valdez, R. (2016). Spanish-language consumer health information technology interventions: A systematic review. *Journal of Medical Internet Research, 18*(8), e214. DOI: 10.2196/jmir.5794 PMID: 27511437

Chen, L., Chen, T., Lan, T., Chen, C., & Pan, J. (2023). The contributions of population distribution, healthcare resourcing, and transportation infrastructure to spatial accessibility of health care. *Inquiry : a Journal of Medical Care Organization, Provision and Financing, 60*, 00469580221146041. Advance online publication. DOI: 10.1177/00469580221146041 PMID: 36629371

Çiftçi, A., Vural, A., & Ural, M. (2021). Analysis of some concepts related to the environment and health with the n-gram method. *Journal of International Health Sciences and Management, 7*(13), 47–54. DOI: 10.48121/jihsam.796465

Cu, A., Meister, S., Lefebvre, B., & Ridde, V. (2021). Assessing healthcare access using the Levesque's conceptual framework– a scoping review. *International Journal for Equity in Health, 20*(1), 116. Advance online publication. DOI: 10.1186/s12939-021-01416-3 PMID: 33962627

Czermański, E., Oniszczuk-Jastrząbek, A., Laskowicz, T., Badyda, A., Reis, L. A., & Tzanis, C. G. (2024). Editorial: Air pollution as a risk factor affecting human health and economic costs. *Frontiers in Environmental Science, 12*, 1421547. Advance online publication. DOI: 10.3389/fenvs.2024.1421547

da Silva, T. H. R. (2022). Emotional awareness and emotional intelligence. *British Journal of Community Nursing, 27*(12), 573–574. DOI: 10.12968/bjcn.2022.27.12.573 PMID: 36519463

da Silva, T. H. R., & Rodrigues, E. C. P. (2023). Body Image Related Discrimination. In Leal Filho, W., Azul, A. M., Brandli, L., Lange Salvia, A., Özuyar, P. G., & Wall, T. (Eds.), *Reduced Inequalities. Encyclopedia of the UN Sustainable Development Goals*. Springer., DOI: 10.1007/978-3-319-71060-0_61-1

Davis, J., Ohan, J., Gibson, L., Prescott, S., & Finlay-Jones, A. (2022). Understanding engagement in digital mental health and well-being programs for women in the perinatal period: Systematic review without meta-analysis. *Journal of Medical Internet Research, 24*(8), e36620. DOI: 10.2196/36620 PMID: 35943773

Doetsch, J., Schlösser, C., Barros, H., Shaw, D., Krafft, T., & Pilot, E. (2023). A scoping review on the impact of austerity on healthcare access in the European union: Rethinking austerity for the most vulnerable. *International Journal for Equity in Health, 22*(1), 3. Advance online publication. DOI: 10.1186/s12939-022-01806-1 PMID: 36604705

Fathi, S., Sajadzadeh, H., Sheshkal, F., Aram, F., Pintér, G., Felde, I., & Mosavi, A. (2020). The role of urban morphology design on enhancing physical activity and public health. *International Journal of Environmental Research and Public Health, 17*(7), 2359. DOI: 10.3390/ijerph17072359 PMID: 32244358

Gatto, A., Martellozzo, F., Clo', S., Ciulla, L., & Segoni, S. (2024). The downward spiral entangling soil sealing and hydrogeological disasters. *Environmental Research Letters, 19*(8), 084023. DOI: 10.1088/1748-9326/ad5fa1

Ghorani-Azam, A., Riahi-Zanjani, B., & Balali-Mood, M. (2016). Effects of air pollution on human health and practical measures for prevention in Iran. *Journal of Research in Medical Sciences : the Official Journal of Isfahan University of Medical Sciences*, *21*(1), 65. DOI: 10.4103/1735-1995.189646 PMID: 27904610

Grigorieva, E., & Lukyanets, A. (2021). Combined effect of hot weather and outdoor air pollution on respiratory health: Literature review. *Atmosphere (Basel)*, *12*(6), 790. DOI: 10.3390/atmos12060790

Guan, Z., Yiu, T., Samarasinghe, D., & Reddy, R. (2022). Health and safety risk of migrant construction workers–a systematic literature review. *Engineering, Construction, and Architectural Management*, *31*(3), 1081–1099. DOI: 10.1108/ECAM-02-2022-0129

Haque, E. (2023). Towards equitable healthcare: A cross dataset analysis of healthcare and telehealth access. *Proceedings of the Association for Information Science and Technology*, *60*(1), 11–20. DOI: 10.1002/pra2.764

Hou, H., Wang, H., Wang, Y., Yu, J., & Qiu, G. (2022). Construction path of smart health care platform for the elderly in China. *Zhongguo Gongcheng Kexue*, *24*(2), 170. DOI: 10.15302/J-SSCAE-2022.02.023

Hsieh, C., & Shih, Y.-L. (2023). Study on home-based direct care workers' coping responses to workplace sexual harassment and their satisfaction with long-term care preventive strategies. *International Journal of Studies in Nursing*, *8*(3), 6. DOI: 10.20849/ijsn.v8i3.1392

Hussein, F., Stephens, J., & Tiwari, R. (2020). Memory for social sustainability: Recalling cultural memories in Zanqit Alsitat historical street market, Alexandria, Egypt. *Sustainability (Basel)*, *12*(19), 8141. DOI: 10.3390/su12198141

Jian, L., Matthews, T., Clausen, T., & Rugulies, R. (2023). Workplace discrimination and risk of hypertension: Findings from a prospective cohort study in the united states. *Journal of the American Heart Association*, *12*(9), e027374. Advance online publication. DOI: 10.1161/JAHA.122.027374 PMID: 37099326

Jovanović, J., Šarac, I., Đinđić, N., & Jovanović, S. (2017). The influence of working conditions, health status and characteristics of workers on the occurrence of workplace injuries. *Acta Medica Medianae*, *56*(4), 17–24. DOI: 10.5633/amm.2017.0403

Kim, D., Chen, Z., Zhou, L., & Huang, S. (2018). Air pollutants and early origins of respiratory diseases. *Chronic Diseases and Translational Medicine*, *4*(2), 75–94. DOI: 10.1016/j.cdtm.2018.03.003 PMID: 29988883

Kim, Y., Park, J., & Park, M. (2016). Creating a culture of prevention in occupational safety and health practice. *Safety and Health at Work*, *7*(2), 89–96. DOI: 10.1016/j.shaw.2016.02.002 PMID: 27340594

Krishnamoorthy, Y., Rajaa, S., Ramasubramani, P., & Saya, G. (2021). Association between indoor air pollution and cognitive function among nationally representative sample of middle-aged and older adults in India—A multilevel modelling approach. *Indoor Air*, *32*(1). Advance online publication. DOI: 10.1111/ina.12929 PMID: 34510562

Kurt, O., Zhang, J., & Pinkerton, K. (2016). Pulmonary health effects of air pollution. *Current Opinion in Pulmonary Medicine*, *22*(2), 138–143. DOI: 10.1097/MCP.0000000000000248 PMID: 26761628

Larter, N., Jersky, M., Ryan, L., Harding, G., Moore, M., Hamill, L., Caplice, S., Woolfenden, S., & Zwi, K. (2024). Strength-based approaches to providing an aboriginal community child health service. *International Journal of Indigenous Health*, *19*(1). Advance online publication. DOI: 10.32799/ijih.v19i1.41292

Lawani, K. (2023). Exploring mental health challenges and implications for construction safety. Journal of Engineering Design and Technology. DOI: 10.1108/JEDT-07-2023-0327

Lee, H., & Lee, D. (2019). Do sociodemographic factors and urban green space affect mental health outcomes among the urban elderly population? *International Journal of Environmental Research and Public Health*, *16*(5), 789. DOI: 10.3390/ijerph16050789 PMID: 30836691

Li, J., & Zuo, C. (2022). Can the urban growth boundary reduce urban industrial air pollution in China? a study from the perspective of the sustainability of land urbanization. *Polish Journal of Environmental Studies*, *31*(5), 4745–4756. DOI: 10.15244/pjoes/150070

Li, L., Du, T., & Zhang, C. (2020). The impact of air pollution on healthcare expenditure for respiratory diseases: Evidence from the people's republic of China. *Risk Management and Healthcare Policy*, *13*, 1723–1738. DOI: 10.2147/RMHP.S270587 PMID: 33061706

Liu, H., Fan, X., Luo, H., Zhou, Z., Shen, C., Hu, N., & Zhai, X. (2021). Comparison of depressive symptoms and its influencing factors among the elderly in urban and rural areas: Evidence from the China health and retirement longitudinal study (charls). *International Journal of Environmental Research and Public Health*, *18*(8), 3886. DOI: 10.3390/ijerph18083886 PMID: 33917216

Liu, Y., & Ao, C. (2021). Effect of air pollution on health care expenditure: Evidence from respiratory diseases. *Health Economics, 30*(4), 858–875. DOI: 10.1002/hec.4221 PMID: 33556215

Lo, B., Shi, J., Hollenberg, E., Abi-Jaoudé, A., Johnson, A., & Wiljer, D. (2020). Surveying the role of analytics in evaluating digital mental health interventions for transition-aged youth: Scoping review. *JMIR Mental Health, 7*(6), e15942. DOI: 10.2196/15942 PMID: 32348261

Lu, H., Kandilov, I., & Wang, Y. (2022). Heterogeneous impact of social integration on the health of rural-to-urban migrants in China. *International Journal of Environmental Research and Public Health, 19*(16), 9999. DOI: 10.3390/ijerph19169999 PMID: 36011631

Macdonald, W., & Oakman, J. (2024). Changes needed to reduce risk of musculoskeletal disorders. *American Journal of Industrial Medicine, 67*(7), 575–581. DOI: 10.1002/ajim.23613 PMID: 38752696

McEwan, K., Richardson, M., Sheffield, D., Ferguson, F., & Brindley, P. (2019). A smartphone app for improving mental health through connecting with urban nature. *International Journal of Environmental Research and Public Health, 16*(18), 3373. DOI: 10.3390/ijerph16183373 PMID: 31547286

McMaughan, D., Oloruntoba, O., & Smith, M. (2020). Socioeconomic status and access to healthcare: Interrelated drivers for healthy aging. *Frontiers in Public Health, 8*, 231. Advance online publication. DOI: 10.3389/fpubh.2020.00231 PMID: 32626678

Meyer, M., Hendricks, M., Newman, G., Masterson, J., Cooper, J., Sansom, G., Gharaibeh, N., Horney, J., Berke, P., van Zandt, S., & Cousins, T. (2018). Participatory action research: Tools for disaster resilience education. *International Journal of Disaster Resilience in the Built Environment, 9*(4/5), 402–419. DOI: 10.1108/IJDRBE-02-2017-0015 PMID: 30519288

Mialon, M., Swinburn, B., Wate, J., Tukana, I., & Sacks, G. (2016). Analysis of the corporate political activity of major food industry actors in Fiji. *Globalization and Health, 12*(1), 18. Advance online publication. DOI: 10.1186/s12992-016-0158-8 PMID: 27160250

Moll, R., Cepek, J., Lorch, P., Dennis, P., Tans, E., Robison, T., Millspaugh, J. J., & Montgomery, R. (2019). What does urbanization actually mean? a framework for urban metrics in wildlife research. *Journal of Applied Ecology, 56*(5), 1289–1300. DOI: 10.1111/1365-2664.13358

Mucchielli, L. (2023). Environmental and corporate crimes., 520-534. DOI: 10.4018/979-8-3693-2045-7.ch028

Mutono, N., Wright, J., Mutunga, M., Mutembei, H., & Thumbi, S. (2022). Impact of traffic congestion on spatial access to healthcare services in Nairobi. *Frontiers in Health Services*, *2*, 788173. Advance online publication. DOI: 10.3389/frhs.2022.788173 PMID: 36925766

Ndejjo, R., Musinguzi, G., Yu, X., Buregyeya, E., Musoke, D., Wang, J., Halage, A. A., Whalen, C., Bazeyo, W., Williams, P., & Ssempebwa, J. (2015). Occupational health hazards among healthcare workers in Kampala, Uganda. *Journal of Environmental and Public Health*, *2015*, 1–9. DOI: 10.1155/2015/913741 PMID: 25802531

Oche, O., Nneka, O., Abiola, O., Raji, I., Jessica, A., Bala, H., & Ijapa, A. (2020). Determinants of occupational health hazards among roadside automobile mechanics in Sokoto metropolis, Nigeria. *Annals of African Medicine*, *19*(2), 80. DOI: 10.4103/aam.aam_50_18 PMID: 32499463

Onguto, N., Peterson, W., & Mwanzo, I. (2020). Knowledge about physical hazards and use of personal protective equipment based on demographic characteristics and among small scale welders in Nairobi city, Kenya. *Journal of Scientific Research and Reports*, 120–130. DOI: 10.9734/jsrr/2020/v26i630277

Palla, A., Pezzagno, M., Spadaro, I., & Ermini, R. (2024). Participatory approach to planning urban resilience to climate change: Brescia, Genoa, and Matera—three case studies from Italy compared. *Sustainability (Basel)*, *16*(5), 2170. DOI: 10.3390/su16052170

Parak, Y., Davis, R., Barnard, M., Fernandez, A., Cloete, K., Mukosi, M., & Pitcher, R. (2022). A 6-year audit of public-sector mr utilisation in the western cape province of south Africa. *SA Journal of Radiology*, *26*(1). Advance online publication. DOI: 10.4102/sajr.v26i1.2464 PMID: 35936227

Peponi, A., & Morgado, P. (2020). Smart and regenerative urban growth: A literature network analysis. *International Journal of Environmental Research and Public Health*, *17*(7), 2463. DOI: 10.3390/ijerph17072463 PMID: 32260315

Prior, J., Legg, R., & McIntyre, E. (2023). A participatory system map of the adverse influence of urban environments on population health: Integrating urban development and preventive health expertise. *Public Health Research & Practice*, *33*(4). Advance online publication. DOI: 10.17061/phrp3342335 PMID: 38052202

Priyankara, S., Senarathna, M., Jayaratne, R., Morawska, L., Abeysundara, S., Weerasooriya, R., Knibbs, L. D., Dharmage, S. C., Yasaratne, D., & Bowatte, G. (2021). Ambient pm2.5 and pm10 exposure and respiratory disease hospitalization in Kandy, Sri Lanka. *International Journal of Environmental Research and Public Health, 18*(18), 9617. DOI: 10.3390/ijerph18189617 PMID: 34574538

Puig-Ribera, A., Rofin, M., Bort-Roig, J., Aumatell, E., Pujol, A., Pedro, M., & Geli, M. (2022). Integrating health into the urban master plan of vic, barcelona: A comprehensive approach. *Urban Planning, 7*(4). Advance online publication. DOI: 10.17645/up.v7i4.5492

Qiu, L., Chen, Q., & Gao, T. (2021). The effects of urban natural environments on preference and self-reported psychological restoration of the elderly. *International Journal of Environmental Research and Public Health, 18*(2), 509. DOI: 10.3390/ijerph18020509 PMID: 33435508

Rahaman, M., Kalam, A., & Al-Mamun, M. (2023). Unplanned urbanization and health risks of Dhaka city in Bangladesh: Uncovering the associations between urban environment and public health. *Frontiers in Public Health, 11*, 1269362. Advance online publication. DOI: 10.3389/fpubh.2023.1269362 PMID: 37927876

Ramírez, C. (2024). Impact of air quality on respiratory health in children in Mexico. *Global Journal of Health Science, 9*(2), 1–10. DOI: 10.47604/gjhs.2575

Ramírez-Rubio, O., Daher, C., Fanjul, G., Gascón, M., Mueller, N., Pajín, L., Plasencia, A., Rojas-Rueda, D., Thondoo, M., & Nieuwenhuijsen, M. (2019). Urban health: An example of a "health in all policies" approach in the context of SDGS implementation. *Globalization and Health, 15*(1), 87. Advance online publication. DOI: 10.1186/s12992-019-0529-z PMID: 31856877

Reaver, K. (2023). Augmented reality as a participation tool for youth in urban planning processes: Case study in Oslo, Norway. *Frontiers in Virtual Reality, 4*, 1055930. Advance online publication. DOI: 10.3389/frvir.2023.1055930

Reis da Silva, T. H. (2023a). Moving and Handling in the Community. *British Journal of Community Nursing, 28*(8), 369. DOI: 10.12968/bjcn.2023.28.8.369 PMID: 37527217

Reis da Silva, T. H. (2023b). Falls assessment and prevention in the nursing home and community. *British Journal of Community Nursing, 28*(2), 68–72. DOI: 10.12968/bjcn.2023.28.2.68 PMID: 36735363

Reis da Silva, T. H. (2023c). Ageing in place: Ageing at home and in the community. *British Journal of Community Nursing*, *28*(5), 213–214. DOI: 10.12968/bjcn.2023.28.5.213 PMID: 37130715

Reis da Silva, T. H. (2024a). Enhancing the mental health of refugees and asylum seekers through music interventions. *Mental Health Practice*. Advance online publication. DOI: 10.7748/mhp.2024.e1717

Reis da Silva, T. H (2024b). Oncology and Cancer Medicine: Understanding the complexities in Older Patients. *Biomed J Sci & Tech Res*, *55*(3)-2024. DOI: 10.26717/BJSTR.2024.55.008720

Reis da Silva, T. H. (2024c). Falls prevention in older people and the role of nursing. *British Journal of Community Nursing*, *29*(7), 335–339. DOI: 10.12968/bjcn.2024.0005 PMID: 38963269

Reis da Silva, T. H. (2024d). Navigating Healthcare Complexity: Integrating Business Fundamentals into Nursing Leadership. In A. Sedky (Ed.) *Resiliency Strategies for Long-Term Business Success* (pp. 145-168). IGI Global. DOI: 10.4018/979-8-3693-9168-6.ch006

Reis da Silva, T. H. (2024e). Integrating business essentials into Gerontological Nursing: Enhancing Care for Older Adults in Diverse Settings. In A. Sedky (Ed.) *Resiliency Strategies for Long-Term Business Success*. (pp. 283-316). IGI Global. DOI: 10.4018/979-8-3693-9168-6.ch011

Reis da Silva, T. H. (2024f). Loneliness in older adults. *British Journal of Community Nursing*, *29*(2), 60–66. DOI: 10.12968/bjcn.2024.29.2.60 PMID: 38300245

Reis da Silva, T. H. (2024g). Emotional Intelligence in Integrative Medicine: Enhancing Patient-Centred Care Through Humanised Technology. In Tikadar, S. (Ed.), *Liu, H.; Bhattacharya, P.; Bhattacharya, S. Humanizing Technology With Emotional Intelligence*. IGI Global Scientific Publishing., DOI: 10.4018/979-8-3693-7011-7.ch012

Reis da Silva, T. M. (2025a). Designing for Longevity: Economic Perspectives on Age-Friendly Housing and Urban Development. In Gölçek, A. (Ed.), *Perspectives on the Economics of Aging* (pp. 151–176). IGI Global Scientific Publishing., DOI: 10.4018/979-8-3693-7753-6.ch006

Reis da Silva, T. M. (2025b). Cultivating Emotionally Intelligent Leadership: Strategies for Enhancing Authentic Engagement and Organisational Impact. In Sayed, Z. (Ed.), *Emotionally Intelligent Methods for Meaningful Leadership* (pp. 119–148). IGI Global Scientific Publishing., DOI: 10.4018/979-8-3693-7372-9.ch006

Reis da Silva, T. M. H. (2025c). The Role of Emotional Intelligence in Promoting Mental Peace, Healthy Work Environments, and Emotional Well-Being Among Entrepreneurs. In Tunio, M. N. (Ed.), *Supporting Psychological and Emotional Well-being Among Entrepreneurs*. IGI Global Scientific Publishing., DOI: 10.4018/979-8-3693-3673-1.ch21

Reis da Silva, T. M. (2025d). Fostering Emotional Intelligence for Competency Development in Nursing Education. In Aldosemani, T., Lytras, M., & Ordóñez de Pablos, P. (Eds.), *Innovative Educational Frameworks for Future Skills and Competencies* (pp. 39–62). IGI Global Scientific Publishing., DOI: 10.4018/979-8-3693-7555-6.ch002

Reis da Silva, T. H. (2025e). Promoting Emotional Well-Being in Older Adults: The Role of AI in Supporting Emotional Intelligence and Mental Health. In Jermsittiparsert, K., & Marzo, R. R. (Eds.), *Physical Health, Mental Health, and Human Well-Being in the Age of AI* (pp. 137–167). IGI Global Scientific Publishing., DOI: 10.4018/979-8-3693-6190-0.ch8

Reis da Silva, T. M. (2025f). Integrative Approaches to Geriatric Care: Enhancing Physical and Mental Health Through AI-Driven Insights. In Jermsittiparsert, K., & Marzo, R. (Eds.), *Physical Health, Mental Health, and Human Well-Being in the Age of AI* (pp. 113–136). IGI Global Scientific Publishing., DOI: 10.4018/979-8-3693-6190-0.ch007

Reis da Silva, T. H. (2025g). Promoting Emotional Well-Being in Older Adults: The Role of AI in Supporting Emotional Intelligence and Mental Health. In Jermsittiparsert, K., & Marzo, R. R. (Eds.), *Physical Health, Mental Health, and Human Well-Being in the Age of AI* (pp. 137–167). IGI Global Scientific Publishing., DOI: 10.4018/979-8-3693-6190-0.ch8

Reis da Silva, T. H. (2025h). Integrating Artificial Intelligence in Geriatric Care: Enhancing Physical and Mental Health Outcomes. In Jermsittiparsert, K., & Marzo, R. R. (Eds.), *Physical Health, Mental Health, and Human Well-Being in the Age of AI*. IGI Global Scientific Publishing., DOI: 10.4018/979-8-3693-6190-0.ch11

Reis da Silva, T. M. (2025i). Gamification as a Pedagogical Tool in Geriatric Nursing: Engaging and Empowering Future Nurses. In Marcão, R., & Ribeiro Santos, V. (Eds.), *Enhancing Engagement With Gamification: Education, Business, and Healthcare Perspectives* (pp. 103–136). IGI Global Scientific Publishing., DOI: 10.4018/979-8-3693-8322-3.ch005

Reis da Silva, T. H. (2025j). AI-Powered Emotional Intelligence in Nursing: Bridging the Gap in Older People Care. In Jermsittiparsert, K., & Marzo, R. R. (Eds.), *Physical Health, Mental Health, and Human Well-Being in the Age of AI*. IGI Global Scientific Publishing., DOI: 10.4018/979-8-3693-6190-0.ch9

Reis da Silva, T. H. (2025k). Emotional Intelligence and AI in Geriatric Nursing: Bridging Technology and Compassionate Care. In Jermsittiparsert, K., & Marzo, R. R. (Eds.), *Physical Health, Mental Health, and Human Well-Being in the Age of AI*. IGI Global Scientific Publishing., DOI: 10.4018/979-8-3693-6190-0.ch10

Reis da Silva, T. M., Hammett, R., & Low, G. (2025). Emotional Intelligence in Business: Enhancing Leadership, Collaboration, and Performance. In Sedky, A. (Ed.), *Building Business Knowledge for Complex Modern Business Environments* (pp. 149–178). IGI Global Scientific Publishing., DOI: 10.4018/979-8-3693-6447-5.ch006

Ren, J., Guo, X., Lu, Z., Zhang, J., Tang, J., Chen, X., Gao, C. C., Xu, C. X., & Xu, A. (2016). Ideal cardiovascular health status and its association with socioeconomic factors in Chinese adults in Shandong, China. *BMC Public Health*, *16*(1), 942. Advance online publication. DOI: 10.1186/s12889-016-3632-6 PMID: 27605115

Rupprecht, C. (2017). Informal urban green space: Residents' perception, use, and management preferences across four major Japanese shrinking cities. *Land (Basel)*, *6*(3), 59. DOI: 10.3390/land6030059

Ruziyev, S. (2024). Development of measures to reduce air pollutants as much as possible. *SCBMEJ*, *1*(2), 7. DOI: 10.47134/scbmej.v1i2.2400

Sadler, D., Arnold, A., Herrmann, J., Daniele, A., Silva, C., Ghosh, A., Szmit, S., Khan, R. I., Raez, L., Blaes, A., & Brown, S. (2021). Reaching across the aisle: Cardio-oncology advocacy and program building. *Current Oncology Reports*, *23*(6), 64. Advance online publication. DOI: 10.1007/s11912-021-01059-1 PMID: 33855620

Saini, D. K., & Kumar, M.SAINI. (2022). Seasonal changes in respiratory health status of road-side vendors in industrial city Gajraula. *Pollution Research*, •••, 1106–1111. DOI: 10.53550/PR.2022.v41i03.048

Santos, I. (2024). Examining the relationship between air quality and respiratory health in urban environments in Brazil. *AJPS*, *2*(2), 1–12. DOI: 10.47604/ajps.2669

Sazali, M., Dulhamid, H., & Zainol, H. (2022). Elderly's feedback on the service quality of urban green open space in Penang as a catalyst for health and lifestyle resilience. *E-Bangi Journal of Social Science and Humanities*, (4). Advance online publication. DOI: 10.17576/ebangi.2022.1904.12

Sharma, D., Shah, U., & Singh, U. (2021). Epidemiological correlates of well being at work place and hazards identification and risk assessment amongst saw mill workers in Anand, Gujarat. *Indian Journal of Occupational and Environmental Medicine*, *25*(3), 152–156. DOI: 10.4103/ijoem.ijoem_356_20 PMID: 34759602

Shi, L., Sun, C., Liu, C., Jiang, L., Xie, Y., Yan, S., & Zhang, A. (2021). The influence of air pollutants and meteorological conditions on the hospitalization for respiratory diseases in shenzhen city, china. *International Journal of Environmental Research and Public Health*, *18*(10), 5120. DOI: 10.3390/ijerph18105120 PMID: 34065982

Somsopon, W., Kim, S., Nitivattananon, V., Kusakabe, K., & Nguyen, T. (2022). Issues and needs of elderly in community facilities and services: A case study of urban housing projects in Bangkok, Thailand. *Sustainability (Basel)*, *14*(14), 8388. DOI: 10.3390/su14148388

Spencer, B., Jones, T., Carpenter, J., & Brownill, S. (2023). *The potential for public participation in planning healthy urban mobility: the case of Oxford.*, DOI: 10.1108/S2044-994120230000018006

Thondoo, M., Mogo, E. R. I., Tatah, L., Muti, M., van Daalen, K. R., Muzenda, T., Boscott, R., Uwais, O., Farmer, G., Yue, A., Dalzell, S., Mukoma, G., Bhagtani, D., Matina, S., Dambisya, P. M., Okop, K., Ebikeme, C., Micklesfield, L., & Oni, T. (2024). Multisectoral interventions for urban health in Africa: A mixed-methods systematic review. *Global Health Action*, *17*(1), 2325726. Advance online publication. DOI: 10.1080/16549716.2024.2325726 PMID: 38577879

Tolera, S., Assefa, N., Geremew, A., Toseva, E., & Gobena, T. (2024). Magnitude and associated factors of occupational hazard exposures among sanitary workers: Propose rasm model for risk mitigation for the public hospitals, eastern Ethiopia. *BMC Research Notes*, *17*(1), 172. Advance online publication. DOI: 10.1186/s13104-024-06828-2 PMID: 38902762

Tran, B., Vu, G., Pham, K., Vuong, Q., H , M., Vuong, T., Nguyen, H.-K. T., Nguyen, C. T., Latkin, C. A., Ho, C. S. H., & Ho, R. (2019). Depressive symptoms among industrial workers in Vietnam and correlated factors: A multi-site survey. *International Journal of Environmental Research and Public Health*, *16*(9), 1642. DOI: 10.3390/ijerph16091642 PMID: 31083499

Tripathi, V., & Preetha, G. S. (2024). Public health infrastructure and human resources in tribal areas of India: A decadal assessment (2012–2022) with rural health statistics data. *International Journal of Health Governance*, *29*(2), 162–175. DOI: 10.1108/IJHG-03-2024-0025

Tuson, M., Turlach, B., Murray, K., Kok, M., Vickery, A., & Whyatt, D. (2021). Predicting future geographic hotspots of potentially preventable hospitalisations using all subset model selection and repeated k-fold cross-validation. *International Journal of Environmental Research and Public Health, 18*(19), 10253. DOI: 10.3390/ijerph181910253 PMID: 34639555

Uddin, S., Albert, A., Ovid, A., & Alsharef, A. (2023). Leveraging chatgpt to aid construction hazard recognition and support safety education and training. *Sustainability (Basel), 15*(9), 7121. DOI: 10.3390/su15097121

Wang, Y., Timms, F., Li, J., & Yu, H. (2024). Benefits of nature-based intervention in combating the impact of urbanization on psychopathology in industrialized societies. *Current Opinion in Psychiatry, 37*(3), 202–211. DOI: 10.1097/YCO.0000000000000937 PMID: 38415720

Weeks, W., Chang, J. E., Pagán, J. A., Lumpkin, J., Michael, D., Salcido, S., Kim, A., Speyer, P., Aerts, A., Weinstein, J. N., & Lavista, J. M. (2023). Rural-urban disparities in health outcomes, clinical care, health behaviors, and social determinants of health and an action-oriented, dynamic tool for visualizing them. *PLOS Global Public Health, 3*(10), e0002420. DOI: 10.1371/journal.pgph.0002420 PMID: 37788228

Wijaya, R., Permatasari, H., Fitriyani, P., & Setiyadi, A. (2022). Nurses' experiences as worker during the covid-19 pandemic. *The Malaysian Journal of Nursing, 14*(01), 45–52. DOI: 10.31674/mjn.2022.v14i01.007

Yang, X., Chen, M., Du, J., & Wang, Z. (2018). The inequality of inpatient care net benefit under integration of urban-rural medical insurance systems in China. *International Journal for Equity in Health, 17*(1), 173. Advance online publication. DOI: 10.1186/s12939-018-0891-0 PMID: 30466451

Yiga, P., Lippevelde, W., Seghers, J., Ogwok, P., Tafiire, H., Muluuta, S., & Matthys, C. (2022). The conceptual framework for a combined food literacy and physical activity intervention to optimize metabolic health among women of reproductive age in urban uganda. *BMC Public Health, 22*(1), 351. Advance online publication. DOI: 10.1186/s12889-022-12740-w PMID: 35183134

Yu, H., & Ahlgren, E. (2023). Enhancing urban heating systems planning through spatially explicit participatory modeling. *Energies, 16*(11), 4264. DOI: 10.3390/en16114264

Zebrak, K., Yount, N., Sorra, J., Famolaro, T., Gray, L., Carpenter, D., & Caporaso, A. (2022). Development, pilot study, and psychometric analysis of the AHRQ surveys on patient safety culture™ (sops®) workplace safety supplemental items for hospitals. *International Journal of Environmental Research and Public Health*, *19*(11), 6815. DOI: 10.3390/ijerph19116815 PMID: 35682402

Zhao, Q., Wu, G., & Wang, H. (2024). Effect of health rights accessibility on the urban integration of minority rural migrants in China: A cross-sectional study. *BMC Public Health*, *24*(1), 761. Advance online publication. DOI: 10.1186/s12889-024-18294-3 PMID: 38468194

Zhong, S., Yu, Z., & Zhu, W. (2019). Study of the effects of air pollutants on human health based on Baidu indices of disease symptoms and air quality monitoring data in beijing, China. *International Journal of Environmental Research and Public Health*, *16*(6), 1014. DOI: 10.3390/ijerph16061014 PMID: 30897769

Zhou, Z., Gao, J., Lai, S., & Chen, G. (2018). Urban-rural difference in the associations between living arrangements and the health-related quality of life (hrqol) of the elderly in china—Evidence from Shaanxi province. *PLoS One*, *13*(9), e0204118. DOI: 10.1371/journal.pone.0204118 PMID: 30235258

Zulfikri, A. (2023). Effects of pollution and transportation on public health in Jakarta. *West Science Interdisciplinary Studies*, *1*(03), 22–26. DOI: 10.58812/wsis.v1i03.51

Chapter 4
Defining Tuberculosis Notification:
Key Determinants and Associated Factors

Suryanti Chan
https://orcid.org/0009-0008-9978-2511
Universitas Dian Nuswantoro, Indonesia & Lincoln University College, Malaysia

Idris Adewale Ahmed
Lincoln University College, Malaysia

Hamzah Hamzah
University Batam, Indonesia

ABSTRACT

Tuberculosis (TB) remains one of the most deadly infectious diseases worldwide, with accurate notification playing a critical role in its control. This chapter explores the importance of TB notification in public health, focusing on international guidelines from the World Health Organization (WHO) and their implementation in high burden of TB, such as Indonesia. Several factors associated with TB notification, such as patient demographics, healthcare provider characteristics, and notification-system challenges, are discussed. The chapter also highlights the problem of under-notification in private healthcare settings and examines how technological advancements can improve notification systems. Finally, it provides policy recommendations for enhancing TB notification, emphasizing private-public partnerships and regulatory reforms.

DOI: 10.4018/979-8-3693-9755-8.ch004

INTRODUCTION

Globally, tuberculosis (TB) continues to be a major contributor to mortality from infectious diseases. According to the World Health Organization (2023), TB was responsible for roughly 1.3 million deaths worldwide in 2022, solidifying its position as a leading cause of infectious disease-related deaths (World Health Organization, 2023). Even with worldwide efforts spearheaded by the WHO and improvements in diagnosis and treatment strategies, tuberculosis (TB) presents a formidable public health challenge, with a disproportionate impact on high-burden nations like Indonesia, India, and Nigeria. In these settings, constrained health systems, poverty, and limited access to care exacerbate the impact of the disease.

Accurate and timely reporting of diagnosed TB cases is essential for TB control. This process, known as notification, which involves the official reporting of TB cases to public health bodies, allows for disease monitoring, aids in the effective distribution of resources, and promotes the application of specific control measures. A key challenge to effective tuberculosis (TB) management is the persistent issue of under-notification, particularly in private healthcare settings. This is often attributable to deficiencies in knowledge, a lack of motivating incentives, and the fragmented nature of health systems (Rusnoto, Murti, & Reviono, 2022; Suryanti & Ahmed, 2024).

Tuberculosis poses a significant challenge in Indonesia, a country that ranks among those with the highest TB burden in the world, the challenge of under-reporting—especially within the private health sector—continues to hinder national TB control efforts. A recent review highlighted the critical need for stronger integration between public and private systems to improve case detection and reporting (Suryanti & Ahmed IA, 2025).

A wide range of factors influence TB notification practices, including demographic characteristics of patients, such as socioeconomic status, geographic location, and gender, as well as the competencies and motivations of healthcare providers. Operational barriers within health information systems—such as inadequate infrastructure, data fragmentation, and lack of interoperability between public and private sectors—further impede comprehensive reporting. In high-burden countries, the disconnect between public health mandates and the realities of private clinical practice contributes to persistent data gaps and missed opportunities for intervention.

Strengthening TB notification systems requires a multifaceted approach. Policy reforms must be supported by strong regulatory frameworks and public-private collaboration, while frontline healthcare workers need greater support through training, simplified reporting tools, and incentive mechanisms. Addressing TB stigma, enhancing community engagement, and leveraging digital technologies are also essential to improving case detection and reporting accuracy.

This chapter explores the key determinants of TB notification, with a particular focus on challenges within private healthcare. It highlights how systemic and provider-level barriers intersect to produce under-reporting, and outlines strategies to strengthen TB surveillance systems through innovation, collaboration, and inclusive policy design.

TUBERCULOSIS (TB) NOTIFICATION

Tuberculosis (TB) notification denotes the official procedure for reporting confirmed instances of the disease to health authorities, with subsequent transmission of this information to the National Tuberculosis Program (NTP). This process plays a vital role in identifying tuberculosis cases, reducing the spread of the disease, and guiding appropriate public health interventions. The absence of a robust notification system would severely impede efforts to track TB trends, optimize resource allocation, and formulate focused interventions.

"The evolution of tuberculosis (TB) notification has been shaped by advancements in surveillance technologies and the reinforcement of health system infrastructures. Contemporary notification systems facilitate real-time data acquisition, thereby aiding health authorities in the identification of TB hotspots, the evaluation of treatment program efficacy, and the monitoring of national and global TB control strategy progress. Timely and accurate notification also supports early diagnosis and prompt treatment—key components in breaking the chain of transmission. Additionally, notification data inform epidemiological research, policy formulation, and global cooperation in TB elimination efforts (Uplekar et al., 2016; Gawde, 2013; Dirjen, 2023).

In 2014 and 2015, all countries under the World Health Organization (WHO) and the United Nations (UN) endorsed global commitments to eliminate tuberculosis by adopting the WHO's End TB Strategy and the UN's Sustainable Development Goals (SDGs). These strategic frameworks outlined clear milestones for 2020 and 2025, as well as ambitious targets for 2030 and 2035, focusing on significant declines in TB incidence, mortality, and the financial burden faced by patients. The End TB Strategy is built upon three main pillars: (1) integrated, patient-focused care and prevention, (2) bold policies supported by robust systems, and (3) strengthened research and innovation. Within this strategy, mandatory TB case notification is highlighted as a key policy action, especially in countries with a high TB burden (World Health Organization, 2022).

The notification system not only facilitates intervention but also serves as an epidemiological indicator of TB incidence. In countries with mature TB surveillance mechanisms, notification data provide reliable insights into disease trends and program effectiveness. However, many high-incidence countries still lack strong enforcement of mandatory notification policies, leading to persistent under-reporting. Strengthening legal frameworks and improving compliance mechanisms remain critical steps to enhance notification accuracy and coverage (Uplekar et al., 2016; Directorate General of Disease Prevention and Control, 2018).

Recent innovations in digital health have also contributed to improved surveillance, reporting, and treatment adherence. Although numerous tools are developed to assist patients in adhering to TB treatment, they also play an important role in enabling real-time monitoring and improving data collection—both of which are essential for accurate case notification. For example, digital adherence technologies (DATs) such as mobile health (mHealth) apps and smart pillboxes have been shown to improve treatment outcomes and facilitate integrated data reporting (Lee, Rajaguru, Baek, Shin, & Park, 2023).

A large-scale implementation in China further demonstrated the benefits of comprehensive digital innovation for TB control. The China-Gates TB Project successfully scaled electronic medication monitoring systems (EMMs), integrated e-learning modules for TB care providers, and developed automated data exchange within a national TB information system. These efforts contributed significantly to improved notification practices and stronger integration between care delivery and data reporting (Long, Huang, Huan, & Zhao, 2021).

Additionally, recent spatial–temporal analyses have emphasized the importance of contextual and environmental factors in TB trends and notification. A study by Bie et al. (2021) highlighted that TB risk in mainland China varied by region and season, with higher incidence rates influenced by environmental conditions such as precipitation, sunshine duration, and socioeconomic variables like GDP per capita. These findings underscore the need for geographically targeted strategies in TB surveillance and control, especially in regions with structural vulnerabilities (Bie et al., 2021).

TRENDS AND RECENT DEVELOPMENTS IN TB NOTIFICATION

Prior to the onset of the COVID-19 pandemic, global TB notifications experienced a steady upward trend, with a particularly significant rise in reported cases between 2017 and 2019. The culmination of this trend was marked by 7.1 million individuals receiving new TB diagnoses and official notification by 2019. In contrast, the emergence of the COVID-19 pandemic in early 2020 led to a sharp 18% decrease in global TB case notifications between 2019 and 2020, with the number of reported cases falling to 5.8 million in 2020. This decline, representing the nadir of global TB notifications in over a decade, stemmed directly from pandemic-induced disruptions to TB diagnosis, treatment, and care (World Health Organization, 2023).

Several factors contributed to the reduction in TB case detection during this period. Notably, healthcare resources were predominantly reallocated to address the COVID-19 crisis, which consequently diminished the accessibility of TB diagnostic services, encompassing laboratory testing and chest radiography. Second, social distancing measures and lockdowns made it difficult for patients to access healthcare facilities, while fear of contracting COVID-19 in hospitals deterred many from seeking medical attention. Additionally, the global disruption in supply chains affected the availability of diagnostic equipment and medications necessary for TB management.

Partial Recovery in 2021 and Significant Rebound in 2022

Although progress was hindered, global TB notifications started to recover in 2021, though the pace remained slower than anticipated. That year, 6.4 million new TB cases were diagnosed and reported, indicating a partial rebound from the most severe effects of the pandemic. The upward trend continued and gained momentum in 2022, with global notifications reaching 7.5 million cases. This number not only exceeded pre-pandemic levels but also represented a 16% increase from 2021, a 28% rise compared to 2020, and the highest annual number of TB notifications recorded since the WHO began global surveillance in the mid-1990s (World Health Organization, 2023).

The significant recovery in TB notifications in 2022 serves as a positive sign of enhanced access to healthcare services and the restoration of TB care infrastructure in numerous countries. It also implies that a backlog of undiagnosed TB cases—individuals who contracted TB during the pandemic—was gradually cleared as healthcare services resumed more typical operations. However, this increase may also indicate a rise in the incidence of TB itself, as the socioeconomic fallout from the pandemic, including increased poverty, malnutrition, and weakened immune systems, created conditions conducive to the spread of TB.

Regional Variations in Tuberculosis Case Notifications

Despite there is an overall trend of recovery globally, the impact of the COVID-19 pandemic on TB notifications and the subsequent recovery has varied significantly across different regions and countries. These differences highlight variations in healthcare infrastructure, implemented pandemic control measures, and the pre-existing burden of TB.

WHO South-East Asia Region. Mirroring the global trend, the WHO South-East Asia Region, encompassing high TB-burden countries like India, Indonesia, and Bangladesh, saw a substantial 24% reduction in TB notifications from 2019 to 2020, primarily driven by pandemic-associated service interruptions and restricted access to diagnostic resources. Subsequently, the region experienced a partial recovery in 2021 and a robust rebound in 2022, with case notifications surpassing pre-pandemic levels. This notable recovery was propelled by intensified efforts to identify cases, the adoption of digital surveillance technologies, and robust government-led TB control strategies, as illustrated in Figure 1.

Figure 1. TB notification trends in the WHO South-East Asia Region, 2019–2022.

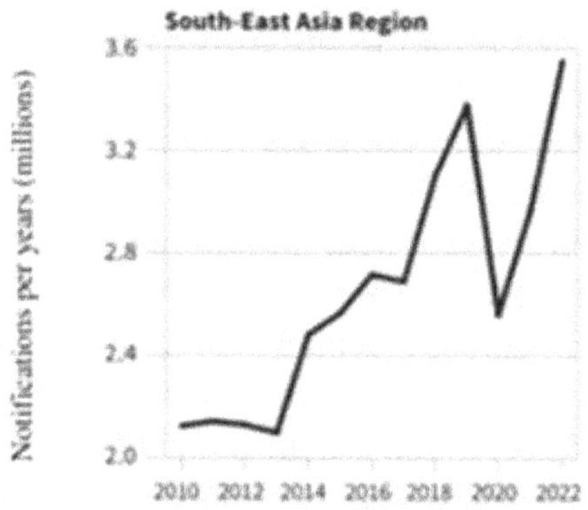

WHO Region of the Americas and Eastern Mediterranean Region. The WHO Region of the Americas experienced a sharp decline in TB notifications in 2020, attributed to widespread lockdowns and the realignment of health system priorities. Subsequently, a gradual improvement occurred in 2021, with notifications rebounding to pre-pandemic levels by 2022. Notably, nations like Brazil and Peru have demonstrated dedication to reinstating TB services and enhancing case detection efforts. In contrast, the WHO Eastern Mediterranean Region, encompassing high-burden countries like Pakistan, exhibited a more rapid recovery. TB notifications in this region reached 2019 levels by 2021 and continued to rise in 2022, potentially due to the early resumption of TB programs and the implementation of adaptive strategies in response to challenging circumstances, such as conflict zones and humanitarian crises (as shown in Figures 2 and 3).

Figure 2. TB notification trends in the WHO Region of the Americas, 2019–2022.

Figure 3. TB notification trends in the WHO Eastern Mediterranean Region, 2019–2022.

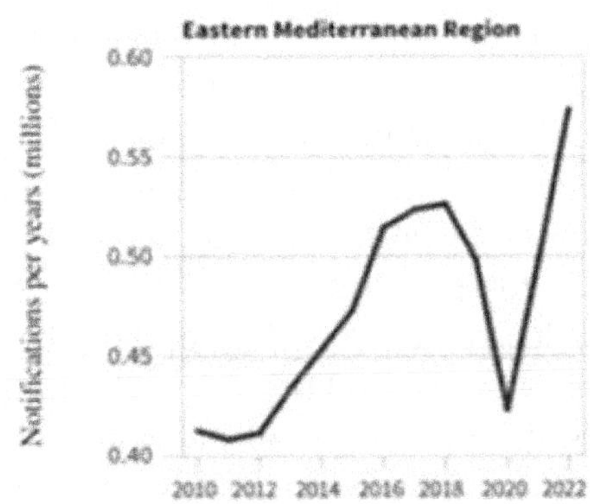

WHO Western Pacific Region. The WHO Western Pacific Region, in contrast, experienced more extended disruptions. In this region, TB notifications decreased significantly in 2020 and continued to decrease in 2021, with only a partial recovery noted in 2022. It is important to highlight that China, which comprises a large share of TB cases in the region, has shown a sustained long-term decline in TB notifications, suggesting continuous advancements in TB control. Nevertheless, other countries within the region, including the Philippines, Vietnam, and Cambodia, encountered sharp reductions in TB notifications during the pandemic. Despite these challenges, these nations achieved a return to near pre-pandemic notification levels by 2022, a recovery attributed to vigorous recovery campaigns and community-based screening initiatives, as depicted in Figure 4.

Figure 4. TB notification trends in the WHO Western Pacific Region, 2019–2022.

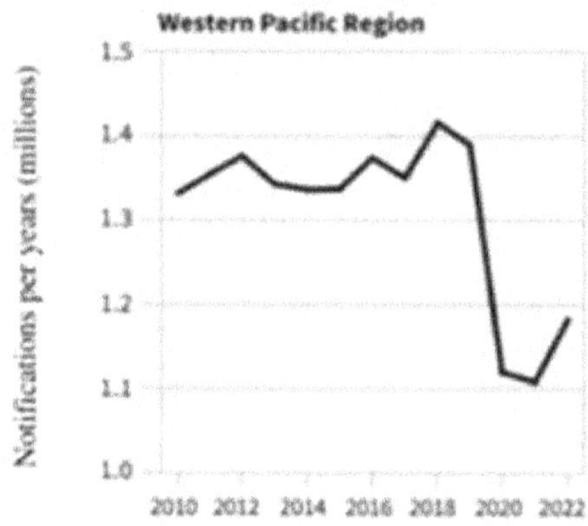

WHO African Region. The WHO African Region presents an intriguing deviation from the global trend, as TB notifications paradoxically rose during the pandemic period. This observation implies that the disruptions caused by COVID-19 may have exerted a comparatively minor influence on TB case detection within numerous African nations. Several factors may account for this trend, including the comparatively limited disruptions to health systems in certain African countries, the resilience and adaptability of established TB programs, and the sustained provision of international support for TB services throughout the pandemic. It is plausible that the historical experience of operating under resource constraints has better equipped many African TB programs to maintain essential services during the crisis, as illustrated in Figure 5.

Figure 5. TB notification trends in the WHO African Region, 2019–2022.

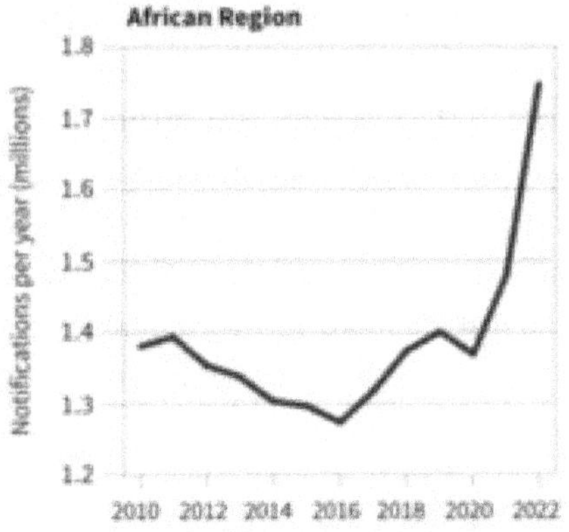

Country-Level Trends

A national-level analysis shows a wide range of trends among the 30 high-burden TB countries and the three countries on the global TB watchlist, both during and after the pandemic. These countries can be grouped into six categories based on the timing and extent of disruptions to TB notifications and their subsequent recovery patterns.

These trends can be divided into six categories. The first group includes thirteen countries, such as India, Indonesia, and the Philippines, which saw significant declines in TB notifications in 2020 or 2021 but fully recovered to 2019 levels or even surpassed them by 2022. Second, six countries saw significant reductions in TB notifications between 2019 and 2021, with only a partial recovery observed in 2022. Third, nine countries reported either continuous increases in TB notifications throughout the pandemic or declines consistent with historical trends, indicating minimal disruptions to TB detection attributable to COVID-19. Finally, a small group of countries exhibited unusual patterns, such as a reduction in 2020, recovery in 2021, and a further decline in 2022, or a decline during the pandemic followed by a sharp increase in 2022 that deviated from pre-pandemic trends..

Persistent Under-Notification

Despite the global recovery in TB notifications, under-notification likely persists in many regions and countries. The pandemic exacerbated pre-existing gaps in TB surveillance and diagnosis, and in some places, these gaps have not been fully addressed. The uneven recovery in TB notifications across regions and countries suggests that under-reporting remains a challenge, particularly in areas where healthcare systems were already strained or where COVID-19 had a prolonged impact on public health services.

Additionally, while the 2022 rebound in notifications indicates that many previously undiagnosed cases have now been detected, there may still be undiagnosed cases from the pandemic period that have yet to be identified. Furthermore, the pandemic's socioeconomic impact—such as increased poverty, malnutrition, and weakened health systems—may have led to an actual increase in TB incidence, which could contribute to future under-reporting if healthcare systems are unable to keep pace with rising case numbers.

DETERMINANTS OF TUBERCULOSIS (TB) NOTIFICATION

Factors associated with tuberculosis notification can be systematically categorized into three main domains: healthcare provider-related factors, patient demographic characteristics, and notification system components. Each domain contributes to the overall performance of TB notification systems and reflects the multifaceted challenges that hinder accurate and timely TB case reporting.

Healthcare Provider-Related Factors

Healthcare providers are crucial in detecting and notifying TB cases, but various obstacles hinder their reporting practices.. Among the most commonly cited issues are low awareness, lack of commitment, administrative burden, fear of stigma, and limited incentives. These factors collectively contribute to inconsistent and delayed reporting.

Awareness and Commitment

A key challenge is insufficient awareness of TB notification protocols, particularly among private healthcare providers. In many countries, notification guidelines are poorly disseminated to providers outside the public system. For example, studies in Indonesia have reported gaps in knowledge and adherence among private practitioners due to limited training and unclear responsibilities (Rusnoto et al., 2022; Stallworthy et al., 2020). Similar patterns were observed in India and China, where awareness, regulatory guidance, and digital infrastructure affect reporting (Rupani et al., 2021; Zhou et al., 2019).

Even when providers are aware of notification procedures, their commitment to comply can be hindered by other factors. Notification tasks are often viewed as time-consuming and outside core clinical responsibilities. The absence of incentives or recognition further reduces motivation, particularly in settings where providers face high patient loads and resource constraints (Duggal et al., 2021).

Stigma and Confidentiality Concerns

Stigma continues to influence provider behavior in TB case reporting. Healthcare workers may avoid reporting cases to protect patient privacy or to avoid damaging trust, especially in private practice. Some providers also fear regulatory consequences or scrutiny related to misreporting. A qualitative study in Indonesia showed that stigma, coupled with concerns about legal liability, significantly reduced reporting among private pediatricians (Suryanti Chan, Ahmed, & Hamzah, 2025).

Administrative and Practical Barriers

The notification process is often seen as burdensome. Forms are detailed, reporting platforms may be non-user-friendly, and digital tools are not always compatible with available infrastructure. A study in Jember, Indonesia found that many private physicians lacked digital literacy or appropriate devices to complete notification tasks (Wadudah et al., 2020; Kurniadi et al., 2021). Moreover, without sufficient administrative support, the additional paperwork becomes a barrier to timely notification.

The lack of standardized formats, inadequate training, and unclear reporting chains all contribute to delays or omission of TB case notification. These issues are compounded in facilities that lack supervision or access to consistent feedback, reducing opportunities for continuous improvement (Li et al., 2019; Lestari BW et al., 2024; Susanti et al., 2022).

Overcoming these provider-related barriers requires targeted interventions that combine education, supportive supervision, simplification of notification procedures, and system-wide incentives to encourage timely and complete TB case reporting.

The Role of Pharmacies and Telemedicine in TB Notification

The expansion of private healthcare services has brought pharmacies and teleconsultation platforms to the frontline of initial TB care. Yet, these actors are often excluded from formal notification processes. Pharmacies may dispense antibiotics suggestive of TB treatment without appropriate referrals or recordkeeping, thus contributing to under-reporting. Moreover, telemedicine services—especially those serving remote areas—often operate outside the purview of TB surveillance mechanisms. Incorporating these stakeholders into TB notification requires policy shifts and system interoperability. India's Nikshay platform, for instance, has piloted integration with pharmacy chains and telehealth providers, which could offer valuable insights for adaptation in Indonesia (Choudhury et al, 2018).

Patients Demographic Characteristics

Factors related to patients, including age, gender, and geographic location, have been found to impact TB notification rates. Elderly individuals often face limited access to care and delayed diagnoses, while pediatric cases may go unrecognized due to atypical symptom presentations and difficulties with diagnostic testing (Fatima et al., 2019; Oliwa et al., 2018; Suryanti & Idris A, 2025).

Patients' Age

Elderly populations (≥65 years) are more vulnerable to under-notification, primarily due to mobility limitations, comorbidities, and diagnostic delays. Pediatric cases, likewise, are frequently underreported due to nonspecific symptoms and diagnostic challenges, including the inability to produce sputum samples (Fatima et al., 2019; Malik et al., 2018).

Patients' gender

Gender disparities also influence TB notification. In low-resource settings, women frequently encounter obstacles to accessing healthcare because of social roles, restricted financial independence, or stigma, which results in delayed diagnoses. Men, conversely, may be overrepresented in notification data due to occupational exposure and healthcare-seeking behaviors (Horton, 2020; Peer et al., 2023).

Geographic location

People residing in rural or underserved areas often encounter systemic obstacles such as limited access to diagnostics, distance from facilities, and weaker health infrastructure. A study in Indonesia revealed that geographical location was strongly associated with under-notification, especially in rural areas with limited digital health infrastructure (Suryanti et al., 2025). Additional evidence from Hainan, China, revealed that not only geography, but also occupation and migration status significantly affected TB notification. For instance, migrant workers from other provinces had higher notification rates, and areas with fewer healthcare resources experienced more underreporting (Zhou et al., 2024).

Critical Components of Notification System

Effective TB notification requires a supportive system structure, including simplified reporting formats, digital tools, supervision, and incentives.

The Format of the Notification System

The format of the notification system is crucial in shaping the efficiency and accuracy of TB reporting procedures.. Traditional manual systems require healthcare providers to manually fill out paper-based forms, which can be labor-intensive and prone to delays in data entry and transmission. In contrast, electronic notification systems leverage digital platforms to streamline reporting, enabling real-time data entry, immediate transmission to centralized databases, and integration with existing healthcare information systems. However, the successful implementation of electronic systems necessitates robust technological infrastructure, adequate provider training in digital literacy, and seamless compatibility with healthcare IT frameworks to optimize their effectiveness.

Research conducted by Wadudah et al. among private practice physicians in Jember has underscored that the complexity of filling out TB notification forms significantly impacts the rate of TB patient notifications. Private practice physicians in Indonesia face challenges in adhering to the TB notification process due to the intricate nature of the notification forms, which often require detailed information about patient demographics, clinical history, laboratory test results, and treatment regimens. This complexity can lead to confusion and delays in completing and submitting the forms, contributing to under-notification of TB cases (Wadudah et al., 2020).

Furthermore, the burden of administrative tasks associated with TB notification forms may deter private practitioners from fully engaging in the notification process. Physicians in private practice often have limited administrative support compared to their counterparts in public healthcare facilities, which can hinder the timely and accurate completion of notification forms and ultimately affect overall notification rates (Wadudah et al., 2020).

Research by Kurniadi et al. (2021) among private physicians in Semarang City highlighted significant barriers to the adoption of electronic notification systems for tuberculosis. The research revealed that a substantial majority, specifically 86.2% of doctors, held a negative perception of using electronic systems or applications for TB notification. One of the primary challenges identified was related to the technological infrastructure required for electronic notifications. In 79.5% of cases, doctors reported that their smartphones did not meet the operational requirements necessary to effectively use the notification application. This limitation could stem from issues such as outdated smartphone models, insufficient storage capacity, or incompatible operating systems, thereby hindering their ability to engage with the electronic notification process.

Additionally, the study found that 78.5% of private physicians were not adequately prepared to conduct TB notifications through the application. This lack of preparedness could encompass various factors, including insufficient training on how to use the application, unfamiliarity with digital reporting processes, or concerns about data security and confidentiality when using electronic platforms. Moreover, the negative perceptions towards electronic notification systems may also be influenced by perceived complexities in integrating these systems into daily clinical workflows. Private physicians often face time constraints and heavy patient loads, making it challenging to adopt new technologies without disrupting existing routines or compromising patient care. These findings underscore the importance of addressing technological barriers and enhancing training and support mechanisms to facilitate the uptake of electronic TB notification systems among private healthcare providers (Kurniadi, 2021).

Supervision mechanism

Supervision mechanisms are essential for maintaining the accuracy and comprehensiveness of tuberculosis notification systems. These mechanisms provide oversight to healthcare providers by establishing protocols that guide the collection, reporting, and verification of TB data. By implementing a structured supervisory framework, healthcare authorities can monitor the consistency and quality of reported cases, ensuring that the data accurately reflects the epidemiological situation of TB in a given area. Supervision mechanisms typically include regular audits of notification data, on-site visits to healthcare facilities, and direct feedback loops to healthcare providers. These actions help mitigate common issues such as underreporting or misclassification of TB cases, which can skew public health responses (Harries, 2016)

A well-functioning supervision system also offers continuous professional development to healthcare providers, ensuring they are well-equipped to handle complex TB reporting protocols. Regular training sessions focus on improving the knowledge and skills required for proper notification, thus enhancing compliance with national and international TB control standards. By providing guidance and technical support, supervision mechanisms foster a culture of accountability, promoting a higher level of engagement in TB notification efforts (Long, Huang, Huan, & Zhao, 2021).

In addition to supportive supervision, penalties for non-compliance are sometimes incorporated into the framework to reinforce the importance of accurate and timely TB reporting. These penalties can range from financial fines to professional disciplinary measures, though they are generally used as a last resort. The threat of penalties serves as a deterrent against negligence in reporting, ensuring that healthcare providers understand their critical role in public health surveillance. While punitive actions may not be frequently applied, their existence underscores the serious public health implications of TB notification and the need for reliable data to guide interventions (Rusnoto, 2022; Thangaraj & Hemalatha, 2021).

UNDER-NOTIFICATION IN PRIVATE HEALTHCARE SETTINGS

Under-reporting of tuberculosis is a critical public health challenge that significantly impedes efforts to control and eliminate the disease. The WHO estimates that approximately 30% of global TB cases, equivalent to around 3.1 million individuals, go unreported or undiagnosed each year (World Health Organization, 2023). This issue presents a significant challenge in low- and middle-income countries, where the private healthcare sector frequently acts as the primary point of contact for patients seeking treatment for TB symptoms.

In countries such as Indonesia, India, and Nigeria, the private healthcare sector is integral to the healthcare system, encompassing private practices, clinics, pharmacies, and laboratories that cater to a large segment of the population. However, these private entities often operate outside national TB surveillance and reporting systems, resulting in a significant number of TB cases going unreported. The consequences of under-reporting are severe, contributing to ongoing TB transmission, rising drug resistance, and increased mortality rates. Research indicates that in India, for example, private pharmacies remain the first point of contact for many individuals with TB symptoms, yet referral for TB testing is still low, and inappropriate medications are commonly dispensed without a prescription. (Svadzian et al., 2023).

Therefore, it is crucial to understand the various factors that contribute to under-reporting, especially in private healthcare settings, in order to design targeted interventions and enhance overall TB management.

The consequences of under-reporting extend beyond the immediate clinical implications for affected individuals. By failing to capture the true burden of TB, under-reporting complicates efforts to allocate resources efficiently, plan public health interventions, and mobilize funding for TB control initiatives. Furthermore, it can perpetuate a cycle of neglect, where unreported cases continue to circulate within communities, increasing the risk of transmission and further entrenching TB as a persistent public health threat. Therefore, addressing the systemic barriers that contribute to under-reporting in private healthcare settings is paramount for achieving effective TB control and ultimately eliminating the disease (Suseela & Shannawaz, 2023)

Definition of Under-Reporting

Under-reporting in the context of TB can be understood as the systematic failure to capture diagnosed cases within health records, resulting in an underrepresentation of the true incidence of the disease. This phenomenon may arise from various factors, including the absence of proper diagnostic procedures, inadequate integration of private healthcare providers into national reporting systems, and a lack of awareness regarding TB notification protocols (World Health Organization, 2023). The effects of under-reporting go beyond individual patient outcomes; they undermine the reliability of TB surveillance data, obstruct public health authorities' capacity to allocate resources efficiently, and hinder the development of evidence-based policies for TB control.

The complexity of under-reporting is further compounded by social, economic, and structural factors that influence healthcare delivery in private settings. Patients may choose private facilities for care due to perceived advantages such as shorter waiting times, enhanced confidentiality, or greater convenience. However, these perceived advantages may come at a cost. As shown in India, despite efforts to engage private healthcare providers in TB control, many continue to function in isolation and often lack the incentives, training, or infrastructure to comply with standardized notification processes (Salve & Porter, 2021). Consequently, even diagnosed cases may never be reported to national TB programs.

Importance of Addressing Under-Reporting in Private Healthcare Settings

The importance of addressing under-reporting in private healthcare settings cannot be overstated, especially given the increasing reliance on private entities for healthcare delivery in many regions. Precisely recording TB incidence is essential for effective public health planning and response. Without a complete picture of the disease burden, public health authorities are unable to allocate resources efficiently or implement interventions in areas with the greatest need.

Data from India show that despite substantial investments aimed at involving the private sector through the National TB Elimination Program (NTEP), under-reporting remains an ongoing issue. Private providers—including pharmacies and clinics—remain under-involved in formal notification mechanisms, and often operate without regulatory oversight or integration into public health reporting systems (Suseela & Shannawaz, 2023).

Furthermore, repeat assessments of pharmacy practices in Patna, India, have revealed a decline in ideal TB management and referral practices over time, underscoring the need for sustained efforts to integrate private sector actors into TB control strategies (Svadzian et al., 2023).

Moreover, addressing under-reporting is essential for improving patient outcomes. Timely and accurate diagnosis and reporting facilitate earlier treatment initiation, which is critical in reducing TB-related morbidity and mortality. Unfortunately, delays caused by fragmented care and poor referral systems remain common. For instance, patients often experience prolonged pathways to diagnosis—visiting multiple providers over several weeks—before receiving appropriate care (Mutalikdesai et al., 2024).

Beyond individual health outcomes, systemic improvements in notification practices can also contribute to reducing the spread of drug-resistant TB. Delays in treatment and incomplete reporting create situations where patients may be prescribed inappropriate regimens, facilitating the development and spread of multidrug-resistant TB (DR-TB). As described by Udwadia and Furin (2019), gaps in quality of care—such as poor treatment monitoring, use of ineffective regimens, and limited access to drug susceptibility testing—are often exacerbated in fragmented systems, particularly when care is accessed through unregulated private providers (Zarir U & Fudin, 2019).

Therefore, strengthening the interface between public and private sectors is vital not only for improving the surveillance and control of TB, but also for building a more accountable, equitable, and effective health system overall..

Systemic Barriers in Private Healthcare Settings

The ongoing under-reporting of tuberculosis (TB) cases in private healthcare settings is not just a consequence of individual provider actions but is rooted in larger systemic challenges. These barriers are multifaceted and often interrelated, encompassing limitations in diagnostic practices, economic disincentives, inadequate provider capacity, weak regulatory oversight, and a general lack of integration between private providers and national health systems.

A recurring challenge is the fragmented nature of service delivery in private healthcare. Despite various government-led engagement initiatives, the private sector remains largely heterogeneous—ranging from small solo practices to unregistered pharmacies—with significant variation in practices and knowledge of TB guidelines (Salve & Porter, 2021). These structural limitations are compounded by resource constraints and low incentives to report, resulting in a landscape where TB notification is inconsistent at best..

Lack of Standardized Diagnostic Practices Across Private Healathcare Providers

One prominent barrier is the absence of standardized diagnostic protocols among private healthcare providers. Many practitioners in the private sector rely heavily on radiological tools such as chest X-rays rather than bacteriological confirmation, which remains the gold standard. This tendency is influenced by cost considerations, patient preferences, and limited access to laboratory services. As a result, misdiagnoses or underdiagnoses become common, exacerbating the problem of under-reporting.

Moreover, private pharmacies and chemists often act as first points of contact, especially in urban centers, yet lack training in appropriate referral pathways. A recent study using standardized patients in India demonstrated that pharmacy staff frequently provided symptomatic medications—including antibiotics and corticosteroids—without initiating proper diagnostic or referral protocols (Svadzian et al., 2023). Such practices delay definitive diagnosis and hinder the inclusion of cases in national TB registries.

Economic Incentives Over Public Health Responsibilities

Profit-driven motivations often dominate practice in private healthcare settings, which can conflict with public health imperatives. For example, providers may avoid initiating referrals or recording TB cases if doing so disrupts client relationships or reduces patient retention. These financial incentives can override adherence to TB notification protocols (Suseela & Shannawaz, 2023). The same study also noted that many private actors operate with limited regulatory scrutiny, allowing economic motivations to go unchecked. This environment fosters practices that, while responsive to market demand, fail to align with the ethical and procedural requirements of TB control programs.

Limited capacity for comprehensive Tuberculosis management

Another systemic constraint is the limited capacity of many private providers to deliver comprehensive TB care. These limitations include a lack of access to advanced diagnostic tools, insufficient training in TB protocols, and absence of support systems for treatment adherence. Awan et al. (2022) emphasized that in low-resource settings, like Pakistan, the fragile healthcare infrastructure—further strained by overlapping crises such as COVID-19—weakens the capacity to provide standardized TB services across various sectors (Awan et al., 2022). This situation is mirrored in India, where integration between vertical programs and general health services remains weak, particularly at the frontline level (Mutalikdesai et al., 2024). The result is a patchwork system where providers function in silos, further complicating surveillance and case detection efforts..

Communication Gaps

Communication barriers between private providers and national TB programs remain a key obstacle to effective notification. Many practitioners, especially in smaller clinics and standalone pharmacies, are either unaware of the TB notification mandate or lack clarity on how to report cases. This information gap is not just a matter of training but also reflects the absence of integrated digital systems and feedback loops between sectors. Findings from a qualitative study in India showed that frontline TB workers often struggled to maintain routine coordination with private actors due to vague roles, lack of trust, and weak referral infrastructure (Salve & Porter, 2021).

Additionally, providers who are inclined to cooperate frequently encounter bureaucratic hurdles or receive little follow-up from the public sector, discouraging sustained engagement. This disconnect leads to a loss of potentially valuable surveillance data and ultimately hinders the continuity of care for TB patients.

Regulatory Challenges

Weak enforcement mechanisms pose another challenge. Although policies exist to mandate TB notification and outline expectations for private sector reporting, implementation remains patchy. Private providers, especially in urban areas, often function autonomously without oversight, leading to variable adherence to guidelines. Moreover, public-private engagement strategies have tended to focus more on purchasing services than building equitable and sustainable partnerships (Suseela & Shannawaz, 2023).

As a result, incentives for notification are often short-lived and do not foster systemic compliance. The lack of accountability and absence of consistent monitoring further entrenches under-reporting as a normalized practice in many private settings.

Patient Factors

From the patient's side, several factors contribute to under-reporting as well. TB remains a stigmatized disease in many communities, and patients often seek care in private settings due to concerns over confidentiality and social judgment. This preference for privacy can reduce the likelihood of engaging with public programs that require formal registration and notification. The level of TB awareness and health-seeking behavior within a population also exerts a significant influence. Insufficient knowledge regarding TB symptoms and transmission pathways can contribute to delayed diagnosis, as individuals may fail to recognize the necessity of seeking medical evaluation. Furthermore, cultural beliefs and practices can shape health-seeking behavior, with some individuals opting for traditional healing methods instead of conventional medical treatment.

Additionally, in some contexts like India, studies show that patients commonly visit multiple providers—including unqualified or informal practitioners—before reaching a TB diagnosis (Mutalikdesai et al., 2024). This "shopping around" behavior not only delays diagnosis but also increases the chances that cases fall through the cracks of the surveillance system..

Social and Cultural Barriers

Social norms and cultural perceptions surrounding TB also shape health-seeking behavior and provider engagement. In many cases, TB is still associated with poverty, moral failing, or contagion, which fuels denial and concealment. These perceptions affect both patient willingness to disclose symptoms and provider readiness to report diagnoses.

Stigma may also be internalized by healthcare providers themselves. Evidence shows that some private providers avoid reporting TB cases to preserve their reputation or to prevent patients from facing discrimination in their communities (Awan et al., 2022). Without targeted community education and culturally sensitive outreach, these entrenched beliefs can remain powerful deterrents to open reporting and treatment.

Furthermore, there is often limited community engagement in TB awareness activities. As noted by Suseela & Shannawaz (2023), public health campaigns frequently overlook the role of local leaders and networks in shaping beliefs about illness and healthcare. Strengthening grassroots communication and leveraging trusted community figures may offer a path forward in addressing these socio-cultural dimensions of under-reporting.

IMPACT OF TECHNOLOGY ON NOTIFICATION SYSTEMS

The rapid progress of technology has significantly reshaped healthcare systems globally, including tuberculosis (TB) notification systems. Timely and accurate reporting of TB cases is essential for effective disease management, as it allows public health authorities to track disease spread, initiate prompt interventions, and allocate resources efficiently. Traditional TB notification systems, which often relied on paper-based records and manual processes, were susceptible to delays, inaccuracies, and under-reporting. However, the incorporation of digital health technologies into these systems has greatly improved the efficiency, precision, and promptness of TB case reporting, particularly in low- and middle-income countries (LMICs), where the TB burden remains high.

Enhancing Data Collection and Reporting Accuracy

One of the major advantages of technology in TB notification systems is the enhancement of data collection and reporting accuracy. Digital tools such as electronic health records (EHRs) and mobile health (mHealth) apps have streamlined the process of documenting and reporting TB cases. These platforms minimize the chances of human error linked to manual data entry and allow for real-time updates on patient diagnoses and treatment progress. Furthermore, digital systems can automatically prompt healthcare providers to submit TB cases to national surveillance systems, ensuring better adherence to reporting requirements. This is especially important in environments where healthcare providers are overwhelmed, as it alleviates the administrative burden of reporting (Rajanandh M G et al., 2020). Moreover, technology has enhanced the ability to collect more detailed patient data, which is invaluable for tracking TB epidemiology. Information such as patient demographics, comorbidities, treatment outcomes, and medication adherence can now be easily integrated into notification systems, allowing for more sophisticated analyses of TB trends and the identification of at-risk populations.

Improving Timeliness and Responsiveness

Timeliness plays a crucial role in the effectiveness of TB notification systems. Delayed reporting can lead to missed opportunities for early intervention, facilitating the further spread of the disease within communities. Digital notification systems have significantly shortened the time required to report TB cases, allowing for quicker public health responses. With electronic systems, healthcare providers can submit TB notifications in real-time, eliminating the prolonged delays that come with manual data entry and transmission. This advancement has been especially valuable in remote or rural areas, where transporting paper records to centralized health offices often caused reporting delays.

In some regions, mobile health (mHealth) applications have been developed to facilitate TB reporting directly from the field. These applications enable healthcare workers in resource-limited settings to report cases via mobile devices, even in areas with limited internet connectivity. The use of mHealth for TB notification has been shown to significantly improve both the speed and coverage of reporting, particularly in LMICs where traditional reporting systems are often less robust (Ashari et al., 2021).

Facilitating Interoperability Between Public and Private Sectors

One of the key challenges in TB control is the divide between public and private healthcare systems, particularly in LMICs, where a large proportion of TB cases are managed in the private sector. Traditionally, private healthcare providers have been less inclined to report TB cases to national notification systems, resulting in significant under-reporting. However, technology has improved the integration of public and private health systems, allowing for more thorough case tracking.

Interoperable digital systems enable private healthcare providers to effortlessly report TB cases to national surveillance databases, removing the requirement for extra administrative procedures. For instance, Indonesia's introduction of a web-based TB notification system has helped bridge the reporting gap between public and private healthcare providers. This system has contributed to a more accurate and complete picture of TB incidence across sectors, ensuring that all cases are accounted for.

Strengthening Monitoring and Supervision

Technology has been instrumental in improving the monitoring and oversight of TB notification systems. Digital platforms enable real-time tracking of case notifications, allowing health authorities to promptly detect discrepancies, observe trends, and ensure adherence to reporting protocols. Automated alerts can be generated when there is a decline in the number of reported cases from specific healthcare facilities, prompting immediate follow-up investigations. This capability is crucial for identifying gaps in reporting, especially in areas where under-notification has been a persistent issue (Ashari et al., 2021).

Furthermore, digital systems provide health authorities with the tools to assess TB control program performance through key performance indicators (KPIs), such as treatment adherence rates and the timeliness of case reporting. This data-driven strategy enables a more focused and efficient allocation of resources, ensuring that TB control programs can respond to evolving public health demands.

Challenges and Considerations

Despite the many advantages of digital technologies in improving TB notification systems, several challenges remain. In many LMICs, the initial costs of implementing digital health systems can be prohibitive, especially in areas with limited infrastructure. Moreover, healthcare providers may require additional training to effectively use these systems, which could hinder widespread adoption. Data privacy and security are also critical concerns, as digital systems must ensure that patient information is protected from unauthorized access (Rajanandh M G et al., 2020).

Additionally, while digital systems have led to significant improvements in reporting, there is still a need for strong regulatory frameworks to ensure full participation by private healthcare providers. In the absence of proper oversight, reporting gaps may continue, particularly in countries where the private sector plays a significant role in TB treatment.

The integration of technology into TB notification systems has significantly improved data accuracy, reporting timeliness, and the interoperability between public and private healthcare sectors. Digital tools, such as EHRs, mHealth applications, and interoperable platforms, have helped strengthen TB surveillance efforts, enhance case reporting, and ultimately improve TB control outcomes. Nevertheless, issues concerning cost, infrastructure, and regulatory oversight must be tackled to fully leverage the potential of these technologies in alleviating the global TB burden.

IMPROVING TUBERCULOSIS NOTIFICATION: STRATEGIES AND APPROACHES

Proper tuberculosis (TB) notification is crucial for disease monitoring, public health intervention, and resource distribution. By officially reporting diagnosed TB cases to national health authorities, health systems can track disease patterns, address outbreaks, and implement suitable treatment and prevention measures. Yet, despite its importance, TB notification remains a challenge in many countries due to issues such as under-reporting, particularly from private healthcare providers, and systemic barriers in health infrastructure (Irawaty, 2023; Ngwatu, 2018; Kelamane et al., 2021; Khanna et.al., 2023; Suseela & Shannawaz, 2023).

Strengthening Healthcare Provider Engagement

A key challenge in TB notification is the inconsistent reporting by healthcare providers, particularly in the private sector. Private providers, who handle a large number of TB cases, are often unaware of the mandatory reporting requirements or lack the incentive to comply. Enhancing provider engagement through awareness campaigns, training sessions, and targeted outreach efforts can help improve adherence. By cultivating a culture of accountability and cooperation, healthcare providers can actively contribute to national TB control initiatives.

Both financial and non-financial incentives can serve as effective motivators for providers. These incentives can encourage compliance while strengthening a collective commitment to public health objectives. However, these efforts should be carefully crafted to ensure sustainability and foster mutual trust between public health authorities and private sector stakeholders (Kelamane et al., 2021; Khanna et al., 2023).

Leveraging Digital Health Technologies

Digital innovations have revolutionized health reporting and can significantly improve TB notification systems. The integration of electronic health records (EHRs), mobile applications, and cloud-based applications can streamline case registration, reduce administrative delays, and ensure data accuracy. In remote and underserved regions, mobile health (mHealth) tools enable frontline workers to report cases in real time, bridging the gap between diagnosis and notification.

These technologies not only improve operational efficiency but also equip healthcare workers with the tools necessary for prompt and accurate reporting. Ensuring digital accessibility and intuitive platforms is crucial to fully realize the benefits of these innovations (Ngwatu et al., 2018; Suseela & Shannawaz, 2023).

Strengthening Public–Private Partnerships (PPPs)

Collaborative engagement between the public and private sectors is vital to ensure that all TB cases, regardless of where they are diagnosed, are reported into national surveillance systems. Effective PPPs foster trust, create shared platforms for case notification, and facilitate coordinated responses. Examples from high-burden countries demonstrate that integrating private providers into national TB programs—supported with tools, training, and incentives—can substantially increase notification rates (Irawaty, 2023; Suseela & Shannawaz, 2023).

However, to build sustainable partnerships, engagement strategies must move beyond transactional arrangements toward long-term, value-based collaboration. Recognizing the diversity within the private sector—ranging from formal hospitals to informal providers—is critical for tailoring effective interventions..

Enhancing Legal and Regulatory Frameworks

Robust legal frameworks form the backbone of effective TB notification. Mandating notification through national regulations ensures that TB reporting is not optional but a professional and legal obligation. Clear guidelines and accountability measures reinforce this requirement and contribute to standardized reporting practices across healthcare systems.

To improve compliance, enforcement should be balanced with support. Educational outreach, clear reporting protocols, and accessible reporting platforms help ensure that regulations are practical and achievable. Moreover, regular monitoring and evaluation mechanisms are necessary to track implementation and identify gaps for improvement (Suseela & Shannawaz, 2023).

Community-Based Interventions and Social Engagement

Community health workers (CHWs) are essential in the early detection and reporting of cases, particularly in areas with limited access to formal healthcare services. As trusted members of the community, CHWs can overcome stigma, cultural barriers, and misinformation that often delay TB diagnosis and reporting.

Community engagement efforts that focus on awareness, early symptoms, and referral systems can improve notification by connecting people with the care they need. Furthermore, by promoting transparency and inclusion, community-level interventions can contribute to broader public health resilience and social trust (Irawaty, 2023; Kelamane et al., 2021).

Recent evidence underscores the impact of mental health on TB treatment adherence. Research by Agustine et al. (2024) showed that the integration of motivational interviewing and progressive muscle relaxation effectively lowered anxiety levels in TB patients, potentially enhancing their adherence to treatment. This suggests the value of embedding non-pharmacological psychosocial interventions into TB care models. Addressing mental health alongside physical treatment could not only support better outcomes but also reduce patient drop-out rates—one of the contributing factors to under-notification (Agustine et al., 2024).

Addressing Systemic Barriers and Strengthening Infrastructure

Challenges such as inadequate infrastructure, limited funding, and workforce constraints often hinder effective TB notification. Strengthening laboratory capacity, investing in information systems, and training healthcare workers are essential components of a well-functioning TB surveillance system.

Governments and international stakeholders must prioritize funding for health system infrastructure, ensuring that notification processes are well-integrated, responsive, and resilient. The use of interoperable digital systems, combined with adequate support and supervision, will ensure that healthcare providers are well-equipped to report cases efficiently and accurately (Stallworthy, 2020; Suseela & Shannawaz, 2023)

Improving TB notification is a multifaceted challenge that demands coordinated strategies across various levels of the health system. Strengthening provider engagement, embracing digital technologies, fostering public–private collaboration, establishing clear legal mandates, and empowering communities are all vital components. Addressing these areas comprehensively will help ensure that TB cases are promptly identified, accurately reported, and effectively managed.

As the global community intensifies its commitment to TB elimination, these strategies—adapted to local contexts and supported by sustained investment—will be key in advancing public health outcomes and achieving universal access to high-quality TB care.

Strengthening Monitoring and Evaluation Systems

Monitoring and evaluation (M&E) is a vital yet often overlooked component in ensuring the effectiveness of tuberculosis (TB) notification programs, particularly in resource-limited settings. Without consistent supervision and structured feedback, under-reporting and data gaps persist, especially in private healthcare settings.

Experiences from TB programs in high-burden, low-resource regions highlight the importance of M&E. For example, the study conducted by Salve and Pangandaman (2024) in Jolo, Sulu, Philippines, showed that the absence of routine follow-up and weak patient tracking systems contributed to high rates of treatment loss to follow-up, with up to 62.5% of patients discontinuing treatment in 2019. These findings underscore how poor monitoring practices can directly impact both treatment outcomes and the integrity of notification data (Salve & Pangandaman, 2024).

To address such gaps, regular supervision, integrated digital recording, and structured data review are essential. Furthermore, tools such as electronic applications—like those evaluated in maternal health contexts by Sugesti and Sansuwito (2025)—demonstrated that systematic data collection using digital tools significantly improved detection accuracy and could be adapted for TB M&E systems as well. These insights suggest that optimizing M&E does not always require sophisticated platforms, but rather committed implementation, clear indicators, and routine feedback to service providers (Sugesti & Sansuwito, 2025).

CONCLUSION

Tuberculosis notification systems are essential for controlling and eventually eliminating TB, especially in high-burden countries. Timely reporting of diagnosed cases allows for tracking disease trends, optimizing resource allocation, and implementing targeted interventions. However, under-notification remains a major challenge, particularly in private healthcare settings, where inconsistent case reporting is driven by inadequate infrastructure, lack of awareness, and insufficient incentives for healthcare providers. Key determinants influencing notification rates include healthcare provider engagement, patient demographics, and structural issues within the notification system, especially in low- and middle-income countries where healthcare systems are often under-resourced.

Enhancing TB notification requires a multifaceted approach, including strengthening public-private partnerships, improving healthcare provider training and incentives, and integrating digital health technologies like electronic health records and mobile applications. These innovations have proven effective in resource-limited settings, where traditional paper-based reporting systems are prone to delays. Countries such as India have demonstrated success through systems like Nikshay, which improve communication between healthcare providers and public health authorities. Ultimately, addressing the barriers to TB notification—whether operational, technical, or social—will enable more effective monitoring and control of TB, contributing to the global effort to eliminate the disease.

REFERENCES

Agustine, U., Putri Santoso, S. D. R., Mugianti, S., & Paju, W. (2024). Motivational Interviewing with Progressive Muscle Relaxation for Anxiety Disorders in Tuberculosis. [MJN]. *The Malaysian Journal of Nursing, 15*(3), 47–53. DOI: 10.31674/mjn.2024.v15i03.006

Ashari, M. R., Apriani, I., Firmansyah, F., & Lanyumba, F. S. (2021). Evaluation of the Tuberculosis Prevention Program in the Discovery of Tuberculosis Cases in Nosara Public Health Center Palu City. *Open Access Macedonian Journal of Medical Sciences, 9*(E), 1200–1206. DOI: 10.3889/oamjms.2021.7185

Awan, H. A., Sahito, A. M., Sukaina, M., Khatri, G., Waheed, S., Sohail, F., & Hasan, M. M. (2022). Tuberculosis amidst COVID-19 in Pakistan: A massive threat of overlapping crises for the fragile healthcare systems. *Epidemiology and Infection, 150*, e41. DOI: 10.1017/S0950268822000358 PMID: 35190004

Bie, S., Wang, Y., & Li, J.. (2021). Influential factors and spatial–temporal distribution of tuberculosis in mainland China. *Scientific Reports, 11*(1), 6520. DOI: 10.1038/s41598-021-85781-7 PMID: 33737676

Choudhury, P., Zulawati, A., Lailatul, I., Ong, K., & Shahnaz, B. (2018). Effectiveness of Pharmacists' Intervention in Improving Patients Knowledge and Attitude Towards Antibiotic Usage in Klinik Kesihatan Seremban, Malaysia. *International Journal of Advancement in Life Sciences Research, 1*(1), 34–42. DOI: 10.31632/ijalsr.2018v01i01.005

Directorate General of Disease Prevention and Control Ministry of Health of the Republic of Indonesia. (2018). Guide-Determining-Burden-and-Target-Coverage-Discovery-and-Treatment-of-TB-2019-2024. In *Ministry of Health of the Republic of Indonesia.*

Dirjen P2P. (2023). Laporan Program Penanggulangan Tuberkulosis Tahun 2022. *Kemenkes RI*, 1–147. https://tbindonesia.or.id/pustaka_tbc/laporan-tahunan-program-tbc-2021/

Duggal, K., Elsy, M., Majella, M. G., Akkilagunta, S., & Sahu, S. K. (2021). Assessing the Status of Mandatory Tuberculosis Case Notification among Private Practitioners in Urban Puducherry. *Indian Journal of Community Medicine : Official Publication of Indian Association of Preventive & Social Medicine, 46*(4), 701–705. DOI: 10.4103/ijcm.IJCM_503_20 PMID: 35068738

Enos, M., Sitienei, J., Ong, J., Mungai, B., Kamene, M., Wambugu, J., Kipruto, H., Manduku, V., Mburu, J., Nyaboke, D., Ngari, F., Omesa, E., Omale, N., Id, N. M., Okallo, G., Id, J. N., Githiomi, M., Mwangi, M., Kirathe, D., . . . Weyenga, H. (2018). Kenya tuberculosis prevalence survey 2016 : Challenges and opportunities of ending TB in Kenya. *PLoS ONE, 13(12): e0*, 1–19. https://doi.org/https://doi.org/ 10.1371/ journal.pone.0209098

Fatima, R., Id, A. Y., Qadeer, E., & Hinderaker, S. G. (2019). Measuring and addressing the childhood tuberculosis reporting gaps in Pakistan : The first ever national inventory study among children. *PLoS ONE, 14(12): e0*, 1–11. DOI: 10.1371/ journal.pone.0227186

Gawde, N. (2013). Do we need notification of tuberculosis? A public health perspective. *Indian Journal of Medical Ethics*, *10*(1), 56–58. DOI: 10.20529/IJME.2013.014 PMID: 23439202

Harries, A. D., Kumar, A. M., Satyanarayana, S., Lin, Y., Zachariah, R., & Lönnroth, K. (2016). Addressing data needs for enhanced tuberculosis surveillance in the context of the global End TB strategy. *The European Respiratory Journal*, *48*(5), 1493–1497. https://doi.org/https://doi.org/10.1183/13993003.01448-2016

Horton, K. C., MacPherson, P., Houben, R. M., White, R. G., & Corbett, E. L. (2020). Sex differences in tuberculosis burden and notifications in low- and middle-income countries: A systematic review and meta-analysis. *PLoS Medicine*, *13*(9), e1002119. https://doi.org/https://doi.org/10.1371/journal.pmed.1002037. DOI: 10.1371/journal. pmed.1002119 PMID: 27598345

Irawaty, L., Manurung, N. S., Darmawan, E., & Ardhani, P. (2023). Improving Tuberculosis Response Strategies By Involving The Private Sector In The Public-Private Mix Scheme: A Systematic Review. *Jurnal Kesehatan Masyarakat*, *7*(2), 1562–1573. DOI: 10.31004/prepotif.v7i1.18316

Kelamane, S., Satyanarayana, S., Nagaraja, S. B., Panibatla, V., Dasari, R., Rajeesham, , Khan, A., & Kamineni, V. (2021). Rajeesham, Khan, A., & Kamineni, V. (2021). Engaging Informal Private Health Care Providers for TB Case Detection: Experiences from RIPEND Project in India. *Tuberculosis Research and Treatment*, *9579167*, 1–10. Advance online publication. DOI: 10.1155/2021/9579167 PMID: 34239728

Kemenkes, R. I. (2020). Strategi Nasional Penanggulangan Tuberkulosis di Indonesia 2020-2024. In *Pertemuan Konsolidasi Nasional Penyusunan STRANAS TB*.

Khanna, A., Saha, R., & Ahmad, N. (2023). National TB elimination programme-What has changed. *Indian Journal of Medical Microbiology*, *42*, 103–107. DOI: 10.1016/j.ijmmb.2022.10.008 PMID: 36402676

Kurniadi, A., Widianawati, E. E. D., & Ernawati, D. (2021). Kajian Faktor Kendala Dokter Tidak Menggunakan Aplikasi Wifi Tb Di Kota Semarang. *VisiKes*, *20*(1). Advance online publication. DOI: 10.33633/visikes.v20i1.4534

Lee, S., Rajaguru, V., Baek, J. S., Shin, J., & Park, Y. (2023). Digital health interventions to enhance tuberculosis treatment adherence: Scoping review. *JMIR mHealth and uHealth*, *11*, e49741. DOI: 10.2196/49741 PMID: 38054471

Lestari, B. W., Hadisoemarto, P. F., Afifah, N., McAllister, S., Fattah, D., Salindri, A. D., van Crevel, R., Murray, M., Hill, P. C., & Alisjahbana, B. (2024). Tuberculosis care provided by private practitioners in an urban setting in Indonesia: Findings from a standardized patient study. *PLOS Global Public Health*, *4*(6), e0003311. DOI: 10.1371/journal.pgph.0003311 PMID: 38833456

Li, T., Shewade, H. D., Soe, K. T., Rainey, J. J., Zhang, H., Du, X., & Wang, L. (2019). Under-reporting of diagnosed tuberculosis to the national surveillance system in China: An inventory study in nine counties in 2015. *BMJ Open*, *9*(1), 1–10. DOI: 10.1136/bmjopen-2018-021529 PMID: 30696665

Long, Q., Huang, F., Huan, S. T., Cheng, S., Wang, W., & Uplekar, M. (2021). Scale-up of a comprehensive model to improve tuberculosis control in China: Lessons learned and the way forward. *Infectious Diseases of Poverty*, *10*(1), 41. DOI: 10.1186/s40249-021-00828-1 PMID: 33766122

Malik, A. A., Amanullah, F., Codlin, A. J., Siddiqui, S., Jaswal, M., Ahmed, J. F., & Saleem, S. (2018). *Improving childhood tuberculosis detection and treatment through facility-based screening in rural Pakistan*. *22*(October 2017), 851–857. https://doi.org/http://dx.doi.org/10.5588/ijtld.17.0736

McLaren, Z. M., Milliken, A. A., Meyer, A. J., & Sharp, A. R. (2015). Does directly observed therapy improve tuberculosis treatment? Evidence from Sub-Saharan Africa. *The International Journal of Tuberculosis and Lung Disease : the Official Journal of the International Union against Tuberculosis and Lung Disease*, *19*(4), 406–416. https://doi.org/https://doi.org/10.5588/ijtld.14.0415 PMID: 25859995

Murti, B., Widyaningsih, V., & Pamungkasari, E. P. (2022). Determinant Indicators of Under-Reporting Case of Tuberculosis (A Mix Method Study). *Journal of Pharmaceutical Negative Results*, *13*(2).

Murti, B., Widyaningsih, V., Pamungkasari, E. P., Kristiyanto, A., Wahyuni, C. U., & Syafiq, A. N. (2021, November). Under-Reported Tuberculosis Cases and Related Factors at the Hospital Level in Kudus, *Central Java. In The International Conference on Public Health Proceeding* (Vol. 6, No. 01, pp. 370-377).

Mutalikdesai, N., Tonde, K., Shinde, K., Kumar, R., Gupta, S., Dayma, G., Krishnan, A., Juvekar, S., Santosa, A., Ng, N., & Patil, R. (2024). Exploring Potential Barriers and Facilitators to Integrate Tuberculosis, Diabetes Mellitus, and Tobacco-Control Programs in India. Exploring Potential Barriers and Facilitators to Integrate Tuberculosis, Diabetes Mellitus, and Tobacco-Control Programs in India. BMJ Yale; *Preprints* version. DOI: 10.1101/2024.03.19.24304558

Ngwatu, B. K., Nsengiyumva, N. P., Oxlade, O., Mappin-Kasirer, B., Nguyen, N. L., Jaramillo, E., Falzon, D., & Schwartzman, K. (2018). The impact of digital health technologies on tuberculosis treatment: A systematic review. *The European Respiratory Journal, 51*(1), 1701596. DOI: 10.1183/13993003.01596-2017 PMID: 29326332

Oliwa, J. N., Maina, J., Ayieko, P., Gathara, D., Kathure, I. A., Masini, E., & Van Hoog, A. H. (2018). Variability in distribution and use of tuberculosis diagnostic tests in Kenya : A cross-sectional survey. *BMC Infectious Diseases, 18*(328), 1–13. DOI: 10.1186/s12879-018-3237-z PMID: 30012092

Rajavardhana, T., Rajanandh, M. G., Geethavani, M., & Sreedhar, V. (2020). Role of mhealth in the management of Tuberculosis: A new approach to improve adherence. *International Journal of Research in Pharmaceutical Sciences, 11*(4), 5560–5568. DOI: 10.26452/ijrps.v11i4.3191

Rupani, M., Shah, C., Dave, J., Trivedi, A., & Mehta, K. (2021). 'We are not aware of notification of tuberculosis': A mixed-methods study among private practitioners from western India. *The International Journal of Health Planning and Management, 36*(4), 1052–1068. Advance online publication. DOI: 10.1002/hpm.3151 PMID: 33735506

Salve, M. M., & Pangandaman, H. (2024). Characteristics and status of treatment for multi-drug-resistant tuberculosis (MDRTB) patients in a TB-DOTS centre in the Province of Jolo, Sulu, Philippines. [MJN]. *The Malaysian Journal of Nursing, 16*(1), 47–59. DOI: 10.31674/mjn.2024.v16i01.006

Salve, S., & Porter, J. D. H. (2021). A qualitative study exploring perspectives and practices of district TB officers and frontline TB workers implementing public-private mix for TB control in India. *SSM. Qualitative Research in Health, 1*, 100008. Advance online publication. DOI: 10.1016/j.ssmqr.2021.100008

Stallworthy, G., Dias, H. M., & Pai, M. (2020). Quality of tuberculosis care in the private health sector. *Journal of Clinical Tuberculosis and Other Mycobacterial Diseases*, *20*, 100171. DOI: 10.1016/j.jctube.2020.100171 PMID: 32642560

Sugesti, R., & Sansuwito, T. B. (2025). Survey on the use of E-application for anaemia in pregnant women at midwifery clinic. [MJMR]. *Malaysian Journal of Medical Research*, *9*(1), 1–10. DOI: 10.31674/mjmr.2025.v09i01.001

Suryanti, S., & Ahmed, I. A. (2024). Under-reporting Tuberculosis Cases At Private Health Sector: A Scoping Review. *Journal of Health Research and Technology*, *2*(2), 137–148. DOI: 10.58439/jhrt.v2i2.223

Suryanti, S., & Ahmed, I. A. (2024). Correlation Between Demographic Factors (Age, Gender, and Living Area) and Tuberculosis Notification Rates in Private Healthcare: A Cross-Sectional Study. iHelis, 1(2). https://ihelis.com/index.php/ihelis/article/view/68

Suryanti, S., & Ahmed, I. A. (2025). Recent Review Tuberculosis in Indonesia: Burden and the Challenge of Under-Reporting. *Iranian Journal of Public Health*, *54*(2), 445–446. DOI: 10.18502/ijph.v54i2.17933 PMID: 40225262

Suryanti Chan, S., Ahmed, I. A., & Hamzah, H. (2025). Addressing barriers in paediatric tuberculosis reporting: A qualitative study of private healthcare providers' perspectives. *South Sudan Medical Journal*, *18*(1), 19–23. DOI: 10.4314/ssmj.v18i1.4

Susanti, A. T. Y., Putra, S., & Endah, A. K. (2022). Empowering the Critical Role of Public Health Center on Communicable Disease Prevention and Control of Drug-Resistant Tuberculosis. *Universal Journal of Public Health*, *10*(5), 439–447. DOI: 10.13189/ujph.2022.100501

Suseela, R. P., & Shannawaz, M. (2023). Engaging the Private Health Service Delivery Sector for TB Care in India—Miles to Go! *Tropical Medicine and Infectious Disease*, *8*(5), 265. DOI: 10.3390/tropicalmed8050265 PMID: 37235313

Svadzian, A., Daniels, B., Sulis, G., Das, J., Daftary, A., Kwan, A., Das, V., Das, R., & Pai, M. (2023). Use of standardised patients to assess tuberculosis case management by private pharmacies in Patna, India: A repeat cross-sectional study. *PLOS Global Public Health*, *3*(5), e0001898. DOI: 10.1371/journal.pgph.0001898 PMID: 37235550

Thangaraj, P., & Hemalatha, K. (2021). Tuberculosis notification: Facilitators and barriers among private practitioners in Trichy, South India. *The Journal of Mahatma Gandhi Institute of Medical Sciences*, *26*(2), 81–85. DOI: 10.4103/jmgims.jmgims_43_21

Udwadia, Z., & Furin, J. (2019). Quality of drug-resistant tuberculosis care: Gaps and solutions. *Journal of Clinical Tuberculosis and Other Mycobacterial Diseases, 16*, 100101. Advance online publication. DOI: 10.1016/j.jctube.2019.100101 PMID: 31720427

Uplekar, M., Atre, S., Wells, W. A., Weil, D., Lopez, R., Battista, G., & Raviglione, M. (2016). In, Mandatory tuberculosis case notification Policy, high tuberculosis-incidence countries: Journal, and practice. *European Respiratory*. https://doi.org/ DOI: DOI: 10.1183/13993003.00956-2016

Wadudah, F., Prasetyowati, I., & Bumi, C. (2020). Pelaksanaan Wajib Notifikasi (WiFi) TB di Dinas Kesehatan Kabupaten Jember. *Pustaka Kesehatan*, *8*(2), 131. DOI: 10.19184/pk.v8i2.20360

World Health Organization. (2022). *Global Tuberculosis Report*. World Health Organinzation. https://www.who.int/teams/global-programme-on-tuberculosis-and-lung-health/tb-reports/global-tuberculosis-report-2022

World Health Organization. (2023). *Global Tuberculosis Report 2023*. World Health Organinzation. https://www.who.int/teams/global-tuberculosis-programme/tb-reports/global-tuberculosis-report-2023

Zhou, D., Pender, M., Jiang, W., Mao, W., & Tang, S. (2019). Under-reporting of TB cases and associated factors: A case study in China. *BMC Public Health*, *19*(1), 1664. DOI: 10.1186/s12889-019-8009-1 PMID: 31829147

Chapter 5
Embracing Change:
Understanding Climate Changes and Diversity Challenges

Oindrilla Ghosh
https://orcid.org/0000-0001-9609-0781
Christ University, India

Binod Kumar
https://orcid.org/0009-0002-9721-1367
Radha Govind University, India

ABSTRACT

Embracing change in the context of climate change and diversity challenges is crucial for fostering resilience and promoting sustainability. Rising temperatures, extreme weather events, and sea-level rise are not just environmental issues; they amplify social inequities and economic disparities, disproportionately affecting marginalized communities. Addressing these challenges requires a commitment to environmental sustainability and the integration of diverse perspectives. Additionally, fostering cultural diversity enhances our collective knowledge and adaptive capacity, allowing for innovative solutions rooted in varied experiences and traditions. Governments and organizations must collaborate to create adaptive policies that prioritize resilience, equity, and inclusivity. Embracing change means recognizing the interconnectedness of climate issues and social dynamics, ultimately fostering a holistic approach to create a sustainable and equitable future for all. By understanding these challenges, we can navigate the complexities of change and emerge stronger together.

DOI: 10.4018/979-8-3693-9755-8.ch005

INTRODUCTION

In the ever-evolving tapestry of our world, two prominent issues (Schlosberg and Collins, 2014) have come to the forefront of global consciousness, climate change and diversity challenges (Harris, 2019). These twin phenomena, each complex and interconnected (Caney, 2014) in its own right, have profound implications for the future (Leach et al., 2021) of our planet and the human civilization that inhabits it (Sultana, 2019). As we stand at a critical juncture in history, it is imperative (Kothari et al., 2019). that we deepen our understanding of these issues and explore the myriad ways (Caney, 2014) in which they shape our collective existence. Climate change has emerged as one of the most pressing challenges (Harris, 2019) of our time, with far-reaching consequences for the environment (Bond, 2010), economies, and societies worldwide. The resulting changes in temperature patterns, sea levels (Mehta et al., 2019), and weather systems are already causing a cascade of impacts (Krause, 2018), from extreme weather events to loss of biodiversity and disruptions to food and water supplies (Schlosberg and Collins, 2014). The climate crisis represents one of the most pressing challenges facing humanity today (Alves and Mariano, 2018). As greenhouse gas emissions continue to rise, global temperatures are escalating (Heffron and McCauley, 2018), leading to a wide array of detrimental impacts on our environment, societies, and economies (Pottier, Godard and Hourcade, 2017).

In parallel, the climate crisis exacerbates existing social disparities (Roberts and Parks, 2006) and inequalities, disproportionately affecting marginalized communities worldwide (Umbers and Moss, 2020). Understanding the interconnected nature of the climate crisis (Okereke, 2008) and diversity challenges is essential in formulating effective strategies to mitigate (Adger et al., 2006) its adverse effects and foster a more equitable and sustainable future (Adelman, 2016). At the heart of the climate change dilemma lies the recognition (Wallimann-Helmer, 2015) that our current trajectory is unsustainable. The need for urgent and decisive action (Smith and Frakenberger, 2018) to mitigate greenhouse gas emissions, transition to renewable energy sources (Bruno, Karliner and Brotsky, 1999), and adapt to the changes already underway has never been more pressing (Bullard and Wright, 1990). As we grapple with the complexities of climate science and the uncertainties (Simms, 2005) of the future, a deeper understanding of the interconnected nature of these challenges (Bond, 2014) is essential for shaping effective responses at local, national, and global scales (Schlosberg and Collins, 2014).

Central to our exploration of climate change and diversity challenges (Hughes and Hoffman, 2020) is the recognition that these issues are not separate and distinct (Alkon and Aygeman, 2011) but deeply interconnected. At the same time, acknowledging the interconnected nature (Srivastava and Mehta, 2017) of climate change and diversity challenges requires us to confront uncomfortable truths (Bachram, 2004) and grapple with power differentials, privilege, and historical injustices (Cavanagh and Benjaminsen, 2014) that have shaped our world. This demands a commitment to introspection, humility (Edstedt and Carton, 2018), and empathy as we seek to build bridges across divides (Corbera and Brown, 2008), amplify marginalized voices, and strive for transformative change that benefits all members of society (Boyd, 2009).

The Climate Crisis

The climate crisis is primarily driven by human activities, particularly (Howson, 2018) the burning of fossil fuels, deforestation, and industrial processes (Milne et al., 2018) that release greenhouse gases into the atmosphere. These gases (Lehtonen and Kern, 2009), such as carbon dioxide and methane, trap heat, leading to the warming (Stirling, 2009) of the planet, a phenomenon known as global warming.

Causes of the Climate Crisis

At the heart of the climate crisis lies the accumulation of greenhouse gases (Paprocki and Huq, 2018) in the Earth's atmosphere, disrupting the planet's energy (Klein and Möhner, 2011) balance and leading to global warming. The primary contributors to this phenomenon (Gajjar et al., 2019) are human activities, notably the burning of fossil fuels, deforestation (Eriksen et al., 2021), industrial processes, and agricultural practices. Carbon dioxide (CO2), methane (CH4), and nitrous oxide (N2O) are among the most prevalent (Eriksen et al., 2011) greenhouse gases emitted through these activities, trapping heat and causing the Earth's temperature (Paprocki and Huq, 2018) to rise. The burning of fossil fuels, such as coal, oil, and natural gas (Caney, 2014), for energy production and transportation is a major source (Moss, 2018) of carbon emissions. Additionally, deforestation and land-use changes release carbon (Roberts and Pelling, 2020) stored in trees and soil, further exacerbating greenhouse gas concentrations in the atmosphere (Roberts and Huq, 2015). Industrial activities, including manufacturing and cement production (Moss, 2018), release various greenhouse gases into the air, contributing to the climate crisis (Fraser, 2000). Moreover, intensive agriculture practices, such as livestock farming (McCauley et al., 2019) and excessive fertilizer use, release methane and nitrous oxide emissions, intensifying (Sovacool et al., 2019) the global warming effect.

Solutions to the Climate Crisis

Addressing the climate crisis requires urgent and coordinated action (Krause, 2018) at the global, national, and local levels to reduce greenhouse gas emissions (Hoare, 2018), enhance resilience to climate impacts, and transition to a low-carbon economy (Rodriguez and Inturias, 2018). Mitigation efforts focus on reducing emissions from key sectors such as energy (Kashwan, 2021), transportation, industry, and agriculture through the adoption (Freire, 1970) of renewable energy sources, energy efficiency measures, and sustainable land-use practices (Visvanathan, 2005). De-carbonizing the economy and phasing out fossil fuels (Forsyth and Sikor, 2013) are essential steps towards achieving net-zero emissions and limiting global warming (Conway and Vincent, 2021) to well below 2°C above pre-industrial levels, as outlined (Rodriguez, 2017) in the Paris Agreement. Adaptation measures are equally important to enhance (Leach and Mearns, 1996) communities' resilience to climate impacts and protect vulnerable populations (Leach et al., 2017) from environmental disasters. Investing in climate-resilient infrastructure, early warning systems (Fischer, 2002), and nature-based solutions can help mitigate the risks associated (Vedwan and Rhoades, 2001) with extreme weather events and sea-level rise. Empowering local communities (Panda, 2016), promoting climate education, and fostering innovation (Carruthers, 1996) in climate technologies are key elements of building adaptive capacity (Figueroa Helland and Lindgren, 2016) and promoting sustainable development in the face of the climate crisis (Mehta et al., 2019). International cooperation and multilateralism play a crucial role (Mehta and Srivastava, 2020) in addressing the climate crisis, as no single country can tackle (Conway et al., 2019) this global challenge alone. The United Nations Framework Convention on Climate Change (UNFCCC) provides a platform (Conway and Vincent, 2021) for countries to negotiate climate agreements, set emission reduction targets (Arora Jonsson, 2011), and mobilize climate finance to support developing countries (Morena, Krause and Stevis, 2020) in their transition to a low-carbon economy. The annual Conference of the Parties (COP) brings together world leaders (Swilling and Annecke, 2012), policymakers, scientists, and civil society to discuss climate action (Newell and Mulvaney, 2013) and share best practices in climate mitigation and adaptation (Newell and Mulvaney, 2013).

The climate crisis represents a defining moment in human history (Sovacool, 2021), demanding collective and decisive action to safeguard the planet (Torres Contreras, 2021) and its inhabitants from the adverse effects of global warming (Newell, 2021). By addressing the root causes of the climate crisis (Erickson et al., 2018), prioritizing climate justice, and fostering international collaboration (Newell and Simms, 2019), we can pave the way for a more sustainable and resilient future (Green and Dennis, 2018) for generations to come. Embracing renewable energy, sustainable practices (Piggot et al., 2018), and inclusive policies is essential in transitioning towards a low-carbon economy (Kartha and Muttit, 2020) and mitigating the impacts of climate change on ecosystems (Isakson, 2015), societies, and economies worldwide. Let us heed the call of science (Ziervogel et al., 2017), elevate ambition, and work together to combat (Gill, 2016), the climate crisis and secure a thriving and equitable planet for all (Willis, 2020).

Diversity Challenges

In addition to its environmental repercussions, the climate crisis (Eckersley, 1995) exacerbates existing social disparities and exposes systemic inequalities (Higgins, 2010) embedded in our societies. Diversity challenges, including racial and economic disparities (Stevenson and Dryzek, 2014), gender inequalities, and disparities in access to resources, further complicate (Newell and Martin, 2020) the impacts of climate change on vulnerable populations (Humphreys, 2009). Marginalized communities are often denied (Beauregard et al., 2021) equal access to decision-making processes, climate adaptation measures (Peel and Lin, 2019), and sustainable resources, perpetuating cycles of poverty and environmental injustice (Moss, 2018).

Understanding Diversity Challenges

Diversity challenges encompass a wide range of structural (Mngumi, 2020) and systemic inequalities that affect individuals based on factors (Jordan, 2015) such as race, ethnicity, gender, sexual orientation, socio-economic status (MacGillivray, 2018), age, ability, and more. These challenges manifest in various forms (Aldrich and Meyer, 2015), including discrimination, prejudice, marginalization, and exclusion (Jacobs and Cramer, 2017), limiting opportunities, access to resources, and participation (Adger, 2003) in social, political, and economic spheres. Understanding the root causes (Pelling et al., 2008) of diversity challenges requires acknowledging historical injustices, power imbalances (Morrison and Ramsey, 2019), and social structures that perpetuate inequality and hinder progress (Aldrich and Meyer, 2015) towards inclusive and equitable societies. One of the key diversity challenges (Rockenbauch and Sakdapolrak, 2017) facing many societies is racial discrimination and systemic racism (Magis, 2010), which disproportionately impact minority communities and perpetuate disparities (Norris et al., 2008) in education, employment, healthcare, and criminal justice systems (Folke, 2006).

Gender inequality is another pervasive diversity challenge that persists (Magis, 2010). in many societies, limiting women's equal rights, opportunities (Jacobs and Cramer, 2017), and representation in various domains. Gender-based discrimination (Folke et al., 2010), stereotypes, and cultural norms constrain women's access to education (Pelling, 2011), employment, leadership positions, and decision-making roles (Urquiza et al., 2021), perpetuating gender disparities and hindering progress towards gender equality (Berkes and Ross, 2016). Empowering women, challenging gender norms, and promoting inclusivity (Fazey et al., 2018) in all sectors of society are essential steps towards breaking down (Walsh-Dilley et al., 2016) barriers and creating a more equitable and diverse world for all (Bourdieu, 1986). Diversity challenges also extend to issues of sexual orientation (Coleman, 1988), and gender identity, with LGBTQ+ individuals facing discrimination (Putnam, 1995), stigmatization, and violence based on their sexual orientation or gender expression (Woolcock, 1998). In many parts of the world, LGBTQ+ rights are not (Tenzin and Natsuda, 2016) fully recognized or protected, leading to marginalization, exclusion (Dzanja et al., 2015), and psychological harm for individuals who do not conform (Lang and Ramırez, 2017) to societal norms of sexuality and gender. Promoting LGBTQ+ inclusion, advocating for equal rights (Akbar and Aldrich, 2018) and protections, and fostering supportive environments are crucial (Habibov and Afand 2017) in addressing diversity challenges related to sexual orientation and gender identity (Phillips, 2016).

Addressing Diversity Challenges

Addressing diversity challenges requires a multifaceted (Carpenter, 2015), and intersectional approach that recognizes the complex interplay (Kim and Marcouiller, 2016) of social identities, power dynamics, and systemic injustices that contribute (Barrett et al., 2011) to inequality and exclusion. By promoting diversity, equity (Cairns-Nagi and Bambra, 2013), and inclusion in all aspects of society, we can create a more just, compassionate (Peters, 2019), and thriving world where all individuals are valued, respected, and empowered (Brown and Sonwa, 2018) to reach their full potential. Education plays a critical role in addressing diversity challenges (Bankoff, 2007) by fostering awareness, understanding, and empathy towards diverse perspectives (Smith and Frankenberger, 2018) and experiences. Incorporating diversity, equity, and inclusion into educational curricula (Wickes et al., 2017), promoting intercultural dialogue, and challenging biases and stereotypes (Kizos et al., 2014) can help create a more inclusive learning environment that celebrates (Carrico et al., 2019) diversity and empowers students to become agents of positive change in their communities (Lisnyj and Dickson-Anderson, 2018).

Climate Justice

Climate justice is a transformative framework that seeks to redress (Beauregard et al., 2021) the social, economic, and political injustices perpetuated by the climate crisis (Peel and Lin, 2019). At its core, climate justice advocates for equitable and inclusive solutions (Moss, 2018) that prioritize the needs and voices of marginalized communities (Leal-Arcas, 2019), centering principles of human rights, equity, and solidarity (Goss et al., 2020). By placing justice at the forefront of climate action, we can address (Steg, 2018) the root causes of inequality and build a more sustainable and resilient world (Brown, 2014) for all. Central to climate justice is the principle (Elmqvist et al., 2019) of "polluter pays," which holds corporations and governments accountable (Patel et al., 2017) for the environmental harm caused by their actions. Fossil fuel companies, agribusinesses (Vaneeckhaute et al., 2017), and other industries that contribute significantly to greenhouse gas emissions (Fazey et al., 2021) bear a moral responsibility to mitigate their impacts, compensate affected communities (Matarrita-Cascante et al., 2017), and transition to more sustainable practices. Climate justice also calls for reparations (Urquiza et al., 2021) for the harms inflicted on communities that have historically borne (Umamaheswari et al., 2021) the brunt of environmental degradation, such as indigenous peoples (Javadpoor et al., 2021), frontline communities, and low-income populations. Climate justice is a term that encapsulates (Tajuddin and Dabrowski, 2021) the intersection of climate change and social justice, emphasizing the need (Pandey et al., 2021) for fair and equitable solutions to address the global climate crisis (Maclean et al., 2014). In recent years, the discourse on climate justice has gained significant traction (Bowser and Cutter, 2015) as the impacts of climate change continue to exacerbate existing inequalities (Gambo Boukary et al., 2016) and injustices around the world. This concept goes beyond mere environmental concerns (Smith and Frankenberger, 2018), recognizing that climate change is not just an ecological issue but also a deeply rooted social (Wilson et al., 2020), economic, and political problem that disproportionately affects marginalized communities and future generations (Mngumi, 2020).

To address these systemic injustices, a climate justice framework calls (Habibov and Afand 2017) for collective action that centers on equity, human rights, and solidarity (Phillips, 2016). This entails not only reducing greenhouse gas emissions and transitioning (Gelder-blom, 2018) to renewable energy but also ensuring that the burden of climate change (Grube and Storr, 2014) is shared fairly and that those most affected receive the necessary support (Babcicky and Seebauer, 2017) and resources to adapt and build resilience. It also requires addressing underlying issues (Saldana, 2016) of poverty, inequality, and discrimination that exacerbate vulnerability (Uekusa and Matthewman, 2016) to climate impacts. Achieving climate justice requires a multi-faceted approach (Vallance and Carlton, 2015) that integrates environmental, social, and economic considerations (Exner et al., 2016). This includes implementing policies that promote sustainable development, renewable energy (Pelling et al., 2015), and conservation efforts, as well as investing in community-led initiatives (Islam and Walkerden, 2014), green infrastructure, and climate-resilient technologies. It also involves supporting (Pare´s et al., 2018) the rights of indigenous peoples and local communities to protect their lands, resources (Carpenter, 2015), and traditional knowledge, as they play a crucial role (Kim and Marcouiller, 2016) in conserving ecosystems and mitigating climate change (Peters, 2019).

Thus, climate justice is not just a lofty ideal but a practical imperative (Bakker et al., 2019) that requires urgent and collective action at all levels of society (Wickes et al., 2017). It calls for a fundamental reorientation of our values, priorities, and systems (Brown and Sonwa, 2018) to ensure that we create a more just and sustainable world for present and future generations (Thompson and Lopez Barrera, 2019). By centering equity, human rights, and solidarity in our response (Bakker et al., 2019) to the climate crisis, we can build a more resilient, inclusive (Thompson and Lopez Barrera, 2019), and equitable society that respects the interdependence of all living beings (Morris et al., 2019) and safeguards the integrity of the natural world (Moreno et al., 2019).

Case Studies

In recent years, climate action has witnessed significant policy breakthroughs and impactful case studies (Leach et al., 2021) that illustrate the urgent need for collaborative global and local efforts to combat climate change (Sultana, 2019). Notably, the United States rejoined the Paris Agreement in 2021, signaling a renewed commitment to international climate goals (Ranganathan and Bratman, 2021). This reintegration has catalyzed a wave of ambitious state-level initiatives (Hughes and Hoffman, 2020), such as California's pledge to achieve carbon neutrality by 2045. The state's comprehensive Climate Action Plan focuses on renewable energy (Delabre et al., 2020), electric vehicles, and stringent emissions regulations, serving as a blueprint for other regions (Newell, 2021a).

On a global scale, the United Nations Climate Change Conference (COP26) held in Glasgow in 2021 was pivotal, resulting in the Glasgow Climate Pact, which urged nations to reconvene in 2022 to accelerate emissions reductions plans (Ghosh & Raj, 2025). The agreement reinforced the necessity of limiting global warming to 1.5 degrees Celsius and led to increased commitments (Sultana, 2020) from countries to phase out coal use and promote greener technologies (Eriksen et al., 2021).

In terms of innovative local initiatives, Bhutan offers a compelling case study (Roberts and Pelling, 2020). This Himalayan kingdom has maintained its status as a carbon-negative nation since 2016 (Sanson and Burke, 2020), absorbing more CO2 than it emits through extensive forest conservation and reforestation efforts (Tschakert, 2020). Bhutan's national development policy prioritizes environmental sustainability (Carrico et al., 2019), demonstrating that economic growth can align harmoniously with climate action (Peters, 2019).

Community-Led Forest Conservation in the Amazon

The Amazon rainforest, often dubbed the "lungs of the planet," is a crucial component of global biodiversity and climate regulation (Wilson et al., 2020). Spanning across multiple countries in South America, this vast ecosystem (Pandey et al., 2021) faces significant threats from deforestation, illegal logging, and climate change (Ghosh, 2023). In response, community-led forest conservation initiatives have emerged (Tajuddin and Dabrowski, 2021) as vital strategies for maintaining these critical environments. These grassroots efforts, often spearheaded (Javadpoor et al., 2021) by Indigenous peoples and local communities, not only contribute to environmental sustainability (Umamaheswari et al., 2021) but also enhance community resilience against climate variability (Fazey et al., 2021).

Indigenous communities in the Amazon have long practiced sustainable land management techniques (Elmqvist et al., 2019) that govern their relationship with the environment (Salman, 2025). These practices include agroforestry, a land use strategy that integrates trees and crops, and rotational hunting and fishing, which preserve biodiversity and ecosystems (Dadhich et al., 2025). By adhering to traditional ecological knowledge, these communities maintain biodiversity while ensuring their survival and cultural identity (Goss et al., 2020). For instance, the Kayapó people in Brazil utilize a mix of plant species for food and medicine that promotes biodiversity while sustaining their livelihood (Beauregard et al., 2021). Their holistic approach reflects a deep understanding of the interconnectedness of all living things (Newell and Martin, 2020).

One landmark initiative showcasing the effectiveness of community-led conservation is the "Forest Guardians" program (Willis, 2020), implemented across various Amazonian regions (Kartha and Muttit, 2020). This program empowers local communities to engage in monitoring and protecting forest landscapes from illegal activities (Newell, 2021). Using tools such as satellite imagery and drone technology, community members track deforestation rates and engage local authorities to enforce environmental laws (Torres Contreras, 2021). By prioritizing local knowledge and ownership, the program instills a sense of responsibility and stewardship, helping to reduce deforestation rates (Sovacool, 2021) by providing an immediate economic incentive to preserve rather than destroy forest resources (Morena, Krause and Stevis, 2020).

Another significant aspect of community-led conservation is its contribution to climate resilience (Conway and Vincent, 2021). Amazonian communities depend on the forest not only for resources (Mehta and Srivastava, 2020) but also as a buffer against climate impacts such as extreme weather events and shifting rainfall patterns (Kashwan, 2021). Through reforestation efforts and sustainable agriculture, these communities enhance soil health and water retention (Ghosh & Raj, 2025), which helps mitigate the effects of droughts and floods (Salman, 2025). For instance, the Matsés people in Peru have developed agroforestry systems (Tower, 2020) that improve soil quality and provide diverse food sources, thus reducing vulnerability to climate change and food insecurity (Dadhich et al., 2025).

The importance of these community-led initiatives extends beyond conservation and resilience (Tschakert, 2020). They also highlight social justice and equity, offering local populations a voice in environmental governance (Sovacool et al., 2019). Indigenous rights to land and resources have been historically undermined (Hughes and Hoffman, 2020), leading to conflicts and environmental degradation (Kenner, 2019). Encouragingly, international frameworks like the United Nations Declaration on the Rights of Indigenous Peoples serve as a backdrop (Sanson and Burke, 2020) to advocate for community rights, acknowledging that empowering local voices is crucial for effective environmental stewardship (Newell, 2021a).

Pathways to a Sustainable and Equitable Future

Addressing the climate crisis and diversity challenges requires a multifaceted (Carrico et al., 2019) approach that integrates environmental, social, and economic dimensions (Peters, 2019). Several key pathways can guide us towards a sustainable and equitable future:

1. Sustainable Development: Sustainable development is a holistic approach (Carrico et al., 2019) that seeks to balance economic growth, social inclusion, and environmental protection (Peters, 2019). This involves transitioning to renewable energy sources, promoting sustainable agriculture (Urquiza et al., 2021) and land use, and ensuring that economic development benefits all segments of society (Morrison and Ramsey, 2019).
2. Social Equity: Ensuring social equity involves addressing the root causes (Mngumi, 2020) of inequality and providing equal access to resources and opportunities (Wilson et al., 2020). This includes implementing policies that promote fair wages, affordable healthcare (Pandey et al., 2021), quality education, and social safety nets. Social equity also requires addressing (Tajuddin and Dabrowski, 2021) systemic discrimination and promoting diversity and inclusion in all aspects of society (Javadpoor et al., 2021).
3. Community Empowerment: Empowering communities to take action on climate and diversity issues (Umamaheswari et al., 2021) is crucial for building resilience and driving change. This involves supporting community-led initiatives (Urquiza et al., 2021), fostering local leadership, and providing resources and training to help communities (Fazey et al., 2021) adapt to and mitigate climate impacts.

4. International Cooperation: The climate crisis and diversity challenges are global issues (Elmqvist et al., 2019) that require international cooperation. Countries must work together to reduce greenhouse gas emissions (Goss et al., 2020), share technology and knowledge, and provide financial support to developing nations (Leal-Arcas, 2019). International agreements, such as the Paris Agreement, play a critical role in fostering (Peel and Lin, 2019) collaboration and accountability.
5. Innovation and Technology: Innovation and technology can provide solutions to both climate and diversity challenges (Beauregard et al., 2021). This includes developing clean energy technologies (Ramesh Kumar et al., 2025), improving climate modeling and forecasting (Newell and Martin, 2020), and using digital tools to enhance social inclusion and equity. However, it is important to ensure that technological advancements (Willis, 2020) are accessible and benefit all communities (Kartha and Muttit, 2020).

CONCLUSION

Climate justice offers a transformative framework for building a more sustainable and inclusive future, grounded in principles of equity, solidarity, and respect for human rights. It is only through collective action, solidarity, and a commitment to justice that we can mitigate the adverse effects of climate change and create a more just and sustainable world for current and future generations.

The urgency of the climate crisis and the persistence of diversity challenges call for immediate and sustained action. It is imperative that governments, businesses, and individuals work together to implement solutions that address both the environmental and social dimensions of these issues. Only through collective effort and a commitment to justice and equity can we ensure a liveable planet for future generations.

Suggestions and Future Research Directions

Embracing change in the context of climate change and diversity challenges necessitates a multifaceted research approach. Future studies should focus on integrating interdisciplinary perspectives that combine climate science, social justice, and cultural studies. This could involve investigating the socio-economic impacts of climate change on diverse communities, ensuring that marginalized voices are heard and included in policy discussions.

Additionally, research should examine adaptive strategies that various cultures employ in response to climate challenges. Understanding traditional ecological knowledge and community resilience can offer valuable insights into sustainable practices that are culturally relevant. Enhancing public awareness and education around the interconnectedness of climate change and social diversity is crucial; thus, studies could explore effective communication strategies that engage various demographics.

Collaboration among scientists, policymakers, and local communities is essential for developing holistic solutions. Future research could focus on participatory methodologies, empowering communities to shape the research agenda and contribute to solutions. Furthermore, evaluating the effectiveness of existing policies in addressing both climate change and diversity issues can inform future interventions. Overall, a commitment to inclusivity, adaptability, and collaborative research will be vital for effectively embracing the complex changes posed by climate dynamics and diversity challenges.

REFERENCES

Adelman, S. (2016). Climate justice, loss and damage and compensation for small island developing states. *Journal of Human Rights and the Environment*, *7*(1), 32–53. DOI: 10.4337/jhre.2016.01.02

Adger, N., Paavola, J., Huq, S., & Mace, M. J. (Eds.). (2006). *Fairness in Adaptation to Climate Change*. MIT Press. DOI: 10.7551/mitpress/2957.001.0001

Adger, W. N. (2003). Social capital, collective action, and adaptation to climate change. *Economic Geography*, *79*(4), 387–404. DOI: 10.1111/j.1944-8287.2003.tb00220.x

Akbar, M. S., & Aldrich, D. P. (2018). Social capital's role in recovery: Evidence from communities affected by the 2010 Pakistan floods. *Disasters*, *42*(3), 475–497. DOI: 10.1111/disa.12259 PMID: 29131374

Aldrich, D. P., & Meyer, M. A. (2015). Social capital and community resilience. *The American Behavioral Scientist*, *59*(2), 254–269. DOI: 10.1177/0002764214550299

Alkon, A. H., & Aygeman, J. (Eds.). (2011). *Cultivating Food Justice: Race, Class, and Sustainability*. MIT Press. DOI: 10.7551/mitpress/8922.001.0001

Alves, M. W. F. M., & Mariano, E. B. (2018). Climate justice and human development: A systematic literature review. *Journal of Cleaner Production*, *202*, 360–375. DOI: 10.1016/j.jclepro.2018.08.091

Arora-Jonsson, S. (2011). Virtue and Vulnerability: Discourses on Women, Gender and Climate Change. *Global Environmental Change*, *21*(2), 744–751. DOI: 10.1016/j.gloenvcha.2011.01.005

Babcicky, P., & Seebauer, S. (2017). The two faces of social capital in private flood mitigation: Opposing effects on risk perception, self-efficacy and coping capacity. *Journal of Risk Research*, *20*(8), 1017–1037. DOI: 10.1080/13669877.2016.1147489

Bakker, Y. W., De Koning, J., & Van Tatenhove, J. (2019). Resilience and social capital: The engagement of fisheries communities in marine spatial planning. *Marine Policy*, *99*, 132–139. DOI: 10.1016/j.marpol.2018.09.032

Barrett, G., Vanderplaat, M., Gonzalez, M. E. C., Irmao, J. F., Ampuero, M. C. G., & Vera, C. E. M. (2011). Civic networks and community resilience in Brazil, Canada, Chile, and Cuba. *Journal of Civil Society*, *7*(4), 333–362. DOI: 10.1080/17448689.2011.626197

Beauregard, C., Carlson, D. A., Robinson, S., Cobb, C., & Patton, M. (2021). Climate justice and rights-based litigation in a post-Paris world. *Climate Policy, 21*(5), 652–665. DOI: 10.1080/14693062.2020.1867047

Berkes, F., & Ross, H. (2016). Panarchy and community resilience: Sustainability science and policy implications. *Environmental Science & Policy, 61*, 185–193. DOI: 10.1016/j.envsci.2016.04.004

Bond, P. (2010). Climate Justice Politics Across Space and Scale. *Human Geographies, 3*(2), 49–62. DOI: 10.1177/194277861000300204

Bond, P. (2014). Justice. In Death, C. (Ed.), *Critical Environmental Politics* (pp. 133–145). Routledge.

Bourdieu, P. (1986). The forms of capital. In Richardson, J. G. (Ed.), *Handbook of theory ands research for the sociology of education*. Greenwood Press.

Bowser, G. C., & Cutter, S. L. (2015). Stay or go? Examining decision making and behavior in hurricane evacuations. *Environment, 57*(6), 28–41. DOI: 10.1080/00139157.2015.1089145

Brown, H. C. P., & Sonwa, D. J. (2018). Diversity within village institutions and its implication for resilience in the context of climate change in Cameroon. *Climate and Development, 10*(5), 448–457. DOI: 10.1080/17565529.2017.1291409

Brown, K. (2014). Global environmental change I: A social turn for resilience? *Progress in Human Geography, 38*(1), 107–117. DOI: 10.1177/0309132513498837

Cairns-Nagi, J. M., & Bambra, C. (2013). Defying the odds: A mixed methods study of health resilience in deprived areas of England. *Social Science & Medicine, 91*, 229–237. DOI: 10.1016/j.socscimed.2013.03.014 PMID: 23566672

Carpenter, A. (2015). Resilience in the social and physical realms: Lessons from the Gulf Coast. *International Journal of Disaster Risk Reduction, 14*, 290–301. DOI: 10.1016/j.ijdrr.2014.09.003

Carrico, A. R., Truelove, H. B., & Williams, N. E. (2019). Social capital and resilience to drought among smallholding farmers in Sri Lanka. *Climatic Change, 155*(2), 195–213. DOI: 10.1007/s10584-019-02449-y

Conway, D., Nicholls, R. J., Brown, S., Tebboth, M. G. L., Adger, W. N., Ahmad, B., Biemans, H., Crick, F., Lutz, A. F., De Campos, R. S., Said, M., Singh, C., Zaroug, M. A. H., Ludi, E., New, M., & Wester, P. (2019). The Need for Bottom-up Assessments of Climate Risks and Adaptation in Climate-Sensitive Regions. *Nature Climate Change, 9*(7), 503–511. DOI: 10.1038/s41558-019-0502-0

Conway, D., & Vincent, K. (2021). Conversations About Climate Risk, Adaptation and Resilience in Africa. In Conway, D., & Vincent, K. (Eds.), *Climate risk in Africa: adaptation and resilience* (pp. 147–162). Palgrave Macmillan. DOI: 10.1007/978-3-030-61160-6_9

Dadhich, M., Bhaumik, A., Hiran, K. K., & Janarthanan, M. (2025). Analysis of Climate Change Governance for Enhancing ESG Frameworks for Corporate Success. In Bhaumik, A., Poddar, S., Dadhich, M., Hiran, K., & Doshi, R. (Eds.), *Community Resilience and Climate Change Challenges: Pursuit of Sustainable Development Goals (SDGs)* (pp. 135–146). IGI Global Scientific Publishing., DOI: 10.4018/979-8-3693-6522-9.ch008

Delabre, I., Boyd, E., Brockhaus, M., Carton, W., Krause, T., Newell, P., Wong, G. Y., & Zelli, F. (2020). Unearthing the myths of global sustainable forest governance. *Global Sustainability*, *3*(e16), 1–10. DOI: 10.1017/sus.2020.11

Dzanja, J., Christie, M., Fazey, I., & Hyde, T. (2015). The Role of social capital in rural household food security: The case study of Dowa and Lilongwe Districts in Central Malawi. *Journal of Agricultural Science (Toronto)*, *7*(12), 165–176. DOI: 10.5539/jas.v7n12p165

Edstedt, K., & Carton, W. (2018). The Benefits That (Only) Capital Can See? Resource Access and Degradation in Industrial Carbon Forestry, Lessons from the CDM in Uganda. *Geoforum*, *97*, 315–323. DOI: 10.1016/j.geoforum.2018.09.030

Elmqvist, T., Andersson, E., Frantzeskaki, N., Mcphearson, T., Olsson, P., Gaffney, O., Takeuchi, K., & Folke, C. (2019). Sustainability and resilience for transformation in the urban century. *Nature Sustainability*, *2*(4), 267–273. DOI: 10.1038/s41893-019-0250-1

Erickson, P., Lazarus, M., & Piggot, G. (2018). Limiting fossil fuel production as the next big step in climate policy. *Nature Climate Change*, *8*(12), 1037–1043. DOI: 10.1038/s41558-018-0337-0

Exner, A., Politti, E., Schriefl, E., Erker, S., Stangl, R., Baud, S., Warmuth, H., Matzenberger, J., Kranzl, L., Paulesich, R., Windhaber, M., Supper, S., & Stöglehner, G. (2016). Measuring regional resilience towards fossil fuel supply constraints. Adaptability and vulnerability in socio-ecological Transformations-the case of Austria. *Energy Policy*, *91*, 128–137. DOI: 10.1016/j.enpol.2015.12.031

Fazey, I., Carmen, E., Chapin, F. S.III, Ross, H., Rao-Williams, J., Lyon, C., Connon, I. L. C., Searle, B. A., & Knox, K. (2018). Community resilience for a 1.5°C world. *Current Opinion in Environmental Sustainability*, *31*, 30–40. DOI: 10.1016/j.cosust.2017.12.006

Fazey, I., Carmen, E., Ross, H., Rao-Williams, J., Hodgson, A., Searle, B., Al Waer, H., Kenter, J., Knox, K., Butler, J. R. A., Murray, K., Smith, F. M., Stringer, L. C., & Thankappan, S. (2021). Social dynamics of community resilience building in the face of climate change: The case of three Scottish communities. *Sustainability Science, 16*(5), 1731–1747. DOI: 10.1007/s11625-021-00950-x

Figueroa Helland, L. E., & Lindgren, T. (2016). What Goes Around Comes Around: From The Coloniality of Power to the Crisis of Civilization. *Journal of World-systems Research, 22*(2), 430–462. DOI: 10.5195/jwsr.2016.631

Fischer, F. (2002). *Citizens, Experts, and the Environment: The Politics of Local Knowledge*. Duke University Press.

Folke, C. (2006). Resilience: The emergence of a perspective for social-ecological systems analyses. *Global Environmental Change, 16*(3), 253–267. DOI: 10.1016/j.gloenvcha.2006.04.002

Folke, C., Carpenter, S., Walker, B., Scheffer, M., Chapin, T., & Rockstro¨m, J. (2010). Resilience thinking: Integrating resilience, adaptability and transformability. *Ecology and Society, 15*(4), 15. DOI: 10.5751/ES-03610-150420

Forsyth, T., & Sikor, T. (2013). Forests, Development, and the Globalization of Justice. *The Geographical Journal, 179*(2), 114–121. DOI: 10.1111/geoj.12006

Fraser, N. (2000). Rethinking Recognition. *New Left Review, 3*, 107.

Freire, P. (1970). *Pedagogy of the Oppressed* (Ramos, M. B., Trans.). Herder and Herder.

Gajjar, S. P., Singh, C., & Deshpande, T. (2019). Tracing back to move ahead: A review of development pathways that constrain adaptation futures. *Climate and Development, 11*(3), 223–237. DOI: 10.1080/17565529.2018.1442793

Gambo Boukary, A., Diaw, A., & Wu¨nscher, T. (2016). Factors affecting rural households' resilience to food insecurity in Niger. *Sustainability (Basel), 8*(3), 181. DOI: 10.3390/su8030181

Ghosh, O. (2023). Environmental Hazards And Disasters - A Response Towards Mitigating Disaster Management. *AIP Conference Proceedings, 2763*(1), 050008. https://Doi.Org/10.1063/5.0158892. DOI: 10.1063/5.0158892

Ghosh, O., & Raj, M. S. S. (2025). Empowering Society Through Localized Methods for Addressing Climate Change. In Bhaumik, A., Poddar, S., Dadhich, M., Hiran, K., & Doshi, R. (Eds.), *Community Resilience and Climate Change Challenges: Pursuit of Sustainable Development Goals (SDGs)* (pp. 93–108). IGI Global Scientific Publishing., DOI: 10.4018/979-8-3693-6522-9.ch012

Gill, B. (2016). 'Can the River Speak? Epistemological Confrontation in the Rise and Fall of the Land Grab in Gambella, Ethiopia', *Environment and Planning A. Economy and Space*, *48*(4), 699–717.

Goss, M., Swain, D. L., Abatzoglou, J. T., Sarhadi, A., Kolden, C. A., Williams, A. P., & Diffenbaugh, N. S. (2020). Climate change is increasing the likelihood of extreme autumn wildfire conditions across California. *Environmental Research Letters*, *15*(9), 094016. DOI: 10.1088/1748-9326/ab83a7

Green, F., & Dennis, R. (2018). Cutting with Both Arms of the Scissors: The Economic and Political Case for Restrictive Supply-Side Climate Policies. *Climatic Change*, *150*(1-2), 73–87. DOI: 10.1007/s10584-018-2162-x

Grube, L., & Storr, V. (2014). The capacity for self-governance and post-disaster resiliency. *The Review of Austrian Economics*, *27*(3), 301–324. DOI: 10.1007/s11138-013-0210-3

Habibov, N., & Afand, I. E. (2017). Community-level social capital and household strategies for coping with global crisis in transitional countries. *Social Indicators Research*, *130*(2), 687–710. DOI: 10.1007/s11205-015-1197-x

Harris, P. (Ed.). (2019). *A Research Agenda for Climate Justice*. Edward Elgar. DOI: 10.4337/9781788118170

Heffron, R. J., & McCauley, D. (2018). 'What is the 'just transition'?'. *Geoforum*, *88*, 74–77. DOI: 10.1016/j.geoforum.2017.11.016

Higgins, P. (2010). *Eradicating Ecocide*. Shepheard-Walwyn.

Hoare, N. (2018). *Activists, Defenders, Investigators: These are the Women Who Inspire Us*. Global Witness.

Howson, P. (2018). Slippery Violence in the REDD+ Forests of Central Kalimantan, Indonesia. *Conservation & Society*, *16*(2), 136–146. DOI: 10.4103/cs.cs_16_150

Hughes, S., & Hoffmann, M. (2020). Just urban transitions: Toward a research agenda. *Wiley Interdisciplinary Reviews: Climate Change*, *11*(3), e640. DOI: 10.1002/wcc.640

Humphreys, S. (Ed.). (2009). *Human Rights and Climate Change*. CUP. DOI: 10.1017/CBO9780511770722

Isakson, R. (2015). Derivatives for Development? Small-Farmer Vulnerability and the Financialization of Climate Risk Management. *Journal of Agrarian Change, 15*(4), 569–580. DOI: 10.1111/joac.12124

Islam, R., & Walkerden, G. (2014). How bonding and bridging networks contribute to disaster resilience and recovery on the Bangladeshi coast. *International Journal of Disaster Risk Reduction, 10*, 281–291. DOI: 10.1016/j.ijdrr.2014.09.016

Jacobs, D. B., & Cramer, L. A. (2017). Applying information network analysis to fire-prone landscapes: Implications for community resilience. *Ecology and Society, 22*(1), 20. DOI: 10.5751/ES-09119-220152

Javadpoor, M., Sharifi, A., & Roosta, M. (2021). An adaptation of the Baseline Resilience Indicators for Communities (BRIC) for assessing resilience of Iranian provinces. *International Journal of Disaster Risk Reduction, 66*, 102609. DOI: 10.1016/j.ijdrr.2021.102609

Jordan, J. C. (2015). Swimming alone? The role of social capital in enhancing local resilience to climate stress: A case study from Bangladesh. *Climate and Development, 7*(2), 110–123. DOI: 10.1080/17565529.2014.934771

Kashwan, P. (2021). Climate Justice in the Global North: An Introduction. *Case Studies in the Environment, 5*(1), 1–13. DOI: 10.1525/cse.2021.1125003

Kenner, D. (2019). *Carbon Inequality: The Role of the Richest in Climate Change*. Routledge. DOI: 10.4324/9781351171328

Kim, H., & Marcouiller, D. W. (2016). Natural disaster response, community resilience, and economic capacity: A case study of Coastal Florida. *Society & Natural Resources, 29*(8), 981–997. DOI: 10.1080/08941920.2015.1080336

Kizos, T., Detsis, V., Iosifides, T., & Metaxakis, M. (2014). Social capital and social-ecological resilience in the Asteroussia Mountains, Southern Crete, Greece. *Ecology and Society, 19*(1), 11. DOI: 10.5751/ES-06208-190140

Klein, R. J., & Möhner, A. (2011). The Political Dimension of Vulnerability: Implications for the Green Climate Fund. *IDS Bulletin, 42*(3), 15–22. DOI: 10.1111/j.1759-5436.2011.00218.x

Kothari, A., Salleh, A., Escobar, A., Demaria, F., and Acosta, A. (2019). pluriverse. A Post Development Dictionary. *New Dehli: Tulika Books*.

Krause, D. (2018). Transformative Approaches to Address Climate Change and Achieve Climate Justice. In Jafry, T. (Ed.), *Routledge Handbook of Climate Justice* (pp. 509–520). Routledge. DOI: 10.4324/9781315537689-37

Lang, T., & Ramı'rez, R. (2017). Building new social capital with scenario planning. *Technological Forecasting and Social Change*, *124*, 51–65. DOI: 10.1016/j.techfore.2017.06.011

Leach, M., MacGregor, H., Scoones, I., & Wilkinson, A. (2021). Post-pandemic transformations: How and why COVID-19 requires us to rethink development. *World Development*, *138*, 105233. DOI: 10.1016/j.worlddev.2020.105233 PMID: 33100478

Leach, M., & Mearns, R. (1996). *Lie of the Land: Challenging Received Wisdom on the African Environment*. James Currey.

Leach, M., Mehta, L., & Prabhakaran, P. (2017). Sustainable Development: A Gendered Pathways Approach. In Leach, M. (Ed.), *Gender Equality and Sustainable Development* (pp. 1–33). Routledge.

Leach, M., & Scoones, I. (Eds.). (2015). *Carbon Conflicts and Forest Landscapes in Africa*. Routledge. DOI: 10.4324/9781315740416

Leal-Arcas, R., Papadea, D., & Richardson, R. (2019). Aiming at Sustainable Trade in the Context of the Rule of Law: What Role for Citizens and How International Trade Can Help Reduce Fossil-Fuel Consumption. *SSRN*, *11*(2), 193–238. DOI: 10.2139/ssrn.3501569

Lehtonen, M., & Kern, F. (2009). Deliberative Socio-Technical Transitions. In Scarse, I., & MacKerron, G. (Eds.), *Energy for the Future: A New Agenda* (pp. 103–122). Palgrave. DOI: 10.1057/9780230235441_7

Lisnyj, K. T., & Dickson-Anderson, S. E. (2018). Community resilience in Walkerton, Canada: Sixteen years post-outbreak. *International Journal of Disaster Risk Reduction*, *31*, 196–202. DOI: 10.1016/j.ijdrr.2018.05.001

Macgillivray, B. H. (2018). Beyond social capital: The norms, belief systems, and agency embedded in social networks shape resilience to climatic and geophysical hazards. *Environmental Science & Policy*, *89*, 116–125. DOI: 10.1016/j.envsci.2018.07.014

Maclean, K., Cuthill, M., & Ross, H. (2014). Six attributes of social resilience. *Journal of Environmental Planning and Management*, *57*(1), 144–156. DOI: 10.1080/09640568.2013.763774

Magis, K. (2010). Community resilience: An indicator of social sustainability. *Society & Natural Resources*, *23*(5), 401–416. DOI: 10.1080/08941920903305674

Matarrita-Cascante, D., Trejos, B., Qin, H., Joo, D., & Debner, S. (2017). Conceptualizing community resilience: Revisiting conceptual distinctions. *Community Development (Columbus, Ohio)*, *48*(1), 105–123. DOI: 10.1080/15575330.2016.1248458

McCauley, D., Ramasar, V., Heffron, R. J., Sovacool, B. K., Mebratu, D., & Mundaca, L. (2019). Energy justice in the transition to low carbon energy systems: Exploring key themes in interdisciplinary research. *Applied Energy*, *233-234*, 916–921. DOI: 10.1016/j.apenergy.2018.10.005

Mehta, L., & Srivastava, S. (2020). 'Uncertainty in Modelling Climate Change: The possibilities of co-production through knowledge pluralism', in I. Scoones and A. Stirling (Eds), The Politics of Uncertainty: Challenges of Transformation, (pp. 99-112), 1 st edition. *London: Routledge*.

Mehta, L., Srivastava, S., Adam, H. N., Alankar, , Bose, S., Ghosh, U., & Kumar, V. V. (2019). Climate Change and Uncertainty from "Above" and "Below": Perspectives from India. *Regional Environmental Change*, *19*(6), 1533–1547. DOI: 10.1007/s10113-019-01479-7

Milne, S.. (2018). Learning from "Actually Existing" REDD+: A Synthesis of Ethnographic Findings. *Conservation & Society*, *•••*, 1–12.

Mngumi, L. E. (2020). Exploring the contribution of social capital in building resilience for climate change effects in peri-urban areas, Dar es Salaam, Tanzania. *GeoJournal*, *86*(6), 2671–2689. DOI: 10.1007/s10708-020-10214-3 PMID: 32836701

Morena, E., Krause, D., & Stevis, D. (Eds.). (2020). *Just Transitions Social Justice in the Shift Towards a Low-Carbon World*. Pluto.

Moreno, J., Lara, A., & Torres, M. (2019). Community resilience in response to the 2010 tsunami in Chile: The survival of a small-scale fishing community. *International Journal of Disaster Risk Reduction*, *33*, 376–384. DOI: 10.1016/j.ijdrr.2018.10.024

Morris, J. C., McNamara, M. W., & Belcher, A. (2019). Building resilience through collaboration between grassroots citizen groups and governments: Two case studies. *Public Works Management & Policy*, *24*(1), 50–62. DOI: 10.1177/1087724X18803116

Morrison, C., & Ramsey, E. (2019). Power to the people: Developing networks through rural community energy schemes. *Journal of Rural Studies*, *70*, 169–178. DOI: 10.1016/j.jrurstud.2018.07.006

Moss, J. (Ed.). (2018). *Climate Change and Justice*. CUP.

Newell, P. (2021). Race and the politics of energy transitions. *Energy Research & Social Science*, *71*, 101839. DOI: 10.1016/j.erss.2020.101839

Newell, P. (2021a). *Power Shift: The Global Political Economy of Energy Transitions*. CUP. DOI: 10.1017/9781108966184

Newell, P., & Martin, A. (2020). '*The Role of the State in the Politics of Disruption & Acceleration*', EIT Climate KIC Working Paper February 2020, Background thinking and research for Climate Innovation Insights Series, 5.

Newell, P., & Mulvaney, D. (2013). The Political Economy of the Just Transition. *The Geographical Journal*, *197*(2), 132–140. DOI: 10.1111/geoj.12008

Newell, P., & Simms, A. (2019). Towards a Fossil Fuel Non-Proliferation Treaty. *Climate Policy*, •••, 1–12.

Norris, F. H., Stevens, S. P., Pfefferbaum, B., Wyche, K. F., & Pfefferbaum, R. L. (2008). Community resilience as a metaphor, theory, set of capacities, and strategy for disaster readiness. *American Journal of Community Psychology*, *41*(1-2), 127–150. DOI: 10.1007/s10464-007-9156-6 PMID: 18157631

Okereke, C. (2008). *Global Justice and Neoliberal Environmental Governance: Sustainable Development, Ethics and International Cooperation*. Routledge.

Panda, A. (2016). Exploring Climate Change Perceptions, Rainfall Trends and Perceived Barriers to Adaptation in a Drought Affected Region in India. *Natural Hazards*, *84*(2), 777–796. DOI: 10.1007/s11069-016-2456-0

Pandey, A., Prakash, A., & Werners, S. E. (2021). Matches, mismatches and priorities of pathways from a climate-resilient development perspective in the mountains of Nepal. *Environmental Science & Policy*, *125*, 135–145. DOI: 10.1016/j.envsci.2021.08.013

Paprocki, K., & Huq, S. (2018). Shrimp and Coastal Adaptation: On the Politics of Climate Justice. *Climate and Development*, *10*(1), 1–3. DOI: 10.1080/17565529.2017.1301871

Patel, S. S., Rogers, M. B., Amlo^t, R., & Rubin, G. J. (2017). What do we mean by "community resilience"? A systematic literature review of how it is defined in the literature. *PLoS Currents*, •••, 9. PMID: 29188132

Peel, J., & Lin, J. (2019). Transnational climate litigation: The contribution of the global South. *The American Journal of International Law*, *113*(4), 679–726. DOI: 10.1017/ajil.2019.48

Pelling, M. (2011). *Adaptation to climate change: From resilience to transformation*. Routledge.

Pelling, M., High, C., Dearing, J., & Smith, D. (2008). Shadow spaces for social learning: A relational understanding of adaptive capacity to climate change within organisations. *Environment & Planning A*, *40*(4), 867–884. DOI: 10.1068/a39148

Pelling, M., O'brien, K., & Matyas, D. (2015). Adaptation and transformation. *Climatic Change*, *133*(1), 113–127. DOI: 10.1007/s10584-014-1303-0

Phillips, M. (2016). Assets and affect in the study of social capital in rural communities. *Sociologia Ruralis*, *56*(2), 220–247. DOI: 10.1111/soru.12085 PMID: 27563158

Piggot, G., Erickson, P., van Asselt, H., & Lazarus, M. (2018). Swimming Upstream: Addressing Fossil Fuel Supply Under the UNFCCC. *Climate Policy*, *18*(9), 1189–1202. DOI: 10.1080/14693062.2018.1494535

Pottier, A., Méjean, A., Godard, O., & Hourcade, J. C. (2017). A survey of global climate justice: From negotiation stances to moral stakes and back. *International Review of Environmental and Resource Economics*, *11*(1), 1–53. DOI: 10.1561/101.00000090

Ramesh Kumar, K. C., Bexci, M. S., Bhaumik, A., & Ojha, S. K. (2025). Educating and Promoting Climate Sustainability. In Bhaumik, A., Poddar, S., Dadhich, M., Hiran, K., & Doshi, R. (Eds.), *Community Resilience and Climate Change Challenges: Pursuit of Sustainable Development Goals (SDGs)* (pp. 183–202). IGI Global Scientific Publishing., DOI: 10.4018/979-8-3693-6522-9.ch010

Ranganathan, M., & Bratman, E. (2021). From urban resilience to abolitionist climate justice in Washington, DC. *Antipode*, *53*(1), 115–137. DOI: 10.1111/anti.12555

Roberts, E., & Huq, S. (2015). Coming Full Circle: The History of Loss and Damage Under the UNFCCC. *International Journal of Global Warming*, *8*(2), 141–157. DOI: 10.1504/IJGW.2015.071964

Roberts, E., & Pelling, M. (2020). Loss and Damage: An Opportunity for Transformation? *Climate Policy*, *20*(6), 758–771. DOI: 10.1080/14693062.2019.1680336

Roberts, J. T., & Parks, B. (2006). *A Climate of Injustice: Global Inequality, North-South Politics and Climate Policy*. MIT Press.

Rockenbauch, T., & Sakdapolrak, P. (2017). Social networks and the resilience of rural communities in the Global South: A critical review and conceptual reflections. *Ecology and Society*, *22*(1), 10. DOI: 10.5751/ES-09009-220110

Rodriguez, I. (2017). Linking Well-Being with Cultural Revitalization for Greater Cognitive Justice in Conservation: Lessons from Venezuela in Canaima National Park. *Ecology and Society*, *22*(4), art24. DOI: 10.5751/ES-09758-220424

Rodriguez, I., & Inturias, M. L. (2018). 'Conflict Transformation in Indigenous' Peoples Territories: Doing Environmental Justice with a 'Decolonial Turn''. *Development Studies Research*, *5*(1), 90–105. DOI: 10.1080/21665095.2018.1486220

Saldana, J. (2016). The coding manual for qualitative researchers. Thousand Oaks, *CA. Sage (Atlanta, Ga.).*

Salman, S. A. (2025). Community Resilience and Climate Change: Challenges Assessing Sustainable Development Objectives. In Bhaumik, A., Poddar, S., Dadhich, M., Hiran, K., & Doshi, R. (Eds.), *Community Resilience and Climate Change Challenges: Pursuit of Sustainable Development Goals (SDGs)* (pp. 93–108). IGI Global Scientific Publishing., DOI: 10.4018/979-8-3693-6522-9.ch006

Sanson, A. V., & Burke, S. E. (2020). Climate Change and Children: An Issue of Intergenerational Justice. In Balvin, N., & Christie, D. (Eds.), *Children and Peace* (pp. 343–362). Springer. DOI: 10.1007/978-3-030-22176-8_21

Schlosberg, D., & Collins, L. (2014). From Environmental to Climate Justice: Climate Change and the Discourse of Environmental Justice. *Wiley Interdisciplinary Reviews: Climate Change*, *5*(3), 359–374. DOI: 10.1002/wcc.275

Simms, A. (2005). *Ecological Debt: The Health of the Planet and the Wealth of Nations*. Pluto Press.

Smith, L. C., & Frankenberger, T. R. (2018). Does resilience capacity reduce the negative impact of shocks on household food security? Evidence from the 2014 floods in Northern Bangladesh. *World Development*, *102*, 358–376. DOI: 10.1016/j.worlddev.2017.07.003

Sovacool, B. K. (2021). Who are the victims of low-carbon transitions? Towards a political ecology of climate change mitigation. *Energy Research & Social Science*, *73*, 101916. DOI: 10.1016/j.erss.2021.101916

Sovacool, B. K., Hook, A., Martiskainen, M., & Baker, L. H. (2019). Decarbonisation and its Discontents: A Critical Energy Justice Perspective on Four Low-Carbon Transitions. *Climatic Change*, *155*(4), 581–619. DOI: 10.1007/s10584-019-02521-7

Srivastava, S., & Mehta, L. (2017). The Social Life of Mangroves: Market-Driven Enclosures, Resource Complexes and Contestations on the Industrial Coastline of Kutch, India, STEPS Working Paper 99, *Brighton: IDS.*

Steg, L. (2018). Limiting climate change requires research on climate action. *Nature Climate Change*, *8*(9), 759–761. DOI: 10.1038/s41558-018-0269-8

Stevenson, H., & Dryzek, J. (2014). *Democratizing Global Climate Governance*. Cambridge University Press. DOI: 10.1017/CBO9781139208628

Stirling, A. (2009). Afterword: Sustainable Energy- The Challenge of Choice. In Scarse, I., & MacKerron, G. (Eds.), *Energy for the Future: A New Agenda* (pp. 251–260). Palgrave MacMillan.

Sultana, F. (2019). Decolonizing Development and the Pursuit of Social Justice. *Human Geographies*, *12*(3), 31–46. DOI: 10.1177/194277861901200305

Sultana, F. (2020). Intersectionality and climate justice An emancipatory research agenda. https://www.youtube.com/watch?v=BkjpRrps7D8&ab_channel=CentreforClimateJustice

Swilling, M., & Annecke, E. (2012). *Just Transitions: Explorations of Unsustainability in an Unfair World*. UCT Press.

Tajuddin, N., & Da̧browski, M. (2021). Enabling Socio-Ecological Resilience in the Global South: Insights from Chennai, India. *Sustainability (Basel)*, *13*(19), 10522. DOI: 10.3390/su131910522

Tenzin, G., & Natsuda, K. (2016). Social capital, household income, and community development in Bhutan: A case study of a dairy cooperative. *Development in Practice*, *26*(4), 467–480. DOI: 10.1080/09614524.2016.1161731

Thompson, D., & Lopez Barrera, S. (2019). Community resilience and collective agency under significant changes in the natural and built environment: A community capitals framework approach. *Local Environment*, *24*(12), 1156–1177. DOI: 10.1080/13549839.2019.1683723

Torres Contreras, G. A. (2021). Twenty-five Years under the Wind Turbines in La Venta, Mexico: Social Difference, Land Control and Agrarian Change. *The Journal of Peasant Studies*.

Tower, A. (2020). We Need to Talk about Climate Migration as a Justice Issue https://www.climate-refugees.org/perspectives/2020/7/29/we-need-to-talk-about climate-migration-as-a-justice-issue

Tschakert, P. (2020). More-than-human solidarity and multispecies justice in the climate crisis. *Environmental Politics*, •••, 1–20.

Uekusa, S., & Matthewman, S. (2016). Vulnerable and resilient? Immigrants and refugees in the 2010–2011 Canterbury and Tohoku disasters. *International Journal of Disaster Risk Reduction*, *22*, 355–361. DOI: 10.1016/j.ijdrr.2017.02.006

Umamaheswari, T., Sugumar, G., Krishnan, P., Ananthan, P. S., Anand, A., Jeevamani, J. J. J., Mahendra, R. S., & Infantina, J. A. (2021). Vulnerability assessment of coastal fishing communities for building resilience and adaptation: Evidences from Tamil Nadu, India. *Environmental Science & Policy*, *123*, 114–130. DOI: 10.1016/j.envsci.2021.05.009

Umbers, L., & Moss, J. (2020). *Climate Justice Beyond the State*. Routledge. DOI: 10.4324/9781003052562

Urquiza, A., C. Amigo, M. Billi, R. Calvo, L. Gallardo, C.I. Neira, and M. Rojas. (2021) An integrated framework to streamline resilience in the context of urban climate risk assessment. *Earth's Future*, 9, e2020EF001508.

Vallance, S., & Carlton, S. (2015). First to respond, last to leave: Communities' roles and resilience across the "4Rs.". *International Journal of Disaster Risk Reduction*, *14*, 27–36. DOI: 10.1016/j.ijdrr.2014.10.010

Vaneeckhaute, L. E., Vanwing, T., Jacquet, W., Abelshausen, B., & Meurs, P. (2017). Community resilience 2.0: Toward a comprehensive conception of community-level resilience. *Community Development (Columbus, Ohio)*, *48*(5), 735–751. DOI: 10.1080/15575330.2017.1369443

Vedwan, N., & Rhoades, R. E. (2001). Climate Change in the Western Himalayas of India: A Study of Local Perception and Response. *Climate Research*, *19*(2), 109–117. DOI: 10.3354/cr019109

Wallimann-Helmer, I. (2015). Justice for climate loss and damage. *Climatic Change*, *133*(3), 469–480. DOI: 10.1007/s10584-015-1483-2

Walsh-Dilley, M., Wolford, W., & Mcccarthy, J. (2016). Rights for resilience: Food sovereignty, power and resilience in development practice. *Ecology and Society*, *21*(1), 11. DOI: 10.5751/ES-07981-210111

Wickes, R., Britt, C., & Broidy, L. (2017). The resilience of neighborhood social processes: A case study of the 2011 Brisbane flood. *Social Science Research*, *62*, 96–119. DOI: 10.1016/j.ssresearch.2016.07.006 PMID: 28126116

Willis, R. (2020). *Too Hot to Handle? The Democratic Challenge of Climate Change*. Bristol University Press.

Wilson, R. S., Herziger, A., Hamilton, M., & Brooks, J. S. (2020). From incremental to transformative adaptation in individual responses to climate-exacerbated hazards. *Nature Climate Change*, *10*(3), 200–208. DOI: 10.1038/s41558-020-0691-6

Ziervogel, G., Pelling, M., Cartwright, A., Chu, E., Deshpande, T., Harris, L., Hyams, K., Kaunda, J., Klaus, B., Michael, K., Pasquini, L., Pharoah, R., Rodina, L., Scott, D., & Zweig, P. (2017). Inserting Rights and Justice into Urban Resilience: A Focus on Everyday Risk. *Environment and Urbanization*, *29*(1), 123–138. DOI: 10.1177/0956247816686905

KEY TERMS AND DEFINITIONS

Climate Adaptation: Climate adaptation refers to strategies and measures implemented to help communities and ecosystems adjust to the adverse effects of climate change.

Climate Justice: Environmental justice is a social movement and legal principle that advocates for fair treatment and meaningful involvement of all individuals, particularly marginalized communities, in environmental decision-making.

Health Equity: Health equity refers to the principle that everyone should have a fair opportunity to attain their highest level of health, regardless of social or economic status.

Indigenous Rights: Indigenous rights refer to the collective and individual entitlements of Indigenous peoples, recognizing their unique cultural identities, traditional lands, and ways of life.

Chapter 6

Evaluating the Role of Industry 5.0 in Achieving Sustainable Development Goal 3: "Good Health and Well-Being"

Piyush Kumar
https://orcid.org/0000-0002-1288-9201
IILM University, Gurguram, India

Kirti Udayai
https://orcid.org/0000-0003-2741-4396
Max Healthcare, India

Ragini Sharma
https://orcid.org/0009-0003-9667-5562
JLL MENA, India

ABSTRACT

Industry 5.0 is on the horizon representing a big change, focusing on combining advanced technologies with a people-centred approach. Industry 5.0 incorporates technologies such as artificial intelligence (AI), big data analytics (BDA), the Internet of Things (IoT), machine learning (ML), robotics, and virtualization to pave the way for innovative ways of doing things. The goal is to attain equilibrium between humans and machines, all while ensuring our growth occurs in an environmentally sustainable manner. In healthcare, Industry 5.0 aspires to build resource-efficient and user-friendly solutions. In this chapter, we explore how Industry 5.0 can work together with Sustainable Development Goal 3 – Good Health and Well-being by

DOI: 10.4018/979-8-3693-9755-8.ch006

analysing the optimal use and the collective potential of numerous technologies that might aid in achieving the targets of SDG 3. We examine the optimal utilization of various technologies to attain the objectives of this goal.

1. INTRODUCTION

The Industrial Revolution had a profound impact on how companies and society operated. With advancements in digital technologies, manufacturing techniques underwent substantial modifications. The focus changed from mechanical engineering and steam power in Industry 1.0 to electrical engineering in Industry 2.0, which brought large-scale assembly lines and electric power systems, revolutionizing industries and people's lives. Industry 3.0 marked the integration of electronics, computers, and information technology into production processes and was superseded by Industry 4.0 with the automation of industrial operations, propelling us to a new level of production efficiency and now making headway for Industry 5.0.

The convergence of Industry 5.0 and the Sustainable Development Goals (SDGs) marks a crucial juncture in the global industrial landscape, blending technological innovation with socio-environmental responsibilities. Industry 5.0, an evolution of Industry 4.0, envisions a future where technological advancements not just improve efficiency but also contribute significantly to achieving sustainable development goals. Unlike its predecessors, Industry 5.0 responds actively to global sustainability challenges. Its emphasis on a human-centric approach prioritizes the well-being of the workforce, aligning with the overarching objective of the SDGs, which is to ensure that no one is left behind. In the face of post-pandemic complexities and disruptions in supply chains, Industry 5.0 becomes crucial for steering toward a more inclusive and sustainable future through resilience, sustainability, and collaborative efforts. Industry 5.0 acknowledges the potential of the industrial sector to contribute to societal goals beyond mere job creation and economic growth. It aspires to transform production into a resilient source of prosperity by adhering to the planet's limits and placing the well-being of industry workers at the forefront of the production process. (Nielsen & Brix, 2023).

The next section discusses Industry 5.0 with the Sustainable Development Goals. We also discuss Industry 5.0 and Sustainable Development Goal 3 of Good Health and Well-being. In the later section, we deeply analyze the integration of Industry 5.0 technologies and how it could help to achieve SDG 3 while also focusing on the challenges and barriers in the implementation. Finally, we conclude the study with a brief discussion of future research opportunities.

2. UNDERSTANDING INDUSTRY 5.0

Figure 1. Evolution from Industry 1.0 to 5.0

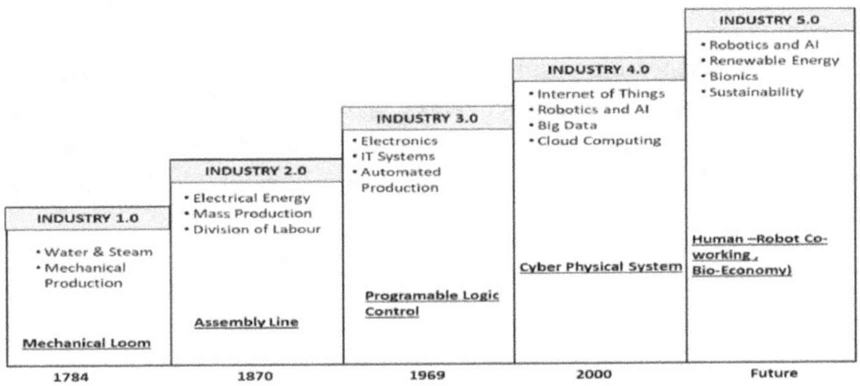

Source: https://www.researchgate.net/figure/Industrial-revolutions-from-Industry-10-to-Industry-50-adapted-from-29-27_fig1_366960759

As depicted in the Figure 1, Industry 5.0 surpasses its predecessor, using advanced technologies that find a balance between humans and machines, focusing on long-term growth. It goes beyond just manufacturing, expanding on the fourth industrial revolution (Industry 4.0), and relies on developments in IT, like artificial intelligence, automation, big data analytics, the Internet of Things (IoT), machine learning, robotics, smart systems, and virtualization. (*Handbook of Research on Innovative Management Using AI in Industry 5.0*, 2022).

Industry 5.0 humanizes the notion of digital transformation via collaborative usage of these technologies. Industry 5.0, seen as the next industrial revolution, aims to achieve resource-efficient and user-preferred manufacturing solutions by leveraging the creativity of human specialists in partnership with efficient, intelligent, and precise machines (Maddikunta et al., 2022). Industry 4.0 is characterized (and supported) by technological adoption (IoT, smart robots, artificial intelligence, 3D printing, connectivity 4G/5G, Digital Twins), however, the move to Industry 5.0 has three characteristics as "attractors" (Saracco, 2022)

The Industry 4.0 was primarily driven by internal imperatives focusing on the pursuit of increased efficiency, adaptability, and cost efficiency through the incorporation of flexible production tools such as intelligent robotics. The emergence of Industry 5.0 is heavily influenced by external forces with three defining characteristics- resilience, sustainability and human centricity (Verma, 2024), as shown in figure 2 below. In contrast to its forerunner, Industry 5.0 is shaped in response to global imperatives for sustainability, endeavoring to curtail raw material consumption, mitigate CO_2 emissions, and accentuate the principles of recycling and reusing resources. Furthermore, Industry 5.0 places a pronounced emphasis on a human-centric paradigm, diverging from a purely business-centric perspective. This approach prioritizes the well-being and developmental trajectory of the workforce, acknowledging the significance of human capital in the industrial landscape. The imperative for resilience has assumed heightened importance in the aftermath of pivotal events such as the pandemic, energy crises, and disruptions in the supply chain. These events have necessitated a thorough reassessment of industrial methodologies to effectively confront and surmount these challenges (Goel & Gupta, 2019).

Figure 2. The three defining characteristics of Industry 5.0

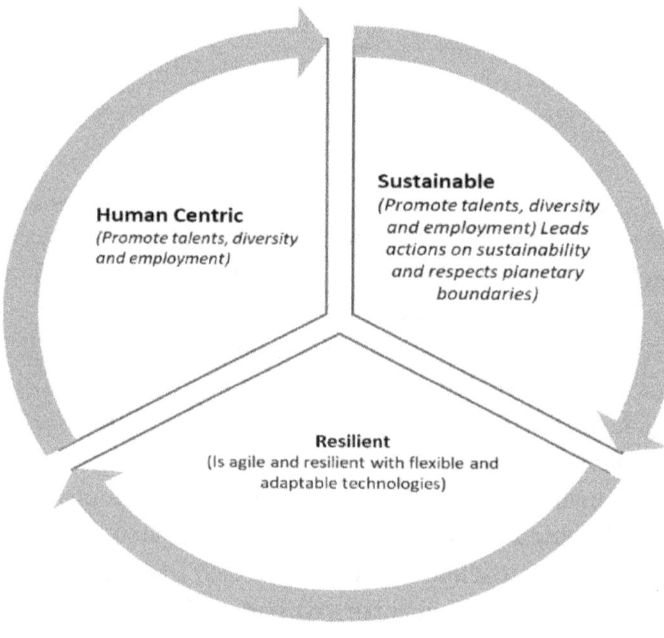

Source: https://cmte.ieee.org/futuredirections/2022/09/19/from-industry-4-0-to-industry-5-0-ii/

Amidst this transformation, either we chose to metamorphose for the better or remain cocooned to watch the transformation happening in front of our eyes and regret it later. The healthcare industry is also rapidly trying to adapt to technology and ensure that it grows with it. The choice is ours and the time is now. What we learned a decade or two ago is fast becoming obsolete with the fundamental paradigm shift in technology impacting almost every sphere of our lives. "Over the past 150 years, breakthroughs in technology—which are the long-term outcomes of scientific advancements—have contributed significantly to improvements in human well-being (including those in economics, health, longevity, life satisfaction, and a variety of options). Even in democracies, the distribution of these gains has not been equitable. There's a lot of room for getting better over the long term in computer science, information science, statistics, and computational social science. These fields are just starting to see big improvements. (The Future of Well-Being in a Tech-Saturated World | Pew Research Center, 2022).

3. INDUSTRY 5.0 ROLE IN HEALTHCARE:

In context of healthcare, the industry 4.0 era aligned with the digitalization focusing on the innovative business models, personalization in healthcare and also enabled predictive healthcare. The technologies like big-data, IoT and cloud facilitated the real time customization of healthcare and transforming healthcare into a cyber -physical system integrated with wearables, robots and other smart devices. The integration of industry 5.0 technologies in healthcare could lay down the path to the convergence of human and technology, offering holistic healthcare and patient wellness by enhancing services quality reducing the cost of care. Dedicated to integrating sophisticated technology with human cooperation, Industry 5.0 has the capability to profoundly affect health and well-being. (Kasinathan et al., 2022). Incorporating Industry 5.0 can promote cooperation among humans and advanced technologies, resulting in enhanced healthcare delivery, medical progress, and overall well-being. (Kumar et al., 2023). This plays a crucial role in achieving Sustainable Development Goals as well. (Gomathi et al., 2023).

Industry 5.0 technologies have proven to be successful in bridging Healthcare Inequalities and enhancing personalised care. AI driven tools like Babyl and ThinkMD enable healthcare workers to deliver quality healthcare in the resource limited and overburdened healthcare ecosystem dealing with the shortage of healthcare workers. Tool like qXR AI tool accelerates tuberculosis diagnosis, surpassing traditional methods and thus accelerating the treatment.

Integration of smart wearables and devices in healthcare has remote patient monitoring, online consultation and real time preventive healthcare a reality, particularly benefitting the uninsured and rural populations. Devices such as Omron's blood pressure monitors sync with apps to offer real-time health insights, promoting early intervention and continuous monitoring. Further, there are AI powered virtual assistants also known as virtual health assistants (VHAs) that offer personalized health advice based on individual data analysis. VHAs like Docus, can manage appointments, provide health advice, track symptoms, monitor health conditions, and more, offering personalized and accessible care.

4. SDG AND THE EVOLVING NEED OF TECHNOLOGY

In September 2015, the United Nations Sustainable Development Summit endorsed the Sustainable Development Goals (SDGs), a UN project with 17 objectives and 169 targets to combat climate change, relieve poverty, and eliminate inequality and injustice by 2030. Unlike the Millennium Development Goals, these objectives are universal and apply to all countries, both developed and developing, as shown in figure 3. The suggested objectives and targets may be seen as a network, with linkages between goals established by targets that relate to numerous goals. (Le Blanc 2015).

Figure 3. The Sustainable Development Goals

Source: https://www.un.org/development/desa/pd/content/sustainable-development-goals-2

"Transforming Our World: The Agenda", often known as the 2030 Agenda is a worldwide agreement among UN members that focuses on a broad variety of linked economic, social, and environmental goals. The plan is to achieve these objectives through multi-sector global partnerships that tackle the most pressing issues affecting the world today and even the UN has recognized how important it will be for their efforts to use technology successfully. Digital technology is major enabling factor in achieving Sustainable Development Goals (SDGs) by enhancing efficiency, transparency, and inclusivity across sectors such as education, health, economy, and the environment. (Ariansyah et al., 2024)

According to the 2030 Agenda of the United Nations General Assembly, "the spread of information and communications technology and global interconnectedness has great potential to accelerate human progress, bridge the digital divide, and develop knowledge societies." To do this, ICT infrastructure is a critical "means of implementation" that allows all goals to be realized. The agenda's 17 goals are universally applicable and represented in the three main dimensions of sustainable development: economic, social, and environmental.

Figure 4. The Aggregation of SDGs into the Three Pillars

Source: https://www.mdpi.com/2071-1050/11/7/1961

As shown in the figure 4, the three main dimensions of sustainable development—social inclusion, economic prosperity, and environmental preservation—all rely on technology to succeed. The 17 SDGs can be met, but only with major increases in the rate, scope, and equality of development. The SDGs cannot be met through economic development in the framework of business as usual. Only technology can sustain this exponential growth. Digitalization has revolutionized the way an organization runs and gives value to its clients.

5. SDG 3: GOOD HEALTH AND WELL-BEING

Throughout all life stages, everyone needs to enjoy access to health and well-being, according to the guidelines set by Sustainable Development Goal 3. This goal tackles critical health concerns, including the universal availability of safe, effective, high-quality, and affordable medications and vaccinations. It also addresses aspects such as reproductive, maternal, and child health, communicable and non-communicable diseases, and environmental health issues, while recognizing evolving consumer needs and healthcare delivery systems. The health goal (SDG) 3 articulates the objective as: 'Ensure healthy lives and promote well-being for all at all ages.' The SDG declaration underscores the importance of achieving universal health coverage (UHC) and ensuring access to top-notch healthcare to fulfill the overarching health goal. The inclusion of everyone is imperative. (*Universal Health Coverage (UHC)*, 2023). In the context of Goal 3 and health, the key terms are defined as follows:

- **'Health':** 'Every individual, regardless of race, religion, political belief, economic or social condition, has the fundamental right to enjoy a state of total physical, mental, and social well-being. This extends beyond the mere absence of disease or infirmity, and the pursuit of the highest possible level of health is considered a basic human entitlement.'
- **'Well-being':** A multi-factorial concept that is based on the satisfaction of material, physical, affective, and psychological needs. While well-being extends beyond physical and mental health, physical and mental health is clearly the key to the notion of well-being. Well-being is the antithesis of illness.
- **'For all at all ages':** The World Health Organisation (WHO) promotes a holistic approach to health. LCAH emphasises health from a time and societal perspective, looking back across an individual's or a social group's life experiences or across generations for indicators of current trends in wellness and illness, while acknowledging that both historical and contemporary experiences are shaped by the larger social, economic, and cultural contexts.

These three terms cannot be taken up separately. They overlap and co-exist. The sustainability goals cannot be met unless all three are pursued concurrently. The three have been defined individually for clarity, but it is important to note that they are linked and form the cornerstone of UHC as well as the foundation for achieving the sustainability goal.

Figure 5. Emphasis of SDG3

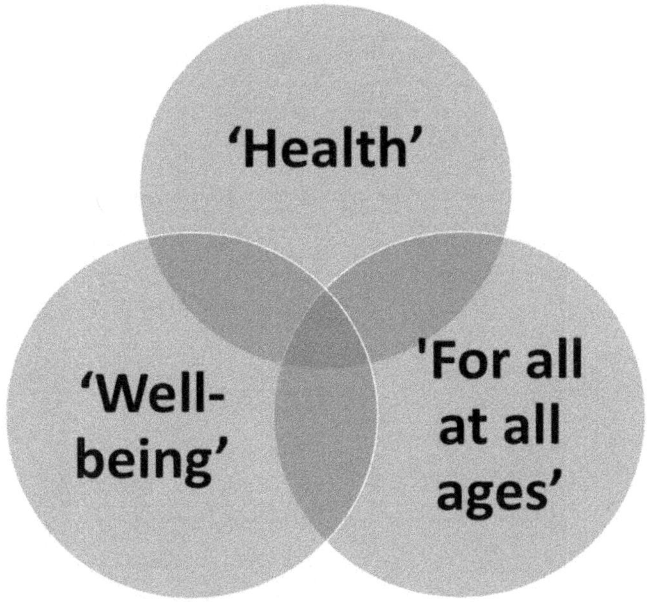

> *'The notion of universal health care is also crucial here, as it is described as "all communities and all people receiving the services they need and being protected from health threats, while also ensuring that they are protected from financial hardship.'*

4.1 Targets to be achieved under SDG 3:

Sustainable Development Goal 3 has 13 targets with 21 indicators (*Goal 3 | Department of Economic and Social Affairs*, n.d.):

Figure 6. SGD Targets and Indicators

SDG3	Target	Indicator
3.1	By 2030, reduce the global maternal mortality ratio to less than 70 per 100,000 live births	3.1.1 Maternal mortality ratio 3.1.2 Proportion of births attended by skilled health personnel
3.2	All countries should aim to end preventable deaths of new-borns and children <5 years of age, reduce neonatal mortality to at least 12/1,000 live births and under-5 mortality to at least 15/1,000 live births, by 2030	3.2.1 Under-five mortality rate 3.2.2 Neonatal mortality rate
3.3	By 2030, end the epidemics of AIDS, tuberculosis, malaria, and neglected tropical diseases and combat hepatitis, water-borne diseases, and other communicable diseases	3.3.1 Number of new HIV infections per 1,000 uninfected population, by sex, age and key populations 3.3.2 Tuberculosis incidence per 100,000 population 3.3.3 Malaria incidence per 1,000 population 3.3.4 Hepatitis B incidence per 100,000 population 3.3.5 Number of people requiring interventions against neglected tropical diseases
3.4	By 2030, reduce premature mortality from non-communicable diseases by 1/3rd through prevention and treatment and promote mental health and well-being	3.4.1 Mortality rate attributed to cardiovascular disease, cancer, diabetes or chronic respiratory disease 3.4.2 Suicide mortality rate
3.5	Strengthen the prevention and treatment of substance abuse, including narcotic drug abuse and harmful use of alcohol.	3.5.1 Coverage of treatment interventions (pharmacological, psychosocial and rehabilitation and aftercare services) for substance use disorders 3.5.2 Alcohol per capita consumption (aged 15 years and older) within a calendar year in litres of pure alcohol
3.6	By 2030, reduce the number of global deaths and injuries, due to road traffic accidents, to half	3.6.1 Death rate due to road traffic injuries
3.7	Sexual and reproductive healthcare services, including for	3.7.1 Proportion of women of reproductive age (aged 15-49 years) who have their

6. INDUSTRY 5.0 & SDG 3 INTERPLAY - EXPLORING SYNERGIES FOR SUCCESS

The provision of healthy life and well-being is a basic human right (Abbas, 2024). SDG 3, also referred to as “Good Health and Well-being,” strives for universal accessibility to healthy lives and well-being across all ages. The integration of technology is crucial in achieving this goal by improving healthcare delivery, preventing illnesses, and promoting overall health. Digital technologies such as artificial intelligence, machine learning, and big data analytics offer valuable tools for strengthening disease surveillance and responding to outbreaks. Utilizing these technologies enables the swift identification of disease outbreaks and real-time tracking of their spread, facilitating quicker and more effective responses. Digital innovations like health apps and wearables can empower patients to take control of their health and make healthier lifestyle choices. Health apps can provide details on a wholesome diet, exercise, and disease prevention, while wearables can track physical exercise and keep an eye on critical indicators including heart rate and blood pressure. Improving public health research and data analysis enables more accurate and comprehensive studies of disease prevalence, risk factors, and treatment outcomes. This information can be employed to formulate well-informed public health policies and interventions, aiming to enhance health outcomes. According to studies recently, it is shown that digitalization and sustainability cannot exist in silos. In this section, we will explore how Industry 5.0 could be leveraged to achieve the targets of Sustainable Development Goal 3.

6.1 Possible implementation of Industry 5.0 to attain targets of SDG 3

6.1.1 Enhancing Telemedicine and Remote monitoring to bridge the healthcare accessibility gap

Telemedicine is a promising approach to providing global access to high-quality healthcare services and could be a useful tool for achieving the targets of Sustainable Development Goals (SDGs) (Palozzi et al., 2020). The use of technology in telemedicine is to provide healthcare services remotely allowing healthcare professionals to reach people in remote areas, lightening the load of travel and associated costs. It has become particularly relevant during the pandemic of COVID-19, enabling remote consultations and patient monitoring. The integration of telemedicine platforms with Hospital Information Systems and Telehealth solutions can provide patients with seamless integration of medical records for advanced decision support and medical support services (MerrellRonald & Doarn, 2016). Digital health technologies, such as mHealth and telehealth, can help bridge healthcare gaps in conflict-affected areas and support humanitarian efforts to realize sustained progress in SDG 3 outcomes (Asi & Williams, 2018).

This could be further improved by embedding IoT devices in medical wearables (e.g., smartwatches, health patches, helmets, ambulances) to continuously monitor vital signs such as heart rate, blood pressure, and glucose levels allowing real-time data transmission through high-speed 5G networks to ensure timely detection of health issues, enabling healthcare providers to intervene promptly whereas Augmented Realty technology could facilitate a more immersive experience of the virtual consultation. Further, AI algorithms can be integrated into Telemedicine platforms for analyzing medical images, lab results, and patient data assisting healthcare professionals in making accurate and timely assessments, generating personalized health insights, and delivering personalized healthcare supported by AI-powered Virtual assistants/Chatbots to provide immediate responses to patient queries and improving accessibility of the information.

Besides being an effective approach for receiving counseling and mental health evaluation in the home environment, Telemedicine also enables effective recruitment, development and training of the workforce.

SGD 3 Targets under impact:

- Target 3.3
- Target 3.6.
- Target 3. C

6.1.2 **Effective Disease surveillance:**

The Covid-19 pandemic brought today's society a different perspective on how vulnerable Humanity is to unknown diseases. However, it also demonstrated the capability of technology to enhance our understanding of the matter and, on top of that, how to safeguard your population with disease surveillance (*an information-based activity involving the ongoing systematic collection, analysis, and interpretation of large volumes of health data originating from a variety of sources*) (What Is Disease Surveillance - Health Protection Surveillance Centre, n.d.).

In public health, it is essential to plan, implement, and evaluate public health practices, and closely integrate them with the timely dissemination of these data to those who need to know (Wagle, 2018). Progress to achieve this is relatively slow as there is not enough granularity in the available data to guide program planning and improvements - one of the few significant obstacles in achieving this target by many countries. MMR continues to be one of the key global public health issues.

To expedite the process, it is crucial to advocate and incentivize the utilization of surveillance systems, such as those for maternal and perinatal death surveillance and response activities, to elevate the quality of care and accountability. By employing AI algorithms to analyze vast datasets, including historical health records, weather patterns, and population movements, to predict and model disease spread, Early warning systems can be established, aiding public health authorities in preparing for and mitigating the impact of disease outbreaks. IoT sensors could be deployed in various locations to monitor environmental factors, vector populations, and other indicators relevant to disease transmission enabling real-time data collection utilizing 5G networks for early detection of potential disease outbreaks, and timely intervention.

SGD 3 Targets under impact:

- Target 3.3
- Target 3.D

6.1.3 **Personalized and Precision Medicine for enhancing the treatment efficacy**:

The goal is to create a foundation for practical health management by using a variety of information. Advances in precision medicine include keeping track of healthy individuals over time to understand how they go from being not sick to being sick. This helps accurately identify those at risk for diseases and customize treatments using detailed data from individual trials and studies involving larger populations (Hamburg & Collins, 2010). Precision medicine depends significantly on extensive population-level data collected from various clinical sources of large-scale information. This data is crucial for making personalized treatment decisions for individuals.

In contrast, Personalized medicine treats each patient as a unique individual throughout the entire treatment process, independent of large datasets, like precision medicine. It has gained traction by integrating augmented artificial intelligence (AI) to personalize combination therapies, thereby enhancing treatment safety and effectiveness (Lim et al., 2019). AI and machine learning (ML) can analyze a patient's medical history, genetic composition, and lifestyle factors to personalize treatment plans, improving effectiveness and minimizing the risk of adverse reactions. Clinical trials are currently being conducted to explore phenotypic personalized medicine (PPM) for different conditions like tuberculosis, HIV, liver and kidney transplant immunosuppression, hematologic cancers, and more. The goal is to offer patient-specific, more effective, and tailored treatments. The integration of personalized and precision medicine, backed by enabling technologies and considerate policy decisions, holds the promise of transforming how we approach disease prevention, monitoring, and overall human well-being.

SGD 3 Targets under impact:

- Target 3. B

6.1.4 **Real-time Health monitoring and measurement of health indicators:**

Information systems do not routinely collect the detailed data required to understand and address the health issue. The use of appropriate technology could help strengthen the monitoring and measurement capacities of health indicators. The IoMT-enabled collection of real-time personal health data from an individual remotely to enable monitoring outside of conventional clinical settings, in addition to providing care and related support has opened a sea of possibilities for healthcare professionals. As doctor-patient interactions have gotten simpler and more effective, it has raised patient involvement and satisfaction. Additionally, remote patient monitoring shortens hospital stays and avoids readmissions by keeping an eye on patients' health. For instance, indicators such as the number of newborn and maternal deaths and stillbirths if gathered, analyzed, and monitored on a real-time basis help in decision-making. Sensors-based wearable devices and other medical equipment can provide continuous monitoring of health indicators such as heart rate, blood pressure, and blood glucose levels. This can help individuals improve the management of chronic illnesses and guard against health issues.

IoT has a huge impact on lowering healthcare expenses of patient care besides improving health outcomes. Insurance firms can use the information gathered by health monitoring devices for screening and claims processing, and they can also reward their clients for using and sharing IoT-generated personal health data. Customers who use IoT devices to track their regular activities, adhere to treatment regimens, and use preventative healthcare measures can receive rewards. This will significantly lower the number of claims that insurers must pay. By integrating sensors into the vehicles, IoT could play a vital role in preventing road traffic accidents by enabling real-time monitoring of the vehicle state and aiding in quick corrective steps.

SGD 3 Targets under impact:

- Target 3.6
- Target 3.8
- Target 3.3
- Target 3.4

6.1.5 **Electronic Health Record:**

EHRs can help provide patients with higher-quality, safer care. A robust EHR acts as the first step towards modernizing healthcare and helps providers provide better care by enhancing all facets of patient care, such as equity, communication, patient-centeredness, safety, efficiency, effectiveness, and efficacy. Implementing blockchain to secure the storage and sharing of genomic and health records, ensuring data integrity, privacy, and interoperability, facilitating secure data exchange among the stakeholders including healthcare providers, researchers, and patients, and fostering collaborative efforts in medicine research and care delivery. Providers are better able to diagnose patients, prevent medical mistakes, and deliver safer care when they have quick access to accurate, full, and up-to-date patient information at the point of care and the freedom to share that information electronically with patients and other doctors.

While this enables a safer and more reliable medicine and vaccine prescription, it also ensures legible, complete, and accurate documentation, streamlined coding, and billing which helps in better clinical decision-making and improved efficiencies. Additionally, the widespread acceptance and implementation of EHRs aid in the promotion of preventative medicine and better coordination of healthcare services, as well as by lowering waste and unnecessary testing, improving services, and lowering costs—key factors in achieving universal health coverage.

SGD 3 Targets under impact:

- Target 3.8
- Target 3.D

6.1.6 **Online Learning and Conferencing Solutions:** The COVID-19 pandemic rushed many of us – from students and teachers to professionals – to online learning platforms. Though it cannot completely replicate the in-person learning environment, it can help in keeping pace with the ever-evolving upskilling needs, online counseling especially in developing countries at a relatively lower cost. A modern learning platform powered by artificial intelligence can be a deal breaker in improving the process of upskilling, reskilling, and training of healthcare workers helping to quickly eliminate the skill gap and increasing efficiency along with counseling for substance abuse. It could further aid the financing and recruitment process by enabling real-time conversations, thus expediting the process and reducing the need to travel and reducing the overall cost of the process.

SGD 3 Targets under impact:

- Target 3.5
- Target 3.7
- Target 3. c

7. CHALLENGES

While Industry 5.0 offers an unprecedented path toward sustainable development, integrating its technologies presents hurdles that cannot be ignored. Few of the challenges are:

Lack of integration among researchers:

A significant challenge lies in the lack of awareness among organizations about the immense potential these technologies hold, coupled with a limited understanding of specific options available (Varriale et al., 2023). Despite the availability of technologies, their implementation to address the specific SDG targets has not been focussed upon. The implementation of the technology for the healthcare purpose needs to be carefully and synergistically planned by the researcher to avoid duplication and enhance efficiency of the technology.

Rising cost of technology: Though, we have been moving towards a tech-based future on a very fast pace, the increasing cost of the technology alongside could not be ignored.

The hefty investment costs of implementing new technologies act as a deterrent, particularly for smaller enterprises (Fan et al., 2023). Further, since the technology becomes obsolete very fast with the introduction of new technology, the fear of losing investment looms among the stakeholders. There has to be an affordable pricing mechanism for implementing the innovative technologies to increase the adoption and safeguard out the stakeholder's interest. Governments can ease the financial challenges linked to the adoption of these technologies, especially for smaller entities, by providing financial incentives and establishing dedicated funding programs (Danish, 2023).

Skills gaps and training needs:

The skills gap and the need for a workforce fluent in these technologies pose another obstacle, demanding extensive reskilling and upskilling initiatives. A large fleet of workforce needs to be skilled in the areas of AI, robotics, data analytics, cybersecurity and IoT. Tech companies and more importantly healthcare organisations shall work together towards upskilling and reskilling of existing workforce on the necessary skills needed to thrive in the era of Industry 5.0. Increasing awareness via education and training programs can illuminate the benefits of Industry 5.0 for sustainable development, empowering organizations to embrace this transformative approach (Danish, 2023). Fostering collaboration among organizations, governments, and academic institutions can facilitate knowledge and resource sharing, paving the way for smoother implementation (Fan et al., 2023).

Lack of streamlined Data availability:

A key hurdle to the accomplishment of Sustainable Development Goal 3 (SDG 3) targets is the lack of streamlined data availability for effective health monitoring systems in many nations. The definition of indicators and their relevance in local contexts remains unclear. Insufficient disaggregated data, limited access to non-health sector data, and disparities between global estimates and nationally reported values further compound the issue. Survey data, a significant portion of SDG health indicators, are often not routinely stratified by equitable dimensions in many countries, particularly in the South-East Asia Region (SEAR).

Data Integration and Security concerns:

Successfully integrating Industry 5.0 for sustainable development hinges on a collective effort. We must harness the combined forces of governments, organizations, and individuals to overcome these challenges and make way for a future where technology and sustainability go hand-in-hand. This collective responsibility represents the key to unlocking the true potential of Industry 5.0 and ensuring a thriving, sustainable future for all. Further, the heavy reliance on data necessitates robust data management and security infrastructure to address privacy concerns and cyber threats. Effectively managing data concerns involves implementing strong data management and security protocols to safeguard privacy and mitigate cyber risks.

Resistance to Technology Adoption:

Healthcare experts and patients may show resistance to the appropriation of keen healthcare advances. There is a common concern that AI and automation could replace human roles rather than augment them, especially in radiology, diagnostics, and administrative tasks. Many healthcare professionals, especially those trained in pre-digital eras, may lack the skills or confidence to operate new technologies such as AI diagnostic tools, telemedicine platforms, or digital twins. Further, adopting new technologies often involves a **steep learning curve**, increased documentation tasks, and system bugs — adding to already high workloads. The Mount Sinai Health System has been an early adopter of artificial intelligence (AI) in improving patient care and health over the past few years, innovating in various clinical areas such as in imaging and patient monitoring.

However, gradually the scenario is changing with hospitals actively leading the AI initiatives with Mount Sinai opening the Hamilton and Amabel James Center for Artificial Intelligence and Human Health designed to centralize Mount Sinai's AI initiatives, promoting collaboration and innovation within the field.

8. ETHICAL CONSIDERATIONS FOR USING ADVANCE TECHNOLOGY IN HEALTHCARE

Healthcare professionals are concerned about **accountability** when technology goes wrong. Questions about who is legally responsible — the doctor, the software provider, or the hospital — are often unclear. In cases of AI misdiagnosis, clinicians fear litigation despite not being in full control of the diagnosis tool.

The utilization of AI calculations in decision-making forms presents moral problems. Issues such as algorithmic predisposition, reasonableness, and straightforwardness must be tended to guarantee that AI applications don't excessively affect certain populations or propagate existing healthcare incongruities (Jagadeeswari et al. 2018). Moral contemplations encompassing assent, responsibility, and the interpretability of AI choices are vital.

9. CONCLUSION

Despite considerable advancements in digitalization and innovation worldwide, there persists a considerable gap between targeted goals and the current situation. Sustainable growth is contingent upon ensuring the health and well-being of all individuals. The global health crisis, aggravated by the current pandemic, has not only severely damaged the global economy but also presented challenges to the physical and emotional well-being of billions. The pivotal role of healthcare professionals, the importance of preparedness, and technological advancements in the healthcare sector have been underscored by the pandemic. The United Nations has made commendable progress in reducing major causes of death and disease, improving life expectancy, and addressing HIV and malaria-related deaths through increased funding, enhanced hygiene practices, and improved access to medical care. However, numerous challenges persist at the local level.

The successful attainment of SDG 3 will undoubtedly impact the achievement of other targets, and vice versa, given the interconnected nature of health and well-being with all other goals. While the Millennium Development Goals (MDGs) effectively directed attention and funding towards health-related issues, it also inadvertently led to a fragmented institutional landscape and competitive delivery systems at the national level. This competitive environment has prioritized individual interests over collaborative efforts to enhance overall health.

Regardless of age, maintaining global health and well-being remains a formidable challenge. Integrating the global SDG monitoring framework and indicators into each nation's framework is essential to meet SDG 3 targets. A robust data platform is imperative for effective monitoring and decision-making, collecting essential information to generate indicators tracking progress towards health-related SDGs. The use of advanced technology is crucial in achieving this seamlessly and addressing national health priorities.

REFERENCES

Abbas, S. (2024). Pathway for attaining SDG3: The role of ICT infrastructure, natural resources, and environmental sustainability. *Sustainable Futures : An Applied Journal of Technology, Environment and Society*, *100*, 100339. DOI: 10.1016/j.sftr.2024.100339

Ariansyah, A., Prayogi, S., Kurnia, N., Bilad, M. R., & Sutarto, S. (2024). Digital technology to support Sustainable Development Goals (SDGs): Literature review. *Lensa Jurnal Kependidikan Fisika*, *12*(2), 315. DOI: 10.33394/j-lkf.v12i2.13557

Asi, Y. M., & Williams, C. (2018). The role of digital health in making progress toward Sustainable Development Goal (SDG) 3 in conflict-affected populations. *International Journal of Medical Informatics*, *114*, 114–120. DOI: 10.1016/j.ijmedinf.2017.11.003 PMID: 29126701

Danish, M. S. S. (2023). AI in energy: Overcoming unforeseen obstacles. *AI*, *4*(2), 22. Advance online publication. DOI: 10.3390/ai4020022

Fan, M., Liu, J., Tajeddini, K., & Khaskheli, M. B. (2023). Digital technology application and enterprise competitiveness: The mediating role of ESG performance and green technology innovation. *Environment, Development and Sustainability*. Advance online publication. DOI: 10.1007/s10668-023-03979-3

Garg, V., & Goel, R. (Eds.). (2021). *Handbook of Research on Innovative Management Using AI in Industry 5.0*. IGI Global.

Goel, R., & Gupta, P. (2019). Robotics and Industry 4.0. In *A roadmap to Industry 4.0: Smart production, sharp business and sustainable development* (pp. 157–169). Springer. https://doi.org/DOI: 10.1007/978-3-030-14544-6_9

Gomathi, L., Mishra, A. K., & Tyagi, A. K. (2023). Industry 5.0 for Healthcare 5.0: Opportunities, challenges and future research possibilities. In *2022 6th International Conference on Trends in Electronics and Informatics (ICOEI)* (pp. 204–213). IEEE. https://doi.org/DOI: 10.1109/ICOEI56765.2023.10125660

Hamburg, M. A., & Collins, F. S. (2010). The path to personalized medicine. *The New England Journal of Medicine*, *363*(4), 301–304. DOI: 10.1056/NEJMp1006304 PMID: 20551152

Health Protection Surveillance Centre. (n.d.). What is disease surveillance. https://www.hpsc.ie/abouthpsc/whatisdiseasesurveillance/

Kasinathan, P., Pugazhendhi, R., Elavarasan, R. M., Ramachandaramurthy, V. K., Ramanathan, V., Subramanian, S., Kumar, S., Nandhagopal, K., Raghavan, R. R. V., Rangasamy, S., Devendiran, R., & Alsharif, M. H. (2022). Realization of Sustainable Development Goals with disruptive technologies by integrating Industry 5.0, Society 5.0, smart cities and villages. *Sustainability (Basel), 14*(22), 15258. DOI: 10.3390/su142215258

Kumar, U., Kaswan, M. S., Kumar, R., Chaudhary, R., Garza-Reyes, J. A., Rathi, R., & Joshi, R. (2023). A systematic review of Industry 5.0 from main aspects to the execution status. *The TQM Journal*. Advance online publication. DOI: 10.1108/TQM-06-2023-0183

Le Blanc, D. (2015). Towards integration at last? The Sustainable Development Goals as a network of targets. *Sustainable Development (Bradford), 23*(3), 176–187. DOI: 10.1002/sd.1582

Lim, J. J., Goh, J., Rashid, M. B. M. A., & Chow, E. K. (2019). Maximizing efficiency of artificial intelligence-driven drug combination optimization through minimal resolution experimental design. *Advanced Therapeutics, 3*(4), 1900122. DOI: 10.1002/adtp.201900122

Maddikunta, P. K. R., Pham, Q. V., B, P., Deepa, N., Dev, K., Gadekallu, T. R., Ruby, R., & Liyanage, M. (2022). Industry 5.0: A survey on enabling technologies and potential applications. *Journal of Industrial Information Integration, 26*, 100257. DOI: 10.1016/j.jii.2021.100257

Merrell, R. C., & Doarn, C. R. (2016). Sustainable Development Goals and telemedicine. *Telemedicine Journal and e-Health, 22*(10), 787–788. DOI: 10.1089/tmj.2016.29013.rcm PMID: 27606490

Nielsen, P. C., & Brix, P. J. (2023). Towards Society 5.0: Enabling the European Commission's policy brief 'Towards a sustainable, human-centric and resilient European Industry.'. *Journal of Behavioural Economics and Social Systems, 5*(1). Advance online publication. DOI: 10.54337/ojs.bess.v5i1.8139

Palozzi, G., Schettini, I., & Chirico, A. (2020). Enhancing the sustainable goal of access to healthcare: Findings from a literature review on telemedicine employment in rural areas. *Sustainability (Basel), 12*(8), 3318. DOI: 10.3390/su12083318

Pew Research Center. (2022, September 15). The future of well-being in a tech-saturated world. *Pew Research Center: Internet, Science & Tech*. https://www.pewresearch.org/internet/2018/04/17/the-future-of-well-being-in-a-tech-saturated-world/

Saracco, R. (2022, September 15). From Industry 4.0 to Industry 5.0 – II. *IEEE Future Directions*. https://cmte.ieee.org/futuredirections/2022/09/19/from-industry-4-0-to-industry-5-0-ii/

Varriale, V., Cammarano, A., Michelino, F., & Caputo, M. (2023). Industry 5.0 and triple bottom line approach in supply chain management: The state-of-the-art. *Sustainability (Basel)*, *15*(7), 5712. DOI: 10.3390/su15075712

Verma, D. (2024). Industry 5.0: A human-centric and sustainable approach to industrial development. *International Journal of Social Relevance & Concern*, *12*(5), 17–21. DOI: 10.26821/IJSRC.12.5.2024.120507

Wagle, K. (2018, November 17). Public health surveillance: Importance, types and steps of conducting it! *Public Health Notes*. https://www.publichealthnotes.com/surveillance/

World Health Organization. (2023, October 5). Universal health coverage (UHC). https://www.who.int/news-room/fact-sheets/detail/universal-health-coverage-(uhc)

Chapter 7
Gender Inequality and Health Disparities:
Addressing Social Discrimination and Poverty in the Pursuit of Equitable Healthcare

Tiago Manuel Horta Reis da Silva
https://orcid.org/0000-0001-5220-1718
King's College London, UK

ABSTRACT

Achieving health equity is central to the Sustainable Development Goals (SDGs). This chapter examines how gender inequality and poverty intersect to create systemic barriers to equitable healthcare. It explores the multifaceted impacts of social discrimination and marginalisation on health outcomes, drawing on global and regional data to highlight disparities. Strategies for addressing these issues are discussed, including policy reform, community-based interventions, and the integration of intersectional approaches. The chapter underscores the urgency of addressing gender and socioeconomic inequalities to foster sustainable, inclusive health systems that leave no one behind, aligning with SDG 3 (Good Health and Well-Being) and SDG 5 (Gender Equality).

1. INTRODUCTION

The Sustainable Development Goals (SDGs), established by the United Nations in 2015, represent a global commitment to address various social, economic, and environmental challenges, with health equity being a central theme (da Silva and

DOI: 10.4018/979-8-3693-9755-8.ch007

Rodrigues, 2023). Health equity is defined as the absence of unfair and avoidable differences in health among different population groups, which is essential for achieving the SDGs, particularly Goal 3, which aims to ensure healthy lives and promote well-being for all at all ages (Amri et al., 2023; da Silva and Rodrigues, 2023). The intersection of health equity and gender inequality is particularly critical, as gender disparities significantly influence health outcomes and access to healthcare services. Gender inequality manifests in various forms, including economic disparities, social norms, and cultural practices that disadvantage women and marginalised genders, thereby exacerbating health disparities (Portnoy et al., 2020; Percival et al., 2018; Reis da Silva, 2024a; Reis da Silva, 2024b).

The scope of gender inequality extends beyond mere access to healthcare; it encompasses systemic issues that affect women's health outcomes, including gender-based violence, reproductive health rights, and the social determinants of health. For instance, the COVID-19 pandemic has highlighted and intensified existing gender inequities, with women facing increased rates of domestic violence, unemployment, and unpaid care burdens (Figueroa et al., 2021; Amri, 2024). These challenges are compounded by the fact that health systems often fail to adequately address the specific needs of women and marginalised genders, leading to further health disparities (Percival et al., 2018; Pauly et al., 2017). The need for a comprehensive approach that integrates gender considerations into health policies and practices is thus paramount for achieving health equity and fulfilling the SDGs.

1.1 Overview of SDGs and Health Equity

The SDGs provide a framework for global development that emphasises the importance of health equity as a fundamental human right. Goal 3 specifically calls for ensuring healthy lives and promoting well-being for all, which includes targets aimed at reducing maternal mortality, ensuring universal access to sexual and reproductive health services, and addressing communicable diseases (Zamora et al., 2018). Achieving these targets requires a concerted effort to dismantle the barriers that perpetuate health inequities, particularly those related to gender. For example, the integration of gender-sensitive approaches in health policies can significantly improve health outcomes for women and girls, as evidenced by initiatives aimed at increasing access to reproductive health services and addressing gender-based violence (Portnoy et al., 2020; Shomuyiwa, 2023).

Furthermore, health equity is not only a matter of access to healthcare services but also involves addressing the underlying social determinants of health, such as education, income, and social status, which disproportionately affect women and marginalised groups (Victora et al., 2019; Dean et al., 2019). The SDGs recognise that health is influenced by a complex interplay of factors, and therefore, a multisectoral approach is necessary to address these determinants effectively. This includes engaging various stakeholders, including governments, civil society, and the private sector, to create an enabling environment for health equity (Moalla, 2024).

1.2 Scope of Gender Inequality and Health Disparities

Gender inequality is a pervasive issue that affects health outcomes across the globe. Women and marginalised genders often face systemic barriers that limit their access to healthcare, education, and economic opportunities. For instance, in many low- and middle-income countries, cultural norms and practices restrict women's autonomy and decision-making power, leading to poorer health outcomes (Nakkeeran & Nakkeeran, 2018; Schenkman et al., 2022). Additionally, gender-based violence remains a significant public health issue, with profound implications for women's physical and mental health (Portnoy et al., 2020; Bergen et al., 2020). The intersectionality of gender with other social determinants, such as race, ethnicity, and socioeconomic status, further complicates the landscape of health disparities, necessitating a nuanced understanding of how these factors interact to shape health outcomes (Pauly et al., 2017; Paul et al., 2019).

The COVID-19 pandemic has exacerbated existing gender inequalities, revealing the vulnerabilities faced by women and marginalised groups in times of crisis. Reports indicate that women have experienced increased rates of domestic violence, mental health issues, and economic instability during the pandemic (Figueroa et al., 2021; Amri, 2024). Furthermore, the pandemic has highlighted the critical role of women in the healthcare workforce, where they constitute a significant proportion of frontline workers yet often face discrimination and unequal pay (Bates et al., 2016). Addressing these disparities requires not only immediate interventions but also long-term strategies that promote gender equity in health systems and policies (Percival et al., 2018).

1.3 Addressing Gender Inequality in Health Policies

To effectively address gender inequality and health disparities, it is essential to integrate gender considerations into health policies and programs. This involves adopting a gender-transformative approach that challenges existing power dynamics and promotes equitable access to healthcare services for all genders (Restar et al., 2021). For instance, health systems should prioritise the development of gender-sensitive policies that address the unique health needs of women and marginalised genders, such as reproductive health services, mental health support, and protection against gender-based violence (Portnoy et al., 2020; Dean et al., 2019). Moreover, the involvement of women and marginalised groups in the decision-making processes related to health policies is crucial for ensuring that their voices are heard, and their needs are met. Engaging these groups in policy formulation and implementation can lead to more effective and equitable health outcomes (Moalla, 2024). Additionally, training healthcare providers on gender sensitivity and equity can help reduce biases and improve the quality of care provided to women and marginalised genders (Morgan et al., 2018).

Gender inequality remains a critical obstacle to equitable healthcare globally, particularly when compounded by socioeconomic status, racial discrimination, and other intersecting factors (Reis da Silva, 2024a; Reis da Silva, 2024b). Research consistently illustrates how these social determinants result in enduring health disparities (Reis da Silva, 2025a). For instance, longitudinal data from the Canadian Health Behaviour in School-aged Children (HBSC) study revealed persistent or worsening health inequalities by gender and socioeconomic status between 2002 and 2018 (Hammami et al., 2022), demonstrating that these disparities are not anomalies but systemic public health concerns.

Discrimination within healthcare systems intensifies these inequities. In France, lower socioeconomic groups—particularly women, immigrants, and people of African descent—reported discrimination in healthcare settings at nearly double the national average (Rivenbark & Ichou, 2020). This contributes to a cycle of disadvantage, deterring individuals from seeking care. In conflict-affected regions such as Sudan, socio-cultural norms and economic disparities mean women are systematically deprived of healthcare access (Oke, 2025). In the U.S., structural racism and occupational inequities result in disproportionately higher rates of preventable chronic disease complications and hospitalisations among Black and Latino populations (MacIntosh et al., 2013; Wong et al., 2015).

The COVID-19 pandemic further highlighted gendered dimensions of health inequality. For example, maternal mortality among non-Hispanic Black women increased by 48% between 2018 and 2020 (Mhyre, 2022), reflecting compounding systemic vulnerabilities. Simultaneously, women faced rising unemployment, delayed healthcare access, and increased domestic violence (Su et al., 2022). The economic costs of these disparities are immense. Health inequities in the U.S. alone are estimated to cost over $300 billion annually (Elias et al., 2016), underscoring the need for policies integrating health equity with economic development. The capability approach offers a framework to address these inequalities by focusing on access and functional outcomes rather than resource parity (Mollet & Mollet, 2024).

Moreover, gender minorities face distinct health challenges, including higher rates of depression and substance use, influenced by minority stress (Gonzales & Deal, 2022). Within the health professions, women are underrepresented in leadership and subject to wage disparities, further perpetuating systemic inequality (Yassine et al., 2021). To effectively address these complex issues, inclusive, intersectional, and evidence-based policy interventions are essential. Collaborative public health strategies and sustained advocacy can foster resilience and equity, particularly in vulnerable and underserved communities (Ndzabela & Lukman, 2023).

1.4 The Role of Data and Research in Promoting Health Equity

Data collection and research play a vital role in understanding and addressing health disparities related to gender. Disaggregated data on health outcomes, access to services, and social determinants of health are essential for identifying gaps and informing targeted interventions (Amri et al., 2022). For example, the use of intersectional analysis can help uncover the compounded effects of gender, race, and socioeconomic status on health outcomes, thereby guiding policymakers in developing more effective strategies to promote health equity (Pauly et al., 2017; Dean et al., 2019).

Furthermore, research on the effectiveness of gender-sensitive interventions can provide valuable insights into best practices for improving health outcomes for women and marginalised groups. This includes evaluating programs aimed at increasing access to reproductive health services, addressing gender-based violence, and promoting mental health support (Portnoy et al., 2020; Shomuyiwa, 2023). By leveraging evidence-based approaches, health systems can better address the unique challenges faced by different population groups and work towards achieving health equity.

2. THE INTERSECTION OF GENDER, POVERTY, AND HEALTH

2.1 Gender-Based Barriers to Healthcare Access

Gender-based barriers to healthcare access are a significant concern, particularly for women and marginalised genders who often face systemic obstacles that hinder their ability to obtain necessary medical services (Reis da Silva, 2024a). These barriers can be attributed to a variety of factors, including socio-cultural norms, economic constraints, and inadequate healthcare infrastructure. For instance, women in low-income settings frequently encounter challenges such as lack of transportation, financial limitations, and societal expectations that prioritise male health needs over female health needs (Kabia et al., 2018). The COVID-19 pandemic has further exacerbated these barriers, as many women reported increased difficulties in accessing healthcare services due to lockdowns and resource reallocations within health systems (West et al., 2021).

Moreover, the stigma associated with certain health conditions, particularly reproductive health issues, can deter women from seeking care. This stigma is compounded by gender-based violence, which not only affects women's physical health but also their mental well-being and access to healthcare (Jewkes et al., 2023). For example, women living in poverty may avoid healthcare settings due to fear of judgment or mistreatment, leading to delayed diagnoses and treatment for conditions such as HIV or cervical cancer (Cope et al., 2020). Additionally, the intersection of gender and disability further complicates access, as women with disabilities often face compounded discrimination that limits their healthcare options (Kabia et al., 2018).

The lack of gender-sensitive healthcare policies also contributes to these barriers. Many health systems fail to consider the unique needs of women, particularly in areas such as maternal health and mental health services (Li et al., 2023). This oversight can result in inadequate care provision, leading to poorer health outcomes for women. Addressing these gender-based barriers requires a comprehensive approach that includes policy reforms, community engagement, and targeted interventions aimed at improving healthcare access for women and marginalised genders (Abdi et al., 2020).

2.2 Socioeconomic Determinants of Health Disparities

Socioeconomic determinants play a crucial role in shaping health disparities, particularly among women and marginalised populations. Factors such as income, education, employment status, and social support networks significantly influence health outcomes and access to healthcare services (Harris, 2024). For instance, women living in poverty are more likely to experience poor health outcomes due to limited access to nutritious food, safe housing, and quality healthcare (Jewkes et al., 2023). The relationship between poverty and health is complex, as low-income individuals often face multiple stressors that can exacerbate health issues, including mental health challenges and chronic diseases (Zhou et al., 2022).

Research indicates that women are disproportionately affected by poverty, which can lead to a cycle of disadvantage that impacts their health and well-being. The feminisation of poverty highlights how women, particularly those in marginalised communities, are more likely to experience economic insecurity and lack access to resources that promote health (Garcia et al., 2019). This situation is further complicated by systemic issues such as gender discrimination in the labour market, which limits women's earning potential and economic independence (Jung et al., 2022).

Moreover, the intersectionality of gender, race, and socioeconomic status can create compounded disadvantages for certain groups of women. For example, women of black and brown ethnic group and those from low-income backgrounds may face additional barriers to healthcare access due to systemic racism and discrimination within healthcare systems (Cardoso et al., 2021). This can result in disparities in health outcomes, such as higher rates of maternal mortality and chronic illnesses among these populations (Ahmed, 2024).

Addressing the socioeconomic determinants of health disparities requires a multi-faceted approach that includes improving access to education, employment opportunities, and healthcare services. Policies aimed at reducing poverty and promoting gender equity are essential for creating a more equitable healthcare system that meets the needs of all individuals, regardless of their socioeconomic status (Cardoso et al., 2021). Additionally, community-based interventions that empower women and marginalised groups can help to mitigate the effects of poverty on health and promote better health outcomes (Marí-Klose et al., 2023).

3. SOCIAL DISCRIMINATION IN HEALTHCARE SYSTEMS

3.1 Impacts of Systemic Bias and Marginalisation

Systemic bias and marginalisation within healthcare systems have profound implications for health equity and access to care. Discrimination based on race, ethnicity, gender, sexual orientation, and socioeconomic status can lead to significant disparities in health outcomes and healthcare utilization (Reis da Silva, 2024a). For instance, studies have shown that individuals from marginalised communities often experience discrimination in healthcare settings, which can deter them from seeking necessary medical attention (Singh & Subedi, 2020, Rivenbark & Ichou, 2020). This discrimination manifests in various forms, including biased treatment by healthcare providers, lack of cultural competence, and inadequate access to services tailored to the needs of diverse populations (Bulgarelli et al., 2021).

The consequences of systemic bias are particularly evident in the experiences of racial and ethnic minorities. Research indicates that perceived discrimination in healthcare is associated with increased rates of unmet healthcare needs and poorer health outcomes among these populations (Khalifeh et al., 2023; Goldenberg, 2024). For example, a study conducted in France found that individuals who reported experiences of discrimination were significantly more likely to forego necessary medical care, highlighting the detrimental impact of bias on health-seeking behaviour (Rivenbark & Ichou, 2020). Similarly, marginalised groups such as LGBTQ+ individuals often face barriers to accessing healthcare, including stigma and discrimination from healthcare providers, which can lead to avoidance of care and negative health outcomes (Mulemfo et al., 2023).

Moreover, the intersectionality of various identities—such as race, gender, and socioeconomic status—can compound the effects of discrimination, leading to unique challenges for individuals who belong to multiple marginalised groups. For instance, transgender individuals often encounter discrimination not only based on their gender identity but also due to their socioeconomic status, which can further hinder their access to appropriate healthcare services (Blakey et al., 2022). This systemic bias creates a cycle of disadvantage that perpetuates health inequities and undermines the overall effectiveness of healthcare systems (Senyurek et al., 2021).

3.2 Case Studies: Global and Regional Examples

Numerous case studies illustrate the pervasive nature of discrimination in healthcare systems across different regions and populations. In Nepal, frontline healthcare workers faced significant stigma and discrimination during the COVID-19 pandemic, which not only affected their mental health but also their ability to provide care effectively (Singh & Subedi, 2020). The stigma associated with COVID-19 led to social isolation and discrimination against healthcare providers, highlighting the broader implications of societal attitudes on healthcare delivery.

In France, a nationally representative survey revealed that discrimination in healthcare settings was a significant barrier for socially disadvantaged populations. The study found that experiences of discrimination were robustly linked to an increased likelihood of foregoing care, indicating that systemic bias can directly impact health-seeking behavior and outcomes (Rivenbark & Ichou, 2020). This finding underscores the need for healthcare systems to address discrimination as a critical factor in health equity.

Another poignant example comes from Brazil, where research has shown that social discrimination based on ethnicity and immigration status significantly affects access to healthcare services. Discrimination within healthcare settings has been linked to negative health outcomes, such as increased rates of tooth loss among socially disadvantaged populations (Bulgarelli et al., 2021). This case illustrates how systemic bias can manifest in tangible health disparities, reinforcing the need for targeted interventions to address discrimination in healthcare.

In Lebanon, displaced Syrians experience cultural differences and discrimination that hinder their access to healthcare services. A qualitative study highlighted the challenges faced by this population, including language barriers and negative attitudes from healthcare providers, which contribute to their marginalisation within the healthcare system (Khalifeh et al., 2023). This case study emphasises the importance of cultural competence and sensitivity in healthcare delivery to ensure equitable access for all individuals, regardless of their background.

Furthermore, the experiences of LGBTQ+ individuals in South Africa reveal the intersection of discrimination and healthcare access. A study found that LGBTQ+ individuals faced significant barriers to accessing HIV management services, exacerbated by societal stigma and discrimination (Mulemfo et al., 2023). This case illustrates the need for healthcare systems to adopt inclusive practices that address the unique needs of marginalised populations to improve health outcomes.

In summary, systemic bias and marginalisation within healthcare systems have far-reaching consequences for health equity and access to care. The case studies presented illustrate the various forms of discrimination experienced by different populations, highlighting the urgent need for healthcare systems to implement strategies that promote equity, inclusivity, and cultural competence. By addressing these systemic issues, healthcare providers can work towards creating a more equitable healthcare landscape that serves the needs of all individuals, regardless of their background or identity.

4. IMPACTS ON MARGINALISED POPULATIONS

4.1 Older People Disparities

Older adults often face significant health disparities that are exacerbated by systemic inequities in healthcare access and quality (Reis da Silva, 2025a; Reis da Silva, 2025b). These disparities are influenced by a combination of factors, including socioeconomic status, geographic location, and the presence of chronic health conditions (Reis da Silva, 2024c). For instance, older adults living in poverty are more likely to experience multiple health issues, which can lead to a higher prevalence of chronic diseases such as diabetes, hypertension, and heart disease (Reis da Silva, 2024d). The intersection of age and poverty creates a unique set of challenges, as older adults may lack the financial resources necessary to access quality healthcare services, leading to worse health outcomes (Schmitz et al., 2019).

Moreover, older adults often encounter ageism within healthcare systems, which can result in inadequate treatment and a lack of respect for their autonomy and preferences. This systemic bias can manifest in various ways, such as healthcare providers dismissing the concerns of older patients or failing to provide appropriate pain management. The stigma associated with ageing can further deter older adults from seeking necessary medical care, as they may fear being perceived as burdensome or incapable (Feletto & Sharkey, 2019). Consequently, these factors contribute to a cycle of neglect and marginalisation that adversely affects the health and well-being of older populations (Reis da Silva, 2023a; Reis da Silva, 2024d; Reis da Silva, 2024e; Reis da Silva, 2024f; Reis da Silva, 2025c; Reis da Silva, 2025d).

Additionally, the COVID-19 pandemic has highlighted and intensified existing disparities faced by older adults. Many older individuals experienced increased isolation due to lockdown measures, which exacerbated mental health issues such as depression and anxiety (Reis da Silva, 2024g; Reis da Silva, 2024h). The pandemic also revealed significant gaps in healthcare access for older adults, particularly those living in long-term care facilities, where outbreaks of COVID-19 led to devastating mortality rates (Constante & Bastos, 2020). Addressing these disparities requires a multifaceted approach that includes policy reforms aimed at improving access to healthcare, enhancing social support systems, and combating ageism within healthcare settings (Reis da Silva, 2024i; Reis da Silva, 2024j; Reis da Silva, 2025e).

4.2 Health Outcomes in LGBTQ+ Populations

LGBTQ+ populations experience significant health disparities that are often rooted in systemic discrimination and stigma. Research indicates that individuals who identify as LGBTQ+ are at a higher risk for various health issues, including mental health disorders, substance abuse, and sexually transmitted infections (STIs) (Sing et al., 2020). The minority stress theory posits that the chronic stress associated with societal stigma, discrimination, and rejection contributes to these adverse health outcomes (Murphy et al., 2022). For example, LGBTQ+ individuals are more likely to experience anxiety and depression compared to their heterosexual counterparts, largely due to experiences of discrimination and social isolation (Yip et al., 2021).

Access to healthcare services is another critical area where LGBTQ+ populations face disparities. Many LGBTQ+ individuals report negative experiences with healthcare providers, including discrimination, lack of cultural competence, and inadequate knowledge about LGBTQ+ health issues (Chen et al., 2020). This can lead to avoidance of necessary medical care, resulting in poorer health outcomes. For instance, transgender individuals often face significant barriers to accessing gender-affirming care, which can have profound implications for their mental and physical health (Gunnarsdóttir et al., 2023). The lack of inclusive healthcare policies further exacerbates these disparities, as many health systems fail to adequately address the unique needs of LGBTQ+ populations (Kabia et al., 2018).

Moreover, intersectionality plays a crucial role in understanding the health outcomes of LGBTQ+ individuals. Those who also belong to other marginalised groups, such as racial and ethnic minorities, may experience compounded discrimination that further exacerbates health disparities (Peek, 2023). For example, LGBTQ+ individuals of colour often face unique challenges related to both their sexual orientation and racial identity, leading to increased vulnerability to health issues (Tarshish, 2024). Addressing these disparities requires a comprehensive approach that includes targeted interventions, policy reforms, and the promotion of inclusive healthcare practices that recognise and address the diverse needs of LGBTQ+ populations.

5. POLICY AND ADVOCACY APPROACHES

5.1 Intersectional Frameworks for Addressing Inequalities

Intersectional frameworks are essential for addressing the multifaceted inequalities that marginalised populations face in accessing healthcare. These frameworks recognise that individuals experience overlapping identities—such as race, gender, sexual orientation, and socioeconomic status—that can compound their experiences of discrimination and disadvantage in healthcare settings (Mokua, 2024). By employing an intersectional lens, policymakers and advocates can better understand the unique barriers that different groups encounter, leading to more effective and tailored interventions. For example, research has shown that transgender individuals often face significant barriers to accessing gender-affirming care due to a combination of stigma, lack of provider knowledge, and institutional biases (Nolan et al., 2019). An intersectional approach can help identify how these barriers are exacerbated for transgender people of colour, who may experience both racial and gender discrimination in healthcare settings (Hughto et al., 2018). This understanding can inform the development of policies that not only address gender identity but also consider the racial and ethnic backgrounds of individuals seeking care.

Moreover, intersectional frameworks can guide the design of healthcare services that are inclusive and responsive to the needs of diverse populations. For instance, the incorporation of culturally competent care practices can help mitigate the effects of discrimination and improve health outcomes for marginalised groups (Müller, 2017). By recognising the interconnectedness of various social identities, healthcare systems can create environments that foster equity and inclusivity, ultimately enhancing access to care for all individuals.

5.2 Role of Government, NGOs, and International Agencies

The role of government, non-governmental organisations (NGOs), and international agencies is crucial in promoting health equity and addressing the systemic barriers faced by marginalised populations. Governments have the responsibility to create and implement policies that ensure equitable access to healthcare services for all citizens, particularly those from marginalised backgrounds. This includes enacting legislation that prohibits discrimination in healthcare settings and promoting funding for programs that target health disparities (Arnold et al., 2023).

NGOs play a vital role in advocating for the rights of marginalised populations and providing essential services that may not be adequately addressed by government programs. For example, NGOs often work to raise awareness about the specific healthcare needs of LGBTQ+ individuals and provide resources for accessing gender-affirming care (Floyd & Sakellariou, 2017). Additionally, NGOs can facilitate community engagement and empower marginalised groups to advocate for their own health needs, thereby fostering a sense of agency and ownership over their healthcare experiences (Loeb, 2024).

International agencies, such as the World Health Organization (WHO) and the United Nations (UN), also contribute to addressing health inequalities on a global scale. These organisations provide guidance and support for countries to develop health policies that prioritize equity and inclusivity. For instance, the WHO has emphasised the importance of integrating gender considerations into health policies and programs to ensure that the unique needs of women and marginalised genders are met (Shabalala, 2023). Furthermore, international agencies can facilitate knowledge sharing and best practices among countries, helping to promote effective strategies for addressing health disparities (Arnold et al., 2023).

6. COMMUNITY-BASED INTERVENTIONS

6.1 Empowering Marginalised Communities

Community-based interventions play a crucial role in empowering marginalised communities by addressing specific health needs and fostering resilience. These interventions are designed to be culturally relevant and tailored to the unique circumstances of the communities they serve. By engaging community members in the planning and implementation of health programs, these initiatives not only enhance access to healthcare but also promote a sense of ownership and agency among participants (Ratnayake et al., 2022). For instance, community health workers (CHWs) often serve as vital links between healthcare systems and marginalised populations, facilitating access to services and providing education on health-related issues (Bharadwaj et al., 2021).

Empowerment through community-based interventions can take various forms, including health education, capacity building, and advocacy for policy changes. Programs that focus on health literacy, for example, help individuals understand their health conditions and navigate the healthcare system more effectively (Ungar et al., 2015). This increased knowledge can lead to improved health outcomes and greater engagement in personal health management. Furthermore, community-driven initiatives can address social determinants of health, such as housing stability and food security, which are critical for overall well-being (Shareck, 2024).

One successful example of a community-based intervention is the "Exit Doors Here" integrated care program in Toronto, Canada, which supports women exiting sex work. This program emphasises building trust and providing comprehensive services, including healthcare, mental health support, and social services, tailored to the needs of participants (Shareck, 2024). By addressing the multifaceted challenges faced by these women, the program not only improves their health outcomes but also empowers them to make informed decisions about their lives.

6.2 Case Studies of Successful Programs

Several case studies illustrate the effectiveness of community-based interventions in empowering marginalised populations and improving health outcomes. One notable example is the "Community-Based Wound Care Programs for Unhoused Individuals," which integrates housing services into healthcare delivery for homeless individuals. This program has demonstrated that addressing housing instability alongside medical care significantly enhances the effectiveness of wound care services, as many participants require both medical treatment and assistance in finding stable housing (Goto, 2023). By providing comprehensive support, the program improves health outcomes and fosters a sense of dignity and stability among participants.

Another successful initiative is the "Mobile Clinics in the United States," which serve as a critical avenue for reaching underserved populations, particularly during the COVID-19 pandemic. These mobile clinics provide essential healthcare services directly within communities, reducing barriers to access for individuals who may face challenges in reaching traditional healthcare facilities (Crossen & Wagner, 2023). The flexibility and accessibility of mobile clinics have proven effective in delivering vaccinations, preventive care, and chronic disease management to marginalised populations, thereby improving overall health outcomes.

In Ethiopia, the "Health System Strengthening Program" has focused on improving healthcare access for marginalised populations through a community-based approach. This program emphasises the importance of integrating community health workers into the healthcare system to enhance service delivery and address local health needs (Woldemichael et al., 2019). By fostering partnerships between healthcare providers and community members, the program has successfully increased healthcare utilisation and improved health outcomes in underserved areas.

Additionally, the "Supporting Women Exit Sex Work" program in Toronto highlights the importance of trust-building and comprehensive care for marginalised groups. By providing a range of services, including healthcare, mental health support, and social services, this program empowers women to make informed choices about their lives and health (Shareck, 2024). The success of this initiative demonstrates the potential of community-based interventions to address the unique challenges faced by marginalised populations.

7. INTEGRATING GENDER EQUITY INTO SDGS

7.1 Aligning Healthcare Strategies with SDG 3 and SDG 5

Integrating gender equity into the Sustainable Development Goals (SDGs) is essential for achieving both SDG 3 (Good Health and Well-Being) and SDG 5 (Gender Equality). These two goals are inherently interconnected, as gender disparities significantly impact health outcomes and access to healthcare services. To align healthcare strategies with these goals, it is crucial to adopt a gender-sensitive approach that addresses the unique health needs of women and marginalised genders while also promoting their rights and empowerment (Manandhar et al., 2018).

Healthcare strategies should prioritise the elimination of barriers that prevent women and marginalised groups from accessing essential health services. This includes addressing social determinants of health, such as education, economic stability, and social support, which disproportionately affect these populations (Delvaux, 2023). For instance, initiatives that provide comprehensive sexual and reproductive health services, including family planning and maternal healthcare, are vital for achieving SDG 3 and ensuring that women can make informed choices about their health (Sweileh, 2020). Additionally, integrating gender-sensitive policies into healthcare systems can enhance the quality of care provided to women and marginalised genders, ultimately leading to improved health outcomes (Amoroso, 2024).

Moreover, promoting gender equity in healthcare requires the active involvement of women in decision-making processes related to health policies and programs. This can be achieved through community engagement and advocacy efforts that empower women to voice their needs and concerns (Liu, 2020). By fostering an inclusive environment where women's perspectives are valued, healthcare systems can better address the unique challenges faced by marginalised populations and work towards achieving both SDG 3 and SDG 5.

7.2 Metrics for Evaluating Progress

To effectively evaluate progress towards integrating gender equity into healthcare strategies aligned with SDG 3 and SDG 5, it is essential to establish clear metrics and indicators. These metrics should encompass both quantitative and qualitative measures that capture the multifaceted nature of health equity and gender equality (García-Sánchez et al., 2020). For instance, tracking the percentage of women with access to essential health services, such as prenatal care and family planning, can provide valuable insights into the effectiveness of healthcare interventions (Manandhar et al., 2018).

Additionally, qualitative assessments, such as surveys and focus groups, can help gauge the experiences of women and marginalised genders in accessing healthcare services. Understanding their perceptions of discrimination, quality of care, and overall satisfaction with health services can inform policy adjustments and program improvements (Delvaux, 2023). Furthermore, disaggregating data by gender, age, socioeconomic status, and other relevant factors is crucial for identifying disparities and targeting interventions effectively (Jordan, 2023).

International agencies and governments should collaborate to develop standardised indicators for monitoring progress towards gender equity in healthcare. These indicators can include metrics related to maternal mortality rates, prevalence of gender-based violence, and access to reproductive health services (Raman, 2023). By establishing a robust framework for evaluating progress, stakeholders can ensure accountability and drive meaningful change in healthcare systems, ultimately contributing to the achievement of SDG 3 and SDG 5.

8. RECOMMENDATIONS

8.1 Roadmap to Equitable Healthcare

Achieving equitable healthcare requires a comprehensive roadmap that addresses the multifaceted barriers faced by marginalised populations. This roadmap should prioritise the integration of gender equity into healthcare strategies, aligning with the Sustainable Development Goals (SDGs), particularly SDG 3 (Good Health and Well-Being) and SDG 5 (Gender Equality). Key components of this roadmap include:

1. Policy Reform: Governments must enact and enforce policies that promote gender-sensitive healthcare practices. This includes eliminating discriminatory practices within healthcare systems and ensuring that health services are accessible to all, regardless of gender, socioeconomic status, or geographic location (McMaughan et al., 2020; Chuah et al., 2018).
2. Community Engagement: Empowering communities to participate in the design and implementation of health programs is crucial. Community-based interventions that involve local stakeholders can help identify specific health needs and

barriers, leading to more effective and culturally relevant solutions (Alawa et al., 2019; Babalola, 2024).

3. Capacity Building: Training healthcare providers on cultural competence and gender sensitivity is essential for improving the quality of care delivered to marginalised populations. This training should focus on understanding the unique challenges faced by different groups and fostering an inclusive healthcare environment (Wang et al., 2023).
4. Data Collection and Research: Establishing robust metrics for evaluating progress towards health equity is vital. Disaggregated data by gender, age, and socio-economic status can help identify disparities and inform targeted interventions (Rubenstein et al., 2019; Mavole, 2023). Future research should also explore the intersectionality of various identities and their impact on health outcomes (Woodgate et al., 2023).
5. Resource Allocation: Adequate funding and resources must be directed towards healthcare initiatives that specifically target marginalised populations. This includes investing in infrastructure, technology, and human resources to enhance healthcare access and quality (Allard, 2024; Yousef, 2023).

8.2 Future Research and Advocacy Directions

Future research and advocacy efforts should focus on several key areas to further promote equitable healthcare:

1. Intersectional Research: There is a need for more research that examines the intersectionality of gender, race, socioeconomic status, and other factors in shaping health outcomes. Understanding how these identities interact can inform more effective interventions and policies (Moser & Beiruti, 2023).
2. Advocacy for Policy Change: Advocacy efforts should aim to influence policymakers to prioritize health equity in their agendas. This includes pushing for legislation that addresses social determinants of health and promotes inclusive healthcare practices (Attafuah et al., 2022; Skovdal et al., 2022).
3. Community-Based Solutions: Continued support for community-based interventions is essential. Research should evaluate the effectiveness of these programs and identify best practices for scaling successful initiatives (Al-Ramlawi, 2023).
4. Technology and Innovation: Exploring the role of technology, such as telehealth and digital health solutions, in improving healthcare access for marginalised populations is crucial. Research should assess the effectiveness of these technologies in reaching underserved communities (Sharmake, 2024; Reis da Silva and Mitchell, 2024; Reis da Silva, 2025f; Reis da Silva, 2025g; Reis da Silva, 2025h).

5. Global Collaboration: International cooperation and knowledge sharing among countries can enhance efforts to address health disparities. Collaborative initiatives can facilitate the exchange of successful strategies and best practices for promoting health equity (Kanengoni-Nyatara, 2023; Zuma, 2022).

9. CONCLUSION

The intersection of gender inequality and health disparities is a significant challenge to achieving health equity and fulfilling the Sustainable Development Goals (SDGs). Addressing these issues requires a comprehensive approach that integrates gender considerations into health policies and programs, promotes women and marginalised groups' involvement in decision-making processes, and leverages data and research to inform targeted interventions. By prioritising gender equity in health systems, we can work towards a more just and equitable society where everyone has the opportunity to achieve their full health potential.

Social discrimination in healthcare systems is a critical issue that affects the health and well-being of marginalised populations. To promote health equity, healthcare systems should address these issues through targeted interventions, cultural competence training, and policies that prioritize inclusivity and equity for all individuals. An intersectional framework is essential for understanding and addressing the complex inequalities faced by marginalised populations in healthcare. Collaborative efforts of governments, NGOs, and international agencies are crucial in promoting health equity and ensuring access to the care they need. Community-based interventions are vital for empowering marginalized communities and addressing health disparities.

Integrating gender equity into healthcare strategies aligned with the SDGs is essential for promoting health equity and improving outcomes for marginalised populations. Future research and advocacy efforts should focus on intersectionality, community-based solutions, and the role of technology to ensure all individuals have access to the care they need.

Summary

Integrating gender equity into the SDGs, particularly in the context of healthcare strategies aligned with SDG 3 and SDG 5, is essential for promoting health equity and improving outcomes for women and marginalised populations. By adopting gender-sensitive approaches, actively involving women in decision-making processes, and establishing clear metrics for evaluating progress, stakeholders can work towards creating a more equitable healthcare system that meets the needs of all individuals. The successful implementation of these strategies will not only advance the goals of the SDGs but also contribute to the broader objectives of social justice and human rights.

REFERENCES

Abdi, B., Okal, J., Serour, G., & Temmerman, M. (2020). "Children are a blessing from god" – a qualitative study exploring the socio-cultural factors influencing contraceptive use in two Muslim communities in Kenya. *Reproductive Health, 17*(1), 44. Advance online publication. DOI: 10.1186/s12978-020-0898-z PMID: 32245521

Ahmed, H. (2024). Factors influencing obstetric fistula among women of childbearing age at Banadir hospital, Somalia. *MJHIU, 2*(1), 28–50. DOI: 10.59336/nj8yed06

Al-Ramlawi, D. (2023). Strategies of improvement of access to quality primary healthcare in the united Arab emirates: Lessons to learn. *Smart Medical Journal, 6*(2), 99. DOI: 10.13057/smj.v6i2.74287

Alawa, J., Zarei, P., & Khoshnood, K. (2019). Evaluating the provision of health services and barriers to treatment for chronic diseases among Syrian refugees in turkey: A review of literature and stakeholder interviews. *International Journal of Environmental Research and Public Health, 16*(15), 2660. DOI: 10.3390/ijerph16152660 PMID: 31349639

Allard, E., Dumaine, S., Sasseville, M., Gabet, M., & Duhoux, A. (2024). Quality of palliative and end-of-life care: A qualitative study of experts' recommendations to improve indicators in Quebec (Canada). *BMC Palliative Care, 23*(1), 146. Advance online publication. DOI: 10.1186/s12904-024-01474-8 PMID: 38858720

Amoroso, J., Coelho, L., Boulton, R. A., González-Toro, C. M., Costa, F., Christodoulides, E., Cools, W., Dudley, D., Moore, J. E.Jr, Furtado, G. E., Cheng, M.-Y., & Calmeiro, L. (2024). Assessing ethical behavior and self-control in elite ultimate championships: A cross-sectional study using the spirit of the game scoring system. *Frontiers in Sports and Active Living, 6*, 1297821. Advance online publication. DOI: 10.3389/fspor.2024.1297821 PMID: 38756188

Amri, M., Mohamood, L., Mansilla, C., Barrett, K., & Bump, J. (2023). Conceptual approaches in combating health inequity: A scoping review protocol. *PLoS One, 18*(3), e0282858. DOI: 10.1371/journal.pone.0282858 PMID: 36920932

Amri, M., O'Campo, P., Enright, T., Siddiqi, A., Ruggiero, E., & Bump, J. (2022). Probing key informants' views of health equity within the world health organization's urban heart initiative. *BMC Public Health, 22*(1), 1989. Advance online publication. DOI: 10.1186/s12889-022-14395-z PMID: 36316679

Amri, M., Yang, J., Jessiman-Perreault, G., Haikal, A., Barrett, K., & Bump, J. B. (2024). Equity and gender mainstreaming in public policy: A scoping review protocol. *PLoS One, 19*(2), e0299124. DOI: 10.1371/journal.pone.0299124 PMID: 38394263

Arnold, S., Bruce, G., Weise, J., Mills, C., Trollor, J., & Coxon, K. (2023). Barriers to healthcare for Australian autistic adults. *Autism, 28*(2), 301–315. DOI: 10.1177/13623613231168444 PMID: 37161777

Attafuah, P., Everink, I., Lohrmann, C., Abuosi, A., & Schols, J. (2022). Improving health and social care services for slum-dwelling older adults: Perspectives of health professionals. *Frontiers in Public Health, 10*, 988076. Advance online publication. DOI: 10.3389/fpubh.2022.988076 PMID: 36299759

Babalola, T., Sanguedolce, G., Dipper, L., & Botting, N. (2024). Barriers and facilitators of healthcare access for autistic children in the UK: A systematic review. *Review Journal of Autism and Developmental Disorders*. Advance online publication. DOI: 10.1007/s40489-023-00420-3

Bates, C., Gordon, L., Travis, E., Chatterjee, A., Chaudron, L., Fivush, B., Gulati, M., Jagsi, R., Sharma, P., Gillis, M., Ganetzky, R., Grover, A., Lautenberger, D., & Moses, A. (2016). Striving for gender equity in academic medicine careers: A call to action. *Academic Medicine, 91*(8), 1050–1052. DOI: 10.1097/ACM.0000000000001283 PMID: 27332868

Bergen, N., Zhu, G., Yedenekal, S., Mamo, A., Gebretsadik, L., Sudhakar, M., & Labonté, R. (2020). Promoting equity in maternal, newborn and child health – how does gender factor in? perceptions of public servants in the Ethiopian health sector. *Global Health Action, 13*(1), 1704530. Advance online publication. DOI: 10.1080/16549716.2019.1704530 PMID: 31935164

Bharadwaj, M., Bengtson, M., Golverdingen, M., Waling, L., & Dekker, C. (2021). Diagnosing point-of-care diagnostics for neglected tropical diseases. *PLoS Neglected Tropical Diseases, 15*(6), e0009405. DOI: 10.1371/journal.pntd.0009405 PMID: 34138846

Blakey, A., Lavarin, C., Brochier, A., Amaro, C., Eilenberg, J., Kavanagh, P., Garg, A., Drainoni, M.-L., & Long, K. (2022). Effects of experienced discrimination in pediatric sickle cell disease: Caregiver and provider perspectives. *Journal of Racial and Ethnic Health Disparities, 10*(6), 3095–3106. DOI: 10.1007/s40615-022-01483-4 PMID: 36536165

Bulgarelli, A., Santos, C., Rech, R., Baumgarten, A., & Goulart, B. (2021). Tooth loss condition and social discrimination in Brazilian healthcare services. *International Journal of Public Health, 66*, 586597. Advance online publication. DOI: 10.3389/ijph.2021.586597 PMID: 34744559

Cardoso, L., Scolese, A., Hamidaddin, A., & Gupta, J. (2021). Period poverty and mental health implications among college-aged women in the United States. *BMC Women's Health, 21*(1), 14. Advance online publication. DOI: 10.1186/s12905-020-01149-5 PMID: 33407330

Chen, J., Leng, A., Nicholas, S., Maitland, E., Wang, J., Zhao, Q., & Gong, C. (2020). Multimorbidity and mental health: The role of gender among disease-causing poverty, rural, aged households in China. *International Journal of Environmental Research and Public Health, 17*(23), 8855. DOI: 10.3390/ijerph17238855 PMID: 33260787

Chuah, F., Tan, S., Yeo, J., & Legido-Quigley, H. (2018). The health needs and access barriers among refugees and asylum-seekers in Malaysia: A qualitative study. *International Journal for Equity in Health, 17*(1), 120. Advance online publication. DOI: 10.1186/s12939-018-0833-x PMID: 30111329

Constante, H., & Bastos, J. (2020). Mapping the margins in health services research: How does race intersect with gender and socioeconomic status to shape difficulty accessing healthcare among unequal Brazilian states? *International Journal of Health Services, 51*(2), 155–166. DOI: 10.1177/0020731420979808 PMID: 33323017

Cope, A., Edmonds, A., Ludema, C., Cole, S., Eron, J., Anastos, K., Cocohoba, J., Cohen, M., Ofotokun, I., Golub, E. T., Kassaye, S., Konkle-Parker, D., Metsch, L. R., Wilson, T. E., & Adimora, A. (2020). Neighborhood poverty and control of HIV, hypertension, and diabetes in the women's interagency HIV study. *AIDS and Behavior, 24*(7), 2033–2044. DOI: 10.1007/s10461-019-02757-5 PMID: 31907676

Crossen, S., & Wagner, D. (2023). Narrowing the divide: The role of telehealth in type 1 diabetes care for marginalized communities. *Journal of Diabetes Science and Technology, 17*(4), 901–908. DOI: 10.1177/19322968231157367 PMID: 36896887

da Silva, T. H. R., & Rodrigues, E. C. P. (2023). Body Image Related Discrimination. In Leal Filho, W., Azul, A. M., Brandli, L., Lange Salvia, A., Özuyar, P. G., & Wall, T. (Eds.), *Reduced Inequalities. Encyclopedia of the UN Sustainable Development Goals*. Springer., DOI: 10.1007/978-3-319-71060-0_61-1

Dean, L., Ozano, K., Adekeye, O., Dixon, R., Fung, E., Gyapong, M., Isiyaku, S., Kollie, K., Kukula, V., Lar, L., MacPherson, E., Makia, C., Kouokam Magne, E., Nnamdi, D.-B., Mue Nji, T., Ntuen, U., Oluwole, A., Piotrowski, H., Siping, M., & Theobald, S. (2019). Neglected tropical diseases as a 'litmus test' for universal health coverage? understanding who is left behind and why in mass drug administration: Lessons from four country contexts. *PLoS Neglected Tropical Diseases, 13*(11), e0007847. DOI: 10.1371/journal.pntd.0007847 PMID: 31751336

Delvaux, I., & Van den Broeck, W. (2023). Social marketing and the sustainable development goals: Scoping review (2013–2021). *International Review on Public and Nonprofit Marketing*, *20*(3), 573–603. DOI: 10.1007/s12208-023-00372-8

Elias, T., Williams, K., Hershey, T., Documét, P., Barinas-Mitchell, E., & Gary-Webb, T. (2016). The health equity certificate program: A targeted approach to reducing health disparities and increasing the competence of health professional students. *Pedagogy in Health Promotion*, *3*(3), 187–194. DOI: 10.1177/2373379916665637

Feletto, M., & Sharkey, A. (2019). The influence of gender on immunisation: Using an ecological framework to examine intersecting inequities and pathways to change. *BMJ Global Health*, *4*(5), e001711. DOI: 10.1136/bmjgh-2019-001711 PMID: 31565415

Figueroa, C., Luo, T., Aguilera, A., & Lyles, C. (2021). The need for feminist intersectionality in digital health. *The Lancet. Digital Health*, *3*(8), e526–e533. DOI: 10.1016/S2589-7500(21)00118-7 PMID: 34325855

Floyd, A., & Sakellariou, D. (2017). Healthcare access for refugee women with limited literacy: Layers of disadvantage. *International Journal for Equity in Health*, *16*(1), 195. Advance online publication. DOI: 10.1186/s12939-017-0694-8 PMID: 29126420

Garcia, L., Bernuci, M., Marques, A., Bertolini, S., & Silva, T. (2019). A case study of social vulnerability: Thoughts for the promotion of health. *Revista Bioética*, *27*(3), 430–438. DOI: 10.1590/1983-80422019273326

García-Sánchez, I., Ariza, L., Guzmán, B., & Aibar-Guzmán, C. (2020). Do institutional investors drive corporate transparency regarding business contribution to the sustainable development goals? *Business Strategy and the Environment*, *29*(5), 2019–2036. DOI: 10.1002/bse.2485

Goldenberg, T., Tanner, A. E., McGuire, T., Alonzo, J., Mann-Jackson, L., Refugio Aviles, L., Galindo, C. A., Bessler, P. A., Courtenay-Quirk, C., Garcia, M., Reboussin, B. A., & Rhodes, S. D. (2024). The role of stigma and resilience in healthcare engagement among transgender Latinas in the U.S. south: Baseline findings from the Chicas study. *Journal of Immigrant and Minority Health*, *26*(5), 850–858. DOI: 10.1007/s10903-024-01605-6 PMID: 38809298

Gonzales, G., & Deal, C. (2022). Health risk factors and outcomes among gender minority high school students in 15 US states. *Journal of the American Medical Association*, *327*(15), 1498. DOI: 10.1001/jama.2022.3087 PMID: 35438737

Goto, T., Wang, C., Kwiat, C., Nguyen, C., & Saligan, L. N. (2023). Community-based wound care programs for unhoused individuals. *Journal of Epidemiology and Global Health, 13*(4), 604–614. DOI: 10.1007/s44197-023-00157-6 PMID: 37847465

Gunnarsdóttir, H., Traustadóttir, R., Einarsdóttir, Þ., & Rice, J. (2023). Through an intersectional lens: Prevalence of violence against disabled women in Iceland. *Violence Against Women, 30*(10), 2421–2441. DOI: 10.1177/10778012231155174 PMID: 36775963

Hammami, N., Silva, M., & Elgar, F. (2022). Trends in gender and socioeconomic inequalities in adolescent health over 16 years (2002–2018): Findings from the Canadian health behaviour in school-aged children study. *Health Promotion and Chronic Disease Prevention in Canada : Research, Policy and Practice, 42*(2), 68–78. DOI: 10.24095/hpcdp.42.2.03 PMID: 35170931

Harris, D., & Delcher, C. (2024). Geospatial imprecision with constraints for precision public health: Algorithm development and validation. *Online Journal of Public Health Informatics, 16*, e54958. DOI: 10.2196/54958 PMID: 38772021

Hughto, J., Clark, K., Altice, F., Reisner, S., Kershaw, T., & Pachankis, J. (2018). Creating, reinforcing, and resisting the gender binary: A qualitative study of transgender women's healthcare experiences in sex-segregated jails and prisons. *International Journal of Prisoner Health, 14*(2), 69–88. DOI: 10.1108/IJPH-02-2017-0011 PMID: 29869582

Jewkes, R., Chirwa, E., Alangea, D., Addo-Lartey, A., Christofides, N., Dunkle, K., Ramsoomar, L., & Gibbs, A. (2023). Pooled analysis of the association between food insecurity and violence against women: Evidence from low- and middle-income settings. *Journal of Global Health, 13*, 04021. Advance online publication. DOI: 10.7189/jogh.13.04021 PMID: 36896806

Jordan, Z., & Pilla, B. (2023). From agenda to action: JBI evidence synthesis and the United Nations sustainable development goals. *JBI Evidence Synthesis, 22*(3), 364–377. DOI: 10.11124/JBIES-23-00088 PMID: 37851334

Jung, Y., Jeong, S., Park, S., & Jang, S. (2022). The impact of entering poverty on the unmet medical needs of Korean adults: A 5-year cohort study. *BMC Public Health, 22*(1), 1879. Advance online publication. DOI: 10.1186/s12889-022-14251-0 PMID: 36207716

Kabia, E., Mbau, R., Muraya, K., Morgan, R., Molyneux, S., & Barasa, E. (2018). How do gender and disability influence the ability of the poor to benefit from pro-poor health financing policies in Kenya? an intersectional analysis. *International Journal for Equity in Health, 17*(1), 149. Advance online publication. DOI: 10.1186/s12939-018-0853-6 PMID: 30231887

Kanengoni-Nyatara, B., Watson, K., Galindo, C., Charania, N. A., Mpofu, C., & Holroyd, E. (2023). Barriers to and recommendations for equitable access to healthcare for migrants and refugees in Aotearoa, new Zealand: An integrative review. *Journal of Immigrant and Minority Health, 26*(1), 164–180. DOI: 10.1007/s10903-023-01528-8 PMID: 37665540

Khalifeh, R., D'Hoore, W., Saliba, C., Salameh, P., & Dauvrin, M. (2023). Experiences of cultural differences, discrimination, and healthcare access of displaced Syrians (DS) in Lebanon: A qualitative study. *Health Care, 11*(14), 2013. DOI: 10.3390/healthcare11142013 PMID: 37510454

Li, W., Zhang, L., Yue, M., Ruiz-Menjivar, J., & Zhang, J. (2023). Health vulnerability and health poverty of rice farmers: Evidence from Hubei province in China. *China Agricultural Economic Review, 15*(2), 259–277. DOI: 10.1108/CAER-03-2021-0062

Liu, S. (2020). Higher education and sustainable development goals during covid-19: Coping strategies of a university in Wuhan, China. *Journal of Public Health Research, 9*(1, suppl), jphr.2020.1933. Advance online publication. DOI: 10.4081/jphr.2020.1933 PMID: 33409250

Loeb, T., Murray, S. M., Cooney, E. E., Poteat, T., Althoff, K. N., Cannon, C. M., Schneider, J. S., Mayer, K. H., Haw, J. S., Wawrzyniak, A. J., Radix, A. E., Malone, J., Adams, D., Stevenson, M., Reisner, S. L., & Wirtz, A. L. (2024). Access to healthcare among transgender women living with and without HIV in the United States: Associations with gender minority stress and resilience factors. *BMC Public Health, 24*(1), 243. Advance online publication. DOI: 10.1186/s12889-024-17764-y PMID: 38245684

MacIntosh, T., Desai, M., Lewis, T., Jones, B., & Nuñez-Smith, M. (2013). Socially-assigned race, healthcare discrimination and preventive healthcare services. *PLoS One, 8*(5), e64522. DOI: 10.1371/journal.pone.0064522 PMID: 23704992

Manandhar, M., Hawkes, S., Buse, K., Nosrati, E., & Magar, V. (2018). Gender, health and the 2030 agenda for sustainable development. *Bulletin of the World Health Organization, 96*(9), 644–653. DOI: 10.2471/BLT.18.211607 PMID: 30262946

Marí-Klose, M., Julià, A., Escapa, S., & Gallo, P. (2023). Period poverty and mental health in a representative sample of young women in Barcelona, Spain. *BMC Women's Health*, *23*(1), 201. Advance online publication. DOI: 10.1186/s12905-023-02328-w PMID: 37118714

Mavole, J. (2023). Protection and maintenance of healthcare services for civilians' well-being in conflict affected areas: Comparative analysis of the African situation. *European Journal of Health Sciences*, *9*(2), 1–17. DOI: 10.47672/ejhs.1507

McMaughan, D., Oloruntoba, O., & Smith, M. (2020). Socioeconomic status and access to healthcare: Interrelated drivers for healthy aging. *Frontiers in Public Health*, *8*, 231. Advance online publication. DOI: 10.3389/fpubh.2020.00231 PMID: 32626678

Mhyre, J. (2022). Editorial: Justice, equity, diversity and inclusion in obstetric and gynecological anesthesia. *Current Opinion in Anaesthesiology*, *35*(3), 259. DOI: 10.1097/ACO.0000000000001146 PMID: 35671009

Moalla, K., & Darmstadt, G. L. (2024). Legal pluralism and tribalism: Drivers of gender and health inequalities. *Journal of Global Health*, *14*, 03020. Advance online publication. DOI: 10.7189/jogh.14.03020 PMID: 38813678

Mokua, S., Ombogo, L., Mathu, D., Otambo, P., Nyandieka, L., Onteri, S. N., Mbuka, S. J., Kariuki, J., Ahmed, I., Wanjihia, V., Mutai, J., & Bukania, Z. (2024). "for a man to go to hospital, then that would be his last option": A qualitative study exploring men's experiences, perceptions and healthcare needs in the implementation of universal health coverage in Kenya. *PLOS Global Public Health*, *4*(5), e0002925. DOI: 10.1371/journal.pgph.0002925 PMID: 38713655

Mollet, J., & Mollet, G. (2024). Population and development: Employing the capability approach in family planning policy for women in Indonesia. *International Journal of Applied Business and International Management*, *9*(1), 120–135. DOI: 10.32535/ijabim.v9i1.2917

Morgan, A., Chaiyachati, K., Weissman, G., & Liao, J. (2018). Eliminating gender-based bias in academic medicine: More than naming the "elephant in the room". *Journal of General Internal Medicine*, *33*(6), 966–968. DOI: 10.1007/s11606-018-4411-0 PMID: 29564608

Moser, M., & Beiruti, S. (2023). Healthcare inaccessibility in rural Indiana: A scoping review. *Journal of Student Research*, *12*(1). Advance online publication. DOI: 10.47611/jsrhs.v12i1.3923

Mulemfo, D., Moyo, I., & Mavhandu-Mudzusi, A. (2023). LGBTQI+ experiences of HIV management services at primary healthcare facilities in Gauteng province, south Africa. *Advances in Public Health, 2023*, 1–11. DOI: 10.1155/2023/1279409

Müller, A. (2017). Scrambling for access: Availability, accessibility, acceptability and quality of healthcare for lesbian, gay, bisexual and transgender people in south Africa. *BMC International Health and Human Rights*, *17*(1), 16. Advance online publication. DOI: 10.1186/s12914-017-0124-4 PMID: 28558693

Murphy, C., Davis, M., Evans, M., & Zonderman, A. (2022). Racial discrimination, mental health symptoms, and intimate partner violence perpetration in black adults. *Journal of Consulting and Clinical Psychology*, *90*(3), 209–220. DOI: 10.1037/ccp0000712 PMID: 35201781

Nakkeeran, N., & Nakkeeran, B. (2018). Disability, mental health, sexual orientation and gender identity: Understanding health inequity through experience and difference. *Health Research Policy and Systems*, *16*(S1), 97. Advance online publication. DOI: 10.1186/s12961-018-0366-1 PMID: 30301453

Ndzabela, O., & Lukman, Y. (2023). The impact of gender inequality on economic development. *Insights Into Regional Development*, *5*(4), 49–64. DOI: 10.9770/IRD.2023.5.4(4)

Nolan, I., Kuhner, C., & Dy, G. (2019). Demographic and temporal trends in transgender identities and gender confirming surgery. *Translational Andrology and Urology*, *8*(3), 184–190. DOI: 10.21037/tau.2019.04.09 PMID: 31380225

Oke, G., & Sibomana, O. (2025). Understanding health inequality, disparity and inequity in Africa: A rapid review of concepts, root causes, and strategic solutions. *Public Health Challenges*, *4*(1), e70040. Advance online publication. DOI: 10.1002/puh2.70040

Paul, É., Deville, C., Bodson, O., Sambieni, N., Thiam, I., Bourgeois, M., Ridde, V., & Fecher, F. (2019). How is equity approached in universal health coverage? an analysis of global and country policy documents in Benin and Senegal. *International Journal for Equity in Health*, *18*(1), 195. Advance online publication. DOI: 10.1186/s12939-019-1089-9 PMID: 31847877

Pauly, B., Shahram, S., Dang, P., Marcellus, L., & MacDonald, M. (2017). Health equity talk: Understandings of health equity among health leaders. *AIMS Public Health*, *4*(5), 490–512. DOI: 10.3934/publichealth.2017.5.490 PMID: 30155500

Peek, M., Gottlieb, L. M., Doubeni, C. A., Viswanathan, M., Cartier, Y., Aceves, B., Fichtenberg, C., & Cené, C. W. (2023). Advancing health equity through social care interventions. *Health Services Research, 58*(S3), 318–326. DOI: 10.1111/1475-6773.14244 PMID: 38015863

Percival, V., Dusabe-Richards, E., Wurie, H., Namakula, J., Ssali, S., & Theobald, S. (2018). Are health systems interventions gender blind? examining health system reconstruction in conflict affected states. *Globalization and Health, 14*(1), 90. Advance online publication. DOI: 10.1186/s12992-018-0401-6 PMID: 30157887

Portnoy, A., Clark, S., Ozawa, S., & Jit, M. (2020). The impact of vaccination on gender equity: Conceptual framework and human papillomavirus (HPV) vaccine case study. *International Journal for Equity in Health, 19*(1), 10. Advance online publication. DOI: 10.1186/s12939-019-1090-3 PMID: 31937328

Raman, R., Lathabhai, H., Mandal, S., Kumar, C., & Nedungadi, P. (2023). Contribution of business research to sustainable development goals: Bibliometrics and science mapping analysis. *Sustainability (Basel), 15*(17), 12982. DOI: 10.3390/su151712982

Ratnayake, A., Sayfi, S., Veronis, L., Torres, S., Baek, S., & Pottie, K. (2022). How are non-medical settlement service organizations supporting access to healthcare and mental health services for immigrants: A scoping review. *International Journal of Environmental Research and Public Health, 19*(6), 3616. DOI: 10.3390/ijerph19063616 PMID: 35329303

Reis da Silva, T. H. (2023a). Falls assessment and prevention in the nursing home and community. *British Journal of Community Nursing, 28*(2), 68–72. DOI: 10.12968/bjcn.2023.28.2.68 PMID: 36735363

Reis da Silva, T. H. (2024a). Advancing Gender Equity In Nursing Care For Older Adults: A Pathway To Achieving The United Nations Sustainable Development Goals. *J Comm Med and Pub Health Rep, 5*(12). Advance online publication. DOI: 10.38207/JCMPHR/2024/JUL051201105

Reis da Silva, T. H. (2024b). Gender Equity In Healthcare: Integrating Emotional Intelligence To Achieve The United Nations Sustainable Development Goals. *J Comm Med and Pub Health Rep, 5*(12). Advance online publication. DOI: 10.38207/JCMPHR/2024/JUL051202106

Reis da Silva, T. H. (2024c). Enhancing the mental health of refugees and asylum seekers through music interventions. *Mental Health Practice*. Advance online publication. DOI: 10.7748/mhp.2024.e1717

Reis da Silva, T. H (2024d). Oncology and Cancer Medicine: Understanding the complexities in Older Patients. *Biomed J Sci & Tech Res* 55(3)-2024. DOI: https://doi.org/DOI: 10.26717/BJSTR.2024.55.008720

Reis da Silva, T. H. (2024e). Falls prevention in older people and the role of nursing. *British Journal of Community Nursing*, *29*(7), 335–339. DOI: 10.12968/bjcn.2024.0005 PMID: 38963269

Reis da Silva, T. H. (2024f). Prevalence of elder abuse: A narrative review. *British Journal of Community Nursing*, *29*(9), 442–446. DOI: 10.12968/bjcn.2024.0004 PMID: 39240800

Reis da Silva, T. H. (2024g). Loneliness in older adults. *British Journal of Community Nursing*, *29*(2), 60–66. DOI: 10.12968/bjcn.2024.29.2.60 PMID: 38300245

Reis da Silva, T. H. (2024h). Emotional Intelligence in Teaching Geriatric Nursing: Humanising Technology for Compassionate Care in Higher Education. In S. Tikadar, H. Liu, P. Bhattacharya, S. Bhattacharya, (Eds.) *Humanizing Technology With Emotional Intelligence* (pp. 145-168). IGI Global Scientific Publishing. DOI: 10.4018/979-8-3693-7011-7.ch008

Reis da Silva, T. H. (2024i). Navigating Healthcare Complexity: Integrating Business Fundamentals into Nursing Leadership. In A. Sedky (Ed.) *Resiliency Strategies for Long-Term Business Success* (pp. 145-168). IGI Global. DOI: 10.4018/979-8-3693-9168-6.ch006

Reis da Silva, T. H. (2024j). Integrating business essentials into Gerontological Nursing: Enhancing Care for Older Adults in Diverse Settings. In A. Sedky (Ed.) *Resiliency Strategies for Long-Term Business Success* (pp. 283-316). IGI Global. DOI: 10.4018/979-8-3693-9168-6.ch011

Reis da Silva, T. H. (2025a). Fostering Emotional Intelligence for Competency Development in Nursing Education. In Aldosemani, T., Lytras, M., & Ordóñez de Pablos, P. (Eds.), *Innovative Educational Frameworks for Future Skills and Competencies* (pp. 39–62). IGI Global Scientific Publishing., DOI: 10.4018/979-8-3693-7555-6.ch002

Reis da Silva, T. H. (2025b). Designing for Longevity: Economic Perspectives on Age-Friendly Housing and Urban Development. In Gölçek, A. (Ed.), *Perspectives on the Economics of Aging* (pp. 151–176). IGI Global Scientific Publishing., DOI: 10.4018/979-8-3693-7753-6.ch006

Reis da Silva, T. H. (2025c). Integrative Approaches to Geriatric Care: Enhancing Physical and Mental Health Through AI-Driven Insights. In Jermsittiparsert, K., & Marzo, R. (Eds.), *Physical Health, Mental Health, and Human Well-Being in the Age of AI* (pp. 113–136). IGI Global Scientific Publishing., DOI: 10.4018/979-8-3693-6190-0.ch007

Reis da Silva, T. H. (2025d). Promoting Emotional Well-Being in Older Adults: The Role of AI in Supporting Emotional Intelligence and Mental Health. In Jermsittiparsert, K., & Marzo, R. R. (Eds.), *Physical Health, Mental Health, and Human Well-Being in the Age of AI* (pp. 137–167). IGI Global Scientific Publishing., DOI: 10.4018/979-8-3693-6190-0.ch8

Reis da Silva, T. H. (2025e). The Role of Emotional Intelligence in Promoting Mental Peace, Healthy Work Environments, and Emotional Well-Being Among Entrepreneurs. In Tunio, M. N. (Ed.), *Supporting Psychological and Emotional Wellbeing Among Entrepreneurs*. IGI Global Scientific Publishing., DOI: 10.4018/979-8-3693-3673-1.ch21

Reis da Silva, T. H. (2025f). AI-Powered Emotional Intelligence in Nursing: Bridging the Gap in Older People Care. In Jermsittiparsert, K., & Marzo, R. R. (Eds.), *Physical Health, Mental Health, and Human Well-Being in the Age of AI*. IGI Global Scientific Publishing., DOI: 10.4018/979-8-3693-6190-0.ch9

Reis da Silva, T. H. (2025g). Emotional Intelligence and AI in Geriatric Nursing: Bridging Technology and Compassionate Care. In Jermsittiparsert, K., & Marzo, R. R. (Eds.), *Physical Health, Mental Health, and Human Well-Being in the Age of AI*. IGI Global Scientific Publishing., DOI: 10.4018/979-8-3693-6190-0.ch10

Reis da Silva, T. H. (2025h). Integrating Artificial Intelligence in Geriatric Care: Enhancing Physical and Mental Health Outcomes. In Jermsittiparsert, K., & Marzo, R. R. (Eds.), *Physical Health, Mental Health, and Human Well-Being in the Age of AI*. IGI Global Scientific Publishing., DOI: 10.4018/979-8-3693-6190-0.ch11

Reis da Silva, T. H., & Mitchell, A. (2024). Integrating Digital Transformation in Nursing Education: Best Practices and Challenges in Curriculum Development. In Lytras, M., Serban, A. C., Alkhaldi, A., Malik, S., & Aldosemani, T. (Eds.), *Digital Transformation in Higher Education, Part B Cases, Examples and Good Practices*. Emerald Publishing Limited.

Restar, A., Sherwood, J., Edeza, A., Collins, C., & Operario, D. (2021). Expanding gender-based health equity framework for transgender populations. *Transgender Health*, *6*(1), 1–4. DOI: 10.1089/trgh.2020.0026 PMID: 33644317

Rivenbark, J., & Ichou, M. (2020). Discrimination in healthcare as a barrier to care: Experiences of socially disadvantaged populations in France from a nationally representative survey. *BMC Public Health, 20*(1), 31. Advance online publication. DOI: 10.1186/s12889-019-8124-z PMID: 31918699

Rubenstein, L., Hempel, S., Danz, M., Rose, D., Stockdale, S., Curtis, I., & Kirsh, S. (2019). Eight priorities for improving primary care access management in healthcare organizations: Results of a modified Delphi stakeholder panel. *Journal of General Internal Medicine, 35*(2), 523–530. DOI: 10.1007/s11606-019-05541-2 PMID: 31728895

Schenkman, S., Bousquat, A., & Ferreira, M. (2022). Efficiency analysis in Brazil's Sao Paulo state local unified health system (SUS): From gender-ethnicity-power inequities to the dissolution of health effectiveness. *International Journal of Environmental Research and Public Health, 19*(5), 2990. DOI: 10.3390/ijerph19052990 PMID: 35270683

Schmitz, R., Robinson, B., Tabler, J., Welch, B., & Rafaqut, S. (2019). LGBTQ+ Latino/a young people's interpretations of stigma and mental health: An intersectional minority stress perspective. *Society and Mental Health, 10*(2), 163–179. DOI: 10.1177/2156869319847248

Senyurek, G., Kavas, M., & Ülman, Y. (2021). Lived experiences of people living with hiv: A descriptive qualitative analysis of their perceptions of themselves, their social spheres, healthcare professionals and the challenges they face daily. *BMC Public Health, 21*(1), 904. Advance online publication. DOI: 10.1186/s12889-021-10881-y PMID: 33980195

Shabalala, S., & Campbell, M. M. (2023). The complexities of trans women's access to healthcare in south Africa: Moving health systems beyond the gender binary towards gender equity. *International Journal for Equity in Health, 22*(1), 231. Advance online publication. DOI: 10.1186/s12939-023-02039-6 PMID: 37924085

Shareck, M., Buhariwala, P., Hassan, M., Balla, E., & O'Campo, P. (2024). Supporting women exit sex work: A contribution analysis of the exit doors here integrated care program in Toronto, Canada. *International Journal of Integrated Care, 24*(1), 22. Advance online publication. DOI: 10.5334/ijic.7700 PMID: 38550896

Sharmake, A. (2024). Healthcare disparities among socioeconomic groups. *IJHSS, 2*(5), 50–63. DOI: 10.47941/ijhss.1889

Shomuyiwa, D., George, N. S., Sunday, B. A., Omotayo, F. O., Mwaba, M., David, S. C., Nabiryo, M., & Yangaza, Y. (2023). Addressing neglected tropical diseases in Africa: A gender perspective. *Health Science Reports*, *6*(11), e1726. Advance online publication. DOI: 10.1002/hsr2.1726 PMID: 38028711

Sing, S., Peters, R., Syurina, E., Irwanto, I., Naniche, D., & Zweekhorst, M. (2020). Intersectionality and health-related stigma: Insights from experiences of people living with stigmatized health conditions in Indonesia. *International Journal for Equity in Health*, *19*(1), 206. Advance online publication. DOI: 10.1186/s12939-020-01318-w PMID: 33176809

Singh, R., & Subedi, M. (2020). Covid-19 and stigma: Social discrimination towards frontline healthcare providers and covid-19 recovered patients in Nepal. *Asian Journal of Psychiatry*, *53*, 102222. DOI: 10.1016/j.ajp.2020.102222 PMID: 32570096

Skovdal, M., Magoge-Mandizvidza, P., Dzamatira, F., Maswera, R., Nyamukapa, C., Thomas, R., Mugurungi, O., & Gregson, S. (2022). Improving access to pre-exposure prophylaxis for adolescent girls and young women: Recommendations from healthcare providers in eastern Zimbabwe. *BMC Infectious Diseases*, *22*(1), 399. Advance online publication. DOI: 10.1186/s12879-022-07376-5 PMID: 35461220

Su, Z., Cheshmehzangi, A., McDonnell, D., Šegalo, S., A mad, J., & Bennett, B. (2022). Gender inequality and health disparity amid Covid-19. *Nursing Outlook*, *70*(1), 89–95. DOI: 10.1016/j.outlook.2021.08.004 PMID: 34774306

Sweileh, W. (2020). Bibliometric analysis of scientific publications on "sustainable development goals" with emphasis on "good health and well-being" goal (2015–2019). *Globalization and Health*, *16*(1), 68. Advance online publication. DOI: 10.1186/s12992-020-00602-2 PMID: 32723366

Tarshish, N. (2024). Social work advocacy: Towards a trauma-informed model. *Clinical Social Work Journal*. Advance online publication. DOI: 10.1007/s10615-024-00942-1

Ungar, T., Knaak, S., & Szeto, A. (2015). Theoretical and practical considerations for combating mental illness stigma in health care. *Community Mental Health Journal*, *52*(3), 262–271. DOI: 10.1007/s10597-015-9910-4 PMID: 26173403

Victora, C., Boerma, T., Requejo, J., Mesenburg, M., Joseph, G., Costa, J., Vidaletti, L. P., Ferreira, L. Z., Hosseinpoor, A. R., & Barros, A. (2019). Analyses of inequalities in RMNCH: Rising to the challenge of the SDGS. *BMJ Global Health*, *4*(Suppl 4), e001295. DOI: 10.1136/bmjgh-2018-001295 PMID: 31297251

Wang, W., Weng, F., Chen, Y., & Zhu, M. (2023). Two-stage dual-game model approach to view the difficulty of healthcare accessibility. *Frontiers in Public Health, 11*, 1078675. Advance online publication. DOI: 10.3389/fpubh.2023.1078675 PMID: 36969632

West, N., Ddaaki, W., Nakyanjo, N., Isabirye, D., Nakubulwa, R., Nalugoda, F., Kagaayi, J., & Kennedy, C. (2021). "a double stress": The mental health impacts of the covid-19 pandemic among people living with HIV in Rakai, Uganda. *AIDS and Behavior, 26*(1), 261–265. DOI: 10.1007/s10461-021-03379-6 PMID: 34292428

Woldemichael, A., Takian, A., Sari, A., & Olyaeemanesh, A. (2019). Inequalities in healthcare resources and outcomes threatening sustainable health development in Ethiopia: Panel data analysis. *BMJ Open, 9*(1), e022923. DOI: 10.1136/bmjopen-2018-022923 PMID: 30705237

Wong, W., LaVeist, T., & Sharfstein, J. (2015). Achieving health equity by design. *Journal of the American Medical Association, 313*(14), 1417. DOI: 10.1001/jama.2015.2434 PMID: 25751310

Woodgate, R., González, M., & Tennent, P. (2023). Accessing mental health services for a child living with anxiety: Parents' lived experience and recommendations. *PLoS One, 18*(4), e0283518. DOI: 10.1371/journal.pone.0283518 PMID: 37018182

Yassine, B., Rojewski, J., & Ransom, M. (2021). Gender inequity in the public health workforce. *Journal of Public Health Management and Practice, 28*(2), E390–E396. DOI: 10.1097/PHH.0000000000001374 PMID: 34016906

Yip, T., Cheah, C., Kiang, L., & Hall, G. (2021). Rendered invisible: Are Asian Americans a model or a marginalized minority? *The American Psychologist, 76*(4), 575–581. DOI: 10.1037/amp0000857 PMID: 34410735

Yousef, L., Almatroodi, N., AlAngari, D., AlShehri, R., & Alshammari, S. (2023). Disability inclusion assessment in primary healthcare centers in eastern Saudi Arabia: A way forward. *Journal of Medicine and Life, 16*(12), 1813–1817. DOI: 10.25122/jml-2023-0385 PMID: 38585520

Zamora, G., Koller, T., Thomas, R., Manandhar, M., Lustigova, E., Diop, A., … & Magar, V. (2018). Tools and approaches to operationalize the commitment to equity, gender and human rights: towards leaving no one behind in the sustainable development goals. *Global Health Action*, 11(sup1), 75-81. https://doi.org/DOI: 10.1080/16549716.2018.1463657

Zhou, Z., Jiang, Y., Wu, H., Fan, J., & Yu, Z. (2022). The age of mobility: Can equalization of public health services alleviate the poverty of migrant workers? *International Journal of Environmental Research and Public Health*, *19*(20), 13342. DOI: 10.3390/ijerph192013342 PMID: 36293922

Zuma, S. (2022). Pharmacist assistants' role in medicine supply management at a primary healthcare setting. *Health SA = SA Gesondheid*, *27*. Advance online publication. DOI: 10.4102/hsag.v27i0.2041 PMID: 36483511

Chapter 8
Green Infrastructure Strategies for Ageing Populations:
Enhancing Health and Well-Being Through Sustainable Urban Design

Tiago Manuel Horta Reis da Silva
https://orcid.org/0000-0001-5220-1718
King's College London, UK

ABSTRACT

This chapter explores how green infrastructure strategies can improve health and well-being for ageing populations through sustainable urban design. With a focus on concepts such as ageing in place, the chapter demonstrates how access to green spaces reduces loneliness, enhances mobility, reduces falls and promotes holistic care, including those facing chronic conditions like oncology, chronic kidney disease (CKD), and frailty-related issues requiring specialised moving and handling practices. Aligning with Sustainable Development Goals (SDGs), it addresses equitable access to urban health solutions, sustainability, and social inclusion, proposing innovative urban planning solutions to foster improved mental and physical health outcomes for older adults.

DOI: 10.4018/979-8-3693-9755-8.ch008

1. INTRODUCTION

1.1 Background on Ageing Populations and Urban Challenges

The phenomenon of population ageing is increasingly prominent in urban environments worldwide, presenting a series of complex challenges that necessitate innovative solutions. As urbanisation accelerates, cities are witnessing a demographic shift characterised by a growing proportion of elderly residents (Reis da Silva, 2023a; Reis da Silva, 2024a). By 2050, it is projected that the global population aged 60 years and older will reach 2 billion, with a significant concentration in urban areas (Lehrner, 2022). This demographic transition is compounded by the rapid urbanisation of developing countries, where the urban population is expected to rise from 55% in 2014 to 68% by 2050 (Buerkert & Schlecht, 2019). The implications of this demographic shift are profound, as ageing populations often face increased health risks, social isolation, and a lack of accessible services, particularly in urban settings where infrastructure may not be adequately designed to meet their needs (Hoof et al., 2018).

Urban environments pose unique challenges for older adults, including inadequate public transportation, limited access to healthcare facilities, and insufficient recreational spaces that promote physical activity and social interaction (Isa et al., 2023). Moreover, the intersection of urbanisation and ageing exacerbates health inequalities, as older adults in urban areas may experience disparities in access to resources and services compared to their younger counterparts (Cook et al., 2013). The rapid pace of urbanisation often leads to the neglect of the specific needs of ageing populations, resulting in environments that can hinder their health and well-being (Hoof et al., 2018). Consequently, there is an urgent need for urban planners and policymakers to adopt strategies that prioritise the integration of green infrastructure, which can enhance the quality of life for older adults while addressing the broader challenges posed by urbanization (Azzali et al., 2022).

1.2 Importance of Green Infrastructure for Health and Well-Being

Green infrastructure refers to a strategically planned network of natural and semi-natural areas that provide ecosystem services and enhance urban resilience. The incorporation of green spaces within urban design has been shown to have significant benefits for public health, particularly for ageing populations. Access to green spaces is associated with improved mental health outcomes, reduced stress levels, and increased opportunities for physical activity (Endreny, 2018). Studies have demonstrated that older adults who live in proximity to parks and green areas report higher levels of physical activity and lower rates of depression (Rahman, 2019). Furthermore, green infrastructure contributes to improved air quality and reduced urban heat effects, which are particularly beneficial for vulnerable populations, including the elderly (Mutani & Beltramino, 2022).

The integration of green infrastructure into urban planning can also foster social cohesion among ageing populations. Community gardens, parks, and greenways serve as vital spaces for social interaction, enabling older adults to engage with their neighbours and participate in community activities (Endreny, 2018). This social engagement is crucial for combating loneliness and isolation, which are prevalent among older adults living in urban areas (Hoof et al., 2018; Reis da Silva, 2024b). Additionally, green infrastructure can enhance the aesthetic appeal of neighbourhoods, contributing to a sense of place and belonging for older residents (Azzali et al., 2022). By prioritising green infrastructure, cities can create environments that not only support the physical health of ageing populations but also promote their social and emotional well-being.

1.3 Overview of Sustainable Development Goals

The Sustainable Development Goals (SDGs), established by the United Nations in 2015, provide a comprehensive framework for addressing global challenges, including those related to population ageing and urbanisation (da Silva and Rodrigues, 2023). Goal 11, which focuses on making cities inclusive, safe, resilient, and sustainable, is particularly relevant in the context of ageing populations (Lehrner, 2022). The SDGs emphasise the importance of ensuring access to safe and inclusive green spaces, which can significantly enhance the quality of life for older adults living in urban environments (Jarzebski et al., 2021). Moreover, the SDGs advocate for the integration of sustainable urban planning practices that consider the needs of all residents, particularly the most vulnerable, including the elderly (Azzali et al., 2022).

In addition to Goal 11, other SDGs, such as Goal 3 (Good Health and Well-Being) and Goal 10 (Reduced Inequalities), intersect with the challenges posed by ageing populations in urban settings. The promotion of health and well-being for older adults is essential for achieving these goals, as healthy ageing contributes to the overall sustainability of urban communities (Rahman, 2019). Furthermore, addressing inequalities in access to resources and services is critical for ensuring that all members of society, regardless of age, can thrive in urban environments (Hoof et al., 2018). By aligning urban design strategies with the SDGs, cities can foster inclusive and sustainable environments that enhance the health and well-being of ageing populations while addressing the broader challenges of urbanisation.

Figure 1. Ageing Populations and Urban Challenges

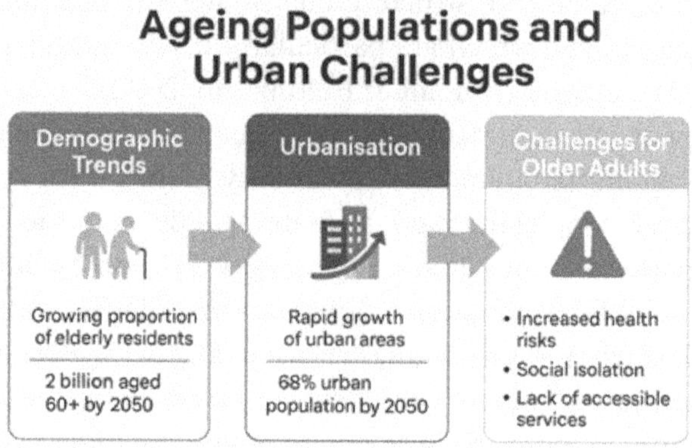

2. GREEN INFRASTRUCTURE: DEFINING THE CONCEPT

2.1 Elements of Green Infrastructure

Green infrastructure (GI) encompasses a variety of natural and semi-natural elements that are strategically integrated into urban environments to enhance ecological functions and improve the quality of life for residents. Key components of green infrastructure include parks, gardens, and eco-corridors, each serving distinct yet interrelated roles in urban ecosystems. Parks and gardens provide essential green spaces that promote biodiversity, offer recreational opportunities, and contribute to the mental and physical well-being of urban dwellers (İnançoğlu et al., 2020). They serve as vital areas for community engagement and social interaction, particularly for ageing populations who may benefit from accessible outdoor environments that encourage physical activity and socialization (Jurković, 2023).

Eco-corridors, or green corridors, are another critical element of green infrastructure. They facilitate the movement of wildlife between fragmented habitats, thereby enhancing biodiversity and ecological resilience (Choi & Lee, 2019). These corridors can connect parks, gardens, and other green spaces, creating a network that supports various species and contributes to the overall health of urban ecosystems (Choi & Lee, 2019). The design and implementation of eco-corridors can also mitigate the effects of urbanisation by providing essential habitats and promoting ecological connectivity (Wildsmith et al., 2013). For instance, in urban areas where natural landscapes have been disrupted, eco-corridors can help restore ecological functions and improve habitat quality for local wildlife (Choi & Lee, 2019).

In addition to parks and eco-corridors, green roofs and walls are increasingly recognized as vital components of green infrastructure. These features not only enhance the aesthetic appeal of urban buildings but also provide insulation, reduce energy consumption, and improve air quality (Yin et al., 2014). The integration of such elements into urban planning can significantly contribute to the sustainability of cities by promoting energy efficiency and reducing the urban heat island effect (Wang & Zhang, 2020). Overall, the diverse elements of green infrastructure work synergistically to create healthier, more sustainable urban environments.

2.2 Role in Urban Planning and Sustainable Cities

The role of green infrastructure in urban planning is pivotal for the development of sustainable cities. As urban areas continue to expand, the need for effective planning that incorporates green spaces becomes increasingly urgent. Green infrastructure provides a framework for integrating ecological considerations into urban development, ensuring that cities can accommodate growth while maintaining environmental integrity (Bibri & Krogstie, 2020). By prioritising the preservation and enhancement of natural systems, urban planners can create resilient cities that are better equipped to withstand the challenges posed by climate change and urbanization (Liu, 2024).

Incorporating green infrastructure into urban planning can also yield significant economic benefits. Studies have shown that well-designed green spaces can increase property values, attract tourism, and reduce healthcare costs associated with urban pollution and sedentary lifestyles (Liu & Feng, 2016). Furthermore, green infrastructure can enhance the overall liveability of urban areas, making them more attractive to residents and businesses alike (Zellmer & Goto, 2022). This economic rationale aligns with the broader goals of sustainable development, which seek to balance environmental, social, and economic considerations in urban planning (Mehta, 2024).

Moreover, the integration of green infrastructure into urban design can facilitate compliance with international sustainability frameworks, such as the United Nations Sustainable Development Goals (SDGs). For instance, Goal 11 emphasises the importance of making cities inclusive, safe, resilient, and sustainable, highlighting the need for accessible green spaces and sustainable urban planning practices (Ito, 2019). By aligning urban development strategies with these global goals, cities can foster environments that promote health, well-being, and social equity among their residents (Lv et al., 2022).

Figure 2. Green Infrastructure

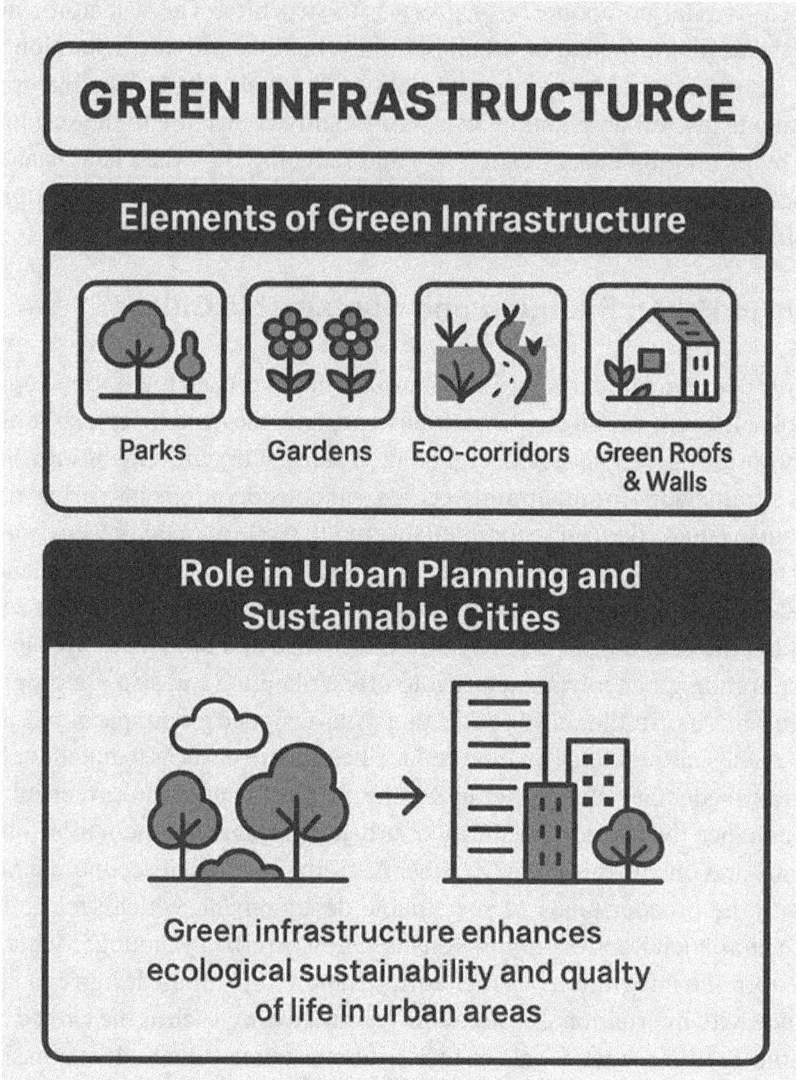

3. LINKING GREEN INFRASTRUCTURE AND AGEING IN PLACE

3.1 Promoting Independence and Community Integration

The integration of green infrastructure within urban environments plays a crucial role in promoting independence and community integration for older adults. Community gardens, parks, and other green spaces provide essential opportunities for older individuals to engage in physical activities, which are vital for maintaining their health and independence (Wang & Glicksman, 2013; Reis da Silva, 2023c). Research indicates that gardening activities not only enhance physical well-being but also foster a sense of belonging and community among participants (Egerer et al., 2018). For older adults, the ability to engage in gardening and other communal activities can significantly contribute to their overall quality of life, as these activities promote social interaction and reduce feelings of isolation (Soga et al., 2017).

Accessibility considerations are paramount in ensuring that green spaces are usable for older adults. Urban planners must prioritise the design of parks and community gardens to accommodate mobility challenges faced by this demographic. Features such as wheelchair-accessible pathways, raised garden beds, and seating areas can enhance the usability of these spaces for older adults (Spliethoff et al., 2016). Furthermore, the presence of community gardens can facilitate intergenerational interactions, where younger community members assist older adults in gardening activities, thereby fostering social bonds and enhancing community cohesion (Anderson et al., 2019). This intergenerational engagement not only benefits older adults but also enriches the community as a whole, creating a supportive environment that values the contributions of all age groups (Harris et al., 2014).

Moreover, community gardens serve as platforms for educational programs that can empower older adults with knowledge about nutrition and sustainable practices. Such initiatives can promote healthier lifestyles and encourage older adults to take an active role in their food production, thereby enhancing their independence (Cepic & Tomićević-Dubljević, 2017). The social networks formed through participation in community gardening can also provide critical support systems for older adults, helping them navigate challenges related to aging and maintaining their independence (Symes et al., 2023). Overall, the integration of green infrastructure in urban planning is essential for fostering environments that support the independence and community integration of ageing populations.

3.2 Reducing Loneliness and Social Isolation

The psychological benefits of communal green spaces, particularly community gardens, are significant in addressing loneliness and social isolation among older adults (Reis da Silva, 2024b). Studies have shown that participation in community gardening can lead to increased social cohesion and a sense of belonging, which are crucial for mental health (White et al., 2023). The act of gardening itself has been associated with various psychological benefits, including reduced stress and anxiety, improved mood, and enhanced overall well-being (Poulsen et al., 2014). For older adults, who may face increased risks of loneliness due to retirement, loss of loved ones, or mobility limitations, communal gardening offers a meaningful way to connect with others and engage in fulfilling activities (Egli et al., 2016).

Case studies of inclusive urban designs highlight the effectiveness of community gardens in promoting social interaction among diverse populations. For instance, community gardens in urban settings have been shown to attract individuals from various backgrounds, fostering cross-cultural exchanges and building social capital (Roberts & Shackleton, 2018). These gardens not only provide fresh produce but also serve as spaces for community gatherings, workshops, and social events, thereby enhancing social ties among participants (Mitchell et al., 2014). The collaborative nature of gardening encourages teamwork and communication, which can further strengthen relationships and reduce feelings of isolation (Mehta et al., 2019).

Additionally, the design of community gardens can be tailored to meet the needs of older adults, ensuring that they are accessible and inviting. Features such as raised beds, accessible pathways, and shaded seating areas can make gardening activities more enjoyable and feasible for older participants (Nimrod, 2012; Reis da Silva, 2023b). By creating inclusive spaces that cater to the needs of all community members, urban planners can facilitate greater participation among older adults, ultimately contributing to their mental health and well-being. The positive impact of community gardens on social connectedness underscores the importance of integrating green infrastructure into urban planning as a strategy to combat loneliness and promote social inclusion for ageing populations.

4. GREEN INFRASTRUCTURE AND CHRONIC CONDITIONS

4.1 Oncology and Access to Therapeutic Natural Spaces

The relationship between green infrastructure and chronic health conditions, particularly in oncology, is increasingly recognised as a vital area of research. Therapeutic natural spaces, such as parks and gardens, have been shown to provide significant psychological and physical benefits for cancer patients (Reis da Silva, 2024c; Reis da Silva, 2024d). Access to these green spaces can enhance recovery by reducing stress and anxiety, which are common among individuals undergoing cancer treatment (Tsokani, 2023). Studies indicate that exposure to nature can lead to improved mood and emotional well-being, which are crucial for patients facing the challenges of chronic illness (Williams, 2023). Furthermore, therapeutic landscapes can serve as settings for rehabilitation programs, promoting physical activity and social interaction among cancer survivors (Tsokani, 2023).

Incorporating green infrastructure into healthcare settings, such as hospitals and treatment centres, can facilitate access to therapeutic natural spaces for oncology patients. For instance, gardens designed specifically for patients can provide a serene environment conducive to relaxation and recovery (Leppold et al., 2023). The presence of greenery has been associated with lower levels of pain and discomfort, contributing to a more positive treatment experience (Williams, 2023). Additionally, the integration of green spaces within healthcare facilities can encourage patients to engage in physical activity, which is essential for maintaining health and preventing the recurrence of cancer (Tsokani, 2023). Thus, the strategic planning of green infrastructure in urban areas can significantly enhance the quality of life for individuals battling chronic conditions like cancer.

4.2 Management of CKD and Other Chronic Diseases through Nature Exposure

Chronic kidney disease (CKD) and other chronic diseases can also benefit from exposure to natural environments (Reis da Silva, 2024e). Research has demonstrated that spending time in green spaces can improve overall health outcomes for individuals with CKD by promoting physical activity and reducing stress levels (Bae et al., 2021). Nature exposure has been linked to lower blood pressure, improved cardiovascular health, and enhanced mental well-being, all of which are critical for managing chronic diseases (Amati & Taylor, 2010). The calming effects of natural environments can help mitigate the psychological burden associated with chronic conditions, thereby improving patients' adherence to treatment regimens and lifestyle modifications (Palantzas, 2024).

Moreover, green infrastructure can play a role in creating supportive environments for individuals managing CKD and other chronic diseases. Community gardens and urban green spaces can serve as venues for health education programs, where individuals can learn about nutrition, exercise, and self-management strategies (Ouyang et al., 2018). These initiatives can foster a sense of community and support among participants, which is essential for promoting healthy behaviours and improving health outcomes (Inoue et al., 2011). By integrating green infrastructure into urban planning, cities can create environments that facilitate the management of chronic diseases and enhance the overall well-being of their residents.

4.3 Integration of Tailored Moving and Handling Practices

The integration of tailored moving and handling practices within green infrastructure can further enhance the health benefits for individuals with chronic conditions (Reis da Silva, 2023b). For instance, designing accessible pathways and spaces within parks and gardens can accommodate individuals with mobility challenges, ensuring that everyone can benefit from nature exposure (Ying et al., 2021). Implementing features such as gentle slopes, handrails, and resting areas can facilitate safe navigation for older adults and individuals with chronic illnesses, promoting their independence and encouraging regular use of these spaces (Horta Reis da Silva, 2022a; Horta Reis da Silva, 2022b; Song, 2024).

Additionally, training healthcare professionals to incorporate nature-based interventions into their practice can enhance the effectiveness of treatment for chronic conditions. For example, physical therapists can develop exercise programs that use green spaces, encouraging patients to engage in physical activity in a natural setting (Li & Lange, 2023). This approach not only improves physical health but also fosters emotional well-being by providing a pleasant and restorative environment for rehabilitation (Lomonaco, 2023). By integrating tailored moving and handling practices into the design and management of green infrastructure, cities can create inclusive spaces that support the health and well-being of individuals with chronic conditions.

4.4 Reducing Loneliness and Social Isolation

The role of green infrastructure in reducing loneliness and social isolation among individuals with chronic conditions cannot be overstated. Access to communal green spaces, such as parks and community gardens, provides opportunities for social interaction and engagement, which are essential for mental health (Suppakittpaisarn et al., 2017). Research has shown that participation in community gardening can foster social connections and create a sense of belonging among individuals facing chronic health challenges (Żarska et al., 2015). These social networks can provide emotional support and encouragement, helping individuals cope with the difficulties associated with their conditions (Calvert et al., 2018).

Moreover, the psychological benefits of communal green spaces extend beyond mere social interaction. Studies indicate that spending time in nature can enhance mood, reduce anxiety, and improve overall mental well-being (Bazán, 2023). For individuals with chronic conditions, these benefits can be particularly significant, as they often experience heightened levels of stress and emotional distress (Wang et al., 2019). By promoting access to green infrastructure, cities can help mitigate the negative psychological impacts of chronic illness and foster a sense of community among residents.

4.5 Case Studies of Inclusive Urban Designs

Several case studies illustrate the positive impact of inclusive urban designs that prioritize green infrastructure for individuals with chronic conditions. For instance, the implementation of community gardens in urban neighbourhoods has been shown to improve social cohesion and enhance the quality of life for residents, particularly for those with chronic illnesses (Drozdowski, 2024). These gardens not only provide fresh produce but also serve as spaces for social interaction and community engagement, thereby reducing feelings of isolation (Ou, 2023).

Another example can be found in cities that have integrated green spaces into healthcare facilities. Hospitals with healing gardens have reported improved patient satisfaction and reduced stress levels among patients undergoing treatment for chronic conditions (Khodadad et al., 2023). These gardens provide a tranquil environment for patients and their families, promoting relaxation and recovery (Dahal, 2024). By prioritising green infrastructure in urban planning, cities can create inclusive environments that support the health and well-being of individuals with chronic conditions.

5. DESIGNING URBAN SPACES FOR FALLS PREVENTION IN OLDER ADULTS

5.1 The Role of Green Spaces in Fall Prevention

Green spaces have been shown to positively influence the physical functioning of older adults, which is crucial for falls prevention. Research indicates that access to green and blue spaces can enhance physical activity levels among older adults, thereby improving balance, strength, and overall mobility (Lehrner, 2022). Regular engagement in physical activities, such as walking or gardening in these spaces, can significantly reduce the risk of falls by enhancing muscle strength and coordination (Hoof et al., 2018). Furthermore, environments that encourage outdoor activity can lead to increased social interactions, which are essential for maintaining mental health and reducing feelings of isolation (Mutani & Beltramino, 2022).

The design of urban green spaces must consider the specific needs of older adults to maximize their benefits. Features such as well-maintained pathways, adequate seating, and clear signage can facilitate safe navigation and encourage older adults to utilize these spaces (Endreny, 2018). Moreover, the incorporation of sensory elements, such as fragrant plants and textured surfaces, can enhance the experience of green spaces, making them more inviting and accessible for older users (Azzali et al., 2022). By prioritising safety and accessibility in the design of green spaces, urban planners can create environments that actively contribute to falls prevention.

5.2 Accessibility Considerations for Older Adults

Accessibility is a critical factor in designing urban spaces that support falls prevention among older adults (Reis da Silva, 2024a). Research has shown that the built environment significantly influences older adults' mobility and willingness to engage in outdoor activities (Buerkert & Schlecht, 2019; Reis da Silva, 2024a). Urban planners must ensure that pathways are smooth, wide, and free of obstacles to accommodate those with mobility aids, such as walkers or canes. Additionally, the installation of handrails, ramps, and non-slip surfaces in public spaces can further enhance safety for older adults (Isa et al., 2023; Reis da Silva, 2023b).

The social environment surrounding green spaces also plays a role in accessibility. Neighbourhoods with a higher proportion of older adults may require tailored interventions to address the unique challenges faced by this demographic (Cook et al., 2013). For instance, creating mixed-age neighbourhoods with diverse amenities can promote social interaction and support networks, which are essential for older adults' well-being (Rahman, 2019). Furthermore, involving older adults in the planning process can ensure that their needs and preferences are adequately addressed, leading to more effective and user-friendly urban designs (Jarzebski et al., 2021).

5.3 Reducing Loneliness and Social Isolation

The psychological benefits of green spaces extend beyond physical health; they also play a crucial role in reducing loneliness and social isolation among older adults (Reis da Silva, 2024b). Access to communal green spaces, such as parks and community gardens, provides opportunities for social interaction and engagement, which are vital for mental health (İnançoğlu et al., 2020). Studies have shown that participation in community gardening can foster social connections and create a sense of belonging among individuals facing chronic health challenges (Jurković, 2023).

These social networks can provide emotional support and encouragement, helping individuals cope with the difficulties associated with aging and maintaining mobility.

Moreover, the design of urban parks should include features that encourage social interaction, such as seating areas, picnic spots, and spaces for group activities. By creating environments that facilitate social engagement, urban planners can help mitigate the negative psychological impacts of loneliness and isolation, which are prevalent among older adults (Choi & Lee, 2019). The integration of green infrastructure into urban planning not only addresses physical health concerns but also promotes mental well-being, ultimately contributing to a higher quality of life for older residents.

5.4 Case Studies of Inclusive Urban Designs

Several case studies illustrate the positive impact of inclusive urban designs that prioritise green infrastructure for falls prevention among older adults. For instance, urban parks designed with the input of older adults have been shown to improve accessibility and usability, leading to increased physical activity and social interaction (Wildsmith et al., 2013). These parks often feature smooth pathways, ample seating, and shaded areas, making them more inviting for older users. Additionally, community gardens have been successful in fostering social connections and providing opportunities for physical activity, thereby reducing the risk of falls (Yin et al., 2014).

Another example can be found in cities that have integrated green spaces into healthcare facilities. Hospitals with healing gardens have reported improved patient satisfaction and reduced stress levels among patients undergoing treatment for chronic conditions (Wang & Zhang, 2020). These gardens provide a tranquil environment for patients and their families, promoting relaxation and recovery. By prioritising green infrastructure in urban planning, cities can create inclusive environments that support the health and well-being of individuals with chronic conditions, including those at risk of falls.

6. DESIGNING URBAN SPACES FOR HOLISTIC CARE

6.1 Integrative Health Approaches: Linking Physical Activity, Nutrition, and Mental Health

The design of urban spaces plays a crucial role in promoting holistic care for individuals, particularly older adults, by integrating physical activity, nutrition, and mental health. Urban environments that encourage physical activity through accessible parks, walking paths, and recreational areas can significantly enhance the overall health of residents. Research indicates that regular physical activity is associated with reduced risks of chronic diseases, improved mental health outcomes, and enhanced quality of life (Buerkert & Schlecht, 2019). For older adults, engaging in physical activities such as walking or gardening not only improves physical health but also fosters social connections, which are essential for mental well-being (Lehrner, 2022).

Moreover, urban spaces can be designed to promote healthy nutrition by incorporating community gardens and farmers' markets. These spaces provide access to fresh produce and encourage healthy eating habits among residents (Hoof et al., 2018). Community gardens, in particular, have been shown to improve food security and promote social interaction, thereby addressing both nutritional needs and social isolation (Isa et al., 2023). The integration of nutrition-focused initiatives within urban design can create environments that support healthy lifestyles and enhance the overall well-being of individuals.

Mental health is another critical component of holistic care that can be supported through thoughtful urban design. Access to green spaces has been linked to reduced levels of stress, anxiety, and depression (Cook et al., 2013). Urban planners can create environments that promote mental health by incorporating elements such as tranquil gardens, seating areas for social interaction, and spaces for mindfulness practices. By fostering environments that support physical activity, nutrition, and mental health, urban spaces can contribute to a comprehensive approach to holistic care.

6.2 Implications for Nursing Care and Patient-Centric Environments

The design of urban spaces has significant implications for nursing care and the development of patient-centric environments. Nurses play a vital role in advocating for the health and well-being of their patients, and understanding the impact of the built environment on health outcomes is essential for effective care delivery. Patient-centric environments that prioritize accessibility, safety, and social interaction can enhance the quality of care provided to individuals, particularly older adults (Azzali et al., 2022).

For instance, healthcare facilities located within or near green spaces can facilitate outdoor activities for patients, promoting physical rehabilitation and mental well-being (Endreny, 2018). Additionally, the integration of community resources, such as nutrition programs and social support networks, can empower nurses to address the holistic needs of their patients (Reis da Silva, 2024f; Reis da Silva, 2024g). By collaborating with urban planners and community organizations, nurses can advocate for the creation of environments that support healthy ageing and improve health outcomes (Rahman, 2019).

Furthermore, the emphasis on social connectedness in urban design aligns with the nursing profession's focus on holistic care. Nurses can leverage community resources to facilitate social interactions among patients, reducing feelings of loneliness and isolation (Mutani & Beltramino, 2022). By fostering connections between patients and their communities, nurses can enhance the overall health and well-being of individuals, ultimately leading to better health outcomes.

7. ALIGNMENT WITH SUSTAINABLE DEVELOPMENT GOALS (SDGS)

The integration of holistic care approaches within urban design aligns closely with the United Nations Sustainable Development Goals (SDGs), particularly those related to health, well-being, sustainable cities, and reduced inequalities. Goal 3 emphasises the importance of ensuring healthy lives and promoting well-being for all individuals, while Goal 11 focuses on making cities inclusive, safe, resilient, and sustainable (Jarzebski et al., 2021). By designing urban spaces that promote physical activity, nutrition, and mental health, cities can contribute to the achievement of these goals.

Moreover, the emphasis on reducing inequalities in access to health resources is critical in the context of urban design. Vulnerable populations, including older adults, often face barriers to accessing healthcare services and healthy food options (İnançoğlu et al., 2020). By creating inclusive urban environments that prioritise accessibility and social support, cities can work towards reducing health disparities and promoting equity in health outcomes (Jurković, 2023). This alignment with the SDGs underscores the importance of integrating holistic care approaches into urban planning and design.

7.1 Cross-Sector Collaboration for Sustainable Urban Interventions

Achieving the goals of holistic care in urban design requires cross-sector collaboration among various stakeholders, including healthcare providers, urban planners, community organizations, and policymakers. Collaborative efforts can facilitate the development of integrated interventions that address the multifaceted needs of individuals living in urban environments (Choi & Lee, 2019). For example, partnerships between healthcare providers and community organisations can lead to the establishment of programs that promote physical activity, nutrition education, and social engagement among residents (Wildsmith et al., 2013).

Additionally, engaging older adults in the planning process can ensure that their needs and preferences are considered in the design of urban spaces. Participatory approaches can empower individuals to take an active role in shaping their environments, leading to more effective and user-friendly designs (Yin et al., 2014). By fostering collaboration across sectors, cities can create sustainable urban interventions that promote holistic care and enhance the quality of life for residents.

8. POLICY RECOMMENDATIONS AND PRACTICAL STRATEGIES FOR DESIGNING URBAN SPACES FOR HOLISTIC CARE

8.1 Enhancing Cross-Disciplinary Collaboration in City Planning

To effectively design urban spaces that promote holistic care, it is essential to enhance cross-disciplinary collaboration among various stakeholders, including urban planners, healthcare professionals, social workers, and community organisations. This collaboration can facilitate the development of integrated urban environments that address the multifaceted needs of older adults and other vulnerable populations. For instance, urban planners can work closely with healthcare providers to identify areas where green spaces can be strategically placed to encourage physical activity and social interaction among older adults (Lehrner, 2022). By fostering partnerships between disciplines, cities can create environments that support health and well-being, ultimately leading to improved health outcomes for residents.

Furthermore, the establishment of interdisciplinary committees can help guide the planning process by ensuring that diverse perspectives are considered. These committees can include representatives from public health, urban design, social services, and community advocacy groups, allowing for a comprehensive approach to urban planning (Buerkert & Schlecht, 2019). Regular workshops and forums can also be organized to facilitate knowledge exchange and collaboration among stakeholders, ensuring that urban spaces are designed with the needs of all residents in mind.

8.2 Frameworks for Inclusive, Green Ageing Cities

Developing frameworks for inclusive, green ageing cities is crucial for promoting the health and well-being of older adults. These frameworks should prioritise accessibility, safety, and social engagement in urban design. For example, incorporating universal design principles can ensure that public spaces are accessible to individuals with varying mobility levels, including those who use wheelchairs or walkers (Hoof et al., 2018). Additionally, creating safe walking paths, well-maintained parks, and community gardens can encourage older adults to engage in physical activity and social interactions, reducing the risk of isolation and loneliness (Isa et al., 2023).

Moreover, urban spaces should be designed to promote healthy nutrition by integrating community gardens and farmers' markets. These initiatives can provide access to fresh produce and encourage healthy eating habits among residents (Cook et al., 2013). By fostering environments that support both physical activity and nutrition, cities can create holistic care frameworks that enhance the overall well-being of older adults and contribute to healthier communities.

8.3 Alignment with Sustainable Development Goals (SDGs)

The design of urban spaces for holistic care aligns closely with the United Nations Sustainable Development Goals (SDGs), particularly those related to health, well-being, sustainable cities, and reduced inequalities. Goal 3 emphasises the importance of ensuring healthy lives and promoting well-being for all individuals, while Goal 11 focuses on making cities inclusive, safe, resilient, and sustainable (Azzali et al., 2022). By designing urban spaces that promote physical activity, nutrition, and mental health, cities can contribute to the achievement of these goals.

Additionally, addressing health inequalities is critical in the context of urban design. Vulnerable populations, including older adults, often face barriers to accessing healthcare services and healthy food options (Endreny, 2018). By creating inclusive urban environments that prioritize accessibility and social support, cities can work towards reducing health disparities and promoting equity in health outcomes (Rahman, 2019). This alignment with the SDGs underscores the importance of integrating holistic care approaches into urban planning and design.

8.4 Cross-Sector Collaboration for Sustainable Urban Interventions

Achieving the goals of holistic care in urban design requires cross-sector collaboration among various stakeholders, including healthcare providers, urban planners, community organizations, and policymakers. Collaborative efforts can facilitate the development of integrated interventions that address the multifaceted needs of individuals living in urban environments (Mutani & Beltramino, 2022). For example, partnerships between healthcare providers and community organisations can lead to the establishment of programs that promote physical activity, nutrition education, and social engagement among residents (Jarzebski et al., 2021).

Furthermore, engaging older adults in the planning process can ensure that their needs and preferences are considered in the design of urban spaces. Participatory approaches can empower individuals to take an active role in shaping their environments, leading to more effective and user-friendly designs (İnançoğlu et al., 2020). By fostering collaboration across sectors, cities can create sustainable urban interventions that promote holistic care and enhance the quality of life for residents.

CONCLUSION

The intersection of population ageing and urbanisation presents significant challenges that require innovative solutions. The integration of green infrastructure into urban design is a promising strategy for enhancing the health and well-being of ageing populations. By prioritising access to green spaces and fostering social cohesion, cities can create environments that support the physical, mental, and emotional health of older adults. Furthermore, aligning urban planning efforts with the Sustainable Development Goals can ensure that the needs of ageing populations are addressed in a holistic and inclusive manner, ultimately contributing to the sustainability and resilience of urban communities.

Green infrastructure represents a multifaceted approach to urban planning that prioritizes ecological health and sustainability. By incorporating elements such as parks, gardens, and eco-corridors into urban design, cities can enhance biodiversity, improve public health, and create more resilient communities. The strategic integration of green infrastructure not only addresses the immediate challenges of urbanisation but also contributes to the long-term sustainability and liveability of urban environments.

The link between green infrastructure and ageing in place is evident through the promotion of independence, community integration, and the reduction of loneliness and social isolation. By prioritising the design and accessibility of community gardens and other green spaces, urban planners can create environments that support the health and well-being of older adults. The psychological benefits associated with communal gardening, coupled with the social connections fostered through these activities, highlight the critical role of green infrastructure in enhancing the quality of life for ageing populations.

The integration of green infrastructure into urban environments offers significant benefits for individuals managing chronic conditions, including oncology and CKD. Access to therapeutic natural spaces can enhance recovery, promote physical activity, and reduce stress levels. Moreover, tailored moving and handling practices can ensure that these spaces are accessible to all, fostering independence and community integration. By addressing loneliness and social isolation through communal green spaces, cities can improve the overall well-being of residents with chronic health challenges. The positive outcomes observed in case studies of inclusive urban designs underscore the importance of prioritizing green infrastructure in urban planning to support the health and quality of life for individuals with chronic conditions.

The design of urban spaces plays a crucial role in falls prevention among older adults. Green infrastructure, including parks, gardens, and accessible pathways, can significantly enhance physical functioning and promote social engagement, ultimately reducing the risk of falls. Accessibility considerations must be prioritised in urban planning to ensure that older adults can safely navigate their environments. By creating inclusive urban designs that foster social connections and support physical activity, cities can improve the quality of life for older residents and promote healthy ageing.

Designing urban spaces for holistic care involves integrating physical activity, nutrition, and mental health into the built environment. The implications for nursing care and patient-centric environments are significant, as nurses can advocate for designs that support the health and well-being of individuals. Furthermore, aligning urban design with the Sustainable Development Goals and fostering cross-sector collaboration can lead to sustainable interventions that address the diverse needs of urban populations. By prioritizing holistic care in urban planning, cities can create environments that promote health, well-being, and social connectedness for all residents.

REFERENCES

Amati, M., & Taylor, L. (2010). From green belts to green infrastructure. *Planning Practice and Research*, *25*(2), 143–155. DOI: 10.1080/02697451003740122

Anderson, E., Egerer, M., Fouch, N., Clarke, M., & Davidson, M. (2019). Comparing community garden typologies of Baltimore, Chicago, and New York city (USA) to understand potential implications for socio-ecological services. *Urban Ecosystems*, *22*(4), 671–681. DOI: 10.1007/s11252-019-00855-9

Azzali, S., Yew, A., Wong, C., & Chaiechi, T. (2022). Silver cities: Planning for an ageing population in Singapore. an urban planning policy case study of kampung admiralty. *Archnet-IJAR*, *16*(2), 281–306. DOI: 10.1108/ARCH-09-2021-0252

Bae, J., Sohn, W., Newman, G., Gu, D., Woodruff, S., Zandt, S., & Tran, T. (2021). A longitudinal analysis of green infrastructure conditions in coastal Texan cities. *Urban Forestry & Urban Greening*, *65*, 127315. DOI: 10.1016/j.ufug.2021.127315

Bazán, R. (2023). Enhancing urban water quality with green infrastructure – a study in Guadalupe, nuevo Leon, Mexico. *Ecological Engineering & Environmental Technology*, *24*(8), 216–224. DOI: 10.12912/27197050/171866

Bibri, S., & Krogstie, J. (2020). Smart eco-city strategies and solutions for sustainability: The cases of royal seaport, Stockholm, and western harbor, Malmö, Sweden. *Urban Science (Basel, Switzerland)*, *4*(1), 11. DOI: 10.3390/urbansci4010011

Buerkert, A., & Schlecht, E. (2019). Rural–urban transformation: A key challenge of the 21st century. *Nutrient Cycling in Agroecosystems*, *115*(2), 137–142. DOI: 10.1007/s10705-019-10008-1

Calvert, T., Sinnett, D., Smith, N., Jerome, G., Burgess, S., & King, L. (2018). Setting the standard for green infrastructure: The need for, and features of, a benchmark in England. *Planning Practice and Research*, *33*(5), 558–573. DOI: 10.1080/02697459.2018.1531580

Cepic, S., & Tomićević-Dubljević, J. (2017). Urban community and allotment gardens: Research trends and a look ahead. *Poljoprivreda i Sumarstvo*, *63*(4). Advance online publication. DOI: 10.17707/AgricultForest.63.4.20

Choi, J., & Lee, S. (2019). Application of habitat evaluation procedure with quantifying the eco-corridor in the process of environmental impact assessment. *International Journal of Environmental Research and Public Health*, *16*(8), 1437. DOI: 10.3390/ijerph16081437 PMID: 31018499

Cook, I., Gu, C., & Halsall, J. (2013). China's growing urban health inequalities: The challenges ahead. *Journal of Management and Sustainability*, *3*(2). Advance online publication. DOI: 10.5539/jms.v3n2p10

da Silva, T. H. R., & Rodrigues, E. C. P. (2023). Body Image Related Discrimination. In Leal Filho, W., Azul, A. M., Brandli, L., Lange Salvia, A., Özuyar, P. G., & Wall, T. (Eds.), *Reduced Inequalities. Encyclopedia of the UN Sustainable Development Goals*. Springer., DOI: 10.1007/978-3-319-71060-0_61-1

Dahal, A., Khatiwada, R., & Lekhak, B. (2024). Green infrastructure solutions for slope stabilization along the Kathmandu terai/Madhesh fast track road project. *KTFT J.*, *4*, 158–165. DOI: 10.3126/ktftj.v4i1.70440

Drozdowski, G., & Dziekański, P. (2024). Deconcentration of infrastructure and spatial diversification of entrepreneur-ship in powiats in Poland in 2010-2020. *Ekonomia I Prawo*, *23*(2). Advance online publication. DOI: 10.12775/EiP.2024.022

Egerer, M., Philpott, S., Bichier, P., Jha, S., Liere, H., & Lin, B. (2018). Gardener well-being along social and biophysical landscape gradients. *Sustainability (Basel)*, *10*(1), 96. DOI: 10.3390/su10010096

Egli, V., Oliver, M., & Tautolo, E. (2016). The development of a model of community garden benefits to wellbeing. *Preventive Medicine Reports*, *3*, 348–352. DOI: 10.1016/j.pmedr.2016.04.005 PMID: 27419035

Endreny, T. (2018). Strategically growing the urban forest will improve our world. *Nature Communications*, *9*(1), 1160. Advance online publication. DOI: 10.1038/s41467-018-03622-0 PMID: 29563541

Harris, N., Minniss, F., & Somerset, S. (2014). Refugees connecting with a new country through community food gardening. *International Journal of Environmental Research and Public Health*, *11*(9), 9202–9216. DOI: 10.3390/ijerph110909202 PMID: 25198684

Hoof, J., Kazak, J., Perek-Białas, J., & Peek, S. (2018). The challenges of urban ageing: Making cities age-friendly in Europe. *International Journal of Environmental Research and Public Health*, *15*(11), 2473. DOI: 10.3390/ijerph15112473 PMID: 30714577

Horta Reis Da Silva, T. (2022a). Moving and Handling. In Curr, S., & Fordham-Clarke, C. (Eds.), *Clinical Skills at Glance* (pp. 20–21). Wiley.

Horta Reis Da Silva, T. (2022b). Moving and Handling: turning in bed, transfer and hoisting. In Curr, S., & Fordham-Clarke, C. (Eds.), *Clinical Skills at Glance* (pp. 22–23). Wiley.

İnançoğlu, S., Özden, Ö., & Kara, C. (2020). Green corridors in urban landscapes, case study Nicosia Pedieos river. *European Journal of Sustainable Development, 9*(1), 1. DOI: 10.14207/ejsd.2020.v9n1p1

Inoue, K., Sugimoto, M., Shimizu, H., Onishi, A., Murayama, A., & Otsuki, A. (2011). Effect of perviousness oriented streets design in Nagoya city applying the concept of green infrastructure. *Journal of Architecture and Planning. Nihon Kenchiku Gakkai Keikaku-Kei Rombunshu, 76*(660), 335–340. DOI: 10.3130/aija.76.335

Isa, W., Suhaimi, A., Noordin, N., Sobri, S., Hamid, N., Salleh, A., & Rosli, N. (2023). It problem solving formalisms for urban ageing. *International Journal of Academic Research in Business & Social Sciences, 13*(1). Advance online publication. DOI: 10.6007/IJARBSS/v13-i1/15167

Ito, H. (2019). Strategies in promoting eco-policies: The case of Toyama city, Japan. *Asian Social Science, 15*(5), 34. DOI: 10.5539/ass.v15n5p34

Jarzebski, M., Elmqvist, T., Gasparatos, A., Fukushi, K., Eckersten, S., Haase, D., Goodness, J., Khoshkar, S., Saito, O., Takeuchi, K., Theorell, T., Dong, N., Kasuga, F., Watanabe, R., Sioen, G. B., Yokohari, M., & Pu, J. (2021). Ageing and population shrinking: Implications for sustainability in the urban century. *NPJ Urban Sustainability, 1*(1), 17. Advance online publication. DOI: 10.1038/s42949-021-00023-z

Jurković, Ž., & Lovoković, D. (2023). Corridor planning–sustainable planning? *Sustainability (Basel), 15*(21), 15502. DOI: 10.3390/su152115502

Khodadad, M., Aguilar-Barajas, I., & Khan, A. (2023). Green infrastructure for urban flood resilience: A review of recent literature on bibliometrics, methodologies, and typologies. *Water (Basel), 15*(3), 523. DOI: 10.3390/w15030523

Lehrner, S. (2022). Sustainable and future-oriented urban development in Vienna & Barcelona. *International Journal of Sustainable Development Research, 8*(2), 25. DOI: 10.11648/j.ijsdr.20220802.11

Leppold, C., Lockery, J., Burns, P., Brady, K., O'Donnell, M., Ryan, J., & Gibbs, L. (2023). Tracking post-disaster chronic disease: Protocol for the recover cohort study. *Prehospital and Disaster Medicine, 38*(S1), s67–s68. DOI: 10.1017/S1049023X23002029

Li, L., & Lange, K. (2023). Assessing the relationship between urban blue-green infrastructure and stress resilience in real settings: A systematic review. *Sustainability (Basel), 15*(12), 9240. DOI: 10.3390/su15129240

Liu, Y., & Feng, Y. (2016). Simulating the impact of economic and environmental strategies on future urban growth scenarios in Ningbo, China. *Sustainability (Basel)*, *8*(10), 1045. DOI: 10.3390/su8101045

Liu, Y., Lu, Y., Xu, D., Zhou, H., & Zhang, S. (2024). Enhancing the MSPA method to incorporate ecological sensitivity: Construction of ecological security patterns in Harbin city. *Sustainability (Basel)*, *16*(7), 2875. DOI: 10.3390/su16072875

Lomonaco, P. (2023). Large scale laboratory observations of wave force reduction on coastal buildings by an idealized mangrove forest. *Coastal Engineering Proceedings*, (37), 87. https://doi.org/DOI: 10.9753/icce.v37.structures.87

Lv, L., Zhang, S., Zhu, J., Wang, Z., Wang, Z., Li, G., & Chen, Y. (2022). Ecological restoration strategies for mountainous cities based on ecological security patterns and circuit theory: A case of central urban areas in Chongqing, China. *International Journal of Environmental Research and Public Health*, *19*(24), 16505. DOI: 10.3390/ijerph192416505 PMID: 36554384

Mehta, A., Rakholia, S., Yosef, R., Bhatt, A., & Shukla, S. (2024). Regional sustainability through dispersal and corridor use of Asiatic lion *Panthera leo persica* in the eastern greater GIR landscape. *Sustainability (Basel)*, *16*(6), 2554. DOI: 10.3390/su16062554

Mehta, K., Lopresti, S., & Thomas, J. (2019). Addressing nutrition and social connection through community gardening: A south Australian study. *Health Promotion Journal of Australia*, *30*(S1), 5–8. DOI: 10.1002/hpja.235 PMID: 30742727

Mitchell, R., Spliethoff, H., Ribaudo, L., Lopp, D., Shayler, H., Marquez-Bravo, L., Lambert, V. T., Ferenz, G. S., Russell-Anelli, J. M., Stone, E. B., & McBride, M. (2014). Lead (pb) and other metals in New York city community garden soils: Factors influencing contaminant distributions. *Environmental Pollution*, *187*, 162–169. DOI: 10.1016/j.envpol.2014.01.007 PMID: 24502997

Mutani, G., & Beltramino, S. (2022). Geospatial assessment and modeling of outdoor thermal comfort at urban scale. *International Journal of Heat and Technology*, *40*(4), 871–878. DOI: 10.18280/ijht.400402

Nimrod, G. (2012). The benefits of and constraints to participation in seniors' online communities. *Leisure Studies*, *33*(3), 247–266. DOI: 10.1080/02614367.2012.697697

Ou, J., Li, J., Li, X., & Zhang, J. (2023). Planning and design strategies for green stormwater infrastructure from an urban design perspective. *Water (Basel)*, *16*(1), 29. DOI: 10.3390/w16010029

Ouyang, Y., Xu, Z., Fan, E., Liu, Y., Miyake, K., Xu, X., & Zhang, L. (2018). Changes in gene expression in chronic allergy mouse model exposed to natural environmental pm2.5-rich ambient air pollution. *Scientific Reports*, *8*(1), 6326. Advance online publication. DOI: 10.1038/s41598-018-24831-z PMID: 29679058

Palantzas, A. (2024). Air pollution and chronic respiratory diseases: a modern challenge for sustainable urban mobility. *E3s Web of Conferences*, 585, 06006. https://doi.org/DOI: 10.1051/e3sconf/202458506006

Poulsen, M., Hulland, K., Gulas, C., Pham, H., Dalglish, S., Wilkinson, R., & Winch, P. (2014). Growing an urban oasis: A qualitative study of the perceived benefits of community gardening in Baltimore, Maryland. *Culture, Agriculture, Food and Environment*, *36*(2), 69–82. DOI: 10.1111/cuag.12035

Rahman, M. (2019). Health care in aged population: A global public health challenge. *Journal of Medicine (Dhaka)*, *20*(2), 95–97. DOI: 10.3329/jom.v20i2.42010

Reis da Silva, T. H. (2023a). Falls assessment and prevention in the nursing home and community. *British Journal of Community Nursing*, *28*(2), 68–72. DOI: 10.12968/bjcn.2023.28.2.68 PMID: 36735363

Reis da Silva, T. H. (2023b). Moving and Handling in the Community. *British Journal of Community Nursing*, *28*(8), 369. DOI: 10.12968/bjcn.2023.28.8.369 PMID: 37527217

Reis da Silva, T. H. (2023c). Ageing in place: Ageing at home and in the community. *British Journal of Community Nursing*, *28*(5), 213–214. DOI: 10.12968/bjcn.2023.28.5.213 PMID: 37130715

Reis da Silva, T. H. (2024a). Falls prevention in older people and the role of nursing. *British Journal of Community Nursing*, *29*(7), 335–339. DOI: 10.12968/bjcn.2024.0005 PMID: 38963269

Reis da Silva, T. H. (2024b). Loneliness in older adults. *British Journal of Community Nursing*, *29*(2), 60–66. DOI: 10.12968/bjcn.2024.29.2.60 PMID: 38300245

Reis da Silva, T. H (2024c). Oncology and Cancer Medicine: Understanding the complexities in Older Patients. *Biomed J Sci & Tech Res* 55(3)-2024. DOI: https://doi.org/DOI: 10.26717/BJSTR.2024.55.008720

Reis da Silva, T. H. (2024d). Death and its significance in Nursing Practice. *Palliative Medicine & Care International Journal*, *4*(3), 1–7.

Reis da Silva, T. H. (2024e). Chronic kidney disease in older adults: Nursing implications for community nurses. *Journal of Kidney Care*, *9*(4), 174–179. DOI: 10.12968/jokc.2024.9.4.174

Reis da Silva, T. H. (2024f). Understanding body fluid balance, dehydration and intravenous fluid therapy. *Emergency Nurse*. Advance online publication. DOI: 10.7748/en.2024.e2201 PMID: 38978385

Reis da Silva, T. H. (2024g). Can supplementing vitamin B12 improve mental health outcomes?: A literature review. *British Journal of Community Nursing*, *29*(3), 137–146. DOI: 10.12968/bjcn.2024.29.3.137 PMID: 38421889

Roberts, S., & Shackleton, C. (2018). Temporal dynamics and motivations for urban community food gardens in medium-sized towns of the eastern cape, south Africa. *Land (Basel)*, *7*(4), 146. DOI: 10.3390/land7040146

Soga, M., Cox, D., Yamaura, Y., Gaston, K., Kurisu, K., & Hanaki, K. (2017). Health benefits of urban allotment gardening: Improved physical and psychological well-being and social integration. *International Journal of Environmental Research and Public Health*, *14*(1), 71. DOI: 10.3390/ijerph14010071 PMID: 28085098

Song, J., Hemingway, J., & Park, C. S. (2024). Perspective swap from central Europe to East Asia: How relevant is urban environmental acupuncture in small-scale green space development in the context of the republic of Korea? *Land (Basel)*, *13*(3), 298. DOI: 10.3390/land13030298

Spliethoff, H., Mitchell, R., Shayler, H., Marquez-Bravo, L., Russell-Anelli, J., Ferenz, G., & McBride, M. (2016). Estimated lead (Pb) exposures for a population of urban community gardeners. *Environmental Geochemistry and Health*, *38*(4), 955–971. DOI: 10.1007/s10653-016-9790-8 PMID: 26753554

Suppakittpaisarn, P., Jiang, X., & Sullivan, W. (2017). Green infrastructure, green stormwater infrastructure, and human health: A review. *Current Landscape Ecology Reports*, *2*(4), 96–110. DOI: 10.1007/s40823-017-0028-y

Symes, L., Hadgraft, N., Marsh, P., Nuttman, S., & Kingsley, J. (2023). 'surrounding yourself with beauty': Exploring the health promotion potential of a rural garden appreciation group. *Health Promotion International*, *38*(2), daad010. Advance online publication. DOI: 10.1093/heapro/daad010 PMID: 36840528

Tsokani, A., Dimopoulos, T., Vourazanis, E., Strimpakos, N., Billis, E., Pepera, G., & Kapreli, E. (2023). Barriers and facilitators for therapeutic green exercise in patients with chronic conditions: A qualitative focus group study. *Applied Sciences (Basel, Switzerland)*, *13*(18), 10077. DOI: 10.3390/app131810077

Wang, D., & Glicksman, A. (2013). “being grounded”: Benefits of gardening for older adults in low-income housing. *Journal of Housing for the Elderly*, *27*(1-2), 89–104. DOI: 10.1080/02763893.2012.754816

Wang, H., Dai, X., Wu, J., Wu, X., & Nie, X. (2019). Influence of urban green open space on residents’ physical activity in China. *BMC Public Health*, *19*(1), 1093. Advance online publication. DOI: 10.1186/s12889-019-7416-7 PMID: 31409316

Wang, H., & Zhang, P. (2020). Urban green corridors analysis for a rapid urbanization city exemplified in Gaoyou city, Jiangsu. *Forests*, *11*(12), 1374. DOI: 10.3390/f11121374

White, M., Hamlin, I., Butler, C., & Richardson, M. (2023). The joy of birds: The effect of rating for joy or counting garden bird species on wellbeing, anxiety, and nature connection. *Urban Ecosystems*, *26*(3), 755–765. DOI: 10.1007/s11252-023-01334-y

Wildsmith, D., Smith, P., Baru, K., & Depok, U. (2013). From bricks to bytes: Digitizing green cities. *International Journal of Technology*, *4*(3), 269. DOI: 10.14716/ijtech.v4i3.114

Williams, A., Goss, D., & Hardman, C. A. (2023). Greening therapeutic spaces - the impact of green infrastructure on people affected by neurological conditions. *Appetite*, *189*, 106698. DOI: 10.1016/j.appet.2023.106698

Yin, K., Wang, R., An, Q., Yao, L., & Liang, J. (2014). Using eco-efficiency as an indicator for sustainable urban development: A case study of Chinese provincial capital cities. *Ecological Indicators*, *36*, 665–671. DOI: 10.1016/j.ecolind.2013.09.003

Ying, J., Zhang, X., Yi-qi, Z., & Bilan, S. (2021). Green infrastructure: Systematic literature review. *Ekonomska Istrazivanja*, *35*(1), 343–366. DOI: 10.1080/1331677X.2021.1893202

Żarska, B., Fornal-Pieniak, B., & Zaras-Januszkiewicz, E. (2015). Shaping the landscape of rural communes in the aspect of green infrastructure creation. *Barometr Regionalny Analizy I Prognozy*, *13*(1), 47–52. DOI: 10.56583/br.962

Zellmer, A., & Goto, B. (2022). Urban wildlife corridors: Building bridges for wildlife and people. *Frontiers in Sustainable Cities*, *4*, 954089. Advance online publication. DOI: 10.3389/frsc.2022.954089

Chapter 9
Harnessing the Power of Digital Transformation to Promote Sustainable Growth Enabling Companies and Societies to Build a Durable and Inclusive Future

Ananya Shukla
https://orcid.org/0009-0000-8578-4382
Christ University, India

Shiv Kumar Singh Pundhir
https://orcid.org/0000-0001-6249-6943
Christ University, India

ABSTRACT

This chapter explores the critical role of digital transformation in fostering sustainable development across various industries. It highlights how advanced technologies such as the Internet of Things, artificial intelligence, and big data analytics enhance environmental sustainability by improving operational efficiency and enabling informed decision-making. Key issues discussed include the connections between digital transformation and environmental sustainability, as well as the challenges organizations face during implementation. The chapter includes case studies demonstrating the successful use of digital technologies to address environmental

DOI: 10.4018/979-8-3693-9755-8.ch009

challenges like air and water pollution and promote resource conservation. It emphasizes the importance of ethical leadership and stakeholder engagement in guiding digital initiatives toward genuine sustainability goals. Finally, the chapter presents a comprehensive framework for leveraging digital transformation to encourage sustainable behaviors and achieve global sustainability objectives.

1.INTRODUCTION

The 21st century marks a pivotal era characterized by the rapid evolution of technology and its profound influence on societal structures.A new age of digitalisation has begun with the introduction of Industry 4.0, fundamentally altering how we live, work, and interact (Vial, 2019). This transformative wave is driven by the integration of digital technology into every facet of society and the economy, making digitalization a pivotal force for change in the digital era. As Businesses aim to maintain their sustainability and competitiveness, digital transformation (DT) has emerged as a strategic priority across various sectors. Defined by Hanelt*etal.,* as "organizational change triggered and shaped by the widespread diffusion of digital technologies," digital transformation encompasses a broad spectrum of technological advancements, including artificial intelligence, big data analytics, cloud computing, and the Internet of Things (IoT) (Hanelt*et al.,* 2020). These technologies enable companies to adapt to shifting customer expectations, disruptive market forces, globalization, and evolving regulatory landscapes (Lyu& Liu, 2021).

The importance of digital transformation has been underscored dramatically by recent global events, particularly the COVID-19 pandemic. This crisis forced organizations to pivot rapidly, adopting digital solutions to maintain operations in an unprecedented environment. Businesses that had previously been hesitant to embrace technology found themselves compelled to transition to remote work and online services. This swift adaptation highlighted technology as a lifeline, demonstrating how digital capabilities could sustain operations amidst significant disruptions. As we emerge from the immediate impacts of the pandemic, it has become clear that many organizations are now adopting hybrid work models that blend remote and in-office work. This shift signifies a broader acceptance of digitalization as a core component of business strategy (Erten& Antonio Ocampo, 2021). The adaptability exhibited by businesses during the pandemic underscores the critical need for digital resilience. Organizations that embraced digital tools demonstrated remarkable agility, navigating market uncertainties with innovative approaches.

For instance, educational institutions that rapidly adopted online learning platforms were able to continue their mission despite physical restrictions, illustrating the importance of digital skills in today's workforce (Alsoud&Harasis, 2021; Dima *et al.,* 2021; Eri *et al.,* 2021). The necessity for organizations to cultivate digital resilience as a key determinant of success in overcoming unforeseen challenges cannot be overstated (Piro că*et al.,* 2021). As businesses reflect on their experiences during the pandemic, the importance of integrating digital transformation into long-term strategies becomes evident. Companies that have invested in digital capabilities are better positioned to respond to future crises and capitalize on emerging opportunities.

Amidst this backdrop of rapid digital transformation, sustainability emerges as a paramount concern for organizations today. The convergence of global challenges—such as the COVID-19 pandemic, energy crises, climate change, and political instability—along with heightened stakeholder expectations, necessitates the development of ongoing competitive advantages in a rapidly evolving market (Reuschl*et al.,* 2022; Jia & Li, 2020). Sustainability, a multifaceted concept encompassing economic, environmental, and social dimensions, aims to satisfy current demands without endangering the capacity of future generations to satisfy their own. (Baumgartner &Rauter, 2017 ; Ghobakhloo, 2020 ; Guandalini, 2022). This delicate balance is particularly relevant in the context of the United Nations' 2030 Agenda, which identifies digital technologies as vital tools for achieving the Sustainable Development Goals (SDGs)

The adoption of the SDGs by the United Nations in September 2015 marked a significant milestone in the global commitment to fostering a sustainable future. These 17 goals, encapsulated within the framework of "a plan of action for people, planet, and prosperity," aim to "shift the world onto a sustainable and resilient path" ("Transforming governance for the Sustainable Development Agenda of 2030," 2015). Within this context, digital transformation emerges as a crucial enabler for achieving sustainability. By leveraging digital technologies, businesses and communities can innovate and create systems that promote economic growth while addressing social and environmental challenges. This interplay between digital transformation and sustainability is not just a theoretical concept; it has practical implications for how organizations operate and engage with stakeholders.

Recent studies have highlighted both the potential benefits and uncertainties associated with the relationship between digital transformation and sustainability (Kiron & Unruh, 2018). While many scholars agree that digital transformation can serve as an effective tool for enhancing sustainability, others raise critical questions about its actual impact on achieving the SDGs (Akande *et al.,* 2019). This divergence of perspectives reflects a broader debate about the implications of digitalization for ecological, economic, and social systems. On one hand, digital technologies offer transformative possibilities. For instance, data analytics can optimize resource use, artificial intelligence can enhance decision-making processes, and the Internet of Things (IoT) can facilitate more efficient operations across industries. These innovations enable organizations to minimize waste, reduce emissions, and improve overall sustainability.

However, as Beier et al. noted, "it remains unclear whether the digital transformation of the economy can be reconciled with the goals of sustainable development" (Dhingra, 2021). This statement highlights the necessity of a nuanced understanding of how digital transformation interacts with sustainability initiatives. Brenner et al. also emphasize the complexities involved in this relationship, stating: "Although digitalization offers new pathways and (unseen) possibilities, its potential to achieve or impede sustainability of ecological, economic, and social human systems remains unclear" (Brenner &Hartl, 2021). This ambivalence underscores the importance of critically examining both the positive and negative ramifications of digital transformation.

The concerns regarding the impact of digitalization on sustainability are particularly relevant in the context of corporate social responsibility (CSR). As organizations strive to align their business strategies with sustainable practices, they must navigate the intricacies of digital transformation. This journey requires a commitment to not only leveraging technology for operational efficiency but also ensuring that these advancements contribute meaningfully to societal and environmental goals. For example, while digital tools can enhance productivity and innovation, they can also lead to increased energy consumption and electronic waste if not managed responsibly.

As such, companies need to adopt a holistic approach to digital transformation—one that integrates sustainability into the core of their operations and decision-making processes (Verhoef *et al.,* 2021). By doing so, businesses can create value not just for themselves but for the communities and ecosystems they are part of. The connection between sustainable business development and digital transformation warrants further exploration. Digitalization empowers corporate innovation, leading to improvements in financial performance, operational efficiency, and environmental stewardship (Fernandez-Vidal *et al.,* 2022) . Organizations that leverage digital tools can streamline processes, reduce waste, and enhance resource management, contributing to more sustainable practices. Furthermore, the integration of green technologies within the framework of digital transformation enhances the potential for achieving the SDGs. Companies that adopt sustainable practices through innovative technologies can mitigate their environmental footprint while simultaneously driving growth and profitability.

This symbiotic relationship between digitalization and sustainability aligns with CSR principles, enabling organizations to fulfill their ethical obligations to stakeholders and society at large. As we look toward the future, the imperative for businesses and communities is clear: leveraging the potential of digital transformation to foster sustainable growth is not merely an option; it is a necessity. By embracing digital technologies, organizations can create resilient and inclusive systems that address the pressing challenges of our time. This transformation empowers businesses to innovate responsibly, engage with their communities meaningfully, and contribute to a sustainable future for all.

In addition to exploring the interplay between digital transformation and sustainability, it is essential to consider the role of localization in achieving the SDGs. Localization involves adapting strategies to fit local contexts, ensuring that digital solutions address the unique challenges faced by communities. For instance, in developing regions, mobile technologies can enhance access to information and services, empowering individuals and fostering economic growth. In urban areas, smart city initiatives can improve resource management and reduce environmental impacts, contributing to more sustainable urban living.

The integration of digital transformation into local governance supports corporate social responsibility initiatives. By leveraging digital tools to enhance CSR efforts, companies can foster stronger relationships with local communities. For example, businesses can utilize technologies that promote sustainability such as renewable energy solutions to demonstrate their commitment to the SDGs while simultaneously driving innovation. This creates a positive feedback loop where businesses not only contribute to sustainable growth but also benefit from the trust and loyalty of consumers who prioritize ethical practices.According to Pareek & Mathur, 2022, green marketing tactics have been used as part of Corporate Social Responsibility (CSR), with a focus on environmental conservation. As we embrace digital transformation to support sustainable growth, CSR, sustainability, and green marketing become more and more entwined. By using digital tools and initiatives, businesses have the opportunity to build more ethical and ecologically sustainable companies that benefit the environment and contribute to a more resilient and inclusive future for everybody.

Furthermore, the integration of digital tools and green technologies can enhance operational efficiencies, which directly contribute to a company's sustainability goals. For instance, smart manufacturing techniques can reduce resource consumption and waste, enabling companies to align their operations with environmental stewardship principles (Ferreira *et al.,* 2019). Utilizing data analytics to monitor and optimize supply chains can lead to significant reductions in carbon footprints, highlighting the potential for technology to drive sustainable practices across industries.

As we delve deeper into the complexities of digital transformation and sustainability, the necessity of inclusivity becomes increasingly evident. The benefits of digital advancements must extend to all members of society, ensuring equitable access to opportunities and resources. By fostering digital literacy and ensuring that marginalized communities have access to technology, organizations can empower these groups, allowing them to participate actively in the digital economy. This empowerment is crucial for creating resilient societies capable of adapting to changes and challenges, making sure nobody is left behind in the pursuit of sustainable growth.

Moreover, the challenges posed by the digital divide underscore the importance of addressing disparities in technology access. Bridging this divide is essential not only for fostering inclusive economic growth but also for achieving broader sustainability goals. Initiatives aimed at improving digital literacy and access to technology in underserved communities can catalyze local development and innovation, further contributing to the attainment of the SDGs. As we look toward a future increasingly defined by digital technologies, the ongoing dialogue around the relationship between digital transformation and sustainability reflects the need for continuous research and innovation.

The implications of these advancements for society and the environment are profound, necessitating a collaborative approach among stakeholders. Governments, businesses, and communities must work together to harness the potential of digital technologies responsibly, ensuring that they contribute to sustainable development in meaningful ways. The confluence of digital transformation and sustainability is not merely an academic interest; it is a critical area of inquiry that can shape the future of global development. By exploring this intersection, we can uncover valuable insights into how organizations can thrive while simultaneously addressing pressing social and environmental issues.

To further illustrate the potential of digital transformation in promoting sustainability, let us examine specific case studies from various sectors. For instance, in the energy sector, companies that utilize smart grids and renewable energy technologies are not only reducing their carbon footprints but are also enhancing energy efficiency. By integrating IoT devices into energy management systems, these organizations can optimize energy usage, lower costs, and contribute to climate action goals. Additionally, digital platforms that facilitate peer-to-peer energy trading empower consumers to participate in the renewable energy economy, fostering greater engagement with sustainability efforts.

In the transportation sector, the rise of electric and autonomous vehicles demonstrates the potential for technology to drive sustainable mobility solutions. Companies investing in electric vehicle infrastructure are contributing to reduced greenhouse gas emissions while also addressing urban congestion challenges. Moreover, ride-sharing platforms leverage digital technologies to optimize transportation networks, promoting efficient use of resources and reducing the overall environmental impact of travel.

The agriculture sector also stands to benefit significantly from digital transformation. Precision agriculture techniques, powered by data analytics and IoT sensors, enable farmers to monitor crop health, optimize resource use, and enhance yields while minimizing environmental impact. This approach not only supports food security but also promotes sustainable agricultural practices, aligning with the SDGs related to hunger and sustainable consumption.

As we reflect on these examples, it becomes evident that the integration of digital transformation into various sectors offers a pathway to achieving sustainability goals. However, this potential is accompanied by complexities and uncertainties that must be addressed. Organizations must navigate the ethical considerations of technology deployment, ensuring that digital tools are used responsibly and inclusively. This requires a commitment to transparency, accountability, and stakeholder engagement throughout the transformation process.

Furthermore, as we explore the relationship between digital transformation and sustainability, it is essential to acknowledge the role of policy and regulation in shaping outcomes. Governments have a crucial part to play in creating an enabling environment for digital innovation while ensuring that sustainability remains a priority. By developing policies that incentivize responsible technology use and sustainable practices, governments can guide organizations toward achieving their sustainability objectives.

In conclusion, the intersection of digital transformation and sustainability presents a powerful opportunity for organizations to redefine their approaches to growth and development. By understanding and harnessing the relationship between these concepts, businesses can position themselves as leaders in the quest for sustainable solutions. This endeavor is essential not only for their success but also for the well-being of future generations, underscoring the critical role of innovation in achieving a more resilient and inclusive world.

The journey toward sustainable development in the digital age requires a collective commitment to embracing the opportunities presented by digital transformation while remaining vigilant about its potential pitfalls. By fostering a culture of responsible innovation, organizations can enhance their operational capabilities and contribute to a more equitable and sustainable world for all. Through collaboration, innovation, and a commitment to sustainability, we can create a future that honors the principles of social responsibility while striving to meet the aspirations set forth in the SDGs. Ultimately, it is through a collaborative and informed approach that we can unlock the full potential of digital transformation in the service of a sustainable world.

1.2 The purpose of the study

This research aims to investigate the vital link between digital transformation and sustainable development, with a special emphasis on how new technologies might improve environmental sustainability. As organisations face growing demand to address environmental issues, this study seeks to discover how digital technologies might be integrated into sustainability practices to increaseboth operational efficiency and environmental stewardship.

The research will look at how various digital technologies, such as artificial intelligence, big data analytics, and the Internet of Things, may be used to achieve sustainability goals. The research aims to identify best practices that organisations may use to efficiently incorporate these technologies while minimising their environmental impact by analysing case studies and industry guidelines.Furthermore, the study will identify possible impediments and problems that businesses may face during their digital transformation journeys, such as resistance to change and the need for upskilling. The study's detailed analysis intends to add to the larger discussion on the role of technology in furthering sustainable development goals. Finally, this study aims to give practical insights for corporate leaders and policymakers on how to use digital transformation to generate positive environmental results, encouraging a future that is more sustainable and resilient for all stakeholders.

1.3 Scope and Limitations

This chapter examines the role of digital transformation in promoting sustainable development, focusing on how technologies like AI, big data, and the Internet of Things can improve environmental sustainability. It explores case studies illustrating successful initiatives and discusses strategic frameworks for integrating digital solutions into sustainability efforts. However, the chapter acknowledges limitations, including the rapid evolution of digital technologies, which may render some information outdated. Additionally, examples may be region-specific, and the qualitative insights provided lack comprehensive quantitative data. Ultimately, the effectiveness of these initiatives depends on the commitment of diverse stakeholders across various contexts.

Figure 1. Conceptual Framework

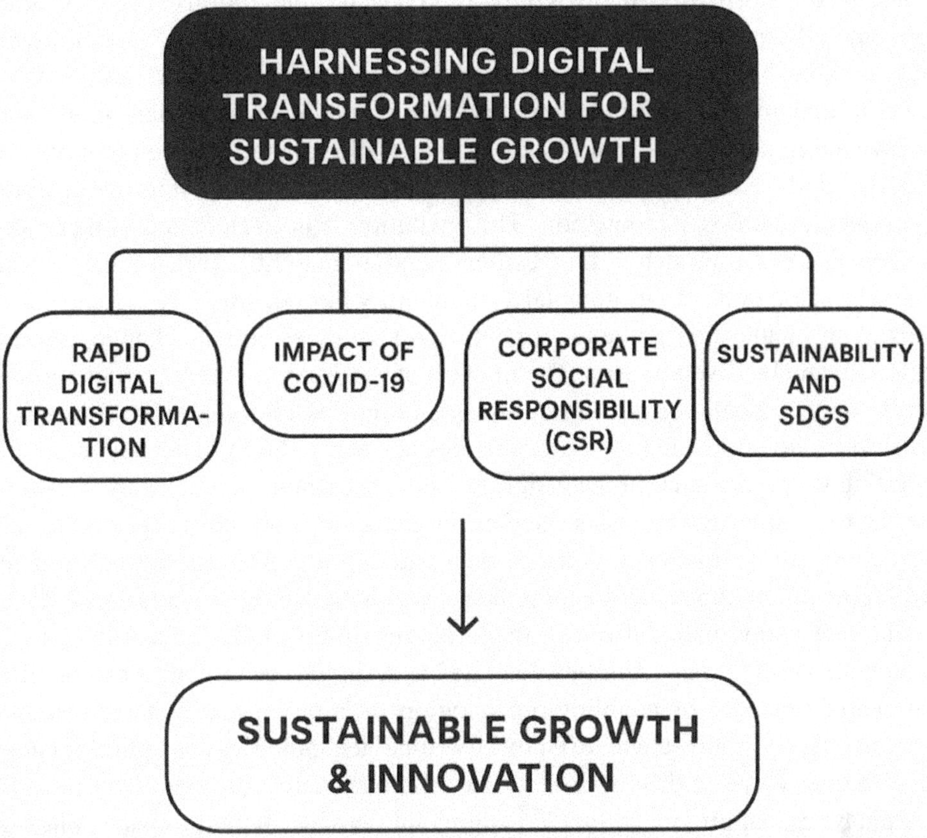

2. LITERATURE REVIEW

In today's rapidly evolving business landscape, digital transformation and environmental sustainability have emerged as crucial elements that organizations must navigate to thrive. The integration of digital technologies fundamentally reshapes operational frameworks, customer interactions, and overall business models. Concurrently, there is an increasing urgency for businesses to adopt sustainable practices in response to escalating environmental challenges and regulatory pressures.

Digital transformation involves the comprehensive integration of digital technologies into all aspects of an organization, significantly altering how it operates and delivers value. This transformation goes beyond technological upgrades; it encompasses a fundamental shift in culture, processes, and business models. Companies are leveraging advanced technologies such as artificial intelligence (AI), big data analytics, and the Internet of Things (IoT) to enhance efficiency, improve customer experiences, and foster innovation. This evolution is not solely about operational efficiency; it is also about building resilience and adaptability in a fast-paced market.

At the same time, environmental sustainability has become a core focus for organizations as they recognize the urgent need to address climate change, resource depletion, and biodiversity loss. The impacts of these environmental challenges are increasingly evident, compelling businesses to rethink their operational practices. Consumers, investors, and regulatory bodies are demanding greater accountability regarding corporate social responsibility, and sustainable practices are becoming integral to long-term business strategies. Organizations are now expected to minimize their environmental footprints, necessitating a commitment to sustainable development that harmonizes economic growth with ecological preservation.

The intersection of digital transformation and environmental sustainability presents both challenges and opportunities. On one hand, digital technologies can facilitate sustainable practices by enabling organizations to monitor and manage resources more effectively. For instance, IoT-powered smart technologies can optimize energy usage, reduce waste, and enhance resource efficiency across various operations. Big data analytics can provide valuable insights into environmental impacts, allowing companies to identify areas for improvement. On the other hand, the environmental implications of digital technologiessuch as energy consumption from data centers and electronic wasteraise critical questions about the sustainability of these innovations.

This literature review aims to explore the complex relationships between digital transformation and environmental sustainability, particularly focusing on the role of emerging technologies in promoting sustainable practices. Key themes will include the implications of big data and analytics for sustainability decision-making, the potential of AI in optimizing resource allocation, and the role of IoT in enhancing operational efficiencies. Additionally, the review will address the adoption of green technologies to mitigate environmental impacts and discuss the barriers organizations face in implementing these solutions.

Moreover, the review will consider the broader context of sustainability through the lens of the Sustainable Development Goals (SDGs) established by the United Nations. Aligning digital transformation strategies with the SDGs allows organizations to contribute to global efforts against pressing challenges, including poverty and climate change, while achieving their business objectives.

Ultimately, this exploration seeks to provide valuable insights for practitioners, scholars, and policymakers in navigating the interconnected realms of digital transformation and environmental sustainability. By understanding and leveraging the synergies between these domains, organizations can position themselves as leaders in creating a sustainable and resilient future, ensuring they meet the needs of the present while safeguarding the planet for generations to come.

2.1 Digital Transformation

Digital transformation represents a profound shift in how organizations leverage technology, integrating digital innovations into all facets of their operations. This transformation is not merely a technology upgrade; it signifies a fundamental change affecting business models, operational efficiencies, and customer engagement [Fitzgerald & Neville, 2002;Hess *et al.,* 2020]. As organizations increasingly rely on digital tools and processes, the significance of digital transformation has grown, compelling businesses to rethink their strategies and operations to remain competitive in a rapidly evolving market.

Definitions and Scope

Definitions of digital transformation vary among scholars and practitioners, but they often emphasize the necessity of new digital technologies in enhancing operational efficiencies, improving customer experiences, and enabling the development of innovative business models (Linderoth*et al.,* 2018). The term encompasses a wide range of initiatives, from adopting cloud computing solutions to implementing artificial intelligence (AI) and the Internet of Things (IoT) to optimize processes and enhance decision-making.For instance, organizations that implement cloud-based services can achieve significant improvements in flexibility and scalability, allowing for a more agile response to market changes. By moving away from traditional on-premises systems, businesses can access resources on-demand, reducing costs and enhancing their ability to innovate (Andriole, 2018;Liere-Netheler*et al.,* 2018). This transition to cloud computing is often seen as a foundational step in the digital transformation journey, setting the stage for further technological advancements.

The Evolutionary Nature of Digital Transformation

Digital transformation is frequently characterized as an evolutionary process wherein the adoption of digital capabilities creates value across multiple dimensions: business models, operational processes, and customer interactions [Morakanyane*et al.,* 2017]. As organizations embark on this journey, they often find that digital technologies enable them to streamline operations, enhance customer engagement, and create new revenue streams. For example, companies leveraging data analytics can gain insights into customer behavior, allowing for more targeted marketing and improved customer satisfaction (Li *et al.,* 2017).Research conducted by (Li *et al.,* 2017) highlights the importance of aligning information technology (IT) with business strategies, particularly for small and medium-sized enterprises (SMEs), which often face resource constraints. SMEs can benefit significantly from digital transformation, as it allows them to compete with larger firms by leveraging technology to improve efficiency and reach new customers. However, this alignment requires careful planning and a commitment to integrating digital solutions into the core of business operations. Legner, 2017 argue that digital transformation often originates from IT initiatives aimed at automating organizational tasks. Automation can enhance productivity and reduce the burden of routine tasks on employees, enabling them to focus on more strategic activities. This aligns with the broader trend of businesses seeking to improve efficiency and reduce costs through technological solutions. As organizations increasingly adopt automation technologies, they must also consider the implications for their workforce and develop strategies for reskilling employees (Legner*et al.,* 2017).Recent semantic analyses by (Vial, 2021) have synthesized definitions of digital transformation, emphasizing its role in instigating substantial changes through the application of various technologies. This perspective underscores that digital transformation is not a linear process but rather a complex interplay of technological advancements and organizational change. As companies adopt new technologies, they must also be prepared to adapt their structures, processes, and cultures to fully leverage the benefits of digital transformation.

Beyond Digitization and Digitalization

It is crucial to differentiate digital transformation from related concepts such as digitization and digitalization. Digitization refers to the conversion of analog information into digital formats, while digitalization involves the adoption of digital technologies to improve existing processes. In contrast, digital transformation encompasses a comprehensive overhaul of business models and practices, driven by digital technologies [Verhoef *et al.,* 2021]. This distinction highlights the transformative potential of digitalization, which can lead to new value creation opportunities rather than merely improving existing functions.As organizations navigate this transformation, it is essential to consider the implications for environmental sustainability. While digital transformation offers numerous advantages, it also presents challenges and mixed outcomes regarding its impact on sustainability practices (Reißig *et al.*, 2023). For example, while increased digitalization can lead to greater efficiency, it may also result in higher energy consumption due to the increased reliance on data centers and cloud computing. Organizations must strive to balance the benefits of digital technologies with their environmental impact, ensuring that their transformation efforts contribute positively to sustainability goals.In conclusion, digital transformation is a multifaceted and dynamic process that requires organizations to rethink their strategies, operations, and cultures. By embracing digital technologies and aligning them with business objectives, organizations can enhance efficiency, improve customer experiences, and drive innovation. However, as they embark on this journey, they must remain mindful of the broader implications for sustainability, striving to create value not only for themselves but also for the environment and society as a whole. As digital transformation continues to evolve, its role in shaping the future of business will remain a critical area of focus for scholars and practitioners alike.

2.2 Environmental Sustainability

In an age where environmental issues are at the forefront of global discussions, the intersection of the circular economy and Industry 4.0 has propelled environmental sustainability into a strategic position within organizational agendas (Sarc*et al.*, 2019). The recognition that sustainability is not just a regulatory obligation but a business imperative has shifted stakeholder expectations, with many demanding sustainable practices from the organizations they engage with (Cohen &Kietzmann, 2014). This shift reflects a growing understanding that environmental stewardship can enhance long-term business viability and competitiveness.

Core Principles of Environmental Sustainability

Environmental sustainability is rooted in the principle that present needs must be met without compromising the ability of future generations to meet their own needs [18]. This foundational concept, often associated with the Brundtland Commission's definition of sustainable development, emphasizes the need for a balanced approach to economic growth, social equity, and environmental protection. In practice, this means that organizations must consider the ecological impacts of their operations and strive to minimize negative effects on the planet.Integrating sustainability principles into organizational practices enhances value creation and amplifies the benefits derived from digital transformation initiatives (Ukko*et al.,* 2019). By embedding sustainability into their core strategies, organizations can not only comply with regulations but also foster innovation, improve operational efficiencies, and create new market opportunities. For instance, businesses that adopt renewable energy sources reduce their carbon footprints while potentially lowering energy costs over time. Additionally, sustainable practices can lead to improved employee morale and engagement, as workers increasingly prefer to be associated with environmentally responsible organizations (Kaswan*et al.,* 2019).

The pressing issues of pollution, resource depletion, and climate change necessitate urgent action from businesses and governments alike to protect the environment. Climate change poses significant risks to global ecosystems and economies, prompting calls for urgent and coordinated responses. Businesses that proactively address environmental concerns can mitigate risks associated with climate impacts, such as supply chain disruptions and resource scarcity. Moreover, engaging in sustainable practices can enhance resilience, allowing organizations to better adapt to changing conditions and regulatory landscapes.

Stakeholder Pressures and Sustainable Practices

The pressures from stakeholdersincluding consumers, investors, and regulatory bodiesare driving the adoption of sustainable practices across various industries (Aron & Molina, 2020). Consumers today are more informed and environmentally conscious, often seeking out products and services that align with their values. This trend has given rise to a growing market for sustainable goods, compelling companies to innovate and adopt greener practices. Research indicates that consumers are willing to pay a premium for products that are environmentally friendly, thereby incentivizing businesses to prioritize sustainability.Investors, too, are increasingly integrating environmental, social, and governance (ESG) criteria into their decision-making processes. Institutional investors are recognizing that companies with robust sustainability practices are often more resilient and better positioned for long-term success (Neutzling*et al.,* 2018). This shift in investment philosophy underscores the notion that sustainable practices can lead to improved financial performance, making a compelling case for organizations to embrace environmental responsibility as part of their strategic objectives.Furthermore, regulatory pressures are intensifying, with governments around the world implementing stricter environmental regulations and promoting sustainability initiatives. Companies that fail to comply with these regulations risk facing penalties, reputational damage, and loss of market access. As such, organizations must navigate a complex landscape of legal requirements while proactively seeking opportunities to exceed compliance and differentiate themselves in the marketplace.Organizations that embrace sustainability often find themselves better positioned in the market, as consumers increasingly prefer brands that prioritize environmental responsibility. Sustainable practices can enhance customer value, strengthen brand reputation, and ultimately lead to competitive advantages in the marketplace. For example, brands that transparently communicate their sustainability efforts and demonstrate a genuine commitment to environmental stewardship are likely to build stronger relationships with consumers, fostering loyalty and trust.

Integrating Sustainability into Digital Transformation

As organizations embark on their digital transformation journeys, weaving environmental sustainability into their operational frameworks becomes imperative. This alignment ensures that technological advancements contribute positively to sustainable development goals (SDGs) and facilitates meaningful impacts across various sectors. By integrating sustainability into their core strategies, organizations can navigate the complexities of the digital landscape while contributing to global sustainability efforts.Digital technologies can play a crucial role in promoting environmental sustainability. For instance, big data analytics can help organizations optimize resource use and minimize waste by providing insights into operational efficiencies. The Internet of Things (IoT) allows for real-time monitoring of energy consumption, enabling companies to identify and rectify inefficiencies swiftly. Moreover, advancements in renewable energy technologies can help organizations transition to greener energy sources, further reducing their environmental impact.

In conclusion, environmental sustainability has emerged as a critical focus for organizations navigating the complexities of the modern business landscape. By recognizing the importance of sustainable practices and integrating them into their core strategies, businesses can respond to stakeholder pressures, drive innovation, and enhance their competitive positioning. As digital transformation continues to evolve, aligning technological advancements with sustainability goals will be essential for fostering long-term success and contributing to a more sustainable future.

2.3: The Impact of Digital Transformation on Environmental Sustainability

Digital transformation is increasingly recognized as a vital component in fostering environmental sustainability. Technologies such as artificial intelligence (AI), big data analytics, the Internet of Things (IoT), and social platforms are now being harnessed not only to enhance business operations but also to contribute significantly to broader societal benefits [Vial, 2019]. Companies are actively developing innovative products and platforms that leverage these digital technologies to promote sustainability, underscoring the transformative potential of the digital landscape in addressing environmental challenges.

AI-Driven Initiatives for Sustainability

Artificial intelligence has emerged as a powerful tool in the quest for sustainability. Initiatives such as Smart Water Management Systems exemplify how AI can optimize resource usage and enhance environmental outcomes. For instance, these systems can monitor water usage in real time, detect leaks, and forecast demand, ultimately leading to significant reductions in water wastage (Goralski& Tan, 2020). Furthermore, AI applications have been developed to detect waterborne diseases, enhancing public health and environmental safety. These AI-driven innovations not only improve operational efficiencies but also contribute to sustainable water management practices that are critical in water-scarce regions.

The Role of Big Data and IoT

Big data analytics and the Internet of Things (IoT) are pivotal in promoting environmental sustainability by enabling organizations to gather and analyze vast amounts of data related to their environmental impacts.Balogun *et al.,* (2020) explored case studies across nine countries, illustrating how the integration of big data and IoT technologies effectively addresses sustainability challenges. For example, IoT sensors can monitor air quality in real time, allowing cities to respond to pollution spikes and implement measures to improve air quality. This data-driven approach empowers organizations to make informed decisions that directly impact their environmental footprints.Moreover, big data analytics has revolutionized how environmental impacts are measured and managed. It provides insights that enhance traceability in food systems, allowing consumers and regulators to certify goods based on their environmental performance (Weersink*et al.,* 2018). This capability not only fosters transparency but also encourages sustainable practices across supply chains, as organizations are held accountable for their environmental impacts.

Digital Workplaces as Enablers of Sustainability

The emergence of digital workplaces has further reinforced the potential for fostering sustainable practices. As organizations transition to remote and hybrid work models, they are discovering new ways to reduce their environmental impacts. Digital tools facilitate collaboration and communication without the need for extensive travel, significantly lowering carbon emissions associated with commuting (Yalina&Rozas, 2020). Additionally, cloud-based platforms allow for more efficient resource allocation and energy use, as they enable organizations to optimize their operations without the physical constraints of traditional office spaces.

Blockchain Technology and Resource Management

Blockchain technology also presents significant opportunities for advancing sustainability. By providing a decentralized and transparent method for tracking products throughout their life cycles, blockchain can maximize resource utilization and minimize carbon emissions (Leng*et al.,* 2022;Esmaeilian*et al.,* 2020). For instance, in the fashion industry, blockchain can trace the environmental impacts of materials from production to end-of-life, allowing consumers to make more informed purchasing decisions. This transparency not only enhances brand accountability but also encourages more sustainable consumer behavior.

National Initiatives and Global Impacts

The intersection of digitalization and environmental sustainability extends beyond individual organizations and industries; it also has profound implications for national and global initiatives.ElMassah&Mohieldin (2020) examined how digital transformation aids countries in achieving sustainable development goals (SDGs), illustrating the broader scope of these technological advancements. Their research emphasizes that digital tools can enhance governmental capabilities in monitoring environmental indicators, developing policy frameworks, and engaging citizens in sustainability initiatives.The potential for digital transformation to facilitate the achievement of SDGs is immense. For instance, by leveraging big data analytics, governments can better understand environmental trends, allocate resources more effectively, and implement targeted policies that promote sustainability. Furthermore, digital platforms can facilitate greater public participation in sustainability efforts, ensuring that diverse voices are included in decision-making processes.

2.4 COVID-19 and the SDGs

The COVID-19 pandemic has ushered in unprecedented changes to global dynamics, reshaping economies, societies, and environments alike. As the world grappled with the crisis, the implications for sustainability and the Sustainable Development Goals (SDGs) became increasingly evident. The pandemic not only exposed vulnerabilities within existing economic and social systems but also highlighted the critical need for resilience, adaptability, and a renewed commitment to sustainable practices (Sirkeci&Yucesahin, 2020)

Impact on Sustainability Goals

The immediate effects of the pandemic were starkly visible. Lockdowns and restrictions implemented worldwide to mitigate the virus's spread led to significant reductions in pollution levels and greenhouse gas emissions. Cities experienced clearer skies, and many regions reported improved air quality, providing a temporary glimpse into a more sustainable future (Barbier& Burgess, 2020).According to various studies, daily carbon dioxide emissions fell dramatically during peak lockdown periods, illustrating the potential for substantial environmental benefits if sustainable practices were adopted more broadly.

However, the economic fallout from the pandemic has been severe, disproportionately affecting vulnerable populations and threatening the progress made toward key SDGs. For instance, the economic downturn has exacerbated poverty levels, pushing millions back into extreme poverty and jeopardizing efforts to achieve SDG 1 (No Poverty). The World Bank estimated that in 2020 alone, an additional 88 million to 115 million people were pushed into extreme poverty as a result of the pandemic's economic impact [Barbier& Burgess, 2020]. Similarly, SDG 10 (Reduced Inequalities) has been negatively impacted, as marginalized groups' "including women, low-wage workers, and informal sector employees have faced heightened risks of unemployment and economic insecurity [Annette, 2021].

Building Back Better

As nations begin to emerge from the pandemic, there exists a unique opportunity to rethink and reshape recovery efforts. The concept of "building back better" has gained traction, emphasizing the need to integrate sustainability principles into economic recovery plans. This approach seeks to ensure that future growth is not only inclusive but also environmentally responsible [Marin, &Rodino, 2021]. By prioritizing sustainable development in recovery strategies, governments and organizations can create a foundation for long-term resilience against future crises. Integrating sustainability into recovery efforts can take many forms. For instance, investments in renewable energy infrastructure not only create jobs but also contribute to reducing greenhouse gas emissions. Similarly, promoting sustainable agricultural practices can enhance food security while also protecting ecosystems. By aligning recovery efforts with the SDGs, countries can address immediate economic challenges while simultaneously working towards long-term sustainability goals.

2.5 Interconnections Between the SDGs

Understanding the interconnections among the Sustainable Development Goals (SDGs) is crucial for effectively addressing the complex global challenges facing humanity today. The COVID-19 pandemic has underscored the fragility of progress towards these goals, particularly as the predicted decline of the global economy exacerbates vulnerabilities among marginalized populations (Barbier& Burgess, 2020). This interconnectedness highlights the need for comprehensive strategies that consider the intricate relationships between different SDGs.

The Importance of Interconnectedness

The SDGs are designed to be interrelated, with progress in one area often influencing outcomes in others. For instance, improving educational opportunities (SDG 4) can lead to enhanced economic growth (SDG 8) and reduced inequalities (SDG 10). Conversely, failure to address one goal can impede progress on others. The pandemic exemplified this, as disruptions in health systems (SDG 3) had cascading effects on economic stability (SDG 8) and social well-being (SDG 1) (Barbier& Burgess, 2020). Understanding these interconnections enables stakeholders to recognize that isolated efforts are often insufficient for achieving sustainable outcomes. A holistic approach that acknowledges the interplay between various goals is essential for fostering resilience and promoting systemic change.

Multidisciplinary Approaches to Achieving the SDGs

To effectively pursue the SDGs, multidisciplinary approaches are necessary. These approaches must integrate environmental health, economic development, and social equity. Collaborative efforts among governments, businesses, and civil society can create synergies that enhance sustainability outcomes (Felappi*et al.,* 2020). For example, partnerships between corporations and non-governmental organizations (NGOs) can drive initiatives that promote responsible consumption and production patterns (SDG 12).Such partnerships can leverage resources, knowledge, and expertise from diverse sectors, leading to innovative solutions that address multiple SDGs simultaneously. For instance, initiatives aimed at reducing food waste can contribute to zero hunger (SDG 2), promote sustainable cities and communities (SDG 11), and mitigate climate change(SDG 13). By fostering collaboration across sectors, stakeholders can maximize the impact of their efforts and create a more sustainable future

Case Studies of Interconnected SDG Initiatives

Several case studies illustrate the benefits of interconnected initiatives. One notable example is the collaboration between governments and private companies in renewable energy projects. Such projects not only contribute to affordable and clean energy (SDG 7) but also promote economic growth (SDG 8) and help combat climate change (SDG13). By investing in renewable energy infrastructure, countries can reduce their carbon emissions while simultaneously creating jobs and boosting local economies.Another example is the integration of gender equality (SDG 5) into agricultural development initiatives. Empowering women in agriculture not only enhances food security (SDG 2) but also supports economic growth (SDG 8) and reduces inequalities (SDG 10). Programs that provide women with access to resources, education, and training can create a positive feedback loop that benefits entire communities.

Future Research Directions

Future research should prioritize identifying and quantifying the interactions among the SDGs, employing diverse methodologies such as systems thinking and network analysis. By understanding how achieving one goal influences others, organizations can develop strategies that maximize positive outcomes across the SDGs [52]. For instance, researchers can utilize systems dynamics models to simulate the impacts of different policy interventions on multiple SDGs, providing valuable insights for decision-makers.Additionally, qualitative research that explores the lived experiences of communities can reveal how local contexts shape the interconnections among the SDGs. Engaging with diverse stakeholder's including marginalized groups can ensure that research reflects a broad range of perspectives and experiences. Achieving the Sustainable Development Goals (SDGs) requires navigating global trends that are influenced by both long-term and dynamic patterns, such as the digital revolution. We must consider how time, technology, governance, direction, and geography all affect the outcomes in order to completely understand the SDGs and their specific objectives (Ray, 2020).

Building Resilience Through Interconnected Strategies

Addressing the interconnections among the SDGs is vital for building resilience against future crises. The COVID-19 pandemic demonstrated the interconnected nature of global challenges and the necessity of adaptive strategies that account for these relationships. Policymakers must recognize that fostering resilience requires a comprehensive understanding of how different goals interact and influence one another.For example, the health sector's response to the pandemic highlighted the need for integrated approaches that consider the social determinants of health, such as education, economic stability, and environmental conditions. Investing in health systems (SDG 3) must go hand-in-hand with efforts to improve education (SDG 4) and reduce poverty (SDG 1) to create a more resilient society.

2.5 Impact of Technology on various industries

2.5.1 The Impact of Technology on Agriculture and Environmental Sustainability

The agricultural industry is undergoing a significant transformation driven by advanced technologies. This shift, often referred to as "smart farming," leverages innovative solutions to enhance farming practices and management. These technologies are increasingly recognized for their potential to address environmental challenges and promote sustainability by reducing energy consumption and greenhouse gas (GHG) emissions, conserving water, minimizing chemical usage, and facilitating remote monitoring and diagnostics of crop health(Finger *et al.,* 2019)

Precision Farming as a Key Approach

Precision farming (PF) is a pivotal aspect of this technological evolution. It enables farmers to apply the right amount of inputs such as water, fertilizers, and pesticides at the right place, time, and manner, ultimately benefiting crops, soils, and groundwater resources. By optimizing the management of fertilizers and pesticides, precision farming can significantly reduce direct nitrous oxide (N2O) emissions from agricultural fields, as well as decrease indirect emissions associated with the production of these inputs.Despite the recognition of the environmental advantages associated with these practices, there remains a gap in the literature regarding comprehensive assessments of their environmental impacts. Many studies touch upon the environmental aspects of smart farming, but few adopt a holistic approach that considers both direct and indirect effects. This gap is often attributed to the qualitative nature of existing research, which frequently lacks robust quantitative data on the actual outcomes enabled by these practices.

Environmental Impacts and Case Studies

Several initiatives illustrate the potential benefits of advanced farming technologies. Various projects have explored different use cases across the agricultural value chain, particularly in relation to machinery and equipment. However, many studies have not investigated the environmental benefits or burdens associated with the implementation of these practices.

For instance, pilot studies on smart farming have indicated that these approaches can yield positive environmental outcomes by improving irrigation efficiency, enabling site-specific pesticide and nutrient applications, and reducing overall energy consumption. These findings suggest that the integration of advanced farming technologies could significantly enhance the sustainability of agricultural practices.

2.5.2Impact of Advancement of technologies in Air Polloution

Air pollution is a significant global challenge that impacts public health, the environment, and quality of life. Recent advancements in technology, particularly artificial intelligence (AI) and blockchain, have the potential to play a critical role in addressing this issue. These technologies can enhance monitoring, prediction, and management of air quality, ultimately contributing to cleaner air.

Role of Artificial Intelligence

AI is rapidly transforming how various industries operate and can significantly impact air quality management. One of its primary applications in this domain is the ability to predict pollution levels several days in advance(Igliński&Babiak, 2017). AI-driven systems can analyze vast amounts of data to forecast air quality and provide alerts to the public. This proactive approach allows individuals and organizations to take necessary precautions when pollution levels are expected to rise.

For instance, AI systems enable real-time monitoring of pollution levels and can identify sources of air pollutants. By utilizing data from various sensors and historical data patterns, AI can provide accurate and timely information about air quality. This capability not only aids in immediate response efforts but also informs long-term strategies for pollution reduction.Furthermore, AI can optimize urban traffic management through autonomous traffic systems. By managing traffic lights intelligently, these systems can reduce vehicle idling and optimize traffic flow, leading to lower emissions. Research has indicated that implementing such systems can decrease air pollution levels by significant margins, improving urban air quality overall.

Several initiatives have demonstrated the effectiveness of AI in air quality management. For example, pollution forecasting tools that incorporate data from traditional monitoring systems and advanced statistical methods have been deployed in major cities, achieving high accuracy in predicting air quality levels. These tools have reported 80% accuracy in three-day forecasts and 75% in seven to ten-day predictions, enabling better preparedness and public health responses.

Blockchain Technology

In addition to AI, blockchain technology offers innovative solutions for addressing air pollution. By facilitating secure, transparent transactions and data sharing, blockchain can enhance environmental monitoring and accountability. This technology allows for the automated collection and management of emissions data, improving the accuracy and reliability of environmental reporting.One practical application of blockchain in promoting cleaner air involves incentivizing environmentally friendly behavior. For example, blockchain-based reward systems can encourage individuals to use public transportation, bicycles, or electric vehicles. Such systems have been piloted successfully, rewarding users for making sustainable choices, thereby reducing overall vehicle emissions.

Satellite Monitoring Innovations

Innovations in satellite technology also contribute to efforts in monitoring air pollution. New satellites designed specifically for measuring methane emissions from oil and gas operations promise to provide more rapid and comprehensive data than traditional multi-purpose satellites. These satellites can cover extensive areas, focusing on regions responsible for a significant proportion of global methane emissions, and the data they generate is intended to be publicly available. This transparency enhances accountability among industries and governments regarding emissions.

Digital Applications for Urban Air Quality Management

Further advancements in digital technology include initiatives aimed at improving air quality in urban environments. Projects focusing on Autonomous Air Quality Management (AAQM) integrate various technologies to provide tailored solutions for air quality issues in public spaces. These systems involve collecting real-time data on air quality, analyzing it, and automating maintenance tasks to ensure optimal air conditions.

Such initiatives aim to increase public awareness about air quality and improve the efficiency of urban management systems. For instance, smart city projects have implemented air quality sensors to gather emissions data, which can inform strategies for pollution control and promote behavioral changes among citizens.

While many of these initiatives are still in the pilot phase, they hold significant promise for improving air quality and addressing pollution challenges. By leveraging advanced technologies like AI and blockchain, cities can enhance their capabilities to monitor, manage, and ultimately reduce air pollution, fostering healthier environments for their residents.The state of our environment is a crucial factor in guaranteeing that the planet will have a sustainable future. However, the shocking rise in carbon dioxide (CO2) emissions poses a serious threat to our path toward sustainable growth (Dang et al., 2021). In 2018, the Sustainable Development Goals (SDGs) were introduced by the United Nations to address pressing global concerns and prevent the world from experiencing further environmental damage.However, our collective progress towards these goals is being slowed down by the ongoing environmental strain, the rapid growth of industrial activities, and our prolonged reliance on non-renewable energy sources(Ghosh *et al.,* 2024)

2.5.3 Addressing Water Pollution through Digital Solutions

Water pollution remains a critical global challenge, affecting ecosystems, public health, and water quality across various bodies of water. In recent years, advancements in digital applications have emerged as powerful tools in the fight against water pollution. By leveraging technologies such as the Internet of Things (IoT) and Big Data analytics, these solutions facilitate real-time monitoring and reporting on water quality, enabling more effective management and remediation efforts.

Real-Time Monitoring with IoT and Big Data

One of the key innovations in water quality management is the integration of IoT technology with Big Data analytics. This combination allows for continuous monitoring of water bodies, providing real-time data on various water quality parameters. Such systems can wirelessly stream collected data to centralized servers, offering reliable, persistent, and fast access to information relevant for water management.

For instance, pilot projects have been initiated in various locations to develop IoT-based solutions specifically aimed at monitoring water quality. These projects have shown promise in capturing comprehensive data about water conditions, including chemical composition, temperature, and pollutant levels(Chowdury*et al.,* 2019) However, challenges remain in translating this data into actionable insights for end-users. Many users find it difficult to understand and interpret the collected data, which can hinder their ability to evaluate changes in water quality effectively. This gap between data collection and practical application highlights the need for improved user interfaces and educational initiatives to ensure that stakeholders can utilize the information effectively.

Collaborative Initiatives and Policy Frameworks

In the European Union, efforts to enhance digital applications in water management have been formalized through initiatives like the Digital Single Market for Water services. This framework aims to promote the integration of digital technologies in the water sector, enhancing efficiency and sustainability. Under this initiative, various research and innovation projects are being funded to explore digital innovations tailored for water management, known collectively as ICT4Water.

These collaborative efforts are designed to encourage the adoption of digital tools across the water sector, from monitoring and reporting to infrastructure management and policy implementation. By bringing together stakeholders from different sectors, including academia, industry, and governmental organizations, these initiatives aim to create a comprehensive approach to managing water quality and addressing pollution.

Challenges and Future Directions

Despite the potential benefits of digital solutions in water quality management, several challenges need to be addressed. First, there is the issue of data standardization and interoperability among different monitoring systems. Ensuring that various devices and platforms can communicate effectively is crucial for creating a cohesive monitoring strategy. Additionally, the sheer volume of data generated by these systems can be overwhelming, necessitating the development of advanced data analytics tools to extract meaningful insights.

Moreover, enhancing public awareness and understanding of water quality issues is vital for the successful implementation of digital solutions. Educating stakeholders about the significance of water quality data and how to interpret it can empower communities to take action against water pollution.

3. CONCLUSION

Finally, integrating digital transformation into sustainable development processes provides a potential road for organisations aiming to solve today's serious environmental concerns. As this chapter has shown, developing technologies like artificial intelligence, big data analytics, and the Internet of Things may greatly improve operational efficiency while also encouraging environmental sustainability. Organisations may use these technologies to lower their carbon footprints, optimise resource utilisation, and increase overall resilience in the face of changing market demand. However, the path to effective digital transformation is not without hurdles.

Organisations must overcome obstacles such as opposition to change, the requirement for digital skills, and the challenges of integrating technological projects with sustainable aims. Leadership commitment and a culture that values innovation and adaptation.Furthermore, the link between digital transformation and sustainability emphasises the value of a comprehensive strategy. Businesses must structure their objectives in terms of larger societal and environmental implications, going beyond cosmetic attempts to actual stewardship.

As organisations continue to investigate and adopt digital solutions, this study emphasises the value of cross-sector and disciplinary collaboration. Stakeholders may increase the benefits of digital transformation on sustainable development by sharing best practices and promoting collaboration. Finally, by committing to a digital-first strategy that prioritises sustainability, organisations may help to create a healthier planet and a more fair future for everyone.

4. KEY FINDINGS

This chapter demonstrates that digital transformation is an important driver of sustainable development, allowing organisations to improve operational efficiencies while addressing environmental issues. Artificial intelligence, big data analytics, and the Internet of Things all play important roles in real-time monitoring and resource optimisation. However, obstacles such as reluctance to change and skill deficiencies must be overcome via strong leadership and a supportive culture. The significance of a comprehensive approach to sustainability is emphasised, with organisations urged to link their digital activities with actual sustainable practices to prevent "greenwashing." Collaboration among stakeholders is critical to maximising the advantages of digital transformation, which fosters new solutions for society and the environment. Finally, a long-term commitment to sustainability in digital strategy is critical for establishing resilience and achieving global sustainability goals.

REFERENCES

Akande, A., Cabral, P., & Casteleyn, S. (2019). Assessing the gap between technology and the environmental sustainability of European cities. *Information Systems Frontiers*, *21*(3), 581–604. DOI: 10.1007/s10796-019-09903-3

Alsoud, A. R., & Harasis, A. A. (2021). undefined. *Journal of Theoretical and Applied Electronic Commerce Research*, *16*(5), 1404–1414. DOI: 10.3390/jtaer16050079

Andriole, S. J. (2018). Five myths about digital transformation. *How to Go Digital*, 13-18. https://doi.org/DOI: 10.7551/mitpress/11633.003.0005

Annette, L. (2021). COVID 19 - Global research roadmap for recovery. *Impact*, *2021*(5), 83–84. DOI: 10.21820/23987073.2021.5.83

Aron, A. S., & Molina, O. (2020). Green innovation in natural resource industries: The case of local suppliers in the Peruvian mining industry. *The Extractive Industries and Society*, *7*(2), 353–365. DOI: 10.1016/j.exis.2019.09.002

Balogun, A., Marks, D., Sharma, R., Shekhar, H., Balmes, C., Maheng, D., Arshad, A., & Salehi, P. (2020). undefined. *Sustainable Cities and Society*, *53*, 101888. DOI: 10.1016/j.scs.2019.101888

Barbier, E. B., & Burgess, J. C. (2020). Sustainability and development after COVID-19. *World Development*, *135*, 105082. DOI: 10.1016/j.worlddev.2020.105082 PMID: 32834381

Baumgartner, R. J., & Rauter, R. (2017). Strategic perspectives of corporate sustainability management to develop a sustainable organization. *Journal of Cleaner Production*, *140*, 81–92. DOI: 10.1016/j.jclepro.2016.04.146

Brenner, B., & Hartl, B. (2021). The perceived relationship between digitalization and ecological, economic, and social sustainability. *Journal of Cleaner Production*, *315*, 128128. DOI: 10.1016/j.jclepro.2021.128128

Chowdury, M. S., Emran, T. B., Ghosh, S., Pathak, A., Alam, M. M., Absar, N., Andersson, K., & Hossain, M. S. (2019). IoT based real-time river water quality monitoring system. *Procedia Computer Science*, *155*, 161–168. DOI: 10.1016/j.procs.2019.08.025

Cohen, B., & Kietzmann, J. (2014). undefined. *Organization & Environment*, *27*(3), 279–296. DOI: 10.1177/1086026614546199

Dhingra, I. C. (2021). Green economy strategies. *Green Economy: Opportunities and Challenges*, 81-99. https://doi.org/DOI: 10.4324/9781003206729-4

Dima, A. M., Point, S., Maassen, M. A., & Jansen, A. (2021). Academic leadership: Agility in the digital revolution. *Proceedings of the International Conference on Business Excellence, 15*(1), 518-529. https://doi.org/DOI: 10.2478/picbe-2021-0047

ElMassah, S., & Mohieldin, M. (2020). Digital transformation and localizing the sustainable development goals (SDGs). *Ecological Economics, 169*, 106490. DOI: 10.1016/j.ecolecon.2019.106490

Eri, R., Gudimetla, P., Star, S., Rowlands, J., Girgla, A., To, L., Li, F., Sochea, N., & Bindal, U. (2021). Digital resilience in higher education in response to COVID-19 pandemic: Student perceptions from Asia and Australia. *Journal of University Teaching & Learning Practice, 18*(5). Advance online publication. DOI: 10.53761/1.18.5.7

Erten, B., & Antonio Ocampo, J. (2021). undefined. *World Development, 137*, 105164. DOI: 10.1016/j.worlddev.2020.105164 PMID: 32929296

Esmaeilian, B., Sarkis, J., Lewis, K., & Behdad, S. (2020). undefined. *Resources, Conservation and Recycling, 163*, 105064. DOI: 10.1016/j.resconrec.2020.105064

Felappi, J. F., Sommer, J. H., Falkenberg, T., Terlau, W., & Kötter, T. (2020). Green infrastructure through the lens of "One health": A systematic review and integrative framework uncovering synergies and trade-offs between mental health and wildlife support in cities. *The Science of the Total Environment, 748*, 141589. DOI: 10.1016/j.scitotenv.2020.141589 PMID: 33113695

Fernandez-Vidal, J., Antonio Perotti, F., Gonzalez, R., & Gasco, J. (2022). Managing digital transformation: The view from the top. *Journal of Business Research, 152*, 29–41. DOI: 10.1016/j.jbusres.2022.07.020

Ferreira, J. J., Fernandes, C. I., & Ferreira, F. A. (2019). *To be or not to be digital, that is the question: Firm innovation and performance, 101*(0148-2963), 583-590. https://doi.org/DOI: 10.1016/j.jbusres.2018.11.013

Finger, R., Swinton, S. M., El Benni, N., & Walter, A. (2019). undefined. *Annual Review of Resource Economics, 11*(1), 313–335. DOI: 10.1146/annurev-resource-100518-093929

Fitzgerald, B., & Neville, K. (2002). Mid-career employees embracing technology (MEET): A case study. *InSITE Conference*. https://doi.org/DOI: 10.28945/2479

Ghobakhloo, M. (2020). Industry 4.0, digitization, and opportunities for sustainability. *Journal of Cleaner Production, 252*, 119869. DOI: 10.1016/j.jclepro.2019.119869

Ghosh, R., Kumar Ghosh, P., Bagchi, B., & Paul, B. (2024). Measuring the impact of technology innovations and renewable energy consumption for enhancing environmental sustainability in India: Empirical evidence from ARDL approach. International Journal on Recent Trends in Business and Tourism, 08(01), 14 28. https://doi.org/DOI: 10.31674/ijrtbt.2024.v08i01.002

Goralski, M. A., & Tan, T. K. (2020). Artificial intelligence and sustainable development. *International Journal of Management Education, 18*(1), 100330. DOI: 10.1016/j.ijme.2019.100330

Guandalini, I. (2022). undefined. *Journal of Business Research, 148*, 456–471. DOI: 10.1016/j.jbusres.2022.05.003

Hanelt, A., Bohnsack, R., Marz, D., & Antunes Marante, C. (2020). A systematic review of the literature on digital transformation: Insights and implications for strategy and organizational change. *Journal of Management Studies, 58*(5), 1159–1197. DOI: 10.1111/joms.12639

Hess, T., Matt, C., Benlian, A., &Wiesböck, F. (2020). Options for formulating a digital transformation strategy. *Strategic Information Management*, 151-173. https://doi.org/DOI: 10.4324/9780429286797-7

Igliński, H., & Babiak, M. (2017). Analysis of the potential of autonomous vehicles in reducing the emissions of greenhouse gases in road transport. *Procedia Engineering, 192*, 353–358. DOI: 10.1016/j.proeng.2017.06.061

Jia, J., & Li, Z. (2020). Does external uncertainty matter in corporate sustainability performance? *Journal of Corporate Finance, 65*, 101743. DOI: 10.1016/j.jcorpfin.2020.101743

Kaswan, V., Choudhary, M., Kumar, P., Kaswan, S., & Bajya, P. (2019). Green production strategies. *Encyclopedia of Food Security and Sustainability*, 492-500. https://doi.org/DOI: 10.1016/B978-0-08-100596-5.22292-0

Kiron, D., & Unruh, G. (2018, January 17). *The convergence of digitalization and sustainability*. MIT Sloan Management Review. https://sloanreview.mit.edu/article/the-convergence-of-digitalization-and-sustainability/

Legner, C., Eymann, T., Hess, T., Matt, C., Böhmann, T., Drews, P., Mädche, A., Urbach, N., & Ahlemann, F. (2017). Digitalization: Opportunity and challenge for the business and information systems engineering community. *Business & Information Systems Engineering, 59*(4), 301–308. DOI: 10.1007/s12599-017-0484-2

Leng, J., Ruan, G., Jiang, P., Xu, K., Liu, Q., Zhou, X., & Liu, C. (2022). Corrigendum to "blockchain-empowered sustainable manufacturing and product lifecycle management in industry 4.0: A survey" [Renew sustain energy rev 132 (2020) 110112]. *Renewable & Sustainable Energy Reviews*, *167*, 112755. DOI: 10.1016/j.rser.2022.112755

Li, L., Su, F., Zhang, W., & Mao, J. (2017). Digital transformation by SME entrepreneurs: A capability perspective. *Information Systems Journal*, *28*(6), 1129–1157. DOI: 10.1111/isj.12153

Liere-Netheler, K., Packmohr, S., & Vogelsang, K. (2018). undefined. *Proceedings of the Annual Hawaii International Conference on System Sciences*. https://doi.org/ DOI: 10.24251/HICSS.2018.493

Linderoth, H. C., Jacobsson, M., & Elbanna, A. (2018). Barriers for digital transformation: The role of industry. *Australasian Conference on Information Systems 2018*. https://doi.org/DOI: 10.5130/acis2018.az

Lyu, W., & Liu, J. (2021). Artificial intelligence and emerging digital technologies in the energy sector. *Applied Energy*, *303*, 117615. DOI: 10.1016/j.apenergy.2021.117615

Marin, A., & Rodino, S. (2021). The impact of the COVID-19 crisis on Romanian tourism. *TOURISM CHALLENGES AMID COVID*, *19*, 46–61. DOI: 10.52370/TISC2146AM

Morakanyane, R., Grace, A., & O'Reilly, P. (2017). undefined. *Digital Transformation – From Connecting Things to Transforming Our Lives*. https://doi.org/DOI: 10.18690/978-961-286-043-1.30

Neutzling, D. M., Land, A., Seuring, S., & Nascimento, L. F. (2018). undefined. *Journal of Cleaner Production*, *172*, 3448–3458. DOI: 10.1016/j.jclepro.2017.11.091

Pareek, A., & Mathur, N. (2022). A study to analysis and identify the behavioral relationship between the attitude and factor affecting consumer towards green behavior. *International Journal on Recent Trends in Business and Tourism, 06*(03), 01-09. https://doi.org/DOI: 10.31674/ijrtbt.2022.v06i03.001

Piro că, G. I., erban-Oprescu, G. L., Badea, L., Stanef-Puică, M., & Valdebenito, C. R. (2021). Digitalization and labor market—A perspective within the framework of pandemic crisis. *Journal of Theoretical and Applied Electronic Commerce Research*, *16*(7), 2843–2857. DOI: 10.3390/jtaer16070156

Ray, D. (2020). A global attitude, a global perspective, a global pledge towards sustainability: An approach of understanding. [IJRTBT]. *International Journal on Recent Trends in Business and Tourism*, *4*(1), 34–37.

Reißig, M., Kunkel, S., Niehoff, S., &Beier, G. (2023). undefined. *Zeitschrift für wirtschaftlichenFabrikbetrieb, 118*(12), 893-897. https://doi.org/DOI: 10.1515/zwf-2023-1166

Reuschl, A. J., Deist, M. K., & Maalaoui, A. (2022). Digital transformation during a pandemic: Stretching the organizational elasticity. *Journal of Business Research*, *144*, 1320–1332. DOI: 10.1016/j.jbusres.2022.01.088 PMID: 36540204

Sarc, R., Curtis, A., Kandlbauer, L., Khodier, K., Lorber, K., & Pomberger, R. (2019). undefined. *Waste Management (New York, N.Y.)*, *95*, 476–492. DOI: 10.1016/j.wasman.2019.06.035 PMID: 31351634

Sirkeci, I., & Yucesahin, M. M. (2020). Coronavirus and migration: Analysis of human mobility and the spread of COVID-19. *Migration Letters : An International Journal of Migration Studies*, *17*(2), 379–398. DOI: 10.33182/ml.v17i2.935

Ukko, J., Nasiri, M., Saunila, M., & Rantala, T. (2019). Sustainability strategy as a moderator in the relationship between digital business strategy and financial performance. *Journal of Cleaner Production*, *236*, 117626. DOI: 10.1016/j.jclepro.2019.117626

Verhoef, P. C., Broekhuizen, T., Bart, Y., Bhattacharya, A., Qi Dong, J., Fabian, N., & Haenlein, M. (2021). undefined. *Journal of Business Research*, *122*, 889–901. DOI: 10.1016/j.jbusres.2019.09.022

Vial, G. (2019). Understanding digital transformation: A review and a research agenda. *The Journal of Strategic Information Systems*, *28*(2), 118–144. DOI: 10.1016/j.jsis.2019.01.003

Vial, G. (2021). Understanding digital transformation. *Managing Digital Transformation*, 13-66. https://doi.org/DOI: 10.4324/9781003008637-4

Weersink, A., Fraser, E., Pannell, D., Duncan, E., & Rotz, S. (2018). Opportunities and challenges for big data in agricultural and environmental analysis. *Annual Review of Resource Economics*, *10*(1), 19–37. DOI: 10.1146/annurev-resource-100516-053654

Yalina, N., & Rozas, I. S. (2020). Digital workplace: Digital transformation for environmental sustainability. *IOP Conference Series. Earth and Environmental Science*, *456*(1), 012022. DOI: 10.1088/1755-1315/456/1/012022

Chapter 10
Health Challenges Caused by Non-Communicable Diseases

Srishti Kumar
https://orcid.org/0009-0000-1059-9166
Banasthali Vidyapith, India

Vibhuti Sirohi
Bansthali Vidyapith, India

Navita Pareek
https://orcid.org/0000-0002-9007-2213
Bansthali Vidyapith, India

ABSTRACT

Non-communicable diseases (NCDs) are a significant global health issue, contributing significantly to morbidity and mortality worldwide. According to the WHO (World Health Organization) Global Action Plan 2013-2020, NCDs cause the deaths of over 36 million people worldwide, 14 million of whom pass away before turning 70. The number of NCDs in India has increased over the past ten years. NCDs require worldwide action in the areas of surveillance, prevention, and control since they represent a major risk to public health. Developing successful preventative and management measures requires understanding the health issues associated with these illnesses. In this chapter four prevalent NCDs namely, cancer, cardiovascular diseases (CVD), respiratory diseases, and diabetes will be discussed. It will provide a comprehensive overview on the consequences of these diseases, including their prevalence, risk factors, healthcare costs, economic effects, health disparities, and societal determinants that increase their occurrence and management.

DOI: 10.4018/979-8-3693-9755-8.ch010

INTRODUCTION

Non-communicable diseases (NCDs) are a significant global health issue, contributing significantly to morbidity and mortality worldwide. According to the WHO (World Health Organization) Global Action Plan 2013-2020, NCDs cause the deaths of over 36 million people worldwide, 14 million of whom pass away before turning 70.The number of NCDs in India has increased over the past ten years (Kastor & Mohanty, 2018; Mahal et al., 2010; Van Minh et al., 2013).NCDs require worldwide action in the areas of surveillance, prevention, and control since they represent a majorrisk to public health. Developing successful preventative and management measures requires understanding the health issues associated with these illnesses. In this chapter four prevalent NCDs namely, cancer, cardiovascular diseases (CVD), respiratory diseases, and diabetes will be discussed. It will provide a comprehensive overview (**Figure 1**) on the consequences of these diseases, including their prevalence, risk factors, healthcare costs, economic burden, health disparities, and societal determinants that increase their occurrence and management.

Along with this, there have been changes in dietary patterns, drinking patterns, smoking, urbanization, and tobacco use, all of which have contributed to the rise in non-communicable diseases in India (Prentice, 2006; Sinha & Kumar, 2010). The two primary focus areas for the National Policy are the rising burden of non-communicable diseases and the increasing prevalence of unsustainable healthcare expenses (MoHFW, 2017).

Figure 1. Health challenges caused by non-communicable diseases

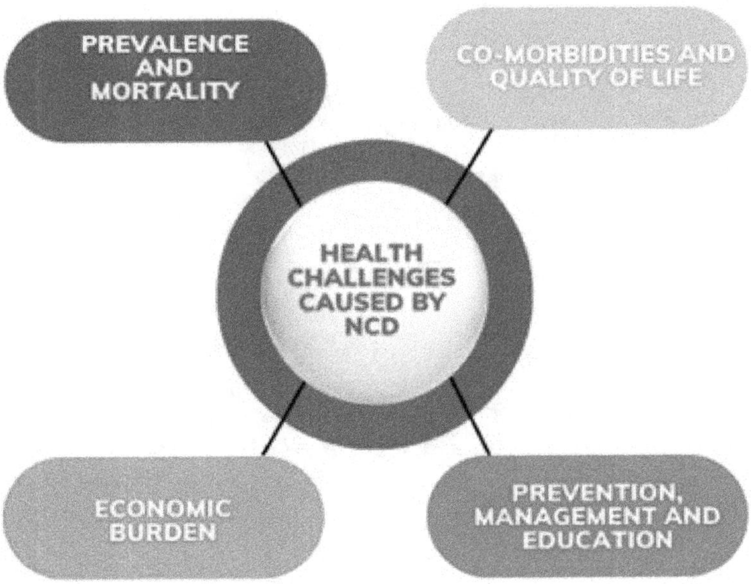

CANCER

"Cancer is a large group of diseases that can start in almost any organ or tissue of the body when abnormal cells grow uncontrollably, go beyond their usual boundaries to invade adjoining of the body or spread to other organs (WHO)." Cancer remains one of the most pressing global health issues of our time, affecting millions of lives and placing a considerable burden on healthcare systems. Defined as a group of diseases characterized by uncontrolled cell growth.It can affect almost any part of the body. This document will explore cancer from various angles, including its prevalence globally and specifically in India, the risk factors associated with its development, the economic burden it imposes, the quality of life for patients, access to care, and prevention and awareness initiatives. Figure 2 illustrates all the aspects at a glance, discussed in the connecting text.

Figure 2. Health aspects of Cancer at a glance

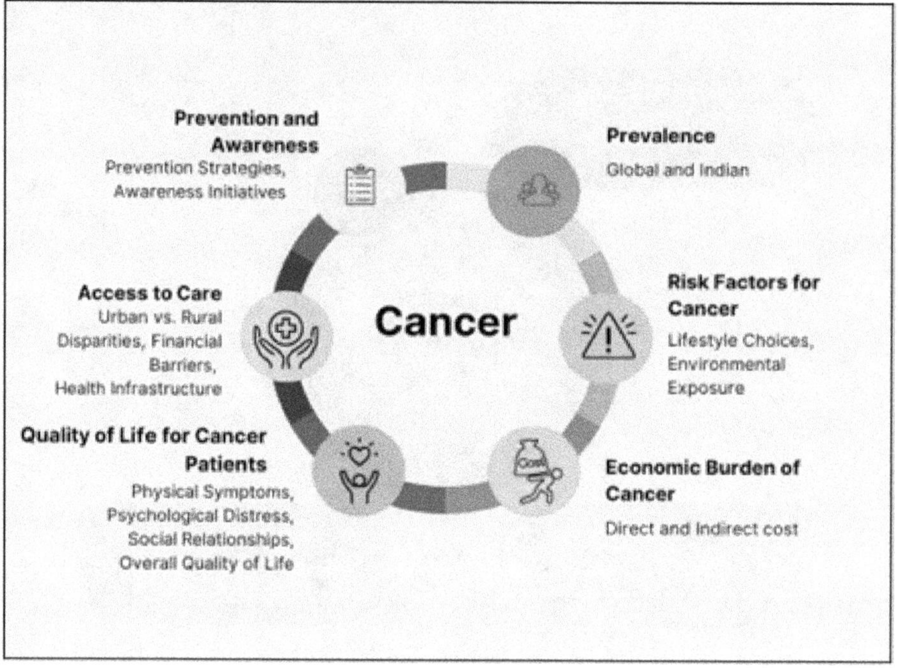

Prevalence of Cancer

Global prevalence

"The World Health Organization (WHO) estimates that cancer accounted for approximately 10 million deaths in 2020, making it the second leading cause of death globally, just behind cardiovascular diseases (WHO, 2021). The International Agency for Research on Cancer (IARC) forecasts that the number of new cancer cases will rise to an estimated 28.4 million by 2040, reflecting a staggering increase of 47% from 2020 levels (Bade and Cruz, 2020)."

Most Common Cancers Globally

1. **Lung Cancer**: "Responsible for the highest number of cancer-related deaths worldwide, with smoking being the primary risk factor."
2. **Breast Cancer**: The most commonly diagnosed cancer among women globally, with increasing incidence rates.

3. **Colorectal Cancer**: Rising prevalence in both men and women, particularly in high-income countries.
4. **Prostate Cancer**: The most commonly diagnosed cancer in men, especially prevalent in North America and Europe.

Prevalence in India

Cancer poses a significant public health challenge in India. According to the National Cancer Registry Programme (NCRP), there are over 1.16 million new cancer cases reported annually (NCRP, 2020). The landscape of cancer in India is influenced by various factors, including lifestyle changes, urbanization, and socio-economic conditions.

Most Common Cancers in India

1. **Breast Cancer**: The leading cancer among women, with increasing incidence particularly in urban areas.
2. **Oral Cavity Cancer**: Prevalent among men, largely due to the high consumption of tobacco and betel nut.
3. **Cervical Cancer**: High incidence rates attributed to limited screening and vaccination.
4. **Lung Cancer**: Increasing rates, particularly in urban areas with high pollution.

Comparative Analysis

The cancer burden in India is characterized by a higher proportion of cancers associated with infectious agents, such as cervical and liver cancers, compared to high-income countries where lifestyle-related cancers are more common (WHO, 2021). The disparities in cancer types reflect differences in public health policies, healthcare access, and socio-economic factors.

Risk Factors for Cancer

It is essential to comprehend the different cancer risk factors in order to create efficient preventative and management plans. These factors can be broadly categorized into lifestyle choices, environmental exposures, and genetic predisposition.

Lifestyle Choices

1. Tobacco Use Tobacco remains the leading cause of preventable cancer deaths worldwide, contributing to approximately 22% of all cancer deaths (Siegel et al, 2021). In India, the extensive use of tobacco products, including cigarettes, bidis, and smokeless tobacco, has led to a high prevalence of oral and lung cancers. Public health campaigns targeting tobacco cessation have been initiated but require further expansion to effectively reduce tobacco-related cancers.
2. Diet and Nutrition Dietary habits significantly influence cancer risk. "Diets high in processed foods, red meats, and low in fruits and vegetables have been linked to increased risks of colorectal and stomach cancers. The World Cancer Research Fund emphasizes the importance of a balanced diet rich in fruits, vegetables, and whole grains for cancer prevention (World Cancer Research Fund, 2018). In India, the shift towards Western dietary patterns, coupled with a decline in traditional diets, raises concerns about rising cancer incidence."
3. Physical Inactivity Sedentary lifestyles are linked to obesity, a major risk factor for various cancers, including breast, endometrial, and colorectal cancers. The National Institutes of Health suggests that regular physical activity can mitigate cancer risk and improve overall health (National Institutes of Health, 2020). Public health initiatives promoting active lifestyles are essential for reducing cancer incidence.
4. Alcohol Consumption Drinking too much alcohol has been linked to a number of malignancies, including esophageal, breast, and liver cancers. Public health campaigns aimed at educating people about the risks associated with alcohol consumption are crucial for cancer prevention (National Cancer Institute, 2021).

Environmental Exposure

1. Pollution Air pollution, particulate matter, is linked to an increased risk of lung cancer. India faces severe air quality issues, especially in urban areas, significantly contributing to the cancer burden (WHO, 2021). Efforts to improve air quality and reduce pollution are essential for cancer prevention.
2. Chemical Exposures Exposure to carcinogenic substances, such as benzene, asbestos, and certain industrial chemicals, can increase cancer risk. Occupational exposure in sectors like construction and manufacturing raises concerns about long-term health effects (Bade and Cruz, 2020). Regulations and safety measures are necessary to protect workers from hazardous exposures.
3. Radiation Both ionizing and non-ionizing radiation can increase cancer risk. Ultraviolet (UV) radiation is a well-known risk factor for skin cancer. Additionally, exposure to radon gas in homes has been linked to increased lung cancer risk

(National Cancer Institute, 2021). Public education on minimizing radiation exposure is vital for cancer prevention.

4. Genetic Predisposition Genetic factors significantly contribute to cancer susceptibility. Certain inherited mutations, such as BRCA1 and BRCA2, are associated with increased risks of breast and ovarian cancers. Family history of cancer is an important factor, with specific cancers exhibiting hereditary components. Genetic counseling and testing are crucial for individuals with a family history of cancer to understand their risks and consider preventive measures (National Cancer Institute, 2021).

Economic Burden of Cancer

The economic burden of cancer is profound, affecting not only patients and families but also healthcare systems. In India, the costs associated with cancer treatment can lead to significant financial distress, often resulting in catastrophic health expenditures.

Direct and Indirect Costs

1. Direct Costs

Direct costs encompass expenses related to diagnosis, treatment, hospitalization, and medications. Cancer treatments, particularly for advanced-stage cancers, can be extremely costly. A study estimated that cancer patients in India spend approximately 30% of their annual household income on treatment (Pandey et al., 2021). This financial burden often leads families to make difficult choices regarding treatment options.

2. Indirect Costs

Indirect costs include lost productivity due to illness, caregiver expenses, and the economic impact of premature death. These costs can significantly outweigh direct medical expenses, particularly in low- and middle-income countries (Pandey et al., 2021). The overall economic impact of cancer extends beyond the healthcare system to include the socio-economic status of families affected by the disease.

Economic Impact on Families

The financial burden of cancer often leads to significant stress and hardship for families. Many patients face difficult decisions regarding treatment options based on their financial situations, potentially leading to delayed care and poorer outcomes (Sharma et al., 2020). The economic impact of cancer on families highlights the need for comprehensive healthcare policies that address financial barriers to care.

Healthcare System Burden

The increasing incidence of cancer places substantial strain on healthcare systems. The demand for cancer care resources, including diagnostic services and treatment facilities, is rising. Policymakers must prioritize investments in cancer care infrastructure to address these challenges (WHO, 2021).

Quality of Life for Cancer Patients

The quality of life (QoL) for cancer patients is influenced by various factors, including physical symptoms, psychological well-being, and social support.

1. Physical Symptoms

Cancer and its treatments often lead to debilitating physical symptoms such as pain, fatigue, nausea, and changes in appetite. Effective management of these symptoms is essential for improving QoL. Palliative care and supportive therapies are crucial components of cancer treatment that focus on alleviating suffering and enhancing the patient's overall well-being (National Comprehensive Cancer Network, 2021).

2. Psychological Distress

The psychological impact of a cancer diagnosis can be profound, leading to anxiety, depression, and fear of recurrence. Mental health support is essential for helping patients cope with their diagnosis and treatment. Research indicates that psychological support and counseling can significantly improve QoL for cancer patients (Hodges et al., 2020).

3. Social Relationships

Cancer can strain relationships with family and friends. Social support plays a vital role in the well-being of cancer patients, with strong social networks associated with better QoL outcomes. Community support groups and family involvement can help mitigate feelings of isolation and enhance coping strategies (La Sala, 2021).

4. Overall Quality of Life

Studies have shown that patients receiving comprehensive cancer care, including psychological and social support, report higher QoL levels compared to those who do not receive such support. Integrating mental health services into cancer care is essential for improving patient outcomes and enhancing QoL (National Comprehensive Cancer Network, 2021).

Access to Care

Access to cancer care remains a critical issue, with disparities based on geographic location, socio-economic status, and healthcare infrastructure.

1. Urban vs. Rural Disparities

In India, urban areas typically have better access to cancer treatment facilities, while rural regions face significant challenges. The lack of healthcare providers and facilities in rural areas often leads to late-stage diagnoses and poorer outcomes for patients (Sharma et al., 2020). Bridging the gap in access to care is crucial for improving cancer outcomes in underserved populations.

2. Financial Barriers

The high cost of cancer treatment can be a barrier for many patients, particularly in low-income groups. Government initiatives and health insurance coverage are vital in improving access to care. However, many families remain uninsured or underinsured, leading to significant financial distress (Pandey et al., 2021). Policies aimed at expanding health insurance coverage and financial assistance programs are necessary to alleviate this burden.

3. Health Infrastructure

The availability of trained oncologists, diagnostic facilities, and treatment centers is essential for effective cancer care. Investments in healthcare infrastructure, including the establishment of more cancer centers and training programs for healthcare providers, are necessary to improve access and outcomes (WHO, 2021). Strengthening health systems is vital for ensuring equitable access to cancer care.

PREVENTION AND AWARENESS

Prevention Strategies

1. Screening Programs

Early identification through screening can greatly enhance the prognosis for cancer. In order to detect cancer in its early stages, when therapy is most successful, programs like Pap screenings for cervical cancer and mammography for breast cancer are crucial (Siegel et al, 2021). For early detection, it is imperative to increase access to screening programs in both urban and rural areas.

2. Vaccination

Vaccines, such as the HPV vaccine, can prevent certain types of cancer, including cervical cancer. Increasing awareness and access to vaccination is crucial for reducing the incidence of vaccine-preventable cancers (National Cancer Institute, 2021). Public health campaigns promoting vaccination can help improve uptake rates, particularly among younger populations.

3. Public Health Campaigns

Raising awareness about risk factors and promoting healthy lifestyles can reduce cancer incidence. Campaigns focusing on tobacco cessation, healthy eating, and physical activity are vital components of cancer prevention strategies (World Cancer Research Fund, 2018). Collaborative efforts between government and non-government organizations can enhance the effectiveness of these campaigns.

Awareness Initiatives

1. Community Engagement Involving communities in awareness programs can help disseminate information about cancer prevention and treatment options. Grassroots efforts can be particularly effective in reaching underserved populations (Sharma et al., 2020). Community health workers can play a pivotal role in delivering information and support to those in need.

2. Educational Resources Providing accessible information through various platforms, including social media and community workshops, can increase awareness and understanding of cancer. Tailored educational materials are essential for addressing the specific needs of different populations (WHO, 2021).
3. Collaboration with NGOs Partnerships with non-governmental organizations can enhance outreach efforts and provide support to cancer patients and their families. Collaborative initiatives can improve access to care and raise awareness in communities (Pandey et al., 2021). NGOs can also assist in providing financial aid and resources to those affected by cancer.

In summary, tackling cancer requires a holistic approach that encompasses prevention, early detection, equitable access to care, and ongoing support for patients and their families. Collective action at local, national, and global levels will be essential to mitigate the burden of this disease and improve health outcomes for all affected individuals.

Cardiovascular Diseases

"According to WHO Cardiovascular diseases (CVDs) is a group of disorders that affects the heart and blood vessels and include coronary heart disease, cerebrovascular disease, rheumatic heart disease and other conditions."CVDsrepresent a group of disorders affecting the heart and blood vessels, leading to significant morbidity and mortality worldwide. CVDs include conditions such as coronary artery disease, heart failure, arrhythmias, and peripheral artery disease. This document aims to provide a thorough exploration of CVDs, covering their prevalence, risk factors, economic impact, co-morbidities, health disparities, access to care, and prevention and education strategies. Figure 3 illustrates all the aspects at a glance, discussed in the connecting text.

Figure 3. Health aspects of Cardiovascular diseases at a glance

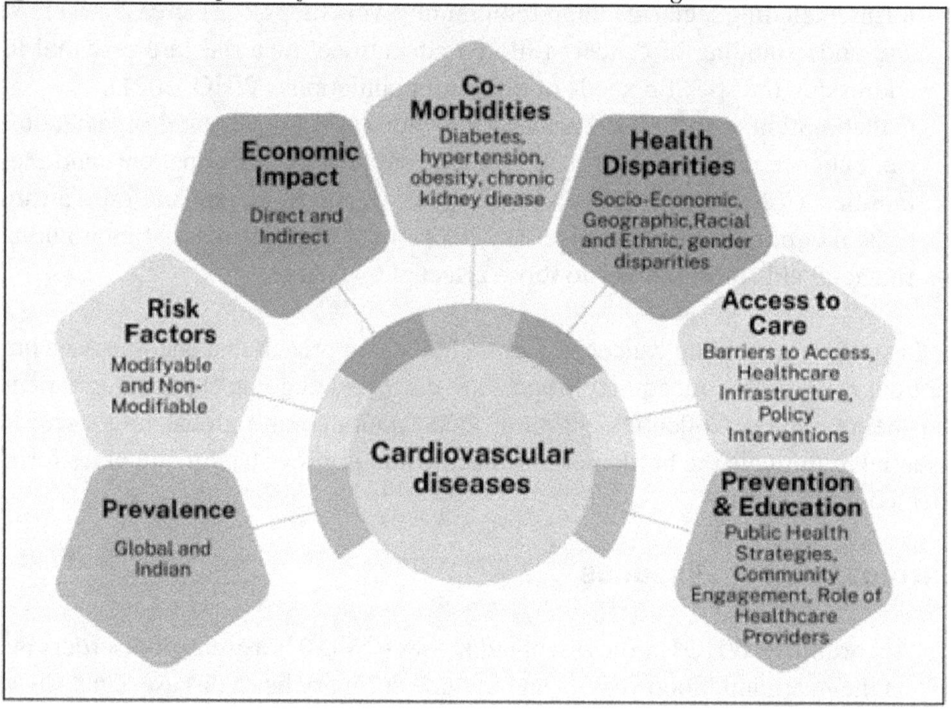

PREVALENCE OF CARDIOVASCULAR DISEASES

Global Prevalence

According to the World Health Organization (WHO), "CVDs are the leading cause of death globally, accounting for approximately 32% of all deaths in 2019. This translates to around 17.9 million deaths annually (WHO, 2021). The most prevalent types of CVDs globally include:"

1. **Ischemic Heart Disease**: Responsible for 9.14 million deaths.
2. **Stroke**: Accountable for 6.2 million deaths.
3. **Heart Failure**: Affecting millions globally, with an increasing incidence due to an aging population and lifestyle factors.

The prevalence of CVDs is rising, particularly in low- and middle-income countries, due to urbanization, lifestyle changes, and an aging population. The Global Burden of Disease Study indicates that the disability-adjusted life years (DALYs) lost due to CVDs have increased significantly over the past few decades (Murray, 2022).

Prevalence in India

In India, CVDs have emerged as a significant public health challenge. According to the Indian Council of Medical Research (ICMR), CVDs account for approximately 28% of all deaths in the country, making it a leading cause of mortality (Anjana et al, 2020). The increasing prevalence of risk factors such as diabetes, hypertension, and obesity has contributed to this alarming trend.

Common Types of CVDs in India

1. **Ischemic Heart Disease**: The most prevalent form of CVD in India, with a rising incidence among younger populations.
2. **Stroke**: The second leading cause of CVD-related mortality, with both ischemic and hemorrhagic strokes being common.
3. **Heart Failure**: Increasingly recognized as a significant health issue due to rising rates of hypertension and diabetes.

Comparative Analysis

The prevalence of CVDs is influenced by socio-economic factors, healthcare access, and lifestyle choices. While high-income countries have seen a decline in CVD-related mortality due to improved healthcare systems and preventive measures, low- and middle-income countries like India are experiencing an alarming rise in CVD cases, necessitating urgent public health interventions.

Risk Factors for Cardiovascular Diseases

Strategies for prevention and management of CVDs require an understanding of the risk factors related to these conditions. It is possible to divide these risk variables into categories that are changeable and non-modifiable.

Modifiable Risk Factors

1. Unhealthy Diet The diet of the West, which is marked by a large intake of processed goods, sugars, and saturated fats, has been linked to increased CVD risk. The Indian diet, although traditionally healthy, has shifted towards higher intake of refined carbohydrates and unhealthy fats due to urbanization and globalization (Misra et al., 2019). Key dietary risk factors include: • **High Sodium Intake**: Linked to hypertension. • **Low Fruit and Vegetable Consumption**: Associated with higher risks of CVD. • **Excessive Sugar and Saturated Fat Intake**: Contributing to obesity and dyslipidemia.
2. Physical Inactivity Sedentary lifestyles are a significant contributor to the global rise of CVDs. According to WHO guidelines, adults should engage in at least 150 minutes of moderate-intensity aerobic activity each week. However, urbanization and technological advancements have led to decreased physical activity levels, particularly in developing countries (WHO, 2021).
3. Smoking Habit Tobacco use is one of the leading modifiable risk factors for CVDs. "The WHO estimates that smoking is responsible for approximately 11% of global deaths from CVDs (WHO, 2021)." In India, the prevalence of tobacco use, particularly among men, remains high, with significant implications for public health.
4. Alcohol Consumption Excessive alcohol consumption raises the risk of CVD by being linked to elevated blood pressure and cardiomyopathy. Heavy drinking is a major risk factor, even if moderate alcohol consumption may have some protective effects (National Institute on Alcohol Abuse and Alcoholism, 2020).

Non-Modifiable Risk Factors

1. Genetic Factors

Genetics play a crucial role in an individual's susceptibility to CVDs. Family history of heart disease is a significant risk factor, with genetic predispositions influencing cholesterol levels, blood pressure, and overall heart health. Specific genetic mutations and markers have been associated with increased risk for certain CVDs (Khera et al., 2016).

2. Age and Gender

The risk of CVDs rises dramatically with age, making aging a non-modifiable risk factor. Although women's risk increases after menopause, men are often more likely than women to acquire CVDs at a younger age (Mosca et al., 2011).

3. Ethnicity

Certain ethnic groups are at a higher risk for CVDs due to genetic, environmental, and socio-economic factors. For example, South Asians have a higher predisposition to heart disease compared to other ethnic groups (Pandey et al., 2021).

ECONOMIC IMPACT OF CARDIOVASCULAR DISEASES

Direct Economic Costs

The economic burden of CVDs is substantial, impacting healthcare systems and economies. Direct costs include:

- **Hospitalization**: CVD patients often require hospitalization for acute episodes, contributing to significant healthcare expenses.
- **Medications**: Long-term management of CVDs necessitates ongoing medication, adding to healthcare costs.
- **Medical Procedures**: Surgical interventions, such as bypass surgeries and angioplasties, entail considerable expenses.

A study estimated that the total direct cost of CVDs in India was around $6 billion in 2015, projected to rise significantly in the coming years (Pandey et al., 2021).

Indirect Economic Costs

Indirect costs related to CVDs include:

- **Lost Productivity**: Patients with CVDs may face decreased work capacity due to illness, leading to lost productivity and income.
- **Caregiver Costs**: Family members often take on caregiving roles, leading to economic impacts on household income.

Overall Economic Impact

The overall economic impact of CVDs can lead to catastrophic health expenditures, particularly in low- and middle-income countries. The burden of CVDs extends beyond healthcare costs, affecting socio-economic conditions and leading to impoverishment for many families (Pandey et al., 2021).

Co-Morbidities Associated with Cardiovascular Diseases

CVDs often co-occur with other chronic conditions, complicating management and increasing healthcare costs. Key co-morbidities include:

1. Diabetes

Diabetes is a major risk factor for cardiovascular diseases (CVDs); people with diabetes have a two to four time's higher risk of heart disease than people without diabetes(American Diabetes Association, 2021). The growing prevalence of diabetes in India poses a substantial public health challenge.

2. Hypertension

Hypertension is both a risk factor and a co-morbidity for CVDs. The increasing incidence of hypertension in India, particularly among urban populations, is concerning (ICMR, 2020). Effective management of blood pressure is crucial for reducing CVD risk.

3. Obesity

Obesity is a significant contributor to the development of CVDs, with excess body weight leading to other risk factors such as diabetes, hypertension, and dyslipidemia. The rise of obesity in India, particularly among children and adolescents, is alarming and necessitates public health interventions (Misra et al., 2019).

4. Chronic Kidney Disease

Chronic kidney disease (CKD) and CVDs share common risk factors, including hypertension and diabetes. Individuals with CKD are at an increased risk of cardiovascular events, complicating their management (Go et al., 2014).

Health Disparities in Cardiovascular Diseases

1. Socio-Economic Disparities Health disparities in CVDs are influenced by socio-economic factors, including income, education, and accessible medical care. Because they have less access to preventative care and treatment, people from poorer socioeconomic backgrounds frequently face higher risks (WHO, 2021).

2. Geographic Disparities Geographic location significantly impacts CVD prevalence and outcomes. Urban areas may have better access to healthcare services, while rural regions often lack necessary resources, leading to delayed diagnoses and treatment (Pandey et al., 2021).
3. Racial and Ethnic Disparities Certain racial and ethnic groups are disproportionately affected by CVDs. In India, South Asians are at a higher risk of developing CVDs compared to other populations, attributed to genetic predispositions and lifestyle factors (Pandey et al., 2021).
4. Gender Disparities Gender differences also play a role in CVD outcomes. While men are generally at a higher risk at younger ages, women's risk increases significantly post-menopause. Additionally, women may experience different symptoms and outcomes related to CVDs, necessitating gender-specific approaches to prevention and treatment (Mosca et al., 2011).

ACCESS TO CARE FOR CARDIOVASCULAR DISEASES

Barriers to Access

Access to cardiovascular care remains a critical issue, particularly in low- and middle-income countries. Barriers to access include:

- **Financial Constraints**: High treatment costs can deter individuals from seeking care.
- **Geographical Barriers**: Limited healthcare infrastructure in rural areas restricts access to timely care.
- **Awareness and Education**: Lack of awareness about CVDs and their symptoms can delay seeking medical attention.

Healthcare Infrastructure

Strengthening healthcare infrastructure is essential for improving access to cardiovascular care. Investment in healthcare facilities, trained healthcare providers, and essential medical equipment is vital for enhancing service delivery (WHO, 2021).

Policy Interventions

Government policies aimed at expanding health insurance coverage, subsidizing medications, and promoting preventive care are essential for improving access to care. Initiatives such as the Ayushman Bharat scheme in India aim to provide financial protection for low-income populations, improving access to essential health services (Ministry of Health and Family Welfare, 2018; Lahariya, 2018).

PREVENTION AND EDUCATION

Public Health Strategies

Preventive measures are crucial in reducing the incidence of CVDs. Public health strategies include:

1. Health Promotion Campaigns Health promotion campaigns focusing on risk factor modification—such as healthy eating, physical activity, and smoking cessation—are vital for preventing CVDs. These campaigns should be culturally sensitive and tailored to specific populations (WHO, 2021).
2. Screening and Early Detection Regular screening for hypertension, diabetes, and dyslipidemia can facilitate early detection and management of risk factors. Community-based screening programs can effectively reach underserved populations (Pandey et al., 2021).
3. Education and Awareness Programs Increasing awareness about the importance of heart health and the risk factors associated with CVDs is crucial. Educational initiatives targeting schools, workplaces, and communities can foster healthier lifestyle choices (ICMR, 2020).

Community Engagement

Community engagement plays a vital role in promoting heart health. Collaborating with local organizations, healthcare providers, and community leaders can enhance the effectiveness of prevention and education initiatives (WHO, 2021).

Role of Healthcare Providers

An essential component of management and prevention is played by healthcare professionals.

Training healthcare professionals to educate patients about risk factors and lifestyle modifications can lead to better outcomes. Incorporating preventive care into routine healthcare visits is essential for early intervention (National Heart, Lung, and Blood Institute, 2021).

In conclusion, cardiovascular diseases (CVDs) represent a critical public health challenge worldwide, with alarming prevalence rates and significant economic implications. Collaborative efforts among governments, healthcare providers, and communities will be paramount in addressing the rising burden of CVDs, promoting heart health, and ultimately reducing mortality and morbidity associated with these diseases.

Respiratory Diseases

"Respiratory diseases encompass a wide range of disorders affecting the lungs and airways, including chronic obstructive pulmonary disease (COPD), asthma, pneumonia, and lung cancer (WHO)." These diseases significantly impact global health, leading to substantial morbidity and mortality. This document provides a detailed analysis of respiratory diseases, including their prevalence, risk factors, economic burden, co-morbidities, health disparities, access to care, healthcare utilization, and prevention and management strategies. Figure 4 illustrates all the aspects at a glance, discussed in the connecting text.

Figure 4. Health aspects of Respiratory diseases at a glance

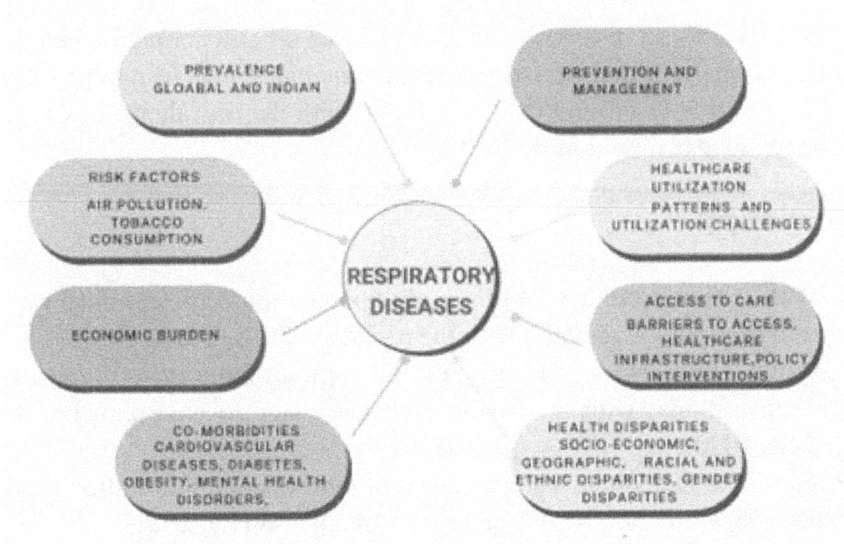

PREVALENCE OF RESPIRATORY DISEASES

Global Prevalence

In the world, respiratory disorders rank among the top causes of mortality and disability. As per the World Health Organization (WHO), respiratory disorders were responsible for about 4 million deaths worldwide in 2019. The most common respiratory diseases were pneumonia and COPD (WHO, 2021). Important figures consist of:

- **Chronic Obstructive Pulmonary Disease (COPD)**: "An estimated 3.23 million deaths annually, making it the third leading cause of death globally (Murray, 2022)."
- **Asthma**: "Affects approximately 300 million people worldwide, with about 250,000 deaths each year (WHO, 2021)."
- **Lung Cancer**: The leading cause of cancer-related deaths, with about 1.8 million fatalities annually (Bade and Cruz, 2020).

Prevalence in India

In India, respiratory diseases have emerged as a significant public health challenge. The Global Burden of Disease Study indicates that respiratory diseases account for about 10% of total deaths in India, with the prevalence of COPD and asthma showing alarming trends.

Key Statistics:

- **COPD**: Affects around 5.6% of the adult population, with significant morbidity and mortality associated with the disease (ICMR, 2020).
- **Asthma**: Approximately 15-20 million people in India are estimated to suffer from asthma, with increasing prevalence due to environmental factors (ICMR, 2020).
- **Pneumonia**: One of the leading causes of morbidity and mortality in children under five, with about 4 million cases annually (WHO, 2021).

Comparative Analysis

The prevalence of respiratory diseases varies significantly between high-income and low- and middle-income countries (LMICs). While developed countries have seen a decline in mortality rates due to improved healthcare access and interventions, LMICs like India face rising incidences of respiratory diseases driven by urbanization, industrialization, and increasing pollution levels.

Risk Factors for Respiratory Diseases

Understanding the risk factors associated with respiratory diseases is crucial for developing effective prevention and management strategies. Key risk factors include:

1. Air Pollution

Air pollution is a significant risk factor for respiratory diseases. According to WHO estimates, air pollution is responsible for about 4.2 million premature deaths annually (WHO, 2021). In India, high levels of particulate matter (PM2.5) from vehicular emissions, industrial discharges, and biomass burning contribute to the burden of respiratory diseases.

Types of Air Pollutants:

- **Particulate Matter (PM2.5 and PM10)**: Small particles that penetrate deep into the lungs, leading to inflammation and respiratory conditions.
- **Nitrogen Dioxide (NO2)**: Emitted from vehicles and industrial activities, associated with increased asthma and COPD exacerbations.
- **Sulfur Dioxide (SO2)**: Released from fossil fuel combustion, contributing to respiratory diseases and aggravating pre-existing conditions.

2. Tobacco Consumption

Tobacco is a significant cause of respiratory illnesses, especially COPD and lung cancer. Approximately 1.2 million fatalities annually are attributed to secondhand smoke exposure, according to WHO projections that tobacco use kills over 8 million people annually (WHO, 2021).

Impact of Tobacco on Respiratory Health:

- **Chronic Obstructive Pulmonary Disease**: Smoking is the primary cause of COPD, with up to 80% of cases attributable to tobacco use (McRobbie & Kwan, 2021).
- **Lung Cancer**: About 85% of lung cancer cases are linked to smoking, highlighting the severe impact of tobacco on respiratory health.
- **Asthma**: Tobacco smoke exposure can trigger asthma attacks and worsen symptoms in children and adults (McRobbie & Kwan, 2021).

Economic Burden of Respiratory Diseases

1. Health Costs

The economic burden of respiratory diseases includes direct healthcare costs, such as hospitalizations, outpatient visits, medications, and diagnostic tests. In India, the total healthcare cost associated with respiratory diseases was estimated to be around $7 billion in 2015 (Pandey et al., 2021). This figure is projected to rise significantly due to increasing prevalence and healthcare inflation.

2. Lost Productivity

Respiratory diseases can lead to lost productivity due to absenteeism and reduced work capacity. The economic impact of lost productivity is substantial, with estimates suggesting that respiratory diseases account for billions in lost economic output each year (Pandey et al., 2021).

3. Long-term Care

Chronic respiratory diseases often require long-term management and care, resulting in significant financial burdens on families and healthcare systems. Individuals with severe COPD or asthma may need ongoing medications, pulmonary rehabilitation, and regular medical consultations, which can be costly.

4. Public Health Investment

Investing in public health initiatives aimed at preventing respiratory diseases can yield substantial economic benefits. Effective interventions, such as anti-smoking campaigns, air quality management, and vaccination programs for pneumonia and influenza, can reduce the incidence of respiratory diseases and associated costs (WHO, 2021).

5. Impact on Quality of Life

Respiratory diseases significantly impact individuals' quality of life. Patients with chronic respiratory conditions often experience symptoms such as breathlessness, fatigue, and reduced physical activity, leading to decreased overall well-being and life satisfaction (Halpin et al, 2021).

6. Indirect Costs

Indirect costs associated with respiratory diseases include caregiver costs, home modifications, and social support services. Families may face financial strain due to the need for assistance in daily activities or modifications to accommodate a family member's condition.

Co-Morbidities Associated with Respiratory Diseases

Respiratory diseases often co-occur with other chronic conditions, complicating their management and increasing healthcare costs. Key co-morbidities include:

1. Cardiovascular Diseases

There is a well-established link between respiratory diseases and cardiovascular conditions. COPD, for instance, is associated with increased risk of heart disease, with shared risk factors such as smoking and systemic inflammation (Sin et al., 2005).

2. Diabetes

Individuals with respiratory diseases, particularly asthma and COPD, are at higher risk for developing diabetes. The chronic inflammation associated with respiratory conditions can contribute to insulin resistance (La Sala, 2020).

3. Obesity

Obesity is both a risk factor and a co-morbidity for respiratory diseases. Excess weight can exacerbate symptoms of asthma and COPD, leading to worse outcomes and increased healthcare utilization (Wang et al., 2020).

4. Mental Health Disorders

Respiratory diseases can have a significant impact on mental health, leading to conditions such as anxiety and depression. The chronic nature of respiratory diseases and the limitations they impose can affect psychological well-being (Fitzgerald et al., 2019).

Health Disparities in Respiratory Diseases

1. Socio-Economic Disparities Health disparities in respiratory diseases are influenced by socio-economic factors, including income, education, and access to medical care. Because they have less access to preventative care and treatment,

people from poorer socioeconomic backgrounds frequently face higher risks (WHO, 2021).

2. Geographic Disparities Geographic location significantly impacts the prevalence and outcomes of respiratory diseases. Urban areas often experience higher pollution levels, leading to increased respiratory illnesses, while rural areas may lack adequate healthcare facilities for timely diagnosis and treatment (Pandey et al., 2021).
3. Racial and Ethnic Disparities Certain racial and ethnic groups are disproportionately affected by respiratory diseases. In India, marginalized communities, particularly those living in slums, are at a higher risk due to exposure to indoor air pollution and limited access to healthcare services (ICMR, 2020).
4. Gender Disparities Gender differences also play a role in respiratory disease outcomes. Men generally have a higher prevalence of smoking-related respiratory diseases, while women may experience more severe asthma symptoms and poorer health outcomes (WHO, 2021).

ACCESS TO CARE FOR RESPIRATORY DISEASES

Barriers to Access

Access to care for respiratory diseases remains a critical issue, particularly in low- and middle-income countries. Barriers to access include:

- **Financial Constraints**: High treatment costs can deter individuals from seeking care, especially in a country like India, where out-of-pocket expenses are significant.
- **Geographical Barriers**: Limited healthcare infrastructure in rural areas restricts access to timely care and specialized services (Pandey et al., 2021).
- **Awareness and Education**: Lack of awareness about respiratory diseases and their symptoms can delay seeking medical attention.

Healthcare Infrastructure

Strengthening healthcare infrastructure is essential for improving access to respiratory care. Investment in healthcare facilities, trained healthcare providers, and essential medical equipment is vital for enhancing service delivery (WHO, 2021).

Policy Interventions

Government policies aimed at expanding health insurance coverage, subsidizing medications, and promoting preventive care are essential for improving access to care. Initiatives such as the Ayushman Bharat scheme in India aim to provide financial protection for low-income populations, improving access to essential health services (Ministry of Health and Family Welfare, 2018; Lahariya, 2018).

HEALTHCARE UTILIZATION FOR RESPIRATORY DISEASES

Patterns of Healthcare Utilization

Understanding healthcare utilization patterns for respiratory diseases is crucial for developing effective management strategies. Key aspects include:

- **Emergency Services**: Individuals with severe respiratory conditions often require emergency care for exacerbations, leading to increased healthcare costs.
- **Outpatient Services**: Regular follow-ups and management for chronic conditions are essential for preventing complications and improving quality of life.
- **Pharmaceuticals**: Access to necessary medications, including bronchodilators and corticosteroids, is critical for effective management.

Utilization Challenges

Challenges in healthcare utilization include:

- **Inconsistent Care**: Patients may experience fragmented care due to a lack of coordination among healthcare providers.
- **Treatment Adherence**: Non-adherence to prescribed medications can result in increased exacerbations and healthcare utilization, complicating management (Bourbeau et al., 2019).

PREVENTION AND MANAGEMENT OF RESPIRATORY DISEASES

Public Health Strategies

Preventive measures are crucial in reducing the incidence of respiratory diseases. Public health strategies include:

1. Health Promotion Campaigns Health promotion campaigns focusing on risk factor modification—such as anti-smoking initiatives, air quality management, and promoting physical activity—are vital for preventing respiratory diseases (WHO, 2021).
2. Screening and Early Detection Regular screening for respiratory diseases can facilitate early detection and management. Community-based screening programs can effectively reach underserved populations, improving outcomes (Pandey et al., 2021).
3. Education and Awareness Programs Increasing awareness about the importance of respiratory health and the risk factors associated with respiratory diseases is crucial. Educational initiatives targeting schools, workplaces, and communities can foster healthier lifestyle choices (ICMR, 2020).

Community Engagement

Community engagement plays a vital role in promoting respiratory health. Collaborating with local organizations, healthcare providers, and community leaders can enhance the effectiveness of prevention and education initiatives (WHO, 2021).

Role of Healthcare Providers

Healthcare providers play a critical role in prevention and management. Training healthcare professionals to educate patients about risk factors and lifestyle modifications can lead to better outcomes. Incorporating preventive care into routine healthcare visits is essential for early intervention (McRobbie & Kwan, 2021).

Management of Chronic Respiratory Diseases

Management of chronic respiratory diseases often includes a combination of pharmacological and non-pharmacological approaches:

- **Pharmacological Management**: Includes bronchodilators, inhaled corticosteroids, and long-acting beta-agonists for asthma and COPD management.
- **Pulmonary Rehabilitation**: A comprehensive program combining exercise, education, and support aimed at improving physical and emotional well-being (Halpin et al, 2021).
- **Vaccination**: Vaccination against influenza and pneumonia is essential for preventing complications in individuals with chronic respiratory diseases.

In conclusion, respiratory diseases constitute a major global health challenge, contributing significantly to morbidity and mortality. Collaborative efforts among governments, healthcare systems, and communities are essential for addressing the rising burden of respiratory diseases. By understanding the underlying risk factors and implementing comprehensive prevention and management strategies, it is possible to significantly improve respiratory health outcomes and reduce the overall impact of these diseases on individuals and society.

Diabetes

"Diabetes mellitus is a chronic metabolic disorder characterized by high blood sugar levels due to insulin deficiency, insulin resistance, or both. It has emerged as a significant global health challenge, affecting millions of individuals and leading to serious complications, reduced quality of life, and increased healthcare costs. This document aims to provide a detailed analysis of diabetes, including its prevalence and mortality rates, risk factors, economic impact, co-morbidities, complications, quality of life, health disparities, access to care, healthcare utilization, prevention, and management strategies." Figure 5 illustrates all the aspects at a glance, discussed in the connecting text.

Figure 5. Health aspects of Diabetes at a glance

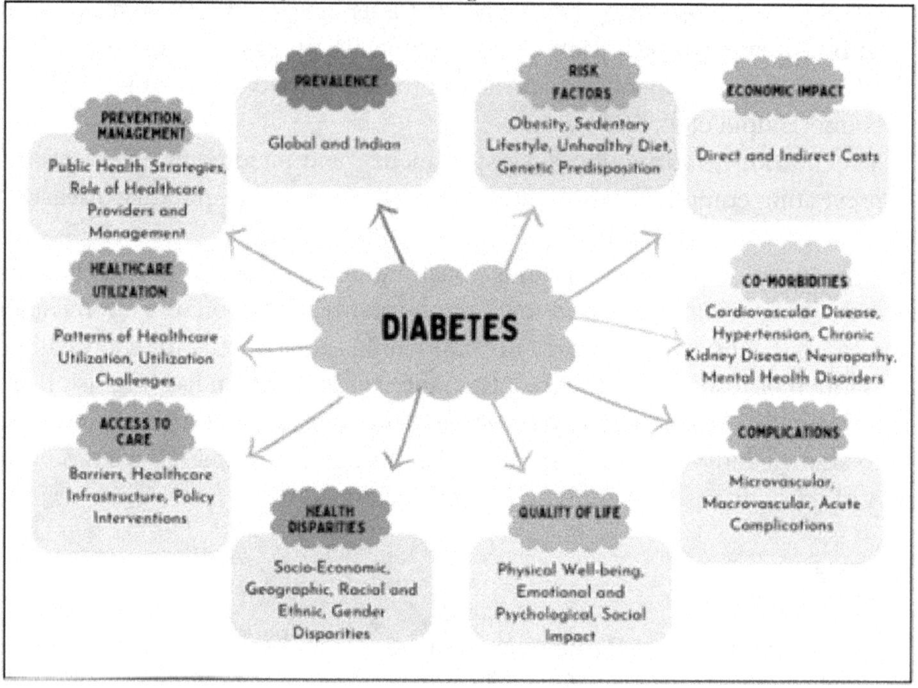

PREVALENCE AND MORTALITY

Global Prevalence

According to the International Diabetes Federation (IDF), 537 million persons worldwide between the ages of 20 and 79 were estimated to have diabetes in 2021. This number is expected to rise to 643 million and 783 million, respectively, between 2030 and 2045 (Magliano, 2022). Important data are as follows:

- **Type 1 Diabetes**: Although less common, Type 1 diabetes affects around 10% of all diabetes cases globally.
- **Type 2 Diabetes**: The most prevalent form, accounting for about 90% of diabetes cases, with rising incidence attributed to lifestyle factors.

Prevalence in India

India has witnessed a dramatic increase in diabetes prevalence, making it one of the countries with the highest number of diabetic individuals. "According to the IDF, approximately 74 million adults aged 20-79 years were living with diabetes in India in 2021, with projections indicating an increase to 101 million by 2030 (Magliano, 2022)."

Key Statistics

- **Urban vs. Rural**: Diabetes prevalence is significantly higher in urban areas (around 12.1%) compared to rural areas (around 4.6%).
- **Age Groups**: The highest prevalence is observed in individuals aged 45-64 years, with increasing rates in younger populations due to lifestyle changes.

Mortality Rates

Diabetes is a leading cause of morbidity and mortality globally. In 2019, it was estimated that diabetes was responsible for 1.5 million deaths worldwide (WHO, 2021). In India, diabetes-related complications contribute significantly to mortality, with estimates indicating that approximately 1 million deaths occur annually due to diabetes-related conditions (Magliano, 2022).

Comparative Analysis

The burden of diabetes is notably higher in low- and middle-income countries (LMICs), where rapid urbanization, lifestyle changes, and limited access to medical care is a contribute to increasing prevalence and mortality rates.

Risk Factors for Diabetes

Understanding the risk factors linked to diabetes is crucial for efficacious prevention and therapy approaches. Important risk variables consist of:

1. Obesity Obesity is a major risk factor for Type 2 diabetes. Insulin resistance, which is made worse by extra body fat, particularly visceral fat, results in elevated blood sugar levels. The World Health Organization (WHO) classifies obesity using the Body Mass Index (BMI): • **BMI ≥ 25**: Overweight • **BMI ≥ 30**: Obesity In India, the prevalence of obesity has risen sharply, with estimates suggesting that approximately 30% of adults are classified as overweight or obese (ICMR, 2020).

2. Sedentary Lifestyle A sedentary lifestyle is a major contributor to the obesity epidemic and is associated with increased risk of Type 2 diabetes. Physical inactivity leads to weight gain and insulin resistance, exacerbating diabetes risk. Data from the WHO indicates that about 31% of adults globally do not meet recommended physical activity levels (WHO, 2021).
3. Unhealthy Diet Diet plays a critical role in the development of diabetes. Diets high in refined carbohydrates, sugars, unhealthy fats, and low in fiber are linked to increased diabetes risk. In India, dietary patterns have shifted towards high-calorie, low-nutrient foods, contributing to rising diabetes prevalence (ICMR, 2020). **Key Dietary Risk Factors: • High Sugar Intake**: "Associated with insulin resistance and Type 2 diabetes." • **Low Fiber Intake**: Reduces glycemic control and contributes to obesity. • **Processed Foods**: Increased consumption of processed and fast foods has been linked to diabetes risk.
4. Genetic Predisposition Diabetes risk is mostly influenced by genetics. Diabetes is more likely to occur in families where the disease has a history. Influencing insulin secretion and action, specific genetic variables are linked to Type 1 and Type 2 diabetes (Gonzalez et al., 2016).

Economic Impact of Diabetes

1.Direct Healthcare Costs

The economic burden of diabetes is substantial, encompassing direct healthcare costs such as hospitalization, medications, and outpatient care. According to the IDF, the global healthcare expenditure on diabetes was estimated at $760 billion in 2019, and this figure is expected to rise (Magliano, 2022).

- **Lost Productivity**

Diabetes significantly impacts productivity due to absenteeism, presenteeism, and premature mortality. In India, the economic cost of lost productivity due to diabetes is estimated to reach billions annually, driven by decreased work capacity and increased healthcare needs (Pandey et al., 2021).

- **Long-term Care Costs**

Chronic complications of diabetes, such as cardiovascular disease, neuropathy, and renal failure, often necessitate long-term care, significantly increasing healthcare costs. The management of complications requires ongoing treatment and monitoring, placing a further financial burden on healthcare systems (Pandey et al., 2020).

- **Public Health Investment**

Investing in public health initiatives aimed at diabetes prevention and management can yield significant economic benefits. Effective interventions, such as health promotion campaigns, screening programs, and education initiatives, can reduce the incidence of diabetes and associated healthcare costs (WHO, 2021).

2. Indirect Costs

Indirect costs related to diabetes include caregiver costs, home modifications, and loss of income due to inability to work. Families often bear a significant financial burden due to the need for assistance in daily activities or modifications to accommodate a family member's condition.

Co-Morbidities Associated with Diabetes

Diabetes is often associated with various co-morbidities that complicate management and worsen outcomes. Key co-morbidities include:

1. Cardiovascular Disease Diabetes increases a person's risk of cardiovascular conditions such as heart failure, stroke, and coronary artery disease. Because diabetes and common risk factors including obesity, dyslipidemia, and hypertension enhance the risk of cardiovascular events, diabetes substantially raises that risk (La Sala, 2020).
2. Hypertension Hypertension is prevalent among individuals with diabetes, often leading to further complications. The coexistence of diabetes and hypertension increases the risk of cardiovascular disease and renal failure (American Diabetes Association, 2020).
3. Chronic Kidney Disease (CKD) Diabetes is a leading cause of chronic kidney disease and end-stage renal disease. Diabetic nephropathy can result in significant morbidity and increased healthcare costs due to the need for dialysis or kidney transplantation (Khan et al., 2020).
4. Neuropathy Diabetic neuropathy is a common complication that can lead to pain, numbness, and weakness, significantly affecting quality of life. Peripheral neuropathy increases the risk of foot ulcers and infections, leading to further complications (American Diabetes Association, 2020).
5. Mental Health Disorders An increased risk of mental health conditions like anxiety and sadness is linked to diabetes. Psychological discomfort can be exacerbated by the chronic nature of diabetes and the difficulties associated with its management (Fitzgerald et al., 2019).

Complications of Diabetes

Diabetes can lead to a range of acute and chronic complications that significantly affect health and quality of life. Key complications include:

1. **Microvascular Complications • Retinopathy**: Diabetes is a leading cause of blindness due to diabetic retinopathy, which results from damage to the blood vessels in the retina (American Diabetes Association, 2020). • **Nephropathy**: As mentioned, diabetic nephropathy can lead to kidney failure and the need for dialysis (Khan et al., 2020). • **Neuropathy**: The effects of neuropathy can lead to foot ulcers and amputations, significantly impacting quality of life.
2. **Macrovascular Complications • Cardiovascular Events**: Individuals with diabetes have a higher risk of heart attacks and strokes, contributing to increased morbidity and mortality (La Sala, 2020). • **Peripheral Arterial Disease**: Diabetes can lead to poor circulation, resulting in pain and potential limb loss.
3. **Acute Complications • Diabetic Ketoacidosis (DKA)**: A life-threatening condition often seen in Type 1 diabetes, characterized by high blood sugar, ketone accumulation, and acidosis (American Diabetes Association, 2020).
    - **Hyperglycemic Hyperosmolar State (HHS)**: A serious condition characterized by extremely high blood sugar levels, typically seen in Type 2 diabetes, leading to dehydration and electrolyte imbalances.

Quality of Life and Diabetes

Diabetes significantly impacts the quality of life of affected individuals. Key factors include:

1. Physical Well-being

Chronic complications and symptoms associated with diabetes can limit physical activity and overall health. Individuals may experience fatigue, pain, and mobility issues, leading to decreased physical functioning (Fitzgerald et al., 2019).

2. Emotional and Psychological Well-being

Managing a chronic condition like diabetes can lead to emotional distress, anxiety, and depression. The burden of constant monitoring, medication adherence, and lifestyle changes can affect mental health and quality of life (Fitzgerald et al., 2019).

3. Social Impact

Social relationships may be impacted due to diabetes management. Dietary restrictions and the need for regular monitoring can lead to feelings of isolation and difficulty participating in social activities (Fitzgerald et al., 2019).

Health Disparities in Diabetes

1. Socio-Economic Disparities Health disparities in diabetes are influenced by socio-economic factors, including income, education, and availability of medical care. Because they have less access to preventative care and treatment, people from poorer socioeconomic backgrounds frequently face higher risks (WHO, 2021).
2. Geographic Disparities Geographic location significantly impacts diabetes prevalence and outcomes. Urban areas often experience higher rates of diabetes due to lifestyle changes, while rural areas may lack adequate healthcare facilities for timely diagnosis and treatment (Pandey et al., 2021).
3. Racial and Ethnic Disparities Certain racial and ethnic groups are disproportionately affected by diabetes. In India, marginalized communities face higher risks due to limited access to healthcare, unhealthy dietary patterns, and socio-economic challenges (ICMR, 2020).
4. Gender Disparities Gender differences also play a role in diabetes outcomes. Women may experience more severe complications and poorer health outcomes due to various biological and social factors (WHO, 2021).

ACCESS TO CARE FOR DIABETES

Barriers to Access

Access to care for diabetes remains a critical issue, particularly in low- and middle-income countries. Barriers to access include:

- **Financial Constraints**: High treatment costs can deter individuals from seeking care, especially in a country like India, where out-of-pocket expenses are significant.
- **Geographical Barriers**: Limited healthcare infrastructure in rural areas restricts access to timely care and specialized services (Pandey et al., 2021).
- **Awareness and Education**: Lack of awareness about diabetes and its symptoms can delay seeking medical attention.

Healthcare Infrastructure

Strengthening healthcare infrastructure is essential for improving access to diabetes care. Investment in healthcare facilities, trained healthcare providers, and essential medical equipment is vital for enhancing service delivery (WHO, 2021).

Policy Interventions

Government policies aimed at expanding health insurance coverage, subsidizing medications, and promoting preventive care are essential for improving access to care. Initiatives such as the Ayushman Bharat scheme in India aim to provide financial protection for low-income populations, improving access to essential health services (Ministry of Health and Family Welfare, 2018; Lahariya, 2018).

HEALTHCARE UTILIZATION FOR DIABETES

Patterns of Healthcare Utilization

Understanding healthcare utilization patterns for diabetes is crucial for developing effective management strategies. Key aspects include:

- **Primary Care Services**: Individuals with diabetes require regular monitoring and management, necessitating frequent visits to healthcare providers.
- **Specialist Care**: Patients may require referrals to specialists for complications related to diabetes, such as cardiologists, nephrologists, and endocrinologists.

Utilization Challenges

Challenges in healthcare utilization include:

- **Inconsistent Care**: Patients may experience fragmented care due to a lack of coordination among healthcare providers.
- **Treatment Adherence**: Non-adherence to prescribed medications can result in increased complications and healthcare utilization, complicating management (American Diabetes Association, 2020).

PREVENTION AND MANAGEMENT OF DIABETES

Public Health Strategies

Preventive measures are crucial in reducing the incidence of diabetes. Public health strategies include:

1. Health Promotion Campaigns Health promotion campaigns focusing on risk factor modification—such as anti-obesity initiatives, dietary education, and promoting physical activity—are vital for preventing diabetes (WHO, 2021).
2. Screening and Early Detection Regular screening for diabetes can facilitate early detection and management. Community-based screening programs can effectively reach underserved populations, improving outcomes (ICMR, 2020).
3. Education and Awareness Programs Increasing awareness about the importance of diabetes prevention and the risk factors associated with the disease is crucial. Educational initiatives targeting schools, workplaces, and communities can foster healthier lifestyle choices (ICMR, 2020).

Role of Healthcare Providers

Healthcare providers play a critical role in prevention and management. Training healthcare professionals to educate patients about risk factors and lifestyle modifications can lead to better outcomes. Incorporating preventive care into routine healthcare visits is essential for early intervention (American Diabetes Association, 2020).

Management of Diabetes

Management of diabetes often includes a combination of pharmacological and non-pharmacological approaches:

- **Pharmacological Management**: Involves the use of oral hypoglycemic agents and insulin for blood sugar control.
- **Lifestyle Modifications**: Emphasizes the importance of a balanced diet, regular physical activity, and weight management in diabetes management (American Diabetes Association, 2020).
- **Monitoring**: Regular monitoring of blood glucose levels is essential for effective management and prevention of complications.

Diabetes is a significant global health challenge with rising prevalence, substantial economic impact, and serious complications. The burden of diabetes is immense, but with coordinated efforts and a commitment to preventive care, we can significantly mitigate its impact. By addressing the underlying risk factors, enhancing access to care, and implementing comprehensive management strategies, we can work towards a healthier future where the prevalence and consequences of diabetes are greatly reduced. The time to act is now, as we strive to improve the health and well-being of individuals and communities around the globe.

CONCLUSION

Non-communicable diseases (NCDs), which include diabetes, cancer, heart disease, and respiratory conditions, pose a serious and expanding global public health threat. These diseases not only pose a substantial burden on healthcare systems but also profoundly affect individuals, families, and communities, leading to a cascade of social, economic, and emotional repercussions.The increasing prevalence of NCDs is alarming. According to the World Health Organization (WHO), NCDs account for approximately 71% of all global deaths, with significant mortality attributed to heart disease, diabetes, cancer, and respiratory illnesses. The rise in these diseases can be linked to demographic transitions, including aging populations, urbanization, and lifestyle changes that promote sedentary behaviors and unhealthy diets. In countries like India, the scenario is particularly concerning. Rapid urbanization and economic development have led to lifestyle shifts, increasing the incidence of NCDs. This trend is compounded by socio-economic disparities, where marginalized populations often face higher risks due to limited access to healthcare and preventive services. The need for urgent intervention and policy reform to address these disparities has never been more critical.

NCDs often coexist, leading to compounded health challenges. For instance, diabetes increases the risk of cardiovascular diseases and respiratory complications. Similarly, cancer survivors frequently face cardiovascular issues as a result of treatment regimens. This interconnectedness not only complicates clinical management but also amplifies the burden on healthcare resources.The economic impact of NCDs is substantial. Healthcare costs associated with treatment, hospitalizations, and management of complications can overwhelm individuals and health systems, particularly in low- and middle-income countries. Additionally, lost productivity due to illness contributes significantly to economic decline. The financial burden extends to families and communities, where care responsibilities often fall on family members, further straining household resources.NCDs severely affect individuals' quality of life. Chronic pain, mobility limitations, and emotional distress stemming from these diseases can lead to isolation, depression, and reduced engagement in social activities. The psychological impact of living with a chronic illness is profound, often resulting in decreased life satisfaction and increased healthcare needs. As such, addressing mental health alongside physical health becomes crucial in the holistic management of NCDs.Access to healthcare remains a significant barrier in managing NCDs. Individuals from disadvantaged backgrounds frequently encounter obstacles such as financial constraints, lack of health insurance, and geographical barriers to accessing quality care. These disparities exacerbate the health crisis, with vulnerable populations facing higher risks of developing NCDs and poorer outcomes. Efforts to improve access to preventive care, early diagnosis, and effective treatment are essential in bridging these gaps.The prevention of NCDs is paramount. Public health initiatives that promote healthy lifestyles—such as physical activity, balanced diets, and tobacco cessation—are crucial in curbing the rise of these diseases. "Education plays a vital role in empowering individuals to make informed choices about their health." Comprehensive health promotion strategies that engage communities, schools, and workplaces can foster environments that support healthier behaviors.Addressing the challenges posed by NCDs requires coordinated global efforts. International cooperation, sharing of best practices, and investment in research and public health infrastructure are essential. Governments must prioritize NCD prevention and management in their health agendas, implementing policies that promote healthier environments and improve access to care.In conclusion, non-communicable diseases present multifaceted challenges that demand urgent attention and action. The interconnectedness of these diseases, combined with their economic and social implications, calls for a comprehensive approach that prioritizes prevention, equitable access to care, and the integration of mental and physical health services. By fostering collaboration among stakeholders—governments, healthcare providers, communities, and individuals—we can work towards reducing the burden of NCDs and enhancing the quality of life for millions. The time for action is now, as we strive for healthier futures in an increasingly complex global health landscape.

REFERENCES

American Diabetes Association. (2011). Standards of medical care in diabetes—2011. *Diabetes Care*, *34*(Supplement_1), S11–S61. DOI: 10.2337/dc11-S011 PMID: 21193625

American Diabetes Association. (2021). Standards of Medical Care in Diabetes—2021. *Diabetes Care*, *44*(Supplement 1), S1–S232. DOI: 10.2337/dc21-Sint PMID: 33298409

Anjana, R. M., Unnikrishnan, R., Deepa, M., Pradeepa, R., Tandon, N., Das, A. K., & Ghosh, S. (2020). Metabolic non-communicable disease health report of India: The ICMR-INDIAB national cross-sectional study (ICMR-INDIAB-17). *The Lancet. Diabetes & Endocrinology*, *11*(7), 474–489. DOI: 10.1016/S2213-8587(23)00119-5 PMID: 37301218

Bade, B. C., & Cruz, C. S. D. (2020). Lung cancer 2020: Epidemiology, etiology, and prevention. *Clinics in Chest Medicine*, *41*(1), 1–24. DOI: 10.1016/j.ccm.2019.10.001 PMID: 32008623

Bourbeau, J., Bourbeau, J., Bhutani, M., Hernandez, P., Aaron, S. D., Balter, M., Beauchesne, M. F., & Marciniuk, D. D. (2019). Self-Management and Behaviour Change in Patients with Chronic Obstructive Pulmonary Disease: A Review of the Literature. *Respiratory Medicine*, *156*, 51–58.

Cohen, J. B., Schrauben, S. J., Zhao, L., Basso, M. D., Cvijic, M. E., Li, Z., & Chirinos, J. A. (2020). Clinical pheno groups in heart failure with preserved ejection fraction: Detailed phenotypes, prognosis, and response to spironolactone. *Heart Failure*, *8*(3), 172–184. PMID: 31926856

Fitzgerald, J. M., Boulet, L. P., Reddel, H. K., & Pedersen, S. (2019). Impact of COPD on Mental Health and Quality of Life. *Chest*, *156*(6), 1157–1166.

Fitzgerald, J. M., Williams, P. A., Dodge, J. A., Quinn, M., Heminger, C. L., Moultrie, R., & Lewis, M. A. (2019). The Psychological Burden of Diabetes. The Lancet Diabetes &amp. *Endocrinology*, *7*(1), 29–36.

. Go, A. S., Mozaffarian, D., Roger, V. L., Benjamin, E. J., Berry, J. D., Blaha, M. J., ... & Turner, M. B. (2014). Heart disease and stroke statistics—2014 update: a report from the American Heart Association. *circulation, 129*(3), e28-e292.

Gonzalez, C. A., Sanz-Anquela, J. M., Companioni, O., Bonet, C., Berdasco, M., López, C., & Gisbert, J. P. (2016). Genetics of Type 2 Diabetes: A Review. *Diabetes*, *65*(3), 659–670.

Halpin, D. M., Criner, G. J., Papi, A., Singh, D., Anzueto, A., Martinez, F. J., Agusti, A. A., & Vogelmeier, C. F. (2021). Global initiative for the diagnosis, management, and prevention of chronic obstructive lung disease. The 2020 GOLD science committee report on COVID-19 and chronic obstructive pulmonary disease. *American Journal of Respiratory and Critical Care Medicine, 203*(1), 24–36. DOI: 10.1164/rccm.202009-3533SO PMID: 33146552

Kastor, A., & Mohanty, S. K. (2018). Disease-specific out-of-pocket and catastrophic health expenditure on hospitalization in India: Do Indian households face distress health financing? *PLoS One, 13*(5), e0196106. DOI: 10.1371/journal.pone.0196106 PMID: 29746481

Khan, M. A., & Atangana, A. (2020). Modeling the dynamics of novel coronavirus (2019-nCov) with fractional derivatives. *Alexandria Engineering Journal, 59*(4), 2379–2389. DOI: 10.1016/j.aej.2020.02.033

Khera, A. V., Emdin, C. A., Drake, I., Natarajan, P., Bick, A. G., Cook, N. R., Chasman, D. I., Baber, U., Mehran, R., Rader, D. J., Fuster, V., Boerwinkle, E., Melander, O., Orho-Melander, M., Ridker, P. M., & Kathiresan, S. (2016). Genetic risk, adherence to a healthy lifestyle, and coronary disease. *The New England Journal of Medicine, 375*(24), 2349–2358. DOI: 10.1056/NEJMoa1605086 PMID: 27959714

Kumar, A. S., & Sinha, N. (2020). Cardiovascular disease in India: A 360 degree overview. *Medical Journal, Armed Forces India, 76*(1), 1–3. DOI: 10.1016/j.mjafi.2019.12.005 PMID: 32020960

Kumar, R., Kaushik, S., Kaushik, S., & Sharma, Y. (2020). The Economic Burden of Diabetes in India: A Systematic Review. *Journal of Health Economics, 70*, 102303.

Kumar, S., & Singh, A., & amp; Gupta, R. (2021). Economic Burden of Cancer in India: A Study. *Journal of Health Economics*.

La Sala, L., & Pontiroli, A. E. (2020). Prevention of diabetes and cardiovascular disease in obesity. *International Journal of Molecular Sciences, 21*(21), 8178. DOI: 10.3390/ijms21218178 PMID: 33142938

Lahariya, C. (2018). 'Ayushman Bharat Program and universal health coverage in India. *Indian Pediatrics, 55*(6), 495–506. DOI: 10.1007/s13312-018-1341-1 PMID: 29978817

Magliano, D. J., & Boyko, E. J. (2022). IDF diabetes atlas.

. Mahal, A., Karan, A., & Engelgau, M. M. (2010). The economic implications of non-communicable disease for India.

McRobbie, H., & Kwan, B. (2021). Tobacco use disorder and the lungs. *Addiction (Abingdon, England)*, *116*(9), 2559–2571. DOI: 10.1111/add.15309 PMID: 33140508

Ministry of Health and Family Welfare, Government of India. (2018). Ayushman

Ministry of Health and Family Welfare (MoHFW). (2017). Available at: https://mohfw.gov.in/

Misra, A., Gopalan, H., Jayawardena, R., Hills, A. P., Soares, M., Reza-Albarrán, A. A., & Ramaiya, K. L. (2019). Diabetes in developing countries. *Journal of Diabetes*, *11*(7), 522–539. DOI: 10.1111/1753-0407.12913 PMID: 30864190

Mosca, L., Benjamin, E. J., Berra, K., Bezanson, J. L., Dolor, R. J., Lloyd-Jones, D. M., Newby, L. K., Piña, I. L., Roger, V. L., Shaw, L. J., Zhao, D., Beckie, T. M., Bushnell, C., D'Armiento, J., Kris-Etherton, P. M., Fang, J., Ganiats, T. G., Gomes, A. S., Gracia, C. R., & Wenger, N. K. (2011). Effectiveness-based guidelines for the prevention of cardiovascular disease in women—2011 update: A guideline from the American Heart Association. *Journal of the American College of Cardiology*, *57*(12), 1404–1423. DOI: 10.1016/j.jacc.2011.02.005 PMID: 21388771

Murray, C. J. (2022). The global burden of disease study at 30 years. *Nature Medicine*, *28*(10), 2019–2026. DOI: 10.1038/s41591-022-01990-1 PMID: 36216939

National Cancer Institute. (2021). *Cancer Statistics*. NCI.

National Cancer Registry Programme. (2020). *Cancer Statistics in India*. NCRP.

National Comprehensive Cancer Network. (2021). *NCCN Guidelines for Patients*. NCCN.

National Heart, Lung, and Blood Institute. (2021). *Heart Health and the Importance of Prevention*. NHLBI.

National Institute on Alcohol Abuse and Alcoholism. (2020). *Alcohol Facts and Statistics*. NIAAA.

National Institutes of Health. (2020). *Physical Activity and Cancer Prevention*. NIH.

Pandey, A., Brauer, M., Cropper, M. L., Balakrishnan, K., Mathur, P., Dey, S., Turkgulu, B., Kumar, G. A., Khare, M., Beig, G., Gupta, T., Krishnankutty, R. P., Causey, K., Cohen, A. J., Bhargava, S., Aggarwal, A. N., Agrawal, A., Awasthi, S., Bennitt, F., & Dandona, L. (2021). Health and economic impact of air pollution in the states of India: The Global Burden of Disease Study 2019. *The Lancet. Planetary Health*, *5*(1), e25–e38. DOI: 10.1016/S2542-5196(20)30298-9 PMID: 33357500

Prentice, R. L., Caan, B., Chlebowski, R. T., Patterson, R., Kuller, L. H., Ockene, J. K., Margolis, K. L., Limacher, M. C., Manson, J. A. E., Parker, L. M., Paskett, E., Phillips, L., Robbins, J., Rossouw, J. E., Sarto, G. E., Shikany, J. M., Stefanick, M. L., Thomson, C. A., Van Horn, L., & Henderson, M. M. (2006). Low-fat dietary pattern and risk of invasive breast cancer: The Women's Health Initiative Randomized Controlled Dietary Modification Trial. *Journal of the American Medical Association, 295*(6), 629–642. DOI: 10.1001/jama.295.6.629 PMID: 16467232

Siegel, R. L., Miller, K. D., Fuchs, H. E., & Jemal, A. (2021). Cancer statistics, 2021. *CA: a Cancer Journal for Clinicians, 71*(1), 7–33. DOI: 10.3322/caac.21654 PMID: 33433946

Sin, D. D., & Man, S. P. (2005). Chronic obstructive pulmonary disease as a risk factor for cardiovascular morbidity and mortality. *Proceedings of the American Thoracic Society, 2*(1), 8–11. DOI: 10.1513/pats.200404-032MS PMID: 16113462

Van Minh, H., Phuong, N. T. K., Saksena, P., James, C. D., & Xu, K. (2013). Financial burden of household out-of-pocket health expenditure in Viet Nam: Findings from the National Living Standard Survey 2002–2010. *Social Science & Medicine, 96*, 258–263. DOI: 10.1016/j.socscimed.2012.11.028 PMID: 23246399

WCRF. A. (2018). Diet, Nutrition, Physical Activity and Cancer: A Global Perspective. Continuous Update Project Expert Report 2018. World Cancer Research Fund. *American Institute for Cancer Research.*

World Health Organization. (2013). Global action plan for the prevention and control of noncommunicable diseases 2013-2020. In the Global *action plan for the prevention and control of noncommunicable diseases 2013-2020.*

World Health Organization. (2021). *Respiratory Diseases Fact Sheet.* World Health Organization.

World Health Organization. (2021). *Cardiovascular Diseases Fact Sheet.* WHO.

World Health Organization. (2021). *Global Diabetes Compact: Progress Report.* WHO.

World Health Organization. (2021). *Cancer Prevention and Control.* WHO.

Chapter 11
Heavy Metals Contamination in River Water and Sediments of Ganga and Hooghly in India

Abantika Ray
https://orcid.org/0009-0008-8155-4027
Jadavpur University, India

Gupinath Bhandari
https://orcid.org/0000-0002-0019-1420
Jadavpur University, India

Waliza Ansar
https://orcid.org/0000-0003-3412-8670
Behala College, India

ABSTRACT

The Ganga River and its tributary Hooghly River in India are distressed by variable levels of heavy metals contamination in river water and sediments by industrial effluents, agricultural runoff, cultural practice, idol immersion and domestic waste. The concentrations of heavy metals (Pb, Hg, Cd & Cr etc) in the river water are repeatedly above the safe limits (above max. admissible & desirable limits) thus making them potentially toxic, hazardous to aquatic lives, ecosystem, biodiversity health and livelihood of people who are using the rivers for drinking, irrigation, pasture and other purposes. The consumption of fish and other aquatic species

DOI: 10.4018/979-8-3693-9755-8.ch011

contaminated with heavy metals poses a risk to food safety and general health of the population including retardation, chronic and acute toxicity, carcinogenic effects, liver and lung damage, neurological & skin diseases, cancer and gastrointestinal disturbances. The result commanding all govt. departments, industries and local communities collaborate to highlight this pollution issues and defend both environmental and human health in India.

INTRODUCTION

Water is one of the most important resources on Earth. India is not only a country of rivers but here rivers were treated as Goddess or Devi. Ganga is treated as the most holy river in India. It is embodied as Mother Ganga. Nearly 25% of the water resources of India, comes from river Ganga (Paul, 2017; Rahaman, 2009; Clayton et al 2025).It is one of the largest rivers in the Indian subcontinent. The water from the Ganga is used for agriculture, industries, domestic purposes, religious rituals and other daily needs. The availability of water in the Ganga is throughout the year, thus it helps in the growth of Indian civilization, culture, rich heritage and Indian economy.

The availability, quality, and quantity of water from this river are rapidly declining, severely impacting flora, fauna, and human life. Waterborne diseases are rising due to poor water quality. In West Bengal, the Ganga and its distributary, the Hooghly River, are heavily contaminated with heavy metals(HMs) in both water and sediments. The agricultural runoff, commercial effluents, urban waste, and idol immersion are some of the causes of massive environmental pollution in Ganga and Hooghly rivers (Maiti et al 2021, Gaur et al 2021) . It has emerged as major environmental issue in India and in densely populated and highly industrialized regions like West Bengal, India (Pandey & Singh, 2017).

The Ganga basin covers most heavily populated areas in the world with an average density of 520 persons/km^2 (Das and Tamminga, 2012). The two major river bodies-the Ganga and Hooghly together sustain millions of people who face serious threats from human activities. Ganga basin in India, Bangladesh and Nepal, sustains more than 300 million people's lives (Gopal, 2000).

The concentration of heavy metals above their normal level is dangerous to aquatic and human health. Contaminated water is not good for drinking, irrigation and other daily uses. The ingestion of fish and other aquatic animals contaminated with HMs poses a danger to food safety and consumption. Frequent consumption of these contaminated foods causes neurological illnesses and cancer (Tchounwou *et al.*, 2012; Dwivedi et al 2018). Another research showed that HMs may produce reactive oxygen species, thereby affecting both terrestrial and aquatic organisms dependent upon these ecosystems as they cause oxidative stress. Besides, polluted water can threaten plant health and agricultural productivity because HMs can slow down growth and decrease crop yields, which risks food security in that area(Samanta, 2013). Outside the immediate ecological damage, HMs contamination has implications that reach far beyond. Chronic exposure to HMs in an aquatic ecosystem can disrupt biological processes, food chain, food web and result in declined species diversity.

HMs contamination in the Ganga and Hooghly rivers has undoubtedly become a multileveled issue, relating to traditions, industrial malpractices, and ecological integrity. This sense of urgency regarding research and action cannot be overemphasized since, health of the rivers relates directly to the welfare of communities. It focuses on the sources, impacts, and potential remediation strategies for HMs contamination in these vital waterways and contributes to a greater discourse on environmental sustainability and public health in Indian states (Das *et al.,* 2023; Kar *et al.,* 2008). Collaboration among stakeholders might help ensure the ecosystem and future of Ganga and Hooghly. Evaluation of the effects of HMs like Lead (Pb), mercury (Hg), Cadmium (Cd) and Chromium (Cr) in Ganga and its distributaries is the focus of this book chapter. This chapter provides an outline of the contamination settings, its causes, detection methods, remediation available in India. Under Sustainable Development Goal (SDG6) this work aligns to target clean water and sanitation.

The National River Ganga: Its Geographical Journey in India

The Ganga river basin (GRB), originates in the Himalayas and flows through northern and eastern regions. The Ganga has two main sources: the Alaknanda and the Bhagirathi. The Alaknanda starts from the snow-capped peaks of Kamet, Nanda Devi and Trisul. The Bhagirathi (main stream of the Ganga) begins at Gomukh ice cave. The Ganga starts in the Garhwal Himalayas at Gomukh($30^0 36'$ N; $79^0 04'$ E; Uttar Kashi district, Uttarakhand) which is the end of the Gangotri Glacier (4,356 meters above mean sea level) (Vass et al., 2010).

So, melting glacier ice forms the clear waters of the Bhagirathi, which meets the Alaknanda River downstream, officially forming the Ganga. The GRB along Brahmaputra and Meghna rivers form the Ganges-Brahmaputra-Meghna (GBM) River Basin. It is the largest river systems in the world(Ganga River System, 2024, NEXT IAS) and is the second-largest river on earth by discharge (average Discharge 12, 037 (m^3/s). Total average annual discharge of Ganga is about 38,000 m^3/s (1,300,000 cu ft/s).

In West Bengal, below the Farakka dam, the Ganga splits into two parts: The Bhagirathi (Hooghly) is on the right, and the Padma is on the left. The Hooghly flows into the Bay of Bengal about 150 km downstream from Kolkata.

Over 400 million people in India reside in the region that supplies water to the river, called the GRB. The GRB is the biggest in India, covering an area of 8, 61,404 square kilometres within the country, which is about 26.2% of the country's total land area (Rahaman,2009; Chauhan *et al,*. 2023; Clayton *et al* 2025, Paul,2017). It flows through 11 different states, 29 class I cities and 23 class II cities, 70 towns, many villages and were drained by Ganga (Agrawal *et al.,* 2010; Biswas *et al.,* 2015; Chauhan *et al.,* 2023).

The tributaries of Ganga (Figure 1) provide fresh water from monsoon rains and the Himalayan snowmelt in the GRB. It receives chilled water sources in Himalayas and uplands and warm water in the downstream plains and deltas (Vass *et al.,* 2010; Singh, 2023). People take a holy dip in the Ganga, starting from Gangotri to pilgrimage like GangaSagar,West Bengal (Singh, 2023). According to popular belief, it purifies the soul and it has antibacterial and medicinal value also (Nautiyal, 2009a; Nautiyal, 2009b; Chauhan *et al.,* 2023).

Figure 1. Main tributaries of river Ganga (adapted from https://www.nextias.com/blog/ganga-river-system/)(2024)

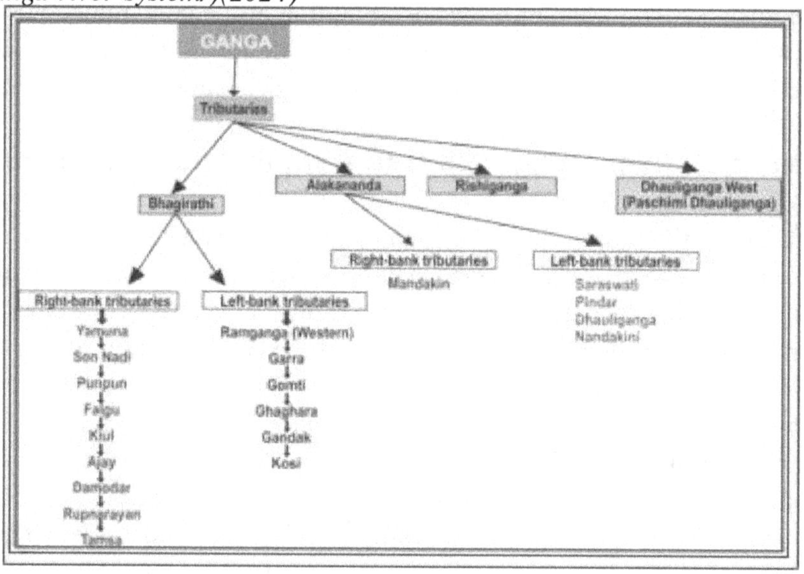

HMs and Ganga River Pollution

HMs pollution is not a newly derived problem in Indian civilization. It initiates from the time, human beings started using processing ores. With the increase in the use of metals, more industrialization, the effect of HMs on environment has also accelerated.

India, being a developing country, the rapid urbanization and industrialization along the banks of this river causing water pollution. Thus deteriorating the quality and quantity of water along the total area of 2525 km of Ganga (Chauhan et al,. 2023). But around 1.3 billion litres per day, of polluted materials discharge in Ganga, thus contaminating the river and disturbing the adjacent settlements (Clayton et al 2025;Rai et al 2010). The quality of water near cities like Allahabad, Kanpur, and Varanasi etc. has become much worst.

The presence of HMs in river has been increasing with growth of industry (like electroplating, mining, rayon, tanning, textile and plating industry), different processes (metal rinse processes, fluidized bed bioreactors, metal smelting, electrolysis applications paper manufacturing, etc), uses of indiscriminate pesticides, batteries, petrochemicals; and diverse human activities (Qasem *et al.,*2021) Out of various types of water pollutants, one of the most important pollutants were HMs pollution because of their toxicological effects. The HMs are not biodegradable in nature and could be carcinogenic (Taseidifar *et al.,* 2017). HMs with degrading nature are Pb, Cu, Ni, Co,, Hg, Mn, Cd, Cr, Fe, As and Zn (Dubey 2021; Clayton *et al.,* 2025). Some metal with positive effects are Cu, Ni, Co and Zn. These HMs even in trace amount are hazardous. They serve as important micronutrients to plants. Cr, Cd, Pb in interaction with Cu, Ni, Co, Zn stabilizes different molecules through electrostatic bonding. Metals like Cr, Cd and Pb have no known physiological activity (Clayton *et al.,*2025). Table 1 summarizes some HMs, focusing on their major sources, health effects, and the permitted quantity in drinking water. Some other metal like boron, calcium, silver, iron, cobalt, molybdenum, antimony etc are also found in rivers and need to be eliminated.

HMs in river came from forest fire, weathering, erosion and leaching of rocks and other natural sources. HMs in sediments deposited due to the precipitation of salts of sulphides, hydroxides, carbonates etc from the leached rocks. Anthropogenic sources includes untreated domestic waste, industrial waste, unsystematic use of HMs containing fertilisers and pesticides, mining industries,etc to the deposition of HMs in ground and drinking water. Some of these HMs gradually leaches from soil to Ganga. Conversely, HMs polluted Ganga traverses the adjoining fields, lands, agricultural patches also. Thus directly exposing animals (during grazing, drinking), aquatic animals and people of different livelihood to this HMs pollution directly or indirectly.

Sources of HMs Pollution in Ganga and Hooghly River:

Wastewater from houses, rapid urbanization, manure release, release from abiotic sources, industrial discharge, agricultural waste, sewage effluents discharge, release of toxic metals including metal chelates from various sources, unsystematic use of HMs containing pesticides and fertilizers and other anthropogenic activities resulted in worsening of water quality, creating threat to human beings and sustaining biodiversity (Figure 2, Table 1). Thousand of animal carcasses mainly cattle are found in Ganga.

The important tributaries of Ganga(Yamuna, Ghaghara, Gandak, etc) while traveling downstream bring several polluting elements and increases the volume of water in the Ganga and also deteriorate its water quality.

Cultural practices such as the immersion of idols during festivals, have enriched the ecosystem with hazardous HMs like Pb,Hg,Cd and Cr in large proportions (Maiti, et al 2021; Ali et al 2019). Along with the effect of industrial effluents, it raises the contamination levels, affecting aquatic biodiversity as well as human health (Maiti, et al 2021; Tover-Sanchez *et al.,* 2018).

HMsfrom industrial discharge have been released from thermal power plants and electroplating industries releases inorganic pollutants(Zn,Hg, Pb, Cr, Cd, and Fe) in water. Large amounts of pesticides are drained from the GRB plainland to the river. To add up to these, there are chlorinated organics, dioxins and organic waste also (Dwivedi*et al.,*2006; Chauhan*et al.,*2023) (Figure 2, Table 1).

HMs pollution along the bank of Hoogly is largely due to industrial activity. Its eastern part, particularly Kolkata and its industrial towns, is so well-known for releasing untreated effluents loaded with HMs directly into the rivers. In general, the north-western Bay of Bengal has been categorized under moderate to high levels of pollution that have been primarily mentioned as due to the higher concentrations of HMs (Hasan et al., 2022).

HMs such as Cd, and Pb are of special concern because they can be bioaccumulating in aquatic organisms and flow up the food chain to finally have impacts on human populations that rely on these water bodies essentially for food and drinking water. The integrity of the rivers is compromised. Pb causes habitat disruption and deterioration of aquatic species critical to the balance of an ecosystem and biodiversity balance.

Figure 2. Sources and effects of HMs pollution in Ganga and its sediments(Figure drawn by author) (Content courtesy: Srivastava et al., 2017; Paul 2017).

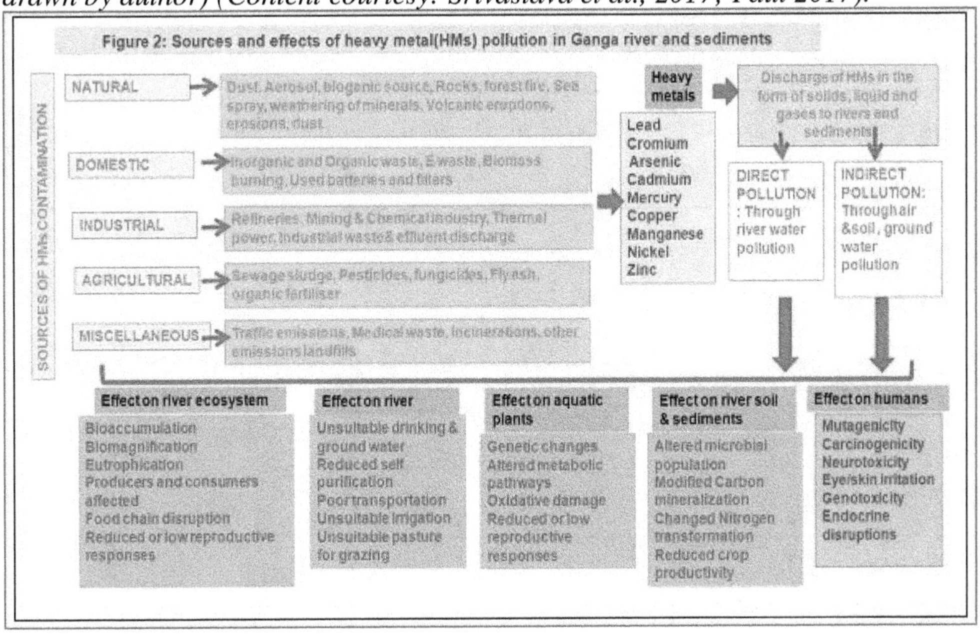

HMs are released into the Ganga and Hooghly through urbanization, chemical industry, municipal sewage and pesticide plants, biomedicals and hazardous agricultural practices (Figure 2, Table 1). For example, Hg releases from combusting coal, electric/light bulb, wood preservatives, leather tanning, ointments, thermometers, adhesives and paints. Cd primarily transpires from manufacturing industries (battery, paint pigments, pesticides, galvanized pipes, and plastics, polyvinyl) and copper refineries. Pb typically originates from materials such as Pb-based paints, gasoline and mobile batteries. Cr is emitted from industrial processes (petroleum refining, electroplating, leather tanning, textile manufacturing), and pulp processing (Das *et al.,* 2023). Rivers waters are also used for the religious activities as immersion of idol, flowers, food offerings, plastic sheets, polythene bags, washing and watering of animals, disposing corpsesand cremation etc(Dwivedi*et al.,* 2018).

Trace metals entering river become part of water and sediments. Distribution of these metals are controlled and maintained by physico-chemical reactions in a dynamic equilibrium. HMs solubility is primarily controlled by pH, various ligands (types and concentration), effects of chelating agents, redox potential and oxidation-state of the mineral components (Beg and Ali, 2008). Natural decomposition of HMs is not possible. The pollution by HMs has both acute and chronic effects on living organisms (Purushothaman andChakrapani, 2007; Baby *et al.,*2019).

Table 1. Sources, exposure pathway, effects in animals and humans of HMs in Ganga

HMs	Sources of HMs in Ganga and Hooghly River	Exposure Pathway	*WHO Max level/ limit (mg/l)	Uses of all these HMs in animals and plants	Effects of HMs (HM) on aquatic animals	Effects of HMs (HM) on human body	Permitted amount in µg*	References
Pb (Pb^{2+})	Paint, glazes, solder, batteries, pesticides, ammunition, alloys, fertilisers, rust inhibitors, automobile emission from Pbed fuel, metal plating, cable sheathing pigments, mining, smelting of ores, burning of coal and plastic stabilizers.	Dietary intake of contaminated water and food through digestive tracts and non-dietary path through muscle and gill kidney>liver>gills>skin>muscle=scales	0.1	In plants affect their metabolic functions, growth, and photosynthetic activity and reduction in the growth of the roots.	Brain damage and behavioural disorders	Neurodegenerative illness, eye yellowing, allergy, decreasing thyroid hormone production, cardiac arrest, autism, Cardiovascular haemolysis, Liver Cirrhosis, cancer, dyslexia, Peripheral vessel disease, Skin yellowing, Infertility Mental disorder involved are kidneys, lungs, spleen, and immunological system.	10	Sankhla *et al.*, 2018; Patel *et al.*, 2021; Rajeshkumar & Li, 2018; Collin*et al.*,2022; Maurya *et al.*, 2019; Paul, D.2017

continued on following page

Table 1. Continued

HMs	Sources of HMs in Ganga and Hooghly River	Exposure Pathway	*WHO Max level/ limit (mg/l)	Uses of all these HMs in animals and plants	Effects of HMs (HM) on aquatic animals	Effects of HMs (HM) on human body	Permitted amount in µg*	References
Hg (Hg^{+})	Runoff from agriculture and landfills, refineries, Hg lamps, pesticides, agricultural industry, electrical appliances, coal combustion, batteries, pharmaceuticals, laboratory apparatus, mining, medical waste, paper & pulp industries	Ingestion--- gill, fish tissue including digestive tracts.	0.00003	No biological functions in plants- Inorganic form of Hgdecreases the mitotic index in the cells of root-tip and alsoincreases the frequency of chromosomal aberrations in direct degrees,	DNA Damage, Lipid peroxidation	Neurodegenerative illness, Eye yellowing, Decreasing thyroid hormone production, Cardiac arrest, Cardiovascular haemolysis, Liver Cirrhosis, kidneyfailure, Skin yellowing, reproductive system	6	Mishra *et al.*, 2022; Sinha *et al.*, 2007; Azevedo and Rodriguez, 2012; Paul, D.2017

continued on following page

Table 1. Continued

HMs	Sources of HMs in Ganga and Hooghly River	Exposure Pathway	*WHO Max level/ limit (mg/l)	Uses of all these HMs in animals and plants	Effects of HMs (HM) on aquatic animals	Effects of HMs (HM) on human body	Permitted amount in µg*	References
Cd (Cd^{2+})	Welding, paints, refineries, electroplating, phosphate fertilizer, coal burning, steel industry, batteries, pigment, plastic industries and stabilisers, ceramic, metal coating batteries, metallurgy, animal supplement, nuclear fission plant, pesticides,, corroded and metal galvanized pipes.	Ingestion of food--- gills and intestine of fish	0.01	If Cd is present in soil, it is causing physiological, chemical, and structural changes in plants.	DNA Damage, Cell death pathways namely apoptosis, autophagy, and inflammation, Enzyme inhibition	Neurodegenerative illness, Eye yellowing, Decreasing thyroid hormone production, Cardiac arrest, Cardiovascular haemolysis, Pulmonary fibrosis, Liver Cirrhosis, Skinyellowing, Infertility, Osteoporosis, renal problem	3	Okocha& Adedeji,2011; Maurya *et al.*,2019; Haider *et al.*, 2021; Paul, D.2017; Das *et al.*,2023

continued on following page

Table 1. Continued

HMs	Sources of HMs in Ganga and Hooghly River	Exposure Pathway	*WHO Max level/ limit (mg/l)	Uses of all these HMs in animals and plants	Effects of HMs (HM) on aquatic animals	Effects of HMs (HM) on human body	Permitted amount in µg*	References
Cr (Cr VI)	Mining, pulp and steel mills electroplating, ferroalloy, textile, metallurgy, fly ash, tanneries.	Dietary intake of contaminated food and water through gill	0.05	Cr (Cr) does not have any recognized biological role in plant physiology; however, high levels of Cr in plant tissues can trigger various morpho-physiological and biochemical processes in plants.	DNA Damage, Cell death pathways (apoptosis), autophagy, inflammation. Growth and reproductive activity of fish by lowering their gonadosomatic index (GSI), fertilization, and hatching rate	Neurodegenerative illness, migraine, Cardiovascular haemolysis, Skin yellowing, puking, reproductive system	50	Kamila *et al.*,2023; Mauryaet *al.*,2019; Sharma et al., 2020; Paul, D.2017; Das *et al.*,2023
Arsenic (As)	Pesticides, animal carcasses, Electronics fungicides, glass production, animal supplements, metal smelters, wood preservatives, biosolids, ore mining, ceramics, geochemical and coals.	Ingestion of contaminated food and water through gill, gastrointestinal tract and skin absorption	0.05	As is non-essential for plants and other organisms.	DNA Damage, Cell death pathways (apoptosis), autophagy, and inflammation.	Eye yellowing, decreasing thyroid hormone production, breathing problems, Cardiac arrest, Cardiovascular haemolysis, metabolic system, Liver Cirrhosis, Peripheral vessel disease, Skin yellowing, Intestinal diarrhoea, Infertility	10	Dwivedi & Singh, 2021; Mauryaet *al.*, 2019; Paul, D.2017; Das *et al.*,2023

continued on following page

Table 1. Continued

HMs	Sources of HMs in Ganga and Hooghly River	Exposure Pathway	*WHO Max level/ limit (mg/l)	Uses of all these HMs in animals and plants	Effects of HMs (HM) on aquatic animals	Effects of HMs (HM) on human body	Permitted amount in µg*	References
Copper (Cu^{2+})	Electroplating, water pipelines and corroded plumbing systems, cables and electronic industry pesticides, alloys mining, pharmaceutical and chemical industries	Ingestion of contaminated water through gill	0.25	Cu plays an important role in plants to maintain enzymatic activities in plants and for chlorophyll and seed production. Cu deficiency causes diseases as ergot.	DNA Damage, Cell death pathways (apoptosis), autophagy, and inflammation. Instigate genotoxicity in aquatic animals,	Cardiovascular, liver disease, Gastrointestinal, Inflammation in the eyes.	2000	Malhotra *et al.*,2020; Maurya et *al.*,2019; La Torre, et al, 2018;Mattsson*et al.*, 2017; Das *et al.*,2023
Manganese (Mn^{2+})	Welding, fuel addition, ferromanganese production	Ingestion of contaminated water through gill	0.4	Mn plays a crucial role in various biological processes, including photosynthesis, respiration, and nitrogen assimilation. It also contributes to pollen germination, the growth of pollen tubes, root cell elongation, and helps plants resist root pathogens.	Cell death	Central nervous system, affect the haematological and biochemical parameters of fish blood	-	Ali *et al*,2021; Lim-Hing, et al 2024; Mattsson*et al.*, 2017; Mukherjee *et al.*, 2022

continued on following page

Table 1. Continued

HMs	Sources of HMs in Ganga and Hooghly River	Exposure Pathway	*WHO Max level/ limit (mg/l)	Uses of all these HMs in animals and plants	Effects of HMs (HM) on aquatic animals	Effects of HMs (HM) on human body	Permitted amount in µg*	References
Nickel (Ni^{2+})	Electroplating, glass batteries, zinc-based casting, Ceramics, Stainless steel production, alloy production, battery industries and nickel alloy production.	Ingestion of contaminated water through gill	0.2	Ni presence in plants can create urea conversion in leaves.	DNA Damage, Cell death pathways (apoptosis), autophagy, and inflammation, hyperplasia, hypertrophy, shortening of secondary lamellae and fusion of adjacent lamellae	Nausea, vomiting, diarrhoea, gastrointestinal distress, headache, pulmonary fibrosis, cardiovascular diseases	70	Al-Attar, 2007; Purushothaman and Chakrapani, 2007;Fabiano*et al.*, 2015;Kumar *et al.*, 2024; Mukherjee *et al.*, 2022
Zinc (Zn^{2+})	Refineries, brass manufacture and coating, aerosol deodorants, rubber products, metal plating, cosmetics, immersion of painted idols, PVC stabilizers, paint industry	liver>kidney>skin>gills>scale=muscle	3	Zn is enzyme component and help in metabolic reactions in plants.	Cell death	Gastrointestinal diseases, skin irritations, anaemia, anxiety, Chest problem, lethargy, nausea and vomiting and convulsions.	3000	Javed, 2012; Maurya*et al.*,2019; Hafeez et al 2013;Kumar *et al.*, 2024

(*Demiral *et al.*, 2021; Mishra*et al.*, 2022; Okocha& Adedeji,2011; Rajeshkumar& Li,,2018; Kamila *et al.*, 2023; Dwivedi& Singh, 2021; Malhotra *et al.*, 2020; Ali *et al.*, 2021; Al-Attar, 2007; Javed, 2012; Collin *et al.*, 2022; Maurya *et al.*, 2019; Purushothaman&Chakrapani, 2007; Azevedo., & Rodriguez, 2012; Haider *et al.*, 2021; Sharma *et al.*, 2020; La Torre et al 2018; Lim-Hing et al 2024; Fabiano *et al.*, 2015; Hafeez et al 2013; Baby *et al.*,2019; Alina *et al.*, 2012; Baby et al., 2022; https://www.betterhealth .vic.gov.au/health/healthyliving/Hg-in-fish; WHO. *Guidelines for Drinking-Water Quality: Fourth Edition Incorporating the First Addendum Quality*; WHO: Geneva, Switzerland, 2017; p. 631).

Effects of HMs on Ecosystems in Ganga and Hooghly:

HMs effects on ecosystems depend on exposure level and duration as well as whether key ecosystem functions necessary for upholding integrity are impacted, such as nutrient cycling and energy flow, biomagnifications, loss of biodiversity (Figure 2, Table 1).

Although hundreds of eco-toxicological studies have measured HMs content in soils, examined their bioavailability and biomagnification, much remains to be learned concerning their biomagnification along the trophic chain and whether this influences ecosystem integrity(Tovar-Sánchez *et al.,* 2018) (Figure 2, Table 1). Factors like turbulence, water acidity, redox potential, seasonal floods, and storms can cause contaminated surface water to move around, can make bottom sediments a possible source of contamination (Sankhla*et al.,* 2018).

Permissible level of HMs pollutants in drinking water according to WHO (World Health Organization, 2007), United States Environmental Protection Agency, Indian Standard Institution, Indian Council of Medical Research, CPCB (Central Pollution Control Board), varies considerably (as mentioned in Paul, 2017).

GROWTH OF TOXIC CONSTITUENTS IN GANGA BY AQUATIC LIFE

The Ganges is home to hundreds of species of fish, phytoplankton and zooplankton, many of which are exotic, and play an important role in the local economy by providing valuable fish stocks. These fish markets are important for livelihood of the adjoining communities. Conversely, increasing pollution has led to severe water degradation and adversely affected health and diversity of fish species. Several fish species such as the dolphin, are now on verge of extinction and number of commercially important fish has declined dramatically.

Toxic substances, especially pesticides, are introduced into the river, causing them to accumulate in fish, causing metabolic disturbances that affects production of various metals and metalloids in fish organs—as in muscles, brain, liver, kidneys, and skin to altering vital metabolic pathways by the way, which are major sites of ingestion of toxic substances that then enter the bloodstream though gills and consumption of contaminated foods, with phytoplankton also have high concentration of metal toxicity. This biomagnifications of toxins not only poses a serious threat to fish health but also to the entire ecosystem and communities that are exposed to these products. Humans consuming sea foods are at risk. Controlling pollution of the Ganga is essential to preserve the ecosystem and ensure sustainable livelihoods for the people who depend on its fisheries (Chauhan et al., 2023).The Hooghly is the key source for the country's inland fish production. Importantly, it serves as a vital area for breeding and raising finfish and shellfish, supports a wide variety of plants and animals, including rare and endangered species, and provides significant benefits to the environment (Mondal *et al.,* 2020).

The WHO (1993) and many other environmental and health safety agencies have set guidelines for ingesting toxic water, organising permissible limits for insecticides and HMs, referred to as "desirable every day intake" (ADI). Inappropriately, concentrations of those dangerous substances inside the Ganga regularly exceed the hooked-up ADI values, making the water deceptive for direct use or consumption.

To make water safe for home use, it should first undergo disinfection and conventional treatment techniques. Though, excessive levels of HMs contamination (of Pb, Cd, Cr, and Hg) pose a huge cancers risk, in keeping with the International Agency for Research on Cancer. These HMs are categorized as group 1 toxicants, pesticides like DDT, HCH, and Pb fall into group 2. Ingesting contaminated toxic food and water increases risk of developing cancers. Furthermore, drinking polluted water causes different waterborne diseases, like cholera, diarrhoea, Hepatitis A, typhoid, food poisoning, and polio. Contaminated water contains bacteria and viruses as well as *E. coli*, hepatitis A, E, etc., which can easily pass from one pathogen to another and affect health.Although another research studies show that toxic chemicals are more poisonous in water though a regular monitoring system, as peoples have lack of interest to know about the high pollution level of Ganga and its remedial measures that indicates the dangerous fatality of Ganga (Chauhan et al., 2023) (WHO, 2022).In Ganga water and sediments, the Pb, Cr, and Cd has no known biological function, but are highly toxic and hazardous elements. These (Pb, Cr and Cd) HMs are not immediately degradable in nature and store in the animal and human bodies to an extremely high amount of toxicityand causing adverse effects beyond a certain limit. These HMs toxicity causes some mortal diseases such as eyelid edema, nephritis, renal tumour, extensive lesions in the kidneys, anuria, nasal mucous membranes and pharynx congestion, increase of blood pressure and cardiovascular diseases,osteoporosis, cancer, headache and malfunctions of different systems of the body, have been reported many times by several authors(Dubey, 2021).These HMs can also affect the production and processing of hormones. Cd is commonly used in making batteries, metals, and in mining and dentistry because it doesn't easily corrode. It can end up in water systems from both natural causes (like weathering and erosion) and human activities (like industry and farming). Pbs exposure can also cause various diseases such as cardiovascular, hypertension, chronic kidney disease, lung and prostate cancer (Samanta, 2013).

Site Selection for Ganga and Hooghly River:

According to CPCB report, 2020; 334 drainsof Ganga were monitored on half yearly basis. Of these 154 drains in Uttar Pradesh and 56 drains in West Bengal were monitored.

From CPCB report,we selected sites both on Ganga and Hooghly based on the presence of drains, pollution sources, population density, possible anthropogenic activities, and the socioeconomic importance of the area.

Varanasi (25° 16′ N latitude, 83° 1′ E longitude), an old city on the left side of the Ganga (Figure 3, created with Arch GIS 10.8 soft ware) was selected. City wastewater (410 MLD; containing inorganic and organic chemicals; 14% being poured into Ganga) mainly changes the water from brownish to nearly black around Varanasi (CPCB, 2013;Singh et al 2024). The city enjoys a humid subtropical climate. Varanasi has ghats/riverbanks as Varunaghat, Dashashwamedh Ghat, Raaj Ghat, and many more. The Varuna is contaminated by the everyday release of domestic and industrial wastewater along with religious practices. Varanasi attracts many pilgrims either as a place for temples or cremation (Trombadore et al 2020). CPCB report revealed water samples collection by consecutive two years, during four seasons: Post Monsoon (September- November), winter (November- January), spring (January- March), and summer (March- May). The sampling locations were Saamne Ghat, the meeting point of Assi Nala with the Ganga, Dashashwamedh Ghat, Raj Ghat, and the confluence of Varuna with the Ganga, as depicted from CPCB report,2020 (Saxena& Singh, 2020; Singh et al 2024). The quality of the Ganga has been reported based on factors like pH, dissolved oxygen, biological oxygen demand, alkalinity, coliform bacteria, chemical oxygen demand, and the presence of HMs (Sankhla*et al.,*2018; Singh et al 2024).

Figure 3. ***Different Varanasi Ghats Polluted withHMs in Ganga River*** *(created with Arch GIS 10.8 soft ware)*

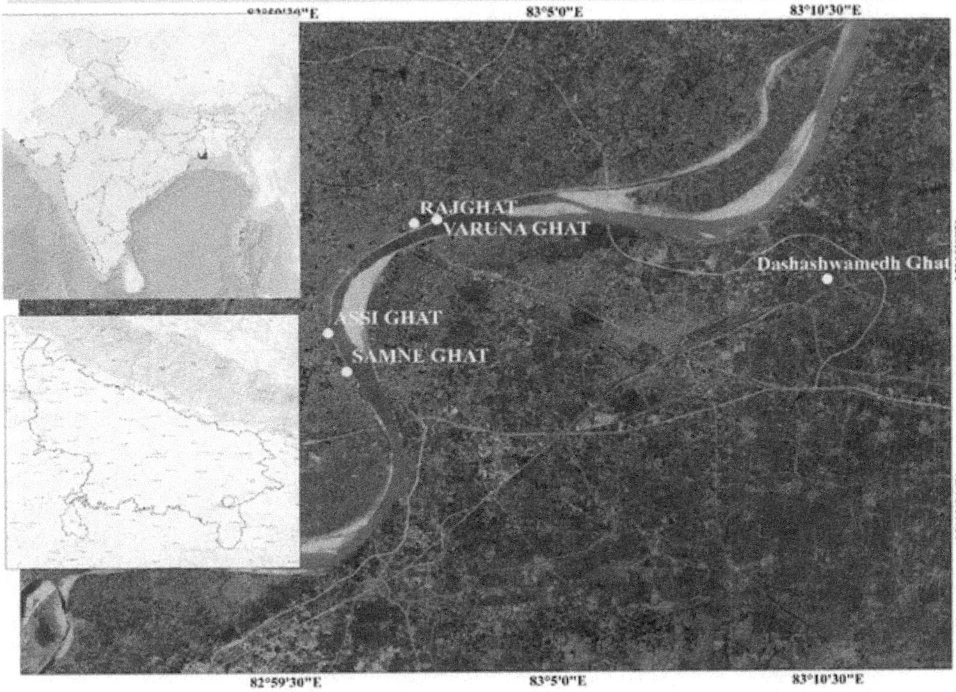

For this study, six immersion ghats of Hooghly have been selected and photographed namelyPanihati Raja Ramchand Ghat, Ariadaha Ghat, Cossipore Ghat, Bagbazar Ghat, Nimtala Thakur Bisarjan Ghat and Babughat(Figure 4-5).

Figure 4. Different Kolkata Ghats Polluted withHMs in river Ganga (created with Arch GIS 10.8 soft ware)

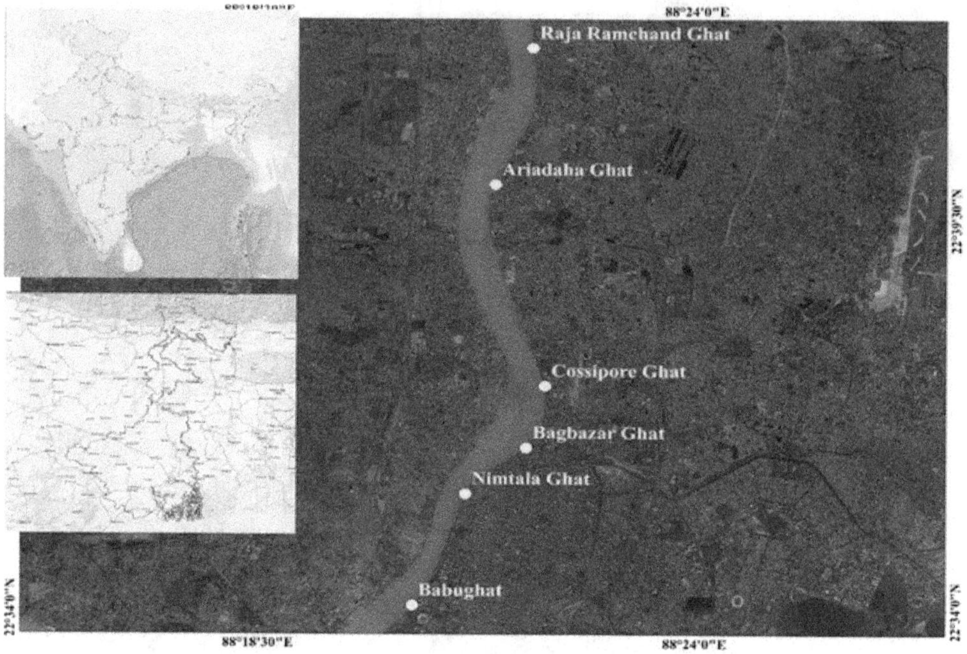

Figure 5. Different Ganga Ghats in West Bengal Showing Pollution(captured by authors)

Drains Discharging Wastewater to Ganga:

In Uttar Pradesh, the Ganges is further subdivided into two regions, the Upper Ganga region (from Sukratal to Anupshar), and second is the Kanpur-Varanasi region (Table 2). The National Green Tribunal noticed that about 128 MLD of wastewater is being released into the Ganga in Varanasi. The Green panel was looking into a case about the release of household and industrial wastewater into the Ganga, which is causing distress to people's religious feelings (CPCB, 2020).

Table 2. Discharge of waste water from different Varanasi Ghats in Ganga (depicted from CPCB report, 2020)

Drain *	Latitude	Longitude	Tapped /Untapped / Interim measures/ STP Outlet	BOD (mg/l)	Flow (MLD)
Samne Ghat Drain	25.272329	83.01551	Untapped	65	29.35
Nagwa/ Asi Drain	25.28305	83.009872	Interim measures	68	177.74
Nakhi Drain/ Dashashwamedh Ghat	25.267417	83.01762	Untapped	60	33.01
Khirkiya/ RajghatNala	25.1934	83.0218	Interim measures	56	53.08
Varuna Drain	25.329262	83.043849	Untapped	8.4	318.92

*All these drains was found in Varanasi town/Catchment with Ganga as their Confluence.

54 drains were found, with 34 situated on the left bank and another 20 on the right bank. The left bank drains contribute 1,179 MLD of wastewater to the Ganga (in West Bengal as Hooghly River), while the right bank drains add 600 MLD. Load, number and flow-wise, left bank drains are higher compared to the right bank drains. The left bank is further divided into 10 zones. These zones are as Kalyani, Naihati, Halisahar, Bhatpara, Titagarg, Barrackpur, Khardaha, Kamarhati, Baranagar, and Kolkata. In total, these drains produce 74,624 kg/day BOD load. Kolkata alone has a high value of 55,443 kg/day or 74% and 6,310 kg/day or 8% BOD load produced by Kamarhati. The right bank drains are divided into six zones. These are Hoogli, Sreerampur, Rishra, Bally, Howrah, and Uluberia.The total BOD load from these drains is 22,514 kg/day. The Hooghly gets 87 million litres of wastewater every day from 22 very polluting industries. It's important to know that different types of industries(like Chemical; Food, dairy and beverage; distillery, sugar, pulp and paper; textile, bleaching and dyeing) are located along the Hooghly. It is noticed that the chemical industry sends out 70% of the total wastewater, followed by the pulp and paper industry, which contributes 20%. Total wastewater generation is 87.2 KLD (Kiloliters per Day) from these industries and the total water consumption is 115.5 KLD.This is different from trend in Upper and middle Ganga (CPCB, 2013 and 2020).

ONGOING RESEARCH AND STUDIES CARRIED OUT ONHMS POLLUTION OF GANGA

Different research on Ganga's tributaries and distributaries that shows anthropogenic sources in some sampling stations, are the fundamental contributors to hazardous HMs pollution (Figure 2). The effect of pollution on ecosystem, flora, fauna and humans were either direct or indirect and fluctuate according to sampling time/season and/or may be followed by some cultural/traditional practices. In Kolkata, the pictures of heavy pollution were depicted (Figure 5) after Durga Puja during idol immersion.

The huge deposit of silts and HMs gradually alters the physicochemical characteristics of the water. The sediment layer, its biota and composition is highly altered. It loses its self-purifying power . Due to HM pollution, microbiota alters and the surge in the growth of pathogenic bacteria increases. Cyclops and Daphnia are highly susceptible to HM pollution. Many aquatic organisms are on the verge of extinction or already extinct. Some of the research work on the effect of HM pollution in Ganga and sediments were depicted in Table 3.

Discussion: Mitigation strategies to curb HMs pollution in Ganga

In case of Ganga and Hooghly, the HMs contamination demands prompt and rigorous action. Remedial measure necessitates government policies, stringent regulation of industrial discharge, household waste and sustainable model on idol immersion(Maiti, et al 2021). Innovative mitigation strategies includes adsorption, membrane filtration, phytoremediation, coagulation and flocculation, ion exchange, immobilisation of metals, biocatalytics which removes HMs from contaminated soil and water. Yet another significant activity is education of communities about the environmental effects, human fitness of HMs contamination through public awareness programs, campaigns, advertisements, pamphlets distribution and block wise implementation. Other methods includes reverse osmosis, electrochemical treatment membrane filtration, photocatalytic based treatment, solvent extraction, chemical precipitation, biochar, hydrogel etc(Figure 6).

Prevention of surged HMs contamination inside the Ganga and Hooghly is important for environmental stability and abundance of freshwater sources(Briffa et al 2020).

Figure 6. Mitigation/remediation strategies of HM removal (Figure drawn by authors) [Content courtesy: Sakakibara et al., 2012; LeDuc and Terry, 2005; Cristaldi et al., 2017; Awa and Hadibarata 2020; Zhou et al. 2016; Bua et al., 2017; Fernández-Martínez et al. 2015; Liu et al. 2017; Desoky et al. 2020; Gururajan and Belur 2018; Gaur et al, . 2021; Zhou 2016].

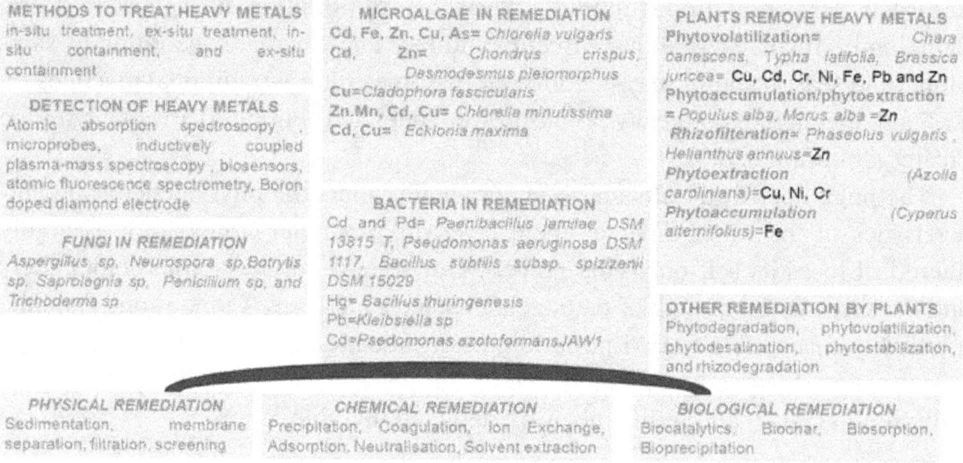

The government of India has taken various initiatives to culminate the level of Ganga pollution. In 1986, Ganga Action Plan was launched to lower sewage discharge directly into the Ganga. Section 3(3) of Environment Protection Act, 1986 was focused on the conservation of Ganga. To clean and conserve Ganga water, the National Ganga River Basin Authority (NGRBA) was established (Dwivedi et al., 2018).

The concentrations of HMs determined from different sampling stations were checked for their maximum admissible and desirable limit when compared with the National and International organizations like CPCB, Indian Standard Institution, Indian Council of Medical Research, WHO and United States Environmental Protection Agency.

Mitigation of HMs in India is quite challenging due to financial constraint and poor technical development. Different traditional methods for the HMs elimination have become old-fashioned because of several shortcomings. Methods like ion exchange, coagulation, adsorption, membrane filtration etc and bioremediation have some drawbacks. Most of these processes have high cost, low public acceptability, incomplete elimination of HMs and generates secondary pollutants. Some also requires additional treatment for complete remediation. Among these, eco-friendly bioremediations is most preferred with certain limitations also. Low contamination sites may be used for bioremediation and subsequent increase in soil fertility.

Furthermore, employing OMICS approach(genomics, transcriptomics, proteomics, and metabolomics) can enhance the bioremediation effectiveness and site implementation. The introduction of genes pertaining to the resistance/ tolerance, and uptake of these contaminants can further increase the bioremediation potential by organisms. An ideal plant with phytoremediation capacity is tolerant of harsh environment, easy to harvest and increased potential to curb HMs by absorption, mobilization, sequestration, and transfer. Genetically modified organisms with their unique sets of enzymes can transform or mineralize these pollutants.

CONCLUSION

The problem of HM pollution(from natural and man made resources) in Ganga causes bioaccumulation and biomagnifications.The toxic effect in ecosystem and related health risk was discussed. Conversion of HMs to different products and by-products has made its remediation(in-situ and ex-situ) a large delay, with the contour of traditional methods. Traditional processes are multi-layered and cumbersome, with extended treatment time and allied secondary pollution. The physical, chemical and plant-microbe bioremediation processes are evolving through adaptive learning to develop cheap and sustainable remediations. Regular monitoring and attenuation of discharge in Ganga, time-regulated sampling at multiple spots, regular monitoring of analytical findings from unified laboratories, rational remediation planning, cost-effective techniques, increased efficiency, heavy metal concentration calculation, tracking different case studies is worthy. Policy formulation in continuity with global regulatory policy, new researches is needed to crib these bottlenecks for the mitigation of HMs contamination in Ganga.In addition, an elaborate future investigation on the microbes, human and plant to pinpoint potential health risks, mitigate exposure routes in metabolism, generation of new GMO, molecular and toxicology studies through clinical trials needed to ensure environment safety(Figure 7).

Figure 7. Limitations and future directives of HM pollution in Ganga river and sediments(Figure drawn by authors) [Content courtesy: Gaur et al,2021].

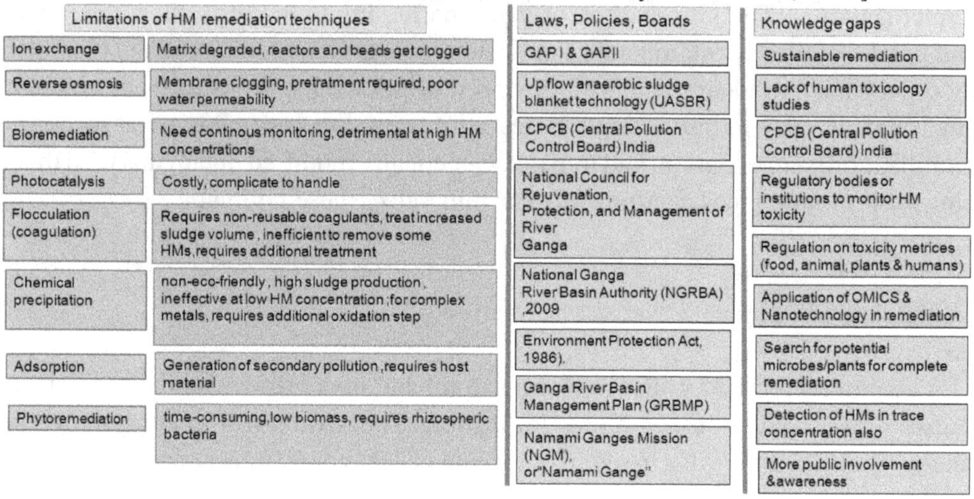

Table 3. Research findings on HMs (HMs) pollution in Ganga

HMs found	Research findings		References
	In Ganga River	In Sediments	
Zn, Cu, Cr, Pb, Cd	I. Occurrence and bioaccumulation of some HMs at Allahabad II. Accumulation of HMs in muscles of 2 species of catfish- a) Channa*punctatus*& b) *Aorichthysaor*)	Zn >Pb> Cu > Cr >Cd level of accumulation. Zinc) Zn was maximally accumulated	Gupta *et al.*,2009
Cu, Pb, Cd, and Zn	I. Ganga River is moderately polluted II. Found HMs in water, fish (*Rita rita*), benthic macro invertebrates (*Thiara lineate*) III. Pb & Cd found above permissible level in tissues of mollusca	Found HMs in sediments also	Nath and Banerjee, 2006
Zn, Mn, Ni, Pb, Cd, Cr, Co, Fe, Cu,	I. Concentrationsandoccurrence of these HMs in Uttar Pradesh II. Concentration varies depending on the sampling station III. Physico-chemical characteristics andanalysis of river water IV. HMs accumulation in *EicchorniaCrassipes* plant &*Heteropnuestesfossilis* fish	Different concentrations these HMs in sediments also	Ajmal *et al.*,1984

continued on following page

Table 3. Continued

HMs found	Research findings		References
	In Ganga River	In Sediments	
Cu, Cr,Ni, Fe, Zn, Cd	I. Concentration of HMs varies depending on the season and pilgrim inflow II. Physico-chemicalparametersanalysis of the river at Vindhyachal Ghat, Varanasi.	ND	Chaturvedi and Pandey, 2006
Cd	I. HMs distribution in the river confluence at Varanasi-Mirzapur	HMs detected insediments also	Prasad et al 1989
Pb	Assessed the effect of Pb in river in West Bengal	ND	Dutta *et al.*,2005
Cu, Zn, Cd, Cr, Fe, Mn, Ni, Co, and Pb	ND	I. Freshly deposited sediments were analysedin 27 locationsfor the geogenic distribution and concentration of baseline II. Northern Indian is enriched with Cu, Fe, Ni, Co& Cr	Singh et *al.*,2003; Singh et *al.*,2002
Cr, Mn, Fe, Co, Ni, Cu, Zn, and Pb	ND	i. From 22 locations, sediments were collected, fractionated and analysed for presence of HMs and total dissolved solids	Purushothaman and Chakrapani, 2007
Cu, Cr, Zn, Ni, and Cd	I. Measured the concentration of HMs in Bhagalpur II. Cd was absent, other 4 metals were present, Cu being the highest concentration in 3 sites for a period of 3 years.	I. Low or negligible concentration level of Ni, Cd and Cu II. High level of concentration of Zn and Cr.	Singh *et al.*,2012
Fe, Mn, Cu, Zn, Hg, Pb	I. The level of dissolved HMs were analysed in the Ganga River ghats of Babughat, Gangasagar and Diamond Harbour of West Bengal II. Pb and Hg's high valueswerereported	ND	Sarkar *et al.*,2007
Hg	I. Hg pollution was studied in 3 seasons in river water, benthic macro invertebrates, aquatic macrophytes fish, and vegetation of the associated floodplains in Varanasi	Hg pollution was noted in sediments also	Sinha *et al.*,2007
Pb, As, Cd, Cr, Fe, Cu,Mn, Ni, Zn and V	I. Lower proportion of free metal ions in water than sediments	I. Sediment quality was assessed fortoxicity bioassay. II. Cr was 30% higher in downstream sediment than in upstream sediment at Kanpur III. Metal levels high in the downstream.	Beg and Ali, 2008

continued on following page

Table 3. Continued

HMs found	Research findings		References
	In Ganga River	**In Sediments**	
Zn, Cr, Cu, Cd, and Pb	I. Concentration and accumulation of HMs in tissues (gill, gonads, skin and muscle tissues) of 6 edible fishes and water in Rishra-Konnagar region, West Bengal were noted for 2 years II. Variation in concentration were noted in different seasons III. Tissue accumulation of HMs is species specific	HMs were also noted in sediments also	Bhattacharya *et al.*,2008
Non-radioactive HMs, (Zn, Pb, Cd, and Cu)	I. Distribution and concentration of these HMs in river from Rishikesh to Allahabad at 5 locations. II. Concentration very high in some locations.	ND	Sharma, et al,2012
Cd, Cu, Cr, Fe, Mn, Ni, Pb and Zn	I. Analysed various HMs of the surface water samples in West Bengal. II. Showed a significant seasonal fluctuation for Fe, Mn, Cd, and Cr. III. Fe, Mn, Zn, Ni, Cr and Pb were found to exist in most samples	ND	Kar *et al.*,2008
Zn, Cu, Cd, Pb, and Cr	I. Very high concentration (above permissible limits) of HMs in Varanasi at 3 sewage plants	ND	Rai, Mishra and Tripath, 2010
Cu, Cr, Cd, Pb and Zn	I. HMs level was studied on quarterly basis at Kanpur and Varanasi II. Concentrations were high at the discharged point and in the effluents III. Concentration low below the discharge zone	ND	Kumar, *Jaiswal and Watal,* 2009
Ni, Cd, Pb, Cr, Cu	I. Cd and Pb levels were high in 5 sampling stations than admissible levels II. Cr and Cu levels stayed below their maximum allowable concentration. III. Ni concentration was very high IV. iv. Metal concentration showed seasonal variations.	ND	Pandey *et al* 2009
Pb, Cr, Fe, Cd, Cu, Mn,Zn, and Ni	I. HM concentrations were analysed in surface water at 4 locations around Kolkata II. metals concentration varied with season III. Fe, Cu, Mn, Zn, and Ni were detected in the many samples. Cr was not detected in any samples	ND	Aktar et al., 2010

continued on following page

Table 3. Continued

HMs found	Research findings		References
	In Ganga River	In Sediments	
Cr, Mn, Fe, Cu, Zn, and Pb	I. Seasonal and site variation of metals in river water at 5 sites of Allahabad II. Concentration of Fe high in all sites. Iii. Mn, Cu and Zn concentration within the permissible limits	ND	Kumar *et al.*,2014
Cd, Cu, Pb, Zn	I. Concentration of HMs were determined from Rishikesh to Allahabad II. Maximum contaminated of Cd and Cu at Narora Barrage III. Pb and Zn were higher at Jajmau Kanpur	I. Sediment were contaminated with HMs and alarming at Jajmau Kanpur and Narora Barrage II. High level of Zinc found	Goswami and Sanjay, 2014
Fe, Ni, Cr, Zn, Mn, Cuand Pb	I. River water contaminated with dissolved metals above the safe limits II. Metal accumulation in the fish blood of *Labeo rohita* was very high for Cr, Fe, Cu, Znand Mn.	ND	Vaseem and Banerjee,2013
Pb, Cr, Cd, Co, Ni, Cuand Zn	I. HM contamination adversely affecting fresh water ecology	I. Total trace metal content in sediments at Buxar, Ghazipurand Ballia urban locations in pre monsoon period were analysed. Level of Cd was very high.	Singh *et al.*, 2013

ND= Not detected. (Singh *et al.*, 2013; Vaseem and Banerjee, 2013; .N. Goswami and Sanjay, 2014; Kumar *et al.*, 2014; Aktar *et al.*, 2010; Pandey et al 2009 ; Kumar et al 2009; Rai, Mishra and Tripath, 2010 ; Gupta *et al.*, 2009; Kar *et al.*, 2008; Sharma, Meher and Mishra, 2012 ; Sinha *et al.*, 2007; Bhattacharya *et al.*,2008; Beg and Ali, 2008; Singh *et al.*, 2012; Sarkar *et al.*,2007; Purushothaman and Chakrapani, 2007; Gupta *et al.*,2009; Nath and Banerjee, 2006; Kumar et al 2024; Ajmal *et al.*, 1984; Singh et *al.*,2003; Singh *et al.*, 2002; Chaturvedi and Pandey, 2006; Prasad, Mathur and Rupaniwar, 1989; Dutta*et al.*, 2005).

REFERENCES

Agrawal, A., Pandey, R. S., & Sharma, B. (2010). Water pollution with special reference to pesticide contamination in India. *Journal of Water Resource and Protection*, *2*(5), 432–448. DOI: 10.4236/jwarp.2010.25050

Ajmal, M., Nomani, A. A., & Khan, M. A. (1984). Pollution in the Ganges River, India. *Water Science and Technology*, *16*(5-7), 347–358. DOI: 10.2166/wst.1984.0142

Al-Attar, A. M. (2007). The influences of nickel exposure on selected physiological parameters and gill structure in the teleost fish, Oreochromisniloticus. *Journal of Biological Sciences (Faisalabad, Pakistan)*, *7*(1), 77–85. DOI: 10.3923/jbs.2007.77.85

Ali, H., Khan, E., &Ilahi, I. (2019). Environmental chemistry and ecotoxicology of hazardous HMs: environmental persistence, toxicity, and bioaccumulation.*Journal of Chemistry, 2019*(1). .DOI: 10.1155/2019/6730305

Ali, Z., Yousafzai, A. M., Sher, N., Muhammad, I., Nayab, G. E., Aqeel, S. A. M., Shah, S. T., Aschner, M., Khan, I., & Khan, H. (2021). Toxicity and bioaccumulation of manganese and Cr in different organs of common carp (Cyprinuscarpio) fish. *Toxicology Reports*, *8*, 343–348. DOI: 10.1016/j.toxrep.2021.02.003 PMID: 33659190

Alina, M., & Azrina, A., MohdYunus, A. S., MohdZakiuddin, S., MohdIzuan Effendi, H., & Muhammad Rizal, R. (2012). HMs (Hg, arsenic, Cd, plumbum) in selected marine fish and shellfish along the Straits of Malacca. *International Food Research Journal*, *19*(1), 135–140.

Awa, S. H., & Hadibarata, T. (2020). Removal of heavy metals in contaminated soil by phytoremediation mechanism: A review. *Water, Air, and Soil Pollution*, *231*(2), 1–15. DOI: 10.1007/s11270-020-4426-0

Azevedo, R., & Rodriguez, E. (2012). Phytotoxicity of Hg in plants: A review. *Journal of Botany (Egypt)*, *1*, 1–6. Advance online publication. DOI: 10.1155/2012/848614

Baby, R., Hussein, M. Z., Abdullah, A. H., & Zainal, Z. (2022). Nanomaterials for the treatment of HMs contaminated water. *Polymers*, *14*(3), 583. DOI: 10.3390/polym14030583 PMID: 35160572

Baby, R., Saifullah, B., & Hussein, M. Z. (2019). Carbon nanomaterials for the treatment of HMs-contaminated water and environmental remediation. *Nanoscale Research Letters*, *14*(1), 341. DOI: 10.1186/s11671-019-3167-8 PMID: 31712991

Beg, K. R., & Ali, S. (2008). Chemical contaminants and toxicity of Ganga River sediment from up and down stream area at Kanpur. *American Journal of Environmental Sciences*, *4*(4), 362–366. DOI: 10.3844/ajessp.2008.362.366

Bhattacharya, A. K., Mandal, S. N., & Das, S. K.A.K. BhattacharyaS.N. MandalS.K. Das. (2008). HMs accumulation in water, sediment and tissues of different edible fishes in upper stretch of Gangetic West Bengal. *Trends in Applied Sciences Research*, *3*(1), 61–68. DOI: 10.3923/tasr.2008.61.68

Biswas, K., Paul, D., & Sinha, S. N. (2015). Prevalence of multiple antibiotic-resistant coliform bacteria in the water of River Ganga. *Frontiers in Environmental Microbiology*, *1*(3), 44–46. DOI: 10.11648/j.fem.20150103.12

Briffa, J., Sinagra, E., & Blundell, R. (2020). HMs pollution in the environment and their toxicological effects on humans. *Heliyon*, *6*(9), e04691. Advance online publication. DOI: 10.1016/j.heliyon.2020.e04691 PMID: 32964150

Bua, D. G., Annuario, G., Albergamo, A., Cicero, N., & Dugo, G. (2017).. . *Environmental Technology & Innovation*, *8*, 309, 326. DOI: 10.1016/j.eti.2017.08.002

Central Pollution Control Board. (2013). Pollution assessment: River Ganga. *(Ministry of Environment and Forests, Govt. of India)*. https://cpcb.nic.in/wqm/pollution-assessment-ganga-2013.pdf

Central Pollution Control Board. (2020). Status of post-monsoon 2020 monitored drains discharging into river Ganga and its Tributaries (BangangaRamganga, Kali-East, Pandu, etc.). *(Ministry of Environment and Forests, Govt. of India)*. https://cpcb.nic.in/ngrba/Identified_drains_postmonsoon-2020.pdf

Chaturvedi, J., & Pandey, N. K. (2006). Physico-chemical analysis of River Ganga at Vindhyachal Ghat. *Current World Environment*, *1*(2), 177–179. DOI: 10.12944/CWE.1.2.14

Chauhan, S., Yadav, A., Kurup, P. M., Li, X., Swarnakar, P., & Gupta, R. K. (2023). Devising a people-friendly test kit for overcoming challenges in the assessment of water quality and analysis of water pollution in the river Ganga. *RSC Sustainability*, *1*(3), 418–431. DOI: 10.1039/D2SU00071G

Clayton, G. E., Richards, L. A., Fox, B. G., Thorn, R. M. S., Bowes, M. J., Read, D. S., Tipper, H. J., Khamis, K., Dutta, T. K., Kumar, A., Hazra, M., Howard, B., Schneidewind, U., Armstrong, L. K., Nicholls, D. J. E., Davies, H., Hannah, D., Nel, H. A., Ghosh, A., & Reynolds, D. M. (2025). Associations of anthropogenic activity and tributaries with the physicochemical, nutrient and microbial composition of the Ganga (Ganges) River, India. *Water Research*, *278*, 123374. Advance online publication. DOI: 10.1016/j.watres.2025.123374 PMID: 40023934

Collin, S., Baskar, A., Geevarghese, D. M., Ali, M. N. V. S., Bahubali, P., Choudhary, R., & Swamiappan, S. (2022). Bioaccumulation of Pb (Pb) and its effects in plants: A review. *Journal of Hazardous Materials Letters*, *3*, 100064. Advance online publication. DOI: 10.1016/j.hazl.2022.100064

Das, P., & Tamminga, K. R. (2012). The Ganges and the GAP: An assessment of efforts to clean a sacred River. *Sustainability (Basel)*, *4*(8), 1647–1668. DOI: 10.3390/su4081647

Das, S., Sultana, K. W., Ndhlala, A. R., Mondal, M., & Chandra, I. (2023). HMs pollution in the environment and its impact on health: Exploring green technology for remediation. *Environmental Health Insights*, *17*, 11786302231201259. Advance online publication. DOI: 10.1177/11786302231201259 PMID: 37808962

Demiral, İ., Samdan, C., & Demiral, H. (2021). Enrichment of the surface functional groups of activated carbon by modification method. *Surfaces and Interfaces*, *22*, 100873. Advance online publication. DOI: 10.1016/j.surfin.2020.100873

Desoky, E.-S. M., Merwad, A.-R. M., Semida, W. M., Ibrahim, S. A., El Saadony, M.-T., & Rady, M. M. (2020). Heavy metals-resistant bacteria (HM-RB): Potential bioremediators of heavy metals-stressed Spinacia oleracea plant. *Ecotoxicology and Environmental Safety*, *198*, 110685. DOI: 10.1016/j.ecoenv.2020.110685 PMID: 32387845

Dubey, I. (2021). Study on the toxic effects of HMs in sediments and water of river Ganga. *International Journal of Biological Sciences*, *12*(2), 89–97. DOI: 10.53390/ijbs.v12i2.7

Dutta, S., Kole, R. K., Ghosh, S., Nath, D., & Vass, K. K. (2005). Impact assessment of Pb on water quality of River Ganga in West Bengal, India. *Bulletin of Environmental Contamination and Toxicology*, *75*(5), 1012–1019. DOI: 10.1007/s00128-005-0850-5 PMID: 16400592

Dwivedi, K., & Singh, S. (2021). Toxicological effect of arsenic on organs of fishes: A review. *Journal of Entomology and Zoology Studies*, *9*(5), 465–473.

Dwivedi, S., Mishra, S., & Tripathi, R. D. (2018). Ganga water pollution: A potential health threat to inhabitants of Ganga basin. *Environment International, 117*, 327–338. DOI: 10.1016/j.envint.2018.05.015 PMID: 29783191

Dwivedi, S., Tripathi, R. D., Rai, U. N., Srivastava, S., Mishra, S., Shukla, M. K., Gupta, D. K., Sinha, S., Baghel, V. S., & Gupta, D. K. (2006). Dominance of algae in Ganga water polluted through fly-ash leaching metal bioaccumulation potential of selected algal species. *Bulletin of Environmental Contamination and Toxicology, 77*(3), 427–436. DOI: 10.1007/s00128-006-1083-y PMID: 17033871

Fabiano, C. C., Tezotto, T., Favarin, J. L., Polacco, J. C., & Mazzafera, P. (2015). Essentiality of nickel in plants: A role in plant stresses. *Frontiers in Plant Science, 6*, 754. DOI: 10.3389/fpls.2015.00754 PMID: 26442067

Fernández-Martínez, R., Rucandio, I., Gómez-Pinilla, I., Borlaf, F., García, F., & Larrea, M. T. (2015). Evaluation of different digestion systems for determination of trace mercury in seaweeds by cold vapour atomic fluorescence spectrometry. *Journal of Food Composition and Analysis, 38*, 7–12. DOI: 10.1016/j.jfca.2014.10.003

Gaur, V. K., Sharma, P., Gaur, P., Varjani, S., Ngo, H. H., Guo, W., & Singhania, R. R. (2021). Sustainable mitigation of heavy metals from effluents: Toxicity and fate with recent technological advancements. *Bioengineered, 12*(1), 7297–7313.

Gopal, B. (2000). *River conservation in the Indian subcontinent. Global Perspectives on River Conservation: Science, Policy and Practice*. John Wiley., DOI: 10.1016/S0006-3207(00)00224-X

Goswami, D. N., & Sanjay, S. S. (2014). Determination of HMs, viz. Cd, copper, Pb and zinc in the different matrices of the Ganges River from Rishikesh to Allahabad through differential pulse anodic striping voltametry. [IJARCS]. *International Journal of Advanced Research in Chemical Science, 1*(5), 7–11.

Gupta, A., Rai, D. K., Pandey, R. S., & Sharma, B. (2009). Analysis of some HMs in the riverine water, sediments and fish from river Ganges at Allahabad. *Environmental Monitoring and Assessment, 157*(1-4), 449–458. DOI: 10.1007/s10661-008-0547-4 PMID: 18850290

Gururajan, K., & Belur, P. D. (2018). Screening and selection of indigenous metal tolerant fungal isolates for heavy metal removal. *Environmental Technology & Innovation, 9*, 91–99. DOI: 10.1016/j.eti.2017.11.001

Hafeez, B. M. K. Y., Khanif, Y. M., & Saleem, M. (2013). Role of zinc in plant nutrition-a review. *American Journal of Experimental Agriculture, 3*(2), 374–391. https://journaljeai.com/index.php/JEAI/article/view/978. DOI: 10.9734/AJEA/2013/2746

Haider, F. U., Liqun, C., Coulter, J. A., Cheema, S. A., Wu, J., Zhang, R., Wenjun, M., & Farooq, M. (2021). Cd toxicity in plants: Impacts and remediation strategies. *Ecotoxicology and Environmental Safety, 211*, 111887. Advance online publication. DOI: 10.1016/j.ecoenv.2020.111887 PMID: 33450535

Hasan, M., Rahman, M., al Ahmed, A., Islam, M. A., & Rahman, M. (2022). HMs pollution and ecological risk assessment in the surface water from a marine protected area, swatch of no ground, north-western part of the Bay of Bengal. *Regional Studies in Marine Science, 52*, 102278. Advance online publication. DOI: 10.1016/j.rsma.2022.102278

Javed, M. (2012). Effects of zinc and Pb toxicity on the growth and their bioaccumulation in fish. *Pakistan Veterinary Journal, 32*(3), 357–362.

Kamila, S., Shaw, P., Islam, S., & Chattopadhyay, A. (2023). Ecotoxicology of hexavalent Cr in fish: An updated review. *The Science of the Total Environment, 890*, 164395. Advance online publication. DOI: 10.1016/j.scitotenv.2023.164395 PMID: 37257624

Kar, D., Sur, P., Mandai, S. K., Saha, T., & Kole, R. K. (2008). Assessment of HMs pollution in surface water. *International Journal of Environmental Science and Technology, 5*(1), 119–124. DOI: 10.1007/BF03326004

Kumar, A. & Mishra, Ashish & Shukla, D.N. (2014). Seasonal HMs concentration variation in the River Ganga at Allahabad. *Journal of the Kalash Science., 2*, 1–7.

Kumar, A., Jaiswal, D., & Watal, G. (2009). Studies on chemical composition and energy transformation in river Ganga at Kanpur and Varanasi due to environmental degradation. *Journal of Environmental Biology, 30*(3), 445–450. PMID: 20120476

Kumar, M., Singh, S., Jain, A., Yadav, S., Dubey, A., & Trivedi, S. P. (2024). A review on heavy metal-induced toxicity in fishes: Bioaccumulation, antioxidant defense system, histopathological manifestations, and transcriptional profiling of genes. *Journal of Trace Elements in Medicine and Biology, 83*, 127377. Advance online publication. DOI: 10.1016/j.jtemb.2023.127377 PMID: 38183919

La Torre, A., Iovino, V., & Caradonia, F. (2018). Copper in plant protection: Current situation and prospects. *Phytopathologia Mediterranea, 57*(2), 201–236. DOI: 10.14601/Phytopathol_Mediterr-23407

LeDuc, D. L., & Terry, N. (2005). Phytoremediation of toxic trace elements in soil and water. *Journal of Industrial Microbiology & Biotechnology, 32*(11-12), 514–520. DOI: 10.1007/s10295-005-0227-0 PMID: 15883830

Lim-Hing, S., Gandhi, K. J., & Villari, C. (2024). The role of manganese in tree defenses against pests and pathogens. *Plant Physiology and Biochemistry*, *210*, 108641. Advance online publication. DOI: 10.1016/j.plaphy.2024.108641 PMID: 38663267

Liu, S.-H., Zeng, G.-M., Niu, Q.-Y., Liu, Y., Zhou, L., Jiang, L.-H., Tan, X., Xu, P., Zhang, C., & Cheng, M. (2017). Bioremediation mechanisms of combined pollution of PAHs and heavy metals by bacteria and fungi: A mini review. *Bioresource Technology*, *224*, 25–33. DOI: 10.1016/j.biortech.2016.11.095 PMID: 27916498

Maiti, M., Chaudhuri, S., & Biswas, A. (2021). Activities of idol immersion Pbs to HMs contamination in river Hooghly in and around the city of Kolkata. *Journal of the Indian Chemical Society*, *98*(11), 100223. Advance online publication. DOI: 10.1016/j.jics.2021.100223

Malhotra, N., Ger, T. R., Uapipatanakul, B., Huang, J. C., Chen, K. H. C., & Hsiao, C. D. (2020). Review of copper and copper nanoparticle toxicity in fish. *Nanomaterials (Basel, Switzerland)*, *10*(6), 1126. DOI: 10.3390/nano10061126 PMID: 32517348

Mattsson, K., Johnson, E. V., Malmendal, A., Linse, S., Hansson, L. A., & Cedervall, T. (2017). Brain damage and behavioural disorders in fish induced by plastic nanoparticles delivered through the food chain. *Scientific Reports*, *7*(1), 11452. DOI: 10.1038/s41598-017-10813-0 PMID: 28904346

Maurya, P. K., Malik, D. S., Yadav, K. K., Kumar, A., Kumar, S., & Kamyab, H. (2019). Bioaccumulation and potential sources of HMs contamination in fish species in River Ganga basin: Possible human health risks evaluation. *Toxicology Reports*, *6*, 472–481. DOI: 10.1016/j.toxrep.2019.05.012 PMID: 31193923

Mishra, B., Gautam, G. J., Chaturvedi, R. K., & Ansari, N. G. (2022). Accumulation of HMs in water, sediment, and different fishes of river Ganga in Varanasi and its health risk assessment. *Research Square*. DOI: 10.21203/rs.3.rs-2367377/v1

Mondal, P., Schintu, M., Marras, B., Bettoschi, A., Marrucci, A., Sarkar, S. K., & Biswas, J. K. (2020). Geochemical fractionation and risk assessment of trace elements in sediments from tide-dominated Hooghly (Ganges) River Estuary, *India. Chemical Geology*, *532*, 119373. Advance online publication. DOI: 10.1016/j.chemgeo.2019.119373

Mukherjee, A. G., Wanjari, U. R., Renu, K., Vellingiri, B., & Gopalakrishnan, A. V. (2022). HMs and metalloid-induced reproductive toxicity. *Environmental Toxicology and Pharmacology*, *92*, 103859. Advance online publication. DOI: 10.1016/j.etap.2022.103859

Nath, A. K., & Banerjee, S. (2006). In-situ accumulation of HMs in the Ganga River system-an overview. *Ecology Environment and Conservation*, *12*(3), 435.

Nautiyal, C. S. (2009a). Scientific validation of incorruptible self-purificatory characteristic of Ganga water. *Asian Agri-History*, *13*(1).

Nautiyal, C. S. (2009b). Self-purificatory Ganga water facilitates death of pathogenic Escherichia coli O157: H7. *Current Microbiology*, *58*(1), 25–29. DOI: 10.1007/s00284-008-9260-3 PMID: 18810537

NEXT IAS Team. (2024). Ganga River system: origin, course & tributaries. https://www.nextias.com/blog/ganga-river-system/#Course_of_Ganga_River

Okocha, R. C., & Adedeji, O. B. (2011). Overview of Cd toxicity in fish. *Journal of Applied Sciences Research*, *7*(7), 1195–1207.

Pandey, J., Shubhashish, K., & Pandey, R. (2009). Metal contamination of GangaRiver (India) as influenced by atmospheric deposition. *Bulletin of Environmental Contamination and Toxicology*, *83*(2), 204–209. DOI: 10.1007/s00128-009-9744-2 PMID: 19434353

Pandey, J., & Singh, R. (2017). HMs in sediments of Ganga River: Up-and downstream urban influences. *Applied Water Science*, *7*(4), 1669–1678. DOI: 10.1007/s13201-015-0334-7

Paul, D. (2017). Research on HMs pollution of river Ganga: A review. *Annals of Agrarian Science*, *15*(2), 278–286. DOI: 10.1016/j.aasci.2017.04.001

Prasad, S., Mathur, A., & Rupainwar, D. D. (1989). HMs distribution in the sediments and sewer-river confluence points of River Ganga in Varanasi-Mirzapur Region. *Asian Environment.*, *11*(2), 73–82.

Purushothaman, P., & Chakrapani, G. J. (2007). HMs fractionation in Ganga River sediments, India. *Environmental Monitoring and Assessment*, *132*(1-3), 475–489. DOI: 10.1007/s10661-006-9550-9 PMID: 17295113

Qasem, N. A., Mohammed, R. H., & Lawal, D. U. (2021). Removal of HMs ions from wastewater: A comprehensive and critical review. *NPJ Clean Water*, *4*(1), 1–15. DOI: 10.1038/s41545-021-00127-0

Rahaman, M. M. (2009). Principles of transboundary water resources management and Ganges treaties: An analysis. *International Journal of Water Resources Development*, *25*(1), 159–173. DOI: 10.1080/07900620802517574

Rai, P. K., Mishra, A., & Tripathi, B. D. (2010). HMs and microbial pollution of the River Ganga: A case study of water quality at Varanasi. *Aquatic Ecosystem Health & Management, 13*(4), 352–361. DOI: 10.1080/14634988.2010.528739

Rajeshkumar, S., & Li, X. (2018). Bioaccumulation of HMs in fish species from the Meiliang Bay, Taihu Lake, China. *Toxicology Reports, 5*, 288–295. DOI: 10.1016/j.toxrep.2018.01.007 PMID: 29511642

Sakakibara, M., Watanabe, A., Inoue, M., Sano, S., & Kaise, T. (2010). Phytoextraction and phytovolatilization of arsenic from As-contaminated soils by Pteris vittata. In: Proceedings of the annual international conference on soils, sediments, water and energy. 26. *University of Massachusetts at Amherst* October 15-18, 2012.

Samanta, S. (2013). Metal and pesticide pollution scenario in Ganga River system. *Aquatic Ecosystem Health & Management, 16*(4), 454–464. DOI: 10.1080/14634988.2013.858587

Sankhla, M. S., Kumari, M., Sharma, K., Kushwah, R. S., & Kumar, R. (2018). HMs pollution of holy River Ganga: A review. *Int. J. Res, 5*(1), 421–436.

Sarkar, S. K., Saha, M., Takada, H., Bhattacharya, A., Mishra, P., & Bhattacharya, B. (2007). Water quality management in the lower stretch of the river Ganges, east coast of India: An approach through environmental education. *Journal of Cleaner Production, 15*(16), 1559–1567. DOI: 10.1016/j.jclepro.2006.07.030

Saxena, S., & Singh, P. K. (2020). Assessment of health of river Ganga at Varanasi, India.Nature Environment and Pollution Technology. *An International Quarterly Scientific Journal, 19*(3), 935–948. DOI: 10.46488/NEPT.2020.v19i03.004

Sharma, A., Kapoor, D., Wang, J., Shahzad, B., Kumar, V., Bali, A. S., Jasrotia, S., Zheng, B., Yuan, H., & Yan, D. (2020). Chromium bioaccumulation and its impacts on plants: An overview. *Plants, 9*(1), 100. DOI: 10.3390/plants9010100 PMID: 31941115

Sharma, P., Meher, P. K., & Mishra, K. P. (2012). Distribution of non-radioactive heavy elements in water of river Ganges from Rishikesh to Allahabad: A study on possible health effects. *Journal of Nehru Gram Bharati University, 1*(1), 52–58.

Singh, D. (2023). A review on the examination of pollution by HMs in the River Ganga. *RP Current Trends in Agriculture and Environmental Sciences, 2*(4), 26–37.

Singh, G., Chaudhary, S., Gupta, D., & Kumar Mishra, V. (2024). Assessing the water quality of River Ganga in Varanasi, India, through WQI, NPI, and multivariate techniques: A comprehensive study. *Water Practice & Technology, 19*(4), 1099–1118. DOI: 10.2166/wpt.2024.027

Singh, H., Yadav, S., Singh, B. K., Dubey, B., Tripathi, K., Srivastava, V., & Shukla, D. N. (2013). Assessment of geochemical environment from study of river sediments in the middle stretch of River Ganga at Ghazipur, Buxar and Ballia area. *Proceedings of the National Academy of Sciences. India. Section B, Biological Sciences*, *83*(3), 371–384. DOI: 10.1007/s40011-012-0134-x

Singh, L., Choudhary, S. K., & Singh, P. K. (2012). Status of HMs concentration in water and sediment of river Ganga at selected sites in the middle Ganga plain. *International Journal of Research in Chemistry and Environment*, *2*(4), 236–243.

Singh, M., Müller, G., & Singh, I. B. (2002). HMs in freshly deposited stream sediments of rivers associated with urbanisation of the Ganga plain, India. *Water, Air, and Soil Pollution*, *141*(1/4), 35–54. DOI: 10.1023/A:1021339917643

Singh, M., Müller, G., & Singh, I. B. (2003). Geogenic distribution and baseline concentration of HMs in sediments of the Ganges River, India. *Journal of Geochemical Exploration*, *80*(1), 1–17. DOI: 10.1016/S0375-6742(03)00016-5

Sinha, R. K., Sinha, S. K., Kedia, D. K., Kumari, A., Rani, N., Sharma, G., & Prasad, K. (2007). A holistic study on Hg pollution in the Ganga River system at Varanasi, India. *Current Science*, *92*(9), 1223–1228. https://www.jstor.org/stable/24097888

Srivastava, V., Sarkar, A., Singh, S., Singh, P., De Araujo, A. S., & Singh, R. P. (2017). Agroecological responses of HMs pollution with special emphasis on soil health and plant performances. *Frontiers in Environmental Science*, *5*, 64. DOI: 10.3389/fenvs.2017.00064

Taseidifar, M., Makavipour, F., Pashley, R. M., & Rahman, A. M. (2017). Removal of HMs ions from water using ion flotation. *Environmental Technology & Innovation*, *8*, 182–190. DOI: 10.1016/j.eti.2017.07.002

Tchounwou, P. B., Yedjou, C. G., Patlolla, A. K., & Sutton, D. J. (2012). HMs toxicity and the environment. *Molecular, clinical and environmental toxicology: Volume 3. Environmental Toxicology*, •••, 133–164. DOI: 10.1007/978-3-7643-8340-4_6 PMID: 22945569

Tovar-Sánchez, E., Hernández-Plata, I., Martinez, M. S., Valencia-Cuevas, L., & Galante, P. M. (2018). HMs pollution as a biodiversity threat. *HMs*, *383*. Advance online publication. DOI: 10.5772/intechopen.74052

Trombadore, O., Nandi, I., & Shah, K. (2020). Effective data convergence, mapping, and pollution categorization of ghats at Ganga River front in Varanasi. *Environmental Science and Pollution Research International*, *27*(13), 15912–15924. DOI: 10.1007/s11356-019-06526-8 PMID: 32172422

Vaseem, H., & Banerjee, T. K. (2013). Contamination of the River Ganga and its toxic implication in the blood parameters of the major carp Labeorohita (Ham). *Environmental Science and Pollution Research International, 20*(8), 5673–5681. DOI: 10.1007/s11356-013-1570-8 PMID: 23456946

Vass, K. K., Mondal, S. K., Samanta, S., Suresh, V. R., & Katiha, P. K. (2010). The environment and fishery status of the River Ganges. *Aquatic Ecosystem Health & Management, 13*(4), 385–394. DOI: 10.1080/14634988.2010.530139

World Health Organization (WHO). (2022). Guidelines for drinking-water quality: fourth edition incorporating the first and second addenda, https://www.who.int/publications/i/item/9789240045064

World Health Organization (WHO). (2017). Guidelines for drinking-water quality*: Fourth edition, incorporating the* [1st] *addendum*. World Health Organization.

Zhou, Y., Tang, L., Zeng, G., Zhang, C., Yi, Z., & Xie, X. (2016). Current progress in biosensors for heavy metal ions based on DNAzymes/DNA molecules functionalized nanostructures: A review. *Sensors and Actuators. B, Chemical, 223*, 280–294. DOI: 10.1016/j.snb.2015.09.090

Chapter 12
Risk Identification and Intervention Strategies in Health, Water, Food Security, and Livestock for Sustainable Development

N. M. A. I. Nikalansooriya
https://orcid.org/0009-0009-6039-4711
Faculty of Agriculture, University of Peradeniya, Sri Lanka

K. P. P. Kopiyawattage
https://orcid.org/0000-0003-1766-9643
Faculty of Agriculture, University of Peradeniya, Sri Lanka

ABSTRACT

This chapter investigates the important relationship of health, water, food security, sanitation, and livestock productivity within the conceptual structure of sustainable development. By aligning with the United Nations Sustainable Development Goals (SDGs), this analysis highlights the importance of risk management and intervention strategies that address these interlinked sectors to ensure a resilient and sustainable future. The chapter is organized into several sections, each focusing on a key area and its associated challenges, risks, and solutions, especially in developing countries where resources are limited and socio-economic and environmental constraints are raised.

DOI: 10.4018/979-8-3693-9755-8.ch012

1. INTRODUCTION

Health and hygiene are integral to sustainable development, as challenges like pandemics, antimicrobial resistance (AMR), and inadequate healthcare and sanitation disproportionately affect low- and middle-income countries (Aslam et al., 2024). The COVID-19 pandemic exposed global healthcare vulnerabilities, emphasizing the need for stronger public health infrastructure and risk management strategies (Benjamin, 2020). Similarly, water scarcity, pollution, and ocean degradation pose severe threats to food security and public health, with case studies such as the Ganges River pollution and the Cape Town water crisis illustrating the consequences of poor water management (Srinivas et al., 2020).

Oceans play a crucial role in climate regulation, yet issues like acidification and overfishing endanger marine ecosystems and food security. Inadequate sanitation further exacerbates public health risks, especially in rural and low-income areas, contributing to the spread of waterborne diseases (Manetu & Karanja, 2021). Examples from India's open defecation crisis and Bangladesh's sanitation improvements highlight both challenges and solutions, such as eco-friendly toilets and decentralized waste management.

Climate change, soil degradation, and unsustainable agricultural practices are increasingly threatening food security, affecting both the quantity and safety of food production (Hossain et al., 2020). Sustainable approaches, such as regenerative farming and agroecology, are essential for building resilient food systems in vulnerable regions like Sub-Saharan Africa and Southeast Asia (Amede et al., 2023).

Additionally, livestock productivity remains crucial for global nutrition and rural economies, yet it faces threats from disease outbreaks, AMR, and environmental degradation due to industrial farming. Sustainable livestock management practices, including rotational grazing and organic feed, offer solutions to mitigate environmental impacts and enhance resilience against climate-related challenges (Erdaw, 2023).

The interconnections between health, hygiene, water resources, food security, and livestock productivity (Figure 1) highlight the complexity of achieving sustainable development (Garcia et al., 2020). Addressing these challenges requires an integrated approach that incorporates risk management, policy interventions, and innovative solutions (Pomaza-Ponomarenko et al., 2023). By strengthening healthcare systems, improving sanitation infrastructure, conserving water resources, promoting sustainable agriculture, and adopting environmentally friendly livestock practices, societies can work toward a more resilient and equitable future (Corvalan et al., 2020). This chapter explores these themes in greater detail, providing insights into effective strategies for mitigating risks and advancing sustainability goals.

Figure 1. Conceptual illustration of interconnected influence of health, water, food security, and livestock

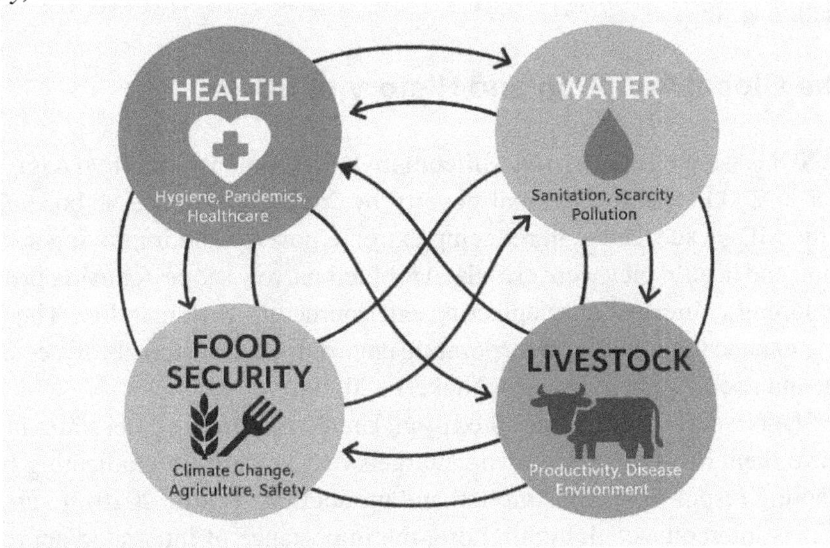

2. SUSTAINABLE DEVELOPMENT

2.1 The Fundamental Aim of the Sustainable Development

Sustainable development represents a multidimensional approach to addressing global challenges while ensuring that future generations can meet their needs (Ghosh & Paul, 2024). The concept, significantly developed following the 1987 Brundtland Report titled "Our Common Future", emphasizes the balance between economic growth, environmental protection, and social equity (Ray, 2020). The UN Sustainable Development Goals (SDGs), adopted in 2015, outline these principles, presenting 17 interconnected global goals that target the most pressing challenges faced by humanity such as poverty, hunger, health crises, water shortages, and climate change (Hassani et al., 2021).

At the core of sustainable development is the idea that these goals cannot be addressed separately. For example, improving food security directly influences health outcomes, while the sustainable management of water resources impacts agricultural productivity and hygiene practices (Young et al., 2021). The interdependence of sectors such as health, hygiene, water, food security, and livestock productivity highlights the importance of integrated approaches to achieving the

SDGs, specifically in developing countries where resources are often constrained, and the challenges are intensified by socio-economic constraints and environmental degradation (Lile et al., 2023).

2.2 The Global Adoption and History of SDGs

The SDGs were built upon the Millennium Development Goals (MDGs), which were set in 2000 to address global poverty by 2015 (Mabuza & Mabuza, 2020). While the MDGs succeeded in reducing extreme poverty and improving access to education and health, they were criticized for their narrow scope, focusing primarily on developing countries and neglecting environmental sustainability. The SDGs sought to expand upon this by incorporating environmental sustainability, economic growth, and social inclusivity (Van Niekerk, 2020).

The SDGs were universally adopted by all United Nations member states in 2015, to achieve them by 2030. They involve targets that range from eradicating hunger to promoting responsible consumption and production (Pelton, 2020). Each of the 17 SDGs is interconnected, highlighting the importance of integrated approaches for global development (Alcamo et al., 2020). For example, SDG 2 (Zero Hunger) focuses not only on increasing food production but also on ensuring that food is nutritious, sustainably origin, and accessible to all. Similarly, SDG 6 (Clean Water and Sanitation) promotes equal access to safe and affordable drinking water, but also highlights the importance of water management in agricultural and industrial sectors to support wider food security and health goals.

2.3 Key SDGs in Health, Water, Food Security, and Livestock Productivity

The interaction between health, hygiene, water, food security, and livestock productivity is deeply embedded in several SDGs. Below are some key goals that align with these important sectors.

- **SDG 2: Zero hunger** – This aims to end hunger, achieve food security, improve nutrition, and promote sustainable agriculture. Livestock productivity, soil health, and agricultural biodiversity play important roles in achieving this goal (M. Tahat et al., 2020).
- **SDG 3: Good health and well-being** – This focuses on ensuring healthy lives and promoting well-being for all. Achieving this requires addressing hygiene, water quality, food safety, and nutrition, all of which are impacted by livestock and agricultural practices (Fernandez, 2020).

- **SDG 6: Clean water and sanitation** – This prioritizes the availability and sustainable management of water and sanitation. Clean water is essential for agriculture, food safety, and hygiene, specifically in regions facing water shortages due to climate change or poor infrastructure (Baskaran, 2022).
- **SDG 12: Responsible consumption and production** – This encourages sustainable consumption and production patterns, which include minimizing food loss, and wastage, and ensuring that food systems do not harm ecosystems or contribute to climate change (Heydari, 2024). Livestock systems must be managed in ways that minimize their environmental impact while meeting food demand.

2.4 Challenges of Achieving SDGs in Developing Countries

While the SDGs are universal strategies for global development, their implementation is accompanied by challenges in developing countries. These nations face a range of socio-economic and environmental constraints that interfere with progress toward the goals.

- **Limited infrastructure and resources:** Inadequate healthcare, poor sanitation, and unreliable water supply hinder progress. Rural areas, especially in Sub-Saharan Africa, struggle with access to clean water, affecting both public health and agriculture (Nkiaka et al., 2021).
- **Economic inequality:** Widespread economic disparities limit access to essentials like food, water, and healthcare. In regions such as South Asia, Sub-Saharan Africa, and the Middle East, gender inequality further restricts women's decision-making power in food production and resource distribution (Njuki et al., 2023).
- **Political instability and conflict:** Wars and conflicts in the Middle East and Africa damage infrastructure, displace populations, and disrupt food systems, slowing progress toward SDG targets (Daher et al., 2021).
- **Environmental degradation and climate change:** Climate change intensifies droughts, floods, and extreme weather, threatening food security and increasing the spread of waterborne diseases. Poor land management and deforestation further exacerbate these challenges (Wassie, 2020).
- **Technological gaps:** Many developing nations lack access to modern technologies, such as precision agriculture or satellite-based water monitoring, leaving them reliant on outdated and unsustainable practices (Foster et al., 2020).

2.5 The Role of Environmental and Health Crises in Risk Management

Environmental and health crises such as pandemics and climate-induced disasters have enhanced the requirement for strong risk management strategies. The COVID-19 pandemic showcased the vulnerabilities of global health systems, particularly in low-income countries where access to healthcare, clean water, and hygiene facilities is limited (Shadmi et al., 2020). The pandemic disrupted food supply chains, worsened food insecurity, and brought out the need for better coordination between sectors such as agriculture, health, and trade.

Similarly, climate change has intensified the frequency and severity of natural disasters such as hurricanes, droughts, and floods which directly impact water quality, food production, and livestock management (Filipe et al., 2020). The unpredictability of these events makes risk management a major component of sustainable development. Developing early warning systems, strengthening health infrastructure, and promoting climate-resilient agricultural practices are critical to mitigating these risks (Mosadeghrad et al., 2023).

2.6 The Complexity of Interconnected Risks across Sectors

The complexity of addressing the SDGs belongs to the interconnectedness of risks across sectors like health, food security, water, and livestock productivity.

For example;

- Water scarcity affects food security, as agriculture is highly water-dependent. At the same time, food production impacts water quality, with agricultural runoff being one of the primary sources of water pollution (Zahoor & Mushtaq, 2023).
- Livestock productivity and food security are complicatedly linked, as livestock provides not only meat but also essential products like milk and eggs. However, livestock farming is a major contributor to greenhouse gas emissions, which accelerates climate change and further disrupts food production systems (Gomez-Zavaglia et al., 2020).
- Hygiene and sanitation are critical for preventing diseases, but without clean water, efforts to improve public health outcomes are significantly weakened. Inadequate sanitation, for example, can lead to the contamination of water sources, exacerbating the spread of infectious diseases and further straining healthcare systems (Andrés et al., 2021).

Therefore, an integrated approach is essential to risk management within the framework of sustainable development. For example, improving water management not only boosts agricultural productivity but also enhances hygiene practices and reduces the spread of waterborne diseases (Shayo et al., 2023).

3. RISK IDENTIFICATION AND INTERVENTION STRATEGIES

3.1 Health and Hygiene

Health and hygiene are fundamental to sustainable development and are deeply interconnected with global challenges, especially in low- and middle-income countries (LMICs) (Cerf, 2023). Addressing these issues is essential for achieving SDG 3 (Good Health and Well-being) and SDG 6 (Clean Water and Sanitation).

3.1.1 The Rising Threat of Pandemics: Case of COVID-19

The COVID-19 pandemic exposed significant vulnerabilities in global healthcare systems, particularly in low- and middle-income countries (LMICs). Weak healthcare infrastructure led to severe shortages of essential medical supplies, as seen in India and Brazil, where oxygen shortages overwhelmed hospitals (Lobo et al., 2022). Inequitable access to healthcare further widened disparities, with wealthier nations securing vaccines more rapidly, leaving poorer countries more vulnerable to prolonged outbreaks. Additionally, insufficient public health surveillance in nations such as Nigeria and Bangladesh hindered early detection and response efforts, exacerbating the crisis (Ahmed et al., 2020). The pandemic also had severe economic consequences, pushing millions into poverty due to lockdowns and job losses, with women and children disproportionately affected. These challenges highlighted the urgent need for stronger healthcare systems, equitable resource distribution, and improved pandemic preparedness worldwide.

3.1.2 Antimicrobial Resistance (AMR): A Growing Global Health Threat

AMR poses a serious threat to medical progress, making common infections increasingly difficult to treat. One of the major contributing factors is the unregulated access to antibiotics, particularly in regions like India and Southeast Asia, where they are available without prescriptions, leading to widespread misuse (Kotwani et al., 2022). Additionally, a lack of public awareness contributes to the problem, as many people mistakenly believe that antibiotics can cure all illnesses, resulting in their inappropriate use. Poor infection prevention in healthcare settings, especially inadequate sanitation in hospitals, further accelerates the spread of resistant bacteria. Moreover, limited diagnostic capacity leads to the overprescription of antibiotics, as healthcare providers are unable to accurately identify bacterial infections (Rose et al., 2021). To combat AMR, several intervention strategies must be implemented, including strengthening regulatory frameworks to control antibiotic distribution, promoting public awareness campaigns to educate communities about responsible antibiotic use, enhancing hospital hygiene to prevent infections, and investing in new antibiotic research to develop effective treatments against resistant strains (Rony et al., 2023). Addressing these challenges is crucial to slowing the spread of AMR and safeguarding global health.

3.1.3 Poor Access to Clean Water and Sanitation

Lack of clean water affects billions of people worldwide, leading to severe health issues such as cholera and typhoid. In Nigeria, around 60 million people lack access to basic water services, increasing the risk of waterborne diseases and poor hygiene (Lee et al., 2020). Similarly, in Bangladesh, arsenic contamination in drinking water has led to stunted growth in children, affecting their long-term health and development (Rahaman et al., 2022). Addressing these challenges requires strategic interventions, including significant investments in water infrastructure to ensure safe and sustainable supply, hygiene education programs to promote proper sanitation practices, and public-private partnerships (PPPs) to fund and implement large-scale sanitation projects (Mundonde & Makoni, 2023). These combined efforts can improve water security, reduce health risks, and enhance overall well-being in vulnerable communities.

3.2 Water Bodies and Oceans

Water scarcity, pollution, and ocean degradation affect food security, health, and environmental sustainability, aligning with SDG 6 (Clean Water and Sanitation) and SDG 14 (Life Below Water).

3.2.1 Water Scarcity and Food Security: Cape Town Water Crisis

In 2018, Cape Town faced "Day Zero" due to prolonged drought and poor water management, leading to severe consequences across various sectors (Millington & Scheba, 2021). The water crisis resulted in reduced crop yields and food shortages, as agricultural production suffered from the lack of irrigation. This scarcity not only increased food prices but also placed economic strain on both farmers and consumers. Additionally, limited access to clean water contributed to a rise in waterborne diseases, posing significant public health risks (Chan et al., 2021). The crisis highlighted the urgent need for sustainable water management and climate-resilient agricultural practices to prevent similar disasters in the future.

3.2.2 Water Pollution and Food Systems: The Ganges River

The Ganges River, a vital resource for agriculture and fishing, faces severe environmental challenges due to industrial and sewage pollution, fertilizer and pesticide contamination, and declining fish populations, which negatively impact agricultural productivity (Srinivas et al., 2020). The unchecked disposal of industrial waste and untreated sewage has led to significant water pollution, posing health risks and reducing the river's ability to sustain ecosystems. Additionally, excessive use of chemical fertilizers and pesticides in farming has further deteriorated water quality, affecting both aquatic life and soil fertility. To address these issues, investing in wastewater treatment facilities is crucial to reducing pollution and ensuring cleaner water for agricultural and domestic use (Mishra et al., 2023). Implementing stricter environmental regulations can help control industrial discharge and encourage responsible waste management practices. Furthermore, promoting sustainable agricultural techniques, such as organic farming, crop rotation, and integrated pest management, can minimize chemical runoff into the river, preserving its ecological balance and supporting long-term food production (Gamage et al., 2023). These intervention strategies, if effectively enforced, can help restore the Ganges River's health and sustain its role as a lifeline for millions of people.

3.2.3 Ocean Degradation: Overfishing and Climate Change

Overfishing depletes marine biodiversity, directly impacting global food security by reducing fish populations that millions rely on for nutrition and livelihoods. In Pacific Island Nations, rising ocean temperatures and unsustainable fishing practices have led to severe fish stock depletion, threatening coastal economies that depend on fisheries for income and food supply (Johnson et al., 2020). This decline not only disrupts local ecosystems but also weakens the resilience of communities that rely on marine resources, making sustainable fisheries management crucial for long-term food security and economic stability.

3.2.4 Ocean Acidification and Climate Change

Oceans absorb about 30% of atmospheric CO_2, causing acidification that disrupts marine ecosystems (Çelekli & Zariç, 2024). This leads to coral reef degradation, reducing biodiversity, and negatively impacting species that rely on these habitats. Additionally, shellfish populations decline as acidification weakens their calcium carbonate shells, disturbing marine food chains. To mitigate these effects, reducing CO_2 emissions through sustainable energy practices is essential. Establishing marine protected areas helps conserve vulnerable ecosystems, while sustainable fisheries management ensures the long-term stability of marine resources (Balata & Williams, 2020).

3.2.5 The Link between Water Quality and Food Production

Agriculture consumes 70% of global freshwater resources, yet water pollution from excessive fertilizer and pesticide use poses a serious threat to food security (Zahoor & Mushtaq, 2023). Regions such as the Middle East, North Africa, and South Asia face severe water shortages, further straining agricultural productivity (Hejazi et al., 2023). Additionally, fertilizer runoff leads to eutrophication, creating dead zones in aquatic ecosystems and disrupting biodiversity. To address these challenges, intervention strategies such as promoting drip irrigation to enhance water efficiency, reducing chemical inputs through sustainable farming practices, and implementing integrated water management approaches are essential for ensuring long-term agricultural sustainability and water security.

3.3 Sanitation

3.3.1 The Global Sanitation Crisis: Open Defecation in India

India historically had high open defecation rates, but the Swachh Bharat Mission (2014) aimed to eliminate this practice by constructing toilets (Chakrabarti et al., 2024). However, infrastructure alone is insufficient, and long-term sustainability depends on behavioral change and proper maintenance.

3.3.2 The Link Between Poor Sanitation and Waterborne Diseases

Poor sanitation contributes to the spread of diseases like cholera, hepatitis A, and dysentery. Rural communities in Africa and South Asia often rely on unprotected water sources, increasing contamination risks (Manetu & Karanja, 2021).

The WHO estimates that inadequate sanitation leads to 485,000 deaths annually (Nada et al., 2025).

3.3.3 Success Stories in Improved Sanitation Infrastructure: Bangladesh

Bangladesh successfully reduced open defecation to below 1% by implementing a Community-Led Total Sanitation (CLTS) approach, which engaged local communities and promoted long-term behavior change in sanitation practices (Mumin et al., 2024).

3.3.4 Innovative Solutions for Sanitation in Low-Income Areas

Eco-friendly toilets, such as composting and biogas toilets, provide a sustainable solution for managing human waste by reducing water usage and generating useful byproducts like fertilizer and energy (Bidira et al., 2024). In informal settlements, decentralized waste management systems, like Kenya's small-scale treatment facilities, improve sanitation by offering localized and efficient waste treatment, reducing reliance on inadequate central infrastructure (Mason et al., 2020).

3.4 Food Security, Safety, and Production

3.4.1 Climate Change and Food Security

Droughts in the Horn of Africa have severely impacted food security, leaving 20 million people facing acute food shortages (Seife et al., 2021). The crisis demands sustainable solutions, including the adoption of drought-resistant crops, improvements in irrigation technology, and the implementation of early warning systems to mitigate future risks.

3.4.2 Food Safety Challenges

Pesticide overuse in Southeast Asia leads to food contamination, impacting consumer health. Vietnam and Thailand implemented safe pesticide use education and monitoring systems (Schreinemachers et al., 2020).

3.4.3 Role of Sustainable Agriculture

Regenerative agriculture in Latin America, such as Brazil's agroforestry, helps restore soil health and biodiversity (Miatton & Karner, 2020). In Central America, practices like crop rotation, cover cropping, and reduced tillage enhance sustainability and long-term agricultural resilience.

3.5 Livestock Productivity

3.5.1 Livestock Diseases and Their Impact on Global Food Chains

African swine fever in China disrupted global pork supplies, driving up prices, while mad cow disease in the UK led to widespread bans and public health concerns, highlighting the impact of livestock diseases on global markets and food safety (You et al., 2021).

3.5.2 Antibiotic Resistance Due to Excessive Use in Livestock

The overuse of antibiotics in farming contributes to antibiotic-resistant bacteria, which can spread through direct contact, food consumption, and environmental contamination, posing serious public health risks (Serwecińska, 2020).

3.5.3 Sustainable Livestock Management Practices and Environmental Impact

Livestock farming accounts for 14.5% of global greenhouse gas emissions, but practices like rotational grazing, integrated pest management, and organic feed help reduce environmental impact while maintaining long-term productivity (Kleppel, 2020).

4. IMPROVING WASTE-TO-ENERGY TECHNOLOGIES

Waste-to-energy (WTE) technologies convert various forms of waste into usable energy, helping in waste management and reducing reliance on fossil fuels. Some advancements and improvements include below (Ali et al., 2020).

4.1 Advanced Thermochemical Processes

Plasma gasification uses extreme temperatures to break down waste into syngas with minimal emissions, while hydrothermal carbonization converts wet waste into biochar for soil enrichment and energy. Supercritical water oxidation efficiently decomposes organic waste, producing energy and clean byproducts (Li et al., 2022).

4.2 Improved Biological Treatment Methods

Enhanced anaerobic digestion utilizes genetically modified microbes to accelerate methane production, improving biogas yield and efficiency (Song et al., 2023). Microbial fuel cells (MFCs) leverage bacteria to generate electricity while simultaneously breaking down organic waste, offering a sustainable solution for energy recovery and waste treatment (Apollon et al., 2022).

4.3 Waste-to-Hydrogen Technologies

Advanced pyrolysis and gasification techniques can improve hydrogen production, providing clean energy from organic waste (Aziz et al., 2021).

4.4 Circular Economy Integration

WTE facilities can be designed to capture CO_2 emissions for carbon sequestration and use waste heat for district heating (Li et al., 2021).

5. FRAMEWORKS FOR HEALTH, WATER, FOOD, AND LIVESTOCK MANAGEMENT

Several global frameworks guide sustainable management in these sectors.

5.1 Health Management

The One Health framework, supported by WHO, FAO, OIE, and UNEP, integrates human, animal, and environmental health to prevent diseases and control AMR. Meanwhile, the International Health Regulations (IHR) under WHO enhance global disease surveillance and response, ensuring coordinated action against health threats (WHO, 2022).

5.2 Water Management

Integrated Water Resources Management (IWRM), promoted by UN-Water, supports sustainable water use by balancing economic, social, and environmental needs (Katusiime & Schütt, 2020). The Safe Sanitation and Water for All (SWA) framework focuses on policy reforms to ensure universal access to clean water and sanitation, improving public health and resilience.

5.3 Food Security Management

FAO's Sustainable Food and Agriculture (SFA) Framework promotes sustainable farming practices and climate resilience, ensuring long-term food security (Mrabet, 2023). The Milan Urban Food Policy Pact (MUFPP) strengthens urban food systems by enhancing resilience and reducing food waste, supporting sustainable and inclusive food policies.

5.4 Livestock Management

The Livestock Environmental Assessment and Performance (LEAP) initiative by FAO establishes metrics for sustainable livestock production (Boulay et al., 2021). The Global Agenda for Sustainable Livestock (GASL) promotes strategies to enhance productivity while minimizing environmental impact, supporting sustainable livestock systems (Mehrabi et al., 2020).

6. ADVANCED BIOTECHNOLOGY TECHNIQUES FOR CROP YIELD AND LIVESTOCK MANAGEMENT

6.1 Crop Yield Enhancement

CRISPR gene editing creates drought- and disease-resistant crops, while RNA interference (RNAi) strengthens plant defenses against pests and viruses (Halder et al., 2022). Microbial biostimulants enhance soil health and crop growth using beneficial microbes, and synthetic biology designs plants with improved nutrient content and stress resistance, advancing agricultural sustainability (Hamid et al., 2021).

6.2 Livestock Management Innovations

Genetic selection and cloning enhance desirable traits like disease resistance and milk production, while lab-grown meat reduces the environmental impact of meat production (Roy et al., 2021). Probiotics and microbiome engineering improve gut health and immunity in livestock, and precision livestock farming (PLF) utilizes AI, sensors, and IoT to monitor animal health and optimize feed efficiency (Hernandez-Patlan et al., 2023).

7. AI AND OTHER TECHNOLOGIES FOR CLIMATE-COMPROMISED SMART AGRICULTURE

As climate change intensifies, smart agriculture technologies play a crucial role in helping farmers adapt and mitigate environmental challenges. Artificial intelligence (AI) and other emerging technologies enable precision farming, resource optimization, and climate resilience, ensuring sustainable food production (Gryshova et al., 2024).

7.1 AI-Powered Precision Agriculture

AI enables data-driven decision-making in agriculture by analyzing vast amounts of data. AI-powered drones and satellite imagery monitor crop health, soil moisture, and pest infestations in real time, allowing early interventions (Mishra & Mishra, 2024). Predictive analytics forecast weather patterns, disease outbreaks, and crop yields, helping farmers plan effectively (Jaber et al., 2022). Automated irrigation systems optimize water use based on real-time soil and weather conditions, reducing waste and enhancing efficiency (Lakhiar et al., 2024).

7.2 Internet of Things (IoT) in Smart Farming

AI helps farmers make data-driven decisions by analyzing vast agricultural data. AI-powered drones and satellite imagery monitor crop health, soil moisture, and pest infestations in real time, enabling early interventions (Mishra & Mishra, 2024). Predictive analytics forecast weather patterns, disease outbreaks, and crop yields, aiding in better planning and loss reduction. AI-driven irrigation systems optimize water use based on real-time soil and weather conditions, improving efficiency and reducing waste.

7.3 Blockchain for Food Traceability

Blockchain technology enhances transparency and trust in the food supply chain by securely recording every stage, from planting to distribution, ensuring food safety and reducing waste (Chandan et al., 2023). Smart contracts automate fair pricing and secure transactions for smallholder farmers, promoting financial inclusion and efficiency.

7.4 Robotics and Automation in Agriculture

AI-powered autonomous machinery, including tractors, robotic harvesters, and automated weeders, reduces labor costs and enhances efficiency (Onteddu et al., 2025). Agri-drones precisely apply pesticides and fertilizers, minimizing chemical runoff and environmental impact while improving crop management.

7.5 CRISPR and Genetic Engineering for Climate-Resilient Crops

CRISPR gene-editing technology enables the development of crops that withstand extreme weather conditions (Ndudzo et al., 2024). Drought-resistant crops with enhanced water retention improve yields in arid regions, while pest-resistant crops reduce the need for chemical pesticides, promoting more sustainable farming practices.

7.6 Vertical and Hydroponic Farming for Urban Resilience

Vertical farms utilize AI-controlled lighting and climate regulation to grow crops in stacked layers, saving space and water (Modu et al., 2020). Hydroponics and aeroponics enable plant growth without soil, using nutrient-rich water or mist, making agriculture feasible in resource-scarce areas.

8. GENDER INEQUALITY IN HEALTH, WATER, AND AGRICULTURAL RESOURCES: IMPACTS AND EMPOWERMENT STRATEGIES

8.1 Impact of Gender Inequality on Health, Water, and Agricultural Resources

Gender inequality significantly affects access to essential resources such as healthcare, clean water, and agricultural inputs, creating widespread resource insecurity (Jeevanasai et al., 2023). Women, particularly in developing countries, face discriminatory socio-cultural norms, limited decision-making power, and economic barriers that restrict their access to and control over these vital resources.

8.1.1 Health Impacts of Gender Inequality

Women in many regions face limited access to healthcare due to financial constraints, cultural restrictions, and gender biases, leading to higher maternal mortality, untreated chronic diseases, and poor reproductive health. Nutritional disparities also exist, with men and boys often receiving priority access to nutritious food, leaving women and girls more vulnerable to malnutrition and anemia (Kumar et al., 2021). This cycle contributes to poor health outcomes, including low-birth-weight infants. Additionally, gender-based violence, economic dependence, and social discrimination result in higher rates of anxiety, depression, and PTSD among women.

8.1.2 Water Insecurity and Gender Inequality

In many developing regions, women and girls are primarily responsible for fetching water, often traveling long distances, which limits their time for education and income-generating activities while exposing them to physical strain and increased risk of harassment. The lack of gender-sensitive sanitation facilities, mainly in schools and workplaces, results in poor menstrual hygiene management, impacting women's health, dignity, and productivity (Tohit & Haque, 2024). Additionally, women are frequently excluded from water governance decisions, leading to policies and infrastructure that fail to meet their specific needs.

8.1.3 Agricultural Resource Inequality and Food Security

Women own less than 20% of the world's land, despite contributing up to 50% of agricultural labor, limiting their access to credit, farming equipment, and subsidies (Glazebrook et al., 2020). Agricultural training and technology often target men, leaving women excluded from climate-smart practices and reducing crop yields. Additionally, women farmers face challenges in accessing markets and financial resources due to limited mobility, financial literacy, and male-dominated supply chains, further hindering their economic opportunities.

8.2 Impacts of Gender Inequality on Resource Insecurity

Gender disparities in health, water, and agriculture exacerbate socio-economic and environmental challenges. Exclusion of women from land ownership, economic opportunities, and education leads to increased poverty, limiting access to food and healthcare (Wei et al., 2021). Poor maternal health and nutrition contribute to intergenerational malnutrition, resulting in stunted growth and cognitive impairments in children. Women's lack of involvement in sustainable agricultural practices contributes to environmental degradation, soil depletion, and food shortages. Additionally, women's economic dependence and vulnerability to climate change-related water and food shortages force families to migrate, driving displacement and social conflicts (Nosheen et al., 2023).

8.3 Strategies to Empower Women and Promote Gender Equality in Resource Management

8.3.1 Policy Reforms and Legal Rights

Governments should enforce land inheritance and ownership laws to ensure women have equal access to property. Women must also be included in water governance bodies to create gender-inclusive water policies that address their needs. Strengthening legislation against gender discrimination, including workplace discrimination, wage gaps, and gender-based violence, enhances women's access to employment and resources (Adeniyi et al., 2024).

8.3.2 Economic Empowerment and Financial Inclusion

Microfinance and credit access enable women to invest in agriculture, small businesses, and community projects through microloans and grants (Ranabahu & Tanima, 2022). Women-led agricultural cooperatives enhance their bargaining power in supply chains, while vocational training and digital literacy improve their business skills, financial literacy, and digital marketing, fostering greater economic independence.

8.3.3 Education and Skill Development

Encouraging girls to pursue careers in science, agriculture, and environmental management strengthens gender representation in resource governance. Providing menstrual health education and gender-responsive sanitation facilities in schools improves female retention rates (Psaki et al., 2022). Additionally, training men and community leaders in gender equality fosters shared responsibility in resource management.

8.3.4 Technological Innovations and Digital Solutions

Mobile banking and digital payment systems enable women to access financial services without physical barriers. Climate-smart agriculture initiatives, such as training women in drought-resistant crops, hydroponics, and sustainable irrigation, ensure food security (Khumalo et al., 2024). Additionally, AI and data-driven solutions, including gender-sensitive big data analytics, help policymakers address inequalities in resource distribution within agriculture and health systems.

8.3.5 Community Engagement and Leadership

Promoting women in decision-making roles, such as in government, community councils, and resource management bodies, ensures more equitable policy-making. Supporting grassroots advocacy groups, including women's self-help groups, strengthens community-driven solutions to resource insecurity (Jabeen & Iqbal, 2020). Public-private partnerships involving NGOs, businesses, and governments can also foster women-led sustainable development projects.

CONCLUSION

This chapter has explored the multifaceted and interconnected approaches required to address the challenges of sustainable development, especially in the contexts of agriculture, health, water, and resource management. The integration of advanced technologies, such as waste-to-energy innovations, biotechnology, and AI-driven solutions, offers immense potential to enhance resilience and productivity in climate-compromised environments. However, these technological advancements must be paired with equitable policies and gender-sensitive strategies to empower women and ensure inclusivity in decision-making, particularly in health and agricultural resource management.

Future research must focus on further integrating these technologies with gender-focused interventions, ensuring that women's voices are central to policy-making and community-driven solutions. Additionally, interdisciplinary frameworks that combine biotechnology, smart agriculture, and sustainability practices should be developed to optimize resource use, mitigate risks, and promote long-term environmental and social stability. There is also a critical need to explore the broader impacts of emerging technologies on gender equality, particularly in agricultural and rural contexts, to ensure that technological advancements benefit all segments of society equitably. By advancing these integrated approaches, we can pave the way for more sustainable, resilient, and inclusive communities worldwide.

ACKNOWLEDGMENT

The authors thank the University of Peradeniya, Sri Lanka as a host university.

REFERENCES

Adeniyi, A. O., Akpuokwe, C. U., Bakare, S. S., & Eneh, N. E. (2024). Gender equality in the workplace: A comparative review of USA and African Practices. *International Journal of Management & Entrepreneurship Research, 6*(3), 526–539. DOI: 10.51594/ijmer.v6i3.842

Ahmed, S. A. S., Ajisola, M., Azeem, K., Bakibinga, P., Chen, Y. F., Choudhury, N. N., Fayehun, O., Griffiths, F., Harris, B., Kibe, P., Lilford, R. J., Omigbodun, A., Rizvi, N., Sartori, J., Smith, S., Watson, S. I., Wilson, R., Yeboah, G., Aujla, N., & Yusuf, R. (2020). Impact of the societal response to COVID-19 on access to healthcare for non-COVID-19 health issues in slum communities of Bangladesh, Kenya, Nigeria and Pakistan: Results of pre-COVID and COVID-19 lockdown stakeholder engagements. *BMJ Global Health, 5*(8), e003042. DOI: 10.1136/bmjgh-2020-003042 PMID: 32819917

Alcamo, J., Thompson, J., Alexander, A., Antoniades, A., Delabre, I., Dolley, J., Marshall, F., Menton, M., Middleton, J., & Scharlemann, J. P. (2020). Analysing interactions among the sustainable development goals: Findings and emerging issues from local and global studies. *Sustainability Science, 15*(6), 1561–1572. DOI: 10.1007/s11625-020-00875-x PMID: 33133296

Ali, J., Rasheed, T., Afreen, M., Anwar, M. T., Nawaz, Z., Anwar, H., & Rizwan, K. (2020). Modalities for conversion of waste to energy—Challenges and perspectives. *The Science of the Total Environment, 727*, 138610. DOI: 10.1016/j.scitotenv.2020.138610 PMID: 32330718

Amede, T., Konde, A. A., Muhinda, J. J., & Bigirwa, G. (2023). Sustainable farming in practice: Building resilient and profitable smallholder agricultural systems in Sub-Saharan Africa. *Sustainability (Basel), 15*(7), 5731. DOI: 10.3390/su15075731

Andrés, L., Joseph, G., & Rana, S. (2021). The economic and health impacts of inadequate sanitation. In *Oxford research encyclopedia of environmental science*. DOI: 10.1093/acrefore/9780199389414.013.561

Apollon, W., Rusyn, I., González-Gamboa, N., Kuleshova, T., Luna-Maldonado, A. I., Vidales-Contreras, J. A., & Kamaraj, S. K. (2022). Improvement of zero waste sustainable recovery using microbial energy generation systems: A comprehensive review. *The Science of the Total Environment*, *817*, 153055. DOI: 10.1016/j.scitotenv.2022.153055 PMID: 35032528

Aslam, B., Asghar, R., Muzammil, S., Shafique, M., Siddique, A. B., Khurshid, M., Ijaz, M., Rasool, M. H., Chaudhry, T. H., Aamir, A., & Baloch, Z. (2024). AMR and Sustainable Development Goals: At a crossroads. *Globalization and Health*, *20*(1), 73. DOI: 10.1186/s12992-024-01046-8 PMID: 39415207

Aziz, M., Darmawan, A., & Juangsa, F. B. (2021). Hydrogen production from biomasses and wastes: A technological review. *International Journal of Hydrogen Energy*, *46*(68), 33756–33781. DOI: 10.1016/j.ijhydene.2021.07.189

Balata, F., & Williams, C. (2020). The role of coastal communities in the sustainable management of marine protected areas. In *Marine protected areas* (pp. 113–129). Elsevier., DOI: 10.1016/B978-0-08-102698-4.00006-X

Baskaran, V., & R, V. (2022). A systematic review on the role of geographical information systems in monitoring and achieving sustainable development goal 6: Clean water and sanitation. *Sustainable Development (Bradford)*, *30*(5), 1417–1425. DOI: 10.1002/sd.2302

Benjamin, G. C. (2020). Ensuring health equity during the COVID-19 pandemic: The role of public health infrastructure. *Revista Panamericana de Salud Pública = Pan American Journal of Public Health*, *44*, e70. DOI: 10.26633/RPSP.2020.70 PMID: 32523608

Bidira, F., Yesuf, M. B., Schaefer, N., Friedle, M., & Alemayehu, E. (2024). Review on dry toilet and management: Brown water (feces) characteristics, composition, and management. *Environmental Health Engineering And Management Journal*, 0-0. .DOI: 10.34172/EHEM.2024.36

Boulay, A. M., Drastig, K., Chapagain, A., Charlon, V., Civit, B., DeCamillis, C., & Pfister, S. (2021). Building consensus on water use assessment of livestock production systems and supply chains: Outcome and recommendations from the FAO LEAP Partnership. *Ecological Indicators*, *124*, 107391. DOI: 10.1016/j.ecolind.2021.107391

Çelekli, A., & Zariç, Ö. E. (2024). Rising tide of ocean acidification. *Environmental Research and Technology*, *7*(4), 605–613. DOI: 10.35208/ert.1407588

Cerf, M. E. (2023). The social-education-economy-health nexus, development and sustainability: Perspectives from low-and middle-income and African countries. *Discover Sustainability*, *4*(1), 37. DOI: 10.1007/s43621-023-00153-7

Chakrabarti, S., Gune, S., Bruckner, T. A., Strominger, J., & Singh, P. (2024). Toilet construction under the Swachh Bharat Mission and infant mortality in India. *Scientific Reports*, *14*(1), 20340. DOI: 10.1038/s41598-024-71268-8 PMID: 39223201

Chan, E. Y. Y., Tong, K. H. Y., Dubois, C., Mc Donnell, K., Kim, J. H., Hung, K. K. C., & Kwok, K. O. (2021). Narrative review of primary preventive interventions against water-borne diseases: Scientific evidence of health-EDRM in contexts with inadequate safe drinking water. *International Journal of Environmental Research and Public Health*, *18*(23), 12268. DOI: 10.3390/ijerph182312268 PMID: 34885995

Chandan, A., John, M., & Potdar, V. (2023). Achieving UN SDGs in food supply chain using blockchain technology. *Sustainability (Basel)*, *15*(3), 2109. DOI: 10.3390/su15032109

Corvalan, C., Villalobos Prats, E., Sena, A., Campbell-Lendrum, D., Karliner, J., Risso, A., Wilburn, S., Slotterback, S., Rathi, M., Stringer, R., Berry, P., Edwards, S., Enright, P., Hayter, A., Howard, G., Lapitan, J., Montgomery, M., Prüss-Ustün, A., Varangu, L., & Vinci, S. (2020). Towards climate resilient and environmentally sustainable health care facilities. *International Journal of Environmental Research and Public Health*, *17*(23), 8849. DOI: 10.3390/ijerph17238849 PMID: 33260752

Daher, B., Hamie, S., Pappas, K., Nahidul Karim, M., & Thomas, T. (2021). Toward resilient water-energy-food systems under shocks: Understanding the impact of migration, pandemics, and natural disasters. *Sustainability (Basel)*, *13*(16), 9402. DOI: 10.3390/su13169402

Erdaw, M. M. (2023). Contribution, prospects and trends of livestock production in sub-Saharan Africa: A review. *International Journal of Agricultural Sustainability*, *21*(1), 2247776. DOI: 10.1080/14735903.2023.2247776

Fernandez, R. M. (2020). SDG3 good health and well-being: integration and connection with other SDGs. *Good Health and Well-Being*, 629–636. DOI: 10.1007/978-3-319-95681-7_64

Filipe, J. F., Herrera, V., Curone, G., Vigo, D., & Riva, F. (2020). Floods, hurricanes, and other catastrophes: A challenge for the immune system of livestock and other animals. *Frontiers in Veterinary Science*, *7*, 16. DOI: 10.3389/fvets.2020.00016 PMID: 32083100

Foster, T., Mieno, T., & Brozović, N. (2020). Satellite-based monitoring of irrigation water use: Assessing measurement errors and their implications for agricultural water management policy. *Water Resources Research, 56*(11), e2020WR028378. DOI: 10.1029/2020WR028378

Gamage, A., Gangahagedara, R., Gamage, J., Jayasinghe, N., Kodikara, N., Suraweera, P., & Merah, O. (2023). Role of organic farming for achieving sustainability in agriculture. *Farming System, 1*(1), 100005. DOI: 10.1016/j.farsys.2023.100005

Garcia, S. N., Osburn, B. I., & Jay-Russell, M. T. (2020). One health for food safety, food security, and sustainable food production. *Frontiers in Sustainable Food Systems, 4*, 1. DOI: 10.3389/fsufs.2020.00001

Ghosh, P. K., & Paul, B. (2024). Influence of Industrialization on Sustainable Development: Evidence from Asian and European Developing Countries. [IJRTBT]. *International Journal on Recent Trends in Business and Tourism, 8*(4), 24–35. DOI: 10.31674/ijrtbt.2024.v08i04.003

Glazebrook, T., Noll, S., & Opoku, E. (2020). Gender matters: Climate change, gender bias, and women's farming in the global South and North. *Agriculture, 10*(7), 267. DOI: 10.3390/agriculture10070267

Gomez-Zavaglia, A., Mejuto, J. C., & Simal-Gandara, J. (2020). Mitigation of emerging implications of climate change on food production systems. *Food Research International, 134*, 109256. DOI: 10.1016/j.foodres.2020.109256 PMID: 32517948

Gryshova, I., Balian, A., Antonik, I., Miniailo, V., Nehodenko, V., & Nyzhnychenko, Y. (2024). Artificial intelligence in climate smart in agricultural: Toward a sustainable farming future. *Access J, 5*(1), 125–140. DOI: 10.46656/access.2024.5.1(8)

Halder, K., Chaudhuri, A., Abdin, M. Z., Majee, M., & Datta, A. (2022). RNA interference for improving disease resistance in plants and its relevance in this clustered regularly interspaced short palindromic repeats-dominated era in terms of dsRNA-based biopesticides. *Frontiers in Plant Science, 13*, 885128. DOI: 10.3389/fpls.2022.885128 PMID: 35645997

Hamid, B., Zaman, M., Farooq, S., Fatima, S., Sayyed, R. Z., Baba, Z. A., Sheikh, T. A., Reddy, M. S., El Enshasy, H., Gafur, A., & Suriani, N. L. (2021). Bacterial plant biostimulants: A sustainable way towards improving growth, productivity, and health of crops. *Sustainability (Basel), 13*(5), 2856. DOI: 10.3390/su13052856

Hassani, H., Huang, X., MacFeely, S., & Entezarian, M. R. (2021). Big data and the united nations sustainable development goals (UN SDGs) at a glance. *Big Data and Cognitive Computing, 5*(3), 28. DOI: 10.3390/bdcc5030028

Hejazi, M., Santos Da Silva, S. R., Miralles-Wilhelm, F., Kim, S., Kyle, P., Liu, Y., Vernon, C., Delgado, A., Edmonds, J., & Clarke, L. (2023). Impacts of water scarcity on agricultural production and electricity generation in the Middle East and North Africa. *Frontiers in Environmental Science*, *11*, 1082930. DOI: 10.3389/fenvs.2023.1082930

Hernandez-Patlan, D., Tellez-Isaias, G., Hernandez-Velasco, X., & Solis-Cruz, B. (2023). Technological strategies to improve animal health and production. *Frontiers in Veterinary Science*, *10*, 1206170. DOI: 10.3389/fvets.2023.1206170 PMID: 37292431

Heydari, M. (2024). Cultivating sustainable global food supply chains: A multifaceted approach to mitigating food loss and waste for climate resilience. *Journal of Cleaner Production*, *442*, 141037. DOI: 10.1016/j.jclepro.2024.141037

Hossain, A., Krupnik, T. J., Timsina, J., Mahboob, M. G., Chaki, A. K., Farooq, M., & Hasanuzzaman, M. (2020). Agricultural land degradation: processes and problems undermining future food security. In *Environment, climate, plant and vegetation growth* (pp. 17–61). Springer International Publishing., DOI: 10.1007/978-3-030-49732-3_2

Jabeen, N., & Iqbal, D. M. Z. (2020). Gender and local governance in Pakistan: Promoting participation through capacity building. *South Asian Studies*, *25*(2). http://111.68.103.26//journals/index.php/IJSAS/article/view/2798

Jaber, M. M., Ali, M. H., Abd, S. K., Jassim, M. M., Alkhayyat, A., Aziz, H. W., & Alkhuwaylidee, A. R. (2022). Predicting climate factors based on big data analytics based agricultural disaster management. *Physics and Chemistry of the Earth Parts A/B/C*, *128*, 103243. DOI: 10.1016/j.pce.2022.103243

Jeevanasai, S. A., Saole, P., Rath, A. G., Singh, S., Rai, S., & Kumar, M. (2023). Shades & shines of gender equality with respect to sustainable development goals (SDGs): The environmental performance perspectives. *Total Environment Research Themes*, *8*, 100082. DOI: 10.1016/j.totert.2023.100082

Johnson, J. E., Allain, V., Basel, B., Bell, J. D., Chin, A., Dutra, L. X., ... & Nicol, S. (2020). Impacts of climate change on marine resources in the Pacific Island region. *Climate change and impacts in the Pacific*, 359-402. DOI: 10.1007/978-3-030-32878-8_10

Katusiime, J., & Schütt, B. (2020). Integrated water resources management approaches to improve water resources governance. *Water (Basel)*, *12*(12), 3424. DOI: 10.3390/w12123424

Khumalo, N. Z., Sibanda, M., & Mdoda, L. (2024). Implications of a climate-smart approach to food and income security for urban Sub-Saharan Africa: A systematic review. *Sustainability (Basel), 16*(5), 1882. DOI: 10.3390/su16051882

Kleppel, G. S. (2020). Do differences in livestock management practices influence environmental impacts? *Frontiers in Sustainable Food Systems, 4*, 141. DOI: 10.3389/fsufs.2020.00141

Kotwani, A., Bhanot, A., Singal, G. L., & Gandra, S. (2022). Marketing and distribution system foster misuse of antibiotics in the community: Insights from drugs wholesalers in India. *Antibiotics (Basel, Switzerland), 11*(1), 95. DOI: 10.3390/antibiotics11010095 PMID: 35052974

Kumar, P., Chauhan, S., Patel, R., Srivastava, S., & Bansod, D. W. (2021). Prevalence and factors associated with triple burden of malnutrition among mother-child pairs in India: A study based on National Family Health Survey 2015–16. *BMC Public Health, 21*(1), 1–12. DOI: 10.1186/s12889-021-10411-w PMID: 33622303

Lakhiar, I. A., Yan, H., Zhang, C., Wang, G., He, B., Hao, B., Han, Y., Wang, B., Bao, R., Syed, T. N., Chauhdary, J. N., & Rakibuzzaman, M. (2024). A review of precision irrigation water-saving technology under changing climate for enhancing water use efficiency, crop yield, and environmental footprints. *Agriculture, 14*(7), 1141. DOI: 10.3390/agriculture14071141

Lee, J., Perera, D., Glickman, T., & Taing, L. (2020). Water-related disasters and their health impacts: A global review. *Progress in Disaster Science, 8*, 100123. DOI: 10.1016/j.pdisas.2020.100123

Li, J., Li, L., Suvarna, M., Pan, L., Tabatabaei, M., Ok, Y. S., & Wang, X. (2022). Wet wastes to bioenergy and biochar: A critical review with future perspectives. *The Science of the Total Environment, 817*, 152921. DOI: 10.1016/j.scitotenv.2022.152921 PMID: 35007594

Li, J., Yang, Z., Li, H., Hu, S., Duan, Y., & Yan, J. (2021). Optimal schemes and benefits of recovering waste heat from data center for district heating by CO2 transcritical heat pumps. *Energy Conversion and Management, 245*, 114591. DOI: 10.1016/j.enconman.2021.114591

Lile, R., Ocnean, M., Balan, I. M., & KIBA, D. (2023). Challenges for Zero Hunger (SDG 2): Links with Other SDGs. *Transitioning to Zero Hunger*. Chapter, MDPI, 9-66. DOI: 10.3390/books978-3-03897-863-3-2

Lobo, S. M., Creutzfeldt, C. J., Maia, I. S., Town, J. A., Amorim, E., Kross, E. K., Çoruh, B., Patel, P. V., Jannotta, G. E., Lewis, A., Greer, D. M., Curtis, J. R., Sharma, M., & Wahlster, S. (2022). Perceptions of critical care shortages, resource use, and provider well-being during the COVID-19 pandemic: A survey of 1,985 health care providers in Brazil. *Chest, 161*(6), 1526–1542. DOI: 10.1016/j.chest.2022.01.057 PMID: 35150658

Mabuza, M. P., & Mabuza, M. P. (2020). The UN Millennium development goals (MDGs) and sustainable development goals (SDGs). *Evaluating International Public Health Issues: Critical Reflections on Diseases and Disasters, Policies and Practices*, 77-103. DOI: 10.1007/978-981-13-9787-5_4

Manetu, W. M., & Karanja, A. M. (2021). Waterborne disease risk factors and intervention practices: A review. *OAlib, 8*(5), 1–11. DOI: 10.4236/oalib.1107401

Mason, N., Oyaya, C., & Boulenouar, J. (2020). Reforming urban sanitation under decentralization: Cross-country learning for Kenya and beyond. *Development Policy Review, 38*(1), 42–63. DOI: 10.1111/dpr.12408

Mehrabi, Z., Gill, M., Wijk, M. V., Herrero, M., & Ramankutty, N. (2020). Livestock policy for sustainable development. *Nature Food, 1*(3), 160–165. DOI: 10.1038/s43016-020-0042-9

Miatton, M., & Karner, M. (2020). *Regenerative Agriculture in Latin America.* Mustardseed Trust Research Reports.

Millington, N., & Scheba, S. (2021). Day zero and the infrastructures of climate change: Water governance, inequality, and infrastructural politics in Cape Town's water crisis. *International Journal of Urban and Regional Research, 45*(1), 116–132. DOI: 10.1111/1468-2427.12899

Mishra, H., & Mishra, D. (2024). AI for Data-Driven Decision-Making in Smart Agriculture: From Field to Farm Management. In *Artificial Intelligence Techniques in Smart Agriculture* (pp. 173-193). Singapore: Springer Nature Singapore. DOI: 10.1007/978-981-97-5878-4_11

Mishra, S., Kumar, R., & Kumar, M. (2023). Use of treated sewage or wastewater as an irrigation water for agricultural purposes-Environmental, health, and economic impacts. *Total Environment Research Themes, 6*, 100051. DOI: 10.1016/j.totert.2023.100051

Modu, F., Adam, A., Aliyu, F., Mabu, A., & Musa, M. (2020). A survey of smart hydroponic systems. *Advances in Science, Technology and Engineering Systems Journal, 5*(1), 233–248. DOI: 10.25046/aj050130

Mosadeghrad, A. M., Isfahani, P., Eslambolchi, L., Zahmatkesh, M., & Afshari, M. (2023). Strategies to strengthen a climate-resilient health system: A scoping review. *Globalization and Health, 19*(1), 62. DOI: 10.1186/s12992-023-00965-2 PMID: 37641052

Mrabet, R. (2023). Sustainable agriculture for food and nutritional security. In *Sustainable agriculture and the environment* (pp. 25–90). Academic Press., DOI: 10.1016/B978-0-323-90500-8.00013-0

Mumin, A. A., Mohammed, A. R., Issahaku, T., & Musah, B. I. (2024). How has community-led total sanitation (CLTS) affected open defecation in urban communities in the Tamale Metropolis? *Environment, Development and Sustainability, 26*(8), 21353–21368. DOI: 10.1007/s10668-023-03533-1

Mundonde, J., & Makoni, P. L. (2023). Public private partnerships and water and sanitation infrastructure development in Zimbabwe: What determines financing? *Environmental Systems Research, 12*(1), 14. DOI: 10.1186/s40068-023-00295-7

Nada, M. J., Najla, B. S. A. S., Othman, Y. A., & Salah, E. M. (2025). Water Contamination and Disinfection: A Review. *Journal of Pioneering Medical Sciences, 14*, 96–102. DOI: 10.47310/jpms2025140215

Ndudzo, A., Makuvise, A. S., Moyo, S., & Bobo, E. D. (2024). CRISPR-Cas9 genome editing in crop breeding for climate change resilience: Implications for smallholder farmers in Africa. *Journal of Agriculture and Food Research, 101132*, 101132. Advance online publication. DOI: 10.1016/j.jafr.2024.101132

Njuki, J., Eissler, S., Malapit, H., Meinzen-Dick, R., Bryan, E., & Quisumbing, A. (2023). A review of evidence on gender equality, women's empowerment, and food systems. *Science and innovations for food systems transformation*, 165. DOI: 10.1007/978-3-031-15703-5_9

Nkiaka, E., Bryant, R. G., Okumah, M., & Gomo, F. F. (2021). Water security in sub-Saharan Africa: Understanding the status of sustainable development goal 6. *WIREs. Water, 8*(6), e1552. DOI: 10.1002/wat2.1552

Nosheen, M., Iqbal, J., & Ahmad, S. (2023). Economic empowerment of women through climate change mitigation. *Journal of Cleaner Production, 421*, 138480. DOI: 10.1016/j.jclepro.2023.138480

Onteddu, A. R., Kundavaram, R. R., Kamisetty, A., Gummadi, J. C. S., & Manikyala, A. (2025). Enhancing Agricultural Efficiency with Robotics and AI-Powered Autonomous Farming Systems. *Malaysian Journal of Medical and Biological Research, 12*(1), 7–22.

Pelton, J. N. (2020). UN Sustainable Development Goals for 2030. In *Handbook of Small Satellites: Technology, Design, Manufacture, Applications, Economics and Regulation* (pp. 1537–1566). Springer International Publishing., DOI: 10.1007/978-3-030-36308-6_84

Pomaza-Ponomarenko, A., Kryvova, S., Hordieiev, A., Hanzyuk, A., & Halunko, O. (2023). Innovative risk management: identification, assessment and management of risks in the context of innovative project management. DOI: 10.7769/gesec.v14i10.2819

Psaki, S., Haberland, N., Mensch, B., Woyczynski, L., & Chuang, E. (2022). Policies and interventions to remove gender-related barriers to girls' school participation and learning in low-and middle-income countries: A systematic review of the evidence. *Campbell Systematic Reviews*, *18*(1), e1207. DOI: 10.1002/cl2.1207 PMID: 36913193

Rahaman, M. S., Mise, N., & Ichihara, S. (2022). Arsenic contamination in food chain in Bangladesh: A review on health hazards, socioeconomic impacts and implications. *Hygiene and Environmental Health Advances*, *2*, 100004. DOI: 10.1016/j.heha.2022.100004

Ranabahu, N., & Tanima, F. A. (2022). Empowering vulnerable microfinance women through entrepreneurship: Opportunities, challenges and the way forward. *International Journal of Gender and Entrepreneurship*, *14*(2), 145–166. DOI: 10.1108/IJGE-01-2021-0020

Ray, D. (2020). A global attitude, a global perspective, a global pledge towards sustainability: An approach of understanding. [IJRTBT]. *International Journal on Recent Trends in Business and Tourism*, *4*(1), 34–37. https://ejournal.lucp.net/index.php/ijrtbt/article/view/954

Rony, M. K. K., Sharmi, P. D., & Alamgir, H. M. (2023). Addressing antimicrobial resistance in low and middle-income countries: Overcoming challenges and implementing effective strategies. *Environmental Science and Pollution Research International*, *30*(45), 101896–101902. DOI: 10.1007/s11356-023-29434-4 PMID: 37610548

Rose, J., Crosbie, M., & Stewart, A. (2021). A qualitative literature review exploring the drivers influencing antibiotic over-prescribing by GPs in primary care and recommendations to reduce unnecessary prescribing. *perspectives in public health*, *141*(1), 19-27. DOI: 10.1177/1757913919879183

Roy, B., Hagappa, A., Ramalingam, Y. D., & Mahalingam, N. (2021). A review on lab-grown meat: Advantages and disadvantages. *Quest International Journal of Medical and Health Sciences*, *4*(1), 19–24. DOI: 10.5281/zenodo.5201528

Schreinemachers, P., Grovermann, C., Praneetvatakul, S., Heng, P., Nguyen, T. T. L., Buntong, B., Le, N. T., & Pinn, T. (2020). How much is too much? Quantifying pesticide overuse in vegetable production in Southeast Asia. *Journal of Cleaner Production, 244*, 118738. DOI: 10.1016/j.jclepro.2019.118738

Seife, T. K. (2021). The impact of climate change on agriculture and food security in the greater horn of Africa. *Politikon: South African Journal of Political Studies, 48*(1), 98–114. DOI: 10.1080/02589346.2020.1861509

Serwecińska, L. (2020). Antimicrobials and antibiotic-resistant bacteria: A risk to the environment and to public health. *Water (Basel), 12*(12), 3313. DOI: 10.3390/w12123313

Shadmi, E., Chen, Y., Dourado, I., Faran-Perach, I., Furler, J., Hangoma, P., Hanvoravongchai, P., Obando, C., Petrosyan, V., Rao, K. D., Ruano, A. L., Shi, L., de Souza, L. E., Spitzer-Shohat, S., Sturgiss, E., Suphanchaimat, R., Uribe, M. V., & Willems, S. (2020). Health equity and COVID-19: Global perspectives. *International Journal for Equity in Health, 19*(1), 1–16. DOI: 10.1186/s12939-020-01218-z PMID: 32586388

Shayo, G. M., Elimbinzi, E., Shao, G. N., & Fabian, C. (2023). Severity of waterborne diseases in developing countries and the effectiveness of ceramic filters for improving water quality. *Bulletin of the National Research Center, 47*(1), 113. DOI: 10.1186/s42269-023-01088-9

Song, Y., Pei, L., Chen, G., Mu, L., Yan, B., Li, H., & Zhou, T. (2023). Recent advancements in strategies to improve anaerobic digestion of perennial energy grasses for enhanced methane production. *The Science of the Total Environment, 861*, 160552. DOI: 10.1016/j.scitotenv.2022.160552 PMID: 36511320

Srinivas, R., Singh, A. P., & Shankar, D. (2020). Understanding the threats and challenges concerning Ganges River basin for effective policy recommendations towards sustainable development. *Environment, Development and Sustainability, 22*(4), 3655–3690. DOI: 10.1007/s10668-019-00361-0

Tahat, M., M., M. Alananbeh, K., A. Othman, Y., & I. Leskovar, D. (2020). Soil health and sustainable agriculture. *Sustainability, 12*(12), 4859.

Tohit, N. F. M., & Haque, M. (2024). Breaking the cycle: Addressing period poverty as a critical public health challenge and its relation to sustainable development goals. *Cureus, 16*(6). Advance online publication. DOI: 10.7759/cureus.62499 PMID: 38887745

Van Niekerk, A. J. (2020). Inclusive economic sustainability: SDGs and global inequality. *Sustainability (Basel), 12*(13), 5427. DOI: 10.3390/su12135427

Wassie, S. B. (2020). Natural resource degradation tendencies in Ethiopia: A review. *Environmental Systems Research, 9*(1), 1–29. DOI: 10.1186/s40068-020-00194-1

Wei, W., Sarker, T., Żukiewicz-Sobczak, W., Roy, R., Alam, G. M. M., Rabbany, M. G., Hossain, M. S., & Aziz, N. (2021). The influence of women's empowerment on poverty reduction in the rural areas of Bangladesh: Focus on health, education and living standard. *International Journal of Environmental Research and Public Health, 18*(13), 6909. DOI: 10.3390/ijerph18136909 PMID: 34199117

World Health Organization. UNEP United Nations Environment Programme, & World Organisation for Animal Health. (2022). *One health joint plan of action (2022–2026): working together for the health of humans, animals, plants and the environment.* World Health Organization.

You, S., Liu, T., Zhang, M., Zhao, X., Dong, Y., Wu, B., Wang, Y., Li, J., Wei, X., & Shi, B. (2021). African swine fever outbreaks in China led to gross domestic product and economic losses. *Nature Food, 2*(10), 802–808. DOI: 10.1038/s43016-021-00362-1 PMID: 37117973

Young, S. L., Frongillo, E. A., Jamaluddine, Z., Melgar-Quiñonez, H., Pérez-Escamilla, R., Ringler, C., & Rosinger, A. Y. (2021). Perspective: The importance of water security for ensuring food security, good nutrition, and well-being. *Advances in Nutrition, 12*(4), 1058–1073. DOI: 10.1093/advances/nmab003 PMID: 33601407

Zahoor, I., & Mushtaq, A. (2023). Water pollution from agricultural activities: A critical global review. *International Journal of Chemical and Biochemical Science, 23*(1), 164–176. https://www.iscientific.org/wp-content/uploads/2023/05/19-IJCBS-23-23-24.pdf

Chapter 13
Silent Struggles:
Revealing the Mental Health Crisis Among Kattunauakan Tribal Adolescents in Kerala, South India

V. K. Aswathy
https://orcid.org/0000-0002-8895-8373
Lovely Professional University, India

Sanjeev Kumar
https://orcid.org/0000-0002-7375-7341
Lovely Professional University, India

ABSTRACT

Kattunayakan, the largest particularly vulnerable tribal group in the state, are facing highest mental health problems and are subjected to higher extend of suicidal rate. This study aims to identify the current state of mental health among Kattunayakan tribal adolescents and explores the reasons and influencing factors behind the mental health deficits among them. A total of 93 tribal adolescents from the Kattunayakan community in Wayanad district, Kerala, were randomly chosen as participants in this study. Data was collected using a self-administered interview questionnaire to assess different aspects of mental health, including self-rated anxiety, mental stress, and social interaction as perceived by the adolescents themselves. The results illuminate the distinctive difficulties that tribal adolescents encounter and offer valuable knowledge for crafting targeted interventions and support systems designed specifically for this demographic.

DOI: 10.4018/979-8-3693-9755-8.ch013

INTRODUCTION

Mental health, according to the World Health Organization (2013), encompasses an individual's emotional, psychological, and social well-being. It reflects their capacity to realize their potential, handle life's stresses, work productively, and contribute to their community. he World Health Organization (WHO) has consistently highlighted the critical need for global mental health reform. In its 2024 and 2025 updates, the WHO emphasized that mental health disorders are a leading cause of disability worldwide, accounting for 15.6% of years lived with disability (YLDs). Despite the prevalence of conditions like depression and anxiety, approximately two-thirds of individuals with mental health conditions do not receive treatment . The WHO's 2025 guidance calls for urgent transformation in mental health policies, advocating for a shift from outdated institutional models to community-based, rights-centered care. This approach aims to address the significant gaps in access and quality of mental health services, ensuring that care is accessible, effective, and aligned with international human rights standards. Mental health deficits refer to limitations or challenges in various aspects of psychological functioning, including cognition, emotional regulation, social interactions, and adaptive behaviors. Assessing these deficits helps identify the specific needs of individuals within a community, guiding the development of tailored mental health programs and services. It informs resource allocation and policy development, supporting mental health promotion, prevention, and treatment. Identifying community-specific mental health deficits enables early intervention, targeting, and the provision of resources tailored to the community's unique needs, increasing the likelihood of successful outcomes.

Mental health deficits can arise from a combination of factors that interact and influence an individual's mental well-being.Genetic predisposition or imbalances in brain chemistry can play a role in the development of mental health deficits. Certain mental health conditions, such as depression, bipolar disorder, and schizophrenia, have been linked to genetic and biological factors. (Proctor, Flanagan, 2009). Adverse experiences or stressful life events can contribute to mental health deficits (Aysheha Yousef Mosallam, et al, 2016). These can include childhood trauma, abuse, neglect, loss of a loved one, relationship difficulties, financial problems, or other significant life stressors. Individual temperament, personality traits, and coping styles can impact mental health (Manuela Pérez-Chacón et al,2023). Factors such as low self-esteem, negative thinking patterns, perfectionism, and poor stress management skills can contribute to mental health deficits (M. Mann et al, 2004). Social support, relationships, and social determinants of health can influence mental well-being (Val Livingston et al. 2022). Isolation, loneliness, discrimination, poverty, inadequate access to healthcare, and lack of social support systems can contribute to mental health deficits. Substance abuse and addiction can significantly impact mental health. Substance use disorders often co-occur with mental health conditions and can exacerbate symptoms or lead to the development of mental health deficits. Cultural expectations, societal pressures, and stigma surrounding mental health can impact individuals' willingness to seek help and contribute to mental health deficits (Ahmedani, 2011).

Scheduled tribes are the ethnic groups of historically disadvantaged people that are given recognition in the constitution of India (Scheduled tribes of Kerala, 2013). Historically, indigenous communities in India have experienced marginalization, discrimination, and socioeconomic disparities, which contributes to mental health issues. Factors such as loss of cultural identity, limited access to healthcare services, and experiences of historical trauma may influence mental health outcomes within these communities (Gopalkrishnan, 2018). The state of Kerala in India is known for its diverse population, which includes various tribal communities. Sadath et al, 2018 conduct an empirical research on the mental health status of tribal communities in Wayanad district of Kerala. The study indicated a high prevalence of mental health issues among tribal communities in that district of Kerala. That study also reported a high incidence of depression, anxiety, and alcohol abuse among the tribal population. A systematic review published by Sadath et al, 2022 examined the prevalence and determinants of substance use among indigenous tribes in south India, which encompasses Kerala. While the study didn't focus solely on Kerala, but it provides insights into the mental health challenges faced by Adivasi communities in the broader region. These studies collectively highlight the higher prevalence of mental health issues among tribal populations in Kerala, including depression, anxiety, and substance abuse.

Kattunayakann community which is the numerically largest among the Scheduled Tribes of Kerala is mainly distributed in Wayanad District (Scheduled tribes of Kerala, 2013). Etymologically 'Kadu' means forest and 'Nayakan' signifies 'King/leader' (Santhosh, Rachel, 2008). According to their oral tradition, they lived freely in Ippimala, a mountain near Banasura Peak in Wayanad and was enslaved by the farming immigrants of the early centuries. Kattunayakans treated as slaves of their respective landlords, were victims of bonded labour system. During the festival of Valliyurkavu near Mananthavady the contract to work as bonded labourer, was renewed annually where the landlord paid an advance called 'Nippu panam'. Kattunayakanns who possessed muscular bodies could carry out any hard physical labour. Kattunayakan families worked under the Nair landlords. They were attached to the *Edoms* (Houses or places) or Devasoms (Temple property) of the landlords. The Chettiyars, the Merchents, Moplahs (the Muslims) also hired the Kattunayakan frequently whom they purchased for a year from a Janmi, the Landlord (Santhosh, Rachel, 2008). Although they have been freed by the enactment of the Abolition of Bonded Labour system since 1976, they still subsist on agriculture labour or any other manual labour. The post-independence rehabilitation measures like land for landless have helped a few families while majority of them lead appallingly low life. Their self-perception is low because of the attitude of others (Scheduled tribes of Kerala, 2013).

The Kattunayakan tribes often face socio-economic disadvantages, including limited access to education, healthcare, employment opportunities, and basic amenities (Mohindra et al.2010). These disparities may contribute to stress, feelings of marginalization, and increased vulnerability to mental health difficulties. Historical marginalization, discrimination, and the loss of traditional lands and resources can have a significant impact on the mental health of the Kattunayakan tribes (Nitheesh Kumar, Hilaria Soundari, 2018). Experiences of discrimination, social exclusion, and a sense of cultural dislocation can contribute to distress and psychological struggles. The Kattunayakan tribes have experienced displacement due to various reasons such as deforestation, land acquisition for development projects, and conflicts (Sreerekha,2010). Limited access to mental health services is a common challenge for marginalized communities (Murthy, 2022), including the Kattunayakan tribes. Factors such as geographic remoteness, language barriers, and lack of culturally appropriate services can contribute to underutilization of mental health resources and hinder timely intervention (Leong, Kalibatseva, 2011). Limited awareness and understanding of mental health issues can contribute to the under-identification and under-treatment of mental health challenges (Colizzi et al,2020) within the Kattunayakan tribes. Promoting mental health literacy and education is crucial for overcoming stigma and encouraging early intervention.

Understanding mental health deficits among the Kattunayakan tribes is indeed important to address the specific needs and challenges faced by this community. The Kattunayakan tribes have distinct cultural beliefs, practices, and social structures that may influence their understanding and perception of mental health. Marginalized communities, including tribal populations, often experience higher levels of socio-economic disparities, discrimination, and limited access to resources. These factors can contribute to mental health challenges within the community and need to be addressed holistically. The Kattunayakan may face unique stressors related to their livelihoods, land rights, displacement, and social integration (Nitheesh Kumar, Hilaria Soundari, 2018). These stressors can impact mental well-being (Birkmann et al, 2022). By understanding the mental health deficits within the Kattunayakan tribes, it becomes possible to empower community members and support their advocacy efforts. Building awareness, reducing stigma, and promoting mental health literacy within the community can foster resilience and well-being. To develop a collaborative approach should help to develop culturally appropriate strategies and interventions that effectively address the mental health needs of the Kattunayakan tribes.

Untreated or unaddressed mental health issues can lead to increased distress, impaired functioning, and reduced quality of life for affected individuals. Mental health deficits can have broader social implications within the Kattunayakan tribes. It can strain relationships, hinder community cohesion, and contribute to social isolation or exclusion. Understanding these effects is essential for promoting supportive and inclusive communities. Understanding these factors associated with mental health deficits among the Kattunayakan tribes may guide the development of culturally sensitive interventions, improve access to mental health services, and address the social, economic, and cultural determinants that contribute to mental health disparities. It is important to involve the Kattunayakan community itself in these efforts, ensuring their voices and perspectives are considered in designing appropriate support systems.

Adolescence, marked by significant physical, cognitive, and emotional changes, is a crucial developmental period (Robert Schlack et al, 2021). Mental health deficits during this stage can have enduring consequences on well-being, education, and future prospects. Studying mental health deficits in tribal adolescents allows for the development of support systems to enhance their development and life outcomes. Untreated deficits can hinder their future roles as parents, potentially perpetuating poor mental health cycles. Early understanding and intervention can break this cycle and promote positive inter-generational mental health. This support system fosters a nurturing environment, encourages help-seeking, and advocates for improved mental health services.

Despite the growing recognition of mental health as a critical aspect of human development, there is a dearth of research specifically examining the mental health challenges experienced by Kattunayakan tribal adolescents in Kerala. Consequently, understanding the nature and extent of mental health deficits in this population is essential for designing targeted interventions and support systems to improve their mental well-being. This study aims to investigate the mental health deficits among Kattunayakan tribal adolescents in Kerala and identify the factors contributing to these challenges, thereby filling the existing research gap and informing evidence-based interventions.

This study aims to achieve two primary objectives. It seeks to assess the prevalence and characterize the nature of mental health deficits within the Kattunayakan tribal adolescent population in the state of Kerala. The research aims to delve into the various contributing factors that exert significant influence on these mental health deficits among Kattunayakan tribal adolescents in the Kerala. By addressing these objectives, the study endeavors to provide a comprehensive understanding of the mental health challenges faced by this specific demographic and the factors that underlie these challenges.

MATERIAL AND METHODS

Study Sample

The Kattunayakan community is one of Kerala's largest tribal communities, primarily residing in Wayanad. The 2001 Census of India reported a total adolescent population of 15,578, with 7,703 males and 7,875 females. A decade later, in the 2011 Census, the Kattunayakan population showed a moderate increase, estimating a total of 17,267 adolescents, including 8,765 males and 8,502 females. Due to the lack of recent data, the study projected the population based on previous growth rates, estimating a total of 20,120 Kattunayakan adolescents, with 10,376 males and 9,755 females in 2021. The study included a sample of 93 Kattunayakan tribal adolescents selected using random sampling, ensuring an unbiased and representative reflection of the expected proportions of the 2021 Kattunayakan tribal population in Wayanad, Kerala. This method enhances the generalizability of the study's findings to the broader Kattunayakan tribal population in the area.

Tools and Techniques

This study employed a prospective cross-sectional survey design and focused on various Kattunayakan settlements within Kerala's Wayanad district. Mental stress and anxiety are self-reported variables in the study. To evaluate anxiety and social phobia, a symptom-based approach was utilized, where the presence and quantity of symptoms related to these conditions were recorded for each participant, enabling the assessment of condition severity. This approach facilitated the determination of anxiety and social phobia levels among the study cohort. In addition to basic descriptive analyses, the study utilized logistic regression and multinomial logistic regression to identify significant factors contributing to mental health deficits among Kattunayakan tribal adolescents. This comprehensive methodology allowed for a thorough exploration of the factors impacting the mental well-being of the studied population.

Conceptual Frame Work

The conceptual framework (Figure 1) for assessing the detrimental effects of mental health defects (anxiety, mental stress, social phobia, depression) among Kattunayakan tribal adolescents on demographic, social, economic, environmental, and physical health backgrounds involves a holistic approach to understanding the multi-faceted impact of these mental health issues.

Figure 1. Conceptual framework on the factors influencing mental health deficits

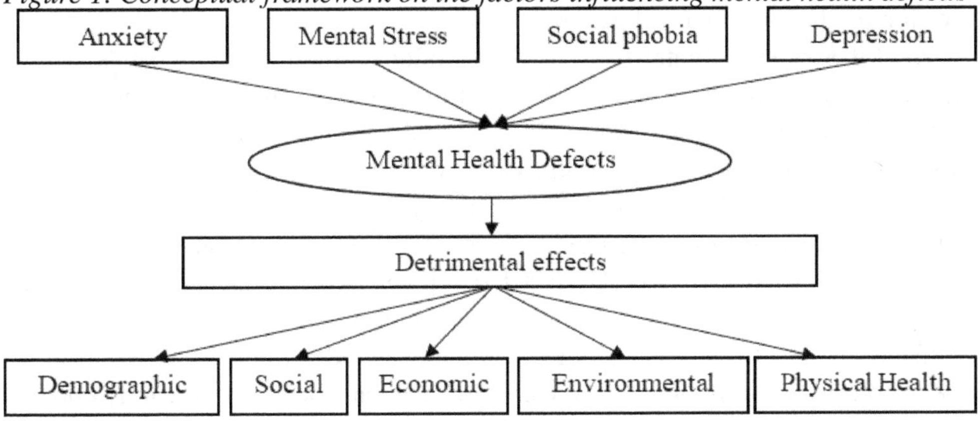

Demographic factors like age and sex influence mental health (Yuan et al, 2016). Adolescents and young adults may have higher rates of anxiety, depression, and eating disorders due to academic stress and identity formation challenges (Chyu & Chen, 2022; Jung et al, 2013). Females often experience higher rates of depression and anxiety, while males may show more externalizing behaviors like aggression or substance use (Malhotra S, Shah R, 2015; Liu, 2004; Winters et al, 2008). Social factors, including family type, dynamics, mobile phone and internet use, friendship issues, and peer disregard, affect mental health. Family structure, stability, and support impact mental health. Problematic family dynamics, like conflict and abuse, can harm mental well-being. Friendship issues, such as isolation and bullying, affect mental health by causing loneliness and low self-esteem. Peer disregard exacerbates mental health deficits by leading to emotional distress and social anxiety. Economic problems, like poverty and parental unemployment, can increase stress, anxiety, and depression among adolescents. Environmental factors, including living conditions, economic stability, healthcare access, educational opportunities, and social dynamics, also influence mental health in tribal adolescents. Limited healthcare access can lead to unaddressed health issues contributing to mental distress.

Explanation of Dependent Variables

Anxiety: - Anxiety is a natural response to stress or perceived threats, characterized by fear, worry, and unease (Prima Vitasari et al, 2010). Excessive, persistent anxiety interfering with daily life suggests an anxiety disorder. In the study, the interviewer assesses anxiety among adolescents from their response of self-rated question on the prevalence of anxiety.

Mental Stress: - Mental stress is the emotional strain when demands exceed coping ability (Schneiderman et al, 2005). In this semi-structured interviews, respondents self rated their mental status and discuss their impact on mental well-being, allowing a detailed exploration of individual experiences.

Social phobia: - Social phobia is an anxiety disorder characterized by intense fear in social situations where individuals fear scrutiny or potential embarrassment (British Psychological Society (UK); 2013). It involves persistent and excessive fear of negative judgment, humiliation, or rejection by others, leading to distress and avoidance of social situations. Common triggers include public speaking, meeting new people, group activities, and conversations. Social phobia significantly impacts daily life, relationships, and overall well-being. In the study, respondents were asked about five social phobia symptoms: fear, high palpitations, excessive shyness, excessive sweating, and nervousness when meeting others. Each symptom was scored as 1, and a Social Phobia index was created. The severity of social phobia was categorized as mild, moderate, or severe based on the index mean and standard deviation.

Depression: - Depression is a mental health disorder marked by persistent feelings of sadness, hopelessness, and a loss of interest or pleasure in activities (Chand SP, 2022). It significantly impacts daily functioning, relationships, and well-being. The study used emotional, behavioral, and cognitive symptoms to identify depression among adolescents, including disappointment, sadness, isolation, loneliness, anger, and self-criticism. A Depression Index assessed the severity of depression, categorizing it as mild, moderate, or severe based on respondents' experiences of isolation, hopelessness, sadness, anger, and vulnerability.

Analytical Approach

Data collected from a sample of 93 Kattunayakan tribal adolescents was subjected to rigorous analysis using IBM SPSS Statistics version 26.0. The initial step encompassed the computation of descriptive statistics for key mental health dimensions, including anxiety, mental stress, social phobia, and depression. Descriptive statistics aided in summarizing and characterizing the study sample. Subsequently, binary logistic regression was employed to examine the factors influencing anxiety and mental stress. This allowed for an exploration of the relationships between various demographic, social, economic, environmental, and physical health-related factors and the likelihood of experiencing anxiety and mental stress. Moreover, multinomial logistic regression was applied to investigate the factors influencing social phobia and depression, two categorical outcomes. By utilizing these analytical methods, the study aimed to unveil the complex web of factors affecting mental health in

Kattunayakan tribal adolescents, thereby offering valuable insights for tailored interventions and support strategies specific to this community in Kerala.

RESULTS

The data presents descriptive statistics related to three variables: Age, Gender, and Type of Family, along with their corresponding categories and sample sizes. The study involves a fairly balanced distribution of participants across the age groups, with slightly more respondents falling within the 10-14 age range. This suggests that both younger (10-14) and older (15-19) individuals are represented in the study. The study has a higher representation of male participants compared to female participants. This gender distribution might have implications on the findings of the study, considering the potential for gender-related differences in responses or behaviors. The study involves a relatively balanced distribution of participants across different family types, with nuclear and joint families being the most common. Extended families are less represented, which might limit the study's ability to draw detailed conclusions about this family type.

Mental Health Deficits

The table 1 presents the prevalence rates of different types of mental health deficits among Kattunayakan tribal adolescents, categorized by Anxiety, Mental Stress, Social Phobia, and Depression. Anxiety appears to be a significant mental health concern among Kattunayakan tribal adolescents, with a high prevalence rate (73.1%) . This suggests that a considerable portion of this demographic is experiencing symptoms of anxiety, which could have implications for their overall well-being. Mental stress is also prevalent among Kattunayakan tribal adolescents, with a significant portion (68.8%) of them reporting symptoms. This reinforces the notion that mental stress is a considerable issue affecting this population. Social phobia is evident among Kattunayakan tribal adolescents, with a varying degree of severity. A significant portion experience mild social phobia (50.5%), while notable percentages experience moderate (25.8%) and severe levels (23.7%), highlighting the need for intervention and support. Depression is a prevailing issue among Kattunayakan tribal adolescents. A substantial proportion experience both mild (40.9%) and moderate (50.5%) levels of depression, with a smaller but notable percentage (8.6%) experiencing severe depression. This suggests a range of depressive symptoms within this demographic.

Table 1. Mental health deficits among Kattunayakan tribal adolescents

Type of mental health deficits	Category	Percentage
Anxiety	Prevalence rate	73.1
Mental stress	Prevalence rate	68.8
Social phobia	Mild	50.5
	Moderate	25.8
	Severe	23.7
Depression	Mild	40.9
	Moderate	50.5
	Severe	8.6

Factors Influencing the Anxiety

Anxiety is a prevalent mental health concern that affects individuals of all ages and backgrounds. Among adolescents, anxiety can manifest in various forms and may be influenced by a multitude of factors. This analysis explores the factors associated with anxiety among tribal adolescents residing in the state of Kerala, India, with a particular focus on their family structure, household conditions, and experiences with animal attacks.

Table 2. Factors influencing anxiety among Kattunayakan tribal adolescents

Variables	B	S.E.	Wald	df	Sig.	Exp(B)
Infestation (®= No)	1.325	.601	4.868	1	.027	3.763
Genital Infection (®= No)	.993	.751	1.749	1	.186	2.699
Dental Infection (®= No)	1.245	.733	2.884	1	.089	3.474
Wildlife Incidents (®= No)	2.513	1.107	5.150	1	.023	12.347
Neglect by Peers (®= No)	1.375	1.117	1.516	1	.218	3.956
Constant	-.885	.541	2.678	1	.102	.413
®= Reference category						

The logistic regression analysis of anxiety factors in tribal adolescents reveals significant results. “Infestation” significantly increases anxiety risk, making those who've experienced it 3.763 times more likely to have anxiety. In contrast, “Genital

Infection" and "Dental Infection" lack statistical significance (p = 0.186 and p = 0.089, respectively) and do not affect anxiety. "Wildlife Incidents" substantially raise anxiety risk, with a 12.347-fold likelihood increase. Conversely, "Neglect by Peers" isn't statistically significant (p = 0.218), indicating it doesn't impact anxiety likelihood significantly among tribal adolescents.

Factors Influencing Mental stress Among Tribal Adolescents

Mental stress among tribal adolescents is a pressing concern that warrants in-depth investigation and understanding. Various factors can significantly influence the mental well-being of these individuals, impacting their overall quality of life and future prospects. From environmental factors like infestations to personal challenges such as learning issues, and the often-overlooked influence of family backgrounds, this multifaceted issue requires a comprehensive analysis to identify the root causes and develop effective strategies for support and intervention. By examining these factors, we can work towards providing the necessary resources and assistance to help tribal adolescents in Kerala manage and reduce mental stress, promoting their mental health and overall well-being.

Table 3. Factors influencing mental stress among Kattunayakan tribal adolescents

Variables	B	S.E.	Wald	df	Sig.	Exp(B)
Infestation *(®= No)*	1.310	.623	4.431	1	.035	3.708
Learning Issues *(®= No)*	1.366	.562	5.916	1	.015	3.919
Family Background *(®=(Fair)*	1.918	.691	7.706	1	.006	6.807
Friendship Issues *(®= No)*	.336	1.179	.081	1	.775	1.400
Negligence of Peer *(®= No)*	.114	.903	.016	1	.900	1.120
Constant	-1.727	.672	6.600	1	.010	.178
®= Reference category						

In examining mental stress factors among tribal adolescents, several findings emerge. "Infestation" significantly contributes to mental stress, with an Exp(B) of 3.708, indicating a 3.708-fold increase in the likelihood of mental stress for those who've experienced it. "Learning Issues" also significantly affect mental stress, with a 3.919-fold likelihood increase. Family background is a substantial influencer, as those with backgrounds other than "Fair" face a 6.807-fold increased likelihood of mental stress. However, "Friendship Issues" and "Negligence of peers" lack statistical significance (p = 0.775 and p = 0.900, respectively), suggesting no significant impact on the likelihood of mental stress among tribal adolescents.

Factors Influencing Social Phobia

Social phobia, also known as social anxiety disorder, is a common mental health condition characterized by an intense and persistent fear of social situations. It can lead to significant distress and impairment in an individual's daily life, affecting their ability to interact with others, participate in social activities, and perform tasks in public settings. Factors influencing social phobia among individuals, particularly in tribal communities, can be multifaceted and complex. Understanding these factors is crucial for developing effective interventions and support systems to alleviate the burden of social phobia and improve the mental well-being of affected individuals. In this context, this analysis aims to explore and identify the factors that contribute to the development and exacerbation of social phobia among tribal adolescents, shedding light on the unique challenges and vulnerabilities within this specific population.

Table 4. Factors influencing social phobia among Kattunayakan tribal adolescents

Social Phobia	Independent Variables	B	Std. Error	Wald	Df	Sig.	Exp(B)
Moderate	Intercept	7.34	1.96	13.97	1	.000	
	Age=10-14 (®= 15-19)	-1.75	.730	5.78	1	.016	.173
	Respiratory Infections = No (®=Yes)	-1.29	.858	2.26	1	.132	.275
	Economic Problem = No (®= Yes)	-2.74	.795	9.70	1	.002	.084
	Family Background = Not Fair (® = Fair)	-.93	.744	1.58	1	.208	.392
	Friendship Issues = No (®= Yes)	-2.17	1.30	2.77	1	.096	.114
	Negligence of Peer = No (®= Yes)	-2.19	.940	5.46	1	.019	.111
	Substance use = No (®=Yes)	.25	1.09	.053	1	.817	1.288
Severe	Intercept	8.18	2.02	16.3	1	.000	
	Age=10-14 (®= 15-19)	-1.29	.874	2.19	1	.138	.274
	Respiratory Infections = No (®=Yes)	-2.59	.901	8.29	1	.004	.075
	Economic Problem = No (®= Yes)	-1.24	.947	1.73	1	.188	.287
	Family Background = Not Fair (® = Fair)	-1.80	.808	4.99	1	.025	.164
	Friendship Issues = No (®= Yes)	-3.68	1.26	8.56	1	.003	.025

continued on following page

Table 4. Continued

Social Phobia	Independent Variables	B	Std. Error	Wald	Df	Sig.	Exp(B)
	Negligence of Peer = No (®= Yes)	-1.39	1.01	1.89	1	.169	.248
	Substance use = No (®=Yes)	-.12	1.14	.012	1	.913	.883

®= Reference category: Mild

The multinomial logistic regression on social phobia in tribal adolescents yields significant insights. Younger age (10-14) is linked to lower risk of "moderate" and "severe" social phobia, suggesting an age-related susceptibility. Economic stability reduces the risk of "moderate" social phobia. Persistent cough lasting over two weeks increases the risk of "severe" social phobia, highlighting physical health's impact on mental well-being. Family background fairness somewhat elevates "severe" social phobia risk for those from "Not Fair" families. Friendship issues are associated with higher "severe" social phobia risk, illustrating the complex link between social interactions and mental health. Peer negligence is linked to "moderate" but not "severe" social phobia, suggesting variable influence across different condition levels. These findings emphasize the multifaceted nature of social phobia in tribal adolescents, requiring tailored interventions addressing economic stability, age, physical health, social dynamics, and family backgrounds to effectively address this mental health issue in this population.

Factors Influencing Depression

Depression is a complex and prevalent mental health concern that affects individuals worldwide, cutting across various demographic and cultural boundaries. Among specific population groups, such as tribal adolescents in Kerala, India, exploring the factors influencing depression is of paramount importance. Understanding the unique determinants of depression within this context can lead to more targeted interventions and support systems.

Table 5. Factors influencing depression among Kattunayakan tribal adolescents

Depression	Independent Variables	B	Std. Error	Wald	df	Sig.	Exp(B)
Moderate	Intercept	1.27	.779	2.66	1	.103	
	Gender = Female (® = Male)	-1.62	.494	10.8	1	.001	.196
	Genital Infection = No ®= Yes	-.815	.603	1.82	1	.176	.443
	Allergy = No (® = yes)	.376	.674	.311	1	.577	1.45
Sever	Intercept	1.43	.973	2.17	1	.140	
	Gender = Female (®= Male)	-.701	.923	.576	1	.448	.496
	Genital Infection = No (®= Yes	-2.79	.985	8.02	1	.005	.061
	Allergy = No (® = yes)	-1.48	.950	2.43®	1	.118	.227

®= Reference category: Mild

In this multinomial logistic regression on depression in tribal adolescents, compared to “Mild” depression, males have a significantly higher risk of “Moderate” depression, while gender doesn't affect transitioning to “Severe” depression. Genital infection and allergies don't significantly impact the shift from “Mild” to “Moderate” depression. The absence of genital infection significantly reduces the risk of “Severe” depression, indicating it's a risk factor for more severe depression. Allergies don't strongly influence the shift to either “Moderate” or “Severe” depression. These findings underscore gender-specific vulnerability to moderate depression in males and the influence of genital infection on more severe depression, while allergies have minimal impact on these transitions.

DISCUSSION ON FINDINGS

Adolescence brings profound physical, emotional, and social changes that can heighten anxiety due to pressures and identity struggles. The high prevalence of anxiety among Kattunayakan tribal adolescents is linked to socio-cultural, economic, and environmental factors, requiring culturally sensitive interventions. Mental stress is also prevalent, fueled by economic hardships, limited resources, and societal expectations. Social phobia, with varying intensities, results from cultural, social, and individual factors. Addressing these issues calls for interventions and supportive environments. Depression, marked by persistent sadness and disinterest, is widespread among Kattunayakan tribal adolescents. The study by Jeyarani and Ramar (2024) presents a critical exploration of mental stress among tribal adolescents, focusing on the effectiveness of positive psychological interventions in the Jawadhu Hills region of Tamil Nadu. The research identifies economic hardship, limited access to resources, and entrenched societal expectations as significant contributors to elevated stress levels among tribal youth. The study utilized a pre-test/post-test control group design and demonstrated a substantial reduction in stress scores among participants who underwent the intervention (from 22.53 to 14.27), underscoring the potential of culturally sensitive, resilience-based psychological programs in mitigating mental distress. Although the study does not focus exclusively on the Kattunayakan tribe, its findings are highly relevant, given the similar socio-cultural and economic conditions faced by Kattunayakan adolescents in Kerala and Tamil Nadu. The authors advocate for professional counseling services and tailored mental health strategies rooted in the cultural context of indigenous communities, calling attention to the urgent need for inclusive and sustainable mental health care delivery in tribal areas.

The logistic regression analysis on anxiety in tribal adolescents reveals significant findings. Infestation significantly impacts anxiety, likely due to its connection to living conditions and hygiene. Similarly, wildlife incidents strongly affect anxiety levels, emphasizing the need for trauma support. These results underscore the importance of addressing these factors to alleviate anxiety in tribal adolescents. The social work intervention like counselling, therapeutic practices are more significant. The study by Hidayati et al. (2024) demonstrates that group therapeutic interventions significantly enhance emotional and psychosocial development among adolescents. Using a quasi-experimental design with pre- and post-tests, the authors found notable improvements in the treatment group compared to the control. The findings support the effectiveness of structured group therapy in adolescent mental health programs.

The statistical analysis reveals that infestation significantly increases the risk of mental stress in tribal adolescents. Infestation, such as pests or parasites, can cause physical discomfort, health issues, and social stigma, contributing to stress. Dealing with infestation incurs financial burdens and disrupts daily routines, further exacerbating stress. Similarly, "Learning Issues" significantly raise the likelihood of mental stress, as they create academic pressures, erode self-esteem, and may lead to bullying or stigmatization. Additionally, a family background other than "Fair" suggests lower socioeconomic status, potential discrimination, and family dysfunction, all of which can contribute to stress and feelings of inadequacy. Adolescents from disadvantaged backgrounds may perceive fewer opportunities, fostering a sense of hopelessness and increased stress. These findings underline the multifaceted nature of mental stress in tribal adolescents, impacted by various factors including infestation, learning issues, and family background.

The analysis indicates several significant findings regarding social phobia in adolescents. Younger adolescents (aged 10-14) are less likely to experience both "moderate" and "severe" social phobia than older counterparts (aged 15-19), suggesting an age-related susceptibility linked to increasing social awareness and peer pressures. Economic stability significantly reduces the risk of "moderate" social phobia, as it provides resources, reducing financial stress and enhancing overall well-being. The presence of a persistent cough lasting more than two weeks is associated with higher risk of "severe" social phobia, likely due to physical discomfort, self-consciousness, and social stigma. Family background fairness, specifically being characterized as "Not Fair," is linked to a somewhat elevated risk of "severe" social phobia, indicating a potential connection between family dynamics and the severity of social phobia. Friendship issues significantly correlate with a higher risk of "severe" social phobia, highlighting the impact of strained social relationships and feelings of rejection on mental health. These findings underscore the complex interplay of various factors contributing to social phobia in adolescents.

The multinomial logistic regression analysis on depression in tribal adolescents reveals important findings. Males are at a higher risk of "Moderate" depression than females, highlighting the need for gender-specific mental health support. Genital infection is a significant risk factor for "Severe" depression, indicating the interplay between physical and mental well-being. This underscores the importance of holistic healthcare to address depression effectively in this population. A 2024 study by the Canadian Men's Health Foundation revealed that young men (19–29 years), racialized men, and those identifying as gay or bisexual are at significantly higher risk of experiencing moderate-to-severe depression compared to the broader male population, emphasizing the urgent need for gender- and identity-specific mental health interventions (Canadian Men's Health Foundation, 2024). Complementing this, research published in the Chinese Medical Journal found that genital infections were significantly associated with severe depression and somatic symptoms in individuals with major depressive disorder, highlighting the critical interplay between physical health and mental well-being (Zhao et al., 2024). Together, these findings stress the importance of holistic, intersectional approaches to mental health care that address both psychosocial and physiological factors.

IMPLICATIONS, LIMITATIONS AND FUTURE DIRECTION

The findings on anxiety among tribal adolescents emphasize the importance of addressing environmental factors like infestations and wildlife incidents. Targeted interventions should improve living conditions, provide mental health services, and promote prevention and resilience. These findings have significant implications for mental stress, suggesting the need for tailored interventions addressing challenges such as infestations and learning issues, family support, and early identification. Social phobia interventions should consider age-specific approaches and economic stability programs. A holistic healthcare approach, integrating physical and mental well-being, is essential, particularly for severe social phobia, and addressing friendship issues requires peer support and conflict resolution strategies. In the context of depression, gender-specific interventions and holistic healthcare are key, along with enhanced mental health awareness and community involvement to reduce stigma and improve support accessibility for tribal adolescents.

CONCLUSION

This comprehensive analysis of mental health deficits among Kattunayakan tribal adolescents in Kerala has illuminated the multifaceted nature of their mental well-being challenges. The prevalence rates of anxiety, mental stress, social phobia, and depression underscore the urgent need for targeted interventions within this community. Anxiety and mental stress are prevalent issues, with infestation, learning issues, and family background emerging as significant contributing factors. Social phobia varies in severity, with age, economic stability, physical health, and family fairness all playing discernible roles. Additionally, depression levels vary, with gender disparities and the presence of genital infection as key determinants. These findings emphasize the complexity of mental health in tribal adolescents and highlight the interplay of demographic, social, economic, environmental, and physical health factors. Tailored interventions encompassing healthcare access, educational support, community awareness, and gender-specific strategies are imperative to alleviate the burden of mental health deficits and ensure the well-being of Kattunayakan tribal adolescents in Kerala. This research provides a valuable foundation for future studies and evidence-based interventions to enhance the mental health outcomes of tribal youth in similar contexts.

REFERENCES

Ahmedani, B. K. (2011). Mental Health Stigma: Society, Individuals, and the Profession. *Journal of Social Work Values and Ethics*, *8*(2), 41–416. PMID: 22211117

Ahn, W., Proctor, C. C., & Flanagan, E. H. (2009). Mental health clinicians' beliefs about the biological, psychological, and environmental bases of mental disorders. *Cognitive Science*, *33*(2), 147–182. DOI: 10.1111/j.1551-6709.2009.01008.x PMID: 20411158

Anandakumar, S. (2020). The Kattunayakan Tribes in Nilgiri Hills of Tamil Nadu. *Learning Community*, *11*(1), 53–61. DOI: 10.30954/2231-458X.01.2020.6

Birkmann, J., Liwenga, E., Pandey, R., Boyd, E., Djalante, R., Gemenne, F., & Wrathall, D. (2022). Poverty, Livelihoods and Sustainable Development. In Pörtner, H.-O., Roberts, D. C., Tignor, M., Poloczanska, E. S., Mintenbeck, K., Alegría, A., Craig, M., Langsdorf, S., Löschke, S., Möller, V., Okem, A., & Rama, B. (Eds.), *Climate Change 2022: Impacts, Adaptation and Vulnerability* (pp. 1171–1274). Cambridge University Press., DOI: 10.1017/9781009325844.010

British Psychological Society. (2013). *Understanding mental health: A guide for the public*. British Psychological Society.

Canadian Men's Health Foundation. (2024, May 30). New study identifies higher risk of depression and anxiety among young men, gay or bisexual and racialized Canadian men. GlobeNewswire. https://www.globenewswire.com/news-release/2024/05/30/2890706/0/en/New-study-identifies-higher-risk-of-depression-and-anxiety-among-young-men-gay-or-bisexual-and-racialized-Canadian-men.html

Chand, S. P., & Arif, H. (2023). Depression. In StatPearls. Treasure Island (FL): StatPearls Publishing. Available from: https://www.ncbi.nlm.nih.gov/books/NBK430847/. (Updated 2022, July 18).

Chyu, E. P. Y., & Chen, J. K. (2022). Associations Between Academic Stress, Mental Distress, Academic Self-Disclosure to Parents, and School Engagement in Hong Kong. *Frontiers in Psychiatry*, *13*, 911530. DOI: 10.3389/fpsyt.2022.911530 PMID: 35928778

Colizzi, M., Lasalvia, A., & Ruggeri, M. (2020). Prevention and early intervention in youth mental health: Is it time for a multidisciplinary and trans-diagnostic model for care? *International Journal of Mental Health Systems*, *14*(23), 23. Advance online publication. DOI: 10.1186/s13033-020-00356-9 PMID: 32226481

Gopalkrishnan, N. (2018). Cultural diversity and mental health: Considerations for policy and practice. *Frontiers in Public Health*, *6*, 179. DOI: 10.3389/fpubh.2018.00179 PMID: 29971226

Hidayati, E., Ben Olina, Y., da Costa Freitas, A. F., & Martins, A. X. (2024). The Influence of Group Therapeutic Intervention on the Enhancement of Emotional and Psychosocial Development in Adolescents. [MJN]. *The Malaysian Journal of Nursing*, *16*(1), 169–177. DOI: 10.31674/mjn.2024.v16i01.017

International Bank for Reconstruction and Development / The World Bank. (2022). Social Cohesion and Forced Displacement: A Synthesis of New Research.

Jeyarani, J., & Ramar, L. (2024). Effectiveness of positive psychological intervention on mental stress among tribal adolescents in Jawadhu Hills. *Journal of Positive School Psychology*, *8*(2), 1453–1460.

Jung, E., Pick, O., Schlüter-Müller, S., Schmeck, K., & Goth, K. (2013). Identity Development in Adolescents with Mental Problems. *Child and Adolescent Psychiatry and Mental Health*, *7*(1), 26. DOI: 10.1186/1753-2000-7-26 PMID: 23899433

Kerala State Planning Board. (2013). *Scheduled Tribes of Kerala: Report on the socio-economic status*. Government of Kerala. https://spb.kerala.gov.in

Kumar, N., & Soundari, H. (2018). Female Subaltern: Double Marginalization of Kattunayakan Women. *IJCRT* Volume 6(2), April 2018, ISSN: 2320-2882.

Kumar, N., & Soundari, H. (2021). The burden of mental health illnesses in Kerala: A secondary analysis of reported data from 2002 to 2018. *BMC Public Health*, *21*(1), 1–10. DOI: 10.1186/s12889-021-11101-7 PMID: 33388037

Leong, F. T., & Kalibatseva, Z. (2011). Cross-Cultural Barriers to Mental Health Services in the United States. *Cerebrum*, 2011(5). https://doi.org/.DOI: 10.1036/cerebrum.2011.0005

Liu, J. (2004). Childhood Externalizing Behavior: Theory and Implications. *Journal of Child and Adolescent Psychiatric Nursing*, *17*(3), 93–103. DOI: 10.1111/j.1744-6171.2004.tb00003.x PMID: 15535385

Livingston, V., Jackson-Nevels, B., & Reddy, V. V. (2022). Social, Cultural, and Economic Determinants of Well-Being. *Encyclopedia*, *2*(3), 1183–1199. DOI: 10.3390/encyclopedia2030079

Malhotra, S., & Shah, R. (2015). Women and Mental Health in India: An Overview. *Indian Journal of Psychiatry*, *57*(6, Suppl 2), S205–S211. DOI: 10.4103/0019-5545.161479 PMID: 26330636

Mann, M., Hosman, C., Schaalma, H., & Vries, N. (2004). Self-esteem in a broad-spectrum approach for mental health promotion. *Health Education Research, 19*(4), 357–372. DOI: 10.1093/her/cyg041 PMID: 15199011

Mohindra, K., Narayana, D., Harikrishnadas, C., Anushreedha, S. S., & Haddad, S. (2010). Kattunayakan Voices: A Participatory Poverty and Health Assessment among a Marginalized South Indian Tribal Population. *BMC Public Health, 10*(149), 149. Advance online publication. DOI: 10.1186/1471-2458-10-149 PMID: 20307290

Mosallam, A., & Aziz, A. (2016). Coping With Stressful Life Events and Mental Health Disorders among University Students. *BAOJ Psychology, 1*(3). Advance online publication. DOI: 10.24947/baojp/1/3/00111

Mudunna, C., Weerasinghe, M., Tran, T., Antoniades, J., Romero, L., Chandradasa, M., & Fisher, J. (2025). Nature, prevalence and determinants of mental health problems experienced by adolescents in south Asia: A systematic review. *The Lancet Regional Health. Southeast Asia, 33*, 100532. Advance online publication. DOI: 10.1016/j.lansea.2025.100532 PMID: 39902294

Murthy, V. H. (2022). The Mental Health of Minority and Marginalized Young People: An Opportunity for Action. *Public Health Reports, 137*(4), 613–616. DOI: 10.1177/00333549221102390 PMID: 35674401

Pérez-Chacón, M., Borda-Mas, M., Chacón, A., & Avargues-Navarro, M. L. (2023). Personality Traits and Coping Strategies as Psychological Factors Associated with Health-Related Quality of Life in Highly Sensitive Persons. *International Journal of Environmental Research and Public Health, 20*(5644), 5644. Advance online publication. DOI: 10.3390/ijerph20095644 PMID: 37174164

Pérez-Chacón, M., Borda-Mas, M., Chacón, A., & Avargues-Navarro, M. L. (2023). Personality traits and coping strategies as psychological factors associated with health-related quality of life in highly sensitive persons. *International Journal of Environmental Research and Public Health, 20*(9), 5644. DOI: 10.3390/ijerph20095644 PMID: 37174164

Putri, A., & Sansuwito, T. (2025). Developing Knowledge of Sexual and Reproductive Health Among Adolescent Girls Through a Peer Mentoring Approach in Nursing. [MJN]. *The Malaysian Journal of Nursing, 16*(3), 205–214. DOI: 10.31674/mjn.2025.v16i03.020

Sadath, A., Jose, K., Jiji, K. M., Mercy, V. T., Ragesh, G., & Arensman, E. (2022). Prevalence and Determinants of Substance Use Among Indigenous Tribes in South India: Findings from a Tribal Household Survey. *Journal of Racial and Ethnic Health Disparities, 9*(1), 356–366. DOI: 10.1007/s40615-021-00964-2 PMID: 33495925

Sadath, A., Uthaman, S. P., & Shibu Kumar, T. M. (2018). Mental Health in Tribes: A Case Report. *Indian Journal of Social Psychiatry*, *34*(2), 187–188. DOI: 10.4103/ijsp.ijsp_56_17

Santhosh, R. (2008). Mapping of an Ethnohistory of the Kattunayakann: Some Preliminary Reflections. [Retrieved from JSTOR.]. *Indian Anthropologist*, *38*(1), 61–76.

Schlack, R., Peerenboom, N., Neuperdt, L., Junker, S., & Beyer, A. K. (2021). The Effects of Mental Health Problems in Childhood and Adolescence in Young Adults: Results of the KiGGS Cohort. *Journal of Health Monitoring*, *6*(4), 3–19. DOI: 10.25646/8863 PMID: 35146318

Schneiderman, N., Ironson, G., & Siegel, S. D. (2005). Stress and health: Psychological, behavioral, and biological determinants. *Annual Review of Clinical Psychology*, *1*(1), 607–628. DOI: 10.1146/annurev.clinpsy.1.102803.144141 PMID: 17716101

Sreerekha, M. S. (2010). Challenges before Kerala's Landless: The Story of Aralam Farm. *Economic and Political Weekly*, *45*(21), 55–62.

United Nations Development Programme Democratic Governance Group. (2010). Marginalized Minorities in Development Programming.

U.S. Department of Health and Human Services. (2001). Mental Health: Culture, Race, and Ethnicity—A Supplement to Mental Health: A Report of the Surgeon General. Rockville, MD: U.S. Department of Health and Human Services, Substance Abuse and Mental Health Services Administration, Center for Mental Health Services. Available from: https://www.ncbi.nlm.nih.gov/books/NBK44249/

Winters, K. C., Stinchfield, R. D., Latimer, W. W., & Stone, A. (2008). Internalizing and Externalizing Behaviors and Their Association with the Treatment of Adolescents with Substance Use Disorder. *Journal of Substance Abuse Treatment*, *35*(3), 269–278. DOI: 10.1016/j.jsat.2007.11.002 PMID: 18328664

World Health Organization. (2013). What is mental health? [Web page]. Retrieved from https://www.who.int/features/qa/62/en/

World Health Organization. (2024). Mental health: Strengthening our response. https://www.who.int/observatories/global-observatory-on-health-research-and-development/analyses-and-syntheses/mental-health/global-strategic-direction

World Health Organization. (2025, March 25). New WHO guidance calls for urgent transformation of mental health policies. https://www.who.int/news/item/25-03-2025-new-who-guidance-calls-for-urgent-transformation-of-mental-health-policies

Yousef, A. Y., & Mosallam, E. A. (2016). Mental health problems among youth in India and its correlates. *International Journal of Human Rights in Healthcare*, *9*(2), 97–108. DOI: 10.1108/IJHRH-07-2015-0018

Yuan, Q., Abdin, E., Picco, L., Vaingankar, J. A., Shahwan, S., Jeyagurunathan, A., Sagayadevan, V., Shafie, S., Tay, J., Chong, S. A., & Subramaniam, M. (2016). Attitudes to Mental Illness and Its Demographic Correlates among the General Population in Singapore. *PLoS One*, *11*(11), e0167297. DOI: 10.1371/journal.pone.0167297 PMID: 27893796

Zhao, J., Zhang, J., Li, Y., Chen, L., & Wang, H. (2024). Clinical features and treatment outcomes of major depressive disorder with genital symptoms: A comparative study. *Chinese Medical Journal*, *137*(5), 550–556. https://journals.lww.com/cmj/fulltext/2024/03050/clinical_features_and_treatment_outcomes_of_major.17.aspx PMID: 37646139

Chapter 14

Solid Waste Management: E-Waste Management for Environmental Sustainability – Issues and Strategies

Sunil Sankathala
https://orcid.org/0009-0004-7809-7647
Ajeenkya D.Y. Patil University, India

Aditya Shrivastav
https://orcid.org/0009-0000-8461-8171
Ajeenkya D.Y. Patil University, India

Devanshi Soni
Ajeenkya D.Y. Patil University, India

Yadnyesh Khapekar
Ajeenkya D.Y. Patil University, India

Kashvi Chaturvedi
https://orcid.org/0009-0005-3192-3400
Ajeenkya D.Y. Patil University, India

Susanta Das
https://orcid.org/0000-0002-9314-3988
Ajeenkya D.Y. Patil University, India

Rakesh Kumar Jain
https://orcid.org/0000-0002-0216-5437
Ajeenkya D.Y. Patil University, India

ABSTRACT

The global market for recycling electronics is expected to grow to ~ $66 billion by 2026, owing to the growing volume of electronic waste (e-waste), generated by electrical & electronic devices. Significant environmental & health issues result from the fact that only ~18% of this waste is collected & recycled in developing nations. E-waste contains useful materials that can be recycled, reducing need for natural resources & supporting renewable energy technologies. This chapter discusses different kinds of e-waste, recycling techniques, & the possibility of repurposing valuable materials in environmentally friendly technologies. It examines how e-waste is managed in major producing nations, pointing out areas that need improvement and offering best practices. Many nations lack recycling infrastructure & specific

DOI: 10.4018/979-8-3693-9755-8.ch014

policies, which makes managing e-waste particularly difficult. Community education & stricter regulations are demanded. A concerted worldwide strategy is needed to properly manage e-waste, lessen its negative effects on the environment, & promote sustainable development.

INTRODUCTION

The large technological advancements and economic expansion of the electronics and telecommunications industries have led to the widespread usage of electronic gadgets. However, if these devices are discarded without being repurposed, they become electronic trash, or e-waste, which is crucial for promoting sustainability and a circular economy. It is anticipated that the e-waste industry would reach ~ 75 million tons by 2030, with a projected yearly growth rate of 2 million tons (Seif et al., 2023). Disposing of e-waste can have long-term repercussions on the ecosystem due to landfill pollution and hazardous uncontrolled recycling processes. The Green Climate Fund aims to support developing countries in addressing climate change, and the 2015 Paris Agreement emphasizes the necessity of renewable energy sources (Seif et al., 2023).

One major problem with waste management in the EU and throughout the world is the growing volume of e-waste, which includes computers, TVs, refrigerators, cell phones, and power tools. The continuous armed confrontation in Northeastern Europe, together with digitalization and the advancement of information technology, are the main causes of the explosive development of e-waste (Constantinescu et al., 2022). As a result, there is now a demand for more efficient electronic equipment recycling and reuse. E-waste may be recycled more successfully since it contains precious elements like rare metals.

Unauthorized recycling methods are damaging the environment. Sustainable growth, particularly in emerging nations like China and India, depends on efficient e-waste management (Soesanto et al., 2023). Scholars have conducted a thorough investigation of the management of e-waste, including bibliometric analysis to pinpoint important themes and trends. This study looks for current trends, potential paths forward, and essential components that facilitate effective e-waste management in order to enhance procedures and advance sustainable development goals (Soesanto et al., 2023). Figure 1 presents a systematic framework for solid waste management, beginning with the generation of waste from primary sources such as kitchen waste (organic and inorganic), electronic waste (e-waste), and other solid materials including plastics, metals, and glass (Poddar et al., 2023; Yang et al., 2024; Mallick & Poddar, 2025). Following generation, the waste is directed through a collection and segregation process, wherein it is classified as either biodegradable or non-biodegradable. Biodegradable waste is managed through environmentally sustainable methods such as composting and biogas production (Poddar et al., 2023) whereas, non-biodegradable waste majorly E-waste and plastic, which are harmful for our environment are managed through recycling or safe dismantling procedures. This structured approach facilitates efficient waste handling, resource recovery, and environmental protection (Yang et al., 2024; Mallick & Poddar, 2025). In this chapter, we have briefly discussed the current status of e-waste management.

Figure 1. Flowchart of Solid Waste Management Process

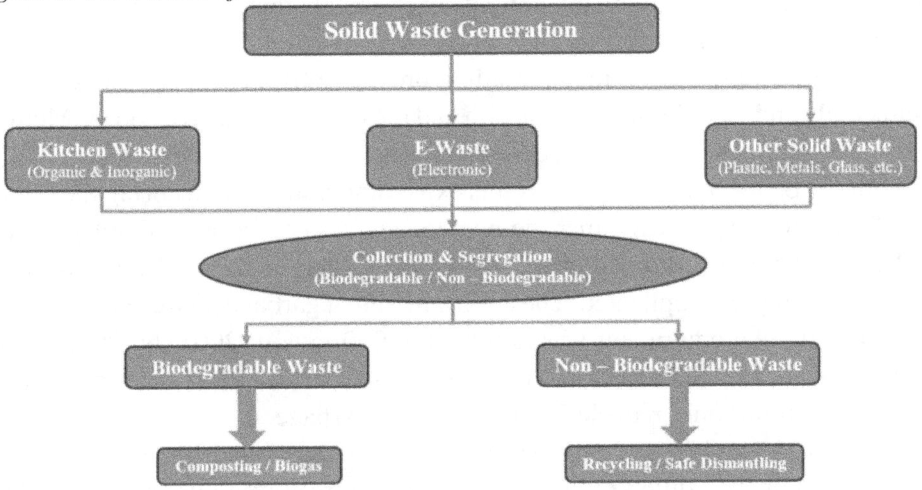

A Brief Overview of Status of e-waste Management and India's Roles in e-waste Management

Electronic trash, sometimes known as "e-waste," is a significant worldwide issue that presents significant risks to human health and the environment. It is divided into six categories, all of which contain dangerous substances. Poor disposal practices can affect human health and contaminate natural resources. Since a sizable portion are imported or exported as used goods, informal management makes monitoring more difficult (Madkhali et al., 2023).

It is crucial to take a safe, economical, and ecologically responsible strategy that incorporates appropriate recycling, metal recovery, transportation, and disposal techniques. In Saudi Arabia, a study of the literature examined the economic, environmental, and social implications of e-waste's categorization, management, recycling, and forecasting. In 2021, approximately 54 million metric tons of e-waste were generated worldwide; estimates indicate that this amount will continue to rise (Madkhali et al., 2023). In order to maximize the financial benefits of recycling programs and protect the environment and public health, it is imperative that e-waste management challenges be resolved (Madkhali et al., 2023).

An international environmental and public health concern, electronic garbage (e-waste) is becoming a bigger problem in India. Devices that are wasted, redundant, outdated, or damaged are referred to as e-waste, or Waste Electrical and Electronic Equipment (WEEE). Many Indian homes hang onto outdated electronics because they are unsure of how to properly dispose of them. According to Kishore and Monika (2010), the trash is complex and contains rich metals that may be recovered and utilized again in manufacturing, such as copper, silver, and gold.

Although e-waste recycling and trading provide jobs, improper processing and disassembly endanger both human health and the environment (Kishore & Monika, 2010). The public health dangers connected with e-waste are being evaluated, and methods are being created to address this expanding issue, underscoring the critical need for appropriate e-waste management techniques (Kishore & Monika, 2010).

The growth of electronic garbage, or "e-waste," has made solid waste management in India more complicated. The entire amount of garbage produced by obsolete or malfunctioning equipment was around 146,000 tons in 2005; by 2012, it was expected to surpass 800,000 tons (Kishore & Monika, 2010). However, approved recycling facilities only recycle 3 percent of this garbage.

Between 50% and 80% of the e-waste collected in the United States is transported to India, making it a dumping ground for e-waste from wealthy nations (Kishore & Monika, 2010). India, one of the nations with the quickest rates of economic growth, has witnessed a notable surge in domestic demand for consumer products, as evidenced by the ~ 53.1% rise in worldwide sales of household appliances between 1998 and 2002. Furthermore, 10% of e-waste is produced in India each year, which is predicted to have a detrimental effect on environmental health (Kishore & Monika, 2010).

The way people live has changed dramatically as a result of the development of information and communication technology (ICT). According to the United Nations' Global E-trash Monitor, there were 53 million tons of electronic waste in 2019. This amount is predicted to rise to 74 million tons by 2030 and 120 million tons by 2050 (Farida et al., 2023). Approximately 17 percent of this electronic waste consists of valuable and hazardous elements that may be properly gathered, processed, and reused. Approximately 56% of Indonesia's anticipated 2 million tons of electronic waste in 2021 came from Java Island (Farida et al., 2023). The government has allocated twenty to fifty percent of its budget to waste management.

In 2020, Indonesia produced approximately 1,600 kilotons of electronic garbage, making it the biggest generator in Southeast Asia. Because it contains heavy elements such mercury, lead, chromium, cadmium, arsenic, silver, cobalt, palladium, and copper, electronic trash is categorized as B3 waste (toxic hazardous materials) (Farida et al., 2023). The Nexus3 Foundation's Toxics Program Officer stressed that in order to protect the environment, electronic waste had to be managed differently from conventional garbage. While burying electronic garbage can contaminate soil and water, burning it can damage the environment.

Electronic waste management in Indonesia entails gathering, classifying, fixing, and recycling. By selecting durable devices, buying items with manufacturer warranties, choosing eco-friendly solutions, and encouraging repair over replacement, households may limit the amount of electronic trash they produce. According to Farida et al. (2023), household electronic trash is divided into three categories: big devices, small devices, and accessories. Household trash disposal behaviours are influenced by a number of factors, including education, employment, income, and environment. In order to educate the public about electronic waste management in Indonesia, this study attempts to determine how families in developing nations handle electronic garbage (Farida et al., 2023).

Excess e-waste is frequently sent to underdeveloped countries by countries with inadequate recycling facilities, where workers may be put in danger by unofficial recycling methods. In a regulated area of the green and circular economy, improving e-waste management in EU nations might lead to income and employment creation (Constantinescu et al., 2022). In order to enhance e-waste management, this study intends to investigate the causal links between e-waste statistical indicators and other circular economy indicators at the global level (Constantinescu et al., 2022).

Approximately 17% of electronic garbage, or "e-waste," is properly handled, making it a major worldwide problem. According to the 2019 Global E-waste Monitor, e-waste creation has increased, with Europe exhibiting the highest efficiency at ~ 42%. Approximately 1.7 million tons of e-waste are disposed of by India, the country with the fifth-largest e-waste production (Sharma et al., 2024). The issues that nations confront worldwide, such as dangerous byproducts and behavioural variables throughout the buying and usage stages, are the main focus of research on e-waste management. Supply chain management and handling may be enhanced by using e-waste management techniques and software. For real-time tracking and monitoring of the e-waste management process, blockchain technology is suggested (Sharma et al., 2024).

The production of e-waste is increased by frequent gadget updates and rapid technical breakthroughs, yet consumer behaviour is not directly regulated. Safe disposal may be enhanced by social norms and open communication. Using the circular economy to address e-waste issues might reduce health hazards and generate long-term employment. The purpose of this research is to showcase the contributions made by different writers to the management of e-waste, with a focus on new developments in India (Sharma et al., 2024).

Electronic rubbish, or "e-waste" covers gadgets that are getting close to the end of their useful life or abandoned objects. The rapid expansion and technological advancements in the electronics sector have led to a large increase in the generation of e-waste, which peaked in 2019 at ~ 54 million metric tons (Mt) (Nandan et al., 2023). Abuse and improper disposal of e-waste cause environmental harm in addition to serious health risks like cancer, arthritis, and birth issues. E-waste comes from a variety of sources, including residences, businesses, and consumers. In the EU, residential appliances account for ~ 53% of all e-waste, whereas businesses and industries worldwide generated 56.3 Mt in 2019 (Nandan et al., 2023).

Significant ecological deterioration as well as health hazards including cancer, infertility, and developmental problems can result from this pollution. By 2025, India, one of the economies with the quickest rate of growth, is predicted to overtake all other countries as the greatest producer of e-waste. India produced more than 3 Mt of e-waste in 2019, growing at a pace of 21% per year. Just 10% of this garbage is recycled formally; the rest is recycled at landfills, incinerators, or locations that oversee the unofficial recycling process (Nandan et al., 2023).

Government, business, and communities must work together to handle e-waste effectively. While public education and awareness efforts are required to encourage responsible e-waste control, dumping may be reduced by establishing thorough legislation and promoting recycling and reconstruction. With more than 25 Mt of e-waste produced by 2022, Asia leads the world in e-waste production, followed by China, the US, and India (Nandan et al., 2023).

Due to variables including market diffusion, replacement markets, and high obsolescence rates, e-waste which includes undesired or unsuitable materials—is growing at a pace of 20–25% annually. Legal hazards, operating expenses, and transportation and disposal costs may all be decreased using efficient waste management techniques (Mor et al., 2021). The bulk of India's e-waste is composed of residential e-scrap, medical equipment, electrical devices, telecom equipment, and computer accessories. While precious elements like lanthanum, neodymium, silver, palladium, and platinum are recovered from e-waste, electronic gadgets need over 320 tons of gold and 7,500 tons of silver annually (Mor et al., 2021).

According to estimates, mining e-waste in metropolitan areas, particularly for precious metals like gold and silver, may generate approximately $21 billion yearly. Only 15% of these valuable components are being recovered, however. E-waste contains hazardous compounds that pose a major risk to human health, including lead, mercury, cadmium, and hexavalent chromium (Mor et al., 2021). Improper urban mining of e-waste affects a wide range of communities by causing air pollution, soil and water contamination, and major health hazards. As a result, it is critical to gauge public concern for environmental preservation and e-waste management (Mor et al., 2021).

India is one of the top five countries in the world for producing "e-waste," or electronic trash. The unorganized sector handles almost 90% of waste, including valuable materials like plastics, rare earth metals, and precious metals. Uncontrolled processing methods pose major risks to human health and the environment. To solve these problems, strategies have been implemented in both developed and developing countries. A common strategy for reducing e-waste is Extended Producer Responsibility (EPR), which puts manufacturers in responsible of how their goods are handled at the end of their useful lives. EPR may be implemented in four ways: Economic Responsibility, Physical Responsibility, Information Responsibility, and Liability Rules. The EPR concept was incorporated into India's initial e-waste regulations, the E-waste (Management and Handling) Rules of 2011, however early evaluations revealed its lack of effectiveness. In two regulatory modifications, the government established take-back goals for producers (Turaga et al., 2019). Over the past eight years, there have been significant changes in India's e-waste sector, including an increase in the formal waste management sector, a rise in producer responsibility organizations (PROs), improved domestic e-waste processing technologies, and heightened producer efforts. The primary focus of several publications is integrating the unorganized sector into a formal e-waste management system that safeguards and enhances livelihoods while lowering external costs (Turaga et al., 2019).

Electronic rubbish (e-waste) has sharply increased as a result of technological advancements and product obsolescence. E-waste includes things like home appliances, small kitchen appliances, IT equipment, and consumer electronics. Even though it may include valuable minerals like copper and gold, improperly handled e-waste poses serious environmental risks since it contains dangerous substances like lead, mercury, and cadmium (Fawole et al., 2023).

Approximately six million metric tons of e-waste were created, a 21% increase over the previous five years. Only a small percentage of e-waste is properly recycled; the bulk is burnt or thrown away, harming the environment and making climate change worse. According to statistics, only 20% of e-waste is successfully recycled, which results in the loss of vital minerals and further environmental damage (Fawole et al., 2023). This article is to investigate the environmental impacts of e-waste, particularly with regard to greenhouse gas emissions and the release of hazardous substances, in addition to evaluating current treatment strategies. Promoting longer discussions on e-waste and its increasing significance in the battle against climate change is the aim (Fawole et al., 2023).

According to (Voskergian and Ishaq, 2023), a smart city is an advanced urban setting where information and communication technologies (ICT) are seamlessly integrated to increase environmental sustainability and people' quality of life. In order to create more intelligent and sustainable cities, applications like waste management, smart grids, traffic control, and remote patient monitoring are essential. Many electrical equipment swiftly approaches the end of their life cycle due to increased customer demand and fast technical improvements. In order to effectively manage e-waste and lessen its negative impacts, intelligent solutions are desperately needed. Technological innovations, especially Deep Learning (DL) and the Internet of Things (IoT), present potential ways to improve systems and infrastructure, particularly in the management of e-waste (Voskergian and Ishaq, 2023). The suggested system better manages e-waste by utilizing IoT and DL-based item recognition, which is in line with sustainability objectives and green city programs. This cutting-edge method might greatly improve e-waste management, improving public health and environmental sustainability (Voskergian and Ishaq, 2023).

Rapid growth in ICT use and the shortening lifespan of digital devices have contributed to the problem of ICT-related e-waste in developing countries. Due to faster ICT adoption, a lack of formal recycling facilities, greater dangers from inappropriate handling, and lax or non-existent legislation, developing countries face higher rates of e-waste generation than developed ones (Heeks et al., 2014). These difficulties lead to a more pressing sustainability problem in the global south, which is made worse by a significant lack of understanding about managing e-waste. Few studies have been conducted on e-waste in poor nations, and those that have been conducted have frequently concentrated on the global trade of e-waste rather than regional management strategies. Local e-waste management has become a topic that requires more attention due to the sharp rise in ICT usage in these areas (Heeks et al., 2014). While previous research has mostly focused on the responsibilities of producers, recyclers, and legislators, this study focuses on ICT consumers in particular—organizational ICT users who are in charge of producing the bulk of e-waste (Heeks et al., 2014). The absence of data on bulk ICT consumers, who are the biggest producers of e-waste, the lack of knowledge about e-waste in developing nations, and the lack of knowledge about locally created e-waste are the three major knowledge gaps that this study seeks to fill. The study intends to improve e-waste management procedures, especially recycling rates, and assist in the formulation of policy by examining these issues (Heeks et al., 2014). The emphasis is on India, where it is believed that almost 30% of the country's e-waste comes from the ICT services industry. An explanation of the research approach follows a survey of the literature to create conceptual models of e-waste management methods and their causes (Heeks et al., 2014).

Problems with e-waste management include growing quantities, inadequate infrastructure, illicit trade, and a lack of knowledge about the negative effects on the environment and human health. Although informal recycling persists because it saves money, it is bad for the environment and human health. The antiquated methods of burning, dumping, and landfilling release pollutants and waste materials. Effective solutions must cooperate with stakeholders, optimize recovery procedures, and adhere to criteria in order to ensure sustainability (Bhat et al., 2021).

Due to contaminants like heavy metals, electronics with shorter lifespans including TVs and laptops produce 40 million tons of e-waste annually, endangering human health and the environment. Resource shortages can be lessened and precious materials recovered with the use of recycling. High disposal costs in wealthy nations push recycling to nations like China and India, where dangerous, unofficial methods are more common (Zhang et al., 2012).

The issue is made worse by lax implementation of agreements such as the Basel Convention. China is the world's largest recycler of e-waste, and their approach offers important insights for the sustainability of e-waste treatment worldwide. More than 70% of the world's e-waste is handled in China, with the provinces of Guangdong and Zhejiang acting as important recycling centres because of their close proximity to import routes and electronics industries. China is expected to become the world's second-largest producer of e-waste by 2020 due to its rapid growth in this area (Zhang et al., 2012).

E-waste, which includes computers, phones, and medical devices, has increased as a result of ICT expansion, posing serious risks to human health and the environment. Asia was the largest contributor to the world's 53.6 million tons of e-waste in 2019. However, because of complicated and dangerous procedures, only 17% of it is recycled correctly. E-waste management is a global problem since improper recycling releases harmful substances (Shahabuddin et al., 2022). Despite the financial benefits, advancement is hampered by outdated technology and infrastructure. To enhance regulations and management procedures, further in-depth research on e-waste recycling technologies and methods is needed (Shahabuddin et al., 2022).

Electronic rubbish (e-waste), which includes all abandoned electrical and electronic gadgets, has increased as a result of consumer purchasing power and technological advancements. In addition to device failure or end-of-life, customer behaviour and obsolescence can also result in e-waste (Halim et al., 2019). Only 15% of the e-waste is recycled, despite its yearly growth of 3-4%, raising worries about its hazardous components and their effects on the environment and human health (Halim et al., 2019). Research on e-waste has advanced significantly since 2002, including topics such as management, material recovery, and potential health effects. In order to highlight future challenges and research opportunities, this paper analyzes e-waste research conducted between 2004 and 2020 (Halim et al., 2019).

In the UAE, urbanization and the use of technology have made industrial effects like e-waste and global warming more significant issues. Both valuable and hazardous metals can be found in e-waste. The UAE's capacity to handle e-waste (EWM) is being hindered by infrastructural shortcomings and stakeholder disputes. The value of stakeholder cooperation in enhancing management and recycling (Alblooshi et al., 2022). It is anticipated that the global electronics recycling market would reach $65.8 billion by 2026, growing at a compound annual growth rate of 12.7%. At a 13.3% CAGR, the metals segment is expected to reach around $54 billion. According to estimates, the electronics recycling industry was valued at $7.5 billion in 2021. China is expected to reach $15.3 billion by 2026 at an annual growth rate of 16.3% (Seif et al., 2023). Canada and Japan are also expected to increase. Germany is expected to expand at a 12.5% CAGR, while other European markets are expected to reach $6.1 billion. The consumer electronics industry is expected to develop at a compound annual growth rate of 12% (Seif et al., 2023). Electronic trash, which accounts for 5% of global solid waste, is a growing concern. In the EU, phones, TVs, and computers produce around 9 million tons of e-waste a year. Just 17.4% of the 53.6 million tons of e-waste produced globally in 2019 was successfully recycled (Seif et al., 2023). The ten categories into which e-waste may be separated include information technology, consumer electronics, home appliances, lighting fixtures, toys, sporting goods, non-infected medical equipment, control and monitoring units, and automated dispensers. The composition of e-waste is influenced by the item's age, manufacturer, model, kind, and year of creation. Rapid technological advancements make it more challenging to develop effective e-waste management methods (Seif et al., 2023).

As part of the recycling process for e-waste, precious metals such as copper, aluminium, gold, lead, mercury, cadmium, palladium, platinum, and others are gathered, pre-treated, and recovered. According to Seif et al. (2023), only 15% to 20% of Egypt's electronic waste is recycled domestically. To address this issue, national policies and legislation, the development of an e-waste database, and more technological recycling capabilities are all required (Seif et al., 2023). Refining, upgrading, and dismantling are crucial stages in the recycling of electronic trash. Pyrometallurgical and hydrometallurgical processes are used to remove impurities since mechanical recycling methods usually fall short of recovering precious metals. Precious metals like gold and silver are commonly extracted from mobile phones via hydrometallurgical processing, which uses a range of chemicals, including cyanide (Seif et al., 2023). Copper is recovered from printed circuit boards (PCBs) via pyrometallurgy, hydrometallurgy, and mechanical techniques; hydrometallurgical processes are particularly favoured because of their high selectivity and lower costs (Seif et al., 2023). Recent studies have focused on innovative methods for recovering copper resources to raise the value of discarded PCBs. The recycling of lithium-ion batteries (LIBs), which include valuable metals like cobalt, nickel, and lithium, is expected to increase significantly as a result of the rising demand for electric vehicles (Seif et al., 2023).

At the worldwide volume expected to reach 74.4 million metric tons by 2030, managing electronic garbage, or "e-waste," is a major concern (Seif et al., 2023). Methane, which is produced by conventional disposal techniques like landfilling, has 21 times the global warming potential of carbon dioxide over a century. Conventional disposal techniques including landfilling, incineration, and trash exporting are no longer practical choices because of stringent environmental restrictions (Seif et al., 2023). The environmental risks connected to the hazardous elements included in electronic trash are also lessened by this sustainable recycling strategy. Since burning hydrogen produces only water vapor and is therefore a clean substitute for fossil fuels, it is a promising use of metals recovered from e-waste. However, only a small portion of hydrogen produced today comes from renewable sources, with the majority originating from fossil fuels. Water electrolysis and green energy storage technologies, such as copper recovered from used electrical cables and materials recovered from used lithium-ion batteries and electronic components, are examples of green methods for producing hydrogen. Recycling e-waste not only lowers expenses but also promotes sustainability by supplying useful materials for energy storage and conversion technologies. (Seif et al., 2023).

Research looks at the literature on managing e-waste using bibliometric analysis. The researchers analysed 441 publications from the Scopus database published between 2012 and 2021 using the Bibliometric R-package and VOS viewer (Soesanto et al., 2023). Knowledge structures, sources, keywords, and author information were all included in the data. The results were presented using descriptive statistics (Soesanto et al., 2023). The researchers also looked at article dissemination and the evolution of e-waste management studies throughout time. evaluates the quantity of publications, citations, and original sources, among other aspects of publishing performance. To determine the variables impacting the implementation of e-waste management, the top ten publications were analysed. Analysis offered a thorough grasp of the subject's present situation by offering a complete picture of trends and changes in the area (Soesanto et al., 2023). The amount of e-waste produced worldwide rose by 20% between 2014 and 2021, reaching 53.6 million metric tons. The United States was the largest producer of e-waste, with 13.1 million tons created year, or 13.3 kg per person. However, according to Madkhali et al. (2023), only 1.2 million tons of this e-waste are properly managed by formal collection and recycling methods. Europe is known for its effective e-waste management, with 42.3% of its total e-waste being treated lawfully. Asia generated the highest e-waste, with 24 million tons produced, while only 2.9 million tons were recycled (Madkhali et al., 2023).

Europe also leads the globe in this area, with each individual producing an average of 16.2 kg of e-waste. Over the past nine years, the quantity of e-waste created globally has surged by 58%. E-waste production may increase by 121% between 2020 and 2030 due to the correlation between GDP growth and e-waste generation (Madkhali et al., 2023). India created the least amount of e-waste in Asia in 2019 roughly 2 kg per person while most other countries produced 20 to 25 kg per person. An ecosystem strategy that considers social, economic, and environmental factors is necessary to manage e-waste efficiently and sustainably. Implementing models for accurate e-waste projections can improve preparation and management strategies (Madkhali et al., 2023). Since the informal sector is labour-intensive and unregulated, the supply chain plays a crucial role in managing electronic waste. In Saudi Arabia, a significant amount of e-waste is generated and handled by the unorganized sector. Ineffective processes including acid leaching, disassembly, and improper landfill disposal hinder the treatment of sustainable e-waste. Despite its potential, Extended Producer Responsibility (EPR) is not being used effectively (Madkhali et al., 2023). The Analytical Hierarchy Process (AHP) and Quality Function Deployment (QFD) may improve e-waste management. Research indicates that for every $1,000 increase in GDP, 0.5 kg more e-waste is produced (Madkhali et al., 2023).

According to Madkhali et al. (2023), e-waste management techniques such as Value-Belief-Norm Theory (VBNT), Life Cycle Assessment (LCA), Material Flow Analysis (MFA), Multi-Criteria Analysis (MCA), Extended Producer Responsibility (EPR), and others aim to recover valuable metals through proper collection and sorting, minimize environmental impact, and ensure safe recycling. LCA has gained international recognition for its beneficial impacts on the economy and ecology, particularly in regions such as Europe, Asia, Northeast Africa, and Switzerland (Madkhali et al., 2023). Countries including India, China, Indonesia, Australia, Japan, and Nigeria have embraced MFA to map E-waste flows and track collection and recycling initiatives because it offers insights on the movement of E-waste during collection, recycling, and disposal (Madkhali et al., 2023). Decision assistance systems have been implemented in the United States, Spain, and Cyprus, and Multi-Criteria Analysis (MCA) is advised for integrating social elements into e-waste management. EPR is a nationwide strategy that makes producers responsible for returning goods at the end of their useful lives. Smart cars, robotics, artificial intelligence (AI) tools, sensors, and real-time monitoring are examples of digital technologies that are becoming useful for managing e-waste (Madkhali et al., 2023).

Physical processes including pyrometallurgy, hydrometallurgy, biohydrometallurgy, and pyrolysis are effective pre-treatment techniques for recycling electronic waste (E-waste). Non-chemical methods may now be used to prepare e-waste for recycling or treatment (Madkhali et al., 2023). Pyrometallurgical methods employ eddy currents, air currents, magnetic separation, and vacuum metallurgical separation.

Hydrometallurgy use chemical techniques to recover metals, whereas biohydrometallurgy uses microorganisms (Madkhali et al., 2023). A new technique called pyrolysis involves thermally breaking or transforming e-waste. This innovative technique is crucial for improving recycling practices and promoting environmental sustainability (Madkhali et al., 2023). The recovery process typically starts with mechanical separation and moves on to pyrometallurgical treatment in order to eliminate nonferrous metals and extract valuable metallic components. Before being released into the environment, acidic wastewater is neutralized and processed, and electrometallurgical procedures are used to treat metallic items (Madkhali et al., 2023). We are used to efficiently and sustainably handling electronic trash. These models use data from the past and present to forecast trash volume and metal recovery. Studies on e-waste quantities, end-of-life, and material flow analysis have been carried out in Vietnam, South Korea, Australia, the United States, and the United Kingdom using a variety of techniques. Grey modelling has been used to forecast the production of e-waste in Botswana and to measure the amount of e-waste from gadgets like PCs, cell phones, and televisions in India (Madkhali et al., 2023). Although their accuracy may vary based on the characteristics of the data, these models are well known for their accuracy, especially when properly adjusted. Other studies have used distribution delay models, regression analysis, and material flow analysis to estimate the volumes of e-waste in various firms. Grey forecasting models, particularly the univariate grey forecasting model GM (1.1) and its improved variations, are known for their accuracy when properly adjusted (Madkhali et al., 2023).

E-waste management, which includes procedures for collection, segregation, and recycling, is essential for environmental preservation and sustainable development. Research and technological developments have shown certain recycling and recovery strategies that may be paired with analytical and forecasting methodologies (Madkhali et al., 2023). Systematic research, a holistic methodology, government efforts, private and social media participation, real-time monitoring, data management, public awareness, and a well-optimized supply chain are all necessary to improve e-waste collection, segregation, and recycling. Consumer responsibility, economic viability, security, and recycling system feasibility should all be part of the waste management regulation framework (Madkhali et al., 2023). To improve garbage disposal efficiency and health advantages in poor nations, an integrated strategy including artificial intelligence for collection logistics and route optimization is suggested (Madkhali et al., 2023). Due to foreign investments, the Asia Pacific area is rapidly industrializing, which is increasing the amount of electronic garbage, or "e-waste" (Andeobu et al., 2021). Because inappropriate disposal can release hazardous compounds and cause the loss of important metals, this presents a serious threat to the environment and nearby populations (Andeobu et al., 2021). With nearly 50 million tons of e-waste created worldwide in 2019, including 24.9

million tons in the Asia Pacific area alone, the yearly production of e-waste is concerning (Andeobu et al., 2021).

Recycling efforts are not keeping up with the estimated 74 million tons of e-waste that will be generated worldwide by 2030. Ineffective collection and recycling methods and a lack of producer accountability for product disposal are major problems with the way e-waste is currently managed (Andeobu et al., 2021). Three primary research needs are identified by this study: Despite decades of research into e-waste generation and management, 1) few studies have specifically looked at the impact of e-waste generated in specific Asia Pacific countries and its effects on human health and the environment; 2) many countries are not managing their e-waste effectively, indicating a need for smarter and more sustainable production, consumption, and disposal practices; and 3) challenges still exist (Andeobu et al., 2021). More than 95% of India's e-waste is handled in urban slums, making the country mostly dependent on the unorganized sector for recycling. Untrained personnel frequently do dangerous disassembly tasks without personal protective equipment, putting both the environment and their health at risk (Kishore & Monika, 2010). It takes a lot of money to set up official recycling facilities, and many individuals are paid very little for their labour, frequently endangering their health in the process (Kishore & Monika, 2010).

The e-waste issue is still getting worse in spite of national trade restrictions and some media attention. To estimate the effects of inadequate e-waste management in underdeveloped nations, health risk evaluations are required (Kishore & Monika, 2010). To encourage customers to properly dispose of their e-waste, some electronic businesses, such as Apple, Dell, and HP, have launched recycling programs (Kishore & Monika, 2010). Ragpickers are also being included in trash management initiatives by the Delhi government, which is offering them resources and training to enhance their working circumstances (Kishore & Monika, 2010). Additional environmental epidemiology studies are required to evaluate the present status of e-waste management in India, including the amounts of e-waste created and the effects of the informal recycling industry (Kishore & Monika, 2010). Such studies will yield useful information to support the development of an e-waste management action plan. India ought to set up a monitoring system to keep an eye on health problems brought on by exposure to e-waste. Sustainable e-waste management requires better collection and recycling methods, and public-private partnerships may make it easier to set up drop-off or buy-back locations. Sustainability initiatives may also benefit from the use of advance recycling fees (Kishore & Monika, 2010). Future expansion will depend on locating and implementing the top e-waste management solutions available worldwide (Kishore & Monika, 2010).

Government regulations pertaining to the treatment of electronic trash are still loose in nations like Singapore, Malaysia, and Indonesia. The negative effects of inadequate electronic waste management on society and the environment require better approaches. To avert more environmental damage, recommendations include tightening laws controlling electronic trash. With data gathered from surveys in the United Arab Emirates showing the problem of home electronic trash, other research has observed that the rise in mobile phone usage is an important signal of technological improvement (Kishore & Monika, 2010). The way that communities handle electronic trash varies greatly between those with effective public waste management systems and those with low recycling rates (Kishore & Monika, 2010). In places like Dubai, the legal frameworks established serve as models for sustainable waste management practices. The impact of handling electronic waste on human health and the environment, particularly in China, has been the subject of several studies. The increase in electrical and electronic waste is partly a result of population growth (Kishore & Monika, 2010).

The management of e-waste in Europe and beyond is examined by Farida et al. (2023), with an emphasis on important elements and incentives for sustainable development. Effective waste electrical and electronic equipment (WEEE) management procedures, Serbian legal and logistical deficiencies, and changes to electronic device costs brought about by European regulations are important considerations. Additionally, the study emphasizes the difficulties in recycling rare metals and the significance of raising recycling rates for the growth of the business (Farida et al., 2023). Economic performance in the EU's WEEE recycling sector is positively impacted by regulation and competition. 23 important facilitators for sustainable WEEE management have been identified by recent studies, with a focus on environmental rules, digitalization, and research and development. The usage of digital technology has increased in developing nations due to the knowledge economy, creating problems for the management of e-waste. Poor communities now depend on used electrical and electronic equipment (EEE) because computer lifespans have shortened (Maphosa & Maphosa, 2020). Developed nations have put rules in place to efficiently handle e-waste, such the Extended Producer Responsibility (EPR) legislation. Nonetheless, it is anticipated that the world would produce more than 53 million metric tons of e-waste by 2021, of which 25.4 million will come from emerging nations (Maphosa & Maphosa, 2020). The environment and public health are at serious risk due to the increasing amount of e-waste. More than 700 million outdated computers will be disposed away by emerging nations by 2030.

However, research on managing e-waste in Africa is lacking (Maphosa & Maphosa, 2020). Because of improper handling, wealthy nations have put rules in place to manage it. Pregnant women, children, locals, and informal e-waste workers are among the vulnerable groups that are impacted by the crude processing of e-waste in many poor countries. Illegal exports to the Global South account for over 80% of the e-waste produced in the Global North. More nations must enact laws to stop environmental deterioration and detrimental effects on human health (Maphosa & Maphosa, 2020). Based on the data gathered, the study produced visual maps using VOS Viewer and Atlas Ti software. Using a network visualization approach, things were represented by labels, and their weight was shown by circles. By analysing factors including authorship, co-authorship, and citations, Atlas Ti produced idea maps of keywords discovered in several publications (Sharma et al., 2024). After conducting a qualitative review of the literature, the research chose 211 pertinent e-waste management papers. According to their labels and related circles, the network visualization approach was utilized to show the connections and significance of the objects (Sharma et al., 2024).

According to the literature, e-waste is being dealt with creative solutions that turn it from a problem into an opportunity. E-waste is acknowledged as a major worldwide crisis. Researchers are looking at ways to recover metals efficiently, find important rare earth elements, and see if e-waste can be used as a source of energy (Nandan et al., 2023). Innovative projects that rethink the lifetime of these materials include e-waste art. Reducing waste and prolonging product lifespans need the adoption of a circular economy strategy that prioritizes recycling, refurbishing, and repairing electronics (Nandan et al., 2023). The supply of protective gear and appropriate training can improve worker safety. To stop the illicit movement of dangerous e-waste to underdeveloped countries, international collaboration is essential (Nandan et al., 2023). By taking these steps, the hazards that e-waste poses to the environment, human health, and safety may be reduced, opening the door to a more sustainable and healthful future. The growing production of electronic garbage is a major problem for India's e-waste management (Nandan et al., 2023). The nation generated 3.2 million metric tons of e-waste in 2019, and estimates indicate that by 2025, that amount would rise to 5.2 million metric tons. India's infrastructure is still insufficient to manage this expanding waste stream, even after the E-Waste (Management) Rules were introduced in 2016 (Nandan et al., 2023).

The informal sector handles a sizable amount of e-waste and uses antiquated and dangerous disposal techniques, which present major threats to human health and the environment. The growing demand cannot be satisfied by the few permitted recycling plants because of a lack of government incentives, poor infrastructure, and insufficient investments. The government, commercial businesses, and non-governmental organizations have taken a number of steps to improve the e-waste management situation in order to solve these issues (Nandan et al., 2023). In order to encourage appropriate disposal, organizations such as Toxics Link have created collection centres and increased awareness. To improve recycling efforts, public-private partnerships (PPPs) have installed e-waste collecting systems (Nandan et al.,

2023). E-waste collection services have been made more efficient by technological advancements such mobile applications like "Eco E-Waste," and other programs seek to incorporate the unorganized sector by offering required equipment and training. Nonetheless, the system as a whole continues to suffer from a lack of infrastructure and regulation required for ecologically responsible behaviours (Nandan et al., 2023). Globally, poor nations are disproportionately impacted by the e-waste problem since they frequently act as disposal sites for e-waste from wealthier countries. There are several advantages to managing e-waste effectively, such as lowering pollution, conserving resources, and advancing sustainability. By 2025, the e-waste management industry in India is projected to generate over 120,000 employment and reach a value of Rs 30 billion (Nandan et al., 2023).

According to medical research, exposure to chemicals found in e-waste has been connected to cancer, neurological disorders, respiratory ailments, skin concerns, and developmental issues. Exposure to these toxic compounds increases the health concerns for communities around informal recycling centres. A number of Sustainable Development Goals (SDGs), including responsible consumption and production, health and well-being, and climate action, are in line with efficient e-waste management (Nandan et al., 2023). Effective management efforts are hampered by the absence of trustworthy statistics on the creation of e-waste. Tracking e-waste is made more difficult by illegal imports. Despite giving many people a living, the informal sector engages in ecologically unsustainable behaviours (Turaga et al., 2019). Consumer preferences and a lack of knowledge about recycling technology make it difficult for the formal sector to get enough e-waste for recycling. E-waste management practices have not been considerably enhanced by the legislative framework's mandated take-back mechanism for producers (Turaga et al., 2019).

By establishing collection objectives, the 2016 amendments sought to solve this issue; nonetheless, underfunded agencies find it difficult to handle the regulatory load. Enforcement operations are hampered by problems including regulatory capture and a lack of openness. To create more effective markets for the management of e-waste, public policy might need to take a more active role (Turaga et al., 2019). All things considered, there are still several barriers preventing India's e-waste management system from making significant progress. The government must acknowledge the informal sector as a critical stakeholder and regularly review and modify rules in order to develop a robust e-waste management system (Turaga et al., 2019). Developing cooperative solutions requires interacting with employees, NGOs, PROs, and recyclers. Platforms for national and state-level stakeholder meetings can promote collaboration and confidence (Turaga et al., 2019). Economic tools like an advanced recycling charge (ARF) or advanced disposal fee (ADF) are more successful, hence policy instruments under the Extended Producer Responsibility (EPR) approach need to be reevaluated. Customers, recyclers, and workers in the unorganized sector can all benefit from these payments (Turaga et al., 2019). Agencies' regulatory burden would be lessened by switching to economic tools like the ADF (Turaga et al., 2019).

To increase public knowledge of the effects of e-waste and proper disposal techniques, stronger laws governing awareness efforts are also required. To solve the problem of inadequate recycling infrastructure, India could have to outlaw the importation of all e-waste for recycling and reuse. Research on effective messaging should be done, and public awareness efforts should be included with other waste management activities (Turaga et al., 2019). An important first step in addressing the e-waste situation was India's 2011 e-waste management regulations, which were founded on the Extended Producer Responsibility (EPR) concept. But putting these rules into effect has been difficult (Turaga et al., 2019). Despite being essential to waste processing, the informal sector acts outside of the legal framework, making it more difficult for the formal sector to comply with its EPR duties. In addition to posing a threat to the environment and public health, the unregulated activities of the informal sector also make it more difficult for the formal sector to get e-waste for processing (Turaga et al., 2019). The operations of the informal sector continue to be unlawful and unrecognized despite its crucial significance, which makes regulatory measures more difficult (Turaga et al., 2019).

In India, 90-95% of e-waste is managed by the unorganized sector, while there are issues with its operational inefficiencies and environmental effect. Due to a lack of collaboration with the informal sector, the formal sector finds it difficult to reach collection objectives, which encourages corruption and unlawful activity. Transparency and resource recovery can be improved by incorporating informal into the formal system (Turaga et al., 2019). The government must acknowledge and assist efforts to legalize informal systems in order to close the funding gap between them and official ones with improved cooperation between collection networks, PROs, and recyclers, forming informal-formal partnerships can result in a more effective e-waste management system. To increase overall efficiency, it is essential to assist informal recyclers in switching to safer processing techniques (Turaga et al., 2019). Collaboration, formalizing recycling methods, and supporting facility upgrades are all part of the vision for informal-form partnerships. A more open and sustainable e-waste management system in India may result from these collaborations (Turaga et al., 2019).

E-waste recycling may be enhanced by utilizing technology to monitor resource movements and foster transparency. Informal workers must be empowered by information and safer procedures. Sustainable e-waste processing requires the establishment of precise standards and monitoring mechanisms (Turaga et al., 2019). Formal and informal sectors must work together to identify stakeholders, create cooperative models, and offer assistance and training. According to Turaga et al. (2019), incorporating informal players into formal systems can improve resource recovery, provide employment, and lessen environmental damage. Government, producers, civic society, and the unorganized sector are just a few of the stakeholders that must put out effort to accomplish this. India can transition to a circular economy with increased recycling rates and sustainable e-waste management by encouraging collaborations (Turaga et al., 2019). This strategy promotes the lives of informal workers in addition to addressing the issues associated with e-waste, paving the way for a more sustainable and equitable future (Turaga et al., 2019). Due to antiquated technology and inappropriate disposal techniques, the electronics industry's explosive expansion has resulted in an increase of electronic garbage, or "e-waste," particularly in nations like India. E-waste is primarily recycled informally in India using hazardous methods, putting both the environment and human health at risk (Turaga et al., 2019). Despite the availability of indigenous technology by MeitY and CSIR, the informal sector processes over 90% of India's two million metric tons of e-waste. This sector lacks the necessary equipment and depends on foreign smelters for additional processing (Turaga et al., 2019).

The creation of skill-training programs is essential to the shift to safer e-waste management techniques. With government assistance, eco-parks that integrate the official and informal sectors may maximize recycling procedures and establish a healthy ecosystem (Turaga et al., 2019). Micro factories have the potential to completely transform the processing of e-waste, reducing expenses and emissions while promoting a circular economy. Sustainability might be further improved by local solutions for recycling dangerous parts like lithium-ion batteries (Turaga et al., 2019).

In order to handle e-waste effectively, the government encourages innovation, facilitates sector integration, offers financial support, and promotes cost-effective recycling solutions (Turaga et al., 2019). Converting unofficial e-waste processors into environmentally friendly micro factories supports government programs like "Make in India" and "Swachh Bharat," which encourage job development and economic expansion. Nonetheless, there are still issues with controlling the unorganized sector and guaranteeing equitable access to important resources (Turaga et al., 2019).

Turaga et al. (2019) discussed the difficulties in creating a safe and effective e-waste disposal system in India. According to Turaga et al. (2019), these difficulties include ineffective recycling techniques, technical developments that impact profitability, low compliance attitudes, consumer compensation expectations, monitoring shortcomings, logistical problems, and selective recycling practices. Implementing comprehensive cost pricing through an Extended Producer Responsibility framework, broadening the product scope to include new e-waste streams, encouraging competitive market dynamics, offering proactive financing for recycling companies, and improving monitoring systems with technology are some recommendations made to address these issues (Turaga et al., 2019). By guaranteeing correct compliance, minimizing material loss, and supporting cutting-edge recycling technology, these actions seek to increase the overall efficacy and sustainability of e-waste management in India. Because of the complex interactions between technical, economic, and regulatory issues affecting the industry, efforts to improve e-waste management in India are essential (Turaga et al., 2019). A number of milestones must be met in order to develop a strong e-waste system. A well-defined financing structure to guarantee financial stability, extensive data systems to enhance decision-making, technology-driven monitoring to enhance control, and well-defined standards to guarantee adherence and reduce inequalities are a few of these. It is possible to create an efficient and sustainable e-waste management system that will solve environmental issues, spur economic expansion, and generate employment possibilities in the recycling industry (Turaga et al., 2019). It is difficult to create an open and efficient e-waste management system in India, particularly when it comes to making sure that old electronics are disposed of and recycled safely (Turaga et al., 2019). Like successful foreign models, India might successfully solve these issues by implementing a mix of voluntary and regulatory norms. Globally, regulations such as the EU's WEEE and RoHS Directives have enhanced waste management and product design (Turaga et al., 2019).

Globally, hazardous waste and emissions have decreased as a result of cooperative initiatives like the IEEE 1680.1 standard. Measures like mass balance reporting and financial frameworks, in addition to tougher rules for dismantlers, recyclers, and PROs, might improve accountability and encourage ecologically friendly business practices in India (Turaga et al., 2019). To guarantee the sustainability of e-waste management in the nation, issues including poor traceability, a lack of official recycling capacity, and the prevalence of informal methods must be addressed (Turaga et al., 2019). By expanding on current programs like as the CII Green Co rating, voluntary standards may promote innovation and capacity building in the industry even more. Strong tracking and reporting procedures might be required by regulatory requirements to solve e-waste management issues (Turaga et al., 2019). By upskilling employees and encouraging safer recycling methods, voluntary norms may encourage cooperation between the formal and informal sectors (Turaga et al., 2019). Creating demand for official recycling services requires raising awareness and encouraging circularity. Through resource efficiency measures like leasing programs and product take-back plans, India should improve circularity in its electronics industry (Turaga et al., 2019). In order to promote sustainable e-waste disposal, bulk buyers and procurement regulations are essential. Stakeholder collaboration is crucial, with voluntary standards encouraging innovation and regulated standards addressing pressing issues. A sustainable e-waste management system may be established in India by coordinating voluntary and regulatory measures (Turaga et al., 2019). India can enhance its e-waste procedures and transition to a circular economy in the electronics industry by utilizing both kinds of standards (Turaga et al., 2019).

To foster accountability and transparency, PROs oversee the collection and channelization of e-waste. However, there are obstacles in the way of PROs managing e-waste effectively. Long-term commitment from producers to help PROs build recycling ecosystems is lacking. Criteria for selection Prioritize cost effectiveness over systemic changes, promoting inferior methods such as selective recycling. Uncertain frameworks for choosing PROs based on quality and accountability lead to inconsistent performance (Turaga et al., 2019). There is a lack of consumer knowledge and involvement; large customers are unwilling to interact with professionals and are not aware of their legal responsibilities. PROs are not integrated into platforms such as Metal Scrap Trading Corporation, and domestic customer engagement requires financial incentives. The integrity of the e-waste industry is compromised by malpractices such illicit trades and double accounting of e-waste (Turaga et al., 2019). The informal sector leaks important components as a result of e-waste management malpractices that are sustained by a lack of verification methods for producer sales data and inadequate regulatory control. This damages the credibility of the official system and calls into question the efficacy of authorized recyclers (Turaga et al., 2019).

In order to overcome these obstacles, it is advised that regulatory frameworks be strengthened, bulk users be required to utilize PROs, pricing and classification be standardized, the EPR process be digitized, and international standards like Weetabix and R2 be adopted. Enforcing rules, encouraging cooperation, and obtaining sustained commitment from manufacturers and regulators are all necessary for the successful management of e-waste in India (Turaga et al., 2019). India can create a sustainable e-waste management ecosystem that supports both economic and environmental objectives and guarantees a safer and cleaner environment for all by strengthening the role of PROs and increasing operational frameworks (Turaga et al., 2019).

CONCLUSION

The global electrical and electronic equipment (EEE) market is growing rapidly, yet as the lifespans of these products decrease, the quantity of electronic trash, or "e-waste," is increasing dramatically. Lawmakers and governments are searching for solutions to handle hazardous components and recycle important materials for renewable energy technologies. Scholars are exploring methods like hydrometallurgy to extract parts from printed circuit boards and batteries in an attempt to recover high-quality materials from a range of e-waste types. In subsequent research, copper and precious metals may be employed as catalysts to purify water and create green hydrogen. According to a recent study that looked at international academic articles on e-waste management from 2012 to 2021, the five key elements for effective management are policy, economy, social concerns, environment, and technology. It was emphasized that institutions in developing countries are competitive in this field, and notable authors and papers were acknowledged. However, the study was limited to the Scopus database, suggesting that future research should explore more sources. Many Asia Pacific countries choose to illegal dumping and unofficial routes because they lack effective e-waste management programs. Due to the increasing market for old electronics, developed nations are increasingly dumping their e-waste in China, Indonesia, India, and Malaysia. Formal recycling is the most efficient way to handle e-waste, reducing greenhouse gas emissions and contaminants. The effective treatment of e-waste depends on organized rules and infrastructure that are tailored to the demands of each country. In order to protect the health of those involved in the unregulated disassembly of e-waste, the research emphasizes the urgent necessity for preventative measures in India. There are technical solutions available, but their successful implementation requires trained personnel and related laws. The authors recommend that laws be passed by African countries to promote eco-friendly recycling practices. Research on the management of e-waste has increased, particularly in India, despite the fact that thorough life cycle analysis and informal collecting methods are still lacking. Future studies should focus on the health impacts and the locations of e-waste disposal in order to emphasize the significance of proper management. The study found that e-waste poses significant risks to human health and the environment, thus effective treatment methods are needed. Open recycling programs and public awareness campaigns are crucial for motivating individuals and businesses to embrace sustainable practices. A comprehensive approach that includes enhanced recycling technology, eco-design, regulatory measures, and international collaboration is necessary to address the challenges of handling e-waste. The study also looks at innovative technologies that can encourage proper disposal practices, such as real-time e-waste bin monitoring systems and smartphone apps that locate disposal sites.

REFERENCES

Alblooshi, B. G. K. M., Ahmad, S. Z., Hussain, M., & Singh, S. K. (2022). Sustainable management of electronic waste: Empirical evidences from a stakeholders' perspective. *Business Strategy and the Environment, 31*(4), 1856–1874. DOI: 10.1002/bse.2987

Andeobu, L., Wibowo, S., & Grandhi, S. (2021). A Systematic Review of E-Waste Generation and Environmental Management of Asia Pacific Countries. *International Journal of Environmental Research and Public Health, 18*(17), 9051. DOI: 10.3390/ijerph18179051 PMID: 34501640

Bhat, V., & Patil, Y. (2021). An Integrated and Sustainable Model for E-Waste Management for Pune City Households. *Journal of Physics: Conference Series, 1964*(6), 062111. DOI: 10.1088/1742-6596/1964/6/062111

Constantinescu, A., Platon, V., Surugiu, M., Frone, S., Antonescu, D., & Mazilescu, R. (2022). The Influence of Eco-Investment on E-Waste Recycling-Evidence from EU Countries. *Frontiers in Environmental Science, 10*, 928955. Advance online publication. DOI: 10.3389/fenvs.2022.928955

Farida, A., Marjono, M., Siwindarto, P., & Yanuwiadi, B. (2023). A literature study on electronic waste management in indonesia and other developing countries: Challenges and opportunities. *International Research Journal of Modernization in Engineering Technology and Science*. Advance online publication. DOI: 10.56726/IRJMETS42873

Fawole, A. A., Orikpete, O. F., Ehiobu, N. N., & Ewim, D. R. E. (2023). Climate change implications of electronic waste: Strategies for sustainable management. *Bulletin of the National Research Centre. Bulletin of the National Research Center, 47*(1), 147. Advance online publication. DOI: 10.1186/s42269-023-01124-8

Halim, L., & Suharyanti, Y. (2019). E-Waste: Current Research and Future Perspective on Developing Countries. *International Journal of Industrial Engineering and Engineering Management, 1*(2), 25–42. DOI: 10.24002/ijieem.v1i2.3214

Heeks, R., Subramanian, L., & Jones, C. (2014). Understanding e-Waste Management in Developing Countries: Strategies, Determinants, and Policy Implications in the Indian ICT Sector. *Information Technology for Development, 21*(4), 653–667. DOI: 10.1080/02681102.2014.886547

Kishore, J., & Monika, N. (2010). E-Waste management: As a challenge to public health in India. *Indian Journal of Community Medicine : Official Publication of Indian Association of Preventive & Social Medicine*, *35*(3), 382. DOI: 10.4103/0970-0218.69251 PMID: 21031101

Madkhali, H., Duraib, S., Nguyen, L., Prasad, M., Sharma, M., & Joshi, S. (2023). A Comprehensive Review on E-Waste Management Strategies and Prediction Methods: A Saudi Arabia Perspective. *Knowledge (Beverly Hills, Calif.)*, *3*(2), 163–179. DOI: 10.3390/knowledge3020012

Mallick, R., & Poddar, S. (2025). Electronic wastes, occupational exposure, and safety measures. In *CRC Press eBooks* (pp. 160–165). https://doi.org/DOI: 10.1201/9781003582311-20

Maphosa, V., & Maphosa, M. (2020). E-waste management in Sub-Saharan Africa: A systematic literature review. *Cogent Business & Management*, *7*(1), 1814503. DOI: 10.1080/23311975.2020.1814503

Mor, R. S., Sangwan, K. S., Singh, S., Singh, A., & Kharub, M. (2021). E-waste Management for Environmental Sustainability: An Exploratory Study. *Procedia CIRP*, *98*, 193–198. DOI: 10.1016/j.procir.2021.01.029

Nandan, A., Suresh, A., Saole, P., Jeevanasai, S., Chandrasekaran, R., Meili, L., Azelee, N. W., & Selvasembian, R. (2023). An Integrated Approach for Electronic Waste Management—Overview of Sources of Generation, Toxicological Effects, Assessment, Governance, and Mitigation Approaches. *Sustainability (Basel)*, *15*(24), 16946. DOI: 10.3390/su152416946

Poddar, R., Bose, D., Nambiar, N., & Poddar, S. (2023). Sustainable use of kitchen waste in advanced microbial enzyme production. In *Advances in civil and industrial engineering book series* (pp. 229–247). https://doi.org/DOI: 10.4018/979-8-3693-0044-2.ch013

Seif, R., Salem, F. Z., & Allam, N. K. (2023). E-waste recycled materials as efficient catalysts for renewable energy technologies and better environmental sustainability. *Environment, Development and Sustainability*, *26*(3), 5473–5508. Advance online publication. DOI: 10.1007/s10668-023-02925-7 PMID: 36691418

Shahabuddin, M., Uddin, M. N., Chowdhury, J. I., Ahmed, S. F., Uddin, M. N., Mofijur, M., & Uddin, M. A. (2022). A review of the recent development, challenges, and opportunities of electronic waste (e-waste). *International Journal of Environmental Science and Technology*, *20*(4), 4513–4520. DOI: 10.1007/s13762-022-04274-w

Sharma, S., Mehta, A., & Sharma, S. (2024). A Bibliometric Analysis of Electronic Waste Management: Issues and Challenges. *Current World Environment*, *18*(3), 1265–1276. DOI: 10.12944/CWE.18.3.28

Soesanto, H., Maarif, M. S., Anwar, S., & Yurianto, Y. (2023). Current Trend, Future Direction, and Enablers of e-Waste Management: Bibliometric Analysis and Literature Review. *Polish Journal of Environmental Studies*, *32*(4), 3455–3465. DOI: 10.15244/pjoes/163607

Turaga, R. M. R., Bhaskar, K., Sinha, S., Hinchliffe, D., Hemkhaus, M., Arora, R., Chatterjee, S., Khetriwal, D. S., Radulovic, V., Singhal, P., & Sharma, H. (2019). E-Waste Management in India: Issues and Strategies. *Vikalpa*, *44*(3), 127–162. DOI: 10.1177/0256090919880655

Voskergian, D., & Ishaq, I. (2023). Smart e-waste management system utilizing Internet of Things and Deep Learning approaches. *Journal of Smart Cities and Society*, *2*(2), 77–98. DOI: 10.3233/SCS-230007

Yang, B., Lee, C., & Suryawan, I. W. K. (2024). Resilient socio-technical systems for adaptive consumer e-waste management. *Sustainable Cities and Society*, *106026*. Advance online publication. DOI: 10.1016/j.scs.2024.106026

Zhang, K., Schnoor, J. L., & Zeng, E. Y. (2012). E-Waste Recycling: Where Does It Go from Here? *Environmental Science & Technology*, *46*(20), 10861–10867. DOI: 10.1021/es303166s PMID: 22998401

ADDITIONAL READING

Kumar, A., Gaur, D., Liu, Y., & Sharma, D. (2022). Sustainable waste electrical and electronic equipment management guide in emerging economies context: A structural model approach. *Journal of Cleaner Production*, *336*, 130391. DOI: 10.1016/j.jclepro.2022.130391

Maurice, A. A., Dinh, K. N., Charpentier, N. M., Brambilla, A., & Gabriel, J. P. (2021). Dismantling of printed circuit boards enabling electronic components sorting and their subsequent treatment open improved elemental sustainability opportunities. *Sustainability (Basel)*, *13*(18), 10357. DOI: 10.3390/su131810357

Nowakowski, P., Kuśnierz, S., Płoszaj, J., & Sosna, P. (2021). Collecting Small-Waste electrical and electronic equipment in Poland—How can containers help in disposal of E-Waste by individuals? *Sustainability (Basel)*, *13*(22), 12422. DOI: 10.3390/su132212422

Román, E. (2012). WEEE management in Europe: learning from best practice. In *Elsevier eBooks* (pp. 493–525). https://doi.org/DOI: 10.1533/9780857096333.5.493

Wang, Q., Kong, L., Li, J., Li, B., & Wang, F. (2020). Behavioral Evolutionary Analysis between the Government and Uncertified Recycler in China's E-Waste Recycling Management. *International Journal of Environmental Research and Public Health, 17*(19), 7221. DOI: 10.3390/ijerph17197221 PMID: 33023179

Xavier, L. H., Ottoni, M., & Lepawsky, J. (2021). Circular economy and e-waste management in the Americas: Brazilian and Canadian frameworks. *Journal of Cleaner Production, 297*, 126570. DOI: 10.1016/j.jclepro.2021.126570

KEY TERMS AND DEFINITIONS

Electronic waste: The main word used to describe electronic trash, which includes abandoned electrical and electronic devices. Another name for e-waste that is sometimes used interchangeably is electronic garbage.

E-scrap: An acronym that is frequently used to refer to abandoned electronics is electronic scrap.

WEEE: Represents Waste Electrical and Electronic Equipment, a European Union rule that governs e-waste disposal.

Recycling: The process of limiting environmental effect, lowering the requirement for new resources, and recovering valuable materials from e-waste.

Management of e-waste: The entire procedure for gathering, classifying, processing, and getting rid of e-waste in an eco-friendly way.

Chapter 15
Spiritual Well-Being Index for Incarcerated Populations:
An Exploratory Study

S. Srinivasan
https://orcid.org/0009-0002-0179-9849
Department of Humanities and Social Sciences, Graphic Era University, Dehradun, India

R. Vallipriya
https://orcid.org/0009-0008-6692-603X
Department of Physical Science, Institute of Education, Tamil Nadu Teacher Education University, India

Ajay Kumar Singh
https://orcid.org/0000-0003-0429-0925
Department of Humanities and Social Sciences, Graphic Era University, Dehradun, India

ABSTRACT

This study explores the spiritual well-being of incarcerated individuals, a topic less examined compared to the relationship between criminality and religiosity. Data were collected from 259 inmates in Tamil Nadu's Central Prisons, Special Prisons for Women, and Open Air Prisons, using the Spiritual Well-Being Scale. This tool encompasses five dimensions: Divine Connectedness (DC), Self Connectedness (SC), Other Connectedness (OC), Nature Connectedness (NC), and the Spirituality Rating Index (SRI). Employing a descriptive research design, the study combined qualitative and quantitative methods, with SPSS version 23 used for analysis. Statistical

DOI: 10.4018/979-8-3693-9755-8.ch015

techniques included descriptive and multivariate methods such as frequency, mean, standard deviation, and correlation, focusing on the Spiritual Rating Scale across dimensions.

INTRODUCTION

Thus, spirituality is a response to the Divine Spirit, and a spiritual person is one who is led by the Divine Spirit, transforming oneself and one's relationship to day-to-day life and concrete human contexts (Parameshwar, 2005; Srinivasan & Rajavel, 2025). Recent studies have highlighted the positive role of spirituality in promoting the general well-being of individuals and communities (Siddiqui, 2025). Spirituality represents a specific form of work-related feeling that energizes action (Appiah, 2022). Research studies have also revealed the important implications of spirituality on mental health, psychological problem, and substance abuse, parenting condition, marital life, and coping with stress, morbidity, and mortality (Dev et al., 2025; Srinivasan & Rajavel, 2025; Mahmoudi-Dehak et al., 2025). Thus, there are many reasons for psychologists to pay attention to the spiritual dimension of people's lives during therapeutic interventions (Snyder et al., 2011). Another analysis of spiritual striving proposes that spirituality leads to purpose and meaning in life. A higher level of spirituality is also found to result in optimism and hope (Snyder et al., 2011).

Understanding Spirituality

Derived from the Latin *Spiritualitas*, spirituality relates to *Pneuma* (spirit) and is seen as a response to the Divine. A spiritual person is guided by the Divine, leading to personal transformation and meaningful living (Martin, 2002). Unlike religion, which is organizational and ritualistic, spirituality is personal, experiential, and reflective (Dougall, 2024; Siddiqui, 2025).

Gandhi and Spiritual Strength in Prison

Mahatma Gandhi, seen as a political offender by the British, was imprisoned multiple times. He used incarceration as a period of reflection and spiritual growth, writing *Search for Truth* in prison. He equated centralized power with violence and upheld *sarvodaya* (welfare of all) as true religion (Pratt, 2013; Raju, 2010; Valmiki, 2015).

Cultural and Psychological Views

Despite belief differences, most cultures recognize a divine force (Saroglou, 2011). Psychologists now acknowledge spirituality's role in therapy, linking it to purpose, meaning, hope, and optimism (Vieten et al., 2013; Snyder et al., 2011).

Spiritual Strength Through Adversity

Encounters shape inner strength. Seligman found inspiration from his daughter's self-awareness, shifting his parenting philosophy to nurturing the soul. Csikszentmihalyi drew strength from observing war survivors who maintained integrity and serenity amidst chaos (Seligman et al., 2000).

The Spiritual Well-being Index for Incarcerated Populations is a progressive approach to enhancing the holistic health of prison inmates. Spiritual well-being—encompassing inner peace, purpose, and hope—is often overlooked in correctional settings (Pharm, 2013). This index can help assess and strengthen inmates' resilience, mental health, and chances of successful reintegration. This initiative supports the UN Sustainable Development Goals (SDGs), particularly SDG 3 (Good Health and Well-being) by promoting mental wellness and reducing emotional distress, self-harm, and trauma among inmates. It also aligns with SDG 16 (Peace, Justice, and Strong Institutions) by encouraging non-violence, empathy, and rehabilitation-focused environments. Overall, the Spiritual Well-being Index contributes to humane incarceration and sustainable development through health and justice-based interventions (Haghes, 2023).

SPIRITUAL WELL BEING

Spirituality, as per this study, is a 'search for the sacred' marked by a set of beliefs, feelings of consolation/desolation, and actions leading to divine connectedness, self-connectedness, other-connectedness, and nature-connectedness that give real happiness, meaning, and purpose in life, as measured by the Spirituality Rating Index (SRI), an index developed by the researcher. It is assumed that a spirituality leading to a right relationship with God and all living beings results in spiritual well-being.

Rationale for the development of the Index

The idea of developing an index on spirituality of prison inmates emerged from the researcher's own religious and professional experiences, discussion with subject experts and review of literature (Melvin, 2021). The researcher observed during her interaction with prison inmates that discovering and experiencing of unconditional love and acceptance of God lifted up the hearts of many a prison inmate, their life satisfaction and even work performance even when bound by feelings of guilt and rejection. Prison is a place where an individual finds himself or herself with unfamiliar persons and locations. Prisonisation is a process that can result in certain characteristic behaviour and thought patterns among the prison inmates when they spend a longer period in the prison (Bondeson, 2017). According to a prison official, many of the prison inmates develop a search for God as they experience the tension and trauma of arrest, legal procedures and imprisonment; they come to a realization that only God might accept and support them (Maruna et al., 2015). Hence a Four-Dimensional Spirituality Rating Index (SRI) for assessing the spirituality of prison inmates was developed by the researcher during her study on the psychological general well-being of prison inmates (Kumar, 2022).

Some of the existing measurement instruments of spirituality are given below which can raise a question on the rationale behind the index validation.

1. The Spiritual Well-Being Scale (SWBS, 1991/2009), a 20 item scale covering two dimensions of religious well-being and existential well-being, with Cronbach's alpha ranging from .89 to .94, developed by (Paloutzian & Ellison, 1991).
2. The Spirituality Index of Well-Being (SIWB, 2004), a 12-item instrument consisting of 6-item self efficacy domain and 6-item life scheme domain with Cronbach's alpha of .91 and test-retest coefficient of .79 developed by Timothy P. Daaleman, DO and Bruce B. Frey among adult outpatient population of Kansas City. The instrument was designed to measure the effect of spirituality upon subjective well-being (Daaleman & Frey, 2004).
3. 10 item shortened version of SWBS as developed with a Cronbach's alpha of .87 (Malinakova et al., 2017)

There are indices and scales measuring spirituality and spiritual well-being among general populations including clinical population. The researcher aims to develop a Four-Dimensional Spiritual Well-Being Index for measuring specifically the spiritual well-being of inmates of correctional settings. A look at the characteristics of an Index and Scale can further clarify the features of the tool selected for validation. Both index and scale are ordinal measures of variables. A person's score on the Four Dimensional Spirituality Index gives an indication of the strength of his/her spirituality in relation to other people and thus is an ordinal measure. Both index and scale are composite measures. Spirituality is an abstract concept which cannot be adequately, accurately and comprehensively measured by a single indicator. Physical objects are rather easily measured in concrete terms of height, weight and quality. Scales and indices are generally utilized in survey method; the present study has used survey method in developing the Spirituality Rating Index (SRI).

Significant of the Study

Spiritual values are on the decline, and the importance spirituality and well-being of persons in prison inmates in particular has been evidenced through various research studies. Few studies have been conducted on the understanding of spirituality and well-being for incarcerated population in recent times (Deuchar et al., 2016). The studies in correctional settings have mostly focused only on the factors influencing the well-being of prison inmates in general.

Research Gap and Research Objectives

The research gap for spiritual well-being recognizes it as an important factor to improve the overall rehabilitation of incarcerated populations. It can focus on various aspects such as spiritual, mental health, coping mechanisms, and quality of life in the incarcerated population. These are specific topics and research gaps that need to be addressed for further research studies. There is a gap in the spiritual well-being literature regarding a universally accepted definition for incarcerated populations. It needs to capture the unique spiritual needs of prison inmates (Maschi et al., 2013). There is much existing literature that provides spiritual well-being but does not account for the cultural aspects of the religions and their backgrounds for the incarcerated populations. Future research can focus on culturally sensitive tools that can enhance further study (Selman et al., 2011). There is a longitudinal study that can improve the mental health outcomes among the incarcerated population, which can include spiritual well-being and mental health. This area is still underexplored; it can provide comprehensive results for mental health outcomes and identify the recidivism rates of the inmates (Duncan et al., 2018). Further studies can focus on spirituality and coping mechanisms among the incarcerated population; this can help address the stress, trauma, and isolation experienced by prison inmates (Srinivasan et al., 2025). The comparative study is more useful to address significant importance for further research. The research study addresses the impact of prison inmates on their spiritual well-being and their rehabilitation for reintegration into society. Research can look into the problems that prison inmates face regarding spirituality and how it can improve institutional policies to provide resources for dynamic prison inmates (Ndung'u, 2021). What are the personal challenges that inhibit spiritual expression, such as trauma and mental health issues? Understanding these challenges can provide more information for interventions that enhance spiritual well-being among the incarcerated population.

Objective of the Study

1. To understand the factors associated with spirituality of the prison inmates
2. To develop and validate a four dimensional Spirituality Rating Index (SRI) for application in correctional settings.

Aim of the Study

This study presents the scientific process followed in validating a spirituality rating index for application in correctional settings in general and to assess the spirituality of the prison inmates of Tamil Nadu in particular.

BACKGROUND OF THE STUDY

Spiritual well-being has emerged as a vital dimension of holistic health, encompassing a sense of meaning, purpose, and connection that transcends the material aspects of life. Among incarcerated populations, where isolation, loss of autonomy, and psychological distress are prevalent, spiritual well-being may serve as a crucial coping mechanism and a pathway to rehabilitation (Srinivasan & Rajavel, 2025). The prison environment, marked by rigid structures, limited freedom, and social stigma, often contributes to a deterioration of mental and emotional health. In such contexts, spiritual resources may offer inmates a sense of inner peace, hope, and personal transformation (Kazemian, 2019). Research has shown that spirituality and religious engagement can play a positive role in improving inmates' mental health, reducing recidivism, and supporting reintegration into society. However, there remains a lack of standardized tools to measure spiritual well-being specifically within correctional settings. Most existing indices have been developed for the general population and may not adequately capture the unique experiences and spiritual needs of incarcerated individuals (Muller & Bukten, 2019). This exploratory study seeks to address this gap by developing and validating a Spiritual Well-being Index tailored for incarcerated populations. By examining the components of spiritual well-being within this context—such as forgiveness, transcendence, inner peace, and connection to a higher power—the study aims to offer insights into how spiritual health can be nurtured in prisons and how it may contribute to more humane and rehabilitative correctional practices (Amitay & Ronel, 2023).

LITERATURE REVIEW

Development and Validation of Four Dimensional Spirituality Index

The study specifically identified four main steps in the construction of an index, namely, *item selection, examination of empirical relationships, index scoring and index validation.* Various authors have also provided guidelines on design tools of measurement (Clark & Watson, 2019; Kalkbrenner, 2021; Moradi, 2019). The researcher followed four steps of tool development by combining the steps recommended by (Kothari, 2004; Lambert & Newman, 2023) in developing the spirituality rating index.

1. Concept development (Identifying the construct and dimensions)
2. Item Selection
3. Index Scoring
4. Index validation

Concept Development (Identifying the Construct and Dimensions)

A concept reveals the meanings and characteristics of objects, events, situations and behaviors associated with it. A construct is an abstract concept or idea specifically invented for a research and theory-building purpose. It is a focused abstract idea inferred from observable phenomena. The researcher identified the construct of 'spirituality' and its dimensions through an extensive review of literature. Inductive approach by gathering the already existing general concepts on spirituality. The operational concept or construct of spirituality was derived by the researcher by looking into the meanings and characteristics attached to the term by dictionaries, social scientists, social reformers as well as by the three major religions in Tamil Nadu, namely, Hinduism, Islam and Christianity.

Table 1. Concept Development - Spirituality

Sl No.	Source	Concept of Spirituality	Thematic Clusters (Dimensions)
1	Oxford dictionary	The quality or condition of being spiritual; attachment to or regard for things of the spirit as opposed to material or worldly interests	Divine connectedness
2	Wiktionary	Concern for that which is unseen and intangible, as opposed to physical or mundane and as appreciation for religious values.	Divine connectedness
3	(McSherry & Cash, 2004)	Spirituality designates a range of spiritual forms. It evokes a cluster of attitudes present in comparable forms of spirituality and is a theosophy based on the triangle – God, humanity and nature.	Divine connectedness, Other connectedness, Nature connectedness
4	(Yust, 2016)	Spirituality is about multi-faceted integral development explored by persons in relation. It can be achieved through relational forms of practice that unveil the spirituality implicit in them.	Connectedness
5	(Mazour-Matusevic, 2006)	· **Relational:** Relationship with God, self, and others, with God as the foundation. · **Holistic:** Integrating all aspects of daily life, avoiding compartmentalization. · **Experiential:** Based on personal experiences. · **Personal:** Individual-centered spirituality. · **Idealistic and Realistic:** Balancing aspirations with practicality. · **Contemplative and Active:** Combining reflection with action. · **Communal and Individualistic:** Blending private and public practices. · **Religious:** Biblical, Christological, Historical, and Ecumenical perspectives.	Divine connectedness, Self connectedness, Other connectedness,
6	(Walker, 2019)	Spirituality is the 'Search for the Sacred' and people can take different pathways of traditional organised religions and more individualised worldviews.	Divine connectedness
7	(Van Niekerk, 2018)	Spirituality is universal. Although the belief systems vary, every culture has a concept of the sacred or the ultimate.	Other connectedness
8	(Reave, 2005)	"Spirituality is the way you choose to live in tune with your values. Values are not mere ideals, which you accept as good and true. They are practical norms by which you decide to live."	Way of life Self connectedness
9	(Yang et al., 2010)	Having a subjective feeling of happiness, affirming self worth, managing inter-personal relationships with an open accepting attitude and possessing an internal energy.	Self connectedness Other connectedness
10	(Huber & Huber, 2012)	Identified four attributes of spirituality namely, faith and attachment with God, Connectedness with others, personal life meaning and purpose and Inner strength and peace.	Divine connectedness, Self connectedness, Other connectedness

continued on following page

Table 1. Continued

Sl No.	Source	Concept of Spirituality	Thematic Clusters (Dimensions)
11	(Guimarães et al., 2021)	1. Being religious is associated with reduced unhealthy habits such as smoking and substance abuse and gain better grades. 2. Religious persons are likely to have lesser marital conflicts and lesser conflicts with their teenage children. 3. Religiosity is predictive of virtues such as altruism, volunteerism, kindness and forgiveness. 4. Religious beliefs are associated with the ability to cope with stress.	Self connectedness Other connectedness
12	(Quotes of Nelson Mandela; Panzini et al., 2017)	Mandela emphasized leaving anger, hatred, and bitterness behind to attain true freedom (Mandela, 1994). Hatred is learned; people can also be taught love, as it aligns naturally with the human heart. Solitude, like in a prison cell, is a space for deep self-reflection and understanding one's thoughts and emotions (Mandela, 2011).	Self Connectedness Other connectedness
13	(Dutch, 2002)	True religion is not a narrow dogma. It is not external observance. It is faith in God and living in the presence of God. It means faith in a future life, in truth and ahimsa.	Divine connectedness Other connectedness
14	(Huber & Huber, 2012)	The four attributes of spirituality are faith and attachment with God, connectedness with others, personal life meaning and purpose and inner strength and peace.	Divine connectedness, Other connectedness Self connectedness

The analysis in Table 1 highlights definitions of spirituality by social reformers and scientists, emphasizing relational spirituality with three dimensions: vertical (Divine connectedness), centripetal (Self connectedness), and horizontal (Other and Nature connectedness). The researcher further examined whether these dimensions align with the philosophies of major world religions: Hinduism, Islam, and Christianity. These religions were chosen due to their significance in Tamil Nadu, India, and globally. Key sub-domains of Divine connectedness—God image, religiosity, and divine presence—were considered in scale development. Table 1 also presents the 2016 religion-based population statistics.

Table 2. Religion Based Population Statistics, 2016

Sl. No.	World (2010)	India (2011)	Tamil Nadu (2011)
1	Christianity 31.5%	Hinduism 79.8%	Hinduism 87.58%
2	Islam 23.2%	Islam 14.23%	Christianity 6.12%
3	Hinduism 15%	Christianity 2.3%	Islam 5.86%
Source	www.pewforum.org	www.census2011.co.in	www.census2011.co.in

EXISTENCE OF THE DIMENSION OF DIVINE CONNECTEDNESS IN THE SPIRITUALITY OF THE THREE MAJOR RELIGIONS

God Image - All Powerful, Almighty God

A review of Hinduism, Islam, and Christianity reveals alignment in the God Image domain within the proposed Spirituality Rating Index (SRI).

Across these religions, God is seen as Supreme, Almighty, and Omniscient.

Christianity: Highlights God's divine providence, as in Matthew 6:26, emphasizing care for all beings.

Merciful, forgiving and compassionate God

Hinduism: A compassionate and merciful God is presented in Hinduism as Sri Basavesvara, the Hindu mystic and reformer says, "Compassionate one, effacer of my births, Compassionate one, destroyer of my births … because you burnt my eight-fold pride, I found your gracious feet with confidence". Vishnu is considered the lover and protector of all devotees.

Religiosity

Hinduism, Islam, and Christianity each possess distinct scriptures, teachings, and belief systems that operate at both the knowledge and ideological levels. Despite these differences, religiosity in all three traditions is fundamentally rooted in the experience of the divine, often exemplified through the lives of holy and revered individuals (Fletcher, 2004). These experiences shape the spiritual expressions and practices that manifest in both private and public domains. In Hinduism, spiritual practice may include the study of scriptures, *puja* (worship), yoga, purification rituals, observances related to key life milestones, and the celebration of numerous festivals. In Christianity, religious life is marked by worship services, the reading of sacred scripture, and the observance of sacraments and rituals that accompany an individual from birth to death (Spirago et al., 2014). These traditions offer diverse yet profound pathways to spiritual well-being and a deeper connection with the divine.

Divine presence

"we taught him knowledge from our divine presence", a verse which Sufis give importance to. Sufism is Islamic mysticism (Heck, 2006). They practice reciting the name of God or sayings of the prophet.

Existence of the dimension of Self Connectedness in the Spirituality of the Three Major Religions

In Hinduism, spiritual teachings emphasize the importance of self-awareness and inner reflection as pathways to liberation. *Bhagavad Gita* 7:02 underscores the role of meditation and contemplation in attaining self-knowledge, while the *Upanishads* describe the mind as a powerful tool that can lead either to bondage or to spiritual freedom. Swami Vivekananda articulated this philosophy by defining spirituality as the "science of the soul" (Radhakrishnan et al.,), highlighting its introspective and experiential nature. Similarly, Islamic teachings emphasize the primacy of the inner life. The poet Rumi advocates for nurturing the inner self over the pursuit of worldly power, and the Quran (5:105) calls upon believers to cultivate self-awareness and live righteously. This theme is further echoed in the Hadith, "Whoever knows himself knows his Lord," illustrating the profound connection between self-knowledge and a deeper understanding of the divine.

Existence of the dimension of Other Connectedness in the Spirituality of the three major religions

Ferrer (2011) emphasizes the concept of participatory spirituality, which encourages individuals to actively engage in their spiritual journeys through diverse paths and practices. Across various religious traditions, spiritual well-being is deeply rooted in ethical and compassionate living. In Hinduism, the principle of *Vasudhaiva Kutumbakam* ("The world is one family") from the Mahopanishad highlights values of non-violence, mutual respect, and the interconnectedness of all life. Similarly, Islam upholds justice as a fundamental value, complemented by benevolence, equality, compassion, and mercy (Clammer & Clammer, 2016). The practice of *Zakat*, or obligatory almsgiving, reflects the spiritual duty to share personal wealth and resources with those in need. Christianity centers on love and forgiveness, as seen in the teachings of Jesus in John 15:12-15, where believers are urged to "love one another as I have loved you," and in his prayer for forgiveness even during crucifixion. The prayer of St. Francis of Assisi further exemplifies this ethos, invoking the desire to become an instrument of peace and healing in the world.

RESEARCH METHODLOGY

Operational Definition of Spirituality

Spirituality as per this study is a 'search for the sacred' marked by a set of beliefs, feelings of consolation/desolation and actions leading to divine connectedness, self connectedness, other connectedness and nature connectedness that gives a real happiness, meaning and purpose in life. It is assumed that a spirituality leading to a right relationship with God and all the living beings results in spiritual well-being.

Tools used for the proposed research study

The Four-Dimensional Spirituality Rating Index (SRI) was developed to assess the spirituality of prison inmates, focusing on their psychological well-being.

Existing spirituality measurement tools include:

- **Spiritual Well-Being Scale (SWBS, 1991/2009):** A 20-item scale measuring religious and existential well-being (Cronbach's alpha: .89–.94).
- **Spirituality Index of Well-Being (SIWB, 2004):** A 12-item scale measuring self-efficacy and life scheme domains (Cronbach's alpha: .91) (Daaleman & Frey, 2004))..
- **Shortened SWBS (2005):** A 10-item version with a Cronbach's alpha of .87 (Malinakova et al., 2017).

Current scales address general and clinical populations, but the Four-Dimensional SRI is tailored for inmates in correctional settings.

Methodology

This study presents the scientific process followed in validating a spirituality rating index for application in correctional settings in general and to assess the spirituality of prison inmates in Tamil Nadu in particular. Development and Validation of the Spirituality Rating Index (SRI): This study presents the scientific process followed in validating a spirituality rating index for application in correctional settings in general and to assess the spirituality of prison inmates in Tamil Nadu in particular. The study uses qualitative and quantitative methods; it is a mixed-methods approach that adopted a purposive sample with a total sample size of 259 from various prisons such as Central Prisons, Special Prisons for Women and Open Air Prisons of Tamil Nadu with specific reference to spirituality (Srinivasan et al., 2025). The Spirituality Rating Index (SRI), which was validated during the process of the study, demonstrated good predictive validity for each item and item reproducibility coefficients. Cronbach's Alpha, the index of internal consistency, showed a good level of reliability for the index and its four dimensions. Split-half analysis and the parallel forms method also revealed a good level of reliability.

Statistical Analysis

The descriptive research study used SPSS version 23 to analyze various statistical methods, including simple frequency, mean, standard deviations, and correlation values, to analyze all the variables, especially in the spiritual rating scale and its dimensions.

Limitation of the study

The study conducted with incarcerated population convicts in central prisons, special prisons for women, and open-air prisons of Tamil Nadu. The inclusion criteria mainly focused on the Spirituality Rating Index.

FINDING OF THE STUDY

Item Selection Item Pooling

Once the construct and the dimensions were arrived at, the researcher framed 85 statements with 25 statements expressing divine connectedness, 31 statements indicating self connectedness, 22 statements for other connectedness and 7 statements for nature connectedness. She used her judgment based on her intuitions, religious, field, professional experience and review of literature to ensure face validity of the statements. This preliminary set of items selected were further subject to face validity and content validity with a panel of subject experts as detailed under the section on 'Index Validation'.

Index Scoring

The index consists of Likert type scale items to be responded on 5 point rating scale, with positively worded as well as negatively worded statements. Negatively worded statements are assigned reverse scoring. The scores are Strongly Agree = 5, Agree = 4, Undecided = 3, Disagree = 2, Strongly Disagree = 1

Index Validation - Tests of Measurement (Item Reduction and Establishment of Validity)

A good measuring instrument must meet validity, reliability, and practicality requirements.

Validity: Ensures the instrument measures what it is intended to, including:

Content Validity, Criterion-Related Validity, and Construct Validity.

Face Validity: Items must clearly represent the variable being measured (Kothari, 2004).

The researcher tested validity with an 85-item set, reviewed by a panel of three experts (a research center director, research assistant, and rehabilitation program volunteer).

Items were refined for relevance, clarity, and simplicity, removing redundant or misleading statements.

Table 3. Examples of Items Eliminated Post Round of Content Validation

Sl. No.	Item eliminated	Reason for elimination
1.	2. I trust in the Divine who can make the impossible possible	Repetition of item 1.
2.	16. Religious exercises give me peace and happiness.	Item 8 reframed – I keep to my prayers and religious exercises faithfully.
3.	21- 23 (I experience divine presence when - I pray, I am in difficulty, I am happy, within. I do not experience God' presence)	Reframed as - In my daily activities I feel the support of a sacred presence of peace, hope and optimism that sustains me.

Table 4. Examples of Items Retained Post Round of Content Validation

Sl. No.	Item retained
1.	I spend time reflecting about my life.
2.	I reach out to others in their need.
3.	Working with nature (Gardening, rearing animals) relaxes me.

The panel remarked that the instrument is too lengthy for a population who is undergoing stress and trauma and those repetitive statements need to be avoided. After extensive review and verification, the instrument contained 33 items. The 33-item index was further given to 15 subject experts for intensive content validation wherein the experts rated each of the statements on a 11-point rating score ranging from the least favorable statement to the most favorable statement. Item analysis was done based on the median for each item and standard deviation. The items which scored 8 (73 per cent) and above were maintained in the index. Simultaneously the tool was administered to 15 male prison inmates and 15 female prison inmates to obtain their feedback and suggestions. Based on the evaluation and validation of the experts and the prison inmates the 24-item Four-Dimensional Spiritual Well-Being Index was drafted and administered to 259 prison inmates comprising 201 male and 58 female inmates.

Criterion Related Validity

Criterion related validity refers to the ability of the item to predict some outcome. It can be assessed via predictive validity and concurrent validity. Predictive validity refers to the ability of the instrument to predict a future performance or the ability of the item to predict the total score. Predictive validity of the 24-item instrument was established through item total correlation or item reproducibility coefficient which indicates how much the particular item represents the aggregate spirituality score and thus can predict the overall spirituality. table 5 presents the item reproducibility coefficient of Spirituality Rating Index.

Table 5. Item Reproducibility Coefficient

Sl. No.	Item	Item Score (Mean)	Total Scale Score	Item Total Correlation
1	There is a divine power that masters the universe.	*4.23*	*89.71± 11.611*	*r = .528** p<.01*
2	God loves me, cares for me and accepts me as I am.	*3.99*	*89.71± 11.611*	*r = .641** p<.01*
3	God will not forgive our offences.**	*3.78*	*89.71± 11.611*	*r = .583** p<.01*
4	I do not keep to my personal prayers and religious exercises faithfully.**	*3.48*	*89.71± 11.611*	*r = .720** p<.01*
5	I am not interested in public religious programmes and ceremonies.**	*3.36*	*89.71± 11.611*	r = .638 p<.01
6	I do not like to keep religious symbols with me.**	*2.55*	*89.71± 11.611*	*r = .248** p<.01*
7	In my daily activities I feel the support of a sacred presence of peace, hope and optimism that sustains me.	*3.64*	*89.71± 11.611*	*r = .528** p<.01*
8	I spend time reflecting about my life.	*4.16*	*89.71± 11.611*	*r = .426** p<.01*
9	I do not see a meaning and purpose in my life.**	*2.86*	*89.71± 11.611*	*r = .516 p<.01*
10	I am not aware of the goodness that is within me or my strengths.**	*3.72*	*89.71± 11.611*	*r = .467 p<.01*
11	I am aware of my weaknesses.	*3.93*	*89.71± 11.611*	*r = .454** p<.01*
12	I nurture unpleasant and negative thoughts about myself. **	*3.33*	*89.71± 11.611*	*r = .516** p<.01*
13	I get distracted when I engage in any activity and cannot concentrate.**	*2.86*	*89.71± 11.611*	*r = .525** p<.01*
14	My thoughts, feelings and actions are responsible for what happens in my life.	*4.19*	*89.71± 11.611*	*r = .375 p<.01*
15	I take steps to improve my relationships with others.	*3.88*	*89.71± 11.611*	*r = .565 p<.01*
16	Others do not share their joys and pains with me.**	*3.60*	*89.71± 11.611*	*r = .459 p<.01*
17	I do not have persons to share my feelings with.**	*3.49*	*89.71± 11.611*	*r = .474 p<.01*
18	I reach out to others in their need.	*4.23*	*89.71± 11.611*	*r = .534** p<.01*
19	I feel compassion and mercy when I see people struggling in life.	*4.28*	*89.71± 11.611*	*r = .588 p<.01*
20	I am motivated to forgive and be at peace with others.	*4.06*	*89.71± 11.611*	*r = .588 p<.01*
21	I do not trust people.**	*3.12*	*89.71± 11.611*	*r = .399 p<.01*

continued on following page

Table 5. Continued

Sl. No.	Item	Item Score (Mean)	Total Scale Score	Item Total Correlation
22	I see the Divine in others and respect every life as a gift of God.	4.13	89.71± 11.611	$r_=$ .575 $p<.01$
23	I do not find relaxation in working with nature	4.40	89.71± 11.611	$r_=$ .509 $p<.01$
	(Gardening, rearing animals).**			
24	I respect nature as the source of life.	4.44	89.71± 11.611	$r_=$ .479 $p<.01$

All the items of the index have manifested a positive correlation at a highly significant .01 level with the total score of the index indicating that each item score represents the aggregate spirituality score and thus can predict the overall spirituality indicating the good predictive validity of each item.

Concurrent Validity

Concurrent validity refers to the utility of the instrument in closely relating to instruments of known validity. The score of the Spirituality Rating Index being a widely used instrument among varied populations indicating its high validity.

Table 6. Concurrent validity: Correlation of the Scores on Spirituality Rating Index and on Spiritual Well-Being Scale by (Paloutzian & Ellison, 1991).

Scores	Correlation	Spirituality Rating Index score	Spiritual Well-Being Scale
Spirituality	Pearson	1	
Rating Index	Correlation		
score	Sig. (2-tailed)		
	N	259	
Spiritual Well-	Pearson	.802**	1
Being Scale	Correlation		
(Paloutzian &	Sig. (2-tailed)	.000	
Ellison, 1991) Score	N	259	

**Correlation is significant at .01 level.

Concurrent Validity: The Spirituality Rating Index (SRI) shows a high positive correlation of .802 (significant at .01 level) with the Spiritual Well-Being Scale (SWBS) by (Paloutzian & Ellison, 1991).

SWBS Reliability: Demonstrated test-retest reliability coefficients (.93–.99) and high internal consistency (Cronbach's alpha: .89–.94 across samples).

SWBS has been used in studies on Christian and non-religious sociopathic convicts.

Construct Validity for the SRI was not performed in this study.

Establishment of Reliability

A measurement is considered reliable if it gives dependable results. Though reliability can contribute to validity, a reliable instrument may not be a valid instrument. Reliability of the instrument was established using Cronbach's alpha, Split Half Analysis and Parallel Forms Method.

Table 7. Cronbach's Alpha of the Spirituality Rating Index (SRI)

Sl. No.	Dimension	Cronbach's Alpha Value (N = *219*)
1.	Divine Connectedness (DC)	*.706*
2.	Self Connectedness (SC)	*.754*
3.	Other Connectedness (OC)	*.784*
4.	Nature Connectedness (NC)	*.762*
5	Spirituality Rating Index (SRI)	*.850*

As per the data in table 7, the Spirituality Rating Index has established a Cronbach's Alpha, the index of internal consistency that shows a good level of reliability, that is, .850 as per the data of the present study among the prison inmates of Tamil Nadu. The four dimensions of the Index have also scored Cronbach's alpha which indicate a good level of reliability, that is, .706 (DC), .754 (SC), .784 (OC), and .762 (NC).

Table 8. Split Half Reliability

Cronbach's Alpha	Part 1	Value	*.743*
		Number of items	*12 (a)*
	Part 2	Value	*.811*
		Number of items	*12 (b)*
	Total number of items		*24*
Correlation between forms			*.614*
Spearman-Brown Coefficient			*.761*
Guttmann split Half Coefficient			*.748*

a. The items are: 1-12

b. The items are: 13-24

The Split half reliability depicted in table 8, reveals a good level of reliability of the Spirituality Rating Index (SRI) administered among the prison inmates of Tamil Nadu with a Cronbach's alpha of .743 for part I with 121 items and .811 for part 2 with 12 items. A high level of positive correlation is also found to exist between part 1 and part 2 with Karl Pearson's correlation coefficient at .614, Spearman-Brown coefficient at .761 and Guttmann Split Half coefficient at .748.

PSYCHOMETRIC PROPERTIES OF SPIRITUALITY RATING INDEX (SRI)

The Spirituality Rating Index consists of 24 Likert-type items, with 12 positive and 12 negative statements, scored on a 5-point scale (Strongly Agree = 5, Strongly Disagree = 1).

Scoring: Negative items are reverse scored.

Domains and Content:

Divine Connectedness: Belief in divine power, God image, religiosity, religious practices, and symbols.

Self Connectedness: Self-reflection, self-image, mindfulness, locus of control.

Other Connectedness: Building rapport, sharing experiences, altruism, forgiveness, trust.

Nature Connectedness: Working with nature, eco-centricism, seeing the divine in all beings.

Table 9. Dimensions of Spirituality Rating Index (SRI)

Sl. No.	Dimension	Number of Items	Reversely scored items (Negatively worded items)	Range of score (Can be calculated considering quartiles of raw data)	Level of spiritual well-being
1.	Divine Connectedness	*1-7* *(7 items)*	*3, 4, 5, 6*	*7-22* *23-28* *29-35*	Low Moderate High
2.	Self Connectedness	*8-14* *(7 items)*	*9, 10, 12, 13,*	*7-22* *23-28* *29-35*	Low Moderate High
3.	Other Connectedness	*15-21* *(7 items)*	*16, 17, 21*	*7-22* *23-28* *29-35*	Low Moderate High
4.	Nature Connectedness	*22-24* *(3 items)*	*23*	*4-11* *12-13* *14-15*	Low Moderate High
5	Total Spirituality	*24*	*12*	*24-82* *83-89* *99-120*	Low Moderate High

The Spirituality Rating Index (SRI) has manifested a good level of validity and reliability based on the validation process carried out from the data gathered during the study conducted among the prison inmates of Tamil Nadu.

SPIRITUALITY/RELIGION AND WELL-BEING AMONG PRISON INMATES

Religious Involvement & Prison Behavior: That higher religious involvement in prison is linked to fewer infractions and better prison adjustment (Levitt & Loper, 2009).

Religiosity & Substance Abuse: Inmates with higher religiosity/spirituality report lower levels of alcohol and drug use.

Conversion & Coping: Prisoner conversions to religion provide new social identities and coping strategies, reducing feelings of shame and empowering released inmates (Maruna et al., 2006).

Spirituality & Well-Being: Little difference in spirituality and well-being between prisoners and other groups, despite prisoners having lower trust and personal well-being.

Religion, Spirituality & Health: Positive relationship between religion/spirituality and well-being, with significant benefits in areas like substance abuse, mental health, self-esteem, and social support.

Bible Study & Recidivism: Inmates actively involved in Bible studies were less likely to be re-arrested.

Yoga and Well-Bing:

Experimental study on Yoga among 152 respondents from nine Swedish correctional facilities. Significant improvements were found in 13 of the 16 variables such as less perceived stress, less aggressive and antisocial behavior, better sleep quality, better work performance and an increased psychological and emotional well-being within the yoga group (Kerekes et al., 2017).

Meditation and Well-Being:

Mindfulness-based stress-reduction courses were offered in the drug units of six Massachusetts correctional facilities covering 1350 prison inmates (Edward, 2021). Highly significant pre-course and post-course improvements were found in relation to hostility, self esteem and mood disturbance. Higher level of improvement was found among women than men; further greater level of improvement was found among male inmates in minimum security prisons than those in medium security prisons. The results recommended effective use of mindfulness-based stress-reduction programmes to be organised regularly in correctional institutions (Luckeenarain, 2015).

The effect of Vipasana Mediation on Quality of Life, Subjective well-being and Criminal Propensity among inmates of Tihar Jail, Delhi. The sample of 262 inmates comprised 232 male and 30 female respondents. The study revealed that the rate of criminal propensity came down and the level of subjective well-being went up after attending the Vipasana mediation courses. The researchers had recommended the need for more congenial atmosphere such as maintaining silence, adequate space for avoiding physical proximity and communication between experimental and control groups (Goldberg, 2001).

Formative Spirituality and Well-Being:

Adrian Van Kaam, the Dutch psychologist and spiritual writer is the founder of formative spirituality. Formative spirituality is about beliefs, attitudes and exchanges that can lead to human formation, a transcendent experience that includes an implicit awareness that one is called to an ever higher form of life. This includes formative relationships, training programmes, activities and experiences (Stamm, 2006). The results of counselling, legal support, family contacts and life-skills training programme organised at Central Prison, Palayamkotai by Prison Ministry India. In the words of a prisoner, "Now I have found how the simple principles of life helped me find a new meaning. Now I love life, people and mainly myself'. The verbatim of the inmates reflect the effectiveness of *spirituality and ethics based programmes* to facilitate progressive change among prison inmates (Clear et al., 2000).

The true stories of individuals who create unconsciously inspiring stories from various secondary sources were recorded. The researcher has related the case study of Anburaj, who is serving life imprisonment at Mysore central prison. He had attempted suicide and endured mental imbalance in the initial years of imprisonment indicating a poor level of psychological general well-being. He eventually started finding meaning in life for himself and co-inmates by using his God given talents as a playwright and (Agtong et al., 2023). The spirituality adopted and combined a *spirituality of 'flow'* or immersing oneself in creative work (Albayrak, 2024).

DISCUSSION

Spiritual Characteristics of the Respondents

Suggestions for a Happier Life

Several studies have emphasized nurturing the spiritual self as key to a happier life. Faith and spirituality offer a support system, help shift focus beyond the self, and bring meaning and purpose to life. A significant 69.7% of respondents identified as strong believers in God, 18% reported minimal faith, and 12.9% had no faith. Some expressed anger, feeling abandoned by God, while others became indifferent after unanswered prayers (Levin, 2009). Similarly, 78.8% stated their parents were strong believers, 15.4% said their parents had some faith, and 5.8% reported no parental faith. A majority (67.8%) had strong self-connectedness in their parental families, while 44.8% experienced such bonding in marital families. Regarding other-connectedness, 65.1% described their families as altruistic. In terms of nature connectedness, 75.1% reported their parental families valued nature, suggesting a strong presence of divine, self, other, and nature connectedness in their lives. However, 55.4% said their friends lacked divine connectedness or they had no close friends. On the other hand, 70% stated their friends were helpful, and 51.2% said their friends were nature-friendly—indicating low divine but higher other- and nature-connectedness among inmates' friends. Notably, 63.9% believed that opportunities for divine connection exist in prison. About 50.6% reported somewhat cooperative and positive relationships with staff, and 67.4% acknowledged only moderate opportunities for nature connectedness.

Factors Influencing Spirituality of the Respondents

Influences on Spirituality Among Prison Inmates

The study reveals significant associations between certain variables and the spirituality of inmates, as measured by the Spiritual Well-Being Scale (Paloutzian & Ellison, 1991).

Prayer after imprisonment shows a highly significant association ($p < .01$) with higher levels of overall spiritual well-being (84.74±13.53), religious well-being (51.09±9.24), and existential well-being (33.65±7.88).

Prayer before imprisonment, yoga practice, and type of prison also show strong influence ($p < .01$): Inmates who prayed before imprisonment recorded higher spiritual (82.58±16.54) and religious well-being (49.62±12.55), with existential well-being (32.97±8.14) significant at the $p < .05$ level. Yoga practitioners reported higher spiritual (80.68±16.06), religious (47.85±13.46), and existential well-being (32.83±7.68). Open-air prison inmates had the highest spiritual (84.53±21.06) and existential well-being (40.35±7.78), while the lowest levels were seen among inmates in central (75.68±18.26) and special women's prisons (30.77±6.43), respectively. Religion was significantly associated ($p < .01$) with spiritual and religious well-being. Christian inmates recorded the highest spiritual (89.43±12.14) and religious well-being (55.18±6.45). No significant link was found between religion and existential well-being. Duration of sentence showed no association with spiritual or religious well-being but had a strong link ($p < .01$) with existential well-being. Inmates with determinate sentences scored higher (33.16±8.38). Age had no significant impact on spiritual well-being, which remained consistently high across all age groups.

Age and Spiritual Well-Being

Elderly inmates are often viewed as spiritual resources, as aging brings awareness of life's impermanence (Allen et al., 2008). This study explored whether older inmates exhibit higher spiritual well-being than younger ones. A strong positive correlation was found between overall spiritual well-being and its two dimensions—religious and existential well-being. A moderate but significant correlation was also observed between religious and existential well-being. However, no statistically significant correlation was found between age and:

Spiritual well-being ($r = .019$, $p > .05$)
Religious well-being ($r = .062$, $p > .05$)
Existential well-being ($r = .062$, $p > .05$)

Field observations revealed that most inmates, regardless of age, find hope in their faith and rely on God during distress. While earlier analysis showed age linked to psychological well-being, it is not associated with spiritual well-being. Hence, the null hypothesis is accepted.

Gender and Spiritual Well-Being

A statistically significant difference was found in religious well-being between male and female inmates (t = 2.264; $p < .05$), with women showing higher RWB (Mean: 48.02 ± 13.70) than men (Mean: 44.57 ± 14.73). However, no significant gender difference was found in:

Existential well-being (t = 1.464; $p > .05$), though men scored slightly higher (Mean: 32 ± 8.38) than women (Mean: 30.77 ± 6.42).

Overall spiritual well-being (t = 1.148; $p > .05$), with women slightly ahead (Mean: 78.79 ± 17.37) compared to men (Mean: 76.56 ± 18.72).

Thus, the null hypothesis is accepted.

All items in the Spirituality Rating Index (SRI) showed a strong positive correlation ($p < .01$) with the total score, confirming good predictive validity and item reliability.

Concurrent validity was confirmed through a high correlation (r = .802, $p < .01$) between SRI and the established Spiritual Well-Being Scale (Paloutzian & Ellison, 1991; Koenig & Al Zaben, 2021).

Reliability scores among Tamil Nadu prison inmates:

Overall Cronbach's alpha for SRI: .850

Dimensions:

Divine Connectedness: .706

Self Connectedness: .754

Other Connectedness: .784

Nature Connectedness: .762

Split-half reliability:

Part I (121 items): $\alpha = .743$

Part II (12 items): $\alpha = .811$

Correlation between parts:

Pearson's: .614

Spearman-Brown: .761

Guttman Split-Half: .748

These findings confirm that SRI is a reliable and valid tool to measure spirituality among prison inmates.

Findings Related to Index Validation

All the items of the index have manifested a positive correlation at a highly significant .01 level with the total score of the index indicating that each item score represents the aggregate spirituality score and thus can predict the overall spirituality indicating the good *predictive validity* of each item and *item reproducibility coefficient. Concurrent validity* of the Spirituality Rating Index was further established as there exists a high level of positive correlation, that is .802 at a highly significant .01 level between the scores of the Spirituality Rating Index (SRI) under validation and the already established Spiritual Well-Being Scale (SWBS) developed by (Paloutzian & Ellison, 1991).

As per the data of the present study among the prison inmates of Tamil Nadu, the Spirituality Rating Index (SRI) has established a *Cronbach's Alpha*, the index of internal consistency that showed a good level of reliability, that is, .850. The four dimensions of the Index have also scored Cronbach's alpha which indicate a good level of reliability, that is, .706 (Divine Connectedness), .754 (Self Connectedness), .784 (Other Connectedness), and .762 (Nature Connectedness). The *Split half analysis* revealed a good level of reliability of the Spirituality Rating Index (SRI) administered among the prison inmates of Tamil Nadu with a Cronbach's alpha of .743 for part I with 121 items and .811 for part 2 with 12 items. A high level of positive correlation is also found to exist between part 1 and part 2 with Karl Pearson's correlation coefficient at .614, Spearman-Brown coefficient at .761 and Guttmann Split Half coefficient at .748.

Feature Implication for Further Research Study

Future research should explore longitudinal studies to track changes in spiritual well-being among incarcerated individuals over time. Such studies can examine how spiritual practices evolve and identify strategies for effective rehabilitation and reintegration. Research must also consider cultural dimensions of spirituality, focusing on inmates' beliefs and practices (Lun & Bond, 2013), and how these shape spiritual well-being. Comparative studies can analyze differences between central prisons and open-air prisons, while category-specific studies can address the unique spiritual needs of diverse inmate groups. Qualitative research is essential to understand personal experiences and challenges related to spirituality in prison. Future work should evaluate the effectiveness of spiritual interventions such as meditation, prayer, and yoga in improving inmates' overall well-being, aiding correctional efforts, and enhancing quality of life.

The current study revealed that religion, prayer (before and after imprisonment), yoga practice, and type of prison had a highly significant impact on spiritual well-being (Shen, 2024). No significant association was found with age or sentence duration. Spiritual characteristics—personal belief in God, daily prayer, religious/existential/spiritual well-being, and divine/self/other/nature connectedness—were strongly linked to overall spirituality and spiritual well-being. However, parental family's faith and yoga/physical exercise showed no significant link with inmates' psychological general well-being. Religion, prayer (before and after imprisonment), yoga practice, and type of prison had a highly significant impact on inmates' spiritual well-being. In contrast, duration of sentence and age showed no significant association with spiritual well-being. The study revealed a strong correlation between spiritual characteristics (religion, belief in God, daily prayer, religious well-being, existential well-being, divine/self/other/nature connectedness) and psychological general well-being. However, no significant link was found between parental family's faith, yoga/physical exercise, and psychological well-being.

Validity and Reliability of SRI

The Spirituality Rating Index (SRI) showed good predictive validity and strong internal consistency (Cronbach's Alpha). It effectively measured overall spirituality among prison inmates.

Consistency and Reliability

The SRI demonstrated high reliability through split-half and parallel forms analysis, confirming its consistency across different index sections.

Psychological Well-Being Findings

The study found low psychological well-being, especially among older inmates, female inmates, and lifers. These groups require focused spiritual and emotional support.

Ethical Research Approach

The study followed strict ethical safeguards:

1. Oral consent was taken despite mandatory participation.

2. Sensitive questioning ensured trauma was not triggered.
3. Interviews were skipped if inmates were uncomfortable.
4. Confidentiality was strictly maintained.
5. No false promises—only empathetic listening and prayer were offered.

CONCLUSION

The exploratory research study aims to validate the Spiritual Well-being Index for the incarcerated population. The study findings provide insights to enhance the overall well-being of prisoners. The study develops a new index to demonstrate the psychometric properties; it can enhance the reliability and validity, making it a valuable tool for assessing the spiritual well-being of prison inmates. The study can emphasize the spirituality among incarcerated inmates. There are various factors involved, such as religious beliefs, faith in God, and their spiritual involvement, like prayer and yoga. This can be found to correlate with the positive aspects of psychological well-being among inmates. It suggests that spirituality can provide essential support for the rehabilitation efforts in the prison. The research study improves the spiritual well-being among the prison population; it includes the prison environment and their spiritual practices among the prison inmates themselves. The correctional setting should provide facilities that consider the spiritual needs of the inmates and offer an overall rehabilitation strategy for them. Finally, the spiritual well-being index for the incarcerated population provides the foundation for the framework for future research practices in correctional settings. Further research studies can be conducted for the long-term effort toward the spiritual well-being of rehabilitation outcomes. These studies can address the spiritual correction programs and increase the prisoners' mental and overall quality of life.

REFERENCES

Agtong, G. A., Bazer, A., Descuatan, K. A., & Ceballo, E. C. (2023). Life after imprisonment: Exploring the repercussions of jail time on ex-convicts. *Asian Research Journal of Arts & Social Sciences*, *21*(3), 61–77. DOI: 10.9734/arjass/2023/v21i3472

Albayrak, I. (2024). Prison Spirituality and Inner Peace. In *A Contemporary Turkish Prison Diary: Reflections on the Writings of Said Nursi and Aleksander Solzhenitsyn* (pp. 27-51). Singapore: Springer Nature Singapore. DOI: 10.1007/978-981-97-1564-0_2

Allen, R. S., Phillips, L. L., Roff, L. L., Cavanaugh, R., & Day, L. (2008). Religiousness/spirituality and mental health among older male inmates. *The Gerontologist*, *48*(5), 692–697. DOI: 10.1093/geront/48.5.692 PMID: 18981285

Amitay, G., & Ronel, N. (2023). The practice of spiritual criminology: A non-doing companionship for crime desistance. *International Journal of Offender Therapy and Comparative Criminology*, *67*(4), 420–441. DOI: 10.1177/0306624X211066828 PMID: 34994230

Appiah, S. O. (2022). *Work-Life Conflict, Personal Resources and Well-Being of Employees in The Ghana Prisons Service* (Doctoral dissertation, University of Cape Coast). https://ir.ucc.edu.gh/xmlui/handle/123456789/11136

Auty, K. M., Cope, A., & Liebling, A. (2017). A systematic review and meta-analysis of yoga and mindfulness meditation in prison: Effects on psychological well-being and behavioural functioning. *International Journal of Offender Therapy and Comparative Criminology*, *61*(6), 689–710. DOI: 10.1177/0306624X15602514 PMID: 26320031

Bondeson, U. (2017). *Prisoners in prison societies*. Routledge., DOI: 10.4324/9781351308120

Clammer, J., & Clammer, J. (2016). Cultural Resources for Sustainability. *Cultures of Transition and Sustainability: Culture after Capitalism*, 41-64. DOI: 10.1057/978-1-137-52033-3_3

Clark, L. A., & Watson, D. (2019). Constructing validity: New developments in creating objective measuring instruments. *Psychological Assessment*, *31*(12), 1412–1427. https://psycnet.apa.org/buy/2019-14248-001. DOI: 10.1037/pas0000626 PMID: 30896212

Clear, T. R., Hardyman, P. L., Stout, B., Lucken, K., & Dammer, H. R. (2000). The value of religion in prison: An inmate perspective. *Journal of Contemporary Criminal Justice, 16*(1), 53–74. DOI: 10.1177/1043986200016001004

Daaleman, T. P., & Frey, B. B. (2004). The spirituality index of well-being: A new instrument for health-related quality-of-life research. *Annals of Family Medicine, 2*(5), 499–503. DOI: 10.1370/afm.89 PMID: 15506588

Deuchar, R., Mørck, L. L., Matemba, Y. H., McLean, R., & Riaz, N. (2016). 'It's as if you're not in the Jail, as if you're not a Prisoner': Young Male Offenders' Experiences of Incarceration, Prison Chaplaincy, Religion and Spirituality in Scotland and Denmark. *The Howard Journal of Crime and Justice*, *55*(1-2), 131–150. DOI: 10.1111/hojo.12160

Dev, P. S., Eljo, J. J. G., & Srinivasan, S. (2025). Navigating Mental Health Challenges in the Care of Elderly With Disabilities in Kerala: A Gerontological Social Work Perspective. In *Modern Digital Approaches to Care Technologies for Individuals With Disabilities* (pp. 33-56). IGI Global Scientific Publishing. DOI: 10.4018/979-8-3693-7560-0.ch003

Dougall, M. (2024). *"Personal Relationship With God": A Mixed-Methods Exploration of Religion and Spirituality Within Formerly Incarcerated Peoples' Desistance Process* (Master's thesis, University of Maryland, College Park). https://www.proquest.com/openview/94aca2149d2ac7b1fba4b04b2802f975/1?cbl=18750&diss=y&pq-origsite=gscholar

Duncan, J., Stansfield, R., Hall, S., & O'Connor, T. (2018). Women's engagement with humanist, spiritual and religious meaning-making in prison: A longitudinal study of its impact on recidivism. *Religions*, *9*(6), 171. DOI: 10.3390/rel9060171

Dutch, S. I. (2002). Religion as belief versus religion as fact. *Journal of Geoscience Education*, *50*(2), 137–144. DOI: 10.5408/1089-9995-50.2.137

Edward, M. (2021). *Mindfulness-based stress reduction in a correctional facility: A systematic literature review and meta-analysis on the impact of violent behaviour* (Doctoral dissertation, The University of Waikato). https://researchcommons.waikato.ac.nz/entities/publication/9b6daac6-117d-45a3-89ce-4c4adcce8e25

Ferrer, J. N. (2011). Participatory spirituality and transpersonal theory: A ten-year retrospective. *Journal of Transpersonal Psychology*, *43*(1), 1–34. https://psycnet.apa.org/record/2012-06273-001

Fletcher, S. K. (2004). Religion and life meaning: Differentiating between religious beliefs and religious community in constructing life meaning. *Journal of Aging Studies*, *18*(2), 171–185. DOI: 10.1016/j.jaging.2004.01.005

Goldberg, K. (2001). Inside-out: a study of Vipassana meditation as taught by SN Goenka and its social contribution. https://escholarship.mcgill.ca/concern/theses/p5547t26d

Guimarães, N. S., de Paula, W., de Aguiar, A. S., & Meireles, A. L. (2021). Absence of religious beliefs, unhealthy eating habits, illicit drug abuse, and self-rated health is associated with alcohol and tobacco use among college students—PADu study. *Journal of Public Health*, •••, 1–9. DOI: 10.1007/s10389-020-01440-7

Heck, P. L. (2006). Mysticism as morality: The case of Sufism. *The Journal of Religious Ethics*, *34*(2), 253–286. DOI: 10.1111/j.1467-9795.2006.00268.x

Huber, S., & Huber, O. W. (2012). The centrality of religiosity scale (CRS). *Religions*, *3*(3), 710–724. DOI: 10.3390/rel3030710

Hughes, Q. A. (2023). *The Implementation of Trauma Informed Design in the United States Prison Campus: A Standardized Design Methodology*. Rochester Institute of Technology. https://www.proquest.com/openview/540602144dacec9d8786474a61f21c00/1?cbl=18750&diss=y&pq-origsite=gscholar

Kalkbrenner, M. T. (2021). A Practical Guide to Instrument Development and Score Validation in the Social Sciences: The MEASURE Approach. *Practical Assessment, Research & Evaluation*, *26*, 1. https://eric.ed.gov/?id=EJ1311131

Kazemian, L. (2019). *Positive growth and redemption in prison: Finding light behind bars and beyond*. Routledge., DOI: 10.4324/9780429458149

Kerekes, N., Fielding, C., & Apelqvist, S. (2017). Yoga in correctional settings: A randomized controlled study. *Frontiers in Psychiatry*, *8*, 204. DOI: 10.3389/fpsyt.2017.00204 PMID: 29085307

Koenig, H. G., & Al Zaben, F. (2021). Psychometric validation and translation of religious and spiritual measures. *Journal of Religion and Health*, *60*(5), 3467–3483. DOI: 10.1007/s10943-021-01373-9 PMID: 34331172

Kothari, C. R. (2004). Research methodology: Methods and techniques. *New Age International*. https://qnamuni.dspace.vn/bitstream/QNA/1934/1/1.%20Research_methodology_methods_and_techniq.pdf

Kumar, N. (2022). *Mental health and well-being: an Indian psychology perspective*. Routledge India., DOI: 10.4324/9781003350651

Lambert, L. S., & Newman, D. A. (2023). Construct development and validation in three practical steps: Recommendations for reviewers, editors, and authors. *Organizational Research Methods, 26*(4), 574-607. https://doi.org/DOI: 10.1177/10944281221115374

Levin, J. (2009). How faith heals: A theoretical model. *Explore (New York, N.Y.), 5*(2), 77–96. DOI: 10.1016/j.explore.2008.12.003 PMID: 19272579

Levitt, L., & Loper, A. B. (2009). The influence of religious participation on the adjustment of female inmates. *The American Journal of Orthopsychiatry, 79*(1), 1–7. DOI: 10.1037/a0015429 PMID: 19290720

Luckeenarain, R. D. (2015). *A Pilot Feasibility Study of Mindfulness Training for Young People* (Doctoral dissertation, King's College, London). https://kclpure.kcl.ac.uk/ws/portalfiles/portal/42430510/2015_Luckeenarain_Ruma_0959412_ethesis.pdf

Lun, V. M. C., & Bond, M. H. (2013). Examining the relation of religion and spirituality to subjective well-being across national cultures. *Psychology of Religion and Spirituality, 5*(4), 304–315. DOI: 10.1037/a0033641

Mahmoudi-Dehaki, M., Nasr-Esfahani, N., & Vasan, S. (2025). The Transformative Role of Assistive Technology in Enhancing Quality of Life for Individuals With Disabilities. In *Assistive Technology Solutions for Aging Adults and Individuals With Disabilities* (pp. 45–72). IGI Global Scientific Publishing., DOI: 10.4018/979-8-3693-6308-9.ch003

Malinakova, K., Kopcakova, J., Kolarcik, P., Geckova, A. M., Solcova, I. P., Husek, V., Kracmarova, L. H., Dubovska, E., Kalman, M., Puzova, Z., Van Dijk, J. P., & Tavel, P. (2017). The Spiritual Well-Being Scale: Psychometric evaluation of the shortened version in Czech adolescents. *Journal of Religion and Health, 56*(2), 697–705. DOI: 10.1007/s10943-016-0318-4 PMID: 27787695

Martin, D. (2002). Dialogue and spirituality: The art of being human in a changing world. In *Dialogue as a means of collective communication* (pp. 71–103). Springer US., DOI: 10.1007/0-306-48690-3_5

Maruna, S., Wilson, L., & Curran, K. (2015). Why God is often found behind bars: Prison conversions and the crisis of self-narrative. In *Second Chances As Transformative Stories Rhd V3 2&3* (pp. 161–184). Psychology Press., https://www.taylorfrancis.com/chapters/edit/10.4324/9780203764022-6/god-often-found-behind-bars-prison-conversions-crisis-self-narrative-shadd-maruna-louise-wilson-kathryn-curran

Maschi, T., Viola, D., & Sun, F. (2013). The high cost of the international aging prisoner crisis: Well-being as the common denominator for action. *The Gerontologist*, *53*(4), 543–554. DOI: 10.1093/geront/gns125 PMID: 23042691

Mazour-Matusevich, Y. (2006). Gerson's Legacy. *A Companion to Jean Gerson*, 357-399. https://doi.org/DOI: 10.1163/9789047409076_011

McSherry, W., & Cash, K. (2004). The language of spirituality: An emerging taxonomy. *International Journal of Nursing Studies*, *41*(2), 151–161. DOI: 10.1016/S0020-7489(03)00114-7 PMID: 14725779

Melvin, A. T. (2021). *An Analysis of Growth in Spirituality as a Means of Evaluating the Effectiveness of the Columbia International University Prison Initiative*. Columbia International University. https://www.proquest.com/openview/95bb07db545dbd10655dd505a8fae240/1?cbl=18750&diss=y&pq-origsite=gscholar

Moradi, H. (2019). *Review of Tests*. Measurements and Research Methods in Behavioural Sciences., DOI: 10.32601/ejal.543793

Muller, A. E., & Bukten, A. (2019). Measuring the quality of life of incarcerated individuals. *International Journal of Prisoner Health*, *15*(1), 1–13. DOI: 10.1108/IJPH-02-2018-0005 PMID: 30827162

Ndung'u, M. P. (2021). The role of religious strategies in coping with stress, and enhancement of the psychological well being of life sentenced inmates in maximum prisons in Kenya. *Journal of African Interdisciplinary Studies*, *5*(4), 81–97. https://kenyasocialscienceforum.wordpress.com/wp-content/uploads/2021/05/pdf-ndungu-the-role-of-religious-strategies-in-coping-with-stress.pdf

Nelson, J. M. (2009). *Religion, Spirituality and Public Health. Psychology, Religion and Spirituality. New York: Springer*. The Guilford Press.

Oxford Dictionary. Definition of Prison. Oxford University Press. Retrieved from https://en.oxforddictionaries.com/definition/spirituality

Paloutzian, R. F., & Ellison, C. W. (1991). Manual for the spiritual well-being scale. *Nyack, NY: Life Advance, 9*, 35-48. https://www.westmont.edu/sites/default/files/users/user401/SWBS%20Manual%202.0_0.pdf

Panzini, R. G., Mosqueiro, B. P., Zimpel, R. R., Bandeira, D. R., Rocha, N. S., & Fleck, M. P. (2017). Quality-of-life and spirituality. *International Review of Psychiatry (Abingdon, England)*, *29*(3), 263–282. DOI: 10.1080/09540261.2017.1285553 PMID: 28587554

Parameshwar, S. (2005). Spiritual leadership through ego-transcendence: Exceptional responses to challenging circumstances. *The Leadership Quarterly*, *16*(5), 689–722. DOI: 10.1016/j.leaqua.2005.07.004

Pham, K. H. (2013). *Outcomes of a recreation therapy yoga meditation intervention on prison inmates' spiritual well-being*. San Jose State University. https://www.proquest.com/openview/ccf3423ad72ffe79c0f34555808478f2/1?cbl=18750&pq-origsite=gscholar

Pratt, J. (2013). The acceptable prison: official discourse, truth and legitimacy in the nineteenth century. In *Crime, Truth and Justice* (pp. 71-88). Willan. https://www.taylorfrancis.com/chapters/edit/10.4324/9781843924388-7/acceptable-prison-official-discourse-truth-legitimacy-nineteenth-century-john-pratt

Radhakrishnan, S., Allien, G., & AT, C. Ramakrishna Mission Vidyamandira. *HISTORY, 5*, 6. https://vidyamandira.ac.in/pdfs/libDB/philo.pdf

Raju, M. L. (2010). *Gandhi and His Resistance to Hegemony. Social Work Journal. 1 (2)*. Department of Social Work, Assam University.

Reave, L. (2005). Spiritual values and practices related to leadership effectiveness. *The Leadership Quarterly*, *16*(5), 655–687. DOI: 10.1016/j.leaqua.2005.07.003

Saroglou, V. (2011). Believing, bonding, behaving, and belonging: The big four religious dimensions and cultural variation. *Journal of Cross-Cultural Psychology*, *42*(8), 1320–1340. DOI: 10.1177/0022022111412267

Seligman, M. E., & Csikszentmihalyi, M. (2000). *No. 1* (Vol. 55). Positive psychology: An introduction. American Psychological Association.

Selman, L., Harding, R., Gysels, M., Speck, P., & Higginson, I. J. (2011). The measurement of spirituality in palliative care and the content of tools validated cross-culturally: A systematic review. *Journal of Pain and Symptom Management*, *41*(4), 728–753. DOI: 10.1016/j.jpainsymman.2010.06.023 PMID: 21306866

Shen, A. (2024). Mental Health and Yoga in Prisons. *Journal of Criminal Law*, *88*(4), 258–281. DOI: 10.1177/00220183241265170

Siddiqui, R. N. (2025). Diversity, Cultural Bonding and Social Resilience. In *Building a Resilient and Responsible World: Psychological Perspectives from India* (pp. 87-97). Singapore: Springer Nature Singapore. https://doi.org/DOI: 10.1007/978-981-96-0108-0_5

Snyder, C. R., & Lopez, J. Shane & Pedrotti, Jennifer Teramoto (2011). *Positive Psychology – The Scientific and Practical Explorations of Human Strengths.* New Delhi: Sage Publications. pp: 19-26; 58-67; 261

Spirago, F., & Clarke, R. (2014). *The Catechism Explained.* Benziger Brothers, Inc., New York, pp: 4. Retrieved from https://catholicebooks.wordpress.com/2014/09/17/free-ebook

Srinivasan, S., & Rajavel, N. (2025). A Study of the Psychological Well-Being of Tamil Nadu Prison Inmates With Special Reference of AI. In Wongmahesak, K., & Marzo, R. (Eds.), *AI Technologies and Advancements for Psychological Well-Being and Healthcare* (pp. 219–254). IGI Global Scientific Publishing., DOI: 10.4018/979-8-3693-9158-7.ch009

Srinivasan, S., & Rajavel, N. (2025). Artificial Intelligence Approach to Psychological Wellbeing Among the Ageing Population. In Wongmahesak, K., & Marzo, R. (Eds.), *AI Technologies and Advancements for Psychological Well-Being and Healthcare* (pp. 187–218). IGI Global Scientific Publishing., DOI: 10.4018/979-8-3693-9158-7.ch008

Srinivasan, S., & Rajavel, N. (2025). Technology Improves the Quality of Life for Elderly People. In *Perspectives on the Economics of Aging* (pp. 109–150). IGI Global Scientific Publishing., DOI: 10.4018/979-8-3693-7753-6.ch005

Srinivasan, S., Rajavel, N., & Mahmoudi-Dehaki, M. (2025). Elderly Inmates Living With Dementia in Central Prisons. In *Assistive Technology Solutions for Aging Adults and Individuals With Disabilities* (pp. 343–404). IGI Global Scientific Publishing., DOI: 10.4018/979-8-3693-6308-9.ch015

Srinivasan, S., Rajavel, N., & Sanchez, N. K. (2025). The Impact of AI on Elderly Inmates in Central Prison. In *Exploration of AI in Contemporary Legal Systems* (pp. 281–314). IGI Global Scientific Publishing., DOI: 10.4018/979-8-3693-7205-0.ch013

Stamm, L. (2006). The dynamics of spirituality and the religious experience. *Religious Education (Chicago, Ill.), 33*(2), 91–113. DOI: 10.1080/15507394.2006.10012378

Valmiki, A. (2015). M.K. Gandhi's concept of religion: a philosophical introspection. *West East Journal of Social Sciences, 4*(1/2), 52.https://westeastinstitute.com/journals/wp-content/uploads/2015/11/6Amita-Valmiki.pdf

Van Niekerk, B. (2018). Religion and spirituality: What are the fundamental differences? *Hervormde Teologiese Studies, 74*(3), 1–11. https://journals.co.za/doi/abs/10.4102/hts.v74i3.4933. DOI: 10.4102/hts.v74i3.4933

Vieten, C., Scammell, S., Pilato, R., Ammondson, I., Pargament, K. I., & Lukoff, D. (2013). Spiritual and religious competencies for psychologists. *Psychology of Religion and Spirituality*, *5*(3), 129–144. DOI: 10.1037/a0032699

Walker, J. K. (2019). *The contribution of informal learning to spiritual development in later life* (Doctoral dissertation, University of Southampton). https://eprints.soton.ac.uk/442176/

Wiktionary (2017). Spirituality. Retrieve from https://en.m.wiktionary.org

Yang, C. T., Yen, S. Y., & Chen, J. O. (2010). Spiritual well-being: A concept analysis. *Hu li za zhi. Journal of Nursing (Luton, England)*, *57*(3), 99–104. https://europepmc.org/article/med/20535684 PMID: 20535684

Yust, K. M. (2016). Adolescent spirituality and education. *Spirituality across Disciplines: Research and Practice:*, 81-93. DOI: 10.1007/978-3-319-31380-1_7

Chapter 16
Technology, Artificial Intelligence, and the Era of Information in Healthcare and Allied Sciences

Sudrita Roy Choudhury
https://orcid.org/0000-0002-5205-0590
Swami Vivekananda University, India

Khusboo Singh
https://orcid.org/0000-0001-6374-0485
Swami Vivekananda University, India

Samarpita Koner
Swami Vivekananda University, India

Joyeta Ghosh
https://orcid.org/0000-0001-9619-1793
Amity University, Kolkata, India

ABSTRACT

This chapter examines the transformative impact of technology, artificial intelligence (AI), and information proliferation on healthcare and allied sciences. It explores advancements in telemedicine, wearable devices, and AI applications in diagnostics and drug discovery. The role of big data analytics in identifying health trends and informing policy is discussed, alongside ethical considerations of AI-driven health-

DOI: 10.4018/979-8-3693-9755-8.ch016

care. The chapter also addresses future trends, including genomics-AI integration and quantum computing in drug development. This overview illuminates how these interconnected forces are reshaping healthcare, driving precision medicine, and evolving the roles of healthcare professionals in an increasingly tech-driven landscape.

1. INTRODUCTION

The 21st century saw an unprecedented combination of technology, AI, and healthcare. This partnership has ushered in information-centric medicine, changing healthcare delivery, research, and experience. AI and advanced technology in healthcare and related sectors have opened new doors for diagnosis, treatment, and patient care, but they have also presented new ethical challenges. Due to an aging population and increased rates of chronic diseases, global societies require better healthcare (Ghosh et al., 2024ab; Taneja et al.,2025;Shakil et al.,2024). Because of growing demand and financial constraints that cannot be resolved by resource augmentation, society must provide healthcare in a sustainable manner. Innovation and quality enhancement lead to better health outcomes without increasing expenditures (Bergman et al. 2015; Ghosh et al., 2024b).

In this chapter, the intersection of information systems, technology, and artificial intelligence in healthcare and related fields is examined. It uses the Technological Innovation Systems (TIS) paradigm to identify systemic difficulties in AI integration, analyzes current applications of AI, and assesses the transformative potential of AI across clinical, administrative, and organizational dimensions. Data-driven decision-making, robots, machine learning, and natural language processing are all discussed, with an emphasis on the advantages and disadvantages of each. Digital health, medical practice, diagnostics, medical equipment, and life sciences innovation are all included in the scope.

AI might accelerate healthcare innovation. Healthcare is data-intensive, and the availability of large amounts of data, processing capacity, and artificial intelligence methods have created promising opportunities. AI-driven advancements aim to mimic human cognitive powers, and robots using large volumes of data may be swiftly interpreted and managed by AI systems. AI can algorithmically identify tiny patterns and correlations in data in the big data age, eliminating the need for more healthcare professionals to examine it. The development of intelligent artificial prostheses (Ortiz-Catalan et al. 2013), the prediction of cardiac surgery mortality (Nilsson et al. 2006), and the diagnosis of skin cancer with an efficacy on par with or superior to dermatologists (Esteva et al. 2017; Haenssle et al. 2018) are just a few of the numerous healthcare applications of AI. However, compared to other industries, the healthcare sector has a low level of digitalization and AI integration (Apell, P., et al 2023). and there are macro, meso, and micro barriers.

According to Ghosh (2023), healthcare is a dynamic, complex socio-technical system with interconnected functional components. For evaluating the form and functioning of innovation systems, the socio-technical analytical framework of Technological Innovation Systems (TIS) is crucial (Bergek, A. 2019). Functional dynamics have been applied in several TIS investigations, such as offshore wind technologies and biorefinery development (Reichardt, K.et al. 2016). To the authors' knowledge, there are few TIS studies in the healthcare business, but no research study or review has used TIS to assess AI healthcare technology innovation systems. Our goal is to contribute to this subject by researching the possible expansion of the TIS framework into additional domains and finding flaws and development prospects. To provide a comprehensive understanding of healthcare innovation processes,(Markard, J., et al 2015) the researchers employed TIS to investigate the effectiveness and systemic obstacles of AI healthcare technology advancements pertinent to the life sciences organization.

Figure 1. Applications of AI in Healthcare (Bergman et al. 2015)

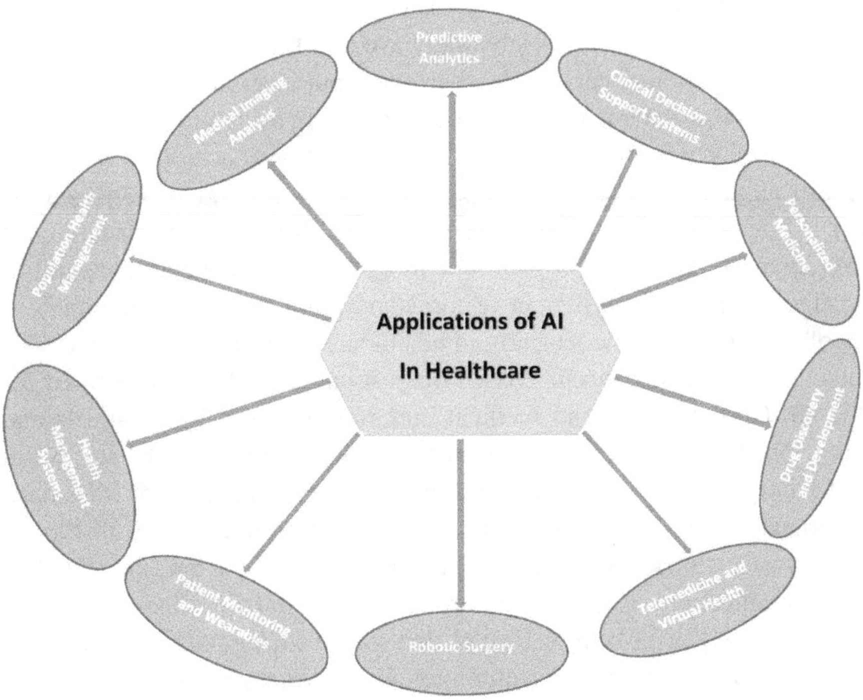

Patients benefit substantially from artificial intelligence in healthcare. In order to detect and differentiate between sick and reasonably healthy people and to improve their comprehension of biological indicators of health changes, researchers must examine large amounts of patient data as well as more general criteria (Guyatt, G. H et al 2002; Banka et al.,2025). AI might manage supplier, payer, and pharmaceutical company patient care and administrative operations. AI gadgets are beating radiologists in identifying critical cancers and advising researchers on pricey clinical trial consortia (Sharma, P., et al 2024;Taneja et al.,2025). Our healthcare system uses AI and robotics. AI devices will complement doctors' and other healthcare workers' work. Healthcare workers may find AI useful for image analysis, medical device management, clinical documentation, patient outreach, administrative duties, and patient monitoring. Therefore, it is necessary to keep an eye on AI advances (Catania, L. J., et al. 2018;). Medical diagnosis, robotic-assisted surgery, clinical trials, training, fraud detection, and drug development are among the twelve main healthcare AI applications depicted in Figure 1. Stroke management, artificial neurons, spinal cord surgery, organ transplantation, plastic surgery, and cardiac tissue chips. AI in healthcare and related goods and applications are examined in this paper.

Like the human brain, artificial neural networks (ANN) have non-linear correlations between input and output variables . Artificial neural networks were created in 1958 and became popular because of data capacity and complexity (Singh, A. K.,et al. 2023). Artificial Neural Networks have input, hidden, and output layers. Implementing a function at each node gives the input layer data. The hidden layer nodes receive a balanced linear mixture of inputs from all input layer components and apply a non-linear activation function. The output layer acts like the concealed layer. It uses an activation function to output buried layer signals (Sharma, S., et al. 2017). AI devices have two main categories: (a) ML analyzes structured data including genetic, electrophysiological, and imaging data. Therapeutically, machine learning algorithms evaluate patient features and predict sickness outcomes. The majority of classical machine learning in healthcare is used in precision medicine to evaluate therapeutic approaches based on past patient outcomes (Ahmed, Z., et al. 2020). (b) Clinical notes and medical literature are used by natural language processing (NLP) to enrich standardized medical data (Sheikhalishahi, S., et al 2019). NLP converts texts into structured, machine-readable data for ML analysis. Natural Language Processing focuses on human-computer interaction. NLP systems quickly analyze scientific data and filter out irrelevant spam from files. NLP helps healthcare organizations isolate complex data. Artificial Intelligence in Natural Language Processing gives healthcare real-time data from reputable sources. Virtual healthcare assistants use medical terminology-activated natural language processing models (Zhou, B., et al. 2022).

2. REVOLUTIONARY EFFECTS OF WEARABLES, AI, AND TELEMEDICINE ON DRUG DISCOVERY AND DIAGNOSTICS

Modern healthcare is being revolutionized by the combination of wearable technology, telemedicine, and artificial intelligence (AI) in drug discovery and diagnostics. In-person consultations, laborious data collection, and trial-and-error methods in medication development and diagnostics have been major components of traditional healthcare methods. According to Baig, Z. A. (2012), these traditional solutions are frequently time-consuming, reactive rather than preventive, and constrained by infrastructure and geographic limitations. By enabling real-time data interpretation, predictive analytics, and remote patient monitoring via telemedicine platforms and smart wearables, AI-driven solutions, on the other hand, have brought about a paradigm shift (Majeed, A., et al., 2024,Ghosh et al.,2024d). Smartwatches and biosensors are examples of wearables that continually monitor vital indicators, allowing for proactive health treatments, early anomaly detection, and more individualized treatment strategies. According to Barbosa, W., et al (2021), telemedicine improves access to healthcare services, particularly in underserved or rural areas, and cuts down on delays in diagnosis and treatment. Additionally, by predicting drug efficacy and toxicity, identifying molecular targets, and improving compound screening, AI speeds up drug development while drastically cutting down on the time and expense associated with conventional pharmaceutical research (Sarkar, C., et al 2023;Ghosh 2024). In addition to enhancing clinical results, these developments support a more patient-centered, data-driven, and effective healthcare system. By integrating AI technologies, the healthcare industry is undergoing a major transformation from reactive to predictive and from generalized to individualized care.

3. AI IN DIAGNOSTIC IMAGING AND RADIOLOGY

AI is used extensively in diagnostic imaging and radiology. Machine learning algorithms, particularly deep learning models, can estimate medical images with accuracy comparable to or better than human professionals. Diagnostic radiography is a graduate career in the UK and worldwide that requires sophisticated practical and critical thinking abilities to maximize picture capture and coordinate patient care alongside medical radiologists. Radiography relies on imaging. Radiography and radiology depend on image acquisition and analysis technologies. The field of radiography has changed to accommodate new technology and its enhanced imaging capabilities (Cowen, A. R., et al 2007).However, creative imaging techniques have not been the emphasis of recent technology advancements. It is necessary to look at how their employment of sophisticated machine learning algorithms and artificial intelligence systems in image processing and equipment operation has affected radiography practice. (Nichols, J. A., etal.2019) The theory and creation of computer systems that are capable of human-like functions, such as voice recognition, visual perception, prediction, and decision-making, are all included in artificial intelligence (AI).(Asensio, J. M. L., et al 2014) It is a data-dependent paradigm that works well with contemporary medical imaging technologies, particularly those using computer vision. There has been a recent surge in industry and academic concepts for AI uses in diagnostic imaging. The majority have concentrated on radiologists and their support, but a new field is tied to radiography. Cowling, C. (2008)

Radiographers have long used automated technologies, which some may view as reducing their skills, responsibilities, and independence. Digitization and automation have improved imaging department efficiency and throughput.(Hanna, M. G., et al. 2019) However, evidence suggests that increased patient workloads and faster examinations may lower radiographer morale, job satisfaction, and burnout. Parker, S. K., et al. (2022). Professional leaders and employers that fail to examine the effects of developing automation technologies on professional and workplace cultures and job flexibility are to blame. In order to close this gap, we look at how the position of the radiographer can change in response to advances in intelligent technology, the opportunities they provide, and the actions that should be taken to maintain the radiography profession's active participation in the development and use of AI systems. (Parker, S. K., et al 2022) AI has been a part of visual technology for decades. automated exposure device in general radiography for the first time in the 1980s. (Holzinger, A., et al 2022)The apparatus calculated the final mAs for each exposure by sensing when enough quanta reached the film to provide a diagnostic image, while the radiographer selected the kV value for X-ray imaging. Assuming the machine could make these judgments more correctly than the radiographer, this procedure transferred decision-making from the radiographer to the machine rather than diagnosing or interpreting pictures. Both the organization and the patient benefited from the decreased number of repeat photos brought on by improper exposure and the optimum dose of the examination. Radiographers employed this method to take pictures and treat patients, particularly when the patient's body habitus affected the quality of the images. Because of the shortcomings in the technology, human oversight was still required. (Blaxter, M. 2009).

Similar to prior technologies, AI systems that automate radiographic decision-making need clinical demonstration and radiographer approval before general adoption. However, modern AI systems can automate a greater range of complex cognitive activities, thus they require more inspection and justification before usage. AI has been studied in mammography, ultrasound (Rodríguez-Ruiz, A., et al 2019), and nuclear medicine (Seifert, R., et al 2021), but projectional radiography and cross-sectional imaging image acquisition methodologies have not. Given the growing need for these modalities, we believe AI will have the most influence on radiography practice going forward (Bergman et al. 2015) .Given the variety of cross-sectional imaging tasks radiographers perform (Figure 1) and identified areas for AI automation, AI will greatly improve their function. However, full implementation of such technologies may reduce radiographers' duties (Matilainen, K., et al 2017). Therefore, healthcare companies must properly understand and manage the risks and liabilities while also looking at how AI technology might increase the throughput and efficiency of the radiology department. Current rules require human oversight and auditing of AI systems used in clinical settings (Matilainen, K., et al 2017).Thus, providers may only create systems and promote them as requiring human oversight. This requires radiography professionalstobe skilled at managing AI-driven semi-automated procedures. Radiographers have seldom discussed the professional constraints of integrating AI technology and increasing picture capturing automation in professional and industrial literature ((Matilainen, K., et al 2017). This may indicate a resigned acceptance of AI's inevitable growth, professional difficulty in understanding its huge consequences, or a developed indifference as a buffer against change or anxiety (Parker, S. K et al 2022). This contrasts with radiologists' debates on diagnostic AI as a solution to radiology reporting backlogs. Since 2015, radiology journal articles addressing, debating, and assessing AI have increased dramatically (Cowling, C. 2008), as radiologists quickly addressed initial concerns about job displacement and obsolescence by arguing that AI automation is a supportive and enhancing technology. Mazurowski, M. A. (2019). This increase in interest and discussion among radiologists may be the result of protectionism and role preservation, but it has also brought attention to the value of the human worker in the imaging process, which is usually disregarded in the pursuit of cost and service reductions. (Barbosa, W., et al 2021)

3.1 Enhancing Accuracy and Efficiency

In order to aid in diagnosis, AI-powered image analysis systems may be able to swiftly identify anomalies in medical pictures such as MRIs, CT scans, and X-rays. A deep learning system was able to classify skin cancer like dermatologists, according to Akhter, Y., et al 2023. AI systems may also detect diabetic retinopathy, breast cancer in mammograms, and lung nodules in chest X-rays. AI may increase diagnosis accuracy, patient outcomes, and staff efficiency. CT and MR imaging exams in the UK increased 54% and 48% from 2013 to 2018, while the radiology workforce grew 19% (Konstantinidis, K. 2024). . The number of diagnostic imaging procedures and advances in slice amount, reconstructions, and sequences have increased the number of images evaluated each patient. Reducing examination reading time may reduce pediatric radiologists' burnout. (Ayyala, R. S., et al2019).Computer-aided detection (CAD) simplifies diagnosis, saving reading time. Research suggests that using CAD tools reduced reading time for usual cases and somewhat increased it for pathological ones (Sharma, P., et al 2024).In addition to AI system quality, workflow integration is crucial to this software's success. Enemosah, A. (2025).found that vascular suppression in CT thorax imaging reduced reading time for pulmonary metastasis by 21%. Images can be enhanced to speed up collection and detection.

Customized diagnostics

AI algorithms can improve precision medicine by predicting risks and outcomes based on individual features instead of population data. This may improve health outcomes and help allocate resources like therapy or testing to those most likely to benefit. AI-generated brain volume measurements were used to predict the need for invasive Alzheimer's disease testing in neurology, and this model achieved high diagnostic accuracy with only 26% of the population (level 4) undergoing biomarker testing. In a similar vein, researchers showed prospectively that ultrasonography may be used to evaluate thyroid lesions without biopsies when malignancy risk was predicted using a commercial AI tool (level 4). Breast density classification in breast cancer screening personalizes the approach. Women with dense breast tissue have a higher cancer risk (Gastounioti, A., et al 2016). Automated screening allows women with large breasts to have more frequent exams or use magnetic resonance imaging. A Dutch study of over 40,000 women with dense breast tissue used commercial AI software to show that supplemental MR screening (level 5) reduced interval tumors. Abdallah, S., et al. (2023). Clinical characteristics and genetic data may improve tailored predictions. This is rare in commercial AI-driven radiography software.

3.2 Workflow Optimization

Besides enhancing diagnosis accuracy, AI streamlines radiologists' procedures. AI techniques can assist radiologists prioritize critical patients and identify problems, lowering burnout and enhancing productivity (Bhandari, A et al., 2024).

3.2.1. More efficient workflow

As global health care costs rise, finite resources must be used efficiently. AI may help clinically and non-clinically. To maximize scheduling efficiency, AI software can schedule imaging sessions and anticipate no-shows before a patient arrives in radiology (Al Serkal et al., 2025) created a model to predict which patients will miss appointments most. No-show rates dropped from 19.3% to 15.9% for patients who received phone calls (Chong LR et al 2020). Most of these methods address border circumstances like patient management, not patient identification or diagnosis. Thus, the applications are safer and require less regulations before clinical usage. However, such software is limited in accessibility and execution, offering corporate growth chances. Modifying the diagnosis method using AI can improve workflow. AI for chest radiography TB detection is a proven application (Qin, Z. et al 2021). AI-assisted TB detection is especially useful in developing countries with limited manpower, knowledge, and funds. This can replace time-consuming and expensive microbiological testing (levels 2, 3, 6) as an independent pre-screening tool (Gunter, H et al 2023). One of the first AI radiology programs, the software performs radiologist duties independently. AI for process optimization is being studied in numerous use cases, but not in clinical practice. An alternate workflow for mammography screening uses an AI risk score to determine the number of radiological interpretations (none, single, or double), reducing reading time (level 3) (Schaffter et al., 2020). To improve CT lung nodule diagnosis, technicians might use AI, shifting some of the work to radiologists (level 3). Artificial intelligence allows computers to perform tasks that humans can . AI can forecast, reduce dimensionality, integrate data, reason about basic processes, and turn large datasets into clinically useful insights from optimum datasets. Learning capacity was increased by optimizing the identification task using performance indicators appropriate to the situation. Machine learning and deep learning are now essential to the analysis of biological data because of the expansion of medical data and the quick development of analytical tools (Mahmud, M. et al., 2021). Artificial intelligence is currently used to automate data extraction, summarization, integration, and cloud storage .ANN, machine learning, and deep learning are all components of artificial intelligence. We can evaluate the probability of illness using AI and high-performance computers with patient data. AI and machine learning transform vast volumes of data into clinical information. According to studies, these methods have enhanced the prediction of illness risk. Precision AI and genomic medicine have the potential to greatly benefit companies and advance knowledge of chronic illnesses (Subramanian, M. et al,. 2020)

4. PHARMACOGENOMICS

Figure 2. Machine learning and artificial intelligence in precision and genomic medicine.

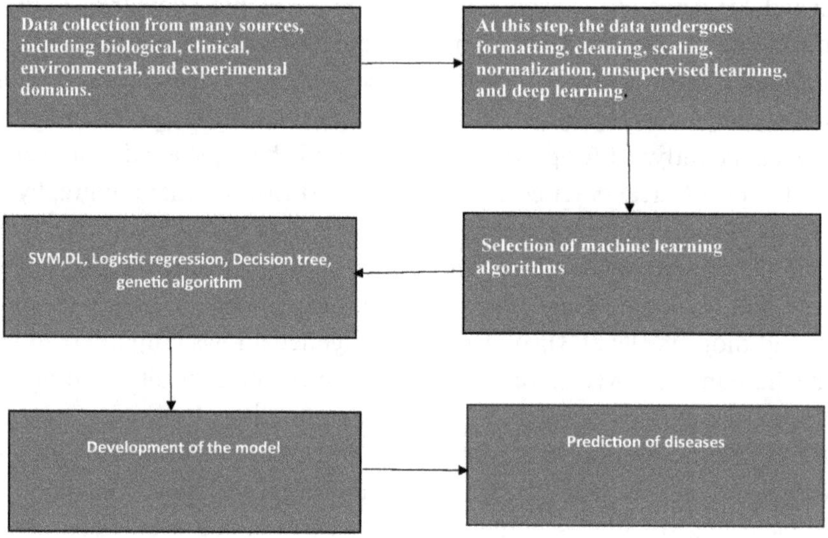

Because it can enable individualized mental health therapy, precision psychiatry—a multidisciplinary discipline that blends psychiatry, precision medicine, and pharmacogenomics—is growing in importance in the medical profession. Precision medicine and pharmacogenomics are commonly conflated. Precision psychiatry is enhanced by pharmacogenomics, the study of how genes and their activities affect drug responses. Patients with mental illnesses can receive customized medical treatments, therapies, and practices through precision psychiatry (Scala, J. et al., 2023).Precision psychiatry uses multi-omics and neuroimaging datasets to classify all mental illness patients by biomarkers. Genetic biomarkers and imaging features can be used to personalize medications for each patient . More genetic biomarkers and imaging features may improve mental disease prediction and treatment response (Abi-Dargham et al., 2016). SNPs and gene expression profiles have long been used to evaluate clinical treatment responses to antidepressants and adverse drug reactions in patients with major depressive disorder (MDD) . To identify intricate patterns in observational datasets, precision psychiatry employs multi-omics and neuroimaging data in conjunction with potent artificial intelligence and machine learning algorithms (Tanaka, M. 2024). Multi-omics and neuroimaging data are used as biomarkers (or predicting variables) in precision psychiatry, together with machine learning and artificial intelligence algorithms.To address precision psychiatry's major challenges, software tools using artificial intelligence and machine learning frameworks to predict quantitative and categorical phenotypes in clinical settings using next-generation multi-omics and neuroimaging datasets are needed. Scientists have made significant advances in AI, machine learning, precision psychiatry, pharmacogenomics, multi-omics, and neuroimaging (Lin et al., 2020). A data-driven system that can learn from past and current data and predict future events is the goal of an artificial intelligence and machine learning approach (Solomatine et al 2008). There are three primary steps in an artificial intelligence and machine learning methodology: Using the initial input data, we construct the prediction model, refine and assess it in the intermediate stage, then utilize the model to estimate the result in the last stage. Complex and nonlinear hierarchical patterns may be found and learned in huge experimental data using AI and machine learning, particularly deep learning algorithms . Deep learning algorithms may now function effectively in a variety of medical applications, including precision psychiatry, thanks to recently developed general-purpose computing on graphics processing units (Bzdoket al., 2018). Artificial neural networks and other abstractions are utilized in deep learning approaches to create hierarchical data representations . Multi-layered artificial neural networks are used by deep learning algorithms for classification tasks, such as precision psychiatric diagnostic prediction, in place of single-layer networks in order to determine the optimal hypothesis. Due to advancements in multi-omics and neuroimaging technology, precision psychiatry offers a significant deal of promise to address the demand for novel diagnostic tools and pharmacological therapy (Stolfi et al 2024). Biomarkers are crucial in AI and machine learning-based precision psychiatry. Precision psychiatric disorders and treatments, utilizing AI and machine learning, have been the subject of several recent academic articles. It would be exciting to create machine learning and artificial intelligence algorithms that can predict the outcomes of medication treatments and the state of illness in individuals with mental disorders (Chekroud et al. 2021).

Table 1. Overview of ML Algorithms and its Impact

ML (Machine learning)algorithms	**Contributions**
In-depth Education	In medicine, this method is widely used. Oncology is the field that employs deep learning the most for analyzing healthcare photographs (Li, M,. et al. 2023). Lung cancer, abdominal and pelvic CT and MRI scans, colonoscopy, mammography, brain tumor scans, radiation oncology, skin cancer, biopsy sample visualization, prostate tumor ultrasound, radiographs of malignant lung nodules, histopathological scanning of gliomas, biomarker data, and sequencing were all analyzed using the algorithm. (Mahmood, A., & Srivastava, R. 2022).Diabetic retinopathy, nodular BCC, histological anticipation in women with cytological deformations, cutaneous nevus and seborrheic keratosis, cardiac abnormalities, and cardiac muscle failure were all diagnosed using magnetic resonance imaging (MRI) of the heart ventricles. (Shashikiran 2016)
Discriminant analysis	Discriminant analysis is used in medicine to classify patients for surgery, symptom-relief satisfaction, primary immunodeficiencies, BOLD MRI response to protein-coding areas, sadness in cancer patients, and realistic movie stimuli.(Quazi, S. 2022).
Naïve Bayes	Mucopolysaccharidosis type II is used to predict risks, censored and time-to-event data are used to classify EHRs, clinical diagnosis is shaped for decision support, genome-wide data is extracted to identify Alzheimer's disease (Ahmed, Z..,et al 2020), cardiovascular disease decisions are modeled, healthcare quality is measured, and a predictive model for brain, asthma, prostate, and breast cancer is constructed.(Ahmed, Z et al 2020)
DNA algorithm	It has made a significant contribution to medicine. Oncology, radiography, endocrinology, pediatrics, cardiology, pulmonology, surgery, infectious disease, neurology, orthopedics, gynecology, and many more fields were among those that reported contributions.(Robertson et al 2018)

5. OBSTACLES IN THE APPLICATION PROCESS

Although there are still challenges, precision medicine is becoming better. Challenges include new tools, databases, public health systems, and networking and interoperability strategies for advanced technologies, clinical, laboratory, healthcare, and omics data. Better data management, including consensus and actionable information, is required in this medical field. It takes a lot of time and effort to extract medical data from clinical systems, identify distinct and unknown functional variants, evaluate metabolite penetrance using predetermined features, find correlations between metabolite levels and genomic variations, and analyze biochemical pathways in multimolecular metabolites. In addition to encouraging healthy living, public health creates novel approaches to the identification, avoidance, and management of prevalent illnesses. Population-centric sickness management is being replaced by AI and precision medicine (Mentis et al.,2024).Precision medicine, artificial intelligence, and comprehensive medical condition data can reduce public health strategy and initiative costs. AI improves genomic analysis pipeline predictions, but it has not yet revolutionized clinical genomics analysis. Increased exercise and speed may increase significantly. AI models for large, complicated biological data processing might accelerate genetic medicine. Future biotechnology may use machine learning to improve medicine (Quazi S 2021, Ghosh,2021, Ghosh et al.,2022).). Closing the gap between research and clinical application will be the biggest issue as machine learning and deep learning accelerate discoveries. Despite its potential, AI must overcome some obstacles to change genetic medicine.

6. AI IN DRUG DISCOVERY AND DEVELOPMENT

AI has expanded its use in many industries, including the pharmaceutical business. This paper highlights AI's role in drug discovery, repurposing, pharmaceutical productivity, and clinical trials. AI reduces time to achieve goals by reducing human workload. Pharmaceutical data digitalization has increased in recent years. Digitization makes data collection, analysis, and use for complicated clinical concerns difficult (Tresp, V., et al 2016,Ghosh et al.,2024). AI can automate massive data management, which encourages its use (Smith & Wang, 2022). Artificial intelligence (AI) uses sophisticated tools and networks to analyze and learn from input data and make autonomous decisions to achieve goals. As stated in this paper, pharmaceutical AI applications are growing. McKinsey Global Institute claims that fast AI-driven automation will revolutionize work culture worldwide. AI is revolutionizing drug research and development, potentially accelerating and reducing the cost of novel treatments (Tiwari et al., 2017).

7. FACILITATING COLLABORATION BETWEEN POLICYMAKERS, HEALTHCARE PROFESSIONALS, AND AI DEVELOPERS

A well-organized partnership between AI developers, medical practitioners, and legislators is necessary for the successful integration of AI into healthcare systems. Every stakeholder contributes a different set of skills: policymakers guarantee patient safety, equitable access, and regulatory compliance; healthcare professionals offer clinical insight, ethical considerations, and real-world applicability; and AI developers offer algorithmic capabilities and technical innovations . An advisory board or interdisciplinary task force can act as a focal point for these teams to collaborate on and evaluate AI solutions at every stage of their development, from conception to clinical implementation. According to He et al. (2019), consistent and open communication guarantees that the technology design complies with ethical norms and clinical requirements. Early clinician involvement in algorithm development, for instance, can enhance diagnostic relevance, minimize bias, and optimize datasets. Policymakers must create flexible regulatory frameworks in the meantime to support innovation without jeopardizing patient privacy and safety (Shoghli et al., 2024). Co-funded pilot projects, institutional review boards with representatives from all three industries, and public-private collaborations can all hasten the adoption of responsible AI. In the end, collaborative governance guarantees that AI technologies improve healthcare delivery while upholding accountability, equity, and trust.

Figure 3. Collaboration between AI Developers, Healthcare Professionals and Policymakers

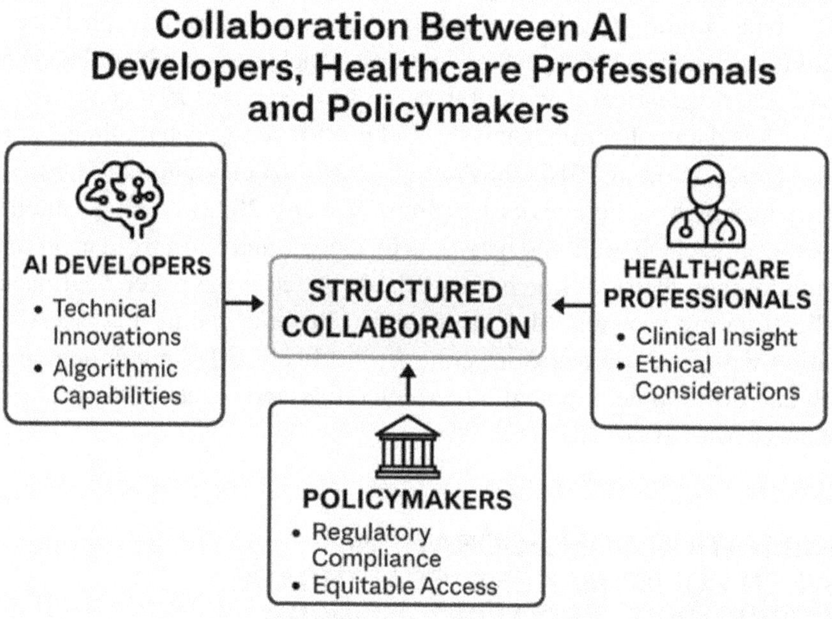

7.1 Structuring Collaboration for Effective AI Implementation in Healthcare

Effective implementation of Artificial Intelligence (AI) in healthcare and allied sciences requires structured collaboration among AI developers, healthcare professionals, and policymakers. Interdisciplinary frameworks that include clinicians during the early stages of algorithm design help ensure clinical relevance and usability, while translational teams comprising data scientists, engineers, and medical experts support real-world validation and continuous refinement of AI tools (Beam &Kohane, 2018; Topol, 2019). Policymakers must engage in this process to develop adaptive regulatory environments and ethical guidelines that ensure patient safety, data privacy, and compliance with legal standards such as HIPAA and GDPR (Khan & Khan, 2020; Mittelstadt et al., 2016). In parallel, collaborative efforts should prioritize data standardization and interoperability to facilitate scalable integration into existing health infrastructures (Raghupathi&Raghupathi, 2014). Cross-disciplinary education and training programs can further bridge knowledge gaps, equipping clinicians with AI literacy and developers with medical context (Jiang et al., 2017). Lastly, ethical governance structures involving all stakeholders, including patient advocacy groups, are essential to address algorithmic bias and promote equitable, transparent deployment of AI in healthcare systems (Morley et al., 2020).

8. CHALLENGES AND ETHICAL CONSIDERATIONS

AI has great potential in drug research, but confirming predictions and preserving transparency in decision-making are difficult. AI bias and the need for human oversight in crucial decisions are ethical issues (Akinrinola O, et al., 2024). According to Yadav S, et al., (2024), artificial intelligence (AI) has transformed a number of fields, including imaging, electronic medical records (EMR), laboratory diagnostics, therapy, physician intelligence, drug development, preventative and precision medicine, biological data analysis, process acceleration, and data storage and access for health organizations.This scientific field faces ethical and legal issues. AI has improved treatment procedures in communities, yet it is still unavailable to many cultures. Many underdeveloped countries lack modern technology (Austin, D et al., 2020). AI difficulties include ethics, privacy, data protection, informed permission, socioeconomic inequalities, medical consultation, empathy, and compassion (Reddy, S &Mathur, P, 2025). The four medical ethical principles—autonomy, beneficence, nonmaleficence, and justice in all facets of healthcare—must be taken into account by professionals and practitioners prior to using artificial intelligence (Gerke, S, et. al., 2020).

Privacy regulations in the US and Canada have been influenced by the European Union's General Data Protection Regulation (GDPR). These regulations mandate that personal data be managed by union-based data processors or controllers, and require enterprises and international communities to take measures to protect individuals' information (Yadav et al., 2023). In the United States, the Genetic Information Nondiscrimination Act (GINA) prohibits companies from discriminating based on genetic health information. Artificial intelligence (AI) accelerates health research, enhances diagnostic accuracy, and analyzes consumer health data and medical device images. AI-powered social media platforms play a significant role in disseminating health information and medical advice, particularly during pandemics.

9. CHALLENGES IN DATA QUALITY AND INTEROPERABILITY

The “quadruple aim” of improving patient care, population health, caregiver satisfaction, and healthcare costs presents a significant challenge for global healthcare systems. Factors such as an aging population, rising chronic disease rates, and escalating healthcare costs necessitate innovation and adaptation in healthcare delivery methods by governments, payers, regulators, and providers. Healthcare systems must not only “perform” by providing high-quality, effective treatment but also “transform” care by integrating real-world data directly into patient care, a shift accelerated by the global pandemic. The pandemic has highlighted disparities in access to care and healthcare workforce challenges, underscoring the need for systemic change (Pittman et al., 2021). Advancements in mobile devices, the Internet of Things (IoT), computing power, and data security, along with expanding access to multi-modal data (including genomics, economics, demographics, clinical, and phenotypic data), signify a critical intersection of technology and healthcare poised to revolutionize healthcare delivery models through AI-enhanced systems. (Bajwa, et al., 2021). Cloud computing facilitates the secure and efficient integration of AI technologies by healthcare providers, enabling the examination of vast volumes of data more quickly and affordably compared to on-premises equipment. Collaborations between technology vendors and healthcare organizations are essential to advance AI-driven medical innovation made possible by cloud computing and technology. However, the potential of big data analytics in healthcare may be hindered by issues related to data quality, interoperability, and the need for specific data formats (Singh et.al., 2022).

10. ETHICAL CONSIDERATIONS AND CHALLENGES

Medicine has changed as a result of AI applications in imaging, EMR, laboratory diagnosis and treatment, physician intelligence, new drug development, biology comprehensive data analysis, preventative and precision medicine, speeding up processes, and data storage and access for health organizations (Topol, 2019). However, there are moral and legal issues in this scientific sector. Though not all cultures can afford it, artificial intelligence (AI) has advanced significantly in communities and has the potential to improve medical results. Modern technology is not readily available in many underdeveloped nations. Moral concerns, informed consent, privacy and data protection, social gaps, medical advice, empathy, and compassion are all brought up by AI (Farhud&Zokaei, 2021). The four medical ethical principles—autonomy, beneficence, nonmaleficence, and justice—should be taken into account in all facets of therapy before implementing artificial intelligence in healthcare (Farhud&Zokaei, 2021).

10.1 Data Privacy and Security

Massive health data collection and analysis generate privacy and security concerns. Strong safeguards and ethical practices are essential to protect sensitive data and maintain public trust (Cohen & Mello, 2018; Price & Cohen, 2019).

In healthcare, **data privacy** and **security** work together to safeguard patient information. Privacy involves informed consent, data minimization, access controls, and transparency, while security includes encryption, network protections, physical safeguards, incident response protocols, and compliance measures (Adjerid et al., 2020). Robust privacy standards foster trust between patients and providers, whereas strong security prevents unauthorized breaches. Despite their interconnection, challenges such as human error, cyber threats, evolving regulations, and technological advancements complicate these efforts (Keshta&Odeh, 2021). Effective management of data privacy and security is critical for maintaining patient trust and complying with the **Health Insurance Portability and Accountability Act (HIPAA)** (Cohen & Mello, 2018).

Enacted in 1996, HIPAA establishes national standards for protecting **protected health information (PHI)**. Key components include:

- **Privacy Rule**: Grants patients rights to access and amend their PHI while restricting unauthorized disclosures.
- **Security Rule**: Mandates technical, administrative, and physical safeguards for **electronic PHI (ePHI)**.
- **Transactions and Code Sets Rule**: Standardizes electronic data exchange in healthcare.
- **Unique Identifiers Rule**: Requires covered entities to use standardized identification codes.
- **Enforcement Rule**: Defines penalties for noncompliance (Adjerid et al., 2020; Keshta&Odeh, 2021).

HIPAA compliance is vital for preserving confidentiality, as violations may result in significant legal and financial repercussions (Price & Cohen, 2019).

10.2 Human-AI Collaboration

Human-AI healthcare collaboration creates ethical concerns and challenges. One challenge is shared decision-making; AI may provide important insights, but healthcare practitioners make patient care decisions. To maintain faith and responsibility in AI, its recommendation process must be transparent to avoid harming patient outcomes (Gerke et al., 2020).

Another major issue is algorithmic prejudice. AI systems educated on biased datasets can prolong healthcare service gaps, harming marginalised people (Belenguer, 2019). Clinicians must recognize these biases and question AI advice to ensure equitable patient treatment. AI in healthcare demands informed consent. AI risks and data use must be disclosed to patients. Transparency fosters patient autonomy and confidence, which is ethical in healthcare. Accountability is another challenge. AI mistakes are hard to attribute to organizations, healthcare practitioners, or developers. Prioritizing patient rights and safety needs clear guidelines (Goktas&Grzybowski, 2025).

Finally, clinicians require ethics training. Healthcare staff must understand AI's shortcomings, biases, and the necessity of human oversight. Training is necessary to ensure that AI complements human judgment rather than replacing it (Topol, 2019). Addressing these ethical challenges would help healthcare institutions adopt AI while maintaining quality and equity.

11. FUTURE PROSPECTS

Although AI and technology in healthcare are relatively young, there remains space for innovation and improvement. Diagnostic imaging and predictive analytics are changing the healthcare business, but there is still much untapped potential (Topol, 2019).

AI may examine lifestyle and genetic features to design individualized treatment regimens that enhance patient outcomes, making personalized medicine a promising topic (By simplifying administrative duties, allocating resources optimally, and scheduling to accommodate patient demand, AI may also increase operational efficiency (Kumar et al., 2020). Telemedicine's real-time data analysis and decision help from AI improves access to treatment, especially in poor areas. However, data privacy, algorithmic bias, and legal restrictions must be addressed to build patient-clinician trust (Bajwa, et. al., 2021).

11.1 Emerging Technologies

With the promise of improved outcomes, new medical technologies are revolutionizing patient care, diagnosis, and treatment. This innovation is fueled by AI, which enhances data analysis and predictive analytics. AI systems can analyze vast volumes of data to improve medical imaging diagnostics by identifying illnesses early and providing therapies (Alowais, et al., 2023). Since the COVID-19 pandemic, telemedicine has become more and more popular.Telemedicine allows video conversations for distant consultations, which benefits underprivileged and rural patients.

Wearable technology like smartwatches lets patients check their health continuously. These gadgets exchange real-time data with doctors to better chronic disease treatment (Piwek et al., 2016). Blockchain is becoming a safe means for healthcare institutions to share data. Streamlining supply chain operations, safeguarding patient privacy, and increasing data quality can reduce fraud and increase trust. (Andrew, et.al., 2023)

VR and AR are being studied for patient education and medical training. Immersive technology can help patients understand difficult surgeries and enhance healthcare professional learning. (Iqbal, et.al., 2024)

CONCLUSION

Technology and artificial intelligence are revolutionizing healthcare by increasing clinical results, increasing efficiency, and improving patient-centered care. Through sophisticated data analysis, AI helps improve diagnostic precision, lower mistakes, and facilitate early disease identification. Particularly in remote areas, technologies like automation and telemedicine enhance access and reduce administrative expenses. But issues like digital inequality, algorithmic prejudice, data privacy, and lax legal protections need to be addressed. Laws ought to encourage innovation while maintaining safety, equity, and transparency. It is essential that developers, physicians, and legislators work together. Safe, efficient adoption will be supported by educating medical practitioners on AI use and incorporating these abilities into medical education. The goal of future research should be to scale AI while preserving compassion in healthcare. Adoption graphs and algorithm infographics are examples of visual aids that might improve comprehension. Developing a tech-driven but humane healthcare system requires a well-rounded, moral, and patient-centered strategy.

REFERENCES

Abdallah, S., Sharifa, M., Almadhoun, M. K. I. K., Khawar, M. M.Sr, Shaikh, U., Balabel, K. M., & Kanwar, M.Sr. (2023). The impact of artificial intelligence on optimizing diagnosis and treatment plans for rare genetic disorders. *Cureus, 15*(10). Advance online publication. DOI: 10.7759/cureus.46860 PMID: 37954711

Abi-Dargham, A., & Horga, G. (2016). The search for imaging biomarkers in psychiatric disorders. *Nature Medicine*, *22*(11), 1248–1255. 1248-1255.doi.org/10.1038/nm.4190. DOI: 10.1038/nm.4190 PMID: 27783066

Adjerid, I., Acquisti, A., Telang, R., Padman, R., & Adler-Milstein, J. (2020). The impact of privacy regulation on technology adoption: The case of health information exchanges. Management Science, *66*(3), 1041–1061. DOI: 10.1287/mnsc.2018.3274

Ahmed, Z., Mohamed, K., Zeeshan, S., & Dong, X. (2020). Artificial intelligence with multi-functional machine learning platform development for better healthcare and precision medicine. *Database : The Journal of Biological Databases and Curation*, *2020*, baaa010. Advance online publication. DOI: 10.1093/database/baaa010 PMID: 32185396

Akhter, Y., Singh, R., & Vatsa, M. (2023). AI-based radiodiagnosis using chest X-rays: A review. *Frontiers in Big Data*, *6*, 1120989. DOI: 10.3389/fdata.2023.1120989 PMID: 37091458

Akinrinola, O., Okoye, C. C., Ofodile, O. C., &Ugochukwu, C. E. (2024). Navigating and reviewing ethical dilemmas in AI development: Strategies for transparency, fairness, and accountability. GSC Advanced Research and Reviews, 18(3), 050-058.

Al Serkal, Y. M., Ibrahim, N. M., Alsereidi, A. S., Ibrahim, M., Kurakula, S., Naqvi, S. A., Khan, Y., & Oottumadathil, N. P. (2025). Real-Time Analytics and AI for Managing No-Show Appointments in Primary Health Care in the United Arab Emirates: Before-and-After Study. *JMIR Formative Research*, *9*, e64936. DOI: 10.2196/64936 PMID: 39763194

Alowais, S. A., Alghamdi, S. S., Alsuhebany, N., Alqahtani, T., Alshaya, A. I., Almohareb, S. N., Aldairem, A., Alrashed, M., Bin Saleh, K., Badreldin, H. A., Al Yami, M. S., Al Harbi, S., & Albekairy, A. M. (2023). Revolutionizing healthcare: The role of artificial intelligence in clinical practice. *BMC Medical Education*, *23*(1), 689. DOI: 10.1186/s12909-023-04698-z PMID: 37740191

Andrew, J., Isravel, D. P., Sagayam, K. M., Bhushan, B., Sei, Y., & Eunice, J. (2023). Blockchain for healthcare systems: Architecture, security challenges, trends and future directions. *Journal of Network and Computer Applications*, *215*, 103633. DOI: 10.1016/j.jnca.2023.103633

Apell, P., & Eriksson, H. (2023). Artificial intelligence (AI) healthcare technology innovations: The current state and challenges from a life science industry perspective. *Technology Analysis and Strategic Management*, *35*(2), 179–193. DOI: 10.1080/09537325.2021.1971188

Asensio, J. M. L., Peralta, J., Arrabales, R., Bedia, M. G., Cortez, P., & Peña, A. L. (2014). Artificial intelligence approaches for the generation and assessment of believable human-like behaviour in virtual characters. *Expert Systems with Applications*, *41*(16), 7281–7290. DOI: 10.1016/j.eswa.2014.05.004

Austin, D., May, J., Andrade, J., & Jones, R. (2021). Delivering digital health: The barriers and facilitators to university-industry collaboration. *Health Policy and Technology*, *10*(1), 104–110. DOI: 10.1016/j.hlpt.2020.10.003

Ayyala, R. S., Baird, G. L., Sze, R. W., Brown, B. P., & Taylor, G. A. (2020). The growing issue of burnout in radiology—A survey-based evaluation of driving factors and potential impacts in pediatric radiologists. *Pediatric Radiology*, *50*(8), 1071–1077. DOI: 10.1007/s00247-020-04693-2 PMID: 32474773

Baig, Z. A. (2012). Multi-agent systems for protecting critical infrastructures: A survey. *Journal of Network and Computer Applications*, *35*(3), 1151–1161. DOI: 10.1016/j.jnca.2012.01.006

Bajwa, J., Munir, U., Nori, A., & Williams, B. (2021). Artificial intelligence in healthcare: Transforming the practice of medicine. *Future Healthcare Journal*, *8*(2), e188–e194. DOI: 10.7861/fhj.2021-0095 PMID: 34286183

Banka, R., Das, P., Das, S., & Ghosh, J. (2025). Tailored nutrition and diet plan using AI and machine learning for precision wellness. In *Harnessing AI and machine learning for precision wellness*. IGI Global., DOI: 10.4018/979-8-3693-9521-9.ch007

Barbosa, W., Zhou, K., Waddell, E., Myers, T., & Dorsey, E. R. (2021). Improving access to care: Telemedicine across medical domains. *Annual Review of Public Health*, *42*(1), 463–481. DOI: 10.1146/annurev-publhealth-090519-093711 PMID: 33798406

Beam, A. L., & Kohane, I. S. (2018). Big data and machine learning in health care. *Journal of the American Medical Association*, *319*(13), 1317–1318. DOI: 10.1001/jama.2017.18391 PMID: 29532063

Belenguer, L. (2022). AI bias: Exploring discriminatory algorithmic decision-making models and the application of possible machine-centric solutions adapted from the pharmaceutical industry. *AI and Ethics, 2*(4), 771–787. DOI: 10.1007/s43681-022-00138-8 PMID: 35194591

Bergek, A. (2019). Technological innovation systems: a review of recent findings and suggestions for future research. Handbook of sustainable innovation, 200-218.

Bergman, B., Hellström, A., Lifvergren, S., & Gustavsson, S. M. (2015). An emerging science of improvement in health care. *Quality Engineering, 27*(1), 17–34. DOI: 10.1080/08982112.2015.968042

Bhandari, A. (2024). Revolutionizing Radiology With Artificial Intelligence. *Cureus, 16*(10). Advance online publication. DOI: 10.7759/cureus.72646 PMID: 39474591

Blaxter, M. (2009). The case of the vanishing patient? Image and experience. *Sociology of Health & Illness, 31*(5), 762–778. DOI: 10.1111/j.1467-9566.2009.01178.x PMID: 19659735

Bzdok, D., & Meyer-Lindenberg, A. (2018). Machine learning for precision psychiatry: Opportunities and challenges. *Biological Psychiatry: Cognitive Neuroscience and Neuroimaging, 3*(3), 223–230. DOI: 10.1016/j.bpsc.2017.11.007 PMID: 29486863

Catania, L. J., & Nicolitz, E. (2018). Artificial intelligence and its applications in vision and eye care. *Advances in Ophthalmology and Optometry, 3*(1), 21–38. DOI: 10.1016/j.yaoo.2018.04.001

Chekroud, A. M., Bondar, J., Delgadillo, J., Doherty, G., Wasil, A., Fokkema, M., Cohen, Z., Belgrave, D., DeRubeis, R., Iniesta, R., Dwyer, D., & Choi, K. (2021). The promise of machine learning in predicting treatment outcomes in psychiatry. *World Psychiatry; Official Journal of the World Psychiatric Association (WPA), 20*(2), 154–170. DOI: 10.1002/wps.20882 PMID: 34002503

Chong, L. R., Tsai, K. T., Lee, L. L., Foo, S. G., & Chang, P. C. (2020). Artificial intelligence predictive analytics in the management of outpatient MRI appointment no-shows. *AJR. American Journal of Roentgenology, 215*(5), 1155–1162. DOI: 10.2214/AJR.19.22594 PMID: 32901567

Cohen, I. G., & Mello, M. M. (2018). HIPAA and protecting health information in the 21st century. JAMA, *320*(3), 231–232. DOI: 10.1001/jama.2018.5630

Cowen, A. R., Davies, A. G., & Kengyelics, S. M. (2007). Advances in computed radiography systems and their physical imaging characteristics. *Clinical Radiology, 62*(12), 1132–1141. DOI: 10.1016/j.crad.2007.07.009 PMID: 17981160

Cowling, C. (2008). A global overview of the changing roles of radiographers. *Radiography, 14*, e28–e32. DOI: 10.1016/j.radi.2008.06.001

Enemosah, A. (2025). Enhancing DevOps efficiency through AI-driven predictive models for continuous integration and deployment pipelines. *International Journal of Research Publication and Reviews, 6*(1), 871–887. DOI: 10.55248/gengpi.6.0125.0229

Esteva, A., Kuprel, B., Novoa, R. A., Ko, J., Swetter, S. M., Blau, H. M., & Thrun, S. (2017). Dermatologist-level Classification of Skin Cancer with Deep Neural Networks. *Nature, 542*(7639), 115–118. 115--118.doi.org/10.1038/nature21056. DOI: 10.1038/nature21056 PMID: 28117445

Farhud, D. D., & Zokaei, S. (2021). Ethical Issues of Artificial Intelligence in Medicine and Healthcare. *Iranian Journal of Public Health, 50*(11), i–v. DOI: 10.18502/ijph.v50i11.7600 PMID: 35223619

Gastounioti, A., Conant, E. F., &Kontos, D. (2016). Beyond breast density: a review on the advancing role of parenchymal texture analysis in breast cancer risk assessment. Breast cancer research, 18, 1-12. DOIhttps://DOI: 10.1186/s13058-016-0755-8

Gerke, S., Minssen, T., & Cohen, G. (2020). Ethical and legal challenges of artificial intelligence-driven healthcare. Artificial Intelligence in Healthcare, 295–336. DOI: 10.1016/B978-0-12-818438-7.00012-5

Ghosh, J. (2023). A review on understanding the risk factors for coronary heart disease in Indian college students. *International Journal of Noncommunicable Diseases, 8*(3), 117–128. DOI: 10.4103/jncd.jncd_68_23

Ghosh, J. (2024). Recognizing and predicting the risk of malnutrition in the elderly using artificial intelligence: A systematic review. *International Journal of Advancement in Life Sciences Research, 7*(3), 01–14. Advance online publication. DOI: 10.31632/ijalsr.2024.v07i03.001

Ghosh, J. (2024a). Leveraging data science for personalized nutrition. In *Nutrition controversies and advances in autoimmune disease* (pp. 572–605). IGI Global., DOI: 10.4018/979-8-3693-5528-2.ch022

Ghosh, J., Choudhury, S. R., Singh, K., & Koner, S. (2024b). Application of machine learning algorithm and artificial intelligence in improving metabolic syndrome related complications: A review. *International Journal of Advancement in Life Sciences Research, 7*(2), 41–67. DOI: 10.31632/ijalsr.2024.v07i02.004

Ghosh, J., Choudhury, S. R., Singh, K., & Koner, S. (2024c). Application of machine learning algorithm and artificial intelligence in improving metabolic syndrome related complications: A review. *International Journal of Advancement in Life Sciences Research*, *7*(2), 41–67. DOI: 10.31632/ijalsr.2024.v07i02.004

Ghosh, J., & Sanyal, P. (2024d). Development and Evaluation of Machine Learning Models for Predicting Constipation and Its Risk Factors Among College-Aged Females. *Nutrition & Food Science*, *12*(3). https://bit.ly/3MPo6eH

Goktas, P., & Grzybowski, A. (2025). Shaping the Future of Healthcare: Ethical Clinical Challenges and Pathways to Trustworthy AI. *Journal of Clinical Medicine*, *14*(5), 1605. DOI: 10.3390/jcm14051605 PMID: 40095575

Gunter, H., Bradley, C., Hannah, D. M., Manaseki-Holland, S., Stevens, R., & Khamis, K. (2023). Advances in quantifying microbial contamination in potable water: Potential of fluorescence-based sensor technology. *WIREs. Water*, *10*(1), e1622. DOI: 10.1002/wat2.1622

Guyatt, G. H., Osoba, D., Wu, A. W., Wyrwich, K. W., & Norman, G. R.Clinical Significance Consensus Meeting Group. (2002, April). Methods to explain the clinical significance of health status measures. [). Elsevier.]. *Mayo Clinic Proceedings*, *77*(4), 371–383. DOI: 10.4065/77.4.371 PMID: 11936935

Hanna, M. G., Reuter, V. E., Samboy, J., England, C., Corsale, L., Fine, S. W., Agaram, N. P., Stamelos, E., Yagi, Y., Hameed, M., Klimstra, D. S., & Sirintrapun, S. J. (2019). Implementation of digital pathology offers clinical and operational increase in efficiency and cost savings. *Archives of Pathology & Laboratory Medicine*, *143*(12), 1545–1555. DOI: 10.5858/arpa.2018-0514-OA PMID: 31173528

Holzinger, A., Saranti, A., Angerschmid, A., Retzlaff, C. O., Gronauer, A., Pejakovic, V., Medel-Jimenez, F., Krexner, T., Gollob, C., & Stampfer, K. (2022). Digital transformation in smart farm and forest operations needs human-centered AI: Challenges and future directions. *Sensors (Basel)*, *22*(8), 3043. DOI: 10.3390/s22083043 PMID: 35459028

Iqbal, A. I., Aamir, A., Hammad, A., Hafsa, H., Basit, A., Oduoye, M. O., Anis, M. W., Ahmed, S., Younus, M. I., & Jabeen, S. (2024). Immersive Technologies in Healthcare: An In-Depth Exploration of Virtual Reality and Augmented Reality in Enhancing Patient Care, Medical Education, and Training Paradigms. *Journal of Primary Care & Community Health*, *15*, 21501319241293311. DOI: 10.1177/21501319241293311 PMID: 39439304

Jiang, F., Jiang, Y., Zhi, H., Dong, Y., Li, H., Ma, S., Wang, Y., Dong, Q., Shen, H., & Wang, Y. (2017). Artificial intelligence in healthcare: Past, present and future. *Stroke and Vascular Neurology*, *2*(4), 230–243. Advance online publication. DOI: 10.1136/svn-2017-000101 PMID: 29507784

Keshta, I., &Odeh, A. (2021). Security and privacy of electronic health records: Concerns and challenges. Egyptian Informatics Journal, *22*(2), 177–183. DOI: 10.1016/j.eij.2020.07.003

Khan, M. S., & Pasha Khan, S. (2020). Perspectives of healthcare sector with artificial intelligence. In Social Networking and Computational Intelligence: Proceedings of SCI-2018 (pp. 151-159). Springer Singapore.DOI: 10.1007/978-981-15-2071-6_12

Konstantinidis, K. (2024). The shortage of radiographers: A global crisis in healthcare. *Journal of Medical Imaging and Radiation Sciences*, *55*(4), 101333. DOI: 10.1016/j.jmir.2023.10.001 PMID: 37865586

Li, M., Jiang, Y., Zhang, Y., & Zhu, H. (2023). Medical image analysis using deep learning algorithms. *Frontiers in Public Health*, *11*, 1273253. DOI: 10.3389/fpubh.2023.1273253 PMID: 38026291

Lin, E., Lin, C. H., & Lane, H. Y. (2020). Precision psychiatry applications with pharmacogenomics: Artificial intelligence and machine learning approaches. *International Journal of Molecular Sciences*, *21*(3), 969. 969.doi.org/10.3390/ijms21030969. DOI: 10.3390/ijms21030969 PMID: 32024055

Mahmood, A., & Srivastava, R. (2022). Medical diagnosis of cancer. In *Understanding Cancer* (pp. 63 78). Academic Press., DOI: 10.1016/B978-0-323-99883-3.00017-2

Mahmud, M., Kaiser, M. S., McGinnity, T. M., & Hussain, A. (2021). Deep learning in mining biological data. *Cognitive Computation*, *13*(1), 1–33. DOI: 10.1007/s12559-020-09773-x PMID: 33425045

Majeed, A., & Hwang, S. O. (2024). A Data-Centric AI Paradigm for Socio-Industrial and Global Challenges. *Electronics (Basel)*, *13*(11), 2156. DOI: 10.3390/electronics13112156

Markard, J., Hekkert, M., & Jacobsson, S. (2015). The technological innovation systems framework: Response to six criticisms. *Environmental Innovation and Societal Transitions*, *16*, 76–86. DOI: 10.1016/j.eist.2015.07.006

Matilainen, K., Ahonen, S. M., Kankkunen, P., & Kangasniemi, M. (2017). Radiographers' perceptions of their professional rights in diagnostic radiography: A qualitative interview study. *Scandinavian Journal of Caring Sciences*, *31*(1), 139–145. DOI: 10.1111/scs.12335 PMID: 27164407

Mazurowski, M. A. (2019). Artificial intelligence may cause a significant disruption to the radiology workforce. *Journal of the American College of Radiology*, *16*(8), 1077–1082. DOI: 10.1016/j.jacr.2019.01.026 PMID: 30975611

Mentis, A. F. A., & Liu, L. (2024). Global impact and application of Precision Healthcare. In *The New Era of Precision Medicine* (pp. 209–228). Academic Press., DOI: 10.1016/B978-0-443-13963-5.00001-7

Mittelstadt, B. D., Allo, P., Taddeo, M., Wachter, S., & Floridi, L. (2016). The ethics of algorithms: Mapping the debate. *Big Data & Society*, *3*(2), 2053951716679679. DOI: 10.1177/2053951716679679

Morley, J., Machado, C. C., Burr, C., Cowls, J., Joshi, I., Taddeo, M., & Floridi, L. (2020). The ethics of AI in health care: A mapping review. *Social Science & Medicine*, *260*, 113172. DOI: 10.1016/j.socscimed.2020.113172 PMID: 32702587

Nichols, J. A., Herbert Chan, H. W., & Baker, M. A. (2019). Machine learning: applications of artificial intelligence to imaging and diagnosis. Biophysical reviews, 11, 111-118. DOIhttps://DOI: 10.1007/s12551-018-0449-9

Nilsson, J., Ohlsson, M., Thulin, L., Höglund, P., Nashef, S. A. M., & Brandt, J. (2006). Risk Factor Identification and Mortality Prediction in Cardiac Surgery Using Artificial Neural Networks. *The Journal of Thoracic and Cardiovascular Surgery*, *132*(1), 12–19.e1. DOI: 10.1016/j.jtcvs.2005.12.055 PMID: 16798296

Ortiz-Catalan, M., Brånemark, R., & Håkansson, B. (2013). BioPatRec: A modular research platform for the control of artificial limbs based on pattern recognition algorithms. *Source Code for Biology and Medicine*, *8*(1), 1–18. DOI: 10.1186/1751-0473-8-11 PMID: 23597283

Parker, S. K., & Grote, G. (2022). Automation, algorithms, and beyond: Why work design matters more than ever in a digital world. *Applied Psychology*, *71*(4), 1171–1204. DOI: 10.1111/apps.12241

Pittman, P., Chen, C., Erikson, C., Salsberg, E., Luo, Q., Vichare, A., Batra, S., & Burke, G. (2021). Health workforce for health equity. *Medical Care*, *59*(10, Suppl 5), S405–S408. DOI: 10.1097/MLR.0000000000001609 PMID: 34524235

Piwek, L., Ellis, D. A., Andrews, S., & Joinson, A. (2016). The Rise of Consumer Health Wearables: Promises and Barriers. *PLoS Medicine*, *13*(2), e1001953. DOI: 10.1371/journal.pmed.1001953 PMID: 26836780

Price, W. N., & Cohen, I. G. (2019). Privacy in the age of medical big data. Nature Medicine, *25*(1), 37–43. DOI: 10.1038/s41591-018-0272-7

Qin, Z. Z., Ahmed, S., Sarker, M. S., Paul, K., Adel, A. S. S., Naheyan, T., Barrett, R., Banu, S., & Creswell, J. (2021). Tuberculosis detection from chest x-rays for triaging in a high tuberculosis-burden setting: An evaluation of five artificial intelligence algorithms. *The Lancet. Digital Health*, *3*(9), e543–e554. DOI: 10.1016/S2589-7500(21)00116-3 PMID: 34446265

Quazi, S. (2022). Artificial intelligence and machine learning in precision and genomic medicine. *Medical Oncology (Northwood, London, England)*, *39*(8), 120. 120.doi.org/10.1007/s12032-022-01711-1. DOI: 10.1007/s12032-022-01711-1 PMID: 35704152

Raghupathi, W., & Raghupathi, V. (2014). Big data analytics in healthcare: Promise and potential. *Health Information Science and Systems*, *2*(1), 1–10. DOI: 10.1186/2047-2501-2-3 PMID: 25825667

Reddy, S., & Mathur, P. (2025). Translational AI: Bridging the Gap Between Research and Clinical Practice. ScienceOpen *Preprints*. DOI: 10.14293/PR2199.001444.v1

Reichardt, K., Negro, S. O., Rogge, K. S., & Hekkert, M. P. (2016). Analyzing interdependencies between policy mixes and technological innovation systems: The case of offshore wind in Germany. *Technological Forecasting and Social Change*, *106*, 11–21. DOI: 10.1016/j.techfore.2016.01.029

Robertson, F. C., Lepard, J. R., Mekary, R. A., Davis, M. C., Yunusa, I., Gormley, W. B., Baticulon, R. E., Mahmud, M. R., Misra, B. K., Rattani, A., Dewan, M. C., & Park, K. B. (2018). Epidemiology of central nervous system infectious diseases: A meta-analysis and systematic review with implications for neurosurgeons worldwide. *Journal of Neurosurgery*, *130*(4), 1107–1126. DOI: 10.3171/2017.10.JNS17359 PMID: 29905514

Rodríguez-Ruiz, A., Krupinski, E., Mordang, J. J., Schilling, K., Heywang-Köbrunner, S. H., Sechopoulos, I., & Mann, R. M. (2019). Detection of breast cancer with mammography: Effect of an artificial intelligence support system. *Radiology*, *290*(2), 305–314. DOI: 10.1148/radiol.2018181371 PMID: 30457482

Sarkar, C., Das, B., Rawat, V. S., Wahlang, J. B., Nongpiur, A., Tiewsoh, I., Lyngdoh, N. M., Das, D., Bidarolli, M., & Sony, H. T. (2023). Artificial intelligence and machine learning technology driven modern drug discovery and development. *International Journal of Molecular Sciences*, *24*(3), 2026. DOI: 10.3390/ijms24032026 PMID: 36768346

Scala, J. J., Ganz, A. B., & Snyder, M. P. (2023). Precision medicine approaches to mental health care. *Physiology (Bethesda, MD)*, *38*(2), 82–98. DOI: 10.1152/physiol.00013.2022 PMID: 36099270

Schaffter, T., Buist, D. S., Lee, C. I., Nikulin, Y., Ribli, D., Guan, Y., Lotter, W., Jie, Z., Du, H., Wang, S., Feng, J., Feng, M., Kim, H.-E., Albiol, F., Albiol, A., Morrell, S., Wojna, Z., Ahsen, M. E., Asif, U., & Jung, H. (2020). Evaluation of combined artificial intelligence and radiologist assessment to interpret screening mammograms. *JAMA Network Open*, *3*(3), e200265–e200265. DOI: 10.1001/jamanetworkopen.2020.0265 PMID: 32119094

Seifert, R., Weber, M., Kocakavuk, E., Rischpler, C., & Kersting, D. (2021, March). Artificial intelligence and machine learning in nuclear medicine: future perspectives. In Seminars in nuclear medicine (Vol. 51, No. 2, pp. 170-177). WB Saunders.DOI DOI: 10.1053/j.semnuclmed.2020.08.003

Shakil, S., Ghosh, J., Singh, K., & Roy Choudhury, S. (2024). Comparative analysis of nutritional status among institutionalized and community-dwelling elderly women and its association with mental health status and cognitive function. *Journal of Family Medicine and Primary Care*, *13*(8), 3078–3083. Advance online publication. DOI: 10.4103/jfmpc.jfmpc_1932_23 PMID: 39228576

Sharma, P., Pathak, L., Doke, R., & Mane, S. (2024). Artificial Intelligence in Clinical Trials: The Present Scenario and Future Prospects. In AI Innovations in Drug Delivery and Pharmaceutical Sciences; Advancing Therapy through Technology (pp. 229-257). Bentham Science Publishers. DOI: DOI: 10.2174/97898153057531240101

Sharma, S., Sharma, S., & Athaiya, A. (2017). Activation functions in neural networks. Towards Data Sci, 6(12), 310-316. ISSN No. 2455-2143, Shashikiran, A. R. (2016). Clinical Study of Facial Skin Disorders (Doctoral dissertation, Rajiv Gandhi University of Health Sciences (India)). DOI: 10.1148/rg.230093

Sheikhalishahi, S., Miotto, R., Dudley, J. T., Lavelli, A., Rinaldi, F., & Osmani, V. (2019). Natural language processing of clinical notes on chronic diseases: Systematic review. *JMIR Medical Informatics*, *7*(2), e12239. DOI: 10.2196/12239 PMID: 31066697

Shoghli, A., Darvish, M., & Sadeghian, Y. (2024). Balancing Innovation and Privacy: Ethical Challenges in AI-Driven Healthcare. *Journal of Research in Medical Sciences : the Official Journal of Isfahan University of Medical Sciences*, *4*(1), 1–11. DOI: 10.22034/jrms.2024.494112.1034

Singh, A. K., Zubair, S., Malibari, A., Pathak, N., Urooj, S., & Sharma, N. (2023). Design of ANN Based Non-Linear Network Using Interconnection of Parallel Processor. *Computer Systems Science and Engineering*, *46*(3), 3491–3508. DOI: 10.32604/csse.2023.029165

Singh, S., Pankaj, B., Nagarajan, K., Singh, N. P., & Bala, V. (2022). Blockchain with cloud for handling healthcare data: A privacy-friendly platform. *Materials Today: Proceedings*, *62*, 5021–5026. DOI: 10.1016/j.matpr.2022.04.910

Solomatine, D. P., & Ostfeld, A. (2008). Data-driven modelling: Some past experiences and new approaches. *Journal of Hydroinformatics*, *10*(1), 3–22. DOI: 10.2166/hydro.2008.015

Stolfi, F., Abreu, H., Sinella, R., Nembrini, S., Centonze, S., Landra, V., Brasso, C., Cappellano, G., Rocca, P., & Chiocchetti, A. (2024). Omics approaches open new horizons in major depressive disorder: From biomarkers to precision medicine. *Frontiers in Psychiatry*, *15*, 1422939. DOI: 10.3389/fpsyt.2024.1422939 PMID: 38938457

Subramanian, M., Wojtusciszyn, A., Favre, L., Boughorbel, S., Shan, J., Letaief, K. B., Pitteloud, N., & Chouchane, L. (2020). Precision medicine in the era of artificial intelligence: Implications in chronic disease management. *Journal of Translational Medicine*, *18*(1), 472. 1-12.doi.org/10.1186/s12967-020-02658-5. DOI: 10.1186/s12967-020-02658-5 PMID: 33298113

Tanaka, M. (2024). From Serendipity to Precision: Integrating AI, Multi-Omics, and Human Models for Personalized Neuropsychiatric Care. DOI: 10.20944/preprints202412.0679.v1

Taneja, J., Ghosh, J., Kant, R., & Christodoulides, M. (2025). Artificial intelligence in predicting, diagnosing and preventing sexually transmitted infections (STIs). *Venereology*, *4*(2), 5. DOI: 10.3390/venereology4020005

Tiwari, P. C., Pal, R., Chaudhary, M. J., & Nath, R. (2023). Artificial intelligence revolutionizing drug development: Exploring opportunities and challenges. *Drug Development Research*, *84*(8), 1652–1663. DOI: 10.1002/ddr.22115 PMID: 37712494

Topol, E. (2019). *Deep medicine: how artificial intelligence can make healthcare human again.*

Tresp, V., Overhage, J. M., Bundschus, M., Rabizadeh, S., Fasching, P. A., & Yu, S. (2016). Going digital: A survey on digitalization and large-scale data analytics in healthcare. *Proceedings of the IEEE*, *104*(11), 2180–2206. DOI: 10.1109/JPROC.2016.2615052

Yadav, N., Pandey, S., Gupta, A., Dudani, P., Gupta, S., & Rangarajan, K. (2023). Data privacy in healthcare: In the era of artificial intelligence. *Indian Dermatology Online Journal*, *14*(6), 788–792. DOI: 10.4103/idoj.idoj_543_23 PMID: 38099022

Yadav, S., Singh, A., Singhal, R., & Yadav, J. P. (2024). *Revolutionizing drug discovery: The impact of artificial intelligence on advancements in pharmacology and the pharmaceutical industry*. Intelligent Pharmacy., DOI: 10.1016/j.ipha.2024.02.009

Zhou, B., Yang, G., Shi, Z., & Ma, S. (2022). Natural language processing for smart healthcare. *IEEE Reviews in Biomedical Engineering*, *17*, 4–18. DOI: 10.1109/RBME.2022.3210270 PMID: 36170385

Chapter 17
The Role of Sustainable Development Goals (SDGs) in Reducing Health Inequalities

Pınar N. Dalgıç
https://orcid.org/0009-0002-0534-6767
Yozgat Bozok Üniversitesi, Turkey

ABSTRACT

The Sustainable Development Goals (SDGs) play a crucial role in reducing health inequalities. These goals focus on the social, economic, and environmental factors that contribute to health disparities. SDG 3, "Good Health and Well-being," aims to provide universal healthcare access and reduce the disease burden, particularly for disadvantaged groups. SDG 1, "No Poverty," and SDG 10, "Reduced Inequality," target the elimination of economic barriers to healthcare access. SDG 2, "Zero Hunger," addresses malnutrition as a key health determinant. Additionally, SDGs 13 and 6 focus on environmental factors such as climate change and access to clean water, which disproportionately affect marginalized groups. By addressing these interconnected factors, the SDGs provide an inclusive and equitable approach to achieving global health equity.

INTRODUCTION

One of the main drivers of health inequalities, especially among low-income or disadvantaged groups, is the presence of financial barriers that limit access to essential healthcare services. As global healthcare costs rise, these barriers become

DOI: 10.4018/979-8-3693-9755-8.ch017

more severe, preventing many from receiving necessary care and increasing their risk of poor health outcomes and higher mortality rates (World Health Organization [WHO], 2023).Low-income households, in particular, often struggle to afford even basic preventive services. This financial strain, coupled with limited access to treatments, leads to a higher disease burden and deepens existing health disparities (Marmot et al., 2020).In this context, one of the most critical strategies to reduce health inequalities is the reduction of healthcare service costs and the empowerment of disadvantaged groups through targeted financial support. These interventions are vital for ensuring equity in health, as they provide greater opportunities for marginalized populations to access healthcare services that are essential for maintaining good health. The WHO's findings during the global COVID-19 pandemic have further underscored the importance of addressing these inequalities, as crises tend to exacerbate existing health disparities, placing economically disadvantaged populations at even greater risk (WHO, 2023). The pandemic served as a stark reminder that vulnerable populations suffer disproportionately during times of crisis, which necessitates urgent attention from policymakers and healthcare leaders to rectify these systemic inequities. Moreover, policies aimed at reducing health inequalities within the broader context of economic development not only promote equity in health but also contribute to broader societal benefits such as increased workforce participation and enhanced social justice (Marmot et al., 2020).

Addressing health inequalities is inherently tied to the advancement of economic development, as economic growth can help elevate societal welfare by fostering higher levels of value-added production and ensuring a more equitable distribution of wealth. A fair and equitable income distribution is crucial for making healthcare services more accessible to disadvantaged groups. This, in turn, helps to reduce health risks, improve quality of life, and create healthier, more resilient communities (Sen, 1999). Additionally, the process of economic development can be greatly enhanced by improvements in key social determinants such as education, employment, and social protection. When these social determinants are improved, they work in tandem to eliminate inequalities in access to healthcare, thereby providing a solid foundation for sustainable development (Braveman, Egerter, & Williams, 2011). Consequently, the implementation of comprehensive and sustainable economic policies, coupled with increased investments in healthcare infrastructure, and the development of strategies to address social inequalities, is essential to effectively reduce health inequalities (Todaro & Smith, 2020).

Sustainability, in general terms, can be defined as the ability of a society to sustain its living and production systems in the future while minimizing excessive pressure on natural resources and maintaining ecological balances. This concept, central to achieving long-term social and environmental goals, requires a commitment to the preservation of ecosystems, as well as a long-term perspective that ensures the harmonious progression of social, economic, and environmental processes to meet human needs (Gilman, 1992). Sustainability is inherently linked to the broader context of public health, as addressing environmental degradation and ensuring the equitable distribution of resources are key to reducing health disparities and promoting social equity.

The Millennium Development Goals (MDGs), adopted by UN member states in 2000, were founded on the principle of equality and aimed to tackle global inequalities, focusing on areas such as poverty, hunger, gender equality, and universal healthcare access. In 2015, the Sustainable Development Goals (SDGs) succeeded the MDGs as a broader and more comprehensive framework, expanding efforts to improve healthcare access, reduce disease burdens, and ensure quality care for all, regardless of socio-economic status (United Nations, 2015).While the SDGs build on the MDGs' achievements, a major challenge persists: low-income and vulnerable populations continue to face significant barriers to accessing healthcare—an issue that remains a critical obstacle to achieving sustainable development worldwide.

Inequalities in healthcare access arise from various factors, including income, geographic location, inadequate infrastructure, and underinvestment in health systems. In many low-income countries, limited access to care and a shortage of healthcare professionals severely impact individual and community health, worsening the global health crisis (WHO, 2020). These disparities not only affect personal well-being but also undermine societal health and economic stability, posing a serious threat to sustainable development.

The Sustainable Development Report outlines key strategies to address these challenges, such as improving healthcare access for marginalized groups, strengthening infrastructure, and offering financial support to vulnerable populations. These actions are crucial for achieving the SDGs and ensuring equitable, inclusive healthcare. By reducing disparities, societies can advance public health, social equity, and long-term sustainability.This study provides a multidimensional analysis of health inequalities through the lens of social determinants, and presents a comprehensive perspective on how these inequalities can be reduced within the framework of the Sustainable Development Goals (SDGs). By integrating the concept of health inequalities - often discussed at a conceptual level in the literature - with measurable indicators and policy recommendations in the context of sustainable development, this study serves as an important reference for both academic research and decision-makers. It aims to contribute to the restructuring of health policies based on equity by exploring the transformative potential of the SDGs in the health sector across social, economic and governance dimensions.

1. HEALTH INEQUALITIES

One of the most significant challenges confronting societies across the globe is the existence of inequalities that present a considerable threat to health and have a detrimental impact on well-being (Bansal et al.,2022; Gkiouleka et al., 2023). In accordance with the World Health Organization's Commission on Social Determinants of Health, health inequalities are defined as systematic disparities in health status within and between countries that are unfair, unjust, and unacceptable (WHO, 2022). The 2024 guideline published by the WHO proposes a new operational framework for countries to monitor and measure these inequalities. This framework facilitates the monitoring of health inequalities through indicators that encompass social determinants such as income distribution, housing conditions, education level, and geographical accessibility (WHO, 2024).The concept emerged in the 1970s and gained significant international attention towards the end of that decade (Bahar &Aydoğdu, 2015). In 1974, Marc Lalonde, the then Canadian Minister of Health, published the Lalonde Report, which emphasised that the equitable, fair and just distribution of healthcare services to society is of greater importance for improving health than healthcare systems themselves (Lloyd, Newell & Dietrich, 2004).

The Declaration of the Alma-Ata Conference in 1978 is a document that places emphasis on the principles of social justice and human rights in the context of international health policies. The declaration set an objective of "Health for All by the Year 2000" and concentrated on international health policies (Polat & İçağasıoğlu Çoban, 2015). Moreover, the declaration asserted that reducing the disparities between the affluent and impoverished segments of society would facilitate the attainment of a superior level of collective health. In the 1980s, the UK Secretary of State for Health constituted a working group, which was chaired by Sir Douglas Black. The group's objective was to examine national and international health inequalities with a view to informing policy development. The studies indicated that health inequalities could result from a range of socioeconomic factors, including income, unemployment, lifestyle, education, and transportation. By the 1990s, health inequalities had become a significant policy issue, and the resolution of these inequalities became a key focus of public policy.

In 2000, at the United Nations (UN) General Assembly, 147 heads of state and government announced the Millennium Declaration. The declaration delineated eight principal objectives.

- Eradicating hunger and poverty,
- Achieving universal education,
- Promoting gender equality and empowering women,
- Reducing child mortality rates,

- Improving maternal health,
- Combating HIV/AIDS, malaria, and other diseases,
- Ensuring environmental sustainability,
- Fostering global partnerships

The Millennium Development Goals, as set forth by the United Nations in 2000, sought to advance progress in pivotal domains, including poverty alleviation, the expansion of educational opportunities, the advancement of gender equality, and the enhancement of health outcomes. Notwithstanding the considerable headway made in these areas, a considerable number of goals remain unfulfilled. Poverty, gender inequality and global health problems continue to represent significant challenges in many regions.For example, according to a study published in 2023, individuals living in poor neighborhoods in Europe still face significant disparities in life expectancy compared to those living in wealthy neighborhoods (Gkiouleka et al., 2023).In 2015, the Sustainable Development Goals (SDGs) were developed as a continuation and furtherance of the aforementioned objectives. The SDGs seek to reduce inequalities in these areas by providing more inclusive and long-term solutions through international cooperation and collective efforts. The SDGs provide a contemporary and comprehensive framework for addressing the shortcomings of the Millennium Goals in advancing global development (Pınarbaşı & Piyal, 2022).

The concept of health inequalities is defined as systematic, preventable, and unjust differences in health outcomes observed between specific societal groups (Whitehead, 1992). Furthermore, health inequalities can be defined as disruptions that are deemed unacceptable, arising from social factors or inadequacies in healthcare systems that impact the health of individuals or communities. These disruptions and differences are shaped by social, economic, and environmental determinants, manifesting as systematic and unjust disparities in individuals' access to healthcare, disease risks, or health outcomes. The Commission on Social Determinants of Health, which is affiliated with the World Health Organization, has indicated that health inequalities between countries are becoming more pronounced, thereby rendering the attainment of the objectives set out in health policies an increasingly challenging endeavour (Şahman & Gün, 2024).

Moreover, numerous studies conducted in the aftermath of the COVID-19 pandemic have shown that health inequalities not only make low-income individuals more vulnerable to diseases, but also reveal significant fragilities in the area of mental health (Bambra et al., 2020; Williams et al., 2019). This indicates that health inequalities should be addressed holistically—not only in terms of physical health, but also considering mental and social dimensions (Cénat et al., 2020; Jaffe et al., 2020; Mishra et al., 2021; Stennet & Tsakos, 2022).

1.1. Social Determinants of Health and Their Impact on Inequality

The social determinants of health directly influence community well-being, affecting life expectancy, health status, and access to healthcare services. Key determinants include education, income, employment conditions, housing, and the social environment (Braveman et al., 2011). Inequities in these areas lead to poorer health outcomes, greater disease risk, and reduced quality of life for those with low socioeconomic status (Viner et al., 2012).To address these disparities, targeted interventions are essential. In this context, the World Health Organization (WHO) established the Commission on Social Determinants of Health (CSDH) to promote evidence-based policies aimed at improving societal well-being and advancing social justice. The Commission seeks to foster a world in which sustainable, inclusive policies enable all individuals to live healthy and dignified lives (Marmot, 2005; Marmot & Allen, 2014).The following section will explore these determinants in more detail, focusing on factors such as education, gender, socioeconomic status, marital status, genetic background, and occupation.

1.1.1. Education

Education is a pivotal factor among the social determinants of health. Education exerts a direct influence on individuals' health knowledge levels, access to healthcare services, and healthy lifestyle behaviours. Furthermore, it exerts an indirect impact on health by determining income levels and socioeconomic status. As the level of education increases, there is a corresponding improvement in health awareness and greater attainability of access to healthy living conditions. Those with higher levels of education are better equipped to make well-informed and effective decisions regarding the utilisation of healthcare services and the management of disease risks. As stated by the World Health Organization (WHO), an increase in educational attainment has a positive impact on an individual's health status, resulting in an extended average life expectancy and an improvement in overall health standards within a given society. Education is identified as a fundamental factor influencing critical decision-making processes, including career choices, income levels and access to healthcare services. Those with higher levels of education are better equipped to manage health risks in a more informed and conscious manner, due to their superior levels of health knowledge and literacy. This plays a pivotal role in determining key health indicators such as quality of life, well-being, and life expectancy (Cutler & Lleras-Muney, 2006).Recent studies have shown that an increase in the level of education positively affects individuals' health literacy and access to healthcare services (Rasu et al., 2015; Coughlin et al., 2020; Meherali et al., 2020).

1.1.2. Gender

Gender is a principal social determinant of health inequalities, which are shaped by a complex interplay of biological and socio-cultural factors that directly influence health outcomes. Although women are typically expected to live longer than men, it is noteworthy that they frequently encounter a range of health-related challenges that negatively impact their quality of life. The available evidence indicates that women are more prone to developing chronic diseases and are more likely to experience a range of long-term health issues than men (Denton, Prus & Walters, 2004).

The accessibility of healthcare services for women is frequently constrained by socioeconomic factors, including income level, educational attainment, and labour force participation. Furthermore, traditional gender roles and domestic responsibilities place an additional burden on women in terms of safeguarding their health and accessing healthcare. Furthermore, societal expectations and social norms frequently place pressure on women to reconcile work and family responsibilities, which can contribute to elevated stress levels. These gender-based inequalities have a significant impact on women's overall health status, underscoring the necessity of gender-sensitive regulations in health policies (Valentine, Koller & Hosseinpoor, 2016).

1.1.3. Economic Status

An individual's economic status represents a significant social determinant of their health status. Income levels, employment status, financial resources and social support networks exert a direct influence on health outcomes. The influence of economic status on health outcomes is reflected in individuals' access to healthcare services, their capacity to maintain healthy living conditions, and their ability to cope with diseases (Çukur & Bekmez, 2011). Those with high income levels typically have greater access to healthcare services, nutritious food, and housing opportunities, as well as sufficient resources to maintain their livelihoods. Conversely, those with low income levels are more susceptible to elevated stress levels, which have a detrimental impact on health. It is observed that this group is more prone to developing chronic diseases and malnutrition, which serves to illustrate the extent to which socioeconomic status influences health inequalities (Thomson et al, 2022; Keeton et al., 2023). Moreover, the absence of economic resources impedes access to preventive healthcare services for low-income groups, frequently resulting in delayed treatment when health issues emerge. Consequently, the improvement of socioeconomic conditions represents a pivotal strategy for the enhancement of individuals' overall health levels and quality of life, while simultaneously reducing health inequalities (Amarasinghe et al., 2009).

1.1.4. Marital Status

Marital status has been identified as a social determinant with both direct and indirect effects on health. Individuals who are married or in a partnership tend to exhibit superior physical and psychological health outcomes, whereas those who are single, divorced, or widowed are more prone to experiencing health challenges. This is associated with factors such as social support, economic stability, and health behaviours. For example, married individuals have access to a more extensive social support network, which enables them to cope with stress and enhances their resilience in addressing health issues (Robards et al., 2012). The institution of marriage or partnership has been demonstrated to exert a positive influence on individuals' engagement with regular health check-ups, the maintenance of a healthy lifestyle, and the avoidance of risky behaviours. Individuals who are single may be more likely to engage in health-risk behaviours, such as smoking and alcohol consumption, than those who are married. However, those who have the support of a spouse are more likely to maintain healthy living habits. Conversely, the dissolution of a marriage or partnership can result in adverse psychological and physical health outcomes. The experience of stress, anxiety, and depression following divorce or bereavement can have a detrimental impact on the health of individuals. Therefore, the impact of marital status on health should be considered a significant determinant, not only in terms of social support and psychological well-being, but also with regard to lifestyle and health behaviours (Lawrence, Rogers, Zajacova & Wadsworth, 2019).

1.1.5. Genetic Structure

The genetic structure of a population is a critical and often overlooked social determinant of health that exerts a significant influence on the development of health inequalities. Genetic factors, which include hereditary traits and inherited predispositions to certain health conditions, can make some individuals more vulnerable to specific diseases. These genetic predispositions, when combined with other social and environmental factors, can lead to disparities in health outcomes across different population groups. For instance, certain chronic conditions, such as cardiovascular diseases, type 2 diabetes, and various forms of cancer, are closely linked to genetic factors. Individuals who inherit genes that predispose them to these conditions often experience earlier onset, more severe progression, and reduced responsiveness to treatment, which directly impacts their overall health status, life expectancy, and quality of life (Fine, Ibrahim & Thomas, 2005).

The relationship between genetic predisposition and health is complex and multifaceted. While genetic factors play a crucial role in determining an individual's susceptibility to various health conditions, the expression of these genetic traits can be influenced by environmental conditions, lifestyle choices, and socioeconomic status. For example, individuals with a genetic predisposition to heart disease may face exacerbated risks if they also experience poor nutrition, lack of physical activity, or exposure to environmental toxins. Similarly, socioeconomic factors such as limited access to quality healthcare, insufficient education, or inadequate housing can interact with genetic predispositions, amplifying the disparities in health outcomes across different populations (Olshansky et al., 2005). This interaction between genetics, environment, and social determinants highlights the need for a more nuanced understanding of health inequalities, one that recognizes the complex interplay between biological and social factors.

The impact of genetic structure on health disparities underscores the importance of considering genetic factors in public health initiatives and health policy development. However, addressing the influence of genetics alone is insufficient in tackling health inequalities. Public health efforts must take a comprehensive approach that addresses not only genetic predispositions but also the environmental, socioeconomic, and behavioral factors that influence the health of individuals. This holistic approach requires the integration of genetic information with data on environmental exposure, lifestyle behaviors, and access to healthcare resources in order to design effective public health interventions.

Policymakers and healthcare professionals must recognize that health inequalities are not solely the result of individual behaviors or genetic factors but are deeply rooted in social and environmental conditions. Therefore, strategies to mitigate health inequalities should focus on reducing environmental risks, improving access to healthcare services, promoting healthier lifestyles, and addressing the broader social determinants of health. The implementation of policies aimed at reducing these disparities can help to reduce the adverse health impacts associated with genetic predispositions, leading to better health outcomes for all populations, regardless of their genetic makeup. Additionally, genetic research and advancements in personalized medicine offer the potential to improve healthcare outcomes by tailoring interventions to an individual's genetic profile. However, such advancements must be accompanied by policies that ensure equitable access to these innovations for all segments of society, especially for disadvantaged or underserved populations. The goal is to ensure that genetic predispositions do not contribute to widening the gap in health outcomes but rather serve as a tool for more effective, personalized healthcare delivery. Therefore, the inclusion of genetic factors in public health frameworks is essential for creating a more equitable healthcare system that addresses the diverse needs of all individuals and reduces health disparities across populations.

1.1.6. Occupation

Occupation is a significant and widely acknowledged social determinant that plays a crucial role in the emergence and perpetuation of health disparities within societies. The nature of an individual's occupation has far-reaching effects on their physical and mental health outcomes, with various occupational factors influencing an individual's overall well-being. Several aspects of occupation, such as working conditions, work hours, the level of physical and mental demands associated with the job, and the presence of job-related risks, directly impact health. For instance, individuals engaged in physically demanding occupations, such as construction work, mining, or manufacturing, are more vulnerable to occupational accidents and illnesses due to the strenuous nature of their work. Over time, workers in these fields face an increased risk of developing chronic health conditions, such as musculoskeletal disorders, repetitive strain injuries, and other physical ailments that can severely impair their quality of life (Karasek & Theorell, 1990).

The impact of occupation on mental health is equally significant. Jobs that require high levels of mental and emotional labor, such as those in healthcare, education, social services, and customer service, can contribute to the development of stress, burnout, and anxiety. The prolonged exposure to high job demands combined with insufficient control over work processes can lead to mental health challenges, including depression, emotional exhaustion, and a general decline in psychological well-being (Karasek & Theorell, 1990). In high-stress occupations, workers may experience adverse effects on their cognitive functions, relationships, and overall life satisfaction, creating a vicious cycle of poor health outcomes. The mental toll of such jobs is compounded by the often insufficient support systems in place to address the psychological needs of workers, further exacerbating health inequalities in the workforce.

Moreover, occupation is closely linked to income levels and social status, both of which are key determinants of access to healthcare services. Individuals employed in high-income and socially prestigious occupations tend to have greater access to quality healthcare, a healthy living environment, and a higher standard of living. These individuals often have the financial means to afford regular health checkups, preventive care, and access to medical specialists, all of which contribute to better health outcomes. In contrast, those employed in low-income, low-status jobs, particularly in sectors characterized by unstable employment conditions, limited job security, and inadequate healthcare benefits, face substantial barriers to accessing healthcare services. These barriers may include unaffordable health insurance premiums, lack of paid sick leave, or geographic isolation from healthcare facilities. As a result, low-income workers are more likely to delay seeking medical care, suffer from untreated illnesses, and experience poorer health outcomes compared to their higher-income counterparts (Marmot et al., 2008).

The direct correlation between occupation, income, social status, and healthcare access intensifies the existing health inequalities in society. Occupation-based disparities are not merely an issue of income but are also linked to broader social determinants, such as education, community support, and health literacy, which further impact the ability of individuals to maintain good health. For example, individuals in lower-status jobs often lack the resources to engage in health-promoting behaviors, such as regular exercise, nutritious eating, or stress management, which are often more accessible to those with higher incomes. Furthermore, the stressful working conditions faced by low-income workers can contribute to a higher prevalence of chronic diseases, such as hypertension, diabetes, and cardiovascular disease, thereby exacerbating the gap in health outcomes between different occupational groups.

Addressing these occupational health disparities requires comprehensive policies that not only improve the working conditions of vulnerable workers but also ensure equitable access to healthcare services across all sectors of the workforce. It is essential for governments and organizations to implement workplace wellness programs, increase investments in occupational health and safety, and provide support for mental health services to reduce stress and burnout. Additionally, improving job security, providing access to affordable health insurance, and offering financial support for low-income workers can help mitigate the negative health consequences of precarious employment. Ultimately, by improving working conditions, reducing occupational health risks, and enhancing access to healthcare, society can begin to address the occupational determinants of health inequalities and promote greater equity in health outcomes for all workers.

2. SUSTAINABLE DEVELOPMENT AND HEALTH INEQUALITIES

It is estimated that a considerable proportion of the global population is unable to access healthcare services that meet their needs. This situation highlights the necessity of addressing health inequalities, which constitute a significant obstacle to the attainment of global health objectives. In order to achieve health equity, it is essential to undertake a comprehensive analysis of the various social determinants and to develop effective policies that target these determinants. The reduction of inequalities based on health-related factors will not only result in improved individual health outcomes but will also contribute to an enhanced overall health level of society, thereby facilitating the achievement of the "Health for All" goal. The attainment of universal health coverage and the guarantee of access to safe, effective, and affordable medicines and vaccines for all societal segments are of paramount importance for the reduction of global health inequalities. In this context, the Sustainable Development Goals (SDGs), in particular SDG 3, seek to provide all individuals with the opportunity to live a healthy life and to guarantee equal access to healthcare services (United Nations, 2024).

The Sustainable Development Goals (SDGs) represent a global development agenda, accepted by 191 countries that are members of the United Nations, with the objective of achieving them by 2030. The 17 main goals, along with the 169 sub-targets, provide a comprehensive transformation agenda that encompasses economic, social, and environmental dimensions, thereby supporting sustainable development. The SDGs seek to enhance societal welfare across a broad spectrum, from the eradication of poverty to the achievement of environmental sustainability, with the objective of creating a shared development vision for all countries (WHO, 2022).

.SDG 3, entitled “Good Health and Well-Being”, is directly related to the field of health. The objective of this goal is to guarantee the preservation of healthy lives and the advancement of well-being across all age groups. The concept of health is a fundamental aspect of sustainable development, with a complex interrelationship with a multitude of economic, social, and environmental factors. SDG 3, while focusing on health, also integrates with other goals, including SDG 1 (poverty), SDG 4 (quality education), SDG 5 (gender equality), and SDG 13 and SDG 15 (environmental protection). Consequently, the achievement of SDG 3 makes a multifaceted contribution to sustainable development, promoting social equity and welfare across a range of sectors, including poverty reduction, education, and gender equality (WHO, 2022; Marmot, 2005).

The reduction of health inequalities has been demonstrated to enhance the quality of life for individuals and to exert a beneficial influence on societal welfare and sustainable development. In particular, individuals with low incomes or those residing in developing countries encounter considerable obstacles to healthcare access, which serves to exacerbate existing health and social inequalities. The social factors that determine health, including education level, income, employment opportunities and housing, directly influence individuals' access to healthcare and their overall health status(Newman et al., 2015; Penman-Aguilar et al., 2016).For example, Marmot (2005) emphasises the considerable influence of social determinants such as education and income on health, demonstrating how these factors shape public health outcomes.SDG 10, or “Reduced Inequalities,” is of critical importance in the pursuit of social health and justice. Ensuring that disadvantaged groups have access to healthcare not only improves individual health levels but also enhances the sustainable development potential of society as a whole. The reduction of health inequalities is of critical importance for the realisation of sustainable development goals. Equal access to healthcare for all individuals contributes to the enhancement of the overall welfare of society and the advancement of sustainable development (United Nations, 2024; WHO, 2022).

In the view of the World Health Organization (WHO), and in the context of the Sustainable Development Goals, the strengthening of global health systems, the improvement of infrastructure and the allocation of greater investment to poor and disadvantaged regions are essential for the elimination of these inequalities. The success of SDG 10 is contingent upon the implementation of comprehensive interventions that encompass a range of measures, including the guarantee of equal access to healthcare and the empowerment of disadvantaged groups. In this context, the implementation of effective policies that address the social determinants of health and promote the equitable distribution of health resources is crucial for reducing health inequalities. The success of the SDGs is contingent upon the enhancement of the welfare and health standards of all social segments. Consequently, investments in healthcare systems facilitate the attainment of sustainable development goals by communities (Bambra et al., 2005).

2.1. Measurement of Health Inequalities

Measuring health inequalities aims to quantitatively determine and analyze the differences in health statuses between different groups in society. Such measurement is critical for understanding the nature and scope of health inequalities and contributes to the development of more targeted health policies. Commonly used methods to measure health inequalities include mortality and morbidity rates, life expectancy, human development index, disease burden, and self-assessment surveys. Additionally, statistical analysis methods such as the Gini coefficient, Theil index, ordered logistic regression, and odds ratio are also used to understand inequalities in health conditions(Harper et al., 2006; Albert-Ballestar & García-Altés, 2021; Schlotheuber & Hosseinpoor, 2022).

2.1.1. Measurement of General Health

The measurement of health inequalities is of paramount importance for the identification of discrepancies in health status at both the societal and individual levels. This measurement not only assesses individuals' general health but also identifies disparities in access to and utilisation of health services, as well as variations based on socioeconomic and geographical conditions. In this context, the measurement of general health is carried out using a range of parameters, including healthy life expectancy, quality of life, and disease burden. Each of these parameters provides detailed information about the extent to which specific groups benefit from health services or are affected by health issues, thus offering insights into health inequalities. Healthy life expectancy represents a pivotal indicator in the assessment of health inequalities. This measure, which predicts the number of years an individual can expect to live in good health, is employed to assess the impact of disparities in access to health services or environmental factors (Marmot, 2005). The concept of quality of life encompasses individuals' physiological, psychological, and social well-being. It is a multidimensional concept that goes beyond the mere assessment of health status, but also considers the impact of health on an individual's life. The examination of quality of life enables a more comprehensive evaluation of societal inequalities (Murray & Lopez, 1997). The most pertinent indicators utilized to assess health at the societal level encompass life expectancy at birth, mortality, morbidity, quality-adjusted life years (QALY), and disability-adjusted life years (DALY).

2.1.1.1. Life Expectancy at Birth

Life expectancy is a comprehensive indicator of the health and well-being level of a society, and it is a critical metric for assessing the general health of a population. This indicator reflects various factors such as access to health services, living conditions, nutrition, environmental factors, and the effectiveness of social services. Specifically, life expectancy at birth expresses the average number of years a newborn is expected to live, considering the mortality risks they may encounter at each age throughout their life. This measure indirectly reflects the general health risks within the community and the effectiveness of the health system (Marmot, 2005).

The life expectancy at birth indicator is frequently used in national and international health assessments. For instance, organizations like the World Health Organization (WHO) and the United Nations Development Programme (UNDP) use it as a fundamental data point when making cross-country comparisons. This metric also contributes to the evaluation of health policies and the formulation of necessary strategic steps to improve public health (Solar & Irwin, 2010; Lopez vd., 2011).

Table 1. Life Expectancy at Birth in Selected Countries (2021)

Country	**Life Expectancy at Birth (years)**	
	Female	**Male**
Switzerland	**85.1**	**81.8**
Germany	**84.8**	**78.7**
Japan	**86.9**	**81.5**
Russia	**78.0**	**68.2**
Turkey	**80.7**	**76.4**

continued on following page

Table 1. Continued

Country	Life Expectancy at Birth (years)	
	Female	**Male**
Canada	**84.1**	**80.4**
Somalia	**59.2**	**54.0**

Source: **World Health Organization. (2021). Life expectancy and healthy life expectancy, data by country. Accessed on November 7, 2024. Available at:**https://apps.who.int/gho/data/node.main.688.

2.1.1.2. *Mortality*

The term 'mortality' is used to describe the death rates that are caused by specific reasons within a particular geographical area and time period. This statistical measure serves as a crucial indicator for evaluating public health, formulating health policies, and measuring the effectiveness of healthcare services (WHO, 2020). The analysis of mortality provides information not only on the general health of the population but also on the prevalence and lethality of specific diseases, such as infectious diseases, chronic diseases, or deaths due to accidents. This enables comparisons to be made across different age groups, genders, or socio-economic groups (Marmot, 2005).

The analysis of mortality data, disaggregated by age and gender, is of critical importance for the understanding of health inequalities. The social determinants of health, including access to healthcare and living conditions, can contribute to variations in mortality rates across specific population groups. In this context, mortality data provides a valuable basis for monitoring public health and improving healthcare systems. Moreover, international organisations, such as the World Health Organization, employ standardised mortality rates to compile comprehensive reports on global health, facilitating comparisons across countries (Marmot, 2005; WHO, 2020).

2.1.1.3. *Morbidity*

Morbidity is a key public health indicator that reflects the prevalence of disease in a population over a specified period, encompassing both prevalence (total cases) and incidence (new cases). It plays a vital role in health system planning, resource allocation, and evaluating service efficacy. Morbidity rates guide health policy priorities and the organization of healthcare services based on community needs. These rates also account for both physical and mental health issues, providing a more comprehensive view of public health. Analyzing morbidity data, such as chronic diseases or epidemics, informs future health interventions (Di Cesare et al., 2013). In the context of health inequalities, morbidity reveals how disease rates vary across socio-economic groups, highlighting disparities in access to healthcare, living conditions, and nutrition, particularly in lower socio-economic populations

(Marmot, 2005).The existence of health inequalities has an impact not only on the frequency of specific diseases but also on the capacity of individuals to cope with illness. For instance, in the case of chronic and infectious diseases, those belonging to lower socioeconomic groups tend to exhibit higher morbidity rates, largely due to the fact that they often fail to benefit sufficiently from early diagnosis, regular treatment, and quality healthcare services. Social and economic disadvantages have a significant impact on an individual's health status, leading to notable inequalities within the community (Wilkinson ve Marmot, 2003; Di Cesare et al., 2013).

2.1.1.4. Quality Adjusted Life Year (QALY)

The QALY (Quality-Adjusted Life Year) is a frequently utilised measurement instrument within the field of health economics. The QALY (Quality-Adjusted Life Year) is an index that evaluates both life expectancy and quality of life. It is the preferred measure for the effectiveness of healthcare services (Drummond et al., 2015). This measure combines the impact of an intervention on both life expectancy and the quality of an individual's life, thereby enabling the assessment of the value of investments in healthcare (Gold, 1996).

A single QALY is equivalent to a year of perfect health. In the event that an individual experiences a decline in quality of life as a result of chronic illness or disability, the value of that year will be less than one QALY. To illustrate, if an individual's health status declines by 50%, that year would be assigned a value of 0.5 QALY (Weinstein & Stason, 1977). This measurement is employed particularly for the assessment of cost-effectiveness in healthcare services and the optimisation of resource allocation.The Quality-Adjusted Life Year (QALY) provides valuable insights into the social determinants of health (SDH), including factors like income, education, and unemployment, which affect individual health. QALY data helps identify how these factors influence health outcomes, guiding health policies and interventions. By analyzing the impact of SDH on quality of life, QALYs enable the identification of effective interventions to reduce health inequalities (Braveman et al., 2011). The value of QALYs lies in their ability to assess both lifespan and quality of life, facilitating the development of policies aimed at reducing health inequalities (Solar & Irwin, 2010).

2.1.1.5. Disability-Adjusted Life Year (DALY)

The Disability-Adjusted Life Year (DALY) is a metric used to quantify the disease burden in a community, assessing the overall impact of disease and disability on health. A DALY represents the number of healthy years lost due to disease, considering both life expectancy and quality of life. A high DALY indicates significant health issues within a community (Murray & Lopez, 1996). DALYs are crucial for analyzing health inequalities and efficiently allocating healthcare resources, as they provide a numerical representation of the impact of diseases on a community's health. This measurement aids in the evaluation of health disparities and the achievement of Sustainable Development Goals (SDGs).The DALY metric allows for the examination of the differential impact of diseases on different socio-economic groups. A higher DALY value typically indicates a greater prevalence of diseases and health risks among lower socioeconomic groups. This measurement facilitates a more nuanced comprehension of health inequalities and informs the formulation of strategies to address inequities in healthcare access. The implementation of health policies that align with the needs of society encourages the adoption of preventative measures for disadvantaged groups (Murray & Lopez, 1996).

DALY supports the achievement of SDG health-related objectives, such as promoting "healthy individuals" and "reducing inequalities," by helping focus healthcare improvements in high-disease areas. DALY data identifies diseases and risk groups to prioritize, aiding in the creation of sustainable health policies. It informs effective interventions in areas like infectious diseases, malnutrition, and environmental health impacts, providing a solid foundation for achieving SDG targets (Murray & Lopez, 1996).

2.1.2. Human Development Index (HDI)

In 1990, the United Nations Development Programme (UNDP) sought to evaluate human development on a broader scale than merely economic income levels. Instead, the UNDP aimed to assess the quality of life and well-being of individuals through a range of social and economic indicators. In consequence of this approach, the Human Development Index (HDI) was developed, comprising key human factors such as income, education and life expectancy, as a tool for measurement. The HDI places emphasis on elements that enhance the quality of life of individuals and support long-term human development. In addition to promoting economic growth, it also encourages the holistic development of human potential (Human Development Reports, 2010).It is evident that the HDI is not an adequate instrument for evaluating health disparities. Nevertheless, the analysis of public health status can be more comprehensive if other indicators used to measure health inequalities are considered in conjunction with the HDI.

2.1.3. Lorenz Curve and Gini Coefficient

The Lorenz curve is a graphical tool used to visualize the cumulative distribution of a variable, typically income, within a society ordered from lowest to highest. It helps assess the level of inequality in resource distribution. The horizontal axis represents the cumulative percentage of individuals, while the vertical axis represents the cumulative percentage of total income or another variable. In a scenario of perfect equality, the Lorenz curve is a 45-degree line. As inequality increases, the curve becomes more concave, with the degree of concavity reflecting the extent of inequality (Cowell, 2011).In the field of healthcare, the Lorenz curve can be employed to evaluate the extent of inequality in specific health variables within a given society. In this analysis, the horizontal axis represents the cumulative percentage of the population, while the vertical axis represents the cumulative percentage of individuals or groups in the society.

Figure 1. Lorenz Curve

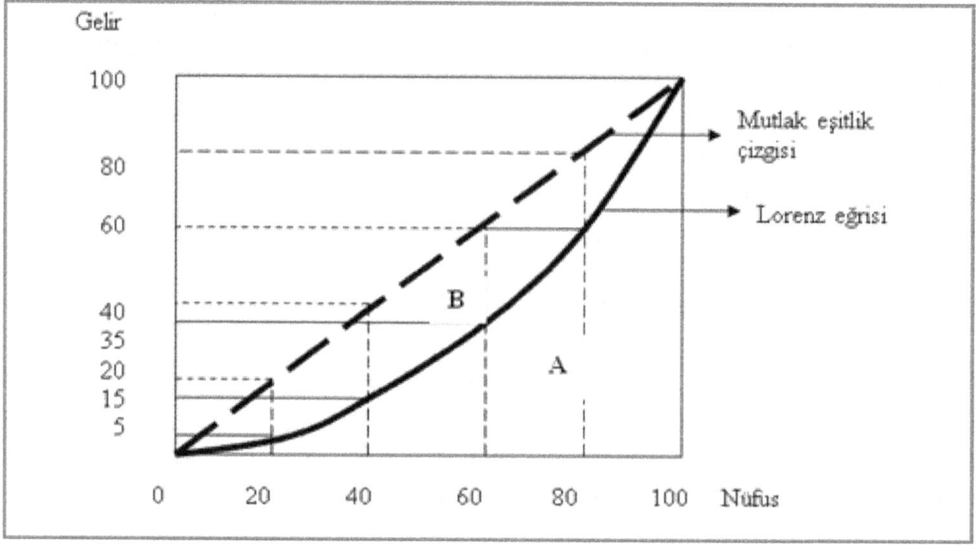

Source: **Gastwirth, J. L. (1972). The estimation of the Lorenz curve and Gini index. The Review of Economics And Statistics, 306-316.***https://doi.org/10.2307/1937992.*

To track the change in inequality over the years between countries or within a country, it is more appropriate to express inequality using a coefficient. The Gini coefficient is a measure that indicates the level of inequality and quantifies its degree.

GINI coefficient = Area A / (Area A + Area B)

In this formula, the larger Area A is (meaning the farther the Lorenz curve is from the line of perfect equality), the higher the Gini coefficient becomes, indicating greater inequality in the distribution of resources (Dinler, 2003).

3. STRATEGIES TO PREVENT AND INTERVENE IN INEQUALITY

The reduction of health inequalities is central to achieving the Sustainable Development Goals (SDGs), particularly SDG1 "No Poverty," SDG2 "Zero Hunger," and SDG3 "Good Health and Well-Being." These goals are linked to strategies that address economic and social empowerment, as factors like poverty, food insecurity, and limited access to healthcare drive health disparities (WHO, 2020; Marmot, 2005). Disadvantaged groups face unequal access to healthcare, which negatively impacts both public health and individual well-being. Addressing these imbalances is crucial for sustainable development (Sen, 1999). Additionally, SDG10 "Reduced Inequalities" can significantly improve healthcare access and community quality of life (UNDP, 2021). Inclusive health policies and practices that enhance societal well-being are essential for advancing sustainability (Solar & Irwin, 2010). Thus, eliminating healthcare access inequalities is vital for social justice and sustainable development.

- *Improving living conditions:* One of the primary ways to reduce health inequalities is by improving individuals' living conditions. Living conditions directly impact individuals' health and well-being, and play a key role in reducing societal inequalities. Good health is not only influenced by genetics or individual behaviors but also depends on social determinants such as safe housing, clean water, healthy nutrition options, a secure environment, and stable income (Solar & Irwin, 2010). Creating healthy living environments, especially for disadvantaged groups, can improve their health levels and reduce social health inequalities.

Ensuring healthy living conditions also contributes to sustainable development across society. For example, improving infrastructure and basic services in low-income areas increases access to healthcare services while also helping individuals lead healthier lives (Marmot, 2005). When social health policies are combined with interventions aimed at improving living conditions, the overall health of the community improves, leading to a healthier society (UNDP, 2021). In this context, policies aimed at reducing poverty and improving education are proposed as effective steps in reducing health inequalities.

- *Providing 'universal' access to healthcare services:* Ensuring that healthcare services are accessible to everyone is a critical approach for enabling equal access to health services based on individuals' needs. This principle aims to ensure that all individuals, regardless of factors like income level, geographical location, or socioeconomic status, have the right to access healthcare services. Equal access to healthcare not only improves public health levels but also facilitates early diagnosis and treatment of diseases, supporting the creation of healthier and more productive societies. Disparities in access to healthcare services for disadvantaged groups negatively affect overall health indicators. Therefore, delivering healthcare services to everyone through effectively planned primary health services and inclusive social policies is regarded as a fundamental strategy in reducing health inequalities (Starfield, 2001). For instance, offering free or low-cost healthcare services ensures that individuals living near the poverty line benefit more from these services (UNDP, 2021). Such inclusive healthcare services are also crucial in achieving the health-related targets of the SDGs. Under SDG3, which calls for "good health and well-being," providing universal access to healthcare supports not only individual health outcomes but also societal welfare and economic development (UNDP, 2021).

- *Strengthening preventive healthcare services:* Strengthening preventive healthcare services involves measures aimed at protecting public health and helping individuals live healthier lives by preventing the onset of diseases. These services include vaccinations, routine health screenings, educational programs, and community projects focused on reducing health risks. Strong preventive healthcare services reduce the burden on healthcare systems by preventing disease, ultimately reducing long-term costs and improving public health (WHO, 2020).

Preventive services support individuals' healthy aging and help reduce health inequalities. Communities with inadequate preventive services become more vulnerable to infectious and chronic diseases, which increases the need for healthcare services among disadvantaged groups (Marmot, 2005). Therefore, an effective preventive healthcare policy not only preserves individual health but also contributes to reducing health inequalities and promoting social justice in line with the SDGs.

- *Developing interventions for disadvantaged and high-risk groups with insufficient use of healthcare services:*Addressing the healthcare access issues for disadvantaged groups is crucial in reducing health inequalities. In this regard, it is necessary to develop strategic interventions for high-risk groups. For instance, individuals living in poor or rural areas often use healthcare services less and encounter more significant barriers in accessing them (Marmot & Wilkinson, 2003).

Increasing access to preventive healthcare services and improving health literacy for groups with insufficient healthcare access are also vital. Innovative solutions, such as social health programs and mobile clinics, are particularly effective for individuals facing transportation issues or living in geographically disadvantaged areas. These interventions contribute to the equitable and efficient distribution of healthcare services, enhancing societal welfare.

In particular, during the COVID-19 pandemic, it was observed that individuals with inadequate access to healthcare services were at greater risk. During this period, the importance of policies that prioritize delivering healthcare services to disadvantaged groups increased (Abrams & Szefler, 2020). To address social health inequalities, continuous support for these groups through public policies and ensuring equal access to healthcare services are essential (Braveman & Gruskin, 2003).

- *Securing the support of civil society organizations (CSOs):* Securing the support of CSOs in increasing disadvantaged groups' access to healthcare services is an effective strategy in reducing health inequalities. CSOs raise awareness about health issues, provide health education, facilitate access to resources, and support the community's access to healthy living conditions (Gilson, 2003). CSOs collaborating with public service providers in the implementation of health policies expand the accessibility of healthcare services and play a key role in ensuring their effective distribution.

CSOs, especially those operating in low-income or rural areas, alleviate health inequalities in these regions by providing mobile health services or free clinics for individuals who do not have adequate access to healthcare services. Additionally, these organizations enhance patients' health literacy, enabling individuals to manage their own health and access preventive healthcare services. For example, international CSOs like MSF (Médecins Sans Frontières) and the Red Cross play a significant role in reducing health inequalities by providing essential healthcare services to communities in humanitarian crises where access to healthcare is limited (Redwood-Campbell & Abrahams, 2011).

CONCLUSİON

The Sustainable Development Goals (SDGs) provide a vital and comprehensive framework for reducing health inequalities and improving global well-being. As is apparent from the analysis, whilst Sustainable Development Goal 3, entitled "Good Health and Well-Being", is explicit in its direct targeting of healthcare access and quality, other key factors affecting health are addressed by other goals, including those entitled "No Poverty", "Zero Hunger" and "Reduced Inequality". Collectively, these objectives underscore the necessity for a comprehensive strategy, emphasising that the reduction of health disparities necessitates the addressing of numerous, interrelated determinants. This integrated effort supports more equitable health outcomes and promotes social justice on a global scale.

One of the key aims of the SDGs in reducing poverty is to eliminate economic barriers that hinder access to essential healthcare, especially for disadvantaged populations. Poverty profoundly impacts health through various social determinants—such as limited access to health insurance, poor nutrition, inadequate housing, and insecure employment—that disproportionately affect low-income communities. By targeting these issues under SDG 1, "No Poverty," the SDGs seek to improve financial stability and, consequently, healthcare access for marginalized groups. Enhancing economic security is thus vital for achieving better health outcomes and reducing disparities at the community level.

As outlined in Sustainable Development Goal 10, income inequalities are not the only social issue addressed; health inequalities resulting from social determinants such as education, gender, age and ethnicity are also encompassed. These determinants are fundamental factors that influence individuals' access to healthcare services and opportunities for a healthy life. The Sustainable Development Goals (SDGs) are a series of international development goals established by the United Nations (UN) in 2015 with the aim of reducing global inequalities through the implementation of social policies and the promotion of social health equity. Moreover, the Sustainable Development Goals (SDGs) of "Climate Action" (SDG 13) and "Clean Water and Sanitation" (SDG 6) have been identified as contributing factors to the reduction of health inequalities. This is achieved through the mitigation of the negative health impacts of environmental factors and the protection of the health of marginalised communities.

The Sustainable Development Goals (SDGs) emphasize environmental sustainability as a crucial determinant of public health, acknowledging that factors such as pollution, climate change, and access to clean water and sanitation significantly impact health outcomes. Marginalized and low-income communities are especially vulnerable to these environmental risks, which can amplify existing health inequalities. SDG 13, "Climate Action," and SDG 6, "Clean Water and Sanitation," directly address these challenges by promoting efforts to mitigate environmental hazards and ensure equitable access to essential resources.More broadly, the SDGs present a multidimensional and integrated framework for reducing health inequalities and enhancing community well-being. While SDG 3, "Good Health and Well-Being," focuses on improving healthcare access and quality, other goals—such as SDG 1 "No Poverty," SDG 2 "Zero Hunger," and SDG 10 "Reduced Inequality"—target the underlying social and economic determinants of health. Together, these goals advocate for a holistic strategy that combines health, social, economic, and environmental interventions.

In conclusion, the SDGs offer a transformative approach to global health equity by addressing the complex interplay of factors that shape health outcomes. Their inclusive and interconnected structure provides a foundation for advancing health justice and building a more resilient, equitable, and sustainable future for all.

REFERENCES

Abrams, E. M., & Szefler, S. J. (2020). COVID-19 and the impact of social determinants of health. *The Lancet. Respiratory Medicine*, *8*(7), 659–661. DOI: 10.1016/S2213-2600(20)30234-4 PMID: 32437646

Albert-Ballestar, S., & García-Altés, A. (2021). Measuring health inequalities: A systematic review of widely used indicators and topics. *International Journal for Equity in Health*, *20*(1), 1–15. DOI: 10.1186/s12939-021-01397-3 PMID: 33691701

Amarasinghe, U., D'Souza, G., Brown, C., Oh, H., & Borisova, T. (2009). The influence of socioeconomic and environmental determinants on health and obesity: A West Virginia case study. *International Journal of Environmental Research and Public Health*, *6*(8), 2271–2287. DOI: 10.3390/ijerph6082271 PMID: 19742160

Bahar, Z., & Aydoğdu, N. G. (2015). Çevre, sağlık, araştırma ve hemşirelik. *Dokuz Eylül Üniversitesi Hemsirelik Fakültesi Elektronik Dergisi*, *8*(2), 119–122.

Bambra, C., Fox, D., & Scott-Samuel, A. (2005). Towards a politics of health. *Health Promotion International*, *20*(2), 187–193. DOI: 10.1093/heapro/dah608 PMID: 15722364

Bambra, C., Riordan, R., Ford, J., & Matthews, F. (2020). The COVID-19 pandemic and health inequalities. *Journal of Epidemiology and Community Health*, *74*(11), 964–968. DOI: 10.1136/jech-2020-214401 PMID: 32535550

Bansal, N., Karlsen, S., Sashidharan, S. P., Cohen, R., Chew-Graham, C. A., & Malpass, A. (2022). Understanding ethnic inequalities in mental healthcare in the UK: A meta-ethnography. *PLoS Medicine*, *19*(12), e1004139. DOI: 10.1371/journal.pmed.1004139 PMID: 36512523

Braveman, P., Egerter, S., & Williams, D. R. (2011). The social determinants of health: Coming of age. *Annual Review of Public Health*, *32*(1), 381–398. DOI: 10.1146/annurev-publhealth-031210-101218 PMID: 21091195

Braveman, P., & Gruskin, S. (2003). Defining equity in health. *Journal of Epidemiology and Community Health*, *57*(4), 254–258. DOI: 10.1136/jech.57.4.254 PMID: 12646539

Cénat, J. M., Dalexis, R. D., Kokou-Kpolou, C. K., Mukunzi, J. N., & Rousseau, C. (2020). Social inequalities and collateral damages of the COVID-19 pandemic: When basic needs challenge mental health care. *International Journal of Public Health*, *65*(6), 717–718. DOI: 10.1007/s00038-020-01426-y PMID: 32651593

Coughlin, S. S., Vernon, M., Hatzigeorgiou, C., & George, V. (2020). Health literacy, social determinants of health, and disease prevention and control. *Journal of Environment and Health Sciences*, *6*(1), 3061. https://pmc.ncbi.nlm.nih.gov/articles/PMC7889072/ PMID: 33604453

Cowell, F. A. (2011). *Measuring Inequality*. Oxford University Press. DOI: 10.1093/acprof:osobl/9780199594030.001.0001

Çukur, A., & Bekmez, S. (2011). Türkiye'de Gelir, Gelir Eşitsizliği ve Sağlık İlişkisi: Panel Veri Analizi Bulguları. *Gaziantep Üniversitesi Sosyal Bilimler Dergisi*, *10*(1), 21–40.

Cutler, D. M., & Lleras-Muney, A. (2006). Education and health: Evaluating theories and evidence. *Natıonal Bureau of Economic Research, 12352*. Advance online publication. DOI: 10.3386/w12352

Denton, M., Prus, S., & Walters, V. (2004). Gender differences in health: A Canadian study of the psychosocial, structural and behavioural determinants of health. *Social Science & Medicine*, *58*(12), 2585–2600. DOI: 10.1016/j.socscimed.2003.09.008 PMID: 15081207

Di Cesare, M., Khang, Y. H., Asaria, P., Blakely, T., Cowan, M. J., Farzadfar, F., Guerrero, R., Ikeda, N., Kyobutungi, C., Msyamboza, K. P., Oum, S., Lynch, J. W., Marmot, M. G., & Ezzati, M. (2013). Inequalities in non-communicable diseases and effective responses. *Lancet*, *381*(9866), 585–597. DOI: 10.1016/S0140-6736(12)61851-0 PMID: 23410608

Dinler, Z. (2003). *İktisada Giriş* (6. baskı). Bursa: Ekin Kitabevi Yayınları.

Drummond, M. F., Sculpher, M. J., Claxton, K., Stoddart, G. L., & Torrance, G. W. (2015). *Methods for the economic evaluation of health care programmes* (4th ed.). Oxford University Press.

Fine, M. J., Ibrahim, S. A., & Thomas, S. B. (2005). The role of race and genetics in health disparities research. *American Journal of Public Health*, *95*(12), 2125–2128. DOI: 10.2105/AJPH.2005.076588 PMID: 16257933

Gilman, R. (1992). The concept of sustainable development. *In Context*, 33, 1–5. https://www.context.org/about/definitions/

Gilson, L. (2003). Trust and the development of health care as a social institution. *Social Science & Medicine*, *56*(7), 1453–1468. DOI: 10.1016/S0277-9536(02)00142-9 PMID: 12614697

Gkiouleka, A., Wong, G., Sowden, S., Bambra, C., Siersbaek, R., Manji, S., Moseley, A., Harmston, R., Kuhn, I., & Ford, J. (2023). Reducing health inequalities through general practice. *The Lancet. Public Health*, *8*(6), e463–e472. DOI: 10.1016/S2468-2667(23)00093-2 PMID: 37244675

Gold, M. R. (1996). *Cost-effectiveness in health and medicine*. Oxford University Press.Retrived from:https://global.oup.com/academic/product/cost-effectiveness-in-health-and-medicine-9780195108248?cc=tr&lang=en&/ dated 10.11.2024

Harper, S., & Lynch, J. (2006) Measuring Health Inequalities. In: Oakes, J. and Kaufman, J., Eds., *Methods in Social Epidemiology*, Wiley, 134-168.Retrived from:https://digital.library.adelaide.edu.au/items/36f387e0-6fdd-4590-b0e4-9615d32ff5c3/ dated 10.12.2024

Human Development Reports. (2010). *The real wealth of nations: Pathways to human development*. United Nations Development Programme.Retrived from:https://www.undp.org/sites/g/files/zskgke326/files/migration/ly/HDR_2010_EN_Complete_reprint-1.pdf /dated 31.12.2024

Jaffe, D. H., Lee, L., Huynh, S., & Haskell, T. P. (2020). Health inequalities in the use of telehealth in the United States in the lens of COVID-19. *Population Health Management*, *23*(5), 368–377. DOI: 10.1089/pop.2020.0186 PMID: 32816644

Karasek, R., & Theorell, T. (1990). *Healthy work: Stress, productivity, and the reconstruction of working life*. Canada: Basic Books. Retired from: https://archive.org/details/healthyworkstres0000kara/ dates 10.10.2024

Keeton, V. F., Bell, J. F., Drake, C., Garcia, E. O. F. Y., Pantell, M., Hessler, D., Wing, H., Silveira, P. P., Donnell, K. J. O., Filho, E. J. M., Meaney, M. J., & Gottlieb, L. M. (2023). Household Social Needs, Emotional Functioning, and Stress in Low-Income Latinx Children and their Mothers. *Journal of Child and Family Studies*, *32*(3), 796–811. DOI: 10.1007/s10826-023-02532-0 PMID: 37143480

Lawrence, E. M., Rogers, R. G., Zajacova, A., & Wadsworth, T. (2019). Marital happiness, marital status, health, and longevity. *Journal of Happiness Studies*, *20*(5), 1539–1561. https://psycnet.apa.org/doi/10.1007/s10902-018-0009-9. DOI: 10.1007/s10902-018-0009-9

Lloyd, D., Newell, S., & Dietrich, U. C. (2004). Health inequity: a review of the literature. *Northern Rivers Area Health Service*.Retired from:https://www.semanticscholar.org/paper/Health-inequity%3A-a-review-of-the-literature-Lloyd-Newell/0d7a855ea44a92ad1b059db62bf394832d6dd4c5/ dated 21.09.2024

Lopez, A. D., Mathers, C. D., Ezzati, M., Jamison, D. T., & Murray, C. J. (2011). Measuring the global burden of disease and risk factors, 1990–2001.*In: Global Burden of Disease and Risk Factors. The International Bank for Reconstruction and Development / The World Bank, Washington (DC);* 2006. PMID: 21250376.

Marmot, M. (2005). Social determinants of health inequalities. *Lancet*, *365*(9464), 1099–1104. DOI: 10.1016/S0140-6736(05)71146-6 PMID: 15781105

Marmot, M., Allen, J., Boyce, T., Goldblatt, P., & Morrison, J. (2020). *Health equity in England: The Marmot review 10 years on.* Institute of Health Equity.https://www.instituteofhealthequity.org/resources-reports/marmot-review-10-years-on/the-marmot-review-10-years-on-full-report.pdf

Marmot, M., & Allen, J. J. (2014). Social determinants of health equity. *American Journal of Public Health*, *104*(4), 517–519. DOI: 10.2105/AJPH.2014.302200 PMID: 25100411

Marmot, M., Friel, S., Bell, R., Houweling, T. A., Taylor, S., & Commission on Social Determinants of Health (2008). Closing the gap in a generation: health equity through action on the social determinants of health. *Lancet (London, England)*, 372(9650), 1661–1669.https://doi.org/.DOI: 10.1016/S0140-6736(08)61690-6

Meherali, S., Punjani, N. S., & Mevawala, A. (2020). Health literacy interventions to improve health outcomes in low-and middle-income countries. *Health Literacy Research and Practice*, *4*(4), e251–e266. DOI: 10.3928/24748307-20201118-01 PMID: 33313935

Mishra, V., Seyedzenouzi, G., Almohtadi, A., Chowdhury, T., Khashkhusha, A., Axiaq, A., Wong, W. Y. E., & Harky, A. (2021). Health inequalities during COVID-19 and their effects on morbidity and mortality. *Journal of Healthcare Leadership*, *13*, 19–26. DOI: 10.2147/JHL.S270175 PMID: 33500676

Murray, C. J., & Lopez, A. D. (1997). Global mortality, disability, and the contribution of risk factors: Global Burden of Disease Study. *Lancet*, *349*(9063), 1436–1442. DOI: 10.1016/S0140-6736(96)07495-8 PMID: 9164317

Murray, C. J. L., & Lopez, A. D. (1996). *The global burden of disease: A comprehensive assessment of mortality and disability from diseases, injuries, and risk factors in 1990 and projected to 2020*. Harvard School of Public Health.

Newman, L., Baum, F., Javanparast, S., O'Rourke, K., & Carlon, L. (2015). Addressing social determinants of health inequities through settings: A rapid review. *Health Promotion International*, *30*(suppl_2), ii126–ii143. DOI: 10.1093/heapro/dav054 PMID: 26420808

Olshansky, S. J., Passaro, D. J., Hershow, R. C., Layden, J., Carnes, B. A., Brody, J., Hayflick, L., Butler, R. N., Allison, D. B., & Ludwig, D. S. (2005). A potential decline in life expectancy in the United States in the 21st century. *The New England Journal of Medicine*, *352*(11), 1138–1145. DOI: 10.1056/NEJMsr043743 PMID: 15784668

Öztek, Z. (2023). *Sürdürülebilir Kalkınma ve Sağlık*. Ankara: Sağlık ve Sosyal Yardım Vakfı. Retrived from: https://ssyv.org.tr/2023/07/11/surdurulebilir-kalkinma-ve-saglik/dated 25.12.2024.

Penman-Aguilar, A., Talih, M., Huang, D., Moonesinghe, R., Bouye, K., & Beckles, G. (2016). Measurement of health disparities, health inequities, and social determinants of health to support the advancement of health equity. *Journal of Public Health Management and Practice*, *22*(Supplement 1), S33–S42. DOI: 10.1097/PHH.0000000000000373 PMID: 26599027

Pınarbaşı, Ş., & Piyal, B. (2022). Sürdürülebilir kalkınma hedefi üç'ün sağlık kapsayıcılığı işlevi. *ESTÜDAM Halk Sağlığı Dergisi*, *7*(2), 379–391. DOI: 10.35232/estudamhsd.1048562

Polat, G., & İçağasıoğlu Çoban, A. (2015). 21.yy'da sağlıkta eşitsizlikler ve eşitsizliğin aşılmasında sosyal hizmetin rolü. *Toplum ve Sosyal Hizmet*, *26*(1), 177–190.

Rasu, R. S., Bawa, W. A., Suminski, R., Snella, K., & Warady, B. (2015). Health literacy impact on national healthcare utilization and expenditure. *International Journal of Health Policy and Management*, *4*(11), 747–755. DOI: 10.15171/ijhpm.2015.151 PMID: 26673335

Redwood-Campbell, L., & Abrahams, J. (2011). Primary health care and disasters—The current state of the literature: What we know, gaps and next steps for research. *Prehospital and Disaster Medicine*, *26*(3), 184–191. DOI: 10.1017/S1049023X11006388 PMID: 22107769

Robards, J., Evandrou, M., Falkingham, J., & Vlachantoni, A. (2012). Marital status, health and mortality. *Maturitas*, *73*(4), 295–299. DOI: 10.1016/j.maturitas.2012.08.007 PMID: 23007006

Şahman, O., & Gün, İ. (2024). Sağlığın sosyal belirleyicilerinin moora yöntemi ile analizi: OECD ülkeleri örneği. *Sosyal Güvence*, *13*(26), 1376–1399. DOI: 10.21441/sosyalguvence.1507454

Schlotheuber, A., & Hosseinpoor, A. R. (2022). Summary measures of health inequality: A review of existing measures and their application. *International Journal of Environmental Research and Public Health, 19*(6), 3697. DOI: 10.3390/ijerph19063697 PMID: 35329383

Sen, A. (1999). *Development as freedom.* Oxford University Press. Retired from: http://www.c3l.uni-oldenburg.de/cde/OMDE625/Sen/Sen-intro.pdf/ dated 23.11.2024

Solar, O., & Irwin, A. (2010). *A conceptual framework for action on the social determinants of health.* WHO Document Production Services.Retired from:https://www.who.int/publications/i/item/9789241500852/ dated 21.12.2024

Starfield, B. (2001). Improving equity in health: A research agenda. *International Journal of Health Services, 31*(3), 545–566. DOI: 10.2190/DGJ8-4MQW-UP9J-LQC1 PMID: 11562005

Stennett, M., & Tsakos, G. (2022). The impact of the COVID-19 pandemic on oral health inequalities and access to oral healthcare in England. *British Dental Journal, 232*(2), 109–114. DOI: 10.1038/s41415-021-3718-0 PMID: 35091614

Thomson, R. M., Igelström, E., Purba, A. K., Shimonovich, M., Thomson, H., McCartney, G., Reeves, A., Leyland, A., Pearce, A., & Katikireddi, S. V. (2022). How do income changes impact on mental health and wellbeing for working-age adults? A systematic review and meta-analysis. *The Lancet. Public Health, 7*(6), e515–e528. DOI: 10.1016/S2468-2667(22)00058-5 PMID: 35660213

Todaro, M. P., & Smith, S. C. (2020). *Economic development* (13th ed.). Pearson Education. Retired from: https://www.pearson.com/en-gb/subject-catalog/p/economic-development/P200000005609/9781292477329/ dated 02.11.2024

United Nations. (2015). *Transforming our world: The 2030 Agenda for Sustainable Development.* United Nations General Assembly.https://sdgs.un.org/2030agenda

United Nations. (2024). *Transforming our world: The 2030 Agenda for Sustainable Development.*https://sdgs.un.org/2030agenda

United Nations Development Programme [UNDP]. (2021). *Leaving no one behind: A UNDP approach to tackling inequality.*https://ses-toolkit.info.undp.org/leave-no-one-behind#:~:text=As%20an%20overarching%20programming%20principle,agents%20of%20the%20development%20process

Valentine, N. B., Koller, T. S., & Hosseinpoor, A. R. (2016). Monitoring health determinants with an equity focus: A key role in addressing social determinants, universal health coverage, and advancing the 2030 sustainable development agenda. *Global Health Action, 9*(1), 34247. DOI: 10.3402/gha.v9.34247 PMID: 27989275

Viner, R. M., Ozer, E. M., Denny, S., Marmot, M., Resnick, M., Fatusi, A., & Currie, C. (2012). Adolescence and the social determinants of health. *Lancet*, *379*(9826), 1641–1652. DOI: 10.1016/S0140-6736(12)60149-4 PMID: 22538179

Weinstein, M. C., & Stason, W. B. (1977). Foundations of cost-effectiveness analysis for health and medical practices. *The New England Journal of Medicine*, *296*(13), 716–721. DOI: 10.1056/NEJM197703312961304 PMID: 402576

Whitehead, M. (1992). The concepts and principles of equity and health. *International Journal of Health Services: Planning, Administration. Evaluation*, *22*(3), 429–445. DOI: 10.2190/986L-LHQ6-2VTE-YRRN PMID: 1644507

Wilkinson, R. G., & Marmot, M. (Eds.). (2003). *Social determinants of health: the solid facts*. World Health Organization. Retired from: https://iris.who.int/handle/10665/326568/ dated 02.10.22024

Williams, D. R., Lawrence, J. A., & Davis, B. A. (2019). Racism and health: Evidence and needed research. *Annual Review of Public Health*, *40*(1), 105–125. DOI: 10.1146/annurev-publhealth-040218-043750 PMID: 30601726

World Health Organization. (2008). *Closing the gap in a generation: Health equity through action on the social determinants of health.* Commission on Social Determinants of Health Final Report. WHO Press. https://iris.who.int/bitstream/handle/10665/43943/9789241563703_eng.pdf

World Health Organization. (2020). *World health statistics 2020: Monitoring health for the SDGs*. World Health Organization.https://www.who.int/publications/i/item/9789240005105

World Health Organization. (2021). *Life expectancy and healthy life expectancy, data by country*.World Health Organization.https://apps.who.int/gho/data/node.main.688

World Health Organization. (2022). *Social determinants of health*.https://www.who.int/publications/i/item/9789240005105

World Health Organization. (2023). *World health statistics 2023: Monitoring health for the SDGs, sustainable development goals.* World Health Organization.https://www.who.int/publications/i/item/9789240074323

World Health Organization. (2024). Operational framework for monitoring social determinants of health equity. World Health Organization. https://www.who.int/publications/i/item/9789240088320

World Health Organization (WHO). (2022). *Health in the sustainable development goals: Where are we now?*https://www.who.int/initiatives/sdg3-global-action-plan

Chapter 18
The Unseen Stressor:
How Pollution Impacts Mental Health – A Narrative Review of Literature

Zainab Hamid
https://orcid.org/0000-0002-3981-1658
J&K Higher Education Department, India

Mohd Muzamil
University of Kashmir, India

ABSTRACT

Global mental health is seriously threatened by environmental pollution, which is also rather increasing. Examining the complex link between several types of environmental pollution and a spectrum of mental diseases, this chapter offers a methodical review of material published mainly between 2007 and 2024. The chapter concludes with emphasizing the critical need of integrated public health policies, strict pollution control measures, sustainable urban planning, and focused interventions to minimize the widespread negative effects of environmental pollution on population mental health and support resilient communities.

INTRODUCTION AND BACKGROUND

Both natural and man-made crises greatly affect the state of the community, particularly mental health, as such, mental disorders have become a major public concern in middle-income nations as well as developing ones. Affecting millions of people worldwide, mental disorders are becoming a major threat to society.

DOI: 10.4018/979-8-3693-9755-8.ch018

According to Krause, et al. (2016), early death and disability globally are mostly caused by mental disorders considerably.

Numerous studies have unequivocally shown a strong relationship between environmental pollution and a spectrum of negative effects on mental health. Pollution exposure has been linked to increased stress, anxiety, depression, cognitive problems including Alzheimer's disease. Moreover, it can raise death rates among people already suffering with chronic mental illness. Particularly arguing that exposure to environmental toxins causes a notable incidence and intensity of mental diseases are Braithwaite et al. (2019) and Zhao et al. (2018). Environmental pollution, according to Stiftung (2010), also compromises mental health and might lead to anxiety, insomnia, major depression, hostility, and social dysfunction.

More especially, key risk factors for mental health have been found to be air, water, and solid waste pollution. Extended exposure to high pollution levels can interfere with the normal operation of important brain areas including the prefrontal cortex, amygdala, and hippocampal involved in control of emotions. This disturbance might produce a biological environment fit for the emergence of several mental disorders, including anxiety and major depression (APA, 2023). Studies have shown that environmental pollution seriously compromises emotional and psychological wellbeing, so affecting concentration, poor decision-making, annoyance, anger, boredom, and disturbed sleep (Perveen, et al., 2015). Along with epigenetic processes, the interaction of genes and the surroundings provides important proof on the causes of various psychotic diseases, including schizophrenia (Attademo et al., 2017). Strong levels of particulate matter, nitrogen, sulfur oxides, organic solvents, and other environmental pollutants as well as heavy metals like lead and cadmium could increase the risk of schizophrenia and other psychotic diseases. Environmental factors account for 55%–60% of the risk for major depression, 32% for bipolar disorder, and 23% for schizophrenia, according to Khan et al. (2019). Marangoni et al. (2016) and Bortolato et al. (2017) have similarly suggested that risk factors for psychiatric and neurological diseases are genetic elements, personal traits, behaviors (such as drug abuse), social conditions (such as work stress), and environmental exposure (including pollution). Factors including air quality, water quality, land quality, weather indices, and sociodemographic elements including income and population density significantly influence the beginning and development of psychiatric diseases, claims Khan et al. (2019). Moreover, areas marked by poverty, inadequate access to reasonably priced homes, high unemployment, limited green areas, overcrowding, and other psychosocial challenges are linked to inflammation and, when combined with poor air quality, can lead to both physical and mental health problems (Bhui, et al. 2023). In essence, the data shows that environmental pollution in all its forms seriously compromises mental health in many different age groups and contexts. From aggravating the risk and severity of mental diseases to affecting brain development and cognitive ability, pollution has negative consequences in many different spheres. This emphasizes how urgently environmental policies and interventions that give pollution reduction top priority and the building of better surroundings top importance in preserving public mental health.

AIMS AND SCOPE

This chapter investigates how pollution affects mental health, strives to explore the unique yet increasingly studied connection between human psychology and environmental pollution in a detailed manner. With the mounting threat of environmental deterioration simultaneously contributing to the rising global mental illness burden, exploration of interrelationship between pollution & mental health requires a multidisciplinary focus for the advancement of public health policy and clinical intervention.

Primary Aims

1. To systematically analyze and amalgamate a substantial volume of scientific literature from the years 2007 to 2024 about the relationships between differing types of pollution and mental health issues.
2. To analyze and outline possible biological, psychological, and sociological pathways whereby exposure to pollutants may initiate, intensify, or otherwise facilitate the onset of mental health disorders.
3. To provide evidence regarding the groups that seem to suffer the most from the mental health consequences of pollution, including children, teenagers, the elderly, pregnant women, and those from lower socioeconomic groups, thus pointing out the fairness aspects of this problem.

Scope

The scope of this chapter is broad, reflecting the pervasiveness of pollution and the range of potential mental health effects. It incorporates: Crucial environmental exposures discussed include, but are not limited to, airborne contaminants such as particulate matter (PM2.5 and PM10), nitrogen oxides, sulphur oxides, ozone, volatile organic compounds, heavy metals (lead, arsenic, mercury, cadmium), pesticides, chemical and biological water pollutants, scarcity of water, excessive environmental noise (especially traffic), and distance to the sources of these pollutants.

Search Strategy

A systematic search of PubMed, google scholar, Scopus and other electronic bibliographic databases was conducted from 2007-2024 with an objective of understanding of the mental disorder and an impact of environmental pollution on mental health. To promote specificity and minimalize the repossession of non-relevant articles and research work, terms were searched regarding titles and abstracts. The aim of this approach was to search and find the most relevant results to our mentioned constructs. In addition, we incorporated in our study key terms linked with air pollution, mental health, water pollution, mental disorder symptoms, demographic characteristics etc. A systematic data collection, presenting main details from every eligible study including- first authors, year and month of publication, country/ location of research study, sample socio-demographic characteristics, study design, data collection method, research result and conclusion. Our study aimed to present a complete global summary, without geographic limits, in order to prove diverse impact of the environmental pollution worldwide, ensuring that the results/findings of the various studies are directly applied to healthcare professionals and their challenges and to policy needs. Last but not least inclusion and exclusion criteria were adopted to refine search findings to ensure only relevant and objective focused studies.

Inclusion and Exclusion Criteria

Research articles were selected in our review based on the following criteria: reports presenting information related to effect of components of environmental pollution on various mental health disorders collected between 2007-2024; publications in English language in peer reviewed and high indexing journals and duplicate articles were removed; presentation of authentic and original data on mentioned topic

In light of the search criteria, a detailed review of literature related to the impact of various types of pollution on mental health is presented below.

Table 1. Studies related to Air pollution and Mental Health

Finding	Authors/Source	Year
Air pollution is a prominent environmental risk factor that causes around 7 million deaths each year. It also leads to various health-related economic burdens, including an increase in respiratory infections, pulmonary disease, heart disease, cancer, stroke, type 2 diabetes, Alzheimer's, and other neurological diseases.	World Health Organization	2021
Exposure to air pollution is associated with an increase in psychiatric illnesses such as depression, schizophrenia, bipolar disorder, personality disorder, and neuro-inflammation.	American Psychiatric Association	2023
Approximately 40% of Americans breathe air with unhealthy levels of pollution.	American Lung Association	2021
Elevated levels of CO_2 have a significant impact on a range of health outcomes, including impaired cognitive performance, neurological symptoms, and respiratory effects.	Lowther, et al	2021
Inhaling polluted air has been associated with impaired cognitive function, emotional disturbances, maladaptive coping strategies, sleep disturbances, and diminished mental well-being.	Balakrishnan & Tsaneva	2023
There is a correlation between air containing particulate matter (PM) with a diameter of 2.5 and depression.	Borroni, et al	2022
Heavy metals like nitrogen, sulphur oxides, lead, and organic solvents have been found to contribute to neurodevelopmental disorders such as schizophrenia.	Attademo, et al.	2017
Air pollution reduces subjective wellbeing, and increases depressive symptoms.	Xin Zhang	2017
Increase in temperature and air pollution can have a negative impact on mental health. Conversely, the only way to promote mental health is through the implementation of good environmental laws worldwide, aimed at reducing pollution and greenhouse gas emissions.	Tao Xue, et al.	2019
Those from low-income backgrounds are particularly vulnerable to the negative effects of air pollution.	Yang, et al.	2021
Individuals living near major roads have a significant number of cases of dementia (243,611), Parkinson's disease (31,577), and multiple sclerosis (9,247). Living in close proximity to excessive traffic might have a detrimental impact on one's cognitive abilities.	Chen et al.	2017
Children and teens who reside in areas with high levels of air pollution are more prone to reporting psychiatric disorders.	Oudin et al	2016
Maternal exposure to air contaminated with high levels of particulate matter (>PM 2.5) is a potential cause of Autism.	Raz et al.	2015
There is a correlation between specific PM 2.5 and other pollutants, such as nitric oxides, and the occurrence and worsening of mental disorders, such as depression. Nevertheless, these authors have proposed that when generalizing any of these findings, one must consider retrospective designs, observation periods, comorbidity, and other confounding variables.	Buoli, et al.	2018
Being exposed to PM 2.5 results in the buildup of amyloid-plaques (Aβ), which serves as a primary contributing component to the development of Alzheimer's disease.	Sahu et al.	2021

continued on following page

Table 1. Continued

Finding	Authors/Source	Year
Traffic-related air pollution, such as black carbon, leads to a decrease in cognitive function.	Power, et al	2011
There is a positive correlation between air pollution, specifically nitrogen dioxide and fine particulate matter (PM2.5), and several health conditions including dementia, Alzheimer's disease, anxiety, and depression.	Carey et al.	2018
Air pollution has emerged as a catalyst for neuroinflammation and the production of reactive oxygen species (ROS), which in turn contribute to the development of strokes.	Block & Calderon-Garciduenas	2009
There is a significant correlation between air pollution and the development of mental health conditions such as depression, anxiety, psychoses, and neurocognitive disorders like dementia. Furthermore, this study has also indicated that children and adolescents are more susceptible to experiencing substantial mental health problems as a result of prolonged exposure to air pollution, inadequate housing, overcrowding, lack of green areas, poverty, and various other psychosocial factors.	Kam Bhui	2023
There is a correlation between environmental pollution, particularly air pollution, and mental health issues in children.	Bennett	2022
Mothers who are exposed to NO_2 and other air pollutants during pregnancy are at a higher risk of having children with behavioral disorders, attention deficits, anxiety, depression, and poor academic performance.	Bishop	2022
Long-term and regular exposure to air pollution has a detrimental effect on cognitive performance as individuals get older, especially among males and those who are unable to read or write.	Zhang et al.	2018
There is a notable association between PM 2.5 and PM 10 and mental and behavioral issues in males and older adults, particularly during the cold season.	Lowe et al.	2020
Both short-term and long-term exposure to air pollution can exacerbate mental health problems. Furthermore, this effect is more pronounced in males, individuals in the middle-aged group, and those who are married. Similarly, this study has also demonstrated that individuals with higher income, access to healthcare resources, green spaces, and other amenities experience reduced impacts of air pollution on their mental health.	Cao, et al	2023
The association between air pollution and mental health outcomes is not well-defined due to methodological weaknesses and the influence of confounding factors. Nevertheless, the distribution of green areas, implementation of an active transport system, and the exclusion of polluting enterprises through zoning may enhance mental well-being.	King	2018

The review of studies reflected in Table 1, highlights the important and complex influence of air pollution on mental health, exposing unambiguous relationships with psychiatric diseases, cognitive decline, and neurodevelopmental disorders. With children, pregnant women, and socioeconomically underprivileged groups especially vulnerable, pollutants including PM2.5, nitrogen oxides, and heavy metals lead to depression, anxiety, schizophrenia, dementia, and even autism spectrum disorders. The biological processes including neuroinflammation, oxidative stress, and amyloid plaque development—further confirm the relationship between environmental toxins and mental health decline. Still, differences in resilience and exposure draw attention to the importance of socioeconomic elements since some of these negative consequences can be lessened by better access to healthcare, green areas, and cleaner surroundings. Although methodological restrictions and confusing factors demand more thorough longitudinal studies, the consensus is clear: air pollution is a public health emergency with lot of psychological consequences. Dealing with this problem calls for coordinated worldwide activities including tighter environmental rules, urban planning giving green infrastructure top priority, and focused interventions for at-risk groups. Essential first steps toward preserving psychological as well as physical well-being are lowering emissions, enhancing air quality monitoring, and including mental health issues into environmental policies. In the end, the relationships between mental health and air pollution emphasize the need of multidisciplinary cooperation among researchers, legislators, and healthcare providers to build better, more fair communities for next generations.

Table 2. Studies related to Water pollution and Mental Health

Finding	Authors/source	Year
Despite significant advancements made in the past twenty years, around 650 million individuals worldwide still do not have access to clean and safe water.	Krause, et al.	2016
Both natural and man-made environmental crises have a substantial impact on behavioral health, specifically mental health. It is suggested that water-related problems could be a contributing factor to heightened levels of stress, anxiety, and even depressive symptoms. Over time, these prolonged mental health issues would have a detrimental effect on the entire community, particularly individuals from low socioeconomic backgrounds.	Cuthbertson, et al.	2016
Consuming contaminated water has a negative impact on mental health and can lead to various mental disorders such as stress, anxiety, depression, obsessive-compulsive disorder (OCD), attention deficit/hyperactivity disorder (ADHD), autism, and others. The research also indicated that water with a total dissolved solids (TDS) level above 300 ppm interferes with the functioning of NMDA, a protein receptor in the human brain that is crucial for cognitive functions and other aspects of mental development.	Care Health Insurance	2023
Individuals who regularly consume water contaminated with arsenic experience severe physical ailments, including skin issues, cancer, reproductive disorders, social stigma, deteriorating mental health, increased caregiver responsibilities, depression, poor academic performance, and reduced productivity.	Krause, et al	2016
Environmental pollution has a negative impact on general health and well-being. Both air and water pollutants increase the occurrence of symptoms related to anxiety, depression, psychosis, conduct disorder, and disruptive impulse control.	Theron et al.	2022
Individuals who consume untested tube-well water report lower levels of mental well-being.	Chowdhury et al.	2016

continued on following page

Table 2. Continued

Finding	Authors/source	Year
Consuming water that is contaminated with both metallic and non-metallic components raises the likelihood of developing emotional disorders such as sadness and anxiety. Furthermore, this study supports the notion that water contaminated with viruses, pesticides, fertilizers, arsenic, mercury, uranium, and lead can contribute to the development of cancer, neurological disorders etc. In addition, exposure to heavy metals during early childhood, such as lead, can lead to cognitive and learning difficulties during school years.	Zhou et al.	2024
Children who consume water that is contaminated are highly susceptible to developing mental retardation, neurodevelopmental problems, and other psychiatric diseases	Care Health Insurance	2023
Exposure to environmental pollutants such as lead, mercury, polychlorinated biphenyls, and pesticides has a negative impact on mental health. It disrupts executive functioning, emotional well-being, and behavioral patterns in children, as well as cognitive processes in older adults	Lanoix & Plusquellec	2013
Consuming water contaminated with tetrachloroethylene (PCE) during childhood raises the likelihood of developing bipolar disorder, post-traumatic stress disorder (PTSD), and engaging in the use of illicit drugs like cocaine and hallucinogens later in life. It is important to note that this investigation also emphasized that those employed in dry cleaning and other industries that commonly utilize PCE solvent are more susceptible to experiencing mood changes, anxiety, and even melancholy. Nevertheless, the association between PCE-contaminated drinking water and schizophrenia remains uncertain.	Aschengrau et al.	2012
Water scarcity may contribute to mental disorders, whereas emotionally significant interactions with water can improve various mental health outcomes.	Wutich et al.	2020
Women experience significant levels of stress and depression due to water insecurity. The authors propose that enhancing water security can contribute to the improvement of maternal psychological well-being in developing nations.	Aihara et al.	2016
Lack of access to safe water and adequate sanitation poses significant health challenges in low and middle income countries. These factors are associated with stressors, psychosocial issues, and have an impact on the well-being of individuals and entire communities.	Bisung & Elliot	2016
Water insecurities have negative consequences in five key areas: nutrition, childcare, economic productivity, physical health, and mental health.	Collins et al.	2017
Dealing with insufficient water availability is a difficulty for individuals in implementing coping techniques. Household water insecurity has a profound and notable impact on anxiety and depression.	Chindarkar et al.	2019
There is correlation between environmental factors and emotional well-being. Insufficient access to drinking water results in persistent anxiety and distress.	Cooper et al.	2019
Water insecurity and inadequate access to water are linked to depression in low and middle income countries. This issue particularly affects women and has become a major factor in the high rates of missed schooling among rural children. The relationship between water insecurity and missed schooling is influenced by the presence of depression in caregivers.	Cooper et al.	2017

The table 2 reflects findings from studies carried out in years 2012–2024. These studies present a troubling picture of complex connection between mental health and water issues. Research continuously shows that the contamination of water sources can both have detrimental effects on the mental health of a wide range of people. The direct correlation between drinking polluted water and a higher risk of developing a number of mental health conditions is one of the main themes that emerged from the review of the studies. Numerous studies point to particular pollutants as the cause. The studies place a great emphasis on the psychological toll that water insecurity - the absence of consistent access to enough safe water takes in addition to direct toxicity. Significant stress, anxiety, and depression are frequently associated with this insecurity (Cuthbertson et al., 2016; Wutich et al., 2020; Aihara et al., 2016; Chindarkar et al., 2019; Cooper et al., 2019). Coping strategies are difficult to implement and cause ongoing emotional strain when dealing with limited water availability (Chindarkar et al., 2019; Cooper et al., 2019). Particularly in low- and middle-income nations, a lack of access to clean water and sanitary facilities causes serious psychosocial stressors that affect both individuals and communities (Bisung & Elliot, 2016). The studies also emphasize how unequally these burdens are distributed. People from low socioeconomic backgrounds (Cuthbertson et al., 2016), children (Care Health Insurance, 2023; Zhou et al., 2024; Cooper et al., 2017), women (Aihara et al., 2016; Cooper et al., 2017), and people living in low- or middle-income countries (Aihara et al., 2016; Bisung & Elliot, 2016; Cooper et al., 2017) are among the vulnerable groups that frequently experience a disproportionately high mental health impact. Water insecurity can cause women and children to miss school, which is made worse by caregiver depression (Cooper et al., 2017). Beyond diagnosed disorders, the effects include decreased productivity, increased caregiving responsibilities, and a decline in general mental health (Chowdhury et al., 2016). In summary, the collected research offers strong proof that access to and poor quality of water are important factors influencing mental health. Insufficient access to safe, clean, and dependable water is a major global health and environmental policy concern, whether due to the neurotoxic effects of pollutants or the widespread stress of scarcity.

Table 3. Studies related to Noise pollution and Mental Health

Finding	Authors/Source	Year
Traffic noise is the second most detrimental element of pollution to public health.	World Health Organization	2011
Noise pollution is defined as the presence of unpleasant and unwanted sounds with different wavelengths and magnitudes that are unpleasant to the ear.	Masoudzadeh et al.	2017
The processes of urbanization and human activities have resulted in a substantial increase in noise pollution, leading to elevated levels of cardiovascular disorders, metabolic and respiratory diseases, as well as negative impacts on psychological well-being and overall quality of life.	Tortorella et al.	2022

continued on following page

Table 3. Continued

Finding	Authors/Source	Year
There is significant environmental problem in China caused by growing urbanization and the escalating noise pollution from road traffic, trains, and other commercial activities.	Ma et al.	2018
Noise pollution adversely affects the mental well-being of children and adolescents, especially those from low-income backgrounds. It can lead to internalizing, externalizing, and general behavioral issues.	Kim et al.,	2018
Individuals who work and live in areas with high levels of noise pollution in Iran experience a higher prevalence of mental health disorders. These individuals often report physical health issues, anxiety, sleep disturbances, impaired social functioning, and depression compared to those residing in areas without noise pollution.	Masoudzadeh et al.	2017
Traffic noise has a detrimental impact on mental health, occurrence of depression significantly rises with aircraft noise.	Hegewald et al.	2020
There is a substantial correlation between exposure to noise pollution and the occurrence of psychotic episodes, sadness, and anxiety from adolescence to young adulthood.	Newbury et al.	2024
Noise pollution has significant psychological effects such as stress, frustration, agitation, restlessness, aggravation, mood swings, anxiety, weariness, and sleep problems.	Vasudeva	2024
Pollution from several environmental sources, such as transportation noise and noise from neighbors, has a considerable negative impact on mental health.	Hammersen et al.	2016
Regular exposure to unpleasant noises might induce tension, anxiety, disruptions in sleep patterns, auditory impairment, and various psychological disorders.	Millar et al.	2020
In addition to impacting both auditory and non-auditory well-being, noise pollution has been strongly associated with behavioral issues and overall mental health in children and adolescents, especially those from low-income backgrounds.	Lim, et al.	2018
Being exposed to noise poses a risk to mental well-being and can result in conditions such as depression, anxiety, suicide, and behavioral issues in children and adolescents. This is because continuous exposure to noise leads to neuroinflammation, disruption of immune cells, and disturbance of circadian rhythms, all of which collectively have a detrimental impact on mental health.	Hahad, et al.	2024
Prolonged exposure to noise results in feelings of irritation, disruptions in sleep patterns, elevated blood pressure, cardiovascular ailments, and diminished cognitive abilities in school-age children.	Basner, et al.	2014
Students residing in areas defined by high levels of noise are more susceptible to using nonprescribed medicines, such as psychotropic substances, compared to those living in low noise environments.	Watkins, et al.	1981
Children from louder environments experienced increased heart rate and symptoms of perceived stress.	Evans, et al.	2001
Chronic noise pollution leads to increased levels of irritation and worse reading comprehension in school-age children, but does not have an impact on their mental health. In addition to children, women also expressed greater levels of aggravation and irritation caused by traffic pollution.	Haines, et al	2001

continued on following page

Table 3. Continued

Finding	Authors/Source	Year
Noise pollution has a negative impact on the overall quality of life in the general population	Dratya, et al.	2010
Extended exposure to noise pollution leads to hypertension and tachycardia. It also triggers the release of cortisol and other stress-related chemicals, which in turn negatively impact everyday life, economic productivity, and other measures of a decent quality of life.	Seidman and Standring	2010

As reflected in table 3, series of studies spanning 1981 to 2024 repeatedly shows the major detrimental effects of noise pollution on both mental and physical health. Traffic noise ranks second most harmful environmental pollution to public health according to the World Health Organization (2011). Studies show a clear correlation between negative psychological effects and noise exposure—mostly from urbanization and transportation—especially. Particularly observed in children and teenagers and especially those from low-income backgrounds, these include stress, anxiety, depression, sleep disturbances, irritation, mood swings, and behavioral problems (Kim et al., 2018; Hahad et al., 2024; Vasudeva, 2024). Certain researchers even point to a relationship with more severe effects like psychotic episodes (Newbury et al., 2024). Overall the research generally points to noise pollution as a major environmental stressor that seriously compromises psychological well-being, physical health, and the general quality of life for different populations all around.

Table 4. Studies related to Soil Pollution and Mental Health

Finding	Authors/Source	Year
Pesticides and biological pathogens, such as lead, manganese, mercury, tin, and PCBs, enter rivers and other water bodies, resulting in water pollution. This pollution, in turn, leads to neurodevelopmental impairment, low IQ, behavioral problems, and symptoms similar to Parkinson's disease.	Munzel, et al.	2023
The individuals living in areas contaminated with high levels of heavy metals and polyaromatics report lower mental well-being.	Vandermoere	2007
Children residing in close proximity to garbage recycling sites exhibit elevated levels of emotional and behavioral difficulties, as well as worse test scores, in comparison to those residing at greater distances.	Dumcke et al.	2020
There is heightened risk of elevated mortality, respiratory ailments, and diminished mental well-being among individuals living in close proximity to landfills (such as disposal sites, dumpsites, and areas where trash is openly burned).	Vinti et al.	2021
Individuals residing near municipal solid waste facilities experienced various physical and mental health symptoms, such as sleep disorder, poor mood, lack of appetite, stress, anxiety, depression, thinking and attention problems, and exhaustion.	Peprah et al.	2024

continued on following page

Table 4. Continued

Finding	Authors/Source	Year
Living within a 5 km radius of waste sites has been found to have a strong correlation with the occurrence of asthma, tuberculosis, diabetes, and depression.	Tomita et al.	2020
There is a higher occurrence of negative emotions, feelings of powerlessness, lack of control, and psychological distress among people living in draught hit areas.	Bulled	2017

Emphasizing the importance of environmental contaminants including heavy metals, pesticides, and waste byproducts, the findings of the studies reflected in table 4 show a clear link between soil pollution and negative mental health effects. Munzel et al. (2023) found Parkinson's-like symptoms, behavioral problems, and neurodevelopmental deficits resulting from pesticide and biological pathogen contamination of water bodies lead and mercury. In line with this, Vandermoer (2007) discovered that people living in places with high levels of polyaromatic hydrocarbon and heavy metal contamination reported poorer mental well-being, so highlighting the psychological effects of contaminated surroundings.Studies by Dumcke et al. (2020) and Vinti et al. (2021) concentrated on proximity to waste sites and found that adults near landfills faced increased risk of respiratory diseases and poor mental well-being while children near garbage recycling facilities showed emotional and behavioral problems. Building on these results, Peprah et al. (2024) connected residential proximity to municipal solid waste facilities to sleep disorders, stress, anxiety, depression, and cognitive impairments. Along with physical health issues like asthma and diabetes, Tomita et al. (2020) strengthened these findings by proving a significant link between living near waste sites and rising depression prevalence. These studies taken together show how various mental health problems, from developmental problems in children to chronic psychological conditions in adults, are caused in part by soil pollution and associated environmental degradation. Particularly for underprivileged groups living in contaminated areas, the evidence supports integrated public health policies addressing environmental remediation and mental health support. To lessen these twin loads, future studies should investigate mechanistic pathways and intervention effectiveness.

FUTURE DIRECTIONS

Future studies must give high priority to resolving the limitations identified above to make the evidence base stronger and to inform effective intervention. Strong, well-standardized methodologies for the assessment of both pollutant exposure (including mixed and cumulative exposures) and mental health outcomes over the lifespan are essential in more longitudinal cohort studies. It is essential to investigate the biological mechanisms underlying the effects of pollutants further, using methods such as neuroimaging, epigenetics, and biomarker studies to elucidate the effects on brain structure, function, and inflammation. Encouraging interdisciplinary collaboration among environmental scientists, neuroscientists, psychologists, psychiatrists, public health professionals, and policymakers will be central to the creation of integrated solutions to safeguard population mental health from environmental stressors.

Limitations

Although this chapter integrates studies illustrating the relationship between pollution and deteriorated mental health to create a compelling narrative for environmental pollution, some gaps within the existing literature warrant attention. The first gap, perhaps the most glaring one, is the absence of definitive causation: most studies tend to be observational and therefore struggle to isolate the effect pollution has in the presence of other predominant risk factors such as socio-economic status, lifestyle choices, and existing health status. Methodological diversity within studies is another matter that deserves attention. Finally, while considering biological mechanisms remains crucial, more work elucidating the exact pathways through which specific pollutants impact distinct mental health conditions is essential. These constraints raise caution around drawing concrete conclusions and highlight gaps that need more thorough scrutiny.

CONCLUSION

The systematic assessment of literature has provided compelling evidence and insights into the relationship between environmental pollution and its impact on mental health. Nevertheless, there is a dearth of material regarding the correlation between pollution and the extent to which it exacerbates mental disorders, as well as its potential to significantly amplify social costs and financial burdens inside nations. Implementing policies to mitigate human exposure to environmental pollution, if the causal relationship is shown, has the potential to alleviate the prevalence of mental diseases. It is necessary to conduct studies using appropriate methodology, randomized experiments, and standardized methods to validate the findings of existing literature about the possible impact of environmental pollution on mental health. It is important to note that significant focus should be placed on identifying crucial areas of knowledge that need to be addressed in order to develop and modify intervention models. This includes understanding how the environment might impact an individual's mental health, as well as finding ways to decrease and manage sources of environmental pollution. Promotion of global initiatives is necessary to educate the masses, raise knowledge of the environment and its dynamics, and implement psychoeducational group interventions. The behavioural healthcare system must comprehend the correlation between pollution and mental disorders in order to incorporate it into diagnostics, thereby aiding individuals in safeguarding their mental well-being. Localizing and mobilizing insecure resources in vulnerable environments can be advantageous for the development of community-based initiatives. To address environmental concerns and risks, it is crucial for all sectors to collaborate and improve social networking and cohesiveness.

REFERENCES

Aihara, Y., Shrestha, S., & Sharma, J. (2016). Household water insecurity, depression and quality of life among postnatal women living in urban Nepal. *Journal of Water and Health, 14*(2), 317–324. DOI: 10.2166/wh.2015.166 PMID: 27105416

American Psychiatric Association. (April 12, 2023). Air Pollution's Impact on Mental Health. Psychiatry.org - Air Pollution's Impact on Mental Health

Attademo, L., Bernardini, F., Garinella, R., & Compton, M. T. (2017). Environmental pollution and risk of psychotic disorders: A review of the science to date. *Schizophrenia Research, 181*, 55–59. DOI: 10.1016/j.schres.2016.10.003 PMID: 27720315

Balakrishnan, U., & Tsaneva, M. (2023). Impact of air pollution on mental health in India. *The Journal of Development Studies, 59*(1), 133–147. DOI: 10.1080/00220388.2022.2120804

Basner, M., Babisch, W., Davis, A., Brink, M., Clark, C., Janssen, S., & Stansfeld, S. (2014). Auditory and non-auditory effects of noise on health. *Lancet, 383*(9925), 1325–1332. DOI: 10.1016/S0140-6736(13)61613-X PMID: 24183105

Bisung, E., & Elliott, S. J. (2016). 'Everyone is exhausted and frustrated': Exploring psychosocial impacts of the lack of access to safe water and adequate sanitation in Usoma, Kenya. *Journal of Water, Sanitation, and Hygiene for Development : a Journal of the International Water Association, 6*(2), 205–214. DOI: 10.2166/washdev.2016.122

Block, M. L., & Calderón-Garcidueñas, L. (2009). Air pollution: Mechanisms of neuroinflammation and CNS disease. *Trends in Neurosciences, 32*(9), 506–516. DOI: 10.1016/j.tins.2009.05.009 PMID: 19716187

Borroni, E., Pesatori, A. C., Bollati, V., Buoli, M., & Carugno, M. (2022). Air pollution exposure and depression: A comprehensive updated systematic review and meta-analysis. *Environmental Pollution, 292*, 118245. DOI: 10.1016/j.envpol.2021.118245 PMID: 34600062

Bortolato, B., Köhler, C. A., Evangelou, E., León-Caballero, J., Solmi, M., Stubbs, B., Belbasis, L., Pacchiarotti, I., Kessing, L. V., Berk, M., Vieta, E., & Carvalho, A. F. (2017). Systematic assessment of environmental risk factors for bipolar disorder: An umbrella review of systematic reviews and meta-analyses. *Bipolar Disorders, 19*(2), 84–96. DOI: 10.1111/bdi.12490 PMID: 28470927

Braithwaite, I., Zhang, S., Kirkbride, J. B., Osborn, D. P., & Hayes, J. F. (2019). Air pollution (particulate matter) exposure and associations with depression, anxiety, bipolar, psychosis and suicide risk: A systematic review and meta-analysis. *Environmental Health Perspectives*, *127*(12), 126002. DOI: 10.1289/EHP4595 PMID: 31850801

Bulled, N. (2017). The effects of water insecurity and emotional distress on civic action for improved water infrastructure in rural South Africa. *Medical Anthropology Quarterly*, *31*(1), 133–154. DOI: 10.1111/maq.12270 PMID: 26698378

Buoli, M., Grassi, S., Caldiroli, A., Carnevali, G. S., Mucci, F., Iodice, S., Cantone, L., Pergoli, L., & Bollati, V. (2018). Is there a link between air pollution and mental disorders? *Environment International*, *118*, 154–168. DOI: 10.1016/j.envint.2018.05.044 PMID: 29883762

Cao, Z., Zhou, J., Li, M., Huang, J., & Dou, D. (2023). Urbanites' mental health undermined by air pollution. *Nature Sustainability*, *6*(4), 470–478. DOI: 10.1038/s41893-022-01032-1

Care Health Insurance. (Dec 28, 2023). 10 adverse effects of water pollution on human health.https://www.careinsurance.com/blog/health-insurance-articles/adverse-effects-of-water-pollution-on-human-health

Carey, I. M., Anderson, H. R., Atkinson, R. W., Beevers, S. D., Cook, D. G., Strachan, D. P., Dajnak, D., Gulliver, J., & Kelly, F. J. (2018). Are noise and air pollution related to the incidence of dementia? A cohort study in London, England. *BMJ Open*, *8*(9), e022404. DOI: 10.1136/bmjopen-2018-022404 PMID: 30206085

Chen, H., Kwong, J. C., Copes, R., Tu, K., Villeneuve, P. J., Van Donkelaar, A., Hystad, P., Martin, R. V., Murray, B. J., Jessiman, B., Wilton, A. S., Kopp, A., & Burnett, R. T. (2017). Living near major roads and the incidence of dementia, Parkinson's disease, and multiple sclerosis: A population-based cohort study. *Lancet*, *389*(10070), 718–726. DOI: 10.1016/S0140-6736(16)32399-6 PMID: 28063597

Chindarkar, N., Chen, Y. J., & Gurung, Y. (2019). Subjective well-being effects of coping cost: Evidence from household water supply in Kathmandu Valley, Nepal. *Journal of Happiness Studies*, *20*(8), 2581–2608. DOI: 10.1007/s10902-018-0060-6

Chowdhury, S., Krause-Pilatus, A., & Zimmermann, K. F. (2016). Arsenic contamination of drinking water and mental health. *SSRN*, (222). Advance online publication. DOI: 10.2139/ssrn.2811583

Collins, S. M., Miller, J. D., Mbullo, P., Boateng, G. O., Wekesa, P., Onono, M., & Young, S. L. (2017). You take the cash meant for beans and you buy water": The Multi-Faceted Consequences of Water Insecurity for Pregnant and Postpartum Kenyan Women of Mixed HIV Status. *The FASEB Journal, 31*(S1), 651–654. DOI: 10.1096/fasebj.31.1_supplement.651.4 PMID: 30231793

Cooper, S., Hutchings, P., Butterworth, J., Joseph, S., Kebede, A., Parker, A., Terefe, B., & Van Koppen, B. (2019). Environmental associated emotional distress and the dangers of climate change for pastoralist mental health. *Global Environmental Change, 59*, 101994. DOI: 10.1016/j.gloenvcha.2019.101994

Cooper-Vince, C. E., Kakuhikire, B., Vorechovska, D., McDonough, A. Q., Perkins, J., Venkataramani, A. S., Mushavi, R. C., Baguma, C., Ashaba, S., Bangsberg, D. R., & Tsai, A. C. (2017). Household water insecurity, missed schooling, and the mediating role of caregiver depression in rural Uganda. *Global Mental Health (Cambridge, England), 4*, e15. DOI: 10.1017/gmh.2017.14 PMID: 29230311

Cuthbertson, C. A., Newkirk, C., Ilardo, J., Loveridge, S., & Skidmore, M. (2016). Angry, scared, and unsure: Mental health consequences of contaminated water in Flint, Michigan. *Journal of Urban Health, 93*(6), 899–908. DOI: 10.1007/s11524-016-0089-y PMID: 27807700

Dratva, J., Zemp, E., Dietrich, D. F., Bridevaux, P. O., Rochat, T., Schindler, C., & Gerbase, M. W. (2010). Impact of road traffic noise annoyance on health-related quality of life: Results from a population-based study. *Quality of Life Research: An International Journal of Quality of Life Aspects of Treatment, Care and Rehabilitation, 19*(1), 37–46. DOI: 10.1007/s11136-009-9571-2 PMID: 20044782

Dumcke, T. S., Benedetti, A., Selistre, L. D. S., Camardelo, A. M. P., & Silva, E. R. D. (2020). Association between exposure to urban waste and emotional and behavioral difficulties in schoolchildren. *Jornal de Pediatria, 96*(3), 364–370. DOI: 10.1016/j.jped.2018.11.014 PMID: 30817895

Evans, G. W., Lercher, P., Meis, M., Ising, H., & Kofler, W. W. (2001). Community noise exposure and stress in children. *The Journal of the Acoustical Society of America, 109*(3), 1023–1027. DOI: 10.1121/1.1340642 PMID: 11303916

Hahad, O., Kuntic, M., Al-Kindi, S., Kuntic, I., Gilan, D., Petrowski, K., & Münzel, T. (2024). Noise and mental health: Evidence, mechanisms, and consequences. *Journal of Exposure Science & Environmental Epidemiology*, •••, 1–8. DOI: 10.1038/s41370-024-00642-5 PMID: 38279032

Haines, M. M., Stansfeld, S. A., Job, R. S., Berglund, B., & Head, J. (2001). Chronic aircraft noise exposure, stress responses, mental health and cognitive performance in school children. *Psychological Medicine, 31*(2), 265–277. DOI: 10.1017/S0033291701003282 PMID: 11232914

Hammersen, F., Niemann, H., & Hoebel, J. (2016). Environmental noise annoyance and mental health in adults: Findings from the cross-sectional German Health Update (GEDA) Study 2012. *International Journal of Environmental Research and Public Health, 13*(10), 954. DOI: 10.3390/ijerph13100954 PMID: 27681736

Hegewald, J., Schubert, M., Freiberg, A., Romero Starke, K., Augustin, F., Riedel-Heller, S. G., Zeeb, H., & Seidler, A. (2020). Traffic noise and mental health: A systematic review and meta-analysis. *International Journal of Environmental Research and Public Health, 17*(17), 6175. DOI: 10.3390/ijerph17176175 PMID: 32854453

Khan, A., Plana-Ripoll, O., Antonsen, S., Brandt, J., Geels, C., Landecker, H., Sullivan, P. F., Pedersen, C. B., & Rzhetsky, A. (2019). Environmental pollution is associated with increased risk of psychiatric disorders in the US and Denmark. *PLoS Biology, 17*(8), e3000353. DOI: 10.1371/journal.pbio.3000353 PMID: 31430271

King, J. (2018). Research & Analysis Air pollution, mental health, and implications for urban design: a review. *Research & analysis. Journal of Urban Design and Mental Health, 4*-6. https://www.urbandesignmentalhealth.com/journal-4---air-pollution-and-mental-health.html

Lanoix, D., & Plusquellec, P. (2013). Adverse effects of pollution on mental health: The stress hypothesis. *OA Evidence-Based Medicine, 1*(1), 1–9. DOI: 10.13172/2053-2636-1-1-572

Lim, J., Kweon, K., Kim, H. W., Cho, S. W., Park, J., & Sim, C. S. (2018). Negative impact of noise and noise sensitivity on mental health in childhood. *Noise & Health, 20*(96), 199–211. DOI: 10.4103/nah.NAH_9_18 PMID: 30516173

Lowe, S. R., Wang, C., Ma, Y., & Chen, K. (2021). Particulate matter pollution and risk of outpatient visits for psychological diseases in Nanjing, China. *Environmental Research, 193*, 110601. DOI: 10.1016/j.envres.2020.110601 PMID: 33307087

Lowther, S. D., Dimitroulopoulou, S., Foxall, K., Shrubsole, C., Cheek, E., Gadeberg, B., & Sepai, O. (2021). Low level carbon dioxide indoors—A pollution indicator or a pollutant? A health-based perspective. *Environments (Basel, Switzerland), 8*(11), 125. DOI: 10.3390/environments8110125

Ma, J., Li, C., Kwan, M. P., & Chai, Y. (2018). A multilevel analysis of perceived noise pollution, geographic contexts and mental health in Beijing. *International Journal of Environmental Research and Public Health, 15*(7), 1479. DOI: 10.3390/ijerph15071479 PMID: 30011780

Marangoni, C., Hernandez, M., & Faedda, G. L. (2016). The role of environmental exposures as risk factors for bipolar disorder: A systematic review of longitudinal studies. *Journal of Affective Disorders, 193*, 165–174. DOI: 10.1016/j.jad.2015.12.055 PMID: 26773919

Masoudzadeh, A., Hadinezhad, P., & Gooran, M. (2017). Comparison of mental health status of people exposed to noise pollution with people in non-polluted areas of sari. *Health (Irvine, Calif.), 9*(05), 839–848. DOI: 10.4236/health.2017.95059

Millar, H. (Dec22, 2020). What are the health effects of noise pollution. *Medical News Today*. https://www.medicalnewstoday.com/articles/noise-pollution-health-effects

Münzel, T., Hahad, O., Daiber, A., & Landrigan, P. J. (2023). Soil and water pollution and human health: What should cardiologists worry about? *Cardiovascular Research, 119*(2), 440–449. DOI: 10.1093/cvr/cvac082 PMID: 35772469

Newbury, J. B., Heron, J., Kirkbride, J. B., Fisher, H. L., Bakolis, I., Boyd, A., Thomas, R., & Zammit, S. (2024). Air and noise pollution exposure in early life and mental health from adolescence to young adulthood. *JAMA Network Open, 7*(5), e2412169–e2412169. DOI: 10.1001/jamanetworkopen.2024.12169 PMID: 38805229

Oudin, A., Bråbäck, L., Åström, D. O., Strömgren, M., & Forsberg, B. (2016). Association between neighbourhood air pollution concentrations and dispensed medication for psychiatric disorders in a large longitudinal cohort of Swedish children and adolescents. *BMJ Open, 6*(6), e010004. DOI: 10.1136/bmjopen-2015-010004 PMID: 27259522

Peprah, P., Agyemang-Duah, W., Morgan, A. K., Onyina, E., & Asare, E. S. (2024). Differences in physical and mental health symptoms among residents living near municipal solid waste sites: A cross sectional study in the Ashanti Region, Ghana. *Journal of Health, Population and Nutrition, 43*(1), 34. DOI: 10.1186/s41043-024-00527-1 PMID: 38424610

Perveen, A., Taufiq, I., Hamzah, H. B., & Khan, R. K. B. A. W. (2015).Environment Pollution's Effects on Human Health and Psychological Wellbeing – A Survey study *Asian J. Adv. Basic Sci.: 2015, 4*(1), 52-56. https://www.ajabs.org/articles/environment-pollutions-effects-on-human-health-and-psychological-wellbeing--a-survey-study.pdf

Power, M. C., Weisskopf, M. G., Alexeeff, S. E., Coull, B. A., Spiro, A.III, & Schwartz, J. (2011). Traffic-related air pollution and cognitive function in a cohort of older men. *Environmental Health Perspectives, 119*(5), 682–687. DOI: 10.1289/ehp.1002767 PMID: 21172758

Raz, R., Roberts, A. L., Lyall, K., Hart, J. E., Just, A. C., Laden, F., & Weisskopf, M. G. (2015). Autism spectrum disorder and particulate matter air pollution before, during, and after pregnancy: A nested case-control analysis within the Nurses' Health Study II cohort. *Environmental Health Perspectives, 123*(3), 264–270. DOI: 10.1289/ehp.1408133 PMID: 25522338

Sahu, B., Mackos, A. R., Floden, A. M., Wold, L. E., & Combs, C. K. (2021). Particulate matter exposure exacerbates amyloid- plaque deposition and gliosis in APP/PS1 mice. *Journal of Alzheimer's Disease, 80*(2), 761–774. DOI: 10.3233/JAD-200919 PMID: 33554902

Seidman, M. D., & Standring, R. T. (2010). Noise and quality of life. *International Journal of Environmental Research and Public Health, 7*(10), 3730–3738. DOI: 10.3390/ijerph7103730 PMID: 21139857

Stiftung, H. B. (2010). Observation and Research on: Psycho-physical Effects of Environment Pollution on the Health of Kabul Citizens. Observation and Research on: Psychophysical Effects of Environment Pollution on the Health of Kabul Citizens Implemented by: Fekr Organization of Psychosocial Development Funded | Semantic Scholar

Theron, L. C., Abreu-Villaca, Y., Augusto-Oliveira, M., Brennan, C., Crespo-Lopez, M. E., de Paula Arrifano, G., Glazer, L., Gwata, N., Lin, L., Mareschal, I., Mermelstein, S., Sartori, L., Stieger, L., Trotta, A., & Hadfield, K. (2022). A systematic review of the mental health risks and resilience among pollution-exposed adolescents. *Journal of Psychiatric Research, 146*, 55–66. DOI: 10.1016/j.jpsychires.2021.12.012 PMID: 34953306

Tomita, A., Cuadros, D. F., Burns, J. K., Tanser, F., & Slotow, R. (2020). Exposure to waste sites and their impact on health: A panel and geospatial analysis of nationally representative data from South Africa, 2008-2015. *The Lancet. Planetary Health, 4*(6), e223–e234. DOI: 10.1016/S2542-5196(20)30101-7 PMID: 32559439

Tortorella, A., Menculini, G., Moretti, P., Attademo, L., Balducci, P. M., Bernardini, F., Cirimbilli, F., Chieppa, A. G., Ghiandai, N., & Erfurth, A. (2022). New determinants of mental health: The role of noise pollution. A narrative review. *International Review of Psychiatry (Abingdon, England), 34*(7-8), 783–796. DOI: 10.1080/09540261.2022.2095200 PMID: 36786115

Vandermoere, F. (2008). Psychosocial health of residents exposed to soil pollution in a Flemish neighbourhood. *Social Science & Medicine*, *66*(7), 1646–1657. DOI: 10.1016/j.socscimed.2007.12.031 PMID: 18237836

Vasudeva, S. (Feb 4, 2024). Noise pollution & its effects on mental health. *Deccan Herald*. https://www.deccanherald.com/health/noise-pollution-its-effects-on-mental-health-2-2876693

Vinti, G., Bauza, V., Clasen, T., Medlicott, K., Tudor, T., Zurbrügg, C., & Vaccari, M. (2021). Municipal solid waste management and adverse health outcomes: A systematic review. *International Journal of Environmental Research and Public Health*, *18*(8), 4331. DOI: 10.3390/ijerph18084331 PMID: 33921868

Watkins, G., Tarnopolsky, A., & Jenkins, L. M. (1981). Aircraft noise and mental health: II. Use of medicines and health care services. *Psychological Medicine*, *11*(1), 155–168. DOI: 10.1017/S003329170005337X PMID: 7208739

World Health Organization. (2021). *WHO global air quality guidelines: particulate matter (PM2.5 and PM10), ozone, nitrogen dioxide, sulfur dioxide and carbon monoxide*. https://iris.who.int/handle/10665/345329. License: CC BY-NC-SA 3.0 IGO

Wutich, A., Brewis, A., & Tsai, A. (2020). Water and mental health. *WIREs. Water*, *7*(5), e1461. DOI: 10.1002/wat2.1461

Xue, T., Zhu, T., Zheng, Y., & Zhang, Q. (2019). Declines in mental health associated with air pollution and temperature variability in China. *Nature Communications*, *10*(1), 2165. DOI: 10.1038/s41467-019-10196-y PMID: 31092825

Yang, Z., Song, Q., Li, J., Zhang, Y., Yuan, X. C., Wang, W., & Yu, Q. (2021). Air pollution and mental health: The moderator effect of health behaviors. *Environmental Research Letters*, *16*(4), 044005. DOI: 10.1088/1748-9326/abe88f

Zhang, X., Chen, X., & Zhang, X. (2018). The impact of exposure to air pollution on cognitive performance. *Proceedings of the National Academy of Sciences of the United States of America*, *115*(37), 9193–9197. DOI: 10.1073/pnas.1809474115 PMID: 30150383

Zhang, X., Zhang, X., & Chen, X. (2017). Happiness in the air: How does a dirty sky affect mental health and subjective well-being? *Journal of Environmental Economics and Management*, *85*, 81–94. DOI: 10.1016/j.jeem.2017.04.001 PMID: 29081551

Chapter 19
Toxins in the Food Chain: Understanding Bioaccumulation of Carcinogens in Marine Life and Human Health Risks

Abhisikta Basu
https://orcid.org/0000-0002-2800-2337
IEM's International Institute of Juridical Sciences, India

Keya De Mukhopadhyay
https://orcid.org/0000-0002-0816-841X
University of Engineering and Management, Kolkata, India

Avishikta Chatterjee
https://orcid.org/0009-0004-1873-0527
IEM's International Institute of Juridical Sciences, India

ABSTRACT

Marine ecosystem is facing threats of pollution from heavy metals and pesticides that have the propensity to bioaccumulate and biomagnify through food chains, putting biodiversity and human health at risk. This chapter focuses on bioaccumulation and trophic transfer of heavy metals and carcinogenic effects that have their pathway in marine organisms to humans via seafood consumption. Objectives include examining the mechanisms of bioaccumulation, evaluating ecological disruptions, assessing cancer risks from prolonged exposure, and analysing the shortcomings of current legal frameworks. The chapter underscores the persistence of heavy metals in aquatic ecosystems, their toxic impacts on marine species, and the severe health risks, including cancer, linked to contaminated seafood. The study urges strong discharge controls, improved water quality standards, and integrated monitoring systems to lower heavy metal contamination, preserve biodiversity, and protect

DOI: 10.4018/979-8-3693-9755-8.ch019

human health from carcinogenic risks. It also calls for international cooperation, public awareness, and strong regulations.

1. INTRODUCTION

The word "bioaccumulation" is very commonly associated when discussing environmental pollution and its impact on ecosystems and human health. It describes gradual accumulation of some substances, particularly harmful chemicals in living things to quantities far higher than those found in the surrounding environment. This phenomenon has the potential to disrupt entire food chains and ecosystems, in addition to the individual organisms affected. Numerous exposure pathways may affect the process of the result such as having direct contact with polluted air, water, or soil or ingestion of contaminated food.

Bioaccumulation is commonly quantified using bioaccumulation factors (BAF), which characterize the rise of pollutants from water to biota while taking into account all exposure pathways (Proc et al, 2021). The material is considered bioaccumulation when these parameters value above predetermined criteria, commonly 5000 on a wet weight basis. The bioaccumulation process includes uptake from the environment, diffusion within the body, metabolism to possibly less or more harmful substances, storage in tissues such as bones or fat, and final elimination. The rate and amount of bioaccumulation depends on the habitat, the organism's biological characteristics, and the material's chemical composition. This phenomenon occurs when the substance's rate at which material builds up within an organism surpasses the rate at which it is broken down (metabolization) or eliminated, resulting in a progressive rise in the substance's presence within the organism. Both the properties of the material and the biological qualities of the organism have significant influence over this process. Substances that are stable, fat-soluble, and resistant to metabolic breakdown are more likely to be bioaccumulated. These materials frequently contain persistent organic contaminants and heavy metals like mercury that can enter the food chain and linger in the environment (Md. Nizam Uddin et al, 2021).

However, thinking from the organism perspective, factors such as environment, food habits, and metabolism rate are quite crucial. Organisms with slower metabolisms or those higher up the food chain are more likely to experience bioaccumulation. For instance, predatory animals have higher levels of accumulated toxins than species lower in the food chain due to a similar process called biomagnification, which raises the concentration of toxins at each trophic level.

Bioaccumulation is a major concern because of the persistence of heavy metals, hydrophobic compounds, food chain expansion, and persistent organic pollutants (POPs). People and wildlife may be exposed to persistent pollutants (POPs) including dioxins, PCBs, and DDT for a long time since they are hard to degrade and can linger in the environment. They may bioaccumulate in living things, heavy metals including arsenic, cadmium, lead, and mercury pose serious dangers to human health and the environment. Mining operations, improper waste disposal, and industrial pollutants are the main ways that these metals get into ecosystems. After being discharged, they linger in the environment, penetrating soils, water bodies, and the air to become easily absorbed by plants and animals. Heavy metal buildup mostly takes place in adipose tissues and organs, where they can cause toxicity, interfere with biological processes, and cause a number of health problems (Alharbi et al, 2018).

2. CARCINOGENIC CONTAMINATION OF MARINE ECOSYSTEM

The marine water is contaminated mostly by pollutants like industrial chemicals, heavy metals, POPs or the persistent organic pollutants which directly impacts the marine ecosystem as well as the human health. Upon entering the marine environment, they get accumulated in water and into the aquatic organisms, which is basically the beginning of a cycle that affects the entire food chain through bioaccumulation and biomagnification. The process of bioaccumulation begins when organisms start absorbing toxic substances at a much faster rate than they can actually excrete which results in build up over the time. This impact is further intensified by the process of biomagnification as higher concentrations of toxins accumulate in organisms who are at the top of the food chain including the ones that are consumed by human beings (Starner, n.d.).

2.1 PAHs, PCBs, and Other Heavy Metals entering the Marine Ecosystem

PAHs or Polycyclic Aromatic Hydrocarbons, the PCBs or Polychlorinated Biphenyls and heavy metals such as mercury, cadmium, lead travels to the marine waters in the form of industrial waste, atmospheric deposition. Runoff, agricultural activities. All these contaminants originate from human activities like oil spills, coal combustion, mining, and waste disposal which releases toxins into the marine environment.

PAHs are in general released in the process of incomplete combustion of organic materials like wood, fossil fuels and biomass. These organic materials are mainly sourced from vehicle exhaust, oil combustion and oil spills. The PAHs enters the marine ecosystem through discharges from industries, atmospheric depositions that contain pollutants caused by air pollution which gradually gets settled into the water bodies (Venkataraman et al, 2024). The contaminants then become part of the marine food cycle when they are consumed by smaller fish, who are then consumed by the bigger ones.

PCBs are synthetic chemicals that are used in industries particularly in transformers and coolers. Almost a decade ago its production was banned in many countries because of its chemical stability. These, also similar to the PAHs, enter the marine ecosystem through industrial runoff, atmospheric deposition. Being hydrophobic in nature they attach to organic materials in the form of sediments which are up taken by the bottom dwelling organisms.

Apart from these heavy metals also enter the marine environment. For instance, mercury enters marine water through industrial discharges and once in water it becomes methylmercury due to bacterial reaction, it is a toxin that bioaccumulates into the fish. Similar to this, cadmium and lead also settle in sediments and enter the food chain (Dave, 2021).

After these toxins enter the marine ecosystem, they either bind themselves into sediments or they simply get dissolved into the water bodies. Then they are taken up by organisms who are at the base of the food web like the small invertebrates, microorganisms and planktons. Who are then consumed by the bigger fish. And through the process of biomagnification the toxins keep moving upwards the food chain. These can particularly be seen in big fish like Tuna, Salmon, etc. These big fishes are mostly consumed by human beings, and thus the contaminants that were present inside the fish enters the human body that accumulates over time in their body tissue which have the potential to cause adverse effects like cancer and other neurological issues and organ damage. Historical events very strongly depict the far-reaching and lasting effects of contaminants on marine environments as well as human health. These events outline the relationship between environmental degradation and public health by explaining how noxious contamination alters sensitive ecological equilibria. Such cases not only focus on the immediate effects for the affected communities but also put pressure on broader implications for global environmental policies and human well-being.

2.2 Minamata Disease Case

The Minamata disease case is one of the significant instances of industrial pollution which caused widespread environmental contamination along with human suffering. It originated in the Minamata City of Japan, where Chisso Corporation, a chemical manufacturer, discharged methylmercury waste into the Minamata Bay from 1932 to 1968. This toxic compound, a byproduct of Chisso's acetaldehyde production, contaminated fish and shellfish, causing hundreds of residents to unknowingly consume mercury-contaminated seafood. The symptoms of Minamata disease first appeared in the 1950s, causing neurological symptoms such as muscle weakness, loss of motor control, visual and auditory disturbances, and, in severe cases, paralysis and death (Collaborative for Health & Environment, n.d.). The most vulnerable were children and fetuses exposed to mercury in the womb, resulting in congenital Minamata disease. Over time, the disease affected nearly 3,000 people, with thousands more suspected of suffering from long-term effects. Discovery and cover-up occurred in 1956, but Chisso and government authorities initially denied responsibility, leading to delayed recognition and action. Scientific investigation by Dr. Hajime Hosokawa connected the neurological symptoms to methylmercury poisoning, but Chisso continued to release mercury into the bay until 1968. A landmark ruling in 1973 held Chisso liable for compensation, citing negligence in protecting public health. The Minamata case became a catalyst for environmental reform in Japan, leading to more stringent environmental protection laws and pollution regulations. Internationally, it inspired the 2013 Minamata Convention on Mercury, a global treaty aimed at reducing mercury emissions and mitigating its impact on health and the environment (Ministry of the Environment, Government of Japan, n.d.). The way how mercury pollution changed international environmental policies, several other disasters have highlighted the urgent need for better protective measures against ecological disasters. An example of this is the large-scale oil spill into marine ecosystems, which shows the massive impact of human activities on the environment and marine life.

2.3 Exxon Valdez Oil Spill

This oil spill case is one of the most devastating environmental disasters in the history of the US. It occurred in March 1989 when the oil tanker owned by the Exxon shipping company, known as Exxon Valdex struck a reef in Alaska's Prince William Sound. An approximate amount of 11 million gallons of crude oil got spilled into the pristine waters which had spread across 1,300 miles. The oil spill contaminated the habitat of numerous marine species of the water body and due to its quick spreading, it impacted delicate ecosystems and further caused extensive harm to the wildlife like thousands of otters, sea bird, and fish etc. (History, 2021).

The root cause of the event was a series of operational and systematic failures. Further investigations have revealed that the captain was intoxicated and had left the control of the ship to an inexperienced mate while the ship was passing through hazardous waters. Also it was found that the company had not been providing proper training to its workers and used to run on outdated navigating systems. It was also pointed out that there was a lack of effective government oversight and regulations that could have prevented the occurrence of the disaster. The oil spill had a long-lasting environmental impact. The Prince William Sound is known to have a fragile ecosystem which faced extensive damage as the thick oil destroyed breeding grounds and fish habitats, sea birds and otters, seals and other marine life (Encyclopedia Britannica, 2024).

In response to this event the US congress had passed the Oil Pollution act in 1990 which mandated double hulls for oil tankers ensuring more stringent oil spill prevention protocols.

3. IMPACT OF TOXIN BIOACCUMULATION ON MARINE BIODIVERSITY

Toxin bioaccumulation is known to have a profound impact on marine biodiversity, as it affects the species ranging from microscopic planktons to the apex predators. Heavy metals, PCBs, lead etc get accumulated directly into the tissues of the smaller organisms from water or sediments and then are transferred when consumed by bigger fishes.

3.1 Scientific Evidence of Cancer-Causing Agents

Scientific evidence shows that the bioaccumulated toxic substances richly found in organisms and ecosystems through extended exposure lead to carcinogenic risks. The agents include POPs, heavy metals, and any other toxic substance. Among these, the main POPs dioxins, PCBs, and pesticides like DDT are especially dangerous because they are lipophilic. They concentrate in body fats of living organisms and multiply up the food chain through biomagnification, leading to higher exposure in top predators, including humans. Since they have a strong carcinogenic association, IARC classifies dioxins as Group 1 carcinogens. Extended exposure to PCBs has been related to liver cancer, melanoma, and a variety of other cancers. They interfere with cellular mechanisms, cause oxidative stress, and alter the action of hormones, thereby promoting the actual oncogenic process (Maji, Samanta & Mondal 2024).

Epidemiological studies have established that the risk of cancer is higher at higher levels of POPs in exposed populations. Industrial workers or populations living near contaminated sites are likely to have a higher incidence of cancers of the liver, breast, and other sites. Understanding the carcinogenic potential of bioaccumulated agents underlines the need for strict environmental regulations and remediation and public health interventions to minimize long-term risks of cancer caused by these persistent toxin (Steenland et al., 2004).

Generally, heavy metals such as arsenic, cadmium, mercury, and lead, which are known to stay long in the environment and bioaccumulate in human tissues, pose a serious hazard to health. Oxidative stress, interference with cellular homeostasis, and DNA damage caused by these metals promote carcinogenesis. Their persistence and interaction with biological systems emphasize their toxic effects. Arsenic exposure, particularly through contaminated water and food, is highly correlated with skin, lung, and bladder cancer conditions. It causes ROS production and interference with DNA repair mechanisms. Cadmium, also being known as a carcinogen, is present in tobacco smoke and industrial emission, and relates to lung and prostate cancer conditions. Cadmium worsens oxidative stress and plays an interference role with cell signaling, further allowing tumor growth.

Clinical studies confirm the role of heavy metals in bioaccumulation and cancer initiation. This evidence calls for the critical need for monitoring heavy metal exposure and the implementation of preventive strategies to reduce the global burden of heavy metal-induced cancers (Biswas & Poddar 2024; Speer et al., 2022; Verougstraete et al., 2003).

PAHs are extremely toxic chemicals products of partial combustion of organic materials. Such chemicals include benzo[a]pyrene. They can easily bind to DNA through formation of adducts that interfere with genetic integrity leading to mutations and eventually cancer. The persistence of PAHs in the environment makes them bio-accumulate in aquatic organisms and humans. Bioaccumulation is especially prevalent in highly polluted urban centers.

There is adequate evidence that skin and lung malignancies are caused by high levels of PAH exposure. Urban residents who are heavily exposed to PAHs from industrial operations, car emissions, and tobacco use have higher cancer risks. For instance, benzo[a]pyrene is a very strong carcinogen that has been well investigated for its ability to create DNA damages, which in turn lead to the development of tumours. Because exposure to PAHs is strongly linked to an elevated risk of cancer, environmental pollution must be controlled, and PAH emissions must be strictly regulated, in order to protect public health (Wang et al., 2021).

Endocrine Disrupting Chemicals that affect hormone balance, such as phthalates and bisphenol A (BPA), negatively impacts cell proliferation and raise the risk of cancer. They are present in industrial goods, plastics, and cosmetics. Over time, they bioaccumulate in human tissues and interfere with regular hormonal processes. By attaching itself to hormone receptors, BPA replicates the effects of oestrogen and encourages unchecked cell proliferation. Experimental models have directly demonstrated a connection between BPA exposure and prostate and breast malignancies. In a similar vein, phthalates, which are frequently used as plasticisers, disrupt hormone pathways and cause cellular alterations that promote the growth of tumours.

High levels of phthalates have been shown to have very strong correlations with hormone-related cancers, such as breast and testicular cancers, in epidemiological studies. Cumulative evidence further underlines the carcinogenic potential of EDCs, requiring stricter regulatory measures to reduce exposure. Public awareness and alternatives are crucial in reducing long-term risks of cancer and preserving hormonal health (Salamanca-Fernández et al., 2021).

Some important case studies, like populations exposed to contaminated fish (e.g., the Great Lakes region) show higher cancer incidences due to bioaccumulated mercury and POPs. (Ramish et al., 2024) Industrial workers exposed to carcinogenic substances (e.g., vinyl chloride, benzene) face elevated risks of cancer due to bioaccumulation. Continuous environmental monitoring of carcinogens is crucial to mitigate their impact. The evidence clearly links bioaccumulation of certain substances to increased cancer risks. Preventive measures like reduced exposure, and stricter environmental controls are essential to minimize the impact of these agents.

3.2 Biodiversity Loss

Bioaccumulation and biomagnification are a significant environmental concern as it leads to biodiversity loss. The process begins when organisms start absorbing toxins, heavy metals and persistent organic pollutants at a much faster rate than they can excrete them which further leads to a buildup of harmful substances within their tissues. These toxins then gradually move up the food chain due to biomagnification which becomes more concentrated in higher trophic levels and causes severe impacts on predators and apex species. As highlighted by the precious research, bioaccumulation affects the biological functions such as reproduction, immunity among various marine species and neurological systems. Studies show that PCBs accumulated in marine species impairs reproductive success in top predators like the seals and seabirds (Ross et al, 2000). The mercury contamination in fishes have been linked to altered behaviors that reduce survival rates which affect both predators and the prey (Lavoie et al, 2013). Heavy metals like lead and cadmium also inhibit enzyme activities essential for physiological processes which impacts the growth, reproduction and lifespan in aquatic species (Burger & Gochfeld, 2004). These create a ripple effect across the ecosystems which leads to biodiversity loss as the sensitive species becomes extinct along with disrupting the food webs and the stability of the ecosystem (Gray, 2002). This decline in species due to bioaccumulation ultimately weakens the ecosystem, reducing their resilience and ability to recover from environmental stressors. And this constant exposure ultimately affects the ecosystem and the human communities reliant on them (Letcher et al, 2010). Certain regulatory measures have been adopted globally for the protection of biodiversity so that the ecosystem can be preserved.

3.3 Regulating Frameworks Protecting Marine Ecosystem

The growing concerns towards the protection of the environment has led to the adaptation of a number of regulatory frameworks both nationally as well as internationally in order to preserve biodiversity and for the preservation of life on earth.

3.3.1 United Nations Convention on the law of the Seas

The UNCLOS or the "Constitution of the Oceans" was adopted in 1982 in order to provide a comprehensive legal regulatory framework for the sustainable management of ocean waters. It deals with the disputes over marine boundaries, along with use of resources, and ensures environmental protection. The convention was adopted as a response to the growing conflicts and pressures relating to marine resources. It identifies rights as well as the responsibilities of the states with regards to the ocean resources and also provides regulating guidelines for protecting the environment, equitable use of the resources along with scientific research. The convention plays an important role by designating specific zones like EEZ or the Exclusive Economic Zone where the states have the right to manage resources along with protecting the environment. It has made it mandatory for the states to prevent marine pollution, ensure conservation of marine life and to regulate activities that cause damage to the ecosystem (Agreement Relating to the Implementation of Part XI of the United Nations Convention on the Law of the Sea). The initiatives undertaken includes the establishment of the International Seabed Authority which regulates mineral related activities, the adoption of the "Part IX Implementation agreement" which promotes sustainable use of seabed resources which protects marine habitats.

India is a signatory to this convention since 1995, and has tried to implement its provisions through various initiatives. The Ministry of Earth Sciences and the Ministry of Environment, Forest and Climate Change (MoEFCC) lead initiatives aligned with UNCLOS to protect marine biodiversity, manage pollution and regulate India's territorial waters (Ministry of Environment, Forest and Climate Change, 2018).

3.3.2 Convention on Biological Diversity (CBD)

The convention was adopted at the 1992 Earth Summit to address the loss of global biodiversity and to ensure the sustainable as well as equitable use of the biological resources. Along with the focus on conserving biodiversity CBD also promotes sustainable practices and frameworks in order to protect the ecosystem from threats like water pollution and habitat degradation. It includes the Aichi Biodiversity targets, specifically target 6 that prevents adverse effects on the marine ecosystem from pollution. To protect the marine diversity from pollution the convention encourages signatories to establish Marine Protected Areas to protect and conserve marine biodiversity. It has also taken initiatives like the strategic plan for biodiversity 2011-2020 which encourages countries to reduce land-based pollutants to enter the marine environments and adapt to sustainable fishing practices. India being a signatory has established MPAs such as the Gulf of Mannar biosphere reserve, for the conservation of marine biodiversity. Along with this India's National Biodiversity Action Plan aligns with the CBD goals to mitigate the impact of the water pollution on the marine ecosystem, supporting habitat restoration (National Biodiversity Authority, 2019).

3.3.3 The International Convention for the Prevention of Pollution from Ships

The convention was adopted in the year 1973 for preventing the pollution of marine environment from human activities especially ships. Keeping in mind the growing global trade and increasing ship traffic, MARPOL addressed pollution risks from oil spills, hazardous cargo, sewage, garbage and air emissions ultimately safeguarding the marine ecosystem from harmful pollutants. It has six key annexes each of which regulates different types of pollutants. The MARPOL's initiatives include mandating proper disposal facilities of wastes in ports and the enforcement of the double hull designs for the oil tankers to minimize the spills. It had also established "Special Areas" like the Mediterranean Sea where the discharge of the harmful pollutants are strictly regulated.

India being a signatory had undertaken many steps to enforce its provisions. The government of India through the Director General of shipping, has mandated the Indian ports to have waste reception facilities so that ships can offload waste safely. And has also designated certain areas as sensitive zones under the convention guidelines enhancing marine projection and minimizing water pollution (Directorate General of Shipping, India, 2021).

3.3.4 Other International Conventions Regulation Marine Water Pollution.

In 1972 the London convention also known as the Convention on the Prevention of Marine Pollution by Dumping of Wastes and Other Matter, was adopted to prevent marine pollution caused by dumping of hazardous materials into the seas. The convention addresses human activities that impact the marine ecosystem by prohibiting the dumping of harmful substances which had adverse effects on marine life. Apart from this the Regional Seas convention and Action plans under the UNEP addresses unique environmental issues faced by specific marine regions like the Helsinki Convention for the Baltic Sea and the Barcelona Convention for the Mediterranean Sea.

3.3.5 Legal frameworks in India

India has adopted many environmental frameworks for safeguarding the biodiversity and prevention of water pollution. The Wildlife (Protection) Act, 1972 laid an early foundation by protecting the marine habitats. It shields water bodies from pollution caused by human encroachments and exploitations. Responding to the environmental crisis like the Bhopal disaster the Environmental (Protection) Act, 1986 was passed to provide a comprehensive legal framework to set pollution standards with specific provisions for the maintenance of the water quality across the rivers, lakes and coastal zones. In accordance with the global biodiversity goals the National Biodiversity Act, 2002 was also implemented for the regulation of the biological resources and foster conservation of the ecosystem. It ensures sustainable use to prevent degradation and pollution (National Biodiversity Authority, 2002). Additionally the Water (Prevention and Control of Pollution) Act, 1974 marks India's first focused initiative against water pollution. It established regulatory bodies to monitor and maintain water quality standards and also restricts harmful industrial discharges into the water bodies. In order to further enhance the conservation efforts the National Plan for Conservation Of Aquatic Ecosystem was implemented which aims at restoring wetlands and preserving aquatic animals and plays a crucial role in improving the water quality (Ministry of Environment, Forest and Climate Change, 2016). All of these collectively aim at reinforcing India's commitments towards protecting its diverse aquatic ecosystems.

4. IMPACTS ON HUMAN HEALTH DUE TO THE CONSUMPTION OF CONTAMINATED FISH.

Consumption of contaminated fish with harmful toxins like the lead, mercury, arsenic, PCBs and other heavy metals poses significant health risks on human health. The pollutants accumulate into the tissues of marine organisms through the process of bioaccumulation. The concentration of these toxins is much higher in larger fishes that are generally consumed by humans. The intake of these contaminants leads to severe health risks like cancer, neurological damages along with kidney damage and weakening of the immune system.

4.1 Analysis trophic transfer and bioaccumulation in the marine food web.

The trophic transfer and bioaccumulation both are crucial processes that put focus on how toxins enter and amplify within the aquatic ecosystem and eventually impact human health. The marine food web comprises various trophic levels, the primary level consists of phytoplanktons who are the foundational producers. They generate energy through the process of photosynthesis. Zooplanktons are considered as the primary consumers who feed on the phytoplanktons and are the main conduit responsible for the transfer of pollutants to other marine organisms.

Moving upwards the food chain then comes the small fishes who feed on the zooplanktons which in turn are fed by the larger fish. In this entire upward movement of the toxins the pollutants that were present at the primary level become more concentrated due to biomagnification.

The process of bioaccumulation and biomagnification are interconnected and they facilitate the buildup of pollutants in marine organisms. In bioaccumulation heavy metals accumulate into the tissues of the organisms over time and when they begin to absorb a higher proportion of pollutants than they can actually excrete (Anderson et al, 2015). On the other hand biomagnification refers to the increasing concentration of toxin concentration at the higher trophic level which affects the apex predators who retain the toxins in their fatty tissues (Gray, 2002).

This poses consequences on the marine animals as they face reproductive issues, immune suppression, organ damage etc. which ultimately affect the ecosystem(Goutte et al, 2013).

4.2 Carcinogenic risks associated with bioaccumulation.

Bioaccumulation occurs when different toxic substances, including carcinogens, accumulate in the living organisms faster than they can be metabolized by the system or excreted. Over time, the concentration of these substances reaches a harmful level in tissues, and this leads to significant public health hazards, including cancer. Here are the key carcinogenic risks factors and the mechanisms associated with bioaccumulation:

i. *Persistent Exposure to Toxic Substances*

Continuous exposure to bioaccumulated toxic substances has drastically increased the risk of carcinogenesis. Chronic cellular stress, DNA damage, and continued inflammation have been identified as the mechanism for carcinogenesis. Ultimately, such factors alter normal cellular function and result in mutations leading to malignant transformation. The genomic instability due to interference of the DNA repair pathway by persistent toxins and chronic inflammation create a favorable microenvironment for tumor initiation and progression (Reuter et al., 2010).

Bioaccumulation of arsenic in the skin, liver, and kidneys is perhaps the best-studied example. Chronic exposure to arsenic-contaminated drinking water or industrial pollutants has been clinically proven to be a cause of skin, bladder, and lung cancers. Arsenic impairs signaling pathways within cells, triggers oxidative stress, and blocks apoptosis, thereby enabling damaged cells to continue multiplying without regulation. This shows the critical demand for monitoring environmental toxicants, with subsequent minimization of exposures, in a bid to ensure the long-term health effects of exposure and further cancer prevention.

ii. *Biomagnification of toxins in the Food Chain*

Biomagnification is the increase in concentration of toxins as they move up the food chain, thereby posing higher risks to top predators, including humans. These are usually persistent organic pollutants or heavy metals that cannot easily be broken down and are stored in tissues of organisms. Humans ingest these concentrated toxins in the form of contaminated fish, meat, or plants, thus greatly increasing their exposure to carcinogens (Montano et al., 2010).

One good example is methylmercury and polychlorinated biphenyls (PCBs) in aquatic ecosystems. These toxins bioaccumulate in small organisms such as plankton and magnify through each trophic level to reach peak concentrations in fish and marine mammals. Humans who consume seafood contaminated with methylmercury or PCBs are associated with increased risks of developing cancer, particularly liver and breast cancers, among others. This happens because these substances disrupt cellular processes, cause oxidative stress, and affect control over hormonal regulation. Knowledge and application about biomagnification are critical to ensuring human health and a balanced ecosystem.

iii. *Endocrine Disruption*

The endocrine disrupting chemicals pose very significant risk in interference of the hormone signaling pathways and thus increase chances of hormone-related cancers. Slowly accumulated toxins act like a mimic, blocker, or modifier of functions related to hormones and cause disturbances in the growth and proliferation of cells. Such disturbances risk disrupting cellular homeostasis and promote tumorigenesis in due course.

The compound Bisphenol A is another EDC commonly used in plastics and food containers. Its action mimics the effect of estrogen, making it responsible for some breast and prostate cancers. Persistent organic pollutants produced as byproducts of industrial processes are known to cause reproductive organ cancers, with dioxins being the examples. Dioxins influence the hormonal pathways and affect immune responses. The condition also results in chronic inflammation that supports cancer formation (Eve et al., 2020).

The pervasiveness of EDCs in the environment has increased the demand for stricter regulatory measures and awareness about reducing exposure to prevent hormone-driven cancers.

iv. *Genotoxic Effects*

Bioaccumulated carcinogens directly affect genomic integrity because they cause DNA damage, resulting in mutations that drive tumor formation. These persistent environmental toxins, often in the form of reactive intermediates, bind to DNA to form adducts or disrupt repair mechanisms, and their gradual accumulation over time fosters genetic instability and permits cancer development.

One of the mechanisms is DNA adduct formation: reactive carcinogenic intermediates covalently bind to DNA bases, changing their structure and function. Meanwhile, other toxicants block the repair pathways, either base excision repair or nucleotide excision repair, that would correct damage. The combined damage induction and inhibition of repair provide a fertile soil for carcinogenesis.

Polycyclic aromatic hydrocarbons, or PAHs, are paradigmatic bio-accumulated carcinogens. PAHs are a ubiquitous pollutant in industrial emission effluents and tobacco smoke whose concentration increases inside fatty tissues and lungs. PAH intermediates can rearrange and cross-link to DNA, causing mutations that are directly associated with lung, bladder, and skin cancers. The changes at the molecular level caused by PAHs typify the pivotal role played by DNA damage in the initiation of cancer. This will illustrate the necessity for avoiding exposure to carcinogenic toxicants and moving forward with targeted therapies for DNA damage in treating cancer (Huang Zhou, 2021).

v. *Oxidative Stress*

Toxicity-induced oxidative stress Bioaccumulated toxins trigger the production of ROS responsible for oxidative DNA, protein, and lipid damage within cells. These chronic inflamed and mutagenic alterations as a result of oxidative stress can create the conducive environment needed to induce cancer.

It involves an imbalance of ROS generation in the cell and antioxidant defenses that protect the body from damage. The elevated levels of ROS damage DNA, which results in mutations; oxidative stress disrupts signaling pathways and activates pro-inflammatory mediators, thus promoting all phases of tumor initiation, progression, and metastasis. Cadmium is a heavy metal in industrial waste, and it is a strong inducer of ROS, associated with lung and prostate cancers. Similarly, arsenic exposure from polluted water or an industrial source produces oxidative stress. This has resulted in the cause of several types of cancers like skin, bladder, and lung cancers. Of course, the linkage between oxidative stress, inflammation, and carcinogenesis would suggest a potential relevance of toxin exposure mitigation. For a more detailed review of the processes involved, see (Reuter et al., 2010), who carefully detail the complicated interplay between oxidative stress, inflammation, and cancer. Such knowledge provides a foundation upon which to work toward preemptive strategies and targeted therapies that counteract toxin-induced carcinogenesis (Reuter et al., 2010).

vi. *Chronic Inflammation*

Long-term exposure to bioaccumulated substances usually leads to chronic inflammation, which is an important driver of carcinogenesis. Chronic inflammatory responses damage tissues, disrupt cellular homeostasis, and create a tumor-supportive microenvironment through the release of pro-inflammatory cytokines, chemokines, and ROS, which facilitate DNA damage, angiogenesis, and immune evasion.

For example, asbestos fibers accumulate in lung tissues, leading to prolonged inflammation and cellular damage. This chronic inflammatory condition gives rise to mesothelioma, the extremely rare and aggressive type of cancer. Silica dust again is inhaled leading to persistent lung inflammation that furthers stimulates the onset of lung cancer.

These inflammatory processes initiate cancer but are also known to support tumor growth and metastasis by changing the composition of the microenvironment. Learning about the interaction between chronic inflammation and carcinogenesis, as defined by Casey et al., helps appreciate the need for limiting exposure and exploring anti-inflammatory strategies to address cancer risks (Casey et al., 2015)

vii. *Synergistic Effects*

Bioaccumulated carcinogens may interact synergistically with environmental or genetic factors, thereby synergistically amplifying the risk for cancer. Often, exposure to many toxicants creates synergistic effects in which genotoxic and cytotoxic impacts produced by combined exposure are greater than those of individual exposures. These synergies enhance the impact of DNA damage, overwhelm cellular repair machinery, and activate signaling pathways whose dysregulation compromises cellular integrity.

As the best example for such association between exposure to asbestos and smoking, the case of lung cancer is also quite common. In the lungs, asbestos fibers remain in place because they cannot be cleared and are thus chronically inflamed and mechanically injured; cigarette smoke delivers an entire category of carcinogens to cells in the lung, including PAHs and nitrosamines. In summary, this results in an additive insult to cellular defenses, accelerates genetic mutations, and promotes cancer development. This phenomenon underlines the complexity of carcinogenesis by which environmental exposures dynamically interact in concert with each individual's genetic susceptibilities. It highlights the synergistic risks arising from combined exposures to toxicants and the necessity for all-inclusive controls on combined exposures to reduce further exposure and frame prevention strategies uniquely to high-risk populations, among them industrial employees. The following table 1 categorizes the carcinogens that are linked with the specific type of cancer and the targeted organs.

Table 1. Key Carcinogens Linked to Bioaccumulation

Carcinogen	Source	Bioaccumulation on Target	Cancer Types
Arsenic	Contaminated water	Skin Lungs Liver	Skin, Bladder, Lung cancers
Cadmium	Industrial emissions, Tobacco	Kidneys, Bones	Prostate, Lung cancers
PCBs	Industrial Pollutants	Fatty tissues	Breast, Liver cancers
PAHs	Combustion of fossil fuels	Lungs Liver	Lung, Bladder cancers
Dioxins	Industrial byproducts	Fatty tissues	Soft tissue sarcoma
Asbestos	Construction material	Lungs	Mesothelioma, Lung cancers

Prevention and Mitigation Strategies include reducing Exposure by avoiding consumption of fish from contaminated water bodies, as well as limiting exposure to industrial pollutants and pesticides, Regulatory Actions such as enforcing stricter limits on emissions of carcinogens like PCBs and heavy metals, Environmental Cleanups by remediating contaminated ecosystems to reduce bioaccumulation risks and Increasing public Awareness by educating communities on the sources and risks of bioaccumulated carcinogens are all effective strategies for the prevention and mitigation. The carcinogenic risks that exist in bioaccumulation come from the extended exposure of such toxins, biomagnification, and interference with various cellular processes. All these would be taken care of by measures involving regulatory actions, protection at the environmental level, and public health.

4.3 Public Health Policy

The SDG goals undertaken for prioritizing public health encompasses a broad range of objectives which aim to eradicate poverty and to enhance the access to clean water and ensure good health. SDG 3 deals with Good Health and Well-being and aims to reduce the per mature mortality of the non-communicable diseases and it promotes the well-being of mankind. Progress shows that challenges exist in proper management to diseases which are influenced by environmental pollution, due bioaccumulation which stands out to be a persistent problem due to the constant exposure to the heavy metals and pollutants that accumulate into the tissues of the aquatic organisms which gradually affect the humans via seafood leading to chronic health issues like cancer. Instead of such goals they face issues in proper implementation. Similarly, the SDG 6 deals with clean water and sanitation which puts focus on the need for effective water management systems which will prevent the pollutants from entering into the water bodies. Its objectives include improvement of the water quality, reduce pollution. As per the UN 2023 progress report inadequate sanitation still continues to be a threat to human health (United Nations Statistics Division, n.d.). Both of these SDGs are very integral in ensuring public health as well as environmental sustainability and require intensive effort policy enforcement. And the regulatory gaps become one of the main reasons for its failures ultimately exposing mankind to the harmful toxins.

To address the impacts caused by bioaccumulation a number of international frameworks have been implemented. The Stockholm Convention on Persistent Organic Pollutants aims to protect both the environment as well as the human health from chemicals that persist in the environment and gradually bioaccumulates and pose health risks (UNIDO, n.d.). It identifies industrial chemicals, pesticides and other POPs that majorly contribute to the process of bioaccumulation and tries to ensure their gradual elimination. The Minamata Convention on Mercury additionally targets mercury as it has the ability to bioaccumulate into the tissues of aquatic organisms (Moon, et al, 2013). It calls for the reduction as well as possible elimination of the said heavy metal as far as possible along with the promotion of proper and safe management of water. Further the Basel convention on the Control of Transboundary Movements of Hazardous wastes and their disposal was adopted on 22 March 1989. It has a pivotal role in the controlling bioaccumulation by controlling the movements of the harmful hazardous wastes. The parties to the convention are under obligation to regulate its waste exports and ensure safe disposal. All of them advocate for stronger global efforts but proper implementation remains to be a challenge due to lack of proper regulatory frameworks.

In India there are also several legislations that aim to address pollution and protect the public health. The Water (Prevention and Control of Pollution) Act, 1974 was the first comprehensive regulatory framework that provided for the prevention and control of water pollution. Central and State boards have been established under the provisions of the act to oversee and undertake pollution control measures. Further amendment in the year 1988 increased the regulatory power along with stricter enforcement for and penalties in case of breach. However there have been gaps in enforcement mechanisms and the limited power of the boards have hindered the effective regulation.

The Environment (Protection) Act, 1986 further regulates various types of pollution and ensures immediate governmental actions for the prevention and mitigation of environmental damages. With the increasing threats the act has gone under several amendments to address the issues like the Environment (Protection) Amendment Rules, 1993 which introduces the standard of emission for the industries. The 2002 amendment aimed to strengthen proper regulation of the hazardous substances. Still there were lack in the enforcement mechanisms along with poor coordination between the authorities at the center and the state.

The Hazardous Waste (Management and Handling) Rules, 1989 was also implemented for the management of the disposal and handling of the hazardous wastes especially from industries. The act was amended in 2003 and 2008 and addressed for recycling and reuse of the hazardous wastes. In 2016 the rule was renamed as Hazardous and Other Wastes (Management and Transboundary movement) Rules which was more aligned to the Basel convention on the Control of Transboundary Movements of Hazardous wastes. Despite such efforts there have been various loopholes like lack of proper monitoring which ultimately affected the objectives.

5. GAPS IN THE LEGAL FRAMEWORKS

As we have already discussed the different existing regulatory frameworks it is evident that proper control of water pollution is still needed. Not only global but also regional and local activities are also to be taken care of as they are directly or indirectly causing pollution. Thus, lack of proper comprehensive legal frameworks can be seen along with limited international cooperation in the end poses significant challenges.

5.1 Addressing the gaps in the Indian legal frameworks and international cooperation.

Due to the absence of proper comprehensive frameworks India faces significant challenges in addressing the water pollution and controlling bioaccumulation and its carcinogenic impacts. As the existing frameworks do not specifically address bioaccumulation as a threat to mankind and along with this, they also fail to control the root cause of the contamination which affect both the ecosystem as well as the human beings. India's standards for the maintenance of the water quality are also seen to be insufficient in addressing the bioaccumulation of contaminants. Although the Bureau of Indian Standards or BIS regulates some contaminants like arsenic and mercury, the limit set is often found to be inadequate leaving loopholes that allow toxic contaminants to accumulate and remain unchecked. Along with this the lack in the monitoring mechanism also hampers the ability of the government to effectively regulate the contaminants and to mitigate their long term carcinogenic impacts of the contaminants (Varun, 2024).

The present monitoring system has underperformed because of many reasons and among them the lack of proper data is one of the prominent causes. This lack of data undermines the ability of proper enforcement of the existing standards, and leads to delayed and inadequate responses to the pollution, as effective monitoring of bioaccumulation requires long term data that are consistent in nature (World Health Organization, 2023). On the international sphere the issue gets exacerbated due to lack of cooperation and monitoring at regional levels. The water pollution due to its transboundary nature gets shared through rivers and oceans and one country's pollution easily affects its neighboring countries. Also, there are no specific regulatory measures that targets bioaccumulation, agreements to set proper standards to combat the carcinogenic impacts ultimately resulting in failure of the entire system (Gleick, 1993).

6. CLEANING SEAWATER WITH NANOTECHNOLOGY: A NEW HOPE FOR THE FUTURE

Nanotechnology, working at the atomic and molecular level, has brought forth revolutionary solutions to one of humanity's most significant challenges: safe drinking water. This technology is revolutionizing the conversion of seawater into potable water by effectively removing harmful pollutants such as heavy metals and carcinogens. Specialized nanoparticles and advanced filtration systems are used by nanotechnology to target and eliminate stubborn contaminants like lead, mercury, and arsenic. These substances, often attributed to severe health conditions such as kidney damage and cancer, are notoriously difficult to treat using conventional water treatment methods (Perez, 2023).

Among the exciting materials leading this revolution include graphene oxide as well as carbon nanotubes. These materials not only possess exceptional efficiency in filtering hazardous particles but also have energy efficiency and extraordinary specificity. Unlike most water treatment technologies that are typically very energy-intensive, nanotechnology-based filters are known to require a significantly lesser amount of energy. This aspect has made it environmentally friendly as well as cost-effective, especially for water-scarce regions. With such advanced materials, nanotechnology brings an affordable solution to the water problem of the world at large.

Nanotechnology goes far beyond the desalination of seawater. Industrial wastewater treatment applications have immense potential in these advanced filtration systems as they can ensure prevention of environmental contamination from happening in the first place by removing hazardous substances before their release into natural ecosystems. This is very important because industrial pollution continues to pose a threat to the health of rivers, lakes, and groundwater sources. They also deploy in emergency circumstances, such as natural disasters and humanitarian crises. Nanotech filters can be quickly used to create access to safe drinking water by affected populations, making them easy to use for emergency situations while being efficient at the same time, thus giving clean water under the most severe conditions.

One of the significant features of nanotechnology is that it is very sustainable. Traditional methods of desalination, like thermal distillation or reverse osmosis, usually require large inputs of energy and suffer from difficulties in waste management. Nanotechnology is cleaner and more efficient in this regard. For instance, a graphene oxide membrane filters out salt and contaminants using very little energy and is also extremely durable and cost-effective. This capability places nanotech solutions as a pivotal tool in addressing the growing global demand for clean water, particularly in arid and semi-arid regions where freshwater resources are scarce.

Beyond the immediate applications, nanotechnology in water purification will also open up long-term sustainability avenues by reducing the dependence on freshwater sources and minimizing the environmental impact of desalination. It may change the very fabric of how societies approach water security by transforming the vast reserves of seawater into a reliable and safe source of drinking water (Joseph, 2023).

In conclusion, nanotechnology marks a paradigm shift in how we manage and access clean water. Its ability to remove harmful pollutants with unparalleled precision, coupled with its energy efficiency and versatility, positions it as a cornerstone of future water treatment strategies. Whether it is addressing water scarcity, preventing environmental contamination, or providing rapid relief in disaster-stricken areas, nanotechnology has the potential to ensure that the oceans become not just a symbol of life but a source of health and safety for generations to come.

7. CONCLUSION

To conclude it is highlighted in this chapter that there exists a huge gap in the proper conservation of marine habitats through the national and international legal frameworks. An in-depth study with particular recommendations is required to fill this gap and strengthen the effectiveness of the same. One of the primary reasons for such deficiency is poor implementation and enforcement of international agreements, such as UNCLOS and MARPOL in the national level. Despite ratification of these agreements by many countries, including India, uneven implementation remains a persistent feature, especially in isolated marine regions. A weak monitoring system and a shortage of qualified staff exacerbate the problem, undermining the effectiveness of regulations. The administration inefficiency at the national level is rooted in the local level and diversification of laws, such as the Biodiversity Act, Water Act, and Wildlife Protection Act.

Regional conventions such as the Helsinki and Barcelona Conventions address specific areas but fails to cover vulnerable regions like the Indian Ocean and Arabian Sea. Land-based marine pollution, in addition, continues to pose a threat to marine biodiversity through agricultural runoff and untreated sewage. The existing law is ineffective in curbing pollutants entering the marine environment by way of rivers and estuaries, even though frameworks such as CBD and the Water Act are in place. Yet another challenge facing marine ecosystems is the relatively recent problems like the impacts of climate change, ocean acidification, and sea-level rise that continue to grow but remain unaddressed in existing legal frameworks. Public awareness and community participation are also lacking, reducing both social acceptance and local compliance with marine conservation measures. Coastal populations, which could be an integral part of the process to protect marine ecosystems, are not often involved in the decision-making process. Moreover, majority of the countries, including India, have technological and infrastructural shortcomings such as inferior waste reception facilities, inefficient systems in oil spill management, and inadequate tools for real-time monitoring. Those gaps should be met by governments through enforcing a better outcome: building up mechanistic systems of enforcement.

Advanced monitoring technologies, such as satellite-based systems, and upgrading enforcement agencies' training should be undertaken to ensure complete conformity with regulation; sufficient funding and resources should be allocated for effective implementation of international conventions and national legislation harmonized, with all existing laws integrated into a unified regulatory framework, in order to achieve smooth management without such conflict between jurisdictions. A national marine ecosystem policy might help consolidate a comprehensive approach toward effective governance. Regional cooperation must be widened to include underrepresented regions, such as the Indian Ocean region, to ensure that overall global coverage is instituted for efforts at marine conservation. India may be an example of facilitator leadership for Indian Ocean Rim countries. Regulations must be implemented and tightened with severe penalties in case of violation and investments made in the establishment of wastewater treatment facilities to minimize land-based pollution sources that enter the marine environment.

Existing frameworks must be amended to include measures to address climate change impacts, such as ocean acidification and sea-level rise. Public awareness campaigns and the inclusion of coastal communities in conservation efforts can enhance social acceptance and local enforcement. Incentivizing community-driven initiatives and establishing citizen science programs can further strengthen grassroots conservation efforts. Finally, technological and infrastructural capacities in terms of modern reception facilities for waste and more importantly oil spill response mechanisms should be invested in. By addressing these gaps and implementing the recommendations, nations can ensure the protection of marine ecosystems and fulfil their commitments to biodiversity conservation and sustainable development.

REFERENCES

Alharbi, O. M., Basheer, A. A., Khattab, R. A., & Ali, I. (2018). Health and environmental effects of persistent organic pollutants. *Journal of Molecular Liquids, 263*, 442–453. DOI: 10.1016/j.molliq.2018.05.029

Anderson, C., Moore, C., & Atwood, J. (2015). The persistence and bioaccumulation of pollutants in marine ecosystems. *Marine Pollution Bulletin, 97*(1-2), 12–18.

Biswas, H. S., & Poddar, S. (2024). Heavy Metals in Foodstuffs: Presence, Bioaccumulation, Origins, Health Risk, and Remediation. In Saini, P. (Ed.), *Biosorption Processes for Heavy Metal Removal* (pp. 85–99). IGI Global Scientific Publishing., DOI: 10.4018/979-8-3693-1618-4.ch004

Burger, J., & Gochfeld, M. (2004). Marine birds as sentinels of environmental pollution. *EcoHealth, 1*(3), 263–274. DOI: 10.1007/s10393-004-0096-4

Casey, S. C., Vaccari, M., Al-Mulla, F., Al-Temaimi, R., Amedei, A., Barcellos-Hoff, M. H., Brown, D. G., Chapellier, M., Christopher, J., Curran, C. S., Forte, S., Hamid, R. A., Heneberg, P., Koch, D. C., Krishnakumar, P. K., Laconi, E., Maguer-Satta, V., Marongiu, F., Memeo, L., Mondello, C., … Felsher, D. W. (2015). The effect of environmental chemicals on the tumor microenvironment. *Carcinogenesis, 36 Suppl 1*(Suppl 1), S160–S183. https://doi.org/DOI: 10.1093/carcin/bgv035

Central Pollution Control Board (CPCB). (1974). *Water (Prevention and Control of Pollution) Act.*

Convention on Biological Diversity (CBD). (1992). *Text of the CBD*. Retrieved from https://www.cbd.int/convention/text/

Convention on Biological Diversity (CBD). (2010). *Strategic Plan for Biodiversity 2011-2020 and the Aichi Biodiversity Targets*. Retrieved from https://www.cbd.int/sp/

Dave, P. N., Chaturvedi, S., & Sahu, L. K. (2021). Impact of polychlorinated biphenyls on environment and public health. In *Elsevier eBooks* (pp. 261–280). DOI: 10.1016/B978-0-12-822121-1.00013-8

Directorate General of Shipping. India. (2021). *Implementation of MARPOL in India*. Retrieved from http://dgshipping.gov.in

Eve, L., Fervers, B., Le Romancer, M., & Etienne-Selloum, N. (2020). Exposure to Endocrine Disrupting Chemicals and Risk of Breast Cancer. *International Journal of Molecular Sciences, 21*(23), 9139. DOI: 10.3390/ijms21239139 PMID: 33266302

Gleick, P. H. (1993). Water and Conflict: Fresh water resources and international security. *International Security*, *18*(1), 79. DOI: 10.2307/2539033

Goutte, A., Bustamante P., Barbraud C., Delord K., Weimerskirch H., & Chastel O. (2013). Demographic responses to mercury exposure in two closely-related Antarctic top predators.

Gray, J. S. (2002). Biomagnification in marine systems: The perspective of an ecologist. *Marine Pollution Bulletin*, *45*(1), 46–52. DOI: 10.1016/S0025-326X(01)00323-X PMID: 12398366

History, E. V. O. S. -. 1. E. &. L. |. (2021, March 23). Exxon Valdez Oil Spill - 1989, Effects & Location | HISTORY. *HISTORY*. https://www.history.com/topics/1980s/exxon-valdez-oil-spill

Huang, R., & Zhou, P. K. (2021). DNA damage repair: Historical perspectives, mechanistic pathways and clinical translation for targeted cancer therapy. *Signal Transduction and Targeted Therapy*, *6*(1), 254. DOI: 10.1038/s41392-021-00648-7 PMID: 34238917

International Journal of Advanced Research in Science, Communication and Technology. (2020). *International Journal of Advanced Research in Science Communication and Technology*. https://doi.org/DOI: 10.48175/568

International Maritime Organization (IMO). (1972). *Convention on the Prevention of Marine Pollution by Dumping of Wastes and Other Matter*. Retrieved from https://www.imo.org

International Maritime Organization (IMO). (1973/1978). *International Convention for the Prevention of Pollution from Ships (MARPOL)*. Retrieved from https://www.imo.org

International Maritime Organization (IMO). (2020). *Special Areas Under MARPOL*. Retrieved from https://www.imo.org/en/OurWork/Environment/Pages/Special-Areas-MARPOL

Joseph, T. M., Al-Hazmi, H. E., Śniatała, B., Esmaeili, A., & Habibzadeh, S. (2023). Nanoparticles and nanofiltration for wastewater treatment: From polluted to fresh water. *Environmental Research*, *238*, 117114. DOI: 10.1016/j.envres.2023.117114 PMID: 37716387

Lavoie, R. A., Jardine, T. D., Chumchal, M. M., Kidd, K. A., & Campbell, L. M. (2013). Biomagnification of mercury in aquatic food webs: A worldwide meta-analysis. *Environmental Science & Technology*, *47*(23), 13385–13394. DOI: 10.1021/es403103t PMID: 24151937

Letcher, R. J., Bustnes, J. O., Dietz, R., Jenssen, B. M., Jörundsdóttir, H., Sonne, C., & Gabrielsen, G. W. (2010). Exposure and effects assessment of persistent organohalogen contaminants in arctic wildlife and fish. *The Science of the Total Environment*, *408*(15), 2995–3043. DOI: 10.1016/j.scitotenv.2009.10.038 PMID: 19910021

Maji, S., Samanta, D., & Mondal, S. (2024). Unveiling Eco-Friendly Solutions: A Comprehensive Review on Leveraging Mechanism-Based Pathways for Sustainable Mitigation of Pesticide Metabolite Contamination and Enhanced Public Health. *International Journal of Advancement in Life Sciences Research*, *7*(4), 32–45. DOI: 10.31632/ijalsr.2024.v07i04.004

Mercury: The Tragedy of Minamata Disease. (n.d.). Collaborative for Health & Environment. https://www.healthandenvironment.org/environmental-health/social-context/history/mercury-the-tragedy-of-minamata-disease#:~:text=In%20the%20late%201950s%20Minamata%20Bay%2C%20Japan%20became,bioaccumulated%20and%20biomagnified%20in%20the%20muscle%20of%20fish

Montano, L., Pironti, C., Pinto, G., Ricciardi, M., Buono, A., Brogna, C., Venier, M., Piscopo, M., Amoresano, A., & Motta, O. (2022). Polychlorinated Biphenyls (PCBs) in the Environment: Occupational and Exposure Events, Effects on Human Health and Fertility. *Toxics*, *10*(7), 365. DOI: 10.3390/toxics10070365 PMID: 35878270

National Biodiversity Authority. (2019). *India's National Report on Biodiversity*.

National Biodiversity Authority (NBA). (2002). *National Biodiversity Act*.

Pérez, H., García, O. J. Q., Amezcua-Allieri, M. A., & Vázquez, R. R. (2023). Nanotechnology as an efficient and effective alternative for wastewater treatment: An overview. *Water Science and Technology*, *87*(12), 2971–3001. DOI: 10.2166/wst.2023.179 PMID: 37387425

Proc, K., Bulak, P., Kaczor, M., & Bieganowski, A. (2021). A New Approach to Quantifying Bioaccumulation of Elements in Biological Processes. *Biology (Basel)*, *10*(4), 345. DOI: 10.3390/biology10040345 PMID: 33923892

Ramish, N., Irshad, M. A., Nawaz, R., Nasim, I., Irfan, A., Hussain, A., Al-Mutairi, A. A., Rizwan, M., Al-Hussain, S. A., & Zaki, M. E. (2024). Bioaccumulation of carcinogenic metals in river fish: A quantitative investigation of public health risk. *Ecological Indicators*, *162*, 112057. DOI: 10.1016/j.ecolind.2024.112057

Reuter, S., Gupta, S. C., Chaturvedi, M. M., & Aggarwal, B. B. (2010). Oxidative stress, inflammation, and cancer: How are they linked? *Free Radical Biology & Medicine*, *49*(11), 1603–1616. DOI: 10.1016/j.freeradbiomed.2010.09.006 PMID: 20840865

Ross, P. S., De Swart, R. L., Addison, R. F., Van Loveren, H., Vos, J. G., & Osterhaus, A. D. (2000). Contaminant-induced immunotoxicity in harbour seals: Wildlife at risk? *Toxicology*, *112*(2-3), 157–169. PMID: 8814345

Salamanca-Fernández, E., Rodríguez-Barranco, M., Amiano, P., Delfrade, J., Chirlaque, M. D., Colorado, S., Guevara, M., Jimenez, A., Arrebola, J. P., Vela, F., Olea, N., Agudo, A., & Sánchez, M. J. (2021). Bisphenol-A exposure and risk of breast and prostate cancer in the Spanish European Prospective Investigation into Cancer and Nutrition study. *Environmental Health : A Global Access Science Source*, *20*(1), 88. DOI: 10.1186/s12940-021-00779-y PMID: 34399780

Speer, R. M., Zhou, X., Volk, L. B., Liu, K. J., & Hudson, L. G. (2023). Arsenic and cancer: Evidence and mechanisms. *Advances in Pharmacology (San Diego, Calif.)*, *96*, 151–202. DOI: 10.1016/bs.apha.2022.08.001 PMID: 36858772

Starner, C. (n.d.). *Bioaccumulation | Causes, Effects, and Mitigation Strategies*. Green Living Answers. https://www.greenlivinganswers.com/ecosystem/bioaccumulation

Steenland, K., Bertazzi, P., Baccarelli, A., & Kogevinas, M. (2004). Dioxin revisited: Developments since the 1997 IARC classification of dioxin as a human carcinogen. *Environmental Health Perspectives*, *112*(13), 1265–1268. DOI: 10.1289/ehp.7219 PMID: 15345337

The Editors of Encyclopaedia Britannica. (2024, October 11). *Exxon Valdez oil spill | Response, Animals, & Facts*. Encyclopedia Britannica. https://www.britannica.com/event/Exxon-Valdez-oil-spill

Uddin, M. N., Desai, F., & Asmatulu, E. (2021). Review of Bioaccumulation, Biomagnification, and Biotransformation of Engineered Nanomaterials. In *Environmental chemistry for a sustainable world* (pp. 133–164). DOI: 10.1007/978-3-030-69492-0_6

United Nations. (1982). *United Nations Convention on the Law of the Sea*. Retrieved from https://www.un.org/Depts/los/convention_agreements/texts/unclos/unclos_e.pdf

United Nations. (1994). *Agreement Relating to the Implementation of Part XI of the United Nations Convention on the Law of the Sea.*

United Nations. (2020). Sustainable Development Goals (SDG 3) | United Nations Western Europe. United Nations Western Europe. https://unric.org/en/sdg-3/

United Nations. (2020). *Sustainable Development Goals (SDG 6) | United Nations Western Europe*. United Nations Western Europe. https://unric.org/en/sdg-6/

United Nations Environment Programme (UNEP). (2021). *Regional Seas Conventions and Action Plans*. Retrieved from https://www.unep.org

United Nations Statistics Division. (n.d.). *Progress Chart — SDG Indicators*. https://unstats.un.org/sdgs/report/2023/progress-chart/

Varun, P. K. (2024), A critical legal analysis of recent amendments to the water (Prevention and control of pollution) act, 1974 in India. In International Journal of Law (pp. 13-17)

Venkatraman, G., Giribabu, N., Mohan, P. S., Muttiah, B., Govindarajan, V. K., Alagiri, M., Rahman, P. S. A., & Karsani, S. A. (2024). Environmental impact and human health effects of polycyclic aromatic hydrocarbons and remedial strategies: A detailed review. *Chemosphere*, *351*, 141227. DOI: 10.1016/j.chemosphere.2024.141227 PMID: 38253087

Verougstraete, V., Lison, D., & Hotz, P. (2003). Cadmium, lung and prostate cancer: A systematic review of recent epidemiological data. *Journal of Toxicology and Environmental Health. Part B, Critical Reviews*, *6*(3), 227–255. DOI: 10.1080/10937400306465 PMID: 12746140

Wang, Y., Kuo, Y., Lin, M., & Tsai, P. (2021). Assessing Lung and Skin Cancer Risks for Steel and Iron Manufacturing Industry Workers Exposed to Polycyclic Aromatic Hydrocarbons. *Aerosol and Air Quality Research*, *21*(11), 210160. DOI: 10.4209/aaqr.210160

World Health Organization. (2023). *Bioaccumulation and Water Quality Monitoring*. WHO Environmental Health Reports.

About The Contributors

Sandeep Poddar, Deputy Vice Chancellor (Research & Innovation) also served as Senior Research Director and Executive Editor(Publications), Lincoln University College, Malaysia. Adjunct Faculty (Honorary), Bharat Center Canada. Dr Sandeep has been graduated from University of Calcutta in with Honours in Zoology, he has obtained Post Graduate Diploma in Dietetics from All India Institute of Hygiene and Public Health, Master of Science in Zoology with specialization in Biochemical Genetics from Dayalbagh Educational Institute with distinction. In addition to this he also obtained Master of Business Administration (MBA) from Lincoln University College. He has completed PhD in Zoology from Vivekananda Institute of Medical Sciences (University of Calcutta) on Cytotoxicity. After completing PhD he pursued Post Doctoral Research in different projects on Hemoglobinopathies and Oral Cancer mutation. Associated in establishment of molecular diagnostics laboratory (Neon) at present under Desun Hospitals, Kolkata. Set Biotechnology laboratory at college in Hooghly, West Bengal under University of Burdwan. He has published more than 200 research papers (in reputed Scopus Web of Sc indexed journals and books, filed more than 15 patents, organized international conferences, and also edited books in Malaysia, Australia, India and USA. He is serving as Guest editor of different reputed Scopus indexed journals of Elsevier, Inderscience, Pertanika like publishers. He has initiated the International Journal of Advancement in Life Sciences Research. Dr Sandeep is founder Assistant Secretary of Dr Tarak Nath Podder Memorial Foundation, Kolkata, India. He is active member of different organizations, Indian Science Congress Association, Indian Science News Association, World Academy of Sciences, Mental Health Innovation Network, UK, Malaysian Society for Molecular Biology and Biotechnology, Fellow member of World Researchers Associations.

Waliza Ansar completed her Bachelors (Zoology Honors) with Chemistry and Botany and Master's degree(Zoology) from Calcutta University. She was awarded the National Scholarship in 1994. She was awarded Ph.D degree(2009) from CSIR-

Indian Institute of Chemical Biology, Kolkata,Govt of India, after qualifying for the State Level Eligibility Test (SLET) and National Eligibility Test (NET) conducted by Ministry of CSIR-HRDG, Govt of India . In her Ph.D work, she had demonstrated various biological roles of CRP in Malaria, Leishmania and Tuberculosis. She also completed three years of post doctoral research from CSIR-IICB, India. Previously she has worked as a lecturer (2002-2003) for undergraduate and postgraduate students from Presidency College (presently Presidency University) in Zoology. Currently she is working as Assistant Professor (Zoology) for undergraduate students in Behala College, Kolkata from 2015 to till date. From 2015-2017 and now, she is the Head of the department of Zoology, Behala College. She has worked at Asutosh College, Kolkata as a lecturer of Environmental Science (2009- 2019) and Zoology (2009- 2014) for postgraduate students. She has done excellent research work on dipteran flies of medico-veterinary importance in ZSI, Kolkata. Apart from this, she has published some papers on CRP, therapeutic applications of monoclonal antibodies, a book chapter on nanomedicine from Springer and a book from Springer in 2016 and 2020 on C-reactive protein and a recent book from NOVA. She has presented her work in different international and national symposiums. Someof her publishedpapers are in Glycoconjugate J (2006, 2009), Cellular physiology and Biochemistry (2009), Immunology research (2013), Indian J of Clinical Medicine (2013) and Journal of Stem Cells (2014).

***

Vyshnavi A started her career at Center for management studies after completing post graduation at Bangalore University, pursuing her PhD in finance derivatives and ICWA.Has further completed value addition courses in Finance, Accounting and Tourism from reputed institutions like university of Melbourne, University of Virginia, University of Melbourne to mention a few.She has authored a book on International Finance.Having 10 years of teaching experience she has worked in different capacities as course facilitator, Member of Research & Development cell.

Idris Adewale is a respected academic and researcher at the Faculty of Applied Science, Lincoln University College. His expertise lies primarily in the field of health science, with a particular focus on biomedical research. Throughout his career, Dr. Adewale has made significant contributions through extensive research and publications that explore critical issues in health and biomedical science. His work, marked by scientific rigor and innovation, has advanced knowledge in these fields, solidifying his reputation as a prominent figure in both academia and research.

Abhisikta Basu is currently serving as an Assistant Professor at Department of Law, University of Engineering and Management Kolkata.

Gupinath Bhandari has completed his Bachelor of Engineering in Civil Engineering from Bengal Engineering College, Shibpur, Howrah, India in 1990 and Masters of Civil Engineering in Geotechnical Engineering and PhD in Coastal Engineering, from Jadavpur University, India, in 1992 and 2003 respectively with few years' industrial experience. He has joined as Faculty Member of School of Oceanographic Studies, Jadavpur University in 2000. Presently he is Associate Professor, Department of Civil Engineering, Jadavpur University. One of the major achievements of Dr. Bhandari, is that his PhD output has been implemented at Field to Protect Digha Coast, a Sea Resort. Dr. Bhandari works extensively on Disaster Management for a long time and supervised seven PhD Thesis works, so far and lot of students are working with him, on Disaster Management aspects. He addresses mainly socio-physical aspects in Disasters. With the initiative of Dr. Bhandari, Jadavpur University has established the Centre for Disaster Preparedness & Management (CDPM).

Avishikta Chatterjee, Final-year student at the University of Engineering and Management, Kolkata, with a keen research interest in Environmental Law. Dedicated towards exploring and addressing critical environmental issues through academic research and policy analysis.

Kashvi Chaturvedi is presently enrolled at Ajeenkya DY Patil University to pursue a B.Tech in Artificial Intelligence and Data Science. Her technological skills are demonstrated by her knowledge on languages like Python, C++, C. Her Semiconductors Research Paper examined developments in microchip technology, while her work on the Comparative Analysis of BJT Configurations offered insights into electronic circuits. Kashvi is now researching on Hyperloop's potential to transform high-speed transportation. She recently took part in the IIT Madras-hosted Global Hyperloop Competition 2025, where she offered creative suggestions for this futuristic form of transportation. In addition, she is investigating the possibilities of Small Modular Reactors (SMRs) and Ethical dimensions of AI in sustainable energy solutions.

Susanta Das is a seasoned educator with a proven record of teaching and mentoring diverse students, working at multiple institutions, and providing service to the various initiatives of organizations. He received his Ph.D. and M.A. degrees from Western Michigan University (WMU), USA, and M.Sc. degree from Banaras Hindu University (BHU), India all in Physics. He continued his research as a Marie-Curie post-doctoral fellow at Stockholm University, Stockholm, Sweden on beam diagnostics for the DESIREE (Double ElectroStatic Ion Ring ExpEriment) in the project DITANET (Diagnostic Techniques for particle Accelerators – a Marie-Curie initial training NETwork), at the Indian Institute of Science Education and Research-Kolkata, India on high-pressure physics as a Project Scientist-B, and at the University of Electro-Communications, Tokyo, Japan on ion-surface interactions as a Post-doctoral fellow. Throughout his career, Dr. Das worked and collaborated with many researchers, Ph.D., master, and visiting students from different countries. He further visited many countries to discuss research and an international conference participant (UK, Italy, Germany, Greece, Belgium, Bulgaria, Romania, Brazil etc.). He co-authored several research articles in WoS/Scopus indexed international journals, conference proceedings, and scholarly book chapters published by renowned international publishing houses. Beyond his research endeavors, Dr. Das has a storied history of service to academic and administrative committees, exhibiting his commitment to the growth and development of educational institutions. His experience includes tenure at Central University South Bihar, Sri Sri University, and P.K. University before assuming his current role at Ajeenkya DY Patil University. He received the Marie-Curie post-doctoral fellowship in Sweden, Science Academies' Summer Research Fellowship in India, Gwen Frostic Doctoral Fellowship, Department Graduate Research and Creative Scholar Award by WMU, and Leo R. Parpart Doctoral Fellowship by Dept. of Physics, WMU, among many others, throughout his academic journey. At present, Dr. Das continues to delve into cutting-edge fields, with a keen interest in nanotechnology, UN SDGs, and data science. His multifaceted contributions, spanning teaching, research, and administrative leadership, showcase a dedicated professional who is instrumental in advancing the vision and mission of the institutions he serves.

Keya De Mukhopadhyay Associate Professor Department of Biotechnology Institute of Engineering and Management (IEM) University of Engineering & Management, Kolkata University Area, Plot No. III - B/5, New Town, Action Area - III, Kolkata, West Bengal 700160 India +91 9836361120 (cell)

Joyeta Ghosh is a dedicated faculty member and researcher with a passion for exploring diverse aspects of Nutrition and Dietetics. Her expertise spans areas including Metabolic Syndrome, Cancer Biology, Genomics, Neurophysiology, and Stress Physiology. With a Ph.D. in Nutritional Biochemistry from the University of Calcutta (DST-INSPIRE Fellow)(2021), a Masters in Applied Nutrition from AIIPH, Kolkata, and a Bachelor's in Food and Nutrition (Honors) from the University of Calcutta, Dr. Ghosh has built a strong academic foundation. She further expanded her skillset with an M.Sc. in Data Science from Liverpool John Moores University, UK. Her core skills encompass experimental design with human subjects, fieldwork, statistical data analysis, and a wide range of laboratory techniques. As a consultant and data scientist in Nutrition Artificial Intelligence, Dr. Ghosh continues to push the boundaries of innovation in the field. Her commitment to excellence in teaching and research, coupled with a relentless pursuit of knowledge, drives her contributions to the advancement of science and nutrition.

Oindrilla Ghosh is a Research Scholar hailing from the School of Law at Christ (Deemed to be University) Bangalore, India, focuses her research on health of tribal communities. Her work includes publications on Neuroscience on Organizational Behavior at IGI Global and also Environmental Disasters of which 8 publications that are indexed in SCOPUS and Web of Sciences conference proceedings. She completed her early education at Loreto Day School, Bowbazar and went on to achieve distinction in her undergraduate (B.A/LL.B) and postgraduate (LL.M) studies at Calcutta University. Having served as an Assistant Professor of Law at Kingston Law College,Barasat, Kolkata, Ghosh has actively participated in numerous National Conferences, International Conferences, UN Global Summits, webinars, and seminars organized by prestigious academic institutions. Her expertise lies in health perspectives, environmental studies, human behavior, and related areas. Additionally, she has conducted various workshops, lectures in educational institutions, and is engaged with NGO's to help the needy.

Zainab Hamid works as an Assistant Professor (Psychology), Higher Education Department J&K, India. She is having specialization in organizational psychology & human resource management.

Hamzah, Sp. An-TI, KNA, KIC (K) currently serves as the Deputy Director of Medical Services at Universitas Airlangga Hospital (RS UNAIR) and is the Head of the Cost Management Team (TKMKB) for BPJS Health in East Java Province. He has extensive experience in health system management, particularly in public health and healthcare financing policies at the provincial level. Dr. Hamzah has an educational background in medicine and over 30 years of experience in hospital management and healthcare cost management. As the head of the TKMKB team, he plays a crucial role in designing and managing healthcare cost policies in East Java to ensure the availability and distribution of effective healthcare services. With a deep understanding of healthcare policies, cost management, and healthcare service delivery, Dr. Hamzah has made significant contributions to raising awareness and improving tuberculosis (TB) notification services, particularly in the public health sector.

Tiago Horta Reis da Silva is a Lecturer in Nursing Education (AEP) at King's College London, with a range of qualifications including BSc in Nursing, BSc in

Traditional Chinese Medicine, MSc in Emotional Intelligence, Counselling and NLP, a Master of Business Administration, and MSc in Traditional Chinese Medicine. He has experience in other Higher Education Institutions and NHS and is a member of the Adult Nursing department, assisting with the running, development, and administration of BSc and MSc programmes. He also assists with teaching other modules' content and assists with interviews and assessment matters for other courses. Tiago is a Senior Fellow in Higher Education, a Fellow of the Royal Society of Medicine, and a Fellow for Faculty Nursing and Midwifery at the Royal College of Southern Ireland.

Rakesh Kumar Jain received his B.E. and M.E. in Civil Engineering from R.D. University, Jabalpur, Madhya Pradesh, and the University of Pune, Maharashtra. He earned his Ph.D. in Engineering from Rajiv Gandhi Technical University, Bhopal. He served as the Principal of Dr. D.Y. Patil Institute of Technology, Pune, India, and as the Director of Rajarshi Shahu College of Engineering, Pune, India, before joining Ajeenkya D.Y. Patil University as Vice-Chancellor. He has been associated with the National Board of Accreditation (NBA) and the National Accreditation and Assessment Council (NAAC) for several years. He received the title of "Margdarshak" (Mentor) from the All India Council for Technical Education (AICTE) for guiding institutions through the NBA accreditation process. He was also appointed as an "Ambassador" for mentoring five institutions for NAAC accreditation under the "Paramarsha" (Advisor) scheme sanctioned by the University Grants Commission of India (UGC). Additionally, he was appointed as a "Mentor" by the Directorate of Technical Education, Mumbai, India, to guide institutions for NAAC/NBA accreditation. He has received several prestigious awards, including the Hon. Balasaheb Wagh Memorial "Best Institute Award" by the Association of Management of Unaided Colleges (Maharashtra), the "Best Principal" and "Best College Award" by the Indian Society of Technical Education, New Delhi, the "Best Principal Award" by Savitribai Phule Pune University, Pune, and the "Best Affiliated College Award" by Savitribai Phule Pune University, Pune. Additionally, he was honored with the "Best Teacher and Certificate of Excellence for Leadership" in September 2014 by Dr. D.Y. Patil Vidya Pratishthan Society, Pune, and the Visvesvaraya Construction Excellence Award by Construction & Business Record, Mumbai, India. He has published books with reputed national and international publishers, including Routledge (Taylor & Francis Group, USA) and CRC Press, Boca Raton, USA. He has published or presented more than 144 technical papers on topics related to Geotechnical Engineering and Transportation Engineering in international and national journals, seminars, and conferences. Three of his papers were adjudged as "Best Paper". He holds several patents and has guided numerous doctoral students. He is a member of various professional bodies, including the

American Society of Civil Engineers, the Institution of Engineers (India), and the Indian Society for Technical Education, among others. He was nominated by the Chancellor (Governor of Maharashtra) as a Member of the Academic Council of SPPU, Pune. He has served as a Member of the Board of Studies (BOS) in Civil Engineering under the Faculty of Engineering (FOE), Chairman of BOS in Civil Engineering under FOE, and a Member of the Research & Recognition Committee. Additionally, he has been an Academic Council Member of JSPM University, Pune; Sanjivani College of Engineering, Kopargaon; M.M. College of Engineering, Pune; Sri Venkateswara COE, Tirupati; Shri Ramswaroop University, Lucknow; and the Confederation of Indian Industries (CII) Western Region Committee on Education, Planning & Monitoring Board. He was also part of the Organizing Committee for the Indo-US Conclave and the Internal Quality Assurance Cell (IQAC) of Dr. D.Y. Patil University, Pimpri, Pune. He has visited numerous countries as a delegate, conference participant, and researcher. He has also organized several Faculty Development Programs (FDPs), Short-Term Training Programs (STTPs), Summer and Winter Schools, seminars, and conferences.

Yadnyesh Khapekar, currently pursuing a B.Tech. in Computer Science and Engineering from Ajeenkya D Y Patil University, has a broad spectrum of research interests, ranging from nanoparticles, and aerodynamics to many others. His research not only focuses on the synthesis but also the characterization of nanoparticles. 'How can one minimize the air resistance for a moving object?' is his focus for studying aerodynamics. He aims to research in these fields and make them more applicable for research purposes. He recently participated at the Global Hyperloop Competition (GHC) at IIT Madras as a member of the team Vac-Vectoor. The event took place from 21st February through 24th February 2025. He contributed significantly to the performance of his team. The team Vac-Vectoor achieved 2nd position in Business and Socio-Economic Impact of Hyperloop in the Innoquest category and Special Mention Certificate in Traction sub-system under Design X category.

Binod Kumar is a graduate student known for his academic excellence, with his total 3 scholarly works indexed in Scopus database on Neuroscience in Organizational Behavior, Neuromarketing and AI Applications on Wildlife Conservation. Hailing from Ranchi, Jharkhand in India, Binod is currently pursuing a Master of Laws (LL.M) at the prestigious Radha Govind University. His passion for technology and innovation along with climate changes is evident through his high academic performance and numerous projects. Binod has a keen interest in artificial intelligence, machine learning, neuropsychology, climate changes and disaster management, fields in which he has undertaken several research projects. He is particularly fascinated by the potential of AI to solve real-world problems and is dedicated to learning and applying new techniques in these areas. He volunteers at local NGOs, teaching underprivileged children basic computer skills. With a strong foundation in law and a commitment to making a positive impact, Binod Kumar is poised to become a future leader in the legal industry.

Piyush Kumar is a faculty member in Marketing at IILM, Gurugram. With over 17 years of extensive experience in strategic consulting, operations, and academic leadership across South Asia, the Middle East, and Africa, he is also a certified hospital quality assessor for both the National Health System Resource Centre (Ministry of Health and Family Welfare, Government of India) and the Quality Accreditation Institute (QAI). Additionally, he serves as a mentor for startups under the MAARG initiative by Start-up India. He has been actively engaged in developing the executive education portfolio besides the training programs, workshops, and certificate courses focused on optimizing healthcare quality, managing digital health, and enhancing hospital management practices. His research interests are deeply rooted in healthcare management and the transformative impact of digital healthcare. Throughout his career, he has focused on leveraging innovative tools and cutting-edge technologies to elevate healthcare practices and drive operational excellence in the sector. During 2019 to 2020, Piyush served as an Assistant Professor in the Department of Management at Banasthali Vidyapith (university). Additionally, he was entrusted with the responsibility of developing and overseeing the Annual Refresher Program in Teaching (ARPIT) under the purview of the University Grants Commission. Between 2013 and 2019, he held a pivotal role in healthcare consulting as a Program Manager for the healthcare and life sciences practice, covering the South Asia, Middle East, and Africa region at Frost & Sullivan. During the period from 2007 to 2013, Piyush Kumar also made significant contributions to prominent healthcare chains in India, assuming various strategic leadership roles. Furthermore, he headed the medical services division of the 'Buddh International Circuit,' India's sole Formula One racing track. Piyush Kumar's academic journey commenced with the attainment of a master's degree in health and Hospital Administration from IIHMR University in 2007. Presently, he is actively pursuing his Ph.D. in Management at Banasthali Vidyapith, Rajasthan. His research interests encompass the realms of healthcare management and digital healthcare. Driven by a passion for writing, Piyush has authored numerous articles pertaining to the healthcare industry, which have been featured in esteemed healthcare publications. Additionally, he has presented his research findings at various national and international conferences. His expertise has been recognized by prestigious organizations, leading to invitations to speak at events hosted by the Ministry of Labor in Taiwan, CSR India, and the Consortium of Accredited Healthcare Organizations (CAHO) in India. Much of his work has centred around enhancing healthcare management through the application of diverse tools and cutting-edge technologies.

Sanjeev Kumar is an accomplished expert in Food and Beverage. He currently holds the positions of Professor in Lovely Professional University, Punjab, India. With over a decade of experience in the field, food Service Industry, his research focuses on Alcoholic beverages, Event management and Sustainable Management Practices, Metaverse, AI Machine Learning and Artificial Intelligence. He has published more than 60 research papers, articles and chapters in Scopus Indexed, UGC Approved and peer reviewed Journals and books. Dr. Sanjeev Kumar participated and acted as resource person in various National and International conferences, seminars, session chair, research workshops and industry talks and his work has been widely cited.

Priya Makhija, 18+ years of academic work experience in the areas of Teaching, Research, Team building, Academic administration, faculty development & research enhancement. Contributed to academics by conducting and attending conferences, webinars, seminars, FDPs and MDPs. In the area of research contributed as reviewer, session chair and published research papers and book chapter, nationally and internationally (Scopus Indexed journals). Follow R3 approach i.e Respect, Responsibility and Resilience. Being Awarded Prof. Indira Parikh 50 Women in Education Leaders at the World Education Congress and has been awarded as Distinguish Teacher award by MTC Education Global.

Mohd. Muzamil works as an Assistant Professor at Department of Psychology, University of Kashmir. He is having specialization in Psychometrics, biopsychology & organizational psychology.

Shankar Prasad, An ardent learner and academician with experience working with Corporate and University. Has an experience of 14 years in the field of policy research and analysis. Has successfully guided many students in their major and minor projects.

R Thanga Kumar is an Assistant Professor is an expert in Finance and Accounting with a deep passion for teaching all facets of finance. He includes practice and application of the fundamentals into Corporate and Cost Management Accounting and also his research interest lies in Understanding the Behavioural Pattern of Investment.

Abantika Ray is an accomplished academic and research scholar, with a profound interest in environmental science. She completed Bachelor of Science in

Botany (Honours) from the University of Calcutta (CU), where she laid the foundation for her passion for environmental science. Building on this academic background, she pursued a Master of Science in Environmental Science, from Vidyasagar University, during which she undertook significant research for her dissertation at the Bose Institute, Kolkata. Her dissertation focused on the toxicity induced by Cisplatin, an anti-cancerous drug, which provided critical insights into its environmental impact. Currently, she is a research scholar at Jadavpur University, where she continues to explore and contribute to her field of study, with a focus on environmental science and related areas of research.

Sunil Sankathala is pursuing his B.Tech. degree in computer science at the School of Engineering of Ajeenkya DY Patil University, Pune, Maharashtra, India. His research interests are artificial intelligence, Data science, and UNSDGs. He actively participates in various extracurricular actvities of the University such as House of Arts. He leads the performing arts as the lead. He recently participated at the Global Hyperloop Competition (GHC) at IIT Madras as a member of the team Vac-Vectoor. The event took place from 21st February through 24th February 2025. He contributed significantly to the performance of his team. The team Vac-Vectoor achieved 2nd position in Business and Socio-Economic Impact of Hyperloop in the Innoquest category and Special Mention Certificate in Traction sub-system under Design X category. He actively participates in various extracurricular activities, and he is a member of House of Arts of Ajeenky DY Patil University.

Ragini Sharma has a diverse background in the healthcare sector, combining clinical experience with expertise in hospital management, health technology, and strategic consulting. Her educational qualifications include a Bachelor of Dental Surgery and a Post Graduate Diploma in Hospital Management. Her work experience spans various areas, including clinical practice, health tech, hospital management system optimization, healthcare facility mapping, and healthcare strategy consulting for projects including feasibility study, financial planning, expansion plan, HMS evaluation etc.

Aditya Shrivastav is currently studying B.Tech. in Computer Engineering at the School of Engineering, Ajeenkya DY Patil University. His research interests are centered around nanoparticle biosynthesis, exploring ionic liquids' use in various applications, and applying Artificial Intelligence to different fields. Aditya is particularly focused on understanding how these technologies can be utilized together to solve practical problems. He aims to advance research in these areas and contribute to innovative solutions that address real-world challenges. He recently participated at the Global Hyperloop Competition (GHC) at IIT Madras as a member of the team Vac-Vectoor. The event took place from 21st February through 24th February 2025. He contributed significantly to the performance of his team. The team Vac-Vectoor achieved 2nd position in Business and Socio-Economic Impact of Hyperloop in the Innoquest category and Special Mention Certificate in Traction sub-system under Design X category.

Ananya Shukla is currently pursuing her bachelor's degree from Christ University.

Ajay K. Singh is working as an Associate Professor (Research) in the Department of Humanities and Social Science, Graphic Era (Deemed to be University) Dehradun. He has worked as Assistant Professor (Economics) in the School of Liberal Arts & Management, DIT University Dehradun for 6 years. He did Post-Doctorate Research with EDI of India, Ahmedabad, Gujarat (India). He received MPhil (Economics) from DAVV Indore (India), and PhD (Economics) from IIT Indore (India. He has published several research papers in the diversified area such as climate change, agricultural productivity, assessment of food security; estimation of GFSI, development of environmental sustainability index (ESI) and its association with socio-economic indicators; measurement and determinants of entrepreneurship ecosystem, and dimension of sustainable development and its interlinkages with economic development.

Shiv Kumar Singh Pundhir is currently associated as an Assistant Professor at the School of Business and Management, Christ Deemed to be University India. He has 13 years of teaching experience at PG (MBA) and UG(BBA) labels. His area of specialization is Operations Research, Business Statistics, and Business Analytics. He completed his M.Sc. (Mathematics) from Dr. B R Ambedkar University Agra (U.P.) and an M.Tech. in Operations Research from NIT Durgapur(W.B.). He completed a PG Certificate in Business Analytics from AIMA, New Delhi. He is currently pursuing his Ph.D. in Management from GLA University, Mathura, U.P. India. He is 2007 GATE qualified. He has a total of seven research publications out of which five are Scopus indexed. He has presented research papers at four international conferences and attended eighteen FDP/Workshops to develop subject domain skills.

Devanshi Soni is currently pursuing a B.Tech in Computer Engineering at the School of Engineering, Ajeenkya DY Patil University. Her research interests are metal nanoparticles and their applications and the integration of Artificial Intelligence across various domains. Devanshi is particularly interested in exploring how metal nanoparticles can be combined with AI technologies to address practical challenges and develop innovative solutions. She aims to advance research in these fields and contribute to groundbreaking developments that tackle real-world issues.

Suryanti Chan, MPH, MMEd, PhD, FIHFAA is a medical doctor and a senior lecturer at the Faculty of Medicine, Universitas Dian Nuswantoro. She earned her medical degree from Trisakti University and further advanced her expertise with a Master's in Public Health (MPH) and a Master's in Medical Education (MMEd) from the University of Indonesia's Faculty of Medicine (FK UI). Dr. Suryanti obtained her PhD in Health Sciences from Lincoln University College. Her expertise spans clinical practice, public health, and medical education, positioning her as a prominent figure in the intersection of healthcare delivery and public health strategies. Through her research and teaching, she is committed to improving healthcare outcomes, particularly in the areas of infectious diseases and public health.

Kirti Udayai boasts a remarkable career spanning over 17 years, seamlessly blending expertise in healthcare and academia. Presently, she holds the esteemed position of Associate Professor at IIHMR Bangalore, where she imparts knowledge in Hospital Management, a role she has embraced for over a decade. Dr. Udayai's professional journey pivots around her profound interest in hospital quality and risk management, areas where she has made significant research contributions. Her scholarly endeavors shine through her prolific publication record in both national and international journals. Beyond academia and research, Dr. Udayai's impact extends to the corporate realm, where she actively collaborates with organizations to mentor and enhance workforce skills, particularly in healthcare. Her dedication to bridging the academia-industry gap resonates with her commitment to human resource development within the healthcare sector. On the global stage, Dr. Udayai has left her mark as a leader, having chaired International Conferences on Public Health in Sri Lanka and Malaysia. Her exceptional skills and experience converge in her role as a certified National Assessor for the National Quality Assurance Standard (NQAS), an initiative under the Ministry of Health and Family Welfare. In this capacity, she plays a pivotal role in assessing and ensuring the quality of public healthcare facilities across India, contributing significantly to the nation's healthcare landscape. Acknowledging her contributions, Dr. Udayai has received the prestigious Education Leadership award, a testament to her unwavering dedication to healthcare education excellence. Her multifaceted career epitomizes her unwavering commitment to advancing healthcare quality, research, education, and workforce development, making her a true luminary in the field.

R. Vallipriya has been working in the Department of Physical Sciences at the Institute of Education (Affiliated to Tamilnadu Teacher Education University) as an Assistant Professor. With a wealth of experience, Mrs. R.Vallipriya has accumulated 12 years of extensive teaching. Her scholarly contributions include publishing 7 papers, with 1 peer review in various UGC-CARE, SCOPUS, and peer-reviewed journals.

S. Srinivasan has been working in the Department of Humanities and Social Sciences at Graphic Era (Deemed to be University) as an Assistant Professor. With a wealth of experience, Mr. Srinivasan has accumulated 14 years of extensive teaching and field-level expertise. Prior to his current role, he served in the Ministry of Health and Family Welfare, Government of India, and gained valuable experience. He also contributed as a Guest Faculty at the university level and served for nearly 2 years in the State Government Public Works Department as a Mobilization Training Specialist. In the past year, Mr. S. Srinivasan has enriched his experience by actively participating in a tuberculosis project funded by GFATM and USAID, providing a platform for further exploration of his research and practical field-based knowledge. His scholarly contributions include publishing 35 papers, with 18 more under peer review in various UGC-CARE, SCOPUS, and peer-reviewed journals.

Index

F

G

H

I

L

M

N

O

P